INTERNATIONAL
PROPAGANDA
AND
COMMUNICATIONS

INTERNATIONAL
PROPAGANDA
AND
COMMUNICATIONS

General Editor:

DR. CHRISTOPHER H. STERLING
Temple University

Editorial Advisory Board:

DR. MORRIS JANOWITZ
University of Chicago
DR. JOHN M. KITTROSS
Temple University
DR. BRUCE LANNES SMITH
Michigan State University

INTERNATIONAL PRESS INSTITUTE SURVEYS

Numbers 1-6

ARNO PRESS
A New York Times Company
New York • 1972

Reprint Edition 1972 by Arno Press Inc.

Reprinted by permission of the International
Press Institute

International Propaganda and Communications
ISBN for complete set: 0-405-04740-1
See last pages of this volume for titles.

Manufactured in the United States of America

IPI SURVEY No. I

Improvement

of

Information

Published by

The International Press Institute

Zurich 1952

CONTENTS

INTRODUCTION

A BASIC OBJECTIVE of the International Press Institute is a broadening and strengthening of the flow of news among peoples. Only by having access to an unobstructed flow of news, the Institute's founders believed, could human beings in various parts of the earth ever hope to arrive at the mutual understanding which is essential to peace.

This paramount assumption underlying the Institute's founding has been the motive force behind the first IPI SURVEY. If public opinion in the free countries of the world is sound, the peoples of the free world will act wisely; if it is unsound, the people will act unwisely. But unless public opinion is well informed, it cannot be sound.

How well informed is public opinion in the free nations? If it is not well informed, what can be done about it? For the answers to these questions, the Institute turned to the men who have the daily responsibility for the gathering and publication of news. The newspaper is fundamental in the formation of public opinion, not only because of its own audience, but also because the other important mass media are dependent upon the news instruments created to serve the press.

Last October the Institute drew up a questionnaire entitled " What is Needed to Improve Information on World Affairs? " and sent it to editors in every part of the globe where the press is relatively free from government control. Replies to these questions have come from 248 editors in 41 countries.

A New Era for the Press

The report of these answers which forms this first IPI SURVEY has both moral and professional significance to the editors of the world. The answers support four basic conclusions:

The world press has entered a new era, which has brought with it new tasks. Responsible editors have felt the growing pains, the new professional demands, the new moral demands. The consciousness that every area of the world, given proper interpretation, is vital news in every community, has forced editors to discard time-honoured conceptions of the news budget. And newspaper economics are now seen by the individual editor to affect not only his manager's ledger but the adequacy of his own coverage of the biggest continued story in history.

A cardinal assumption underlying most of the 248 answers to the

Institute's questionnaire is that the real problem is to make the news interesting, that far too many editors have been underestimating the reader. This IPI SURVEY deals heavily in the ways and means of making the daily news report better, brighter, more significant.

Furthermore, this survey has potentially great value for the large news agencies of the world upon whom the vast majority of newspapers rely for the flow of news to their readers.

And finally, the editors' responses show conclusively that the most important project to which an international press institute can devote itself is an exhaustive and continuing study of the flow of the news. This objective the IPI will seek to fulfil in many different ways.

THE QUESTIONNAIRE

The questions directed to the editors by the Institute were these:

1. What, in your opinion, is the most important step that can be taken to promote world understanding through the dissemination of information?

2. In view of the seriousness of the world situation, do you believe your readers show sufficient interest in world affairs? If not, what steps would you advocate to increase that interest?

3. What proportion of your news space and of your news budget is allotted to foreign news? Do you consider these allotments sufficient?

4a. Are you satisfied with the quality of the foreign news you are getting? If not, how would you improve it?

 b. What are the sources of your foreign news — your own correspondents, news agencies, other sources? How do you rate these in comparative value?

5. Do you believe there is a growing tendency toward restriction of information and, if so, what corrective means do you advocate?

Despite countless variations in approach and emphasis, the editors' answers to the above questions showed a broad agreement on the major problems they face in trying to print full and reliable foreign news reports and what steps might be taken to solve the problems. Taken question by question, the responses to the questionnaire can be briefly summarized as follows:

THE ANSWERS

Answer to 1   What is most needed to promote world understanding is the elimination of existing government barriers to the free flow of legitimate news, regardless of whether those barriers occur in democratic or totalitarian countries.

Of almost equal importance in the improvement of information on world affairs is the need for more and more background material in the presentation of news.

Other ways to improve information on world affairs are: a) greater objectivity, b) an increase in the supply of newsprint and a reduction in cable tolls, c) the exchange of journalists between newspapers of different countries and d) better training of journalists.

Answer to 2   The editors believe, by a large majority (133 to 69 answering this question), that the average newspaper reader is "sufficiently" interested in world affairs. But at the same time, the editors are in almost unanimous agreement that there are ways by which this interest could be more thoroughly cultivated by the press.

Answer to 3   Newspapers exhibit great variation in the amount of space they devote to foreign news material. The percentage of foreign news to total news space runs anywhere from 6 to 60 per cent, with the average running at about 25 per cent. The percentage of newspaper budgets earmarked for foreign news usually runs about 5 per cent higher than the percentage of space allotted for that purpose.

Answer to 4a   A majority of the editors (120—77) are in general satisfied with the quality of the foreign news they receive. Their recommendations for improvement are similar to those made in their answers to question 1.

Answer to 4b   The editors' chief sources of foreign news are the big news agencies, which supply them with up to 95 per cent of their material. Next, the editors draw to a varying extent, depending upon the size of their newspaper and its financial position, on their own full time foreign correspondents and on special correspondents and stringers. Finally, and particularly in the United States, come the large newspaper syndi-

— 7 —

cates, such as the *Chicago Daily News* Foreign Service and the *New York Times* Syndicate.

The editors rate the news agencies first in value because of their general world coverage, which cannot be duplicated. At the same time, the editors prefer the style and content of their own correspondents' material because of its special appeal to their particular audience and because of its greater use of background and interpretation. The material provided by the special newspaper syndicates is also rated highly by American editors for its interpretative value. In general, the editors consider all three sources of news extremely important, but consider only the news agencies as indispensable.

Answer to 5   The majority of editors believe that there is a growing tendency, in democratic as well as non-democratic countries, to restrict the free gathering of legitimate news. Their answers often do not do more than state that the general tendency exists, and where specific examples are given, they often differ widely. The answers propose, as a chief corrective measure, vigorous action on the part of editors, individually and collectively, to expose attempts at restriction at their inception, and to destroy them with publicity.

No short summaries such as the above can accurately reflect the wide diversity of opinion, or of approach, found in the editors' answers. Much of the worth of the survey, therefore, lies in the manner as well as the content of the response.

Three Broad Problems

In a general sense the editors' discussions convey a graphic picture of the difficulties they face in printing the news of a world split by international tensions and complicated by delicate political and economic crises. Their problems in trying to improve the flow of the news fall into three broad classifications — the political, the economic and the professional.

I. THE POLITICAL PROBLEM

THE GREATEST OBSTACLE to improving information on world affairs, say the editors, is the disintegration of lines of communication between segments of a politically divided world. They unanimously recognize that it is now almost impossible for the other nations of the earth to obtain trustworthy news from countries under Soviet control, and that this fact is seriously undermining the reliability of every newspaper's foreign news regardless of what steps individual editors may take.

The editors have few recommendations as to how to deal with this problem. Most of them believe that the only answer to this overriding difficulty lies in the final settlement of political differences with Soviet Russia. But a few newspapermen, notably the editor of the *Chicago Sun-Times,* directly dissent from this point of view. His recommendation:

> A much more determined effort on the part of news gathering agencies and newspapers to penetrate the Iron Curtain, even at the risk exposed by the Oatis case. This effort must be accompanied by a much more courageous editorial attitude, i. e., to transmit news about Communist-run countries even when it isn't unfavorable to them. In short, to try for a balanced, truthful news report from the 'other half' of the world.

Because of the major importance of the problem of the nature and the sources of news from behind the Iron Curtain, and the special questions it poses to editors everywhere, the International Press Institute has made it the subject of the second IPI SURVEY. Emphasis in that survey is placed upon an evaluation of the news from Russia, the sources of that news and the methods by which those sources can be better exploited.

A second kind of political interference with the press, not so flagrant and therefore less apparent to the general public, draws decided attention from the editors. A large number of those replying to the Institute's questionnaire find a growing tendency toward government restriction of legitimate news sources even in the democratic countries with a strong tradition of a free press.

The treatment of this subject has, however, been conditioned both by the distribution of the questionnaire and the source of the greatest number of replies. The Institute sent questionnaires only to editors in countries possessing a nominally free press, and the largest number of replies came from the United States, which has the largest number of daily newspapers.

As a result, this IPI SURVEY is inapplicable not only to Russia and Eastern Europe but also to countries like Iran, Egypt, Yugoslavia, Argentina, Spain and others where restrictions on the press exist in varying degrees of severity. A subordinate result is that the number of cited comments on the tendency toward press restrictions in democratic countries is greater for the United States than for many of the other countries with a nominally free press.

The presentation which follows here, therefore, is limited to the editors' opinions about any tendency toward restriction of news sources in the countries where they reside, and generally does not indicate their views on the problem of gathering or publishing news in areas of the world where actual or hidden censorship is in effect.

Government Attitudes

A large number of editors are uneasy about the attitudes of their own public officials toward "news", and are particularly sensitive to a government's use of "security" considerations to justify its restrictions on the release of information. The editor of the Tel-Aviv *Yedioth Chadashot* declares that censorship is "upheld mostly under the pretext of security reasons — ' security ' meaning, in reality, the wish of governments to sit more securely and be able to govern without the interference of a free press." The point is expanded by the editor of the Sydney *Sun,* who believes "there is a residual tendency in federal parliaments to limit reporting to parliamentary debates and to limit the free gathering of news in the lobbies." His colleague on the Sydney *Sunday Sun* makes this observation about the growth of the security complex:

> In the democracies some controls on information which were instituted during World War II still remain. Worse still, security practices which were no doubt necessary during the war created a state of mind among bureaucrats. These men now believe that agencies of news dissemination should rely on the handout. They discourage and avoid on-the-record interviews, actively resent inquiry by newsmen who are seeking after the truth.

This opinion is not shared by the editor of another Australian paper, the *Adelaide Advertiser,* who states he has noticed no signs of governmental restriction. The *Sunday Sun* editor's comments are repeated by editors in many other parts of the world, however. The managing editor of the *Manila Bulletin,* for example, gives this blunt appraisal of the techniques by which government seeks to interfere with the free flow of information:

> In free nations...governments seek to guide and control public opinion with the use of press agents, off-the-record restrictions, open or hidden subsidies to the press on all levels from publisher to reporter...

The editor of the *Helsingin Sanomat* notes a "certain irritability of the government at criticisms of its economic policies" and says that the decision of the Finnish Foreign Ministry to set up an Office of Information is "therefore viewed with suspicion and is opposed by a majority of the press." (Another Finnish paper, the Tampere *Aamulehti,* disagrees.) Similar sounds of alarm come from such scattered sources as the *Aftenposten* (Norway), *Berlingske Tidende* (Denmark), the *Auckland Star* (New Zealand), the Madras *Hindu* and the Lucknow *Pioneer* in India. The editor of the last named reports that:

> Almost all newspapers and newspaper organizations have condemned this new enactment (the Indian government's Press Act) as an encroachment on the right of free expression of news and views. On behalf of the government it was contended that the measure was more precautionary than punitive, and if that is really so, it must be held not to satisfy the 'clear and present danger' test which alone normally justifies such restrictions.

The P. R. O. is Symptomatic

A considerable number of the editors concentrate their fire on a specific target — the government public relations officer. He seems to have become the symbol, in the eyes of many editors, of what they consider to be government obstructionism and official concealment of legitimate news. Consequently, the public relations officer as an institution comes in for a great deal of unfavorable comment. The editor of the Cardiff *Western Mail* writes perhaps the most resounding indictment:

The appointment of public relations officers to act as buffers between ministers, officials and the press is a form of censorship that tends to release for publication only the information that it wishes to reveal... The public relations officer may have a useful function, but insofar as he is an obstacle to direct access by the journalist to the people he wants to see, the P. R. O. is a hindrance to world understanding.

A similar opinion is voiced by the editor of the Port Elizabeth (South Africa) *Evening Post,* who wants to "do away with the tendency towards bureaucratic distribution of news through public relations and publicity officers. We want news, not publicity and propaganda." The same attitude is expressed by the editors of the Hawkes Bay (New Zealand) *Herald Tribune* and the Brisbane *Courier-Mail.*

The United States

American newspapermen also express opposition and resentment at what the executive editor of the *Chicago Daily News* calls "the growing restrictions everywhere being imposed by bureaucratic officials." The editor of the *Christian Science Monitor* (Boston) takes a similar view, declaring that American newsmen are "greatly concerned with the tendency to restrict information within the United States and are battling it vigorously." The Sunday editor of the *New York Times* gives this picture of the situation:

I feel there is a growing tendency towards restriction of information, both for external and internal consumption. There is no doubt that the bonds of censorship are tightening in various parts of the world, and as situations grow more tense, they are likely to tighten still more.

With that has also gone a clamping down on views for domestic consumption. This is true even in the United States, as evidenced by President Truman's recent security order. The excuse given is that security requires these measures; but there is a general feeling — justified I think — that such a program has to be put into effect with the greatest of care.

The "Security Problem"

Several others agree with the *New York Times* editor in criticizing President Truman's 1951 executive order authorizing heads of government agencies to withhold information which in their opinion might adversely affect the national security. Such a directive, it is believed, accelerates what another American editor describes as " a tendency on the part of our public officials and government bureaus to withhold or censor news that might be embarrassing to them." While the President is criticized by name, most of the offenders are seen to be lower level bureaucrats and civil servants who like to work " unhampered by newspaper interference ", as a Danish editor puts it. The foreign editor of the *Chicago Sun-Times,* calling the President's order " relatively harmless though potentially dangerous ", adds the opinion that " it or something like it seems inevitable ... in view of world conditions."

American editors are also concerned by a somewhat different development in the European countries. In the view of the managing editor of the *St. Louis Post-Dispatch,* for example, " There has been an increasing tendency in some foreign countries to try to use news correspondents as propaganda vehicles. Sometimes this succeeds and sometimes it does not. Stories from France, Spain, Italy and sometimes Western Germany, must be evaluated very carefully to determine whether they are solely propaganda or whether they contain some hidden propaganda. This does not mean that the correspondents themselves willingly lend themselves to the dissemination of propaganda material, but rather that supposedly reliable and authentic sources sometimes seek to mislead the reporters. I do not believe they succeed very often."

RECOMMENDATIONS

THE LIVELINESS OF THE EDITORS' INTEREST in fighting restrictions on the flow of news in non-totalitarian countries appears to arise from the feeling that there is something they can do about them, however helpless they may be when confronting the Iron Curtain. They suggest various courses of action pretty well summed up in short phrases provided by three of them: " vigilance " (Sioux Falls, South Dakota, USA, *Argus-Leader),* " organization " *(Manila Chronicle)* and " hammering hell out of those who are restricting the news " *(New York World-Telegram & Sun).*

Many editors appear to believe that their big job is to blast government officials loose from the aforementioned public relations personnel and official spokesmen whom they habitually interpose between themselves and inquisitive reporters. "Make personal contacts with the persons who should actually be quoted," says the editor of a Canadian daily; "don't let governments place a third party between them and the press." The editor of the *Birmingham Post* (England) advocates a "reduction in the number and influence of public relations officers." An Australian editor adds the suggestion that all publicity handouts should be checked against the official source.

Joint Action

Editors should also act in concert, say many of the respondents to the Institute's questionnaire. The editor of the Cagliari (Sardinia) *Unione Sarda,* for example, proposes an international press organization to fight against government restrictions wherever they may occur. The editor of the *Natal Witness* (South Africa) suggests that news agencies and journalists might refuse to serve papers in countries where governments consistently suppress or censor news. Another version of this idea is advanced by the editor of the Hanoi (Vietnam) *Tia-Sang* — an international press organization under the guidance of the United Nations which would have as a mission to promote vigorous action against abuses aimed at the press. This desire for organization is expressed in less concrete terms by scores of other editors. A comment on the aim of one such professional organization already active in the field is offered by the editor of the Louisville (Kentucky, USA) *Courier-Journal:*

> The American Society of Newspaper Editors has exposed many types of news suppression, has organized to fight against restrictive officials and has renewed public faith in the principle that all news of government belongs to the people.

The importance of such "public faith" is underscored by the editor of the Providence (Rhode Island, USA) *Journal and Bulletin,* who recommends:

> Such measures and practices as would convince the citizens of a country that the privilege of a free press is *their* invaluable right and not that of publishers or

editors or journalists as a group. I believe publishers and editors can best bring people to this point of view by realizing that their first duty is the objective pursuit of truth in all their news reports. A press which is primarily a press of opinion cannot, I think, ever win the support of a people of a country that can be achieved by a press which devotes itself to objective news reporting.

A New Searchlight

If editors take active steps to use their collective efforts to beat down restrictions on news gathering, they will have to be provided with detailed information on the nature and political location of any government-sponsored abuses of the privilege of a free press, according to the editor of the *Washington Post,* who suggests that the IPI:

> Provide the press of the world with a periodic survey of the state of press rights in the world, including accurate reports on measures or actions that infringe upon the right to get the news...and summarizing the plight of those punished for the exercise of that right, so that the moral opinion of mankind may be focused upon the gains and losses in the struggle to achieve free access to the news, free transmission of the news and free expression of views.

Proposals for fighting governmental restrictions, the editors believe, would be equally effective in helping to purify the news of inspired partisan propaganda. A Canadian editor offers this rule of thumb: "See that newspapermen handle the news and the politicians handle the politics."

II. THE ECONOMIC PROBLEM

THE RESTRICTION OF INFORMATION that is initiated by governments is of wide general concern. But to a few editors, even that subject loses all sense of immediacy in comparision with one other. " The restriction of information is, of course, involved in the restriction of newsprint ", says the editor of the *Daily Telegraph* in London. " There is no other form of restriction in this country."

A less sharply defined view of the relative importance of these two subjects is given by another London editor, the editor of the *News Chronicle.* " On balance ", he says, " I believe the world newsprint shortage is a more serious barrier to maintenance of informed public opinion than the censorship which exists in too many countries."

Of little apparent concern to editors in countries which have either their own sources of pulp or the foreign credits to purchase it, the newsprint shortage is a matter of desperate anxiety to editors in many parts of the globe. Britain's mass circulation newspapers suffer most severely, and almost all of the British editors replying to the Institute's questionnaire consider scarcity of newsprint as the greatest obstacle to giving their readers suitable foreign news reports. Small editions have forced British journals not only to abandon publishing official texts but to postpone or reject publication of copy from their own full-time writers abroad. " Obviously a paper cannot carry the full texts of documents and speeches," says the editor of the *Manchester Guardian,* " unless it has adequate space for both the text and the interpretation."

The Price of Newsprint

Many British, European and South American editors, as well as some in the Pacific area, take the stand that it is academic for them to discuss ways to improve their coverage of foreign news if they do not have the paper to print such news. The editor of the Danish *Aalborg Stiftstidende* believes that " If the price of newsprint continues to go up ... the time will come when people of ordinary means cannot afford to buy a daily paper, which will be much to the detriment of international understanding." This view is shared by an editor in Vietnam. An Australian editor writes that since 1939 the cost of newsprint has risen 1,000 per cent while newspaper revenues have increased only slightly. An editor in Austria (where large timber areas in the Soviet occupation zone are being appropriated by Russian commercial interests) points out that the "best news report in the world goes into the wastebasket if there isn't any paper to print it on." German editors are just as emphatic in their plea for more and cheaper paper. A South American states the case most simply: the editor of the Rio de Janeiro *Tribuna da Imprensa* uses one word, "newsprint," to describe his most pressing problem. The Rio de Janeiro *Jornal do Commercio* agrees.

The pulp shortage has created much bitterness among Western European editors, who frequently accompany a description of their own plight with comments on the favourable position of American and Canadian papers in the matter of newsprint supplies. Only one editor (*Nord Eclair,* Lille, France) dissents from the thesis that the newsprint shortage directly affects the quality of foreign news coverage, and his dissent is emphatic:

> To give the newsprint problem highest priority is an interesting solution for press problems in general, but it will add nothing to understanding among peoples, for it is proven that, whenever the public has too much news, it is less well informed.

The Barrier of Cable Rates

A second economic difficulty cited by editors in only certain areas, principally Europe and South Africa, is high cable rates. In discussing this problem, editors use much the same phraseology they use with regard to newsprint supplies and newsprint costs — that it is useless for them to worry about how to improve the quality of the reporting of world news until they can afford the cable costs on direct wire reporting from such centres as Washington, London, Tokyo, Paris and others.

The editor of the Amsterdam *De Volkskrant* says that transatlantic telecommunication rates are so high they discourage the use of special correspondents abroad. A Danish newspaper, the *Sorö Amtstidende* of Slagelse, declares that better world understanding could, of course, be achieved by fuller reporting of the United Nations *, but that cable costs prevent it sending its own correspondent to United Nations headquarters. The editors who stress cable costs agree that the problem is so serious as to call for an immediate and drastic reduction in cable charges for newspapers.

* The advisability of fuller reporting on the UN is stressed by several European and Pacific area editors.

What To Do?

RECOMMENDATIONS FOR SOLUTION of the economic problems raised by inadequate and expensive newsprint supplies and high cable rates emphasize the elimination of inequalities. The most commonly advanced solution to the newsprint problem calls for creation of an international pool of newsprint and allocation from the pool on an equitable basis. The editor of the Edinburgh *Scotsman*, for example, proposes that those newspapers which have plentiful stocks of newsprint voluntarily restrict their own consumption so as to make newsprint available to others not in so fortunate a position. Another suggestion is that research be speeded up to develop a synthetic newsprint which could be made accessible in unrestricted quantities to all newspapers at a reasonable price. A more general approach is made by a British editor who declares that the newsprint shortage can be finally cleared up to the satisfaction of all only by an improvement in the economic status of debtor countries.

Although many editors give implicit recognition to the fact that a proposal to place newsprint on a strict allocation system would arouse strenuous opposition, they do not provide any specific suggestions as to how such opposition could be met.

As far as prohibitive cable costs are concerned, the editors have only the one obvious suggestion — get them down. Special telecommunications rates to newspapers would, they say, immeasurably increase the quality and breadth of their foreign coverage. The editor of the London *Observer* says he could "take more news from 'marginal areas' such as Southeast Asia, if cabling rates were lower and costs of maintaining our own coverage were less." Agreement comes from the editor of the London *Star*, who predicts that a substantial cut in cable costs would "work miracles in the improvement of world wide news coverage."

The inability of many newspaper editors to afford the cost of sending their own special correspondents to major news centres abroad is a third economic problem emphasized in many responses to the Institute's questionnaire. The importance of the special correspondent is, however, bound up with the major professional problems facing editors in the new era in which the press finds itself.

III. THE PROFESSIONAL PROBLEM

THE NEWSPAPERS REPRESENTED BY A VAST MAJORITY of the respondents to the Institute's questionnaire depend solely upon the output of the great news agencies; a minority possess their own special correspondents or subscribe to the syndicates maintained by three or four large metropolitan dailies.

Thus the professional problems uppermost in the minds of the editors reporting their views for this survey are 1) the problem of improving the news agency file and 2) the problem of increasing the number of trained correspondents. Existing shortcomings and recommended improvements are treated together in the comments on both problems, and this fact has conditioned the presentation to be made of this basic section of the Institute's report.

Almost all of the editors, including the majority (120 out of 196 replying on this point) who say they are satisfied with their foreign coverage, agree that there is considerable room for improvement. Because the wire services supply by far the greater part of the news, they inevitably inherit the bulk of the criticism.

That criticism must, of course, be understood in the context of this IPI SURVEY and the manner in which it was conducted. The questionnaire on which it is based did not go to the news agencies, and the replies which the agency heads might give to the criticisms to be considered here are not available for presentation.

The International Press Institute will have frequent occasion to evaluate the news agencies' attitudes toward demands made upon them by editors and the use to which editors put the agency material. The first IPI General Assembly is one of those occasions. But the most important of the Institute's projects is a continuing study of the flow of the news, and in that study the attitude of the news agencies themselves will be thoroughly presented.

News Agency Copy

This first IPI SURVEY, however, has been limited to the views of 248 editors in 41 countries, and it is against this background that the assessment of the product of the news agencies must be understood. The editors' main objections to the presentation of news agency copy are these:

1. Agencies tend to sensationalize their copy in an effort to outdo their rivals.
2. They put too great emphasis on spot news, particularly in the political field.
3. They do not supply enough background and interpretation in their news reports.
4. Their copy too often lacks human interest and local colour.
5. In particular cases, their news coverage is too restricted geographically.
6. Their daily reports are too " nationalistic " in approach to suit the tastes of editors in some parts of the world.

All six judgments are made in relative terms, and despite their freely offered criticisms, it would be a mistake to assume that the editors undervalue the service they receive from the news agencies. Several respondents point out that dissatisfaction is an inevitable occupational attitude for a newspaper editor. One writes, for example, that he is " never satisfied " with his foreign news, although he is " very pleased with it." The fact that editors report they draw on the wire services for anywhere from 50 to 100 per cent of all their foreign news is proof of their dependence upon the offerings of the big services, but it is a dependence almost all of them accept with some degree of optimism. " The news agencies provide the daily bread of our news," reports an editor in France, even though he considers it sometimes too dry and tasteless. The editor of a large provincial daily in the United States which strives to give its readers a heavy budget of foreign news says of the principal American agency: " None of us is satisfied, but we know the direction is upward."

Sensationalism

The remarks of two newspapermen, one an American and the other a Swiss, fairly well sum up the editors' case on the sensationalism charge. The editor of the Zurich *Neue Zürcher Zeitung* declares:

> The quality of the news we get from the agencies is unsatisfactory and subject to great fluctuations. This is due to the fact that most agencies show a tendency to present news in a sensational form. This tendency

has increased with the desire of agencies to beat competitors and has led to the creation of artificial sensations, such as the puffing up of purely hypothetical declarations by official departments.

From Pittsburgh (USA) the editor of the *Post Gazette* writes:

> News services tend to evaluate correspondents by the number of exclusive stories they get... Knowing this, correspondents tend to over-dramatize their news accounts, knowing that the 'color' and 'drama' of a story will result in a better display than the lack of such elements, although the story lacking them may be more rounded out and more objective.

To this, the editor of *El Imparcial* (Guatemala City) adds a plea for "strict objectivity and plenty of details."

"Spot" News

In their criticism of overemphasis on "spot" news, a number of editors say the agencies fail to give their readers a comprehensive and properly evaluated picture of miscellaneous world happenings, and that the readers are often left in the dark about important foreign trends taking place below the surface of current events. Writes the editor of the Chattanooga (Tennessee, USA) *Times:*

> We let great and important trends in international affairs develop without being reported until or unless a cork blows out of a bottle somewhere and makes a story on which a more or less exciting news lead can be made. The next great genius in the newspaper world will be someone who can give more continuity to the greatest continued story ever told... the day's news...

The same attitude is expressed from a slightly different angle by the editor of *Ce Matin - Le Pays* (Paris):

> Emphasis on chronology impresses the reader always with the present political conference, but he doesn't know whether the present conference is more or less important than the preceding one or the ones to come... Events of very different dimensions are pre-

sented in the same manner so that the reader often misunderstands their relative importance. Likewise, the reader is often unaware of whether or not the attitudes or statements of a foreign individual or group are simply a platitude or the reflection of an important current of public opinion... A constant effort to classify and observe a scale of relative values in all news stories would be a valuable reform...

Background and Interpretation

Such a view is frequently expressed by editors replying to the Institute's questionnaire without reference to any difficulties a news agency might encounter in trying to supply interpretative copy to subscribers of widely varied editorial bias. Only a very few replies make the point advanced by the editor of the *Christian Science Monitor,* namely that "Interpretation... is also useful and necessary, but the hard core of an effective newspaper is news."

Wherever the subject is extensively discussed, the replies to the Institute's questionnaire make background and interpretation the chief requisite for improvement in the news agency reports. "The press services emasculate their news by lack of interpretation", the editor of the Atlanta (Georgia, USA) *Constitution* says flatly. The editor of *La Prensa Austral* (Punta Arenas, Chile) declares that "too much news without interpretation" destroys reader interest.

The editor of the *Natal Witness* (South Africa) writes:

> The average news agency message, though factually accurate, does not give enough background information to make the events reported intelligible in their contexts. Emphasis is placed on the event and the cause frequently neglected — for example, a political crisis may be reported without reference to the social and economic factors that have produced it. Consequently, the impression is too often given of a series of violent, disconnected happenings without any apparent cause.

Editors should call for more "situationers," says the managing editor of the Philadelphia *Evening Bulletin,* "instead of keeping the emphasis on spot news breaks, which are often badly backgrounded and little understood." The editor of the Trenton (New Jersey, USA) *Times* agrees.

— 22 —

Most news agency reports, he says, are "written as entirely current news without enough attention to the background necessary to its understanding."

Human Interest

The subject matter of foreign news, as well as its treatment, arouses marked dissatisfaction among many editors. Many would like a greater proportion of human interest material. The editor of the New York *Daily News,* referring to the general character of world news reports, asserts that "the emphasis is heavily on the news of diplomatic negotiations, military activity and economic problems. We know little of the problems which confront the average individual in foreign countries." The editor of the Milwaukee (Wisconsin, USA) *Journal* makes a similar remark: "Too much misinformation at the government level, not enough information at the people's level."

The managing editor of the Hartford (Connecticut, USA) *Times* states the problem in very concrete terms:

> Although I am fully aware of the great significance to us of political developments abroad, I cannot believe that the average European eats cabinet crises for breakfast, is completely occupied during the lunch hour with Marshall Plan economy and goes to bed nights with the shadow of the Russian menace disturbing his sleep...
> There are many legitimate and important news fields which are untouched by foreign correspondents, in some cases perhaps due to their lack of qualification for covering them. There is big news in the field of culture which is not given to us by any of the regular news services. The premiere of a Stravinsky opera (in English) in Venice was big news, but the three major wire services passed it up completely. I do not believe that the field of medical science or science in general is combed abroad. I feel the same doubts regarding religion and literature.

The same hope for more cultural and scientific news is voiced by editors in almost all the countries represented in the poll, and emphasized particularly by the São Paulo (Brazil) *Diario Popular*. But most of the replies state the issue in terms of the average man. Writes the editor of the *Sheffield Telegraph* (England):

An unadorned statement of policy on any subject, domestic or foreign, may be read by only about 40 per cent of the buyers of a newspaper. Present the same policy through a man or woman, clearly and colourfully portrayed, and 70 per cent or more of the readers will absorb it.

The editor of the Amsterdam *De Volkskrant* agrees:

Too much official (and therefore prejudiced) opinions are received as big news. Too few data of daily life are received, though these, if properly combined with the official data, would give a much more truthful picture and provide much more reliable news than happens now.

Geographical Restrictions

Not only is the subject matter of foreign news too monotonous, it is also too restricted in geographical scope, say several editors. (Their discussion of this point is distinct from their consideration of barriers to news from the Iron Curtain countries.) They point out, in varying ways, that many countries which offer relative freedom of inquiry to reporters receive only superficial or token coverage, and that the world is almost totally lacking in understanding of these areas as a result. This criticism, emphasized chiefly by European and Near Eastern editors, is offered in most detail by the foreign editor of the *Chicago Sun-Times,* who recommends:

A much more determined, honest effort to report conditions in the 'grey' part of the world — India, the Middle East, Southeast Asia, Spain, Portugal, Yugoslavia and most of Latin America. Aside from occasional summaries and flashy interviews prepared by 'specials' on short survey trips, the agencies and newspapers transmitting world news need to do a far better job in these areas, on a day-to-day basis. Many stringers are used, there is obviously slanted reporting for business reasons (in Spain, for example) and in Latin America sales are clearly more important than news.

Nationalistic Bias

Distaste of European editors for American news agency material in particular and of Indian editors for "Western reporting" in general, is apparent in their charges that news agency copy is too nationalistic or "tendentious" in character, and therefore not convincing to an international audience. "The distributed services are quite exclusively devoted to politics, and they give the impression of being directed very much to Americans living in Europe rather than to the Europeans themselves," says the news editor of *Paris-Presse*. The editor of the *Pakistan Times* (Karachi) adds his estimate:

> Most of the news agencies belong to the Western nations. The nations of the East are now trying to develop their own news agencies, but they must utilize the services of the Western news services. Correspondents of these agencies, while reporting about the affairs of the East, judge everything from their own standard and not that of the East.

As an illustration of this weakness, the editor of *Die Presse* in Vienna remarks that in 1949 Austrian clients of the major wire services received only a bare paragraph announcement of the assassination of the Austrian ambassador to Chile and that full accounts were unobtainable for two weeks. Almost unanimous dissatisfaction with the great news agencies on similar grounds comes from the Near East — Greece, Turkey, Israel and Lebanon. Stories on the 1951 Anglo-Iranian oil crisis, in addition to being criticized for inadequate background material, are also cited more than once as examples of how important news was slanted by "Western reporting." An editor in India fears that "the cold war has invaded the sphere of the news report." This attitude helps to explain the preference, stated by a large number of European editors replying to the Institute's questionnaire, for their own national news agencies (Swiss Telegraph Agency, Ritzau of Denmark, etc.) along with the regret that these agencies do not have adequate resources to cope with the problems of maintaining full world coverage.

Strong dissatisfaction with the agencies on a different score comes from a Latin American source; the editor of the Bogota (Colombia) *La Opinion* warns that they must not be allowed to become "vehicles of pure propaganda."

Recommendations

THE EDITORS' RECOMMENDATIONS TO THE NEWS AGENCIES are part and parcel of the six major criticisms discussed above, the most detailed of which is the criticism of the agencies' emphasis on spot news and inadequate attention to background and interpretation. The discussions of these six points in the responses to the Institute's questionnaire are about equally divided between critical comments and recommendations for improving or adding to the foreign news reports. Approximately two-thirds of the editors did in fact express general satisfaction with the service received.

A somewhat similar treatment is given by the editors to their own foreign correspondents and those of large metropolitan dailies maintaining syndicates. There is one general distinction drawn. The special correspondent for one of the great dailies of the world is believed by many editors to possess either the freedom or the training to do a better job than the agencies in providing background and interpretation for his daily dispatch. A large number of editors make the identical point that they depend upon the news agencies for their over-all daily budget of foreign news and upon their own or another paper's correspondents for the background and interpretation of a few of the day's stories from abroad.

The Problem of the Foreign Correspondent

In all other respects, the editors replying to the Institute's questionnaire discuss the problem of the foreign correspondent without reference to whether he works for a news agency or an individual paper, and often with equal consideration of the shortcomings of editors themselves. In the opinion of many editors, the foreign press corps is not large enough numerically to provide thorough coverage, and they use this fact to explain why foreign news reports are often limited to spot news and lack the interpretative stories which would give the newspaper reader a better idea of important national trends abroad. Added to the numerical scarcity of foreign correspondents, the editors say, is the fact that many reporters representing newspapers or agencies abroad are not properly trained for their job.

Training for a New Task

One distinguished American editor remarks that " today a first-class foreign correspondent needs a degree of training far transcending anything he ever had before." Editors from many parts of the world express the feeling that such a degree of training has not been forthcoming, that the absence of it underlies many of the weaknesses they see in the foreign news picture and that the correspondents themselves are not solely at fault. But the final responsibility for more intelligently evaluated foreign news rests on the editors at home, says the editor of the *San Francisco Chronicle.* The vacuum must be filled by "competent editors through competent and responsible editorial evaluation, interpretation and exposition — based on knowledge (experience) and sound research." The cardinal importance of foreign news in a shrunken world requires an editor nothing short of omniscient, according to the editor of the *Baltimore Sun,* who adds:

> I know of no way in which editors can be authentic reporters of events and interpreters thereof other than by constant study of available material interspersed as frequently as possible with actual trips to other countries... There is no shortcut to learning and, specifically, no way in which the general public can be brought to a full understanding of foreign affairs. The editor's job, it seems to me, is to speak with such obvious knowledge and conviction that his readers accept his conclusions.

The editor of the Tulsa (Oklahoma, USA) *Tribune* wonders if "editors in a given European country might not set aside a sum of their own currency for the subsistence of American editors whom they would elect and invite to visit their own country." American editors would then put up a sum of equal relative purchasing power in dollars for the maintenance of selected editors in European countries who would tour America. Such travel would help to eliminate what the *Tribune* editor calls the "stereotyped" ideas of foreigners which are responsible for errors of judgment in presenting news from abroad.

Turning over the Topsoil

Better training for correspondents, in the minds of many editors, means not only better initial preparation for their task but continued training in the field. The editor of the Vienna *Arbeiter Zeitung* suggests academic training in languages, economics and the other social sciences, perhaps to be given at an international school of journalism. More thorough academic training is stressed by other editors from the United States, from Canada and from Japan. Continued training in the field is emphasized by the editor of the Seattle (Washington, USA) *Post-Intelligencer,* who tells correspondents to " get out in the homes and factories and farms and talk to people and report what they are doing," and by the editor of the Vienna *Neues Oesterreich,* who recommends that foreign correspondents apply some " journalistische Auflockerung " to their work. To an Austrian farmer, " aufzulockern " means going out to his fields and applying the pitchfork to the topsoil.

Some of the editors' recommendations for improving the calibre and increasing the number of foreign correspondents depend on the solution of certain economic problems. An example of this dependency is illustrated by two South African newspaper executives, who believe that correspondents must have more opportunity to travel extensively. The editor of the Johannesburg *Dagbreek en Sondagnuus* says newsmen should be given special travel rates. A South African colleague points out that travel costs have been a serious limitation on Afrikander journalists, and that present editors of four daily Afrikaans papers have " had only one sponsored trip in a period of service averaging over twenty years."

The Problem of the Small Daily

Also of a professional-financial nature are the recommendations of several editors for making special correspondents' material available to newspapers which, under no circumstances, could afford full-time representatives of their own. One of the most common of these suggestions is an exchange of journalists between newspapers on a temporary basis. The newspapermen involved could provide authoritative copy on the affairs of their native country at little added cost to their employers, but equally important, would improve their own professional competence by gaining a better insight into a foreign country. An additional effect of such an exchange system, it is argued, would be to counterbalance what a large proportion of non-American and non-English editors believe is the tendency of worldwide press agencies to " favour the points of view of their respective countries " (*Akropolis,* Athens). The exchange idea is seconded by editors of papers in such widely separated countries as Israel (*Davar*), England (*West Lancashire Evening Gazette*), Switzerland (*Tribune de Genève*) and the United States (Rochester, N. Y., *Times-Union,* New Bedford *Standard-Times* and Peoria *Journal*).

Another active step is recommended by the editor of *L'Alsace* (Mulhouse, France) who asks, "Could there not be established a list of reliable newsmen which could provide middle-sized journals with special correspondents in the principal world centres?" This suggestion is intended to put expert writers at the disposal of editors at only moderate cost. Indian, Danish and Irish editors individually approach the problem from a different direction. They hope for the creation and expansion of news syndicates in their own countries which would interpret and evaluate world news more in accordance with national reader interest. Here again is the editors' wish, which runs throughout the answers to the Institute's questionnaire, to have their own nationals covering and editing foreign news. Says the editor of *Le Maine Libre* (Le Mans, France):

> Background stories on big events ought to be edited
> by a Frenchman — part of the public for which he
> works — a man who sees, comprehends and expresses
> with the reflexes of a Frenchman ...

The editors have a final suggestion for improving the efficiency of the foreign correspondent. They take up the question of government-imposed regulations on international travel which make it difficult for a correspondent to do his job. The editor of *Paris-Normandie* (Rouen, France) states that it "would be useful for correspondents to be given diplomatic-type passports allowing them to circulate freely." His suggestion is repeated in similar language by the editor of the *Norddeutsche Zeitung* (Hanover).

THE PROBLEM OF READER INTEREST

A BASIC ASSUMPTION underlying the great majority of responses to the Institute's questionnaire is that readers of the daily press have too frequently been underestimated, that the press's real problem is to make the news interesting. The opinions of editors cited in this survey suggest that the problem is one shared in common among the news agencies, foreign correspondents and the editors themselves.

Reader interest, the editors appear to agree, is largely dependent upon how well and convincingly the news is presented, and upon the kind of subject matter which is emphasized. Adequate reader interest, they suggest, is latent if not always apparent. The 118 editors who state specifically in their replies that readers show "sufficient" interest in world news, indicate quite clearly that wherever interest appears to lag it can be blamed upon poor presentation of the news rather than upon any constitutional indifference on the reader's part. Few editors report any marked trend toward isolationism in the reader's interests (only the Stockholm *Expressen* finds such a trend worth emphasis), and a significant number of editors (in Germany, Japan, India, Australia, New Zealand and the Middle East) report a noticeable increase of public interest in foreign affairs.

Self-Criticism

"If the reader does not show sufficient interest in world news, it is the fault of the newspaper and not the reader," says the editor of the *Chicago Daily News*. There are exceptions to his attitude. A few responses state that the newspaper public has not gained sufficient comprehension of how developments in far-off places affect their own personal lives. But in most of these responses, again, there is an implied criticism of the newspapers for not sufficiently dramatizing the changing world. In the comments on reader interest provoked by the Institute's questionnaire, there appears a direct relationship between the individual editor's view of his foreign news report and of his readers' reaction. Editors who are satisfied with the quality of their news report usually believe their readers show sufficient interest; those who are not satisfied believe the reader is not satisfied either.

Why does reader interest lag? "Constantly gloomy headlines," answers the editor of the *Aalborg Stiftstidende* (Denmark). The editor of *Paris-Normandie* also finds the tenor of foreign news depressing.

Unfortunately, readers don't attach much interest to international problems. It is because these problems, for the most part, are presented under their 'aspect catastrophique'. The reader's daily life is heavy and difficult. The newspapers present him foreign material only as part of hot or cold wars and in the climate of arguments... Whether he takes an interest in the problems which bind or divide nations depends on whether his curiosity is aroused by the picturesque and by the differing reactions of human beings throughout the world...

Finding the "Picturesque"

Other French editors repeat that the reader is looking for the "picturesque" in his foreign news. From the editor of *Le Maine Libre* (Le Mans):

> News material, while keeping a serious tone in order to hold the reader's confidence, should be presented with a lively and picturesque aspect which illuminates it and makes it attractive.

And from the editor of the Orléans *La République du Centre:*

> To develop understanding among people, serious news stories should be interesting as well. They should touch the average reader with a picturesque, living, stimulating quality, but they must still be objective; and news from abroad (notably statistical or political news) should be scrupulously exact — which is, unfortunately, not always the case.

"The public is tired of too many conferences," says the editor of *Ouest-France* (Rennes). A Peruvian, the editor of the Lima *La Cronica,* agrees, and suggests that there be less space devoted to political argument ("diatriba"). A similar comment comes from a Zurich editor who declares that "endless communiques and explanations, the notes of protest and the answers to the notes, have considerably used up the public will to follow international developments." The editor of the Seattle (Washington, USA) *Post-Intelligencer* is more outspoken: "Most of our reporting of world affairs is on a stratospheric plane of diplomatic double-talk that only a college professor could grasp."

A Problem of Perspective

In short, the answers to the specific question on reader interest point immediately to the editors' basic criticisms of the foreign news reports now available to them and their recommendations for improvement. Reader interest is a product of interpretative writing, greater use of background, avoidance of sensationalism, less dependence upon spot news and more consistent humanizing of the news in personal terms. The achievement of these specific goals, in turn, depends upon better training of correspondents, a wider exchange of journalists among countries and a broadened outlook on the foreign news file by editors themselves.

CONCLUSION

SOME OF THE MOST SERIOUS PROBLEMS described by the editors replying to the Institute's questionnaire are problems they themselves can do little about today. One such problem is the barrier to the flow of news erected by totalitarian countries. Another is the shortage of newsprint and its prohibitive price. A third is the heavy toll of cable charges beyond the scope of newspapers in many countries of the world.

But there are important steps which the editors can take now as individuals and as members of organized groups to improve the state of information on world affairs. One is to maintain that degree of vigilance — and of publicity — necessary to check new restrictions upon the press in the part of the world in which the privilege of a free press, and hence the power of public opinion, have traditionally existed.

The New Era

Another and equally important step, the editors appear to agree, is a general raising of the editorial standards governing the entire newspaper profession, in order to satisfy fully the needs of people living in a complex and rapidly expanding world. The editors not only recognize the necessity for this readjustment. They are also anxious to do something about it.

This is the encouraging fact that emerges from the first IPI SURVEY. A large and representative number of editors throughout the world clearly recognize the new demands brought to them by the era in which they live and are willing to make the effort to fulfil those demands. The motive animating them, however difficult to satisfy, is simple to state: that the people of free lands may have access to the information they need to understand their fellow human beings and live in harmony with them.

The News
from Russia

Published by

The International Press Institute

Zurich 1952

CONTENTS

INTRODUCTION

This report examines and comments upon a problem of the greatest importance to the public in general and to editors in particular—the gathering and presentation of information about the Soviet Union.

This problem is a problem and not merely a routine chore, because, first, the gathering of news about Russia is a task unlike the gathering of news from any center of importance in Western Europe and America; second, the difference in the way the news of Russia must be gathered makes it both important and difficult to be sure that the news obtained is rightly understood; and third, the nature of that news raises the complex issue of how the objective editor deals with propaganda.

By any traditional standard the newspaper editor and his readers have no real picture of the Soviet Union. The fact is more than amazing; it is equally disturbing, since it may easily affect the whole course of the present generation towards war, peace or accommodation with Russia. How does one deal with a problem of such magnitude if one has no facts by which to clarify one's judgment?

The Dangers

For the editor, the propaganda element in the presentation of "news" from Russia is an additional danger. On the one hand, he may find his newspaper serving as a propaganda outlet for the Soviet Union. On the other is the danger of going so far as to provoke hysteria. One American specialist on the Soviet Union writes:

"In reporting on the Soviet Union, we have been and are engaged in colossal contradictions. The vogue, up to a few years ago, was to view the Soviet Union on the verge of collapse. The new approach is to picture the Soviet Union as a massive and powerful military and economic threat. All this is cockeyed. The way in which news is played up prevents us from getting a realistic picture. I am not concerned about the propaganda aspects about the news from the Soviet Union. The real danger lies in the unreality aspect. I am concerned about the loose thinking, editorially and reportorially, which has led and continues to lead to fundamentally mistaken impressions."

The International Press Institute is reporting upon the problem of the news from Russia after direct and indirect inquiry in 16 countries of newspaper editors, correspondents who have served in Moscow, other journalists and experts who have made the USSR their special study. The report is a review of the answers received from these sources to questions addressed to them by the Institute.

The first section is concerned with the background to the problem —the Russian view of the press, the Russian censorship, restrictions on the movements of Moscow correspondents, other regulations which circumscribe the activities of correspondents or affect what they send and the resultant dwindling of the number of non-Communist journalists in Moscow. The second section reviews the news itself, starting with the reports of Moscow correspondents and examining their contents, omissions and general reliability. Other sources of information—correspondents in neighboring countries, refugees, the Russian press and radio (provincial as well as metropolitan)—are then considered.

This leads to the two concluding sections which deal with the editor's two main problems: how he should present the news which he is getting, and how he may be able to improve the service which he gives to his readers.

I. THE BACKGROUND

The Russian View of the Press

In Russian eyes the press is not a vehicle for information and entertainment but an instrument for the attainment of the government's aims. Even as Russian theory and practice differ from Western theory and practice, on, for example, the proper functions of the judiciary, so do Russian ideas about the press differ from Western ideas. It is essential to insist at the outset on the existence of this cleavage.

According to Lenin a newspaper is "not only a collective propagandist and collective agitator; it is also a collective organizer." In carrying out these functions, the Russian press is highly important. "If," said Stalin in 1948, "our propaganda should ever be permitted to go lame ... our entire state would inevitably collapse." This naturally causes Moscow to pay particular attention to the role of the Russian press and to the activities of representatives of the foreign press.

Since the Russian press is an instrument of state, the uses to which the press will be put differ at different times in accordance with the wishes of the rulers and their estimates of priorities. Changes in the content and tone of the Russian press reflect therefore changes in the principal preoccupations of the rulers—from agricultural organization to industrial production, from patriotism in the face of an invader to a "peace campaign" against a new foe.

Lenin to Gromyko

Traditional attitudes to news gathering and reporting are condemned in the USSR partly as misconceived and partly as hypocritical. Lenin wrote: "What the capitalist calls freedom of the press is merely the liberty of the wealthy to buy the press, the liberty to use their wealth in order to fabricate and falsify public opinion." And Gromyko has said: "The objectives of the entire army of foreign correspondents at the service of the big newspaper monopolies were determined by the general policy of the ruling circles of the states which had taken the path of unleashing a new war."

In other words, to Lenin and Gromyko the important difference between the Russian and the democratic view of the press is in the technique of control. It follows that the rulers in Moscow will feel no inclination to smooth the path of the foreign correspondent and will in general make his task as hard as possible within the limits set by the Russian desire to have Russian correspondents in non-Communist countries.

For the Western correspondent is in Russian eyes intent on getting information which he ought not to have—information about (to quote Gromyko again) "the army, industry, agriculture and science of other countries and primarily about the Soviet Union." And his purpose in so doing, though on the face of it harmless and legitimate in Western eyes, is to harm the USSR either by slanderous distortion or by supplying intelligence to enemies. The timehonored device for countering such supposed malevolence is the censorship.

Censorship and Restrictions on Movement

That news from Moscow is censored is well known to all journalists, though some of the details of this censorship may not be so well known and may be completely unfamiliar to a majority of newspaper readers. Nor may it be generally realized that the Russian censorship has become very much more severe during the past five or six years. In addition to the censorship of dispatches there are also extensive restrictions on the foreign correspondent's freedom of movement in the USSR and in Moscow itself.

Correspondents drawing on early experiences in the USSR (up to 1946) stress the comparative freedom of the past—freedom to move more freely about the country, to talk to chance contacts, to argue with censors (sometimes successfully) and even to avoid the censorship by telephoning a story to a point outside the USSR. The period of Russian sacrifice and victory during the second World War presented obvious opportunities which the Russians were, from their own propagandist motives, in no way anxious to obstruct, while the succeeding period of UNRRA aid also opened the way for visits by foreign correspondents to different parts of the Union. Two correspondents, who were working in the USSR in 1946, give glimpses of now vanished opportunities. The one recalls a "six weeks' journey through southern Russia and the Caucasus in 1946—a trip which most of the time was completely unescorted so that I was able to hitchhike for days on Red Army and other trucks through the north Caucasus and stay in dormitories and rest homes ... I was even able to mention (in his dispatches) such 'dangerous' subjects as the deportation of certain north Caucasus nation-alities to the east." The second witness writes: "Once a correspondent leaves Moscow he finds people less afraid to talk and if his Russian is fluent... he learns quite a lot. That's probably the reason for the present restrictions."

When obstacles began to multiply, one skillful correspondent began to dodge the censors by ingenious or ironical phrasing. Thus: "There isn't any racial discrimination in Moscow, and the sexes are equal. This morning, women were out chipping the ice off the streets just like the men." And again: "On the streets the people march along with set faces, grimly determined to get where they are going. Thoughtful observers sometimes wonder why."

Up to this point, however infuriating and galling the obstacles might be, the correspondent still knew who the censors were, could see and argue with them, and could pick a time when a more lenient censor was on duty. Further, he knew what was deleted from his message.

Tightening Control

In March, 1946, the censorship of foreign correspondents' messages was transferred from the Press Department of the Foreign Office to Glavlit, an organization of the Communist Party (Chief Administration for Literary Affairs and Publishing). Thereafter personal contact with the censors ceased. The switch to Glavlit was the beginning of many changes, whose cumulative effect has made the censorship much more strict and rigid. Other changes were:

1. Uncensored telephone calls abroad stopped.
2. Foreign broadcasts by Western correspondents stopped. (No-vember, 1946.)
3. The Soviet State Secrets Law (June, 1947) classed as espionage the passing of information on a wide range of topics—eco-nomic, agricultural and scientific as well as purely military. The ban extended to anything which the Council of Ministers might declare to be "secret."
4. Citizens of the USSR were forbidden (January, 1948) to have dealings with foreigners unless officially authorized to do so. A correspondent would now require special permission, for example, to visit a public library.

5. Russian women married to foreigners were prevented from leaving the country (March, 1947). The effect of this decree on foreign correspondents is discussed on page 14.
6. Decrees (September 30, 1948, and January 1, 1952) greatly extended the prohibited areas. As a result correspondents are excluded from more than one third of Moscow and from many parts of Moscow province, may not travel more than 40 kilometers from the center of the city and may use only four highways for such travel.
7. New regulations were made (January, 1949) governing re-entry permits. A correspondent going on leave can no longer get a re-entry permit in advance.
8. Other measures, including the expulsion of one correspondent and the threatened expulsion of another, have made the lives of foreign correspondents more difficult, and their number has been gradually reduced.
9. Accrediting of new correspondents has been discouraged by outright refusal or dilatory action on visa applications.

The Effect on the Remaining Correspondents

The life of the resident correspondent in Moscow is colored in every way by these developments. If a correspondent transcends the language barrier, there is still—and above all—the barrier of fear and suspicion which makes friendships with individual Russians impossible. "Those of us who ever had friends and contacts have lost them all since the end of the war," writes a correspondent recently returned. The available evidence indicates that a resident correspondent in Moscow is restricted in his social contacts entirely to the members of Moscow's foreign colony. The cultural life of the capital remains open to the correspondent, but what he reports about it will not always pass the censor.

Since the proclamation of the Soviet State Secrets Law in June, 1947, the correspondent has lived every day under the threat of being prosecuted for espionage. To the residents of Moscow he is pictured (in the words of General Ulrich, who presided over the purge trials of the Thirties) as "striving to catch in (his) net those Soviet citizens who are not discriminating about their friendships, who allow careless conversations and like casual friendships."

A journalist recently in Moscow gives this account of a Western correspondent's typical day:

The papers came at breakfast-time—*Pravda, Izvestia* and the rest. They are virtually your only source for stories: the censor will *almost* always pass direct quotations from the Moscow (though not so invariably from the provincial) press, so long as the quotations are exact and within quotation marks. So every morning three of us used to get together and go through the papers. One was the Russian scholar; the others would run through the headlines briskly, decide between us what might make a story, and he would translate for the three of us.

Not, of course, that we'd all necessarily do the same story. We might have half a dozen stories translated, and we'd each do a a different one. In any case, each would handle them in his own way, with varying degrees in the matter of interpretation, each trying his own pet method of making as sure as possible that his stuff would get through censorship in a reasonably intelligible form.

By experience, we knew that certain subjects were completely tabu, even if they had been mentioned in the Moscow press. In practice, for instance, we could not file any details about prices or wages. When prices were cut, we could give the reductions expressed only as percentages, not in exact figures. Any mention of Stalin, however brief or by the way, would cause a hold-up, perhaps for days, at the censor's office, though not always necessarily a cut. The name of Trotsky was completely banned, in any connection whatsoever. In the course of a quite frivolous, non-tendentious piece on the difficulties of learning Russian, I once referred to 'the language of Lermontov and Lenin, Tolstoy and Trotsky.' The word 'Trotsky' was deleted.

The censor is always on the look-out for sly disparagement of anything Russian. I once wrote an atmospheric piece about a country scene in winter, and mentioned the sledges drawn by shaggy ponies. The word 'shaggy' was cut.

The quirks of censorship would fill a book—and so would our own efforts to circumvent them. One result of the rigid censorship is that you begin eventually to censor your own copy—certainly in the case of stories you consider important or urgent, or want for other reasons to get through quickly or unmutilated.

Another result is that in other cases—with frivolous articles, for instance—you give a bias to your own stuff by deliberately trying to hoodwink the censor, and sometimes succeeding.

Anyway, you'd send off your messages (three copies, signed, bearing your press-card number and a rubber stamp) to the telegraph office, probably by your chauffeur, and go off to lunch. You would lunch probably with a colleague, or a friend from one of the Western embassies. No Russian would eat with you, and neither would any diplomat from any of the satellite countries. In the afternoon, you got the translations of that morning's papers provided by the Joint Press Reading Service run by the British, American and Dominion embassies—a useful check on your morning's work, and also a valuable source for articles from the learned magazines.

Then to the telegraph office to see how much and how many of that morning's (or of previous days') pieces had got through. You got back one copy from the three copies you had filed of each cable, with the deletions marked. But the censored cable had already been sent; there was no opportunity to revise a cable, however much its sense might have been mangled. (Some stories, of course, were killed in toto, in which case you got no copy back at all, and could go on asking for it for ever. The girl at the counter would simply tell you that it wasn't yet available.) 'Mailers,' on the other hand, were returned to be retyped, omitting what the censor indicated had to be omitted. The point was that a mailer had to arrive at your office as though no cuts had been made, and yet the retyped copy had to be resubmitted to receive a censor's stamp, or it would not have got through the postal censorship.

Officially there is no press censorship in the Soviet Union, only 'literary guidance.' You may not mention censorship in your stories, and when, in my early days in Moscow, I asked to see the chief censor (in my innocence I thought that one should pay a courtesy call on arrival, and make acquaintance) I was told by the girl at the counter that there was no censor, because there was no censorship. At the time she was accepting my copy in triplicate.

You will notice that in describing a typical day I make no mention of any arranged visits or any official press conferences. There were none. Three times in the course of my stay in Moscow I was summoned, along with all my colleagues, to the Press

Department of the Ministry of Foreign Affairs, but it was only to be given a handout (the text, say, of Stalin's question-and-answer interview with a Chinese journalist) and there was no questioning or discussion. No visits were arranged by any ministry; no organization had a public relations officer. Any question, of any ministry, had to be asked, in writing, through the MFA.

I once wanted to write about caviar and asked the Ministry of Fisheries if they could tell me roughly what the process of production was. They referred me to the MFA. I telephoned that ministry's Press Department and they reminded me that all queries must reach them in writing, and that they would then pass on the letter to the Ministry of Fisheries. I wrote my letter and, as always, received no answer. We all went through the same process in the year before the Olympic Games, when our papers were screaming for stuff about the Soviet team and its personalities. I don't think anybody got a single word about a single athlete.

The same with visits. If I wanted to visit a factory or a collective farm or the ballet school at the Bolshoi Theater or a kindergarten, I had to apply in writing to the MFA. No such organization could or would admit me on its own. I made 24 such requests, and was granted one, a visit to the Kremlin Museum.

I could write much the same about applying for permission to travel outside Moscow—either the long journeys to, say, Tiflis or Leningrad, or the motor trips one was allowed to make through the forbidden zone around Moscow to Tolstoy's home or Tschaikowsky's. Application in writing, giving the number of the car, names of passengers and time of journey; permission granted by telephone (the MFA never put anything in writing); and then— keep going. Police along the route were warned of your journey and patrols saw to it that you didn't stop, not even for a cup of tea.

But I was never followed in Moscow itself (though diplomats were, and especially service attaches). So I could spend my afternoon pottering round the shops, and my evening at the ballet or the theater, and all without any tiresome embarrassment.

I could never make friends with a Russian; I never entered a Russian home; I never saw the inside of a factory or a school or a hospital. But I could forget the frustrations of the day by having caviar with my dinner and then strolling across the square to see

Ulanova (or one of a dozen equally superb ballerinas) dancing at the Bolshoi Theater. Because of the highly artifical rate of exchange, the dinner—without extravagance—would cost some four or five pounds sterling, and my seat at the theater £3. My expenses altogether were some £12,000 a year (my hotel bedroom alone cost £6 a day). Whether the amount a correspondent can get out of Moscow is worth that to any newspaper I doubt very much. But by dinnertime each day the caviar and the glimpse of Ulanova seemed to me to be worth every penny.

Thus the correspondents in Moscow are thrown back on the Russian press for the substance of their censored dispatches. But the Russian press is itself prefabricated. And, a third barrier, the correspondent inevitably, if often unconsciously, acts as his own censor to the extent that he must try to write only what the censor will pass.

The censorship is thus triple. The correspondent draws on a censored Russian press. He writes his own dispatch with half his mind on the censorship system. Finally, the official censor can delete an unspecified part of what is submitted, even if it is information that has appeared in the Moscow press.

Russian Wives

When to these tribulations are added the restrictions on movement and the practical certainty that a correspondent who leaves will not be given a visa to return, the difficulties and dangers can begin to be appreciated. Yet that is not the end of the matter. There are at present (October, 1952) six non-Communist foreign correspondents left in Moscow. One of these works for *The New York Times*. The other five work for agencies—two for Associated Press and one each for United Press, Reuters and Agence France-Presse. The majority have Russian wives, who are not allowed to leave the USSR. It is understandable that the men with Russian wives should constantly have personal considerations to bear in mind when so regulating their behavior as to insure the renewal of their residence permits every few months. One American correspondent who worked in the USSR a few years ago maintains that correspondents sent to Moscow must be married and must be accompanied by their wives.

II. THE NEWS

Such being their circumstances, what do correspondents succeed in sending out from Moscow? And what other sources of information are available to supplement their dispatches?

The Reports of Moscow Correspondents

The Moscow correspondent can send what the rulers of the USSR are willing to let him send. He reads the Russian press and listens to the Russian radio. He transmits extracts from speeches by leading politicians, texts of notes and treaties and the like. He is relatively free to report what may be called political news from a country which no longer has any politics in the ordinary sense. He can also transmit an occasional harmless piece about the ballet. He cannot check or verify most of what he sends.

"The sort of news one gets out of Moscow," writes a British expert on Soviet affairs, "is various but very sparse. Taken by itself it gives no picture at all. Most of the time it refers to highly publicized enterprises like the new canals and dams and hydroelectric stations. To report this straight gives a misleading picture. It has to be related to its background and taken with a large pinch of salt.

"The deliberations leading to policy decisions are never revealed. More often than not the decisions themselves are not revealed and have to be deduced from practice. To one accustomed to reading between the lines and who already has a good first-hand picture of Russia, the official news may be made to go quite a long way. To anyone else it means nothing."

The most obvious gap in Russian reporting is the absence of facts. So successful have the Soviets been in erecting their Iron Curtain that until one makes an objective analysis of the "news" from Russia as compared with the "news" from Washington, London or Rome, for example, one does not properly realize how amazing is the contrast.

The second gap—the absence of human interest—helps to make the resulting picture of Russia unreal, if not hopelessly vague, for the ordinary reader in other parts of the world. A third gap—the absence of economic and cultural news—is irritating for the specialist. A Swiss expert complains of the agencies' coverage of economic and cultural topics. For instance, reports of an important biological debate in the summer of 1948 were "very vague," and the debate on linguistics, which began in May, 1950, and was widely reported in the Moscow press at the time, did not receive comment in Switzerland until the summer "owing both to the lack of competence of the commentators and to the lack of sufficient information sent from Moscow by agencies or correspondents." (The American specialist who first reported in the press the significance of the Soviets' biological debate says, however, that the subject was one of those either forbidden by the censorship or so "distorted" by censorship as to become "meaningless.")

It is necessary to inquire whether the news sent by censored and semi-captive Moscow correspondents is accurate. The general opinion on this point is that it is accurate in the sense that what is written is strictly true; but that at the same time it is misleading. "The reports of resident correspondents," says a British expert, "are, by and large, insufficient and misleading rather than inaccurate. This is inevitable." A Swiss editor is less charitable. He describes agency reports as "too incomplete and fragmentary and sometimes biased."

No Perspective

A former American correspondent writes: "Leaving aside the vast amount of news it is impossible to transmit at all, I think what is transmitted is in general *literally* accurate, but dangerously subject to misinterpretation because background needed to put it in perspective cannot be transmitted at the same time. For example, to report that the U. S. Ambassador has just made an automobile trip to visit a monastery 25 miles distant (I have actually seen such a dispatch from AP) tends to imply that he can get into his car and go where and when he pleases, however remote from Moscow. To the casual reader the recent list of additional cities (Tomsk, Irkutsk and some 20 others) now barred to foreign visitors certainly must have carried the implication that until that order was issued they could have been visited at will.

"To report that a Soviet trade union has adopted a proposal for longer work hours, may be strictly accurate; but it is tendentious, nevertheless, because the correspondent cannot explain that trade unions there bear no relationship to the bodies with freedom of expression and the right of democratic choice that Western readers automatically register when they read the word 'union.' Mere accuracy is therefore quite meaningless."

An observer recently in Moscow has this to say: "First, you have to distinguish between news and information. These days there is a great deal of information coming out in book form as to how the machinery of state works. But it is not news in the journalist's sense. And it is not being used for the education of people outside the Soviet Union. As regards news in the sense accepted by Western journalists, there tends to be less and less... As regards the larger picture, the difficulty is that the USSR has now reached a stage of political stability that seems likely to last as long as Stalin lives. It has practically no internal politics any more—only administration. Its problems are technical, and present little human interest."

Foreign editors receiving news dispatches from correspondents in Moscow put particular qualifications upon their trustworthiness. One writes: "It (the direct report from Moscow) gives a fairly comprehensive picture of the Russian viewpoint: it obviously has many holes in it." Another says: "All copy that comes from the Soviet Union must be approached with caution and an inquiring mind simply because of the censorship, which as likely as not may distort the correspondent's dispatch by the elimination of qualifying words or the elimination of balancing material."

Mixed Reaction

Tributes to the work of the Moscow correspondents are made in many replies to the Institute's survey, but even these are often mixed with severe strictures. (Some of the tributes sound more like expressions of sympathy than of respect.) One Moscow correspondent's reports are described as "tame and harmless"; another's as "well nigh useless"; a third's as "almost without interest." One French view is that they are worse than useless: "I could give the names of journalists who, in order to prolong their stay in Russia, have written tendentiously, admitting as much in private, but remaining in public the prisoners of their half-truths." A second Frenchman accuses the agency correspondents of being below the level of their job. The American agencies in particular, he says, are often tendentious and sometimes make mistakes. A French expert on the USSR, while emphasizing the limitations of direct wire reports from Moscow, says, however, that "the best service" coming out of the Soviet Union is that given by one of the large American news agencies.

Editors, former Moscow correspondents and experts disagree over the question whether it is or is not worthwhile, given the present conditions of their work, to keep correspondents in Russia. Many who are not sharply critical of the way the present correspondents perform their duties are yet clearly aware that, judged by normal journalistic standards, it is not worth having correspondents in Moscow. But, they argue, normal journalistic standards do not apply, and a number of reasons are advanced for keeping correspondents in Moscow and also for attempting to increase their number.

Correspondents in Moscow keep a channel open, however unsatisfactory that channel may be at the present time. The correspondents pick up news from the Russian press, and their reports, if read with the necessary circumspection, supplement the monitoring reports available in newspaper offices. Then too there is always the possibility of a scoop; it is just as well to have someone on the spot when Stalin dies. More cogent perhaps is the argument against breaking continuity: it may become possible at a critical moment to have a correspondent in Moscow and it would be a grave handicap to have to train a new man at that point.

These arguments do not add up to a great deal and those who put them forward do not maintain that they do. There is, however, a different line of argument which is more powerful. Many have pointed out that a correspondent in Moscow cannot fail to learn something about the Russian people and Russian officials and to feel the Russian atmosphere in a way which is quite impossible for the outsider. In other words, there is a case for sending a man to Moscow in order that he may learn enough to act as an expert after his return. His stay in the Russian capital is not to be regarded in the same light as the assignment of a journalist to Washington, London or Paris but rather as part of his training for a special job, which he will be called upon to perform later on.

Other Sources

The editor normally looks to his own correspondents and to the agencies for news from abroad. But news from Moscow does not conform to this normal pattern. The editor is therefore driven to look for other sources. The Russian press and radio are regarded by most of those whose views have been sought as a principal source for information about the USSR. This situation arises not out of the positive merits of the Russian press and radio but out of the limitations of all other sources. Of these other sources two call first for special consideration: correspondents in the so called "listening posts" and refugees.

Peripheral Correspondents

The listening posts most frequently mentioned are Helsinki, Stockholm, Berlin, Vienna, Belgrade and Ankara. In addition it is suggested that Teheran "should be a news gathering center for information about the Caucasian regions and Soviet Central Asia." To some extent this interest in the possibilities of getting news from these capitals is no more than recognition of the fact that if you cannot go to the place itself you might as well get as near to it as possible, but the argument in favor of exploiting the facilities of such capitals for news gathering also goes deeper.

One American correspondent with considerable experience in this field writes: "It is my belief that an experienced correspondent who has been in Russia should be established in one of the listening posts (Vienna, Ankara, Berlin, Belgrade) to amplify coverage of the Soviet Union. The correspondent should deal with all information coming from Russia, he should get the Moscow dailies as soon as possible, he should be on the best terms with the American and British interrogation groups that work with refugees and he should watch in the satellites for action reflecting changing tactics by the Kremlin. This sort of job would supplement and illuminate material coming from Moscow; the two jobs would be complementary."

There is sharp disagreement with this point of view, however. Many persons believe that the principal Western capitals—London, Paris, New York—are better places for the receipt and study of information about the USSR than the smaller, if nearer, capitals. A British editor and a British correspondent express themselves most clearly to this effect. "The Iron Curtain is the Iron Curtain, and a man in Stockholm is no better situated so far as getting Russian news than a man in Paris or New York. The only possible exception to this is Berlin; and I would not rate that as of any real value." And again: "In my experience Vienna, Berlin and Stockholm are quite useless for gathering Russian news. Coverage from outside can be done much better from London or Paris, where at least all the documentation is available."

Observers in the peripheral capitals are generally dubious about the availability in these cities of more complete and more valuable information about the Soviet Union. A Turkish editor writes: "Practically all the news we print concerning Russia ... is compiled through the news agencies in the democratic countries." Vienna, reports an Austrian editor, "is not a particularly good source for Russian news except to the extent that you are able to watch the behavior of the Red Army."

A correspondent in Belgrade doubts that he receives any more information about Russia than his colleagues in Paris or Rome, but believes Belgrade may receive more information about Soviet policies toward the satellites. Most German editors agree, similarly, that Berlin is a source for substantial information on Soviet policies in Eastern Germany, while disagreeing on Berlin's superiority as a source for news from Russia.

The general view can be faithfully summarized in this way: to send a specially trained man to one of the listening posts may prove worthwhile; but to ask a correspondent, assigned to, say, Vienna in the ordinary course of his career to report about Austria, and also to keep an eye open for happenings beyond the Iron Curtain, is likely to lead to more confusion than sense.

Refugees

There is a general wariness and distrust of refugees, though one British correspondent concludes that the reports of refugees must be accurate since these are so similar as to be monotonous. But, whether accurate or not, reports of refugees are regarded by many newspaper men as containing nothing of real value. "What they say is already known," says one Italian editor; and an American correspondent writes: "We have not got a really big fish yet." Some experts take a similar view. One writes that the reports of refugees are only of value if the refugee has had a leading position in the Soviet regime and real knowledge of Communist dictatorship methods. "Most of the refugees," he adds, "are simple people who are able to report little on valuable facts."

Experts on Russia and many journalists emphasize the distortions possible when the press features reports of emigrés without first subjecting them to expert analysis. One expert puts it thus: "The elaborate techniques which are necessary for the interviewing of refugees are not possible for the journalist who is harried by considerations of time. In addition he lacks the requisite background training." Another writes that "newspapers should utilize refugee reports only after they have been sifted thoroughly by responsible agencies capable of evaluating such reports."

The same emphasis on expert analysis comes from those who believe the reports of emigrés a valuable source for the editor of a newspaper. An expert who works in a British university says: "The reports of emigrés and escapees are an important source of information. But with a few exceptions they only have real significance when they can be fitted into information derived from Soviet papers and broadcasts. My own experience is that they are mainly useful as a means of providing detailed examples of some already observable general trend in Soviet development." And from an American university comes the view that refugees "recount their experiences as they see them at the present moment. Although there is little purposeful distortion, there is nevertheless, and it is to be expected, bias. The problem here is not that of eliminating bias but rather of controlling it."

The Russian Press and Radio

Foreign correspondents in Moscow, as we have seen, are limited almost entirely in their reports to material appearing in the Russian press. Much information in the Moscow newspapers and most of that in the provincial press will not, however, pass the official censors when picked up by resident correspondents for their own dispatches.

Outside the borders of the Soviet Union, these same newspapers become more important sources of information. Taken together with monitored Soviet broadcasts, they are the main sources of information about the USSR, in the view of those contributing to the IPI survey. It is significant that an American specialist on Soviet affairs pointed out that the prospect of the October 5, 1952, Communist Party congress first became visible in articles in certain provincial Russian newspapers. It is also significant of the manner in which the Russian press is used by journalists in the West, that commentary on the coming Moscow congress in the press of Western Europe took on a more definite and more comprehensive character as copies of the August 20 issues of *Pravda* and *Izvestia* reached journalists in Western European capitals, although the news agency correspondents in Moscow had sent out long

— 21 —

dispatches concerning the calling of the congress in the evening of August 20.

Those persons responding to the Institute's survey who find the Russian press the most valuable source of *information* about the Soviet Union emphasize, however, its limitations as a source of *news*. It is not, they say, a source of news in the sense that the press in other major countries is a source of news. Writes one observer with recent experience in Moscow:

"The Soviet press is an instrument of policy. The disinterested search for truth is not its job. Its function is to see that the population is told the things the government and party want it to be told, and to mobilize public opinion in such a way as to ensure the proper fulfillment of the task the state has set itself. You can learn from it which aspects of the national economy are lagging behind. You can learn what problems in non-secret branches of production are causing difficulty. You can study the production and indoctrination campaigns. Whenever there is a party congress in one of the republics, you learn a lot about conditions in that republic. Once a year you get a fair idea of the progress of the national economy. And that is all ..."

The Limitations

The same qualification is put upon monitored Soviet broadcasts. The propagandist tone of such material is strong, whether directed at the Russians themselves, at other Communist peoples or at countries considered by the Soviets to be hostile. The very type and incidence of the propaganda in Soviet broadcasts is revealing. But only to the specialist, say the specialists.

An expert on the Soviet Union writing for one of the large American papers defines as follows the general categories of information available through reading the Soviet press:

1. The general Soviet propaganda line, toward both domestic problems and foreign policy.
2. Vague and fragmentary information on economic matters; for example, percentage changes in production, conditions in particular factories, farm areas and the like.
3. Occasional hints on the relative power of different Soviet officials; for example, the order of precedence in the Politburo.
4. Information about cultural trends (movies, plays, books, etc.).

5. Motivated articles praising or attacking certain local conditions (praising the prosperity of some farm areas for one purpose, attacking the poverty of other farms for another purpose).

6. Announcements of particular major events (opening of the Volga—Don Canal, changes in positions held by different officials, etc.).

"Putting it together," writes this American expert, "the picture of the Soviet Union in the Soviet press is one in which certain parts of the country's life are completely or almost completely hidden (military and economic affairs, Politburo activities) and other parts are presented through a complex, distorting glass (standard of living, honesty of officials, etc.). On many matters you have little or no information. On others your information is unrepresentative and dangerously open to misunderstanding."

The Importance

A French expert writes: "In spite of the time lag in receiving them, Soviet newspapers and periodicals furnish three-quarters of the information one can secure on the USSR.* Naturally, one must read them with circumspection: they are part of a state press supplied by one official agency with news carefully controlled by the Communist Party. They contain the news intended for the Soviet public, and thus one learns only what the party believes it opportune to communicate to the people. But even the "silences" of this press are eloquent and significant, and the specialist can draw from them useful deductions.

"One must never forget that the Soviet press makes no distinction whatsoever between information and commentary. The two are inex-

---

* The same French expert considers as "indispensable" for their information on the Soviet Union these newspapers and periodicals: *Pravda,* the central organ of the Communist Party; *Izvestia,* organ of the Praesidium of the Supreme Council; *Trud,* organ of the labor syndicates; *Komsomolskaia Pravda,* organ of the "Young Communists"; *Krasnaia Zvezda,* the Soviet army publication; *Krasny Flot,* its naval counterpart; *Literatournaia Gazeta,* the publication of the Union of Soviet Writers; *Sovietskoe Izkousstvo,* on the arts and the cinema; *Bolshevik,* bimonthly organ of the party's propaganda section; and the newspapers of the principal Soviet provinces.

Of the second rank in importance, according to this expert, are *Ogoniok,* a widely circulated illustrated weekly; *Krokodil,* the most important of the satiric publications; *Teatr* (dramatic art); *Meditsinski Robotnik* (medicine); *Outchitelskaia Gazeta* (pedagogy); *Voprosy Istorii* ("historical questions") and *Voprosy Filosofii* ("philosophical questions").

tricably mixed in whatever way is necessary to serve the party's propaganda. It is also necessary to bear in mind the constant distortion inspired by Soviet neo-nationalism, which since the end of the war has manifested itself in all realms. The Soviet press works on the basis of certain deliberate assumptions, and one of these is that everything is better in the USSR than in the other countries of the world."

The Radio

The importance of monitored reports of Soviet radio broadcasts as a source of information is emphasized by many respondents to the Institute's questionnaire. The French expert previously cited sums up in these words a view shared by many of his colleagues:

"Radio Moscow is a source of official information undeniably valuable. One can even use it direct through listening to the broadcasts in Russian or in foreign languages, and that seems to me to be the better way. One can also use the monitoring reports of the great telegraphic agencies.

"According to my experience, these agencies, though better equipped in the instruments for reception, do not make enough use of the information and the official commentary broadcast by the Soviet radio. The Russian specialist, for example, would be very glad to have supplied to him the material TASS broadcasts on the home service, in particular the daily editorials in *Pravda* or *Izvestia* and the analyses of principal articles from the Moscow papers.

"It would be equally valuable to know the comments of Radio Moscow concerning a given national or international event. These commentaries, inspired directly from the top, are often revealing of a state of mind and throw a certain light on actions of the Kremlin which are obscure or difficult to explain.

"I secure in Paris a radio monitoring bulletin edited by a linguist who receives Radio Moscow every night both in Russian and in several foreign languages. It is very helpful, and the comparisons one can make between the versions of the same event in Russian (or Ukrainian or Georgian) and in German or in English are often quite revealing."

It has been suggested that a distinction should be drawn between the Russian metropolitan press and the Soviet provincial press; and that a similar distinction can also be observed between broadcasts from Moscow and broadcasts from provincial centers.

A Swiss observer complains that the Russian provincial papers are "completely neglected—and wrongly so—by the agencies and also often by the correspondents and Russian experts... Sometimes reports in these papers are more complete and more recent than those found in the metropolitan papers: e.g. in cases of local purges, campaigns against 'national bourgeois deviationism,' etc." A British expert agrees that these papers are "extremely informative," adding that they are difficult to get since they are not available in Moscow and the Russian authorities try to prevent their circulation beyond the localities which they are designed to serve.

Moscow and the Provinces

A third expert—in this case a Scandinavian—writes: "In our opinion there is a considerable distinction as to the acuracy of the news between the Russian metropolitan and the Russian provincial press, a fact which lately (March, 1952) seems to have become evident to the Russians themselves. It has been proved difficult, or even impossible, to get access to Russian provincial papers in Stockholm and the Western missions in Moscow seem to have met with the same contraction." (At a later date in the preparation of the Institute's survey, an American expert on Soviet affairs reported that Russia appeared to have relaxed restrictions on foreign subscriptions to Soviet provincial newspapers.)

This view of the importance of the Russian provincial press is not universally held. A French expert maintains that there is fundamentally no difference between the two and that the provincial press adds only supplemental details which, if interesting, appear sooner or later in the Moscow press also. Commenting on the publication in *Documentation Française* (issued by the Présidence du Conseil) of texts translated from Russian provincial papers, he says that these do not alter the point of view which he has formed by reading the Moscow press.

III. THE VALUE OF THE COMPOSITE PICTURE

Faced with information from these different sources, each of which has its own limitations and pitfalls, how is an editor to judge the value of the best possible picture which he can piece together for his readers? The conclusion is unavoidable that in terms of what he calls "news" from most other major centers of the world, the editor finds the news from Russia defective in almost every respect.

The most favorable view of dispatches from Moscow taken by editors consulted in the Institute's survey is that these reports are highly selective in their permitted topics and therefore misleading. Other sources are also unsatisfactory. Peripheral correspondents and refugees are inadequate for the reasons already given. And the Russian press and radio require the labors of expert criticism before they can be made to yield anything that looks like material for a newspaper.

Some of the Gaps

The composite picture of Russia, writes a Dutch editor, does not give any insight into what the average Russian knows and thinks about the rest of the world. A French expert calls the picture "defective on all points" and particularly on economic questions, where everything has become a state secret. An American expert weighing the view of Russia he finds in his own country's press, states that with one conspicuous exception, American newspapers make apparently no attempt to cover political, economic, cultural and social developments in the Soviet Union.

"In my opinion," writes an Australian editor, "the greatest defect in Russian coverage is its failure to give any comprehensive picture of the life of the people—that is, what sort of people they are, how they think, talk, work and live." A French writer complains in similar vein of the lack of information about differences in conditions in the various regions of the USSR and about the feelings of different social and national groups. Even the most "serious" newspapers, says a British editor, give no picture of economic and social development in Russia, and one of his colleagues adds that both newsmen and the readers lack the elementary background to understand even the few news stories that come from the Soviet Union.

Even to the expert using all possible sources, says a French specialist on the USSR, the composite picture is "incomplete."

"Why? Because the government of the Soviet Union jealously keeps its own secrets on an infinity of things. The daily life of the Soviet citizens escapes all serious investigation, and in this respect the specialist living abroad is neither more nor less at a disadvantage than the correspondent stationed in Moscow or even than the Soviet journalist.

"It is impossible to know, for example, how many crimes, how many thefts, how many accidents there are in Moscow or in the USSR. Are there railway or aviation catastrophes? How many divorces are there in a year? What are the statistics on birth and death? What is the number of drunkards, of beggars, of prostitutes? What diseases bring the greatest toll? How many felons and political prisoners are there in penitentiaries and labor camps?

"I could multiply greatly the questions to which neither the specialist nor the correspondent stationed in Moscow can give any kind of answer. It is equally impossible to know those things one can easily find in an almanac for any country of the West—ship movements and the tonnage going through different ports, the numbers and the names of warships, the tonnage of the river fleet, telephone subscribers in Moscow and the other cities, the extent and routes of air lines, etc.

"When does the Politburo meet? What questions did it discuss on such and such a date? What opinions were then expressed? Are there cliques in this most important group of Stalin's associates? Which are the intransigents or the conciliators with respect to the capitalist countries?"

Profit and Loss

But the same French expert clearly believes that the use of information carefully gleaned from the Soviet press and radio, the reports of refugees and other sources adds significantly to the censored reports coming out of Moscow. His colleagues in other countries agree.

"The composite picture," writes a British specialist on the Soviets, "is remarkably complete in outline, very hazy in detail, except for occasional bright gleams of hard fact, but nothing like as telling as it might be because of the basic difficulty of knowing, first, exactly how the minds of the Russian leaders work (this affects estimates of foreign policy) and, second, the real hidden reactions of the Russian people to the regime."

"And it is here that the real Iron Curtain lies. All the secrecy about facts and happenings can to a remarkable extent be pierced by anyone with a mind to it. What cannot be fathomed is the attitude of government and peoples to these facts and happenings. And so deep is the Russian habit of dissembling, in the common people as well as in the leaders, that even if the physical bars to knowledge were abolished tomorrow and we were able to travel all over that land, we should not be all that wiser."

An American expert has this to say: "I would argue that by proper use of background and of the kinds of material available from Soviet and non-Soviet sources, we can make pretty good estimates of some major areas of Soviet life—standard of living, general level of production for key goods that are non-war, morale, the state's propaganda line and its objectives, etc. On the other hand, these sources are unsatisfactory and we are still very ignorant about such major areas of knowledge as the struggle for succession to Stalin, the levels of military production, the degree to which people accept the 'hate campaign' against the West, etc."

IV. SUGGESTIONS FOR IMPROVEMENT

The Need for Experts

Incomplete as it is, the composite picture of Russia suggested in Section III, it should be remembered, is not the picture in the mind of the average reader of newspapers. It is the picture drawn only by an expert utilizing all possible sources of information on the Soviet Union.

The term "expert" is used in this report to designate a person who has made a special study of the USSR and has established in the eyes of his contemporaries some claim to a respectful and attentive hearing. It is not a term to which the experts themselves lay claim, and indeed one of the most noted of them expressly declares his dislike of it. It is not a precise term, and it sometimes may be accorded on insufficient grounds. Whether a particular person is an expert or not is a matter of opinion, but that does not alter the fact that such experts do exist. The number of generally accepted experts on Soviet affairs is at the present time small.

The Method

How does an expert on Russia work? Fundamentally, in the same manner in which any academic specialist collates evidence from a mass of sources, but with the additional handicap of finding his subject using every possible means of eluding him.

"The whole business," explains an American expert, "is one of continuous searching, sifting, checking and checking again until one hits 'paydirt.' It means collating evidence patiently until a pattern emerges from many small hints, not all of which point always in the same direction."

From a governmental analysis of Soviet agriculture, this expert drew a comprehensive evaluation never found in the Soviet press. From *Moskovskaya Pravda* (a local Moscow paper), he learned of the steps in the formation of super-collectives in the Moscow area of Russia before word of them appeared in the central Moscow press. From a refugee newspaper he obtained new data on synthetic rubber production in Russia, the authenticity of which he was able to check by other evidence. From reports of the monitoring of Soviet radio broadcasts he is regularly able to check "changes in the propaganda line" more quickly, because they are available days and sometimes weeks before the Soviet newspapers reach the United States. And so on.

A British specialist on Russia gives this description of his general working methods and of how these may result in additions to the press' coverage of events within the Soviet Union:

> I start with a firm picture of what Russia was like when I was last there. This is essential, and all new information is referred to it.
>
> At one and the same time, I am developing this first-hand picture and superimposing changes on it. I find on examination that I now have a curious double-take image of Russia: the Russia I saw with my own eyes, and the Russia I visualize when all the little changes have been superimposed. Over vast areas the two pictures coincide exactly; but sometimes there are marked differences.
>
> This provides the general background. I keep up to date on changes partly from reading the Soviet press, and especially the illustrated magazines (above all *Ogoniok*), which, taken with more than a pinch of salt, are helpful; partly from Soviet films (especially street scenes, etc.); but very much more from questioning returned travellers, diplomats, etc.
>
> The thing to do is never to ask general questions but always little detailed questions on some specific point, so that you get "Yes," "No," "Don't know" for an answer. In this way (which is only possible if you know what the detail used to be) you can get far more information than the questionee knows he is giving; and you can also make good use even of the most ardent fellow-travellers.
>
> Whenever I get the chance I ask people who are going to Moscow to look out for small specific points—e.g. how many different dress patterns are the Moscow girls wearing (it used to be three!), have they repaved the Bolshaya Pirogorskaya, are there still queues outside the ice cream shops, can you go into a bookshop and buy *War and Peace* and so on. Also, of course, prices; general condition of clothing; density of traffic; what jobs done by women and so on.
>
> There are times when reading a series of extravagant claims in the Soviet press one wonders if one is not completely out of

touch; but one or two questions to a returned traveller soon dispel that fear.

Without this background one cannot begin. With it, you are halfway there. Sometimes you can get a really hard news story. The amalgamation of the collective farms was a case in point.

In his election speech to the voters of Moscow region a member of the Politburo, Khruschev, announced that the agriculture of Moscow region was to be improved (February, 1950) by rationalization. He talked at length about the impossibility of using the most modern machinery on the small collectives then existing and (to cut a long story short) announced that he wanted to see throughout Moscow region the small collectives getting together and amalgamating in groups of three or four. Apart from a better use of the machinery, this would enable collectives to have better technical advisory staffs.

This struck me as an epoch making statement, and so it turned out to be. On the strength of it, I wrote a piece saying that Russia was on the eve of a new agricultural revolution, almost as radical as the collectivization in 1931. I was right.

Reasons for this boldness were: (1) Khruschev, from another source, was known to have been given agriculture as one of his special spheres of interest; (2) an invitation from the Politburo to one region voluntarily to start a great movement is taken by Russians to be a command to all, and would be so interpreted through the Communist Party (who would, anyway, have secret instructions); (3) the existing collectives were quite large enough to utilize all the machinery they had; (4) the reference to better advisory staffs was phoney because there was nothing to stop the government from setting up district staffs, on the lines of the Machine Tractor Stations, serving a whole group of collectives.

The real reason was not hard to guess. The government, tired of stringing along at the mercy of the villages, was determined to turn the peasants into wage laborers under an impersonal management on land often far from their villages, under close supervision by a reliable party manager. Reports coming in from all over the place about the "demoralization" of the collectives made some such step not unexpected.

All this I said, and it was soon confirmed. Reports of amalgamations started coming in proudly from all over Russia, although Khruschev had spoken only about the Moscow region.

The various republics began competing with one another. Among these reports there were some interesting giveaways. The chairman of a 12,000 acre collective near Tambov was reported on Moscow radio, boasting of the size of his farm and its resources. The resources included practically no machinery and a very large number of horses. (Twelve thousand acres is an uneconomical unit to farm anyway.) It had none of the giant machinery referred to by Khruschev. I forget the exact figures; but it was something like six tractors, five combines and 120 horses. This confirmed that the amalgamation was a political, not an economic conception.

Then came news of the new agricultural towns, which gave the whole game away. Peasants were to be moved from their villages and resettled in small country towns, scientifically laid out, with small back gardens, grouped round administrative offices and central services. There were futuristic drawings of these towns in illustrated papers.

The whole thing made nonsense to me. It only confirmed my idea that the government was trying to break down the individuality of the old stubborn villages which had survived the collectivization intact. I knew that Russia had no resources for such wholesale rural rebuilding. I knew the peasants would cling to their villages for dear life and would prefer their old cottages and two acres among friends to the most handsome council house with only an eighth of an acre among strangers. I said this. I wrote a piece saying that this idea was concerned with breaking the spirit of the peasants, a direct follow up of the amalgamation; with mixing up the villagers so that no one would know whom to trust; with putting them under central and alien supervision; with breaking their ties with the old familiar fields; with supervising the strict delivery of grain, etc.; and, above all, with taking from the peasants their two acre plots on which, according to earlier reports at the time of the Andreyev purge, they had been working harder than they did on the collectives. All this tied in with other actions against the peasants, such as the devaluation of their hoarded roubles, the new agricultural tax on income derived from their own plots, etc.

Further, I questioned the very existence of the new towns. It seemed to me more likely that the peasants would simply be moved into hutments. I said they would resist this bitterly.

The first confirmation came in a curious letter in *Izvestia* in which a collective manager criticized the slowness of many farms in resettling themselves and gave as an example to all an account of what his own farm had done. In the course of this letter he made it quite clear that far from moving into new towns, his fellow *Kholhozniks* had, in their free time, taken down their wooden huts, loaded them on to carts, and conveyed them to the site of the new settlements, where they put them up again. The state, he said, had been most helpful, and the whole operation most neighborly. Able-bodied peasants had, of course, moved their houses in their own time and at their own expense, but the old and sick had been materially helped by the state.

Then, some months later, Arutinian, the Secretary of the Armenian Communist Party, made a violent speech against the excesses of a centralized bureaucracy. As a supreme example of bureaucratic lunacy he instanced the conception of the new agricultural settlements—tearing people up by the roots and pushing them about to satisfy a bureaucrat's dream of tidiness. This confirmed the resistance to the idea of resettlement. All that remained to be seen was whether Arutinian had gone mad and had set himself up against the Politburo (in which case he would be swiftly put away) or whether he had been detailed by the Politburo to make this speech, putting the blame on the so-called bureaucrats, and indicating that no more would be heard about this sort of resettlement. Arutinian was not put away and no more has been heard. The idea has fallen stone dead.

Out of all this I got half a dozen news stories which I think were interesting and informative. They were true stories and fairly elaborate. They were constructed entirely out of reading between the lines of Khruschev's speech and the initial propaganda for the new towns. They were confirmed up to the hilt by the *Izvestia* letter, the Tambov broadcast and the Arutinian speech.

The techniques and the practices required of the journalist specializing in Russian affairs, in sum, are those of the intelligence officer and the research worker. "A pretty good understanding of the total development of the Soviet Union, some knowledge of Marxism and a good knowledge of ideological controls" is how one writer describes the equipment of the specialist required. Another, a former correspondent and now an expert, says what is needed are "persons who know the whole background, have personal experience of Russia, and a real understanding of Russian political philosophy, Soviet economics, and a knowledge of Soviet foreign policy since the Revolution." It takes, in short, a lot of study to become even tolerably knowledgeable and reliable on Soviet affairs.

A Swiss editor writes that "the key to improvement lies in a sounder appreciation of Russian news, especially internal affairs, by Western editors, and in a choice of more well-qualified and unbiased Russian experts." The difficulty is to find them. An American editor says that he knows "of only one man (he writes for the British press) whom I would call an expert in this field. The others may be called more properly language experts or graduate students or instructors whose knowledge of the Soviet Union is limited to what they have learned on the outside. It is not so much a question of using experts more widely but of training experts so that they may be used more widely. This means at least two years' residence in the Soviet Union, and I would guess that the knowledge acquired during this period would last no more than five years, forcing another two-year stay in Moscow (a refresher course)."

Russian Residence

A French specialist on Russia emphasizes the same point. "A specialist on Soviet affairs," he writes, "is before everything else a journalist who knows Russian, who is capable of reading and writing it fluently. It is obvious that a journalist who is incapable of going directly and for himself to the sources, finds himself severely restrained in the scope of this information and risks committing gross errors of interpretation."

"But it is not sufficient merely to know the Russian language... It is necessary to know also the history of Russia before the Revolution of 1917... and if the specialist is too young to have known for himself the old Russia, it is at the very least desirable that he has been able to make several trips to the USSR, that he has known even in a small way Moscow, the cities and the countryside."

Those contributing to the Institute's survey are plainly aware that Russian specialists possessing even a part of these qualifications have not commonly selected journalism as a career, though the majority would disagree with the American editor cited above that the number was limited to one. At the same time, researchers in universities do not as a rule turn out stuff in a form which fits easily into the columns of a newspaper.

More than one respondent to the Institute's survey has advocated the greater use of academic groups (e.g. the Russian Institute at Columbia University in New York), but on the assumption that the necessary changes could be made in the products of these groups, and indeed in their orientation. Hitherto they have not worked specifically for the press, and they would (if willing) have to adapt themselves to the press' requirements, producing regular, perhaps daily commentaries in the sort of language which editors and their readers like. A French correspondent who makes important use of the *Current Digest of the Soviet Press* (a weekly reprint of selected articles from Russian newspapers edited in New York by Slavic Americans) yet considers it too voluminous for daily use. A Dutch editor adds that the *Current Digest* is too expensive, and a French specialist on Russia points out that its contents are necessarily three or more weeks old when circulated. In short, so long as the experts are primarily engaged in academic work, editors wishing to make use of expert knowledge will have to ask the experts to conform to some extent with journalistic requirements.

The Recommendation

At this point the survey of the Institute, reviewing the opinions of newspaper editors, correspondents and experts in Russian affairs, reaches one of its basic conclusions: Strictly speaking, there is no "news" of the Soviet Union as such, but only information indeterminate in quantity and undigested in character. The work of digesting and interpreting the information that can be obtained requires special knowledge and qualifications. Experts possessing those qualifications are ordinarily not journalists and are in any case few in number.

The conclusion therefore—and it is explicitly drawn by many persons consulted by the Institute—is that the press outside the Iron Curtain, confronted with the special problem of inadequate and inaccurate news from Russia, must develop much more extensively the practice of employing its own experts and adapting them to journalistic techniques. At the same time, it must adapt the techniques of journalism to the requirements of the kind of interpretation the news about Russia demands and which only the experts can supply. If it is true, as the Institute's inquiry would suggest, that the number of such experts is at present limited, then the press, in cooperation with the institutions equipped to train writers in Soviet affairs, must also seek to increase the supply.

The «Russian Desk»

Only the largest newspapers of the world can, however, afford the services of a full-time Russian expert, and the vast majority of editors obtain their foreign news, including news of Russia, from the great news agencies. The idea of a "Russian desk" in newspaper or agency offices is put forward by an American correspondent in these words: "I would suggest that every major news agency and newspaper seriously concerned with Russian coverage should establish a research staff or 'Russian desk' to probe for information from all available sources. This should supplement rather than replace on-the-spot correspondents, who would continue to report on-the-spot developments, color and such interpretative stories as they can get past the censors. These first-hand reports also have their obvious value as one of the ingredients for the research pot.

"The research staff or 'Russian desk,' it seems to me, should be run by men qualified both as alert and responsible newspapermen and as serious students of Russia. One man is not enough. He has to have the assistance of at least a small staff of translators and researchers. Detailed files are of vital importance. Liaison with agencies doing research work on Russia is also important. What is even more valuable than the report of one emigré, for example, is a study of the reports made by one hundred emigrés. There are agencies doing such research."

Not all those persons who advocate the use of Russian experts by the press agree with the proposal that the news agencies should help to supply them. "An agency's job," writes a British editor, "is to report things that happen and things that are said, giving the source in all cases. In the conditions which exist today, therefore, an agency is largely tied down to reporting what is printed in Russia newspapers, with an occasional essay on the comings and goings of diplomats in Moscow. The use of specialists to amplify agency coverage is, in my view, to be deplored, for one seeks facts from an agency and not speculation or even intelligent synthesis."

This point of view overlooks perhaps the conclusion reached by many editors that there are in any case few "facts" coming from Russia and that the only substitute for them is actually the "intelligent synthesis" of an expert drawing on all sources, including reports of resident correspondents in Moscow. It also overlooks the fact that, except for the correspondent of *The New York Times,* all other non-Communist correspondents at present in Moscow serve only the news agencies.

At any rate, the leading news agencies of the world believe they have already entered the realm of "intelligent synthesis" in their coverage of news about the Soviet Union. Four such agencies have reported to the Institute that "there is nothing new" in the idea of using a Russian expert. Their conception of the training and the employment of an expert on the Soviet Union is, however, somewhat different from that offered by many respondents to the Institute's survey—particularly the "Russian experts" themselves.

By and large, the news agencies prefer the term "specialist" to that of "expert," insist that this specialist should be drawn from the ranks of practical newsmen rather than from academic circles and tend to seek from the efforts of such specialists the kind of journalistic copy nearest in character to the traditional news report.

THE ASSOCIATED PRESS: The idea of having specialists for the purposes of regularly analyzing, backgrounding or interpreting the news, including the news dealing with Russia and the Communist-controlled areas, is not a new one, and increasing focus has been put upon the explanatory aspect of AP operations in recent years, due to the increasing complexities in the news and the widespread demand for explaining the meaning or significance of news events.

Newspapermen Only

In all specialized fields of news coverage, the AP's conclusion is that development of expert knowledge and capacity among its own reporters and editors is preferable to the employment of non-journalistic specialists, no matter how well-qualified in their particular fields the latter may be.

In the field of Russian news, a number of AP staff men are trained and equipped to appraise developments, handle essential background material and write special analyses.

The chief of these Russian specialists (attached to the AP foreign desk staff in New York) has concentrated in his field for some years. He reads and speaks Russian, regularly inspects Soviet newspapers and other publications, has travelled extensively in Europe and has his own contacts for the specialized work to which he is assigned.

This AP Russian specialist describes his work as "a sort of osmosis process, sopping up and all that, and it is often difficult to show any tangible results. But what I read three months ago may well have a bearing on what I write tomorrow. That is why this is so arduous and exacting a job and why it requires constant attention. We must remember that we get almost nothing factual from behind the Iron Curtain with respect to the things we really want to know about... (but) by constant reading, one begins to acquire a familiarity with the Communist routine, an ability to translate their double talk and Aesopian language, etc. and an idea of the status of their leadership..."

Speculation

"This is where the comment and the interpretation come in. We may be wrong in our viewpoint, but it's the chance we have to take. I would say that if we were right 35 per cent of the time, we would be rendering a great service. Guessing Communist plans is a slippery business. Often the Communists themselves can't... But one can follow a continuous thread on world events, and this is what we are trying to do.

"The role of the specialist is not rigidly defined. It can encompass many things. When, for instance, should a Moscow dispatch... be used without change? When should it be held pending further check? When should it be spotted for pure propaganda and killed? ...

"There is no question but that somebody familiar with Russia— somebody who lived there long—possesses qualifications in the interpretive field. It is most necessary, however, that the job also be approached from a journalistic standpoint, with an alertness for political, economic and social developments which the unschooled 'expert' invariably lacks. I have found that by working with these people, of whom there are many available in New York and Washington, I am often able to crystallize ideas and bring out something newsworthy which might otherwise be overlooked."

REUTERS: When World War II began, Reuters had on its staff a nucleus of trained European observers, men who not only knew Western Europe intimately but also had a firm knowledge of Russian history and political philosophy and ideology, and throughout the war these observers interpreted and commented upon the news from the Soviet Union. When the war ended, the coverage and interpretation of Russian news was placed fairly high on the list of news priorities in Reuters.

Today Reuters has trained staff correspondents in European capitals who, apart from their normal day to day reporting, regularly cover what news is available to them of the Soviet Union and interpret it for Reuter subscribers. In London, among the corps of diplomatic correspondents, one especially looks for and interprets and comments upon events within the Soviet Union, and the London office also has on its staff a former correspondent in Moscow whose duty it is to coordinate the flow of interpretative material about Soviet Russia received from Reuter correspondents, radio sources, the Soviet Union itself and the so-called Iron Curtain countries in general.

From these combined sources, a regular flow of "expert" stories is contained within the overall Reuter news service.

Other Agencies

THE UNITED PRESS: The UP's Russian specialist is attached to its London headquarters, where he has access to two monitoring services purchased by the United Press and to Soviet and satellite publications. Through the monitoring services, this UP Russian specialist has access to TASS broadcasts, the Balkan broadcasts and Radio Peiping.

This specialist reads regularly in their native languages the Soviet dailies—*Pravda, Izvestia, Komsomolskaya Pravda, Trud*—other Soviet journals and periodicals, the official organs of the Communist parties in Eastern Europe and their propaganda publications and two or three selected emigré journals.

The additional coverage of Russian events from London is coordinated with the wire reports from the UP Moscow bureau and with information picked up in Vienna, Belgrade and other centers from radio monitoring reports, refugees and various publications from the satellite countries. All sources from whatever dateline are labelled.

INTERNATIONAL NEWS SERVICE: The key men on the INS cable desk handling the dispatches from and about Russia have had many years' experience in dealing with news from Moscow. The chief of the INS European staff has been in and out of the Soviet Union several times, and he contributes a weekly analysis of the European situation largely concentrating on relations between East and West.

In addition, INS has specialized in obtaining articles on the Russian question from a variety of "experts" including Alexander Kerensky,

Eugene Lyons, Isaac Don Levine, David Dallin, the late Emil Ludwig and others.

The agency also seeks to report on conditions inside the USSR through articles by important refugees, for example, General Alexander Barmine.

AGENCE FRANCE-PRESSE: The editorial staff in Paris utilizes the services of specialists on questions affecting the Soviet Union when presenting any material from the AFP correspondent in Moscow or from its radio monitoring reports, including TASS dispatches and Soviet official texts.

The role of these specialists is to indicate the method of interpreting the information from any source and its reliability and to add necessary explanatory or historical background, drawing on their own special knowledge of the USSR and their reading of the Soviet press.

These statements to the Institute by a group of the largest news agencies indicate what contributions may be made by traditional journalism toward the expert sifting and synthesis of information about Russia, and it is upon the news agencies that most of the world's editors must depend for this service. The question raised by many respondents to the Institute's survey is whether newspaper editors and the agencies must not increase the supply of a new breed which will combine the academic specialization on Russian affairs with the ability to write material suitable for the daily newspaper.

Non-Journalistic Training

The work some of these journalist-specialists are already doing for a few of the principal newspapers of the West receives important attention from editors contributing to the Institute's survey. The very limitations of the news reports direct from Moscow lead the vast majority of respondents to stress the value of other sources of information about Russia, and, in the view of many, these sources cannot be adequately or safely tapped except by experts possessing special background and training.

News agency representatives appear to be least in favor of employing academically trained Russian experts as journalists; experts themselves appear to be most in favor. But, as shown above, even the latter group emphasize (1) that the supply of trained experts available to the press will always be limited and (2) that the composite picture of events in the Soviet Union possible for the expert to construct from all sources yet has serious gaps.

The supply of experts will be limited if, as there is general agreement, a specialist qualified to interpret information on the Soviet Union must have spent some time in that country. For Russia has since 1946 heavily restricted the admission of Western nationals into the Soviet Union, and only one editor from the West contributing to the Institute's survey has suggested that this situation could be changed (see below).

As for the ultimate limits of the contribution to be expected from trained specialists, a French expert on the USSR has this to say:

"A good specialist on Russia is one who has full awareness of the difficulties of his task and the courage to admit to his readers that it is impossible for him to satisfy their curiosity on many questions, despite all his efforts. And his readers ought on their part to be encouraged not to demand too much from the specialist, lest he be driven ultimately to quit altogether the solid ground of fact in order to launch himself into the domain of unverifiable hypotheses and publish articles of mere fantasy."

Other Suggestions

What has beeen written here about the expert constitutes a principal finding of this report and a principal recommendation. It remains to notice some further suggestions which have been made for the improvement of information services about the USSR.

It may be true, as some suggest, that no real improvement is possible without such a change in the Russian regime or in its aims as will secure for foreign correspondents in Russia freedom of expression and freedom of movement. Since, however, no such change is anticipated at this moment, some observers have indicated certain actions which might meanwhile be taken in order to help the getting of news. The non-Communist press is not without weapons. Although the Russian government may wish to exclude non-Communist journalists from the USSR, it may not wish to do this at the cost of having its own emissaries evicted from the United States and other countries.

In the United States at least one editor seems to feel that the impenetrability of the Iron Curtain may have been exaggerated. "U.S. agencies and newspapers do not press constantly for visas to Iron Curtain satellites or to Russia proper. More enterprise might bring unexpected results. There is far too much passive acceptance and even imitation in America of Iron Curtain restrictions. An effort might be made once again to exchange visiting journalists for a few months' tour in respective countries ... On a quid pro quo basis more and better excursions behind the Iron Curtain could be arranged by an enterprising American and Western press."

Indian Coverage

Two suggestions, aimed at overcoming the obstacles presented by the great expense of keeping a correspondent in Moscow, come from India. One Indian editor wants to explore the possibility of arranging periodic "tours of selected groups of journalists from different countries." An Indian expert writes: "Two suggestions may be worth considering. In the first place ... an effort might be made ... to sponsor a correspondent who would serve three or four papers on a regional basis. Along with this arrangement PTI-Reuters might be asked to post an Indian correspondent for coverage to study special Indian requirements. It is not unlikely that an Indian correspondent would be somewhat better placed at present than a British or an American correspondent. Secondly, an experiment might be made with an exchange of delegations representing newspapers in this country and Russia. Presumably, if the arrangement was on a reciprocal basis, the Russian authorities would not withhold the necessary facilities to Indian representatives. Whether such facilities would be respected if some correspondents wrote unfavorable dispatches, only time would show. But the effort seems worthwhile."

Experts take the view that too little use is made of magazines, periodicals and books as sources of newsworthy information on Russia. "Soviet publications abound in information which is not always sufficiently exploited by the Western press," writes a French expert. "Statistics are, it is true, always given in 'relative percentages,' but it is not always impossible to translate these into absolute figures. Moreover ... it is untrue and silly to say that everything which comes from Moscow is by definition 'exaggerated, mendacious, boastful' etc. There are checks which make it possible easily to disentangle the lies and false figures.

The development of the Soviet economy since 1940 is not so difficult to follow."

The same expert also maintains that Russian publications contain much usable material on social and cultural matters. A Swiss expert echoes these opinions: "It seems to us that not enough attention is paid to the periodical press. It would be useful, however, to treat it not as a source that can be of interest only to academicians, but rather as one of great interest to the public at large."

There is a demand for fuller reproduction of the texts of Russian broadcasts and articles in the Russian press. A Dutch editor suggests the pooling of monitoring services: "The Dutch newspapers are listening in to Dutch broadcasts from behind the Iron Curtain. The French are listening to French, the Germans to news from Moscow in German. Exchange of reports will show up trends in propaganda." The same editor also wants "central provision of exact and complete translations of Soviet publications. Why not sometimes make a facsimile translation of *Pravda* or *Izvestia,* giving the world an opportunity to judge those papers as it is doing *The Times* or *Le Monde?* ... The most effective and the most interesting view of Russian news is provided by literal quotes from TASS or Moscow or Peiping radio, reporting certain events abroad which already have been fully quoted and covered in the country where they took place ... Example: Some time ago a small incident took place in Rotterdam harbor. Next day Moscow gave a report of that incident which, literally quoted, showed up to Dutch readers how the Communists twist the news around ... That one quotation, without any commentary, had more effect than a series of editorial articles."

Pooling Resources

A German suggestion is to this effect. "Couldn't one have *Pravda* and *Izvestia* as well as some provincial papers translated at some center, and send such translations to interested editors by subscription?"

A French editor suggests that the IPI should issue a regular review of information on the USSR gleaned by editors in different countries. A Swedish source advocates "centralized criticism" of news services "by an international institute of some kind, which would also undertake some detailed investigations, and so on. After the war the Utrikes-politiske Institutet in Sweden made an attempt to that purpose. It was highly appreciated here but could not go on owing to the rather high expense and the inconsiderable demand in a small country like Sweden. Arranged on an international basis, for instance in Switzerland, and with the support and guarantees of the international press organizations, an attempt might be much more successful."

Sustained Attention

Less sensationalism is the burden of a British reply, and many people in other countries support this plea. A searching criticism of the general attitude of the press is made by a Swiss expert: "In considering the Western press as a whole, the most striking thing is the absence of a spirit of inquiry. People are led to believe in the existence of a Soviet mystery simply because there is no attempt to make the effort needed to dispel it. The daily press, with a few exceptions, limits itself to what is incidental or sensational. It takes account only of 'happenings' and pays attention to a problem only when that problem has reached the point of crisis. It does not follow questions, but is always shifting its attention from one thing to another. Lacking knowledge of the origins of a problem, it resorts to improvised explanations."

This statement points vividly to another principal recommendation of the Institute's survey—the improvement needed in the presentation of the news from Russia. Unless traditional habits of editorial thinking about the difference between "news" and "interpretation" are revised, the available information about Russia cannot be accurately presented. This subject forms the final section of the Institute's report.

V. THE PRESENTATION OF RUSSIAN NEWS

The problem of presentation in the handling of Russian news is the problem of propaganda. Before all sources of information on the Soviet Union hangs the Iron Curtain, and the reports direct from Moscow are subject to an arbitrary censorship. The newspaper editor outside Russia is involved with the problem of propaganda in deciding *whether* to publish news from Moscow. He is involved with it again in deciding *how* to publish such news, in other words, how to "play" it. Finally, since he cannot perform a straight news job in his coverage of the news from Russia, the editor is involved also with the problem of interpretation.

The Problem of «Play»

The question does not end, therefore, with the editor's decision whether or not to publish a censored dispatch from Moscow or an excerpt from the censored Russian press. The question of presentation also involves the editor's decision to publish a rare statement by Stalin on his front page just because statements from Stalin are rarely available to him. A basic assumption of those persons consulted by the Institute is that news about Russia is different both in degree and in kind from other news traditionally received by an editor. And an interview with Stalin or a Stalin answer to a cabled query from the outside world is subject to none of the conditions normally surrounding the gathering of news. Is Stalin to have the leading pages of the world's newspapers opened to him just because the Russian view of the press makes it impossible for Stalin and Russia to be covered like other important topics with which the press is concerned?

A refugee journalist illustrates the problem this way: "The Supreme Soviet of the USSR has voted a budget providing 21 per cent for armaments. The correspondent (in Moscow) can send this news only in an official version, although he is well aware that in fact a much bigger proportion of the budget goes for military purposes. The Western press, following the news received from the correspondent, publishes the figure as 21 per cent, while the Communists' propaganda in various Western countries uses this fact as an argument against their own governments, accusing them of aggressive plans because their budgets provide 33 per cent or more for defense.

"Should, however, the correspondent say briefly that the Supreme Soviet has voted a new budget for all purposes, including military, without giving the 'official' figure, the Western press would have to return to this problem two or three days later and, when the Soviet papers had arrived, would be able to present the whole budget in the proper light by explaining the purposes of particular items in it."

Opinion on the propaganda element in the presentation of news about Russia is divided in practically all countries from which soundings have been taken for the purpose of this report. Many editors, correspondents and experts—the proportion rising perhaps as one moves nearer to the USSR—firmly believe that their readers are aware of the dangers and need no protection. A majority, however, maintain the contrary, holding that even those who believe themselves immune are being constantly affected by Russian propaganda. On this controversial point the editors must be allowed to speak for themselves:

The American View

Editors in the United States are generally concerned by the propaganda aspects of Soviet news, but all are not equally concerned. A Boston editor writes: "We can pretty well safeguard against the propaganda aspect of news coming from Russia by detecting it and identifying it as propaganda." His view is in sharp contrast to that of a southern editor: "Despite all safeguards, a lot of propaganda gets printed."

An editor of a Chicago daily sees the danger elsewhere. "As for handling 'news' from Communist sources," he writes, "very little is published and the American reader is suspicious of it from the start. There is ... no longer a problem of the deceived U. S. reader. On the contrary, so much of the 'news' from non-Communist sources about Russia ... is suspect and misleading, I think it's the bigger of the problems today."

The editor of another Chicago newspaper says that many readers do not understand the true nature of the Russian press and Russian censorship, but a Washington, D. C., editor contends that the job of indoctrinating readers in these facts has been thoroughly performed. An American correspondent says that the American reader of newspapers is a "sloppy" reader and therefore vulnerable to news from Moscow if presented in exactly the same manner as news from countries where censorship does not exist.

Like the editors in the United States, the editors consulted by the

Institute in the United Kingdom are divided in their views of the propaganda dangers in the presentation of news from Russia, but many British editors view them as a subject for concern. The editor of a London daily says: "I am convinced that at any rate in Britain, very few people indeed are aware of the appallingly onesided nature of any and every Communist statement. I believe this to be a real danger and it is one of the many reasons... I don't believe it is wise to keep correspondents behind the Iron Curtain."

A leading British editor writes: "Naturally, we are concerned... and it seems to me that the chief way in which the danger can be guarded against is by having men in the office—preferably men who have served in Russia—who can go carefully through all the material and pick out the substantial items of news." But one of his colleagues says: "From the point of view of the British public there is no need to worry about propaganda in news from Russia. The English public has a very secure knowledge of the value of sources, and if it knows where the thing comes from it usually works out whether it is right or wrong."

A British expert on the USSR writes: "All Soviet official news is propaganda. It is best not touched at all, except straight items like the death of Stalin or the meeting of the Supreme Soviet, unless there is someone sufficiently knowledgeable to sift it."

The Continental View

French editors and experts, like most of those in other countries on the European continent consulted by the Institute, tend to show less concern about any propaganda element in the presentation of Russian news. Of the French press, writes a French expert, "One sector is Communist and deals with the Soviet Union in a lyrical manner. Another is anti-Communist and publishes primarily the accounts of fugitives or accounts more often than not hostile... At times, even the anti-Communist newspapers present news in the form of propaganda.... Generally speaking, French editors do not know well enough the nature of Soviet institutions to append to the news editorial commentary which will bring out the significance of it."

The propaganda element in news of Russia, says an editor in Paris, begins in the choice of the news; the greatest responsibility belongs therefore to the news agencies. The editor of a provincial newspaper states that there is no reason to be alarmed about Soviet propaganda in the French press. "What is more dangerous," he says, "is the lack of documentation to permit an objective interpretation of news from the USSR." A writer on a Parisian paper says: "I believe that the French reader is sufficiently educated politically and, especially since 1940, too sensitive to the lies of various propagandas, to be easily the victim of the too primitive propaganda of the Russians."

This attitude is apparently shared by a majority of editors on the Continent consulted in the Institute's survey. A West German editor writes: "We are too skeptical toward Soviet propaganda to be alarmed by it." From Frankfurt come the judgments that "German opinion is immune" and that the propaganda in news from Russia is "not subtle enough to be effective." A Stuttgart editor says, however, that he is concerned about the propaganda danger and "we spare no effort to expose it whenever possible."

"The factor of alarm is unknown in this country," a Swiss editor writes. Another says "the free press reveals the Soviet point of view, but this propaganda which is tolerated does not represent a real danger." An editor in Vienna: "It is not the news from Russia which needs improvement so much as the comment on such news. Editors are far too inclined to believe in fairy tales and falsifications about Russia." Editors in the Scandinavian countries have a similar view, but observe that much material that is "straight propaganda" out of Moscow is thrown into their wastebaskets.

The Division Elsewhere

The division of opinion most plainly marked in the United States and Great Britain is apparent in a few replies received by the Institute from Latin America and the Pacific area. A Brazilian editor writes: "The reader is not conscious of the amount of propaganda in the news from Russia. In countries like ours, public opinion is not yet so . . . concerned with the subtleties of propaganda." An Australian editor says he is "extremely concerned" and regards it as one of his functions "to counter this propaganda wherever possible." A Japanese writes that "with the exception of a group of people with a leftist inclination, there is hardly any real danger in connection with such news."

The methods used by editors to define the nature of the news from Russia by presentation vary from somewhat mechanical expedients (italic precedes, bracketed inserts, "shirt-tails" and so forth) to major articles of comment and interpretation. Bracketed inserts add facts drawn by the editor from other sources of information, including previous news developments, and are intended to qualify a statement in the body of a dispatch that is either cryptic, obviously distorted or clothed in terms having a particular meaning in propaganda usage. Italic precedes and "shirt-tails" are sometimes used at the beginning or end of a dispatch for the same purpose, but more generally have the character of editorial notes.

The more mechanical devices lead to complications, since the USSR is not the only country to impose a censorship, and the editor who puts a "censored" label on all dispatches which have passed through censorship may find himself having to explain to his readers the differences between censorship in one country and in another. With the exception of a simple "slug" labelling a story "censored," the other more or less mechanical devices all find favor with some of the editors responding to the Institute's survey, and individual news agencies regularly add bracketed inserts to Moscow dispatches.

These devices are used on occasion even by the editors cited above who tend to believe their readers are immune to the propaganda element in dispatches from Russia. One such favors italic precedes, a second bracketed inserts, a third "editorial notes and editorial boxes." A French editor says he uses bracketed inserts only when presenting news "from a Russian source." A British editor with a correspondent recently in Moscow says he had no occasion to use italic precedes on the correspondent's reports "of a sidelight nature," but would use some such device on "an important story which warrants fuller information."

« Informed Analysis »

Finally, since the editor finds it impossible to do a straight news job in the coverage of the Soviet Union, articles of background and interpretation become principal means by which news about Russia, whether or not freighted with the implications of propaganda, can be put into understandable perspectives. Writing of the propaganda danger, a British editor says: "The only sound counter is objective informed analysis. ... It is part of the job of the experts to provide this setting."

An American expert on Soviet affairs concentrates the basic conclusions of the Institute's survey of the news from Russia in these words: "It seems to me—and I hesitate to say this because I am not a newspaper man—that part of the trouble with our coverage of Russia is a failure or lack of inclination to admit that the problem is fundamentally different from the usual one of getting the news. Time is not of the essence under the present circumstances. Interpretive reporting by specialists unhampered by censorship is of the essence."

CONCLUSION

By any traditional standard, the newspaper editor and his readers have no direct reporting of the Soviet Union at all. The tightening of censorship and other restrictions since 1946 have reduced the correspondent in Moscow to handling a very limited range of topics selected for him by Russian officials who consider him a potential or actual spy.

Other sources of information about Russia are also unsatisfactory. Reporters stationed in capitals on the periphery of the Soviet Union have access to additional information about shifts in Russian policies towards nearby satellites but to very little about the Soviet Union itself. The reports of refugees are of dubious value unless sifted by specialized agencies. The censored Russian press and radio are sources of information, but sources requiring the analysis of experts who are customarily not skilled in the techniques of journalism.

Lacking the sources by which he attempts to cover other major news centers, and not being an expert on Russia himself, the editor is confronted with an important problem of presentation. The occasional dispatch he receives from Moscow is completely misleading when he presents it in the traditional manner. For the necessary commentary and interpretation, he must revise, often, his own traditional approach to reporting and must ask the great news agencies to revise theirs.

These, in summary, are the opinions of the majority of those consulted by the International Press Institute on the main lines of an inquiry into the problem of the news from Russia.

The Basic Premise

The inquiry started from the premise that it is more important and more difficult for the press to give its readers an accurate and live picture of the USSR than of any other part of the world. The importance of this task can be taken for granted. It can also be assumed without argument that readers are really anxious to have information of this kind. The challenge to journalism is therefore plain and compelling.

This report is not concerned to allocate praise or blame but to present facts and judgments. The first fact which clearly emerges from the evidence supplied by the answers given to the IPI's questions is that the root of the problem lies in the Russian view of the proper functions of the press and of journalists, and the consequent Russian attitude to foreign correspondents. It is beyond the powers of editors, correspondents or experts to change any of this.

Nevertheless, so our evidence suggests, it is not beyond the powers of journalism to make better use of what is available. While "news" from Russia is scarce, information about Russia is not. The immediate problem therefore is how to devise methods and to train more persons to handle this information in such a way as to make it usable by editors and attractive to the general reader. The marriage of the expert and the journalist, the introduction into journalism of the attitudes and techniques of the intelligence officer and research worker—these are the most promising lines of development.

Next in importance to the problem of providing more information about the USSR, is the important problem of presentation. Although many editors and others discount the propaganda danger, many are gravely concerned lest their publication of stories from Moscow play into Communist hands or cloud the whole subject of the Soviet Union in an atmosphere of unreality. Even if accurate as far as they go, these stories may seriously mislead because of the gaps in the correspondents' coverage. Through articles of background and interpretation, the editor must fill those gaps or plainly indicate to his readers that they exist and cannot be filled, even by the expert.

Faced with the problem of covering a tremendously vital subject with very little help from its traditional operations, the press is challenged both in its sense of responsibility and its capacity for ingenuity.

IPI SURVEY No. III

The News
from the
Middle East

Published by
The International Press Institute
Zurich 1954

Printed for the International Press Institute
by Imprimerie Ganguin & Laubscher S. A., Montreux

CONTENTS

INTRODUCTION

When the International Press Institute conducted its large-scale inquiry into the flow of news in 1952-53,[1] editors in several countries said that one of the areas of the world from which they would welcome a better service of news was the Middle East.

The following study was accordingly undertaken to find out how adequate the existing coverage of that region was in the light of the special conditions governing reporting there. These conditions were summed up by Walton A. Cole, the editor of Reuters, in an address to IPI members in 1953 as "censorship, costs and communications."

As in its previous surveys of international press problems, the Institute has relied for critical judgments primarily on the press itself. The main basis of this report has been the answers to questions addressed to newspaper editors and foreign editors, newspaper and agency correspondents, agency executives and specialists on the area.

The period covered by this study is the year 1953 and the first part of 1954 against a general background of the years following the second world war.

Any study dealing with the Middle East must define its understanding of the geographical term. For this survey it was decided to regard the area as comprising the eight states of the Arab League— Egypt, Iraq, Jordan, Libya, Lebanon, Syria, Saudi Arabia and Yemen—the Sudan, Arabia as a whole, Iran and Israel. Turkey was excluded because, in spite of its close historical ties with the Arab world, the tendency in news coverage today is to link it with Europe rather than with the Middle East.

The Institute wishes to record its gratitude to the many newspapermen and specialists who, by the fullness and frankness of their information, made this study possible.

---

[1] The results were published in December 1953 under the title "The Flow of the News." The study examined the flow of news into and out of the United States, between Germany and seven other countries of Western Europe and between India and the West.

Chapter I

THE BACKGROUND

THE BACKGROUND

The reporter assigned to the Middle East takes on one of the physically largest beats in the world. He has over 2,000 miles to cover from North Africa in the West to Iran in the East and the same distance from the Turkish border in the North to Aden in the South. The area contains seven major Arab states (two of them almost inaccessible desert kingdoms), the Persian empire and a string of desert principalities and sheikdoms. On its fringes are two new states, Libya and the Sudan, on which he must keep a watchful eye. Israel, in the heart of the region, is normally a separate coverage problem because of the formal state of war still existing between it and its Arab neighbours.

Travel facilities, except in the Arab Peninsula, are comparatively good, especially by air, so that the correspondent can move about reasonably fast—if he has the necessary travel documents in order. Cable communications from most of the capitals to the West exist, though they are frequently interrupted for various reasons. Nevertheless, even if he has a clear field of travel and communication for his work, the man who intends to keep his jigsaw of the Middle East story up to date has to be extremely active in a climate which is often against energetic movement.

He must keep active mentally as well as physically. In Europe he usually has the knowledge of the language required and a well-developed local press to keep him informed of main developments. Further, there is normally sufficient in common between the way of life he is reporting and his own background for him to grasp situations quickly.

In the Middle East (at least outside Israel) these signposts are often faulty or missing. The great majority of correspondents there who are not nationals of the country they are reporting are from the West. They find themselves in a civilisation which has few points of contact with their own, working in an atmosphere which affects every story they touch. The absence of common denominators between East and West makes the Middle East story hard for a western correspondent to understand and even harder to communicate to his public at home.

In Western Europe or the United States a correspondent can reasonably be asked to interpret public opinion and trace the interplay between clear-cut political forces. In the Middle East public opinion is usually confined to an articulate minority in the towns and politics is an affair of personalities. In most of the countries the press is sufficiently developed to offer a rough guide but its standards are comparatively low. Since it is in Arabic (apart from a small, untypical European-language press) few correspondents can read it and, even if they could, they would have to be past masters in the art of reading between the lines to know what was going on. Since subsidies are a recognised source of newspaper revenue, the correspondent would also have to know who had paid for what.

But a correspondent is a determined man and gradually he sifts the mysteries of Middle East politics into an intelligible pattern. Then he finds that he has plunged so deeply into detail that the task of telling the story in the simple form required by his editor and readers baffles him. Tedium can overtake the reporting of a Middle East story as fast as any other story in the world, unless the theme is a riot or an assassination, and the interest of the reader outside the area is limited.

Finally, the reporter is up against the same problem as every other correspondent in the world—space in which to tell his story, not only when its own fire and colour carry it into the front page but also when the fire is damped down and his material is grey speculation. The number of newspapers that regard a Middle East dateline as ranking in importance with Washington or Paris or London is very small. Only a handful have the space and the type of readership to carry a Middle East story day in day out. So the run of the mill story, in which the correspondent might explain why leaders are shot and treaties broken, may get a reluctant paragraph if it is not killed completely.

It is, however, important that the Middle East story should be adequately reported. As the editor of a leading newspaper in India said : "The Middle East is obviously of great, and perhaps crucial, importance because the former apparent equilibrium of forces is giving way to a power vacuum at a time when both the strategic and commercial importance of the area seems to be growing."

Another knowledgeable observer said : "Many experts regard

the Middle East as the testing ground where the battle for the adherence of the under-developed nations of Africa and Asia to either the free world or the Soviet Union will be won or lost."

The Middle East is one of the world's main strategic hinges. It is the obvious military base between the West and the Far East. It is an enormous reservoir of oil, the source (until atomic energy overtakes it) of modern power. Two world wars this century have shown how vital a military priority is its defence. Between wars diplomatic manoeuvring for the friendship of its leaders or, failing that, for effective control of their foreign policies is unceasing. Therefore, any significant movement in the relations of the area with the rest of the world is headline news.

During the last half-century a new element has been blurring the simple lines of the strategic story. The rise of Arab nationalism and the complications induced by the parallel rise of Zionist nationalism have increasingly challenged the right of external powers to dictate foreign policy to the Middle East states. In the process new leaders have arisen and new forces been brought into play.

The change in the relations between the Middle East and the rest of the world was accelerated by the second world war. In the past ten years the area has changed so completely, both in mentality and in constitutional structure, that all who have interests there are having to adjust ideas and revise opinions.

The changes derive mainly from certain basic facts. The first is the achievement or near achievement of independence by Egypt, Iraq, Jordan, the Lebanon, Syria, Libya, the Sudan, Israel and Iran ; accompanied by the emergence from feudalism of the Arabian states, Saudi Arabia, Yemen and the Sheikdom of Kuwait.

In general, independence has caused the disappearance of all foreign executive control in Middle East governments ; it has created real (and artificial) Middle East public opinion by means of official propaganda in the press and broadcasting services, both of which are effectively controlled by the governments concerned ; and it has brought about in many countries the realisation of their power and importance as sovereign owners of the land where oil deposits lie or across which oil is piped.

The second major change has been the creation of the Arab League, comprising Egypt, Iraq, Jordan, the Lebanon, Syria, Saudi Arabia, Yemen and Libya. What the League says is getting worldwide publicity, which means that for the first time Arab aspirations and grievances are becoming known in many western countries which previously ignored them.

The third major change is the admission of almost all the newly independent Arab states to the United Nations. This has given them not only parity status, but also access to a hitherto inaccessible rostrum for the ventilation of their aspirations and grievances, particularly on Palestine. Further, membership of the United Nations has brought the Arab states into regular contact with other countries of the eastern world and the result has been the formation in the Assembly of what is known as the Arab-Asian bloc.

All these changes have put the Middle East, and the Arab world which is its heart, in a new position on the map of the world and have vastly increased the responsibilities of the representatives of the world press stationed in the Middle East to record day-to-day developments.

Before we come to examine performance in reporting Middle East news, however, it is necessary to look more closely at the restrictions under which the reporter of the Middle East is working. Unlike the task of reporting from the Soviet Union and the countries behind the Iron and Bamboo Curtains,[1] adverse conditions in the Middle East do not prevent full and critical reporting of the area. But the journey to a story and the dispatch of it to agency or newspaper desk often involve an obstacle race over hurdles put there by Middle East governments to prevent the story from being told. Further, once the story is in the paper, it may have unpleasant repercussions for the man who reported it.

Censorship in all its refinements, visa delays, difficulties of access to news and other restrictions are familiar parts of the Middle East defence mechanism against the unwelcome truth being told.

---

[1] See "The News from Russia" published by the International Press Institute, Zurich, October 1952.

Chapter II

PROBLEMS OF COVERAGE

PROBLEMS OF COVERAGE

A. Restrictions on Newsgathering

The following account of restrictions encountered in the Middle East is based entirely on reports from foreign correspondents with recent experience of working there. It should be noted that many of the general observations do not apply to Israel or countries, such as the Sudan, where British influence is still, or was until recently, predominant. Restrictions met with in Israel are mentioned specifically.

i. Censorship

Censorship in the Middle East is chiefly remarkable for its variability. It varies between country and country and from one time to another within the same country. It runs from complete formal censorship, with the censors sitting in the telegraph office openly checking messages, to absolutely blind controls of which the correspondent is not told. Correspondents agree that, if censorship must operate at all, the formal type is preferable. At least it gives them the opportunity to argue disputed points and possibly compromise on a change of wording ; once the text is agreed, they can fairly assume that transmission will not be delayed abnormally.

But censorship in the Middle East is usually of a more indirect and baffling type. It is exceptional for the authorities to issue a list of "stops" for the reporter's guidance. Often the decision is an absolute ruling by an individual censor to whom the correspondent has no access. Sometimes the ruling behind closed doors is so long delayed that the message is out of date when it arrives at its destination. From several countries correspondents reported occasional delays of up to 24 hours between the time a message was handed in and the time it left the telegraph office. One American who visited the area every year between 1945 and 1952 summed up the obstacles presented by blind censorship by saying : "My difficulties were about the same when there was no censorship. It seems that, with or without it, stories which thoroughly displease the local authorities are difficult to send abroad."

During the past ten years observers have detected, in the general purpose of Middle East censorship, a change which has increased the foreign correspondent's difficulties. They say that, before the Arab-Israeli war over Palestine, censorship was applied largely for local reasons ; the Arab governments were usually more concerned with preventing unfavourable news and comment from coming back into their territory than with stopping an outward message. But the Palestine war discredited the Arab leadership in the world and the various governments, while remaining sensitive to matter published within their countries, also became increasingly concerned about what was being said in the press abroad.

In the same period, however, another factor has tended to operate in the correspondent's favour. Sensibility to comment abroad starts by clamping on censorship, but often ends in relaxing it as outside criticism accumulates. The government concerned sometimes sees that, in spite of its controls, the unpleasant news is out and is being painted in even darker colours than the news deserves (because of the distortions induced by controls), so it decides to seek publicity for its viewpoint.

Experience has taught that "undesirable" news always does get out, usually quickly, thanks to a number of alternative news channels, official and unofficial. For example : when parts of Cairo were set on fire in January 1952, the news went out immediately by air to Rome, because an aircraft took off for there the same afternoon and at least one person aboard had been in Shepheard's Hotel when it was burned. At the same time, at least one correspondent was quickly off the mark with a dispatch which went by car to the Suez Canal Zone, whence it was radioed to London.

As a result, one contributor pointed out, "periods of strict external censorship have been shortlived and their effect on reporting from the area has not been so serious as in other countries with greater perseverance and less public sensibility."

An American agency executive confirmed this by saying : "As of now (December 1953) the censorship situation in the Middle East, outside Saudi Arabia and to a lesser degree Iraq, has been greatly improved."

Nevertheless, the constantly changing pattern of censorship controls — telegraphic, telephonic, postal and photographic — is agreed by correspondents to be an irritating handicap to working in the Middle East, especially on major stories.

Before giving a sketch, country by country, of how censorship has operated in recent years, something must be said of internal press censorship. Although this is not a primary concern of this study, its effects on the foreign correspondent's work must be considered since one of his normal sources of information is the local press.

Most Middle East countries have been subject to internal censorship since 1939 and the intervals since then when local newspapers could be regarded as free have been rare and brief. Once the world war was over, the Arab war with Israel from 1948 onwards was considered as justification for continuing and tightening controls, and, as hostilities and political crises continued to flare up between the two sides, censorship followed suit.

Internal press censorship is usually much more strict than the control on foreign correspondents. There are special reasons for this. First, much of the local press is inclined to behave irresponsibly and invite control.[1] Secondly, most of the countries are undergoing a period of revolutionary change, and democracy, in spite of the outward forms of some administrations, is still far from being firmly established. Even when there is strong attachment to the theoretical virtues of democracy, the existence of vast numbers of illiterates among the population makes its practice difficult. So censorship tends to be used over the political and economic field very much as the Red Indian uses a blanket over a smoky fire—to send out and suppress news according to the government's views on it.

Thus, students' demonstrations, factory strikes, political arrests and official inquiries may take place with no more than a cryptic reference to them in the local press.

Egypt

Censorship in Egypt, as in other Middle East countries, was a legacy from the second world war. After the war it was allowed to run down, but when the Palestine war broke out in May 1948 it was reinstated and has continued more or less in force ever since, although

---

[1] A French contributor commented: "Excessively harsh censorship in Egypt has been followed, during the brief periods when it was lifted, by excessively violent language in the press. During these periods the press has gone to the lengths of public exhortation to murder."

its severity has varied considerably. Often it has required only a change in the chief censor to tighten or relax it. One of the principal difficulties for the foreign correspondent springs from the fact that its regulations have seldom been codified, with the result that each censor has tended to act according to what he thinks a correspondent should write or what the government in power might like him to write.

A British correspondent commented: "Most journalists keep a constant check on the authorities to discover their attitude to news owing to the rapid changes that occur. One difficulty is that uncertainty affects the censors also and makes them super-cautious."

A particular complaint against Egyptian censorship concerns its vagueness. An American correspondent reported: "I had maddening difficulty with Egyptian censors during the second half of 1948. They were so ill-informed that they did not know and could not conceive what information was general knowledge in the world. They had no published list of 'stops' and they refused to tell correspondents what cuts they had made, so that there was no possibility of argument or alternative phrasing. Although the censorship was ostensibly military, the real aim was apparently to cut out whatever seemed displeasing to Egypt. In one case a 1500-word dispatch of mine arrived with only about 200 words left, but I did not know until my office cabled me."

During the Palestine war censorship was used in an attempt to prevent anything but laudatory and victorious news from getting out, and it was so tight that correspondents in Egypt were not even allowed to depart from the exact wording of the war communiqués, although the true progress of the war was being reported factually by correspondents elsewhere and was also available in foreign governments' reports.

The censorship was so strict that it was made mandatory for all messages leaving Egypt, whether they referred to the Palestine war or not. It was a considerable irritation to correspondents because of irreparable delays in transmission and urgent calls to police headquarters to explain elementary press cablese. One correspondent spoke of his surprise at finding a story filed during this period still held up a week later, even though its subject was an Australian beauty queen's return home to fight a divorce case.

Subsequently the Israeli question declined in importance as a censorship matter until today correspondents report that it obtrudes very little. Meanwhile, however, censorship on news of internal affairs had become increasingly severe and during 1949 censors were placed in all newspapers and in the news agency offices. They remained there until late 1950. Censors were put back into newspaper offices early in 1952, when martial law was imposed after the burning of Cairo. Internal censorship was lifted again on March 7, 1954, for three weeks, being restored on March 29.

Although censors were withdrawn from agency offices late in 1950 and did not return, censorship on outgoing news remained until the advent of the military régime under General Neguib in July 1952.

Throughout the confused political period of the years preceding the Neguib coup d'état it was extremely difficult to know exactly what was subject to censorship beyond the fact that Palace news had to be submitted to the Palace and news about the armed forces was virtually banned.

By law any reference to King Farouk had to be passed by the Minister of the Interior, who apparently had standing instructions to cut out not only any unfavourable reference to the Crown but also any news about the role of the King in politics. Since Egyptian news at that time revolved round the struggle between Farouk and the Wafd Party, censorship made it hard for correspondents to tell anything but a lopsided story.

Although there was no appeal from the censor's ruling, most correspondents tackled the problem by taking their dispatches to censorship and arguing debatable points personally when they were allowed. This paid because the severity of censorship varied with the man on duty. There were occasions when a news message which passed in the morning was stopped when presented by another correspondent in the afternoon.

In theory censorship was eased when the Wafd returned to power in 1950, but in practice it was maintained to protect the interests of the Wafd and the Palace. The difficulty of knowing what could be sent was illustrated by one case in which the Foreign Minister issued a statement for dispatch abroad to an agency and the censor stopped it for reference to the Minister of the Interior, who confirmed the 'stop.'

In the autumn of 1951 censorship reached a peak of arbitrariness during the troubles in the Suez Canal Zone, when the censors began to *write additions* into dispatches and make "corrections." The correspondent who reported this said that it was smoothly done and where possible the effect was achieved by elimination.

For example : Serag el Din, then Minister of the Interior, announced that one million people had marched in an anti-British demonstration. Correspondents' own estimates varied between 150,000 and 400,000, but they dutifully carried the official estimate in addition to their own in their dispatches. The censor either cut out the correspondent's own estimate and left in that of the Minister or went further and eliminated the point that one million was an official estimate, thus making it appear to be the correspondent's own figure. Again, the correspondent of a New York newspaper estimated in one dispatch that the number of British military personnel in the Canal Zone was double the number permitted by the Anglo-Egyptian Treaty. The censor changed it to ten times the number.

Censorship pursued its arbitrary and incalculable course into 1952 when the burning of Cairo in January produced a complete 'stop' for some days (which, as was pointed out on page 16, was unsuccessful).

In the weeks immediately before the Neguib coup censorship reflected the political uncertainty of the situation by becoming completely wild. When the military acted in July 1952, the first building to be occupied by the army was Marconi House in Cairo, which housed the state broadcasting station, the cable office and the censors, and a military censorship was instituted, but it worked badly owing to shortage of staff and inexperience.

In August 1952, with the Ali Maher government installed in power under the aegis of the Council of the Revolution, the Egyptian authorities felt strong enough to fulfil their promise to free the press, but whatever the official position real freedom did not last long. Correspondents reported that for three days only were they exempt from censorship and even during that period officials reading their cables began to discuss openly the desirability of clamping down again. Thereafter they were forbidden to mention that there was any censorship on the ground that it did not exist and they were not required to revert to the practice of filing their messages in duplicate, but their dispatches were being closely scrutinised.

It was during this period of official freedom (in August 1952) that a French correspondent recorded the following experience. He obtained a signed interview with General Neguib, but it was cut by the censor in Cairo on the ground that certain passages revealed military secrets, others might have an adverse effect on the national morale and still others might displease certain Egyptian leaders. When the correspondent argued that the text had been signed by the

General and checked by his staff, the censor refused to budge, especially on one point. "Some passages here," he said, "are damaging to Nahas Pasha (leader of the Wafd). If one day he returns to power, it will not be Neguib who will suffer for this dispatch, but myself."

Nevertheless, the controls were beginning to ease, presumably because the new Egyptian régime found that it was receiving a comparatively good press abroad. Writing of this period, another correspondent said that it was only during the immediate aftermath of the coup d'état that he had any real difficulty, but added : "I must admit that I sent some fairly critical material at that time without stoppage."

Official external censorship did not return until January 1953, when rumours of an attempted counter-coup against General Neguib brought it back and it flourished in full official severity for three days. Nevertheless, the government tried to soften the blow by informing foreign correspondents that they would "continue to enjoy full liberty and be told of deletions from messages, if any."

The ban failed to do more than delay the news and resulted in some distorted versions of the story getting out of the country, and one correspondent was of the opinion that it was experience in this affair which encouraged the Neguib régime to end censorship on outgoing and incoming news.

At all events, early in July 1953 the government announced the official end of all restrictions on outgoing and incoming messages on the ground that "it had nothing to hide and nothing to fear." It was believed by correspondents that the decision was taken because of the intention of inviting some seventy foreign journalists to attend the first anniversary celebrations of the régime later the same month.

Since then, there has been no apparent external censorship operating in Egypt. Correspondents who filed news criticising the régime reported that they found themselves somewhat unpopular with the leadership, but no attempt was made to stop them from working. One correspondent, however, while agreeing that "you can file what you like," added the cynical proviso, "for the moment. That does not mean that if a serious crisis arises, the present régime is not going to sit on the cables."

This, in effect, was what happened during the crisis over General Neguib's position in February 1954. Whereas the national press had remained under censorship, foreign press messages were not formally subject to censorship. A correspondent covering the story, however, stated that in the early stages cables could not be dispatched abroad because of "technical difficulties" affecting both cable and telephone services. The effect, in the experience of one agency in Europe, was to delay the arrival of cables from six to nine hours.

Censorship can adopt more subtle forms than the straightforward blue pencil. Several correspondents were of the opinion that, while restrictions were operating in Egypt, the country ran a close second to Iran in its capacity to muzzle. "For example," said one, "correspondents found themselves explaining to the Egyptian Foreign Office why they had written certain things that did not agree with the Egyptian version of the story. I was once told by officialdom that they could find no inaccuracy in my story, but it was not the way they would have presented the case."

On occasions during the past ten years post-censorship in Egypt has gone to the lengths of expelling foreign correspondents for what they have written. In 1946 the *Chicago Tribune*'s Middle East reporter Alex Small was expelled *in absentia*. In 1948 the Cairo office of *Time* magazine was closed and the *Time* and *Life* correspondents, Don Burke and Manfred Gottfried, were given seven days to leave. In 1951 a Swiss correspondent Kurt Emmenegger was expelled and the Associated Press correspondent Fred Zusy was ordered out, but in his case the order was cancelled.

Correspondents' hazards increased during the early months of the régime of the Council of the Revolution, no doubt due to the Council's nervousness about a counter-coup. In August 1952 a French correspondent Roger Vailland was arrested and held for several days. In October of the same year a wide roundup of newspapermen in Cairo brought a British newspaper correspondent, Alan McGregor, who also worked for a local paper, and the representatives of *The New York Times* and the London *Daily Express* into the net for questioning. In May 1953 the Cairo correspondent of the London *Jewish Chronicle*, Jacques Maleh, was expelled. [1]

Syria

Correspondents agreed with a colleague who described censorship in Syria as "absolute and unthinking." Real difficulty was said to

---

[1] For further details of these cases see Appendix B.

date from the coup d'état of the late Hosni Zaim in 1949. Before that Syria was not reckoned to be a hard country to work from except on the Palestine issue. During 1948 the authorities showed themselves extremely sensitive on all matters concerning the Jews and Israel— so sensitive that a Syrian-born American who returned to Syria was reportedly jailed for distributing tracts of the British Israelite Society.

In June 1949, national sensibility reached such a pitch that, according to a correspondent, a paragraph consisting of a violent attack on the Prime Minister of Iraq was written into an agency dispatch after it had gone to the telegraph office.

Correspondents, however, pointed out that the proximity of other Arab capitals made censorship in Damascus (which is unofficial) nothing but an irritation.[1] Measures to keep a check on correspondents, such as passing a copy of each dispatch to the *deuxième bureau* and the insistence on a Syrian press card for filing, do not mean a great deal when Beirut is 2 ½ hours away by taxi and Amman 4 ½ hours. Short of an exhaustive body and car search of every traveller leaving Syria, censorship can achieve little.

Iraq

Censorship is described by correspondents as "incalculable." It can be extremely lax or severe and vary from week to week. One American correspondent summed up its effects as "something that had to be adjusted to but did not generally stop the flow of legitimate news."

Another said : "In Iraq you can generally file what you like, but when things get hot they clamp the lid on. During the coronation of Feisal II in May 1953, *The New York Times* and Associated Press had transmission delays of up to 48 hours. The reason ? The censor was trying to trace a Turk who had filed that a bomb had been placed

---

[1] Controls, however, have been more than an irritant for the Syrian press. Proof that the régime does not have to be a military dictatorship to muzzle the press was provided after the fall of the Shishakly government early in 1954. In May the new Parliament passed a press law providing heavy sanctions against publications supporting anti-constitutional or disobedience movements and leaving the authorities wide discretion in deciding what was an offence. The requirement that every publisher must obtain a new licence for his newspaper made possible the suppression of an opposition press. This political censorship inevitably reacted on the task of the foreign correspondent trying to cover Syria.

near Feisal's palace. Consequently he was not available to do his blue pencil work."

On September 23, 1953, the new government of Fadel al Jawali announced the abolition of censorship of outgoing press cables.

Jordan

In the days of King Abdullah, censorship was largely dictated by the Palace. It concentrated mainly on news concerning Palestine affairs and Israel, security questions and the Palace itself. It was usually not very severe for a visiting correspondent but bore down heavily on residents, particularly local correspondents and stringers, making it hard for them to file dispatches critical of the régime.

An American correspondent who was reporting from Jordan in 1950 described the authorities there as "very sensitive but fair." He explained : "They sometimes made deletions but advised the correspondent before the copy was cleared. One example of Arab sensibilities was the deletion from a Christmas story, during the Palestine war, of a reference to the fact that Bethlehem had been cleared of Egyptian troops. The reason ? Egyptian and Arab Legion troops were constantly quarrelling and the authorities wanted Bethlehem quiet on Christmas day." There was, however, an interesting sequel. The reporter was allowed to take his story across the lines into Israel "because filing facilities were better there." "I was placed on my honour by the Arabs," he said, "not to add the things I had been forbidden to mention."

Correspondents who visited the country in 1953 reported that Amman post office required copy to be filed in triplicate. One correspondent described the censorship as "incalculable but not very stringent." Another said that he had messages held up occasionally, particularly on matters of Jordan-Israeli relations.

Lebanon

For most correspondents Beirut, capital of Lebanon, is a "free port" for the filing of dispatches and few reported any difficulties. There was, however, restriction during the Palestine war and also toward the end of the Bishara el Khoury régime in 1952. As the régime came under increasing criticism abroad for corruption, pressure on correspondents tightened. There seemed to be no particular rules except that censors opposed dispatches "damaging to the Lebanon's good reputation." Of more recent conditions a correspondent commented : "Lebanon still gets touchy when internal affairs are going badly. Then you will generally get a two-hour stop, after which they will release everything unread. This happened in December 1953, when an officer junta was suspected of trying to overthrow the government."

Saudi Arabia and Yemen

Since very few correspondents visit Saudi Arabia, the question of censorship hardly arises. Indeed, one correspondent who went there was under the impression that the only way to file was via Bahrein Island. There are, however, filing facilities from Jedda. The local press is reported to be rigidly controlled and the government to be extremely sensitive to criticism from abroad.

Even fewer correspondents have visited Yemen and nobody reported trying to file from there.

Persian Gulf

No instances of censorship were reported from Bahrein or Kuwait.

Sudan

There has been no censorship in the Sudan.

Iran

Most correspondents regard Iran as the blackest spot in the area from which to move copy. This is largely because interference takes every other form except direct censorship and often leads to more drastic results than cuts in dispatches. Iranian discouragement of news which the government does not like operates on the "loose board" principle. A correspondent meets with official coldness and polite menaces but continues to get his stories over, until one day, out of the blue, comes a call before authority and he is given a few hours to clear out.

Iran bases its drastic action against correspondents on the article in the convention of the International Telecommunication Union [1] by which members reserve the right to stop any communication which appears dangerous to the security of the state or contrary to its laws or to public order and decency. In November 1952 the Governor of Teheran announced that in future correspondents must accept the consequences of what they filed.

Between the moment when the authorities indicate that a correspondent is following a line which they do not like and the day when he is summoned for expulsion, there are many degrees of veiled intimidation. One correspondent reports that "stories were sometimes read aloud at press conferences (with suitable inflections) with the intention of embarrassing the correspondents who filed them." Another said : "I was warned once or twice to be 'nicer' to the Mossadegh régime in my copy, though nothing was ever stopped." A third reported : "Iran had a clever way of pretexting atmospheric difficulties in transmission whenever a story did not coincide entirely with the official version."

A fourth correspondent, who was expelled, said : "One of the troubles was that a correspondent never knew whether, or when, to take official threats seriously. Dr. Hussein Fatemi, Dr. Mossadegh's assistant, threatened to stop any news message which he considered 'unfriendly,' but I never knew of any of my own dispatches failing to get through. His threat, however, served as indirect censorship on Iranian stringers of foreign newspaper and agencies ... I thought I had overcome the difficulties—till I was kicked out."

The experience of Michael Clark, the *New York Times* correspondent expelled from Iran in December 1951, was typical. Clark told the story in his newspaper's house magazine *Times Talk*.

During a riot in Teheran, in which Dimitri Caplanoglu, correspondent of the Athenian newspaper *Eleftheria*, had been beaten to the ground and bayonetted, because he had a camera, and a conservative newspaper had its offices wrecked with impunity, Clark went

---

1 Article 29 of the International Telecommunication Convention (Atlantic City, 1947) states that :

1. Members and Associate Members reserve the right to stop the transmission of any private telegram which may appear dangerous to the security of the State or contrary to their laws, to public order or to decency, provided that they immediately notify the office of origin of the stoppage of any such telegram or any part thereof, except when such notification may appear dangerous to the security of the State.

2. Members and Associate Members also reserve the right to cut off any private telephone or telegraph communication which may appear dangerous to the security of the State or contrary to their laws, to public order or to decency.

along to Dr. Fatemi's daily press conference "to ask a few questions."

"I was told that Dr. Fatemi wanted to see me in his private office," wrote Clark. "Entering, I found the man in a tantrum. He brandished a clipping from *The New York Times*. It was a dispatch I had filed a few days before, describing the atmosphere of terror that prevailed in Iran. Dr. Fatemi asked if I had written the piece. When I acknowledged that I had, he launched into a tirade in French from which I gathered that I had insulted the government, was an agent of the 'former Anglo-Iranian Oil Company' and had 48 hours to leave the country.

" 'My dear doctor,' I said, 'Do you really accuse me of being an agent of the Anglo-Iranian Oil Company ? ' With a magnificent flourish, reminiscent of Emile Zola, he pointed his finger at me and snapped, 'Oui, j'accuse.'

"As soon as I could get another word in, I suggested that the day's events had perhaps confirmed points I had made in the article. The remark was not a judicious one. It only made the good doctor more furious. I thereupon took leave...

"My first concern was to inform the United States Embassy... Within a half-hour Ambassador Loy Henderson was remonstrating with Premier Mossadegh himself. The Ambassador urged the Premier to cancel the expulsion order and make use of his right of denial and rectification if he thought my piece was at variance with the truth ... but Mossadegh was adamant. He held that I was guilty of criminal libel. He said that I might remain in Iran on one of two conditions. The Ambassador might himself issue a public statement repudiating my article or else I would have to publish a formal retraction. Mr. Henderson rejected both conditions and the interview was at an end.

"Later a police lieutenant came to the Ritz Hotel where I kept a room which I used as an office. With utmost politeness he escorted me to the Prefecture of Police. There, he cancelled my residence permit and issued an exit visa valid for 48 hours."

Clark was the third correspondent to be ordered out during 1951, Haig Nicholson of Reuters and Sefton Delmer of the London *Daily Express* having been expelled in June of that year. By the end of January 1954, ten correspondents in all had been ordered out and one stringer had been sent to jail since the beginning of 1951.[1] The

---

[1] The full list is given in Appendix B.

charges on which decisions to expel correspondents were taken were usually of the vaguest. They were summed up in the indictment against Marc Purdue, the Associated Press correspondent expelled in May 1953—"the reporting of false and provocative news against the interests of Iran."

The change of government from Dr. Mossadegh to General Zahedi in August 1953 did not relieve correspondents from the fear of expulsion, although a British correspondent who had experienced considerable difficulty with the Mossadegh régime reported a marked change for the better under Premier Zahedi.

Nevertheless, David Walker, of the London *News Chronicle,* was ordered out in October 1953 and the AFP correspondent Gaston Fournier was expelled in February 1954.

M. Fournier gave a personal account of his expulsion which shows close parallels with the experiences of Mr. Clark. "Two years of representing the AFP in Iran, after three in Prague, had made me sufficiently philosophical not to be too much surprised when two policemen arrived at my home in Teheran on January 24 and asked me to go with them," wrote M. Fournier. "I was in bed with pneumonia and objected, but they insisted. I asked that at least the French consul should go with me to the security chief's office to which I had been called.

"The security chief asked me if it was true that I had sent to my agency, three days before, a message describing incidents during the elections at Abadan. It was true and I pointed out that the news had also been published by the two leading newspapers in Teheran. I added that the Persian press was under the complete control of the government, which indicated that the news was true ; that I had confirmed my own information, for which I accepted full responsibility ; and that I would not reveal the names of my Persian informants.

"After a telephone call to General Zahedi, I was informed that I was being expelled and must leave Iran within forty-eight hours. Later an interview with the chief of police secured a delay, on grounds of my health, sufficient to enable my agency to send somebody to take over from me. This extension was confirmed to the French Ambassador, who had been asked by the French Government to make an energetic protest, but, two days later, three policemen appeared at my home to try to frighten me into leaving immediately.

"When I told them that I was ill, that a 'reasonable' extension had been promised, that, if they insisted, I should inform my press colleagues in Teheran, including the photographers, and that I should leave only in pyjamas, à la Mossadegh, they went away again.

"In an interview with General Farzanegan, who holds the curious combination of the positions of Minister of Propaganda and Minister of Posts and Telegraphs, I asked him to reverse a decision which could only reflect on him. He said that my dispatches had been lacking in objectivity but could not give me a single example.

"I replied that, on the contrary, it was his strict and illegal censorship of the press — and in particular his habits of interfering with postal secrecy and examining foreign reporters' messages handed in for dispatch — which had always forced me to give a more complimentary picture of events in Iran than was justified. He refused to change the expulsion order, but seemed very nervous about the possibility of my writing, once I was out of the country, what I had been prevented from saying while I was in it.

"A final bit of pettiness took place during my departure on February 18. Realising that this time I had no consular official with me, the airport authorities ordered the customs to carry out a detailed examination of my luggage and my papers, as well as those of my wife. This took nearly one hour and in the course of it I had to go to a search room. I was afraid that I was being made the victim of a careful police 'frame up' ; but it was only an effort to humiliate me and I was allowed to catch the plane.

"One remark, made by General Farzanegan to an Iranian journalist who represents a foreign news agency in Teheran, indicates the impossibility of reporting events in Iran fully and accurately. During a press conference the general said to him : 'Between you and prison is the same distance as between my telephone and the office of the chief of the police'."

Israel

Military censorship has operated in Israel ever since the birth of the new state in 1948 because she has been technically or actually at war with her Arab neighbours throughout her short life. All outgoing copy must be submitted to the censors at the public information offices in Tel Aviv or Jerusalem. They stamp the copy and it passes automatically to the dispatch office unless something is to be censored, in which case the correspondent is consulted.

Military censorship was said to be severe while major hostilities were on and while the new state was finding its feet. Some correspondents said that censorship was not always purely military. "Israel," said one, "had economic censorship then as well and at one point would not allow a correspondent to quote even the exchange rate of the Israeli pound. The airlift of the Yemeni Jews from Aden to Israel was kept secret for months."

The end of the shooting war brought a marked change. "Journalists were given every possible facility," said one. "The press setup was excellent," reported another. "Censors are anxious to help correspondents to move everything possible."

One correspondent said that during two years in Israel (1951-53) he did not think that his copy had been cut more than four or five times ; the cuts were irritating but "not grounds for serious complaint."

On the other hand, another correspondent thought that indirect censorship by pressure and non-cooperation did have an effect, particularly on local correspondents of foreign newspapers and agencies. The local papers are also subject to censorship, being required to submit all copy that might be questionable. Items are frequently cut from the extreme left wing or right wing press, according to one informant, who thought that local press censorship did slip over into political matters.

The effect of moral pressure was indicated by the experience of an American correspondent. During the winter of 1950-51, he reported a sit-down strike of 140 Jews from India who demanded and eventually succeeded in obtaining repatriation. The story was extremely embarrassing to the Jewish Agency and this correspondent declared that he was the only one who covered the story fully. There was, however, no censorship of his story.

Photographic Censorship

Correspondents interested in photography complain bitterly of the rigid restrictions against taking pictures existing in several countries. "There is one difficulty," wrote a Swiss correspondent, "of which one can never speak enough—the trouble given to photographers.

"I refer not to the natural hostility of the people, but to the total lack of comprehension of government officials on the subject. It is forbidden to photograph what is generally known as 'the picturesque.' An ass by the roadside near Damascus, a little girl in Syrian costume— they are taboo. Despite a special request to picture the life of the people of the Holy Places in Arab Jerusalem, I was allowed to photograph only the buildings, not the people."

Another European correspondent confirmed that the ban on photography in Syria was rigid and that even an official promise that it would be relaxed was not kept. The ban is equally stringent in Jordan. In Iraq the same correspondent found an official ban on photography, but an appeal for its relaxation met with success.

Contributors suggested two reasons for this ban. One is that representation of human beings is against the Islamic code. The other is that the authorities are not anxious to have certain aspects of life in their countries emphasized in the press abroad, even if they make picturesque material.

ii. Visa and Travel Difficulties

Many correspondents rate the drawbacks of travel restrictions as a greater obstacle to efficient reporting than censorship.

It is undeniable that the coverage of spot news on major stories has often been spoiled by the delays with which correspondents have met in securing visas either to leave or enter Middle East countries. These delays result in the first, most important, coverage being given by stringers, whose work is naturally less satisfactory than that of the chief correspondent. (The calibre of local correspondents and stringers is discussed in greater detail on pages 82-84.)

Egypt, Iraq, Lebanon, Syria and Saudi Arabia, as well as Iran, insist on exit visas, though in most cases it is not normally difficult to obtain them quickly. Nevertheless, "quickly" may mean a day wasted on a spot news story and in Iran, correspondents reported, an exit visa could take "days and days."

Entry visas may also take a considerable time, as many Middle East consulates abroad issue them only after consultation with their capital. A French correspondent, who travels to the area frequently, rated the delays as follows : Egypt, Lebanon, Israel—immediate ; Iraq, Jordan, Syria—after reference to the capital, five to ten days ; Iran—after reference, three weeks ; Saudi Arabia—issued only exceptionally.

Correspondents have a special, and legitimate, grievance on the travel question in that they find that the word "journalist" or "correspondent" or even "editor" on a passport means a delay in clearing their visa which other travellers do not have to suffer. The reason for the reference back to the appropriate foreign office is that most of them have "black lists" of correspondents. Often, correspondents report, the entry on an Arab black list is due to a vague charge of "pro-Zionist reporting in the Palestine war." Since newspapers as well as individual correspondents figure on the black lists, a correspondent may find the alleged sins of a predecessor visited upon him.

"The nationality of the applicant figures importantly in the granting of visas," said an agency chief. "Experience has shown that visas are usually quickly forthcoming for nationals of countries whose support is deemed necessary."

An additional cause of delay is that some countries, like Syria and Jordan, ask for a certificate of the intending visitor's religion, even though, once it is obtained, it may never be referred to.

The degree of difficulty experienced differed from correspondent to correspondent. One commented : "Visas are a real bore but no obstacle except to speed." Another said : "Visa blocks are too whimsical to be overcome by any single approach—one needs luck, friends and hours and hours of time." A third reported : "Getting visas to any Arab country is a matter of knowing someone in power there who will expedite the visa or of softsoaping the local Embassy. If you insist daily and spend money freely on cables to officialdom, you can cut down the time taken. For a correspondent who has been in the country before, a favourable travel article or an innocuous colour piece sent to the right persons also helps to get him in."

The use of the visa as a form of pressure on the foreign correspondent, however, was commented on by several reporters. "In Egypt you may find," said one, "that the ordinarily simple matter of extending your visa becomes a major project requiring many visits to the Foreign Office where you are subjected to long waits and pointed innuendo, if you have offended by your reporting." In 1948 the reason given for refusing an Egyptian visa to an Overseas News Agency correspondent, Richard Mowrer, was that Egypt disapproved of the editorial policy of two newspapers which published his dispatches. Another correspondent said : "The use of the visa as a form of pressure varies. It operates more effectively, of course, against the resident correspondent."

Special difficulties were reported from individual countries as follows.

Iraq : "I have had difficulties only in Iraq," said one correspondent. "The issue of my visa was delayed two months because the Iraqis in Cairo insisted on consulting Baghdad." "I have had some trouble with Iraq," said another. "For instance, I was unable to get an Iraqi visa in Teheran in 1951, whereas I got one without difficulty in Cairo at the beginning of 1953."

For some reason which was never explained, two American correspondents representing the same newspaper were barred from Iraq for months during 1951. They were never actually told of any ban against them ; they just could not get visas.

Syria : "The practice of demanding an exit visa is maddening," said a correspondent. "Once, when I was in transit through Damascus from Teheran to Beirut, I had to get an exit visa in Damascus." "On one occasion," says another, "my passport was taken from me for the three days I spent in Palmyra."

"The Syrians insisted on consulting Damascus before giving me a visa," reported a third. "Apparently, however, they overlooked the fact that I was expelled from Syria in 1948 because of the allegedly pro-Zionist nature of my dispatches. (The expulsion order was withdrawn after intervention by my legation.)"

Saudi Arabia and Yemen : Foreign correspondents are rarely admitted and all applications for Saudi Arabia have to be referred to Riyadh, usually involving a long delay. Visas are restricted to entry at one particular point—usually either Dhahran or Jedda. Exit visas are also required. The difficulties are increased because, according to one correspondent, "Saudi Arabia has an enormous black list."

Another correspondent reported : "Saudi Arabia and Yemen are the worst for travel permits. They are quite irresponsible and inefficient, with little shame about their exclusionist practices." Another commented : "The normal route into Saudi Arabia was through Aramco (the Arabian American Oil Company), but after they had trouble over oil royalties, even that opening became difficult."

"Yemen is impossible," said a third. "Don't believe anyone at the United Nations or an Arab League meeting who invites you to Yemen. When you arrive at the border by arrangement, the authorities have never heard of you or of the man who invited you."

Iran : "The only way to get an Iranian visa is to have your diplomatic mission in Teheran push one through for you—unless you have a local stringer to help," wrote a correspondent. "The Iranian Foreign Office has to instruct the Legation to issue your visa. Though I have had some 30 visas, I have had to go through the same procedure each time."

"I was in Iran during the visit of the Stokes mission on the oil question," reported another correspondent. "Since then I have twice tried to return. First I waited three weeks in Delhi before I got a refusal. Then I applied later from London and received no reply at all."

Another said : "Iran was always difficult in the visa department. If they dislike your copy, it is almost impossible to re-enter the country. On my second trip to Teheran I was denied a visa out of Egypt and got to Iran only by taking a plane for India and leaving the aircraft in Teheran. This caused some trouble with the authorities, but at least I was in the country."

Arab-Israeli Travel Embargo

There is one further serious obstacle to travel and that is the official impossibility of moving between Israel and the Arab countries because the Arab governments observe the Arab League rule that people with Israeli visas on their passports cannot enter an Arab country. Indeed, one correspondent said : "The worst difficulty is the inability to move from the Arab States into Israel along highways or by train."

The rule, like so many others, is not strictly applied in all cases. A correspondent may enter an Arab country even if it is known that he has visited Israel, provided he has no Israeli visa in his passport. Nevertheless, the bar makes it impossible for the same correspondent to cover both Israel and the Arab world regularly and correspondents say that this inability to compare conditions on both sides of the Israeli frontier inevitably affects balanced impartial coverage of the Middle East.

The usual way of overcoming the barrier is to fly to Cyprus and obtain a visa for Israel on a separate sheet of paper—a manœuvre which is readily accepted in Israel. Visas to travel to Israel are said to be obtained without difficulty although one European correspondent reported difficulty at some Israeli legations.

Apart from the difficulties of moving backwards and forwards over the Arab-Israeli frontiers, a further restriction is imposed on movement in the military zones on either side of the frontiers, for which special permits are necessary. Correspondents in Israel reported little difficulty on their side of the frontier, but on the Arab side official reluctance to allow some correspondents to enter the frontier zone was said to be "very harmful to good coverage."

One correspondent pointed out that the real loser is the Arab. For example, after the Quibya incident in October 1953, when 42 Arab villagers were killed in an organized Israeli raid across the frontier into Jordan, correspondents reported great difficulty in obtaining permission to visit the area, and photographers in particular could not get out timely pictures of a story whose effect was to create sympathy for the Arabs in their dispute with Israel.

Difficulties in moving about within other countries were also reported by correspondents. One said that he found it very difficult to get into Eastern Syria towards the river Euphrates as the region was said to be of military interest. In Jordan, areas in which the Arab Legion carries out its manœuvres are generally prohibited.

In Iran, during the oil dispute, Abadan was placed under martial law and a correspondent who wanted to go there from Teheran had to obtain a special permit renewable at short intervals. One correspondent said that it was very difficult to get such a travel pass and another reported that its grant depended on whether the Iranian authorities were satisfied with the line taken in a correspondent's dispatches. Another correspondent reported that a special travel permit was necessary to go anywhere outside a 50-mile radius from Teheran and generally the permit took a week to obtain.

In Saudi Arabia the few correspondents who have been there found it impossible to move away from their point of entry.

In summary, the consensus of correspondents' opinion on visa and general travel difficulties in the Middle East (outside Israel) amounted to this. If a correspondent has time to waste, he can usually get into any Middle East country, provided he does not figure on the current black list, although Saudi Arabia and Yemen present special problems. Once inside a country, he may find his movements restricted and his time taken up by efforts to cope with the problem of getting out again. He will have the least trouble in Egypt and

Lebanon and the countries under British influence ; in Iran and Iraq, he may meet with the maximum delays. But in all cases, much depends on individual contacts and luck, since efforts to hold up travel and even black lists are haphazard and arbitrary.

iii. Access to News

One general obstacle to reporting in the Middle East was noted by several western correspondents. It is the suspicion they encounter in their search for news. Three principal reasons are suggested.

First, the correspondent suffers for the low esteem in which journalism, as a profession, is held in parts of the Arab world (Iraq, for example). Though the commentator is often drawn from the ranks of leading Arab writers and wields considerable influence, the same respect is not accorded to the rank and file newsgatherer, who tends himself to regard journalism not as a public service so much as a path to fortune, financial or political. Nor is the journalist's standing enhanced by the poor quality of much of the Arab and Iranian press.

Secondly, the correspondent is handicapped by the special drawback of belonging to a particular foreign nation and the failure of that nation to give support to the cause of a particular Middle East country often reacts on the individual representative.

An American correspondent reported : "In the Middle East the correspondent is constantly confronted with suspicion. Arabs, too well aware of the bad press they have in America, are loth to give out information for fear it may be used against them in some way.

"In the Iranian oil crisis, Americans were again confronted with suspicion—though the conflict had nothing to do with Israel—because our State Department policy so closely followed the British.

"Any act of the U. S. Government relating to the area affects the correspondent. A speech by Dean Acheson, showing his backing of the British, could close every door in Teheran to American correspondents for a while. Most correspondents have to do fancy footwork to dissociate themselves from the acts and, especially, the general policy of their government."

Of the position of British correspondents a contributor wrote : "Even before the severance of official relations, British journalists in Iran were under increasingly close surveillance and were not allowed to visit Abadan or, in fact, any part of Khuzistan. For news of this vital area the British press had to rely on the rare interview with other foreign correspondents and on rumours crossing the border to Baghdad or the Persian Gulf to Kuwait."

Thirdly, the Arab authorities try to limit the view of the foreign correspondent to as narrow a field of events as possible because they regard the reporting of their area as often unfair. "The picture of Iraq, for example," said a British correspondent, "has been so badly presented to the world since the last war that the authorities (themselves not of a very high educational standard) are afraid of what the foreign press will do to them next."

He added that the war with Israel had done much to increase the difficulties of foreign journalists working in Arab countries because "Israeli propagandists succeeded in putting over such an unjust picture, for example of Iraq in the foreign press, while journalists working there were unable to get space to tell the unsensational truth, that the authorities found it hard to believe that anyone even tried."

Nevertheless, Arabs and Moslems generally were said to be easy to get along with and extremely approachable once they trusted the individual correspondent and little unusual difficulty was reported in obtaining access to leaders of opinion.

Exceptions to this rule seemed to arise chiefly from personal reasons, when a leader thought that some correspondent was unfriendly to himself or his country and refused to see him. On the other hand, there was agreement that there were frequently administrative delays in arranging appointments. Much of the delay was thought to be due not to illwill but to the comparative casualness with which the oriental world treats appointments. One correspondent summed up the question as "one of influence and above all of luck."

Nevertheless, where there is formal democracy in a country and an opposition as well as a government, a correspondent's desire to hear both sides may create problems.

"Police surveillance of foreign correspondents and local stringers," reported one correspondent, "was a common feature of postwar journalism in Egypt and other Middle East countries. Practices which are part of a foreign correspondent's normal assignment—such as interviews with opposition leaders and reporting facts unfavourable to the regime—were, at least until recently, regarded as subversive activity and could have the most unpleasant consequences for the correspondent."

37

Other problems of access to information, which have nothing to do with political prejudice, can create real difficulties. The first is that the machinery for arranging interviews and holding press conferences is usually poor. The second is that even when a Minister or an official is willing to talk, the facts of the situation are simply not available.

"There are such things as government press offices," wrote one correspondent, "but they are usually of absolutely no use to correspondents. The official in charge is always afraid of giving away even the most harmless information because he fears that he might be dismissed."

Press relations are in their infancy as a technique in the Middle East and even in the more advanced countries, such as Egypt, where press conferences are held, correspondents reported unsatisfactory arrangements. "Very often," reported a correspondent in Cairo, "the foreign correspondents are not told that a press conference is taking place. There is no official spokesman at the Foreign Office. At the so-called Ministry of National Guidance, all help is promised but as soon as something important happens the responsible officials have no time for the correspondent."

The praise which the Israeli censors have earned from correspondents for their helpfulness does not extend to the general work done by the public information services in the country, which one correspondent described as "not very efficient, overburdened with work and lacking in the sort of information the correspondent needs." He added that the result of overwork was that prior attention tended to be shown to representatives of the larger world newspapers as being the more influential—but this is a fault of news sources which is by no means confined to Israel, or the Middle East.

In Israel, however, the weakness of the official services is compensated by the fact that, as one correspondent reported, "almost universally, in the government and out, Israelis are eager to talk to foreign newspapermen. This must be qualified only by adding that East European and Communist newspapermen would certainly get the brush-off almost everywhere except in extreme left-wing circles. Equally, an American or other western correspondent is likely to have a cool reception in Kibutzim belonging to the left-wing Mapam Party, unless he has carefully prepared his visit."

Left to the individual as his sole source of news, the reporter is often baffled by the combination of personal charm and lack of information. Of Iran, for example, one correspondent reported : "I found news sources highly accessible but not always reliable. Information is often highly coloured and of dubious validity. There are plenty of rumours but not much factual information. For instance, I found the Minister of Economics very approachable, but he gave me no information whatever, although I had submitted a long list of written questions. The chief difficulty is to get accurate and reliable information, particularly from official government sources which are often willing but unable to supply factual material. Objective comment by public figures is also rare."

Another said : "For access to be easy there should be information centres, but there are not. There is nothing in Amman, almost nothing in Baghdad. In Damascus there is a press and information bureau, but it is very poor."

Of Jordan, another correspondent reported : "On the whole I was pleasantly surprised by the public relations consciousness of the Arab Legion and Jordan authorities. Though the government rarely gives press conferences or makes public statements, high officials including the Prime Minister were fairly easy to see. They were very critical of the West, but there was little personal spite against western correspondents. The government did have a spokesman, but he was told of events too late and was afraid to make substantive statements without official approval."

A reporter who has travelled the Arab world continuously over a long period thought that the situation on access to information was showing steady improvement nearly everywhere, "due partly to the underlying seepage of democratic views and partly to the fear that the other side will get its story in first."

B. The Effects of Restrictions

Some of the immediate effects of restrictive practices on the flow of news from the Middle East have been described in the foregoing pages. Undoubtedly, their combined result is to curtail the quantity and mar the quality of reporting at exactly those moments when events demand the fullest coverage. They can oblige the correspondent to fall back on rumour and secondhand information from dubious sources because he is denied access to official information. They can mangle what he manages to assemble when it passes through censorship. They can keep him away from the scene of the event. They can make him pause to ask himself whether the story is worth a clash with the authorities and possible expulsion.

All these handicaps can be serious, but two points must be remembered. First, the incidence of restrictions is incalculable and the element of personal luck considerable. Correspondents who have been in the same area at the same time have sometimes had completely different experiences. Secondly, the various types of correspondent who serve foreign agencies and newspapers feel the weight of restrictions in different degrees.

The reporter least affected is the rover who is stationed outside the area. If he has difficulties in one country, he can usually file from another country and count on staying out of the offended country long enough to allow memories of his "indiscretion" to fade before returning.

The man next least affected is the correspondent of the large newspaper stationed permanently in the area. If his funds permit, his capacity for manœuvre is considerable and he also can move to a point from which he can cable or telephone freely. If he has trouble on his return, the standing of his newspaper is (usually, not always) a powerful argument against serious interference with him. Often he works for a newspaper which believes in unsensational reporting and which therefore does not ask its representative to risk his tenure for the sake of a strained headline. One contributor underlined this point by remarking : "It is only just to stress the fact that those journalists who have worked honestly and seriously for serious newspapers have usually enjoyed tolerable relations with the Arab authorities."

The influence of restrictions, however, is very different for the correspondent who has special reasons for remaining in one country ; and, since this means principally the agency representative and the bulk of the world press takes its news from the agencies, this aspect of restrictions is important.

A senior correspondent who has been in the Middle East almost continuously since the end of World War II said : "One result of restriction is that it is always the resident correspondent—the man with an interest in and knowledge of the area—who suffers most.

The man who flies in 'for a story' and flies out again is the man who can most easily be irresponsible and get away with it."

Obviously, the easiest victim of official intimidation is the correspondent or stringer who is a national of the country from which he is reporting. As will be seen later, when the problem of the national correspondent is discussed in detail, observers disagree about whether pressure from officialdom or patriotic sentiment is the greater defect of his work, but it is agreed that, if the authorities cannot appeal to his patriotism to stop an awkward item of news, they can effectively frighten him out of strict objectivity by threat of reprisal. This is true, apparently, not only of Arab countries and Iran, where restrictions are generally more onerous, but also, to some extent, of Israel. An American correspondent commented that in the latter country "local men are inclined to close their eyes to things displeasing to their country ... I do not mean to suggest that there is a régime of fear, but I know of cases in which excessively objective Israelis have been made to feel the displeasure of the Public Information Office and of the Foreign Ministry."

Pressure on the foreign-born stringer varies according to his circumstances. Usually his work for the foreign press is secondary to the post he holds in a particular Middle East country, to which he may be bound by strong domestic ties. He is compelled to weigh the possible results of taking a risk against his legitimate personal interests. One roving foreign correspondent criticised these local men for being "too often unwilling to fight for the right to present both sides of a story." But the stakes are very different for the permanent staff correspondent, who will earn nothing but praise and a transfer to another area if he gets into serious trouble for reporting the full facts, and for the foreign-born stringer who may have no claim on his employer abroad if he is expelled.

The considerable difference in the status of the various types of Middle East correspondent must be borne in mind in assessing the effects of restrictions on newsgathering. In sum, it seems fair to say that censorship and kindred obstacles can and do hinder every correspondent at some point in his work ; but the ingenuity of the reporter on the spot and the alternative channels of information that exist combine to nullify the restrictions in most countries. The controls rarely stop all reporting of an event and, even when they do, their only result is to delay and distort the news.

Who loses by the restrictions ? Certainly the world press is affected, but it is the considered view of most observers that restrictions harm the government imposing them more than the world press against which they are imposed. One experienced correspondent said : "Though censorship has never prevented unpleasant news from getting out, it has frequently resulted in distorted news appearing in the world press. It has also often deterred correspondents from making an effort to visit countries where censorship was bad.

"The Arab states would be much better off without censorship. They would also improve coverage of their area in the world press if they simplified visa regulations and the like."

In particular, he thought that the Arab states had lost a great deal by their refusal to allow correspondents to travel freely between their countries and Israel. Because of the barriers, he pointed out, Israel as the smaller area was usually left to local stringers and the Arab world (and Iran) was the normal beat for the foreign-born Middle East correspondent. Inevitably these arrangements meant a contrast in the objectivity with which the two areas were reported. The Israeli stringers tended to present their country's case sympathetically—more sympathetically than those foreign correspondents who visited the country and saw it for themselves. The foreign correspondents moving about the Arab world, on the other hand, reported with great objectivity. If they were free to move across the Arab-Israeli frontiers, it was a reasonable assumption that coverage of the situation on both sides would be better balanced.

The argument that restrictions on reporting do more harm than good to the governments imposing them is supported, as was noted in discussing censorship generally, by the way these governments usually handle their controls.[1] When an event happens which they would like to suppress, they clamp on restrictions. But invariably the news leaks out, often in a distorted and partial form. The government involved then sees that its controls have only resulted in an even less favourable version than the facts merit and takes off the controls. But the damage is done and the government spokesmen find themselves having to adopt a defensive note which makes their explanations (which might have seemed reasonable enough if they had been given immediately) look like an attempt at covering up.

Another point on which observers agree is the undesirable effect

---

[1] See page 16 above.

of restrictions on the reporter. "You can easily become hostile to a country which causes you a thousand difficulties," commented one correspondent. The irritation provoked by unnecessary controls and by the fact that they hamper one type of reporter more than another is bound to reflect itself ultimately in the attitude with which even the most objective reporter approaches his task.

If the resident correspondent is continually hampered in his work, the chain reaction eventually reaches his editor abroad. There is less enthusiasm on the part of a newspaper to maintain its own man in the Middle East.

Whether it is justifiable or not, the suspicion grows that a correspondent who is constantly subject to external censorship ends by exercising unconscious self-censorship.

The roving correspondent also suffers. If perforce he has to spend his time on one side or the other of the Arab-Israeli fence, he cannot obtain a balanced picture of the whole area. If his reporting of the Arab world and Iran is punctuated with minor, and essentially ineffective, restrictions by censorship and visa trouble, he also becomes soured in his attitude.

Of all these difficulties the immediate victim may be the individual reporter, but the ultimate loser is the government that antagonises and hampers the correspondent. One constant complaint by Middle East authorities is that they are reported by foreigners who do not understand them and their ways. But, if they deliberately behave in a manner which invites the 'hit and run' special correspondent and discourages the resident reporter, they can hardly blame the world press.

C. Other Problems of Coverage

Other problems besides censorship and its kindred restrictions affect the reporting of the Middle East. The area is expensive to cover : the basic cost of living is high ; travel distances are great ; and telecommunication rates are considerable in many countries. Telecommunications could also be improved ; where good lines of communication exist, they are sometimes interrupted for political reasons. To a certain extent the problems of costs and communications overlap, but they are discussed separately in the following sections.

i. Costs of Coverage

The problem of the cost involved in reporting the Middle East is essentially one for the world news agencies. It is true that some editors in Europe stated that, if costs could be reduced, they would look again at the idea of having their own correspondent for the area, perhaps on a pool basis, but this possibility affects only a small minority of the editors who take their Middle East service from the agencies.

Those newspapers which are already represented have made arrangements to suit their budgets. The cost of sending out a reporter who is to be permanently based in the area with instructions to file regularly and at length is beyond all but the wealthiest newspapers. "Few newspapers," said an American correspondent, "will want to spend $ 150 a week, plus salary, for a man to stay in the Middle East." But that is not to say that costs in the Middle East are necessarily much beyond those in other parts of the world. Another correspondent said that the cost of maintaining a reporter in the area was generally no higher than in Rome or London and less than in Singapore or Hong Kong.

Costs affect the news agencies in many ways. The agencies face considerable outlay to collect news from Middle East centres and distribute it over their systems from either Cairo or London. If the assembly centre is Cairo, the cost of getting news there from Baghdad, for example, works out at about £ 100 ($ 280) for 2,500 words, according to the calculations of an agency chief in the Middle East. Inevitably, every possible economy in holding down on cabled news and in staffing must be made.

The agencies also suffer from a special handicap in that it is impossible to secure sufficient income in Middle East countries, with few exceptions, to cover the cost of maintaining a large bureau. An agency executive pointed out that a newspaper in Iraq, Jordan, Lebanon, Syria or Iran can rarely afford to pay more than £ 20 ($ 56) a month for a news service and that many of them do not take an agency service at all but monitor news broadcasts themselves if they want world news.

One of the heaviest items in the news agency budget is the daily cable and telephone bill. Press communication rates vary considerably from country to country within the Middle East, but in some countries they are among the highest rates in the world. [1]

For example, a correspondent filing to London from Aden can take advantage of the cheap British Commonwealth press rate (one penny or 1.17 U.S. cents a word) ; but if he files from the same place to Paris, he pays sixpence (seven cents) a word ; to Hamburg he pays 7³/₄d (just over nine cents) ; to New York fourpence (4.68 cents). Anybody filing from Beirut pays a uniformly high press rate, comparatively (between 9.87 and 22.6 cents). The lowest rate at which it is possible to file at press rates from Teheran to any of the six centres chosen for analysis (London, Paris, Rome, Hamburg, New York and New Delhi) is 10.50 cents a word to London ; the highest is 16.7 cents to Paris. Urgent press rates, which correspondents are often compelled to use, can rise as high as 68 cents a word (Baghdad-Rome).

Why should these wide variations exist ? All the rates, by international agreement, have a common denominator in that they are based on the gold franc,[2] but this agreement in practice bears little relation to the actual rate charged in many countries. Governments have agreed that any tax which they impose on the basic gold franc rate must be excluded from accounts rendered for services by one country to another, but this does not affect the freedom of a government to add a fiscal tax to the price at which the service is sold to the user inside the country—that is, the person sending a cable or making a telephone call across the frontier.

This freedom to tax telecommunications is complete. Many governments take advantage of it to raise revenue and they are under no obligation to notify the position—much less defend it—to the International Telecommunication Union, the organisation set up in 1934 to coordinate and regulate world telecommunications.

Comparisons between communication rates from countries within the same area are further complicated by the existence of bilateral

---

[1] In Appendices C and D are given lists of press cable and telephone rates from Middle East centres to six major cities in the rest of the world.

[2] The gold franc is the monetary unit used to calculate the tariffs of international telecommunication services and accounts between them. Defined as "the gold franc of 100 centimes, of a weight of 10/31 of a gramme and of a fineness of 0.900," it is only a money of account and not a medium of payment. Once the accounts have been made up in gold francs, payments due between different governmental and private services are made in real currencies.

agreements within the general international agreement. Thus, for example, the ordinary press cable rate from Teheran to Paris, Rome, Hamburg and New Delhi is one-third of the ordinary commercial rate, in line with the international agreement; but the press cable rate from Teheran to London is reduced to one-fifth of the ordinary rate and from Teheran to New York to one-sixth of the ordinary rate under special reciprocal agreements. Again, the urgent press cable rate from Teheran is normally the same as the ordinary commercial rate (in accordance with the international agreement), but a special arrangement exists with the U. S. A. by which the urgent press cable rate is only one-half the ordinary commercial rate.

Although one of the basic aims of the ITU is to persuade governments and private companies to lower tariffs as far as is consistent with the maintenance of an efficient service, its powers are limited to recommendation. Twice in the past ten years, its plenipotentiary conference has gone on record with "a declaration of opinion" that "members and associate members recognise the desirability of avoiding the imposition of fiscal taxes on any international communications," but it has remained an expression of opinion without a sequel.[1]

As long as rates remain high in the Middle East, they are bound to affect the quantity of news sent out of the area. An agency executive, for example, said that the "prohibitive press cable rates" were "the major factor militating against a fuller flow of news from Middle East countries to India."

The rates also help to govern the amount of background information added to a spot news story by the reporter. J. Kingsbury Smith, European general director of International News Service, gave a personal experience of this when he addressed the General Assembly of the IPI in London in May 1953.[2] He covered the Anglo-Iranian

---

[1] In April 1954, the United Nations interested itself in the question of high communications rates. Its Economic and Social Council passed a unanimous resolution recognising that press messages on telecommunication channels at lower rates and with higher priority would facilitate the free flow of international information. It therefore asked ITU and Unesco to prepare for the Council's nineteenth session (in Spring 1955) a joint study of the problem and to take into account disparities and anomalies in press rates; it also asked governments to look into the question. The ITU administrative council agreed to act on the Ecosoc proposal and circularised its members in June, asking them to furnish the fullest information practicable not later than September 30, 1954. The information will go to Unesco for compilation and analysis.

[2] See *IPI Assembly 1953: The Proceedings*, page 65: published by the International Press Institute, Zurich, July 1953.

negotiations on the oil dispute. At a vital break in the talks he found the backlog of ordinary press traffic in Teheran was so great that there was an estimated delay of 26 hours on messages. Only urgent telegrams, at 75 cents a word, were going out immediately. Faced with this rate, he had filed only spot bulletins and left the backgrounding to the desk in New York.[1] A British correspondent reported that, during the same period, he was cabling up to 1,500 words a day from Teheran or Abadan at the urgent press rate of 3s. 10d. a word, because only urgent messages reached London in time for the next morning paper ; but even this arrangement was not reliable, because some cables were held up till the following day and still put over at the same high rate per word.

ii. Communications

The existing system of telecommunications in the Middle East was described by most western correspondents as reasonably good from the technical point of view, though the network gets into difficulties when a large number of reporters move to one of the less well equipped centres to cover a major story.

"When that happens," said an American correspondent, "the facilities become a nightmare. Even in modern Teheran, when something like 75 correspondents were burdening the wires, it frequently took more than 24 hours to get a cable to New York.

"In this situation," he continued, "the agencies and the few newspapers with money to burn 'urgent' everything or, worse, they telephone London and hold open one or perhaps two long distance lines. Then other correspondents have to 'urgent' too or else confine themselves to writing airmailers which may take a week to reach New York."

---

[1] With Mr. Smith's statement should be compared the comments of Francis Williams in his Unesco study of telecommunications and the press, "Transmitting World News" (1953).

"It is vital to international understanding," wrote Mr. Williams, "that there should be ample and reliable reporting of events in areas of the world which have now become, or are likely to become, the centre of important political, social and economic changes. The Middle East is such an aiea. But cable rates (using the term to cover international messages sent by either line or radio) to and from Middle East countries not only vary enormously from country to country and according to which direction they are sent, but are frequently so high as to preclude anything like a full and regular service of background news."

Within the area, one agency executive pointed out, "there is no doubt that the difficulty of telephoning to any part of the Arab world from Cairo—one might say that from the journalist's point of view telephone facilities do not exist—gravely affects the efficiency of agency services."

Technical facilities are likely to improve. The International Telecommunication Union's administrative council, at a meeting in June 1952, instructed its three consultative committees (concerned respectively with telegraphs, telephones and radio) to prepare a complete scheme "for connecting countries in the Middle East and Southern Asia with the network of major international communication lines in Europe and the Mediterranean Basin by metallic lines or by radio relay links." This is the third stage of a plan for a network of international telecommunications (telegraph and telephone) on which a special committee has been working for some years. The first and second stages covered Europe and the Mediterranean Basin.

The shape of things to come in the Middle East was shown in the plan produced for a trunk switching system at the meeting of a special sub-committee in Lahore in December 1953. Under the plan (which is being considered by the main committee in Geneva in autumn 1954) the Middle and Far East will be linked with the European and Mediterranean system at Ankara, Amman, Akaba and Cairo.

The change will benefit principally countries lying to the east of the Middle East, since at present direct cable and wireless facilities in most cases do not exist and cables filed, for example, by Indian correspondents have to be routed mainly through London. The consequent delay is particularly harmful for agency messages.

It is hoped to implement the plan by 1957, but the speed of progress depends on the authorities operating the existing services, since it is they who are responsible for financing further developments, either out of their own resources or by borrowing.

Technical improvements, however, will not automatically remove the drawbacks arising from political interference, which led an agency executive to describe facilities as "notoriously bad."

"In many of the countries," he explained, "telegraph, radio, cable and telephone service is often suspended for hours at a time. In times of crisis it is not unusual for communications to be shut down altogether, with the explanation that communications have failed."

One grievance expressed by correspondents concerned the

financial guarantees demanded in countries with nationalised services. "Don't think," warned one, "that just because you have a batch of cards from the Radio Corporation of America, Cable and Wireless and so on, you can file in the Middle East. Only in Jordan, Cyprus, Aden and the British Protectorates in the Persian Gulf will an RCA card do you any good. In other countries there is a national cable company which will believe only a cable from your head office's local cable office saying it is good for the charges."

Another correspondent drew attention to the important effects on coverage which restricted filing hours can have for a country. Taking as his example Jordan, he said : "Probably the most irksome aspect of newsgathering here is the early closing hour of the central telegraph office. In Arab Jerusalem it closes at 8 p. m. and in Amman at 9 p. m. These hours are bad for morning newspapermen and Jordan loses many good stories as a result. This is particularly damaging to the country because the Israeli account of an event can be sent out any hour of the day or night."

Several correspondents complained of favouritism in filing priorities being given to local men. "In Iran," said one, "local stringers' copy would be cleared hours ahead of ours. This opened the door for bribery in one form or another."

Chapter III

THE COVERAGE

THE COVERAGE

A. Sources of News

The Middle East is one the areas of the world where coverage is predominantly in the hands of the world news agencies, though some national agencies also have their own correspondents in the more important capitals and the trend among these agencies is to increase direct coverage.

Of the world press, only some leading British and American newspapers are widely represented by permanent staff correspondents sent out from the home base to cable a comprehensive daily service on major news events. Newspapers in several countries in Western Europe and the East also maintain permanent representatives in the area, but few have sufficiently strong coverage to feel independent of the world agencies. It is a common practice to take day-to-day coverage from the agencies and to send rover correspondents either to make periodic tours or to cover major news breaks.

i. Agency Coverage

Of the six world news agencies five maintain their own staff correspondents in the more important Middle East centres. [1] The exception, International News Service, has stringers in the main centres and sends in American staffers from Rome, Paris or London when the news merits it.

The other four western agencies (full details of TASS coverage are not available) are all represented in Cairo (Egypt), where they have their main Middle East bureaus, Teheran (Iran), Tel Aviv

---

[1] See the chart of agency coverage of the area in Appendix A.

and/or Jerusalem (Israel), Beirut (Lebanon), Baghdad (Iraq), Damascus (Syria), Khartoum (Sudan) and Amman (Jordan). Reuters, Associated Press and United Press are represented in Aden, Benghazi (Libya) and Bahrein (Persian Gulf). The agencies are also covered in some important towns which are not capitals—Port Said and Alexandria in Egypt, Basra in Iraq, and so on, and have arrangements to receive news, on the rare occasions when it breaks, from the countries of Arabia.

Of the western agencies Agence France-Presse is exceptional in that its coverage from the six principal centres — Cairo, Teheran, Jerusalem, Baghdad, Beirut and Damascus — is in the hands of French nationals. Only in the smaller capitals does it rely on a stringer who is a national of the country he is reporting.

By contrast, the other western agencies rely more on national correspondents and stringers. Reuters bureau in Cairo is headed by a Briton and the agency has British correspondents or stringers in Teheran, Amman and Aden. An American staffer is in charge of the Cairo bureau of AP which also has American staffers in Beirut and Teheran. The Cairo bureau of UP is headed by a Briton and the agency has "non-national" representation in Dhahran, Bahrein and Israeli Jerusalem. Otherwise the agency men are nationals of the country they are reporting.

Of the national agencies Deutsche Presse-Agentur has two staff correspondents — a German in Egypt and an Israeli in Israel (another German staffer in Istanbul visits the Levant and Iran). Press Trust of India has an Egyptian correspondent in Cairo and an Iranian correspondent in Teheran and plans to be represented in Baghdad and Damascus. The Associated Press of Pakistan has a Pakistani staff correspondent in Cairo and contemplates posting other correspondents in the Middle East. The official Turkish agency, Anadolu Ajansi, plans to establish its own men in the Middle East, and a new private agency, Turk Haberler Ajansi, has correspondents in Amman, Beirut, Cairo and Damascus.

There is a national agency for the Arab world, the British-owned Arab News Agency, which also covers for the British agency Exchange Telegraph. ANA has its central news office in Cairo, under a British manager and staffed partly by Britons and partly by Egyptians; branches in Beirut (where there is also a British manager), Amman, Baghdad, Damascus and Jerusalem; and representatives in Aden, Benghazi, Khartoum, Mecca and Tripoli.

Another specialised agency is the Jewish Telegraphic Agency with offices in Jerusalem and Tel Aviv, serving newspapers outside the Middle East with Israeli news.

Worldwide Press Service, an American agency which replaced the Overseas News Agency in December 1953, has two non-American stringers, one covering Egypt, Sudan, Libya and Ethiopia from Cairo and the other covering Lebanon, Syria, Jordan and the Arabian Peninsula from Beirut; it also receives part-time coverage from Israel. But the agency does not deal in spot news, confining itself to background and situation articles.

Plans by the smaller agencies to expand facilities for direct coverage indicate the growing interest in the area, as well as dissatisfaction in some countries, especially in the East, with existing world agency coverage. [1]

ii. Newspaper Coverage

The British national press is the most solidly represented in the Middle East by its own staff correspondents and stringers, but the provincial newspapers, with the exception of those belonging to the Kemsley group[2], usually take their news from the agencies. Some important provincial papers subscribe to the foreign services syndicated by national newspapers.

Cairo is the headquarters of the corps of British Middle East correspondents as well as stringers for Egypt. Here *The Times* has been consistently represented by a British staff man, who tours the area regularly, and, usually, a British assistant on a part-time basis. The *Daily Telegraph* normally maintains a British staffer in Cairo, though it changes its representative frequently. In terms of staff men sent into the area, the *Telegraph* has led all other newspapers in recent years; during 1953 it had sometimes four men operating between Khartoum and Teheran at the same time and at one point there were five. The *Daily Mail* and *Daily Express* also have British staffers in Cairo. The *Daily Herald* is covered in Egypt by a British

---

[1] See the comments of an Indian editor on page 92.

[2] The Middle East correspondent of Kemsley is stationed in Cyprus, which has become an important junction for travelling correspondents since the Palestine war split the area into two. Like Beirut, Cyprus offers "free port" facilities for filing messages which might be stopped elsewhere.

stringer ; so are Kemsley, the *Manchester Guardian* and *The Observer*. The *News Chronicle* has an Arab stringer.

Outside Egypt direct newspaper representation is much weaker numerically, except in Israel, where all but one of the above list also have their own correspondents or stringers. But, whereas in Egypt most of the correspondents are British nationals, the majority in Israel are Israelis. Only *The Times,* the *Daily Express* and the *Manchester Guardian* have British representation.

In Iraq only two British newspapers are directly represented—*The Times* and the *News Chronicle,* which have arrangements with two British members of the staff of the English-language *Iraq Times,* published in Baghdad.

Diplomatic difficulties between Britain and Iran have complicated the question of representation in Teheran and no newspaper keeps a permanent staffer there, though the *Daily Telegraph* has senior staffers rotating on duty in Teheran. A more common practice is to cover Iran by maintaining a local stringer and sending in the Middle East correspondent at intervals. Three stringers cover for five British papers — *The Times, Daily Telegraph, Daily Mail, Daily Express* and *The Observer.*

Otherwise the British press relies on a handful of stringers in Beirut, Amman, Khartoum and Aden—mostly either nationals of the country they are reporting or Britons contributing as a sideline.

The American press is more thinly represented in the Middle East, though an American newspaper, *The New York Times,* shares with the British *Daily Telegraph* the distinction of making the fullest staff arrangements to obtain comprehensive coverage, having two American staffers to cover the Arab world and Iran and another stationed in Israel. Additionally, it normally has an American stringer in Israel and another covering Syria and Lebanon.

The *Christian Science Monitor* also relies mainly on its own sources, having an American rover correspondent based on Beirut, an Egyptian stringer in Egypt and an Israeli stringer in Israel. In addition, the newspaper has made a practice of sending in rovers but has done so less frequently since it stationed a staff man in Beirut.

The *New York Herald Tribune* relies for its main coverage on the agencies but has its own stringers, virtually all Americans, in most countries. It also sends in rovers.

The *Chicago Daily News* prefers to cover the area with its own American staff correspondents ; it does not maintain a resident staffer but sends in rovers and keeps them constantly moving through the area. The *Cleveland Plain Dealer* supplements the agency reports by sending in a rover occasionally. Some other newspapers have their own informants here and there, but, to an even greater extent than the British press, the American press's sources of news from the smaller Middle East capitals are the agencies.

Of the news weeklies, *Time-Life* maintains a bureau in Beirut with two American staffers and has stringers elsewhere. *Newsweek* has its own correspondent based in Cairo and *U. S. News and World Report* has an American Middle East correspondent.

It would, however, be misleading to estimate newspaper coverage wholly by the number of staff correspondents stationed permanently in the area. As the editor of one newspaper, whose coverage of the Middle East enjoys a considerable reputation but whose direct representation is comparatively small, commented : "We receive a great deal in the course of a year, but it is largely in the nature of special correspondence from staff members and other people, mostly by way of background articles. We also do a fair amount of interpretation through leading articles. In the Middle East what is really wanted is interpretation rather than a flow of spot news."

This comment is especially true when Middle East coverage in the European press is considered. It is only the exceptional newspaper which has one or more permanent correspondents in the area or which orders cable coverage of major events, but several newspapers use a combination of casual correspondence from residents (usually by air mail), series of articles by occasional roving correspondents and syndicated services from other newspapers to build up effective coverage as a supplement to the agencies' daily services. [1]

---

[1] The steadily expanding practice of syndication of their foreign services by newspapers with their own corps of correspondents is an important factor in Middle East coverage in the world press. For example, *The New York Times* syndicates its foreign reports to 29 subscribers in the United States and three in Canada. Its clients abroad include newspapers in South and Central America, Europe, India and Japan. In Australia, the *New York Times* service is taken by the Australian Associated Press and distributed to most Australian and New Zealand papers. *The Times* (London) service goes to some thirty newspapers all over the world. The *Chicago Daily News* service is taken by 46 other U.S. newspapers as well as by papers in Canada and by a Japanese press service. The *Express Newspapers* (London) service is syndicated to some 300 newspapers overseas. *The Observer* (London), though it is a Sunday newspaper, gives a wide range of clients in 25 countries an all-week service ; in addition to provincial subscribers in Britain, it services some sixty newspapers abroad, 23 of them in the United States. In France, *Le Monde* has for several years sold a service of its foreign correspondents' reports to the provincial press, as well as to newspapers in most other European countries.

Of this practice *Le Monde,* of Paris, is a good example. In some centres it has accredited correspondents, in others only unofficial informants. In addition, it makes extensive use of agency messages and on major events sends its own staff specialist to the spot. In Switzerland several newspapers, and in particular the *Neue Zürcher Zeitung,* give full and continuous coverage by the technique of relying for day-to-day news on the agencies and rounding up problems regularly in articles from an expert rover or from correspondents resident in the area. The result in all cases is a high standard of coverage.

Several European newspapers have the services on a pool basis of rover or permanent correspondents and many more have developed to a higher point than the Anglo-Saxon press the technique of building up services of irregular airmailed articles from residents in the Middle East.

In the East one or two leading newspapers, such as *The Times of India* and *Dawn* (Pakistan), have their own correspondents to supplement agency coverage.

Nevertheless, the sources from which the world press as a whole draws its Middle East news are fairly narrow, especially outside Egypt, Iran and Israel. For example, news from Iraq is supplied by nine correspondents and stringers, of whom five are Iraqis and four— two Britons and two Iraqis—are employed on the *Iraq Times.* The news from Aden comes from six correspondents and stringers, half of whom hold from four to six strings ; three are British, three local people. There are nine foreign press representatives in Jordan, all but one of them Arabs. Of seven in Khartoum, one is British and six Sudanese. Coverage in Israel also is interesting statistically. Of the 28 correspondents and stringers who work for foreign agencies and daily papers, 22 are Israelis, three British, two American and one French. In Teheran only the agencies have staff correspondents, and of the seven four are foreign nationals, three are Iranians ; otherwise five British newspapers, the American magazines *Time* and *Life* and *Dawn,* of Karachi, are covered by five Iranian stringers.

These figures are not quoted in disparagement of the local man, who is often a leading member of the local press ; but they indicate the narrowness of the news channels out of the Middle East.

B. Criticisms of Coverage

The "adequacy" of press coverage of any area is a highly relative term. It is relative to the general place of foreign news in each newspaper ; to the news available ; to the interest in a given area ; to the competition each day from events nearer home and between reports from different foreign areas, and so on. For even the largest newspaper the "news hole" is limited and, supposing that every newspaper could double its editorial space tomorrow, there are few editors who would regard wider and deeper coverage of the Middle East as a priority claim on space.

Nevertheless, once an editor grants that the Middle East belongs to his general pattern of foreign coverage, the question of adequacy is reasonable if it means : does his newspaper give as true and complete a picture of the area as seems humanly and technically possible ? Or, to put the same question negatively, does the news of the Middle East that is given mean something to the reader or is it a waste of space ?

This is a large question and permits only partial answers. The International Press Institute has sought representative views from editors, foreign editors, agency and newspaper correspondents, newspapermen who have edited or are still editing newspapers in the area, Middle Easterners resident outside the area and a variety of specialists —university teachers, officials, people in political life—who have a particular interest in what their daily newspaper tells them about the Middle East.

Contrasts in Performance

The western countries most interested in the Middle East are Britain, the United States and France. They are also the headquarters of five of the world news agencies which supply the bulk of foreign news to the rest of the world. Newspapers which syndicate their news services also are published mainly in these countries. This section therefore concentrates on Middle East coverage by the agencies and newspapers of these three countries.

One difficulty arises immediately. It is the contrast in performance (familiar to readers of the IPI study *The Flow of the News*) between newspapers seriously interested in making their foreign report a comprehensive and continuous picture of the world day by day and those which skim the foreign news for the most dramatic and picturesque stories. This difference of approach results in two appreciations of press coverage of the Middle East.

First, it seems to be agreed that in Britain, the U. S. and France anybody really interested in the Middle East can obtain a fairly comprehensive idea of what is happening, at least in the principal centres and in the field of politics, from a handful of newspapers and periodicals.

One American editor, explaining that his own newspaper used a selective "magazine" type of approach to the Middle East in the coverage it ordered from its own correspondents, said : "We feel that one paper of record is essential in America but that this field is pretty adequately covered by *The New York Times.*"

A British correspondent agreed. "The most consistent effort to report the Middle East comprehensively," he said, "is made by *The New York Times* which ... has devoted considerable space to economic, political and social developments. It has the space which few other newspapers enjoy and its method of reporting, though frequently imposing a dullness on the dispatch, is essentially a compilation of facts and Middle East opinion, which is the essence of reporting."

The Times of London gives comprehensive and balanced coverage within greater space limitations. The newspaper regards Cairo as a dateline comparable in importance with any European capital ; but, once it has fully reported the main political events, it has often little space left for non-political articles. Middle East coverage is also an important department of the *Daily Telegraph*'s foreign news service.

In France, *Le Monde* pays special attention to Middle East affairs. A French foreign editor who specialises in the area gave a list of "several excellent non-specialist publications" in English which he used to supplement his information from French sources. They are : from the U. S. *The New York Times*, the *Christian Science Monitor*, the *New York Herald Tribune* and *Time* magazine; and from Britain *The Times*, the *Daily Telegraph*, the *Manchester Guardian*, *The Observer*, *The Economist* and the *New Statesman and Nation*.

An interesting point is raised by this rating. As was shown earlier in the picture of coverage (pp. 55-58), the newspapers mentioned have very different arrangements for reporting the Middle East. They range from the very full staff coverage given by *The New York Times* and the London *Daily Telegraph* to virtually complete reliance on agency services. It therefore appears that quality of coverage does not depend altogether on the amount of money a newspaper has to spend on its correspondents. Much depends also on the use to which a newspaper puts its various sources of information —agency messages, diplomatic sources, special articles from occasional correspondents, press reading and so on. The implication is that, if a newspaper knows how to handle its basic service from the agencies, it can do a good job of coverage.

The second appreciation of Middle East coverage is that, outside this handful of newspapers and periodicals, it has many shortcomings.

The Criticisms Summarised

The most general criticism of the average newspaper's coverage is that it lacks proper interpretation and is patchy. By giving only spasmodic reports of the highlights and crises, but no continuous coverage or adequate background, it leaves its public bewildered by each fresh crisis.

"The British press," said one contributor, "reports only crises and therefore the Middle East is presented to the public in a news vacuum in which the crises explode inexplicably and with monotonous regularity."

"The American press," said another, "does not give a true picture of the Middle East. Generally it covers well spectacular spot news but it skims lightly over, or else uses rarely, the background of the news that is affecting international relations in the area."

"In the French press," said a third, "preoccupation with sensations and crises means that the area's real problems receive less attention than formerly. Though public interest in the area is growing, the French reader is uninformed, or else badly informed, on the Middle East. The French press's treatment of the area resembles that of a geographer who, in describing a country, confines himself to drawing attention to the mountain peaks without adding that there are also valleys and plateaus."

Other criticisms were made. Some of them applied to the "serious" newspaper and its correspondents as well as to the rest of the press. They were that :

Coverage is geographically uneven. It is largely confined to Egypt, Iran and Israel. Iraq, Lebanon, Syria, Jordan, the Sudan and Libya receive little attention except in time of crisis. (Criticism was also offered of the failure to report the countries of the Arab Peninsula, but in view of the difficulties involved most observers agreed that little could be done.)

Reporting is unbalanced, in that coverage everywhere is too heavily weighted toward politics, whereas the economic and social movements which often determine political events are unreported. Coverage is deficient also in human interest news.

Reporting often suffers from bias, either through the reporter's own predilections or through his newspaper's policy. Bias may be political or, more broadly, racial.

The calibre of much reporting from the area is poor. Permanent senior correspondents of newspapers and agencies (mostly non-nationals of the Middle East) are good, but the area is too big for them to do an adequate job because they are thin on the ground. Further, even when they are not hampered by restrictions, their effectiveness is often limited by inadequate knowledge of the languages of the area—Arabic, Persian and Hebrew. Special correspondents sent in to cover big stories (unless they are regular Middle East rovers) know too little and often go after sensational stories only. Local correspondents, usually nationals of the country from which they are reporting, are too often under pressure to be independent observers and are frequently poorly trained.

The men who handle the news on the home desk know little about the Middle East. Consequently the news received is badly handled and mistakes are not always caught. The reporter on the spot suffers from lack of stimulus as a result and lacks good liaison with his home office.

i. Lack of Interpretation

The importance of proper interpretation of the news from such a "strange" area as the Middle East is regarded as fundamental by all specialists and correspondents.

"Full value must be given," said one correspondent, "to the special factors militating against satisfactory reporting of the area. There is a profound difference between oriental and western civilisations and mentalities which has consequences affecting everyday affairs and political life. The absence of a basis of comparison makes Middle East politics particularly hard to follow and the problem of reporting them effectively has defeated many experienced newsmen. But, without proper explanation, the complete remoteness of the Middle East from everything understood in the West merely increases the reader's indifference to news from the area."

Another correspondent who has spent the greater part of the past ten years in the area said : "Some of the best reporting from the area fails when the reporter is debarred from fulfilling the correct function of a correspondent—the application of his intelligence to the production of what I should call the 'reporting assessment' of the situation. This frequently involves interpretation of the hard news. To take a simple example of what I mean : it would have been inaccurate to give a straight report of the Egyptian request for a cancellation of elections in two southern provinces of the Sudan (in November 1953). The Egyptian statement required interpretation to give it perspective.

"This question of reporting styles is fundamental. The agency or newspaper which insists on a source for all its statements, in the interests of objective and accurate reporting, debars itself frequently thereby from a correct presentation of the news. The circumstances may make it impossible for a correspondent to secure a source for a point which he regards as essential and knows to be true.

"This background is essential to understanding the reporting of the Middle East in the outside world. If the agencies are debarred from proper interpretation of the news and if a newspaper does not have full confidence in the ability of its correspondent to assess and judge events, the essential background must inevitably be lost and news presented in a vacuum."

Other contributors made the same point about the difficulty, on present coverage arrangements, of providing adequate background to news events.

An American specialist said : "Insofar as 'spot' news is concerned, I would say that for the most part agencies provide ample coverage. But to the average newspaper reader, who knows relatively little about the Middle East, the 'spot' news rarely tells the whole story. Take, for example, the treason trials held in Cairo in October and November

1953. Extremely few American newspapers carried reports, and the accounts which they did run concerned primarily the 'higher brass.' It would seem to me that a news service should pull all these treason convictions together, show the background and the connections of the defendants and then what their convictions mean under the new form of government.

"Again, American newspapers speak of 'military dictatorship' in Syria,[1] but rarely do they explain to their readers the conditions that brought about the change in the government of Syria and whether the change has been to the ultimate benefit of the Syrian people and the cause of democracy in that country, or otherwise.

"Ample accounts with pictorial displays were carried when King Abdullah of Jordan was assassinated, but they provided relatively little information about the steady stream of causes that brought about that assassination. This is not said in justification of the assassination, but merely to point out that there is another side of the story which was generally ignored, while full coverage was given to the killing itself. King Abdullah—the central figure in the spot news at that time—is no longer important in today's news developments in the Holy Land, but the causes that led to that assassination are even more alive today than when Abdullah lost his life.

"When King Farouk was forced to abdicate his Egyptian throne and exiled, Americans learned from their newspapers that a 'military dictatorship' seized control in the Nile valley. Obviously it was a military coup d'état. But what about the many causes (even excluding the corruption in the royal palaces) that brought about the ending of the monarchy in Egypt ? The latter events do not provide as spectacular a story as the exposing of Farouk's love affairs and his private gallery of nude paintings and statues. True as those things are, they were not the fundamental reasons that brought about a new way of life in Egypt.

"American newspaper coverage of the Middle East lacks an adult, intelligent comprehension of the fundamental movements that are leading to an economic, social and political renaissance in that vital area of the world. Proof of that statement is the frequency with which some reports from the Middle East are cloaked with an 'Arabian Nights' atmosphere. One cannot begin to understand the Middle East

---

[1]The dictatorship of Hosni Zaim lasted from June to August 1949. In November 1951 Col. Shishakly established his régime, which fell in February 1954.

unless one first understands the mentality of the Middle Easterners. That mentality is not hard to probe because it is found openly in the very background of the events that generate today's news stories."

An American correspondent commented : "An essential of reporting the Middle East is interpretation which involves a great deal of history and background. Unhappily, few publications are interested in this necessary material. Editors for instance, were less interested in the development of Premier Mossadegh in Iran as a nationalist and his place in Iranian history than in the fact that he wore pyjamas and stayed in bed much of the time. Not many people are interested in how the extraordinary situations in the Middle East countries got that way."

If correspondents cannot place major news events against their background of the modern Middle East, stereotyped reporting inevitably results. The greatest sufferers from this have been the Arabs and Iranians. Israel gains by comparison since it is a new state governed by men with western ideas.

But who should give this background to the news ? It is easy to criticise the news agencies, as some newspaper correspondents did. For example, one commented : "Those who read the newspapers that rely on agency reports could not possibly take each isolated development that is reported and fit it into the general picture. Interpretive writing is essential to make it understandable. The trouble with most Middle East reporting is that it is either unintelligible agency transmission of bare facts or slanted reporting that is pro-Arab, pro-Israeli, pro-British or pro-American oil company." Another said : "It is sad but true that it is impossible to get a connected picture of developments in Israel, Iran or the Arab countries over a long period by following the agency files. They hit only the high spots. They lack interpretation, background ; in a word, they are lamentably superficial."

The controversial question of how far interpretation of the news was properly an agency task was thoroughly discussed at the second general assembly of the IPI in London in May 1953.[1] Reuters editor, Walton Cole, said that purely situational material was not a primary responsibility of the agencies, though it seemed to him that editors today did want authoritative background explanations. On this limited definition of 'interpretation' Alan Gould, executive editor of

---

[1] See *IPI Assembly 1953 : The Proceedings,* page 54 onwards.

the Associated Press, and George H. Pipal, general European manager of the United Press, agreed that "proper explanation and background," as opposed to "improper editorialising or opinion writing," was part of the agency's job ; but as Mr. Pipal added, the question was still "one of definition."

The task of defining it is not helped, from the agency point of view, by the suspicion with which some editors regard "interpretation." The case against agency "interpretation" was put succinctly by a British editor in the course of his replies to IPI inquiries on the flow of the news.

"Interpretation on an agency tape," he wrote, "is to be deplored for three reasons. First, the agencies are each and all dominated by some particular nationality, and if they indulge in too much interpretation, the feeling will arise that what is being put out is the American or the English or the French or the Indian viewpoint rather than dispassionate interpretation.

"Secondly, a newspaper does not like to receive its interpretation from anonymous sources. It wants to know more than the name of the person who is interpreting. It wants to know his educational standards, his intellectual ability and all those factors which enable one to say that John Doe knows, or does not know, what he is talking about. Therefore it is desirable that interpretation should come from a newspaper's own correspondents, whose strength and weaknesses are known to their departments.

"Thirdly, while the top level of agency workers is usually reasonably high, the lower level, particularly in areas such as the Middle East, is not so high and it is undesirable that small town newspapermen should, by virtue of being attached to a world-renowned news agency, be able to put across ideas which could be quite fallacious."

The agencies have a fair complaint that even the stories sent out with an essential minimum of explanation are being cut on the newspaper desk. This experience has led them to hold down on expensive cabling at the Middle East source and further to cut out at the head office material considered superfluous for the general service. As a French foreign editor pointed out : "As there are few people among the press or public with a great interest in the Middle East, the agencies understandably regard it as superfluous to circulate information which would interest only experts."

Another practical problem about the difficulty of interpretive writing arises from the attitude of the authorities in some Middle East countries. They want anything written about their country to be favourable or at least neutral in tone and are sometimes prepared to take action against the unfavourable critic. Several editors complained that the special articles sent out by agencies and known as "situationers" are few and that those which are provided are too colourless and cautious. One critic added : "Situationers are normally based on government handouts and therefore largely useless. Another of their weaknesses is that, when they are written by local correspondents, they show an unwillingness to ask awkward questions of the persons interviewed or to go back and check a point of fact with them." But a correspondent asked a pertinent question : "How long can a reporter write frank interpretive pieces and get away with it ? You cannot do it consistently about any one country in the Middle East. A visitor may get by with a few such stories, but not for long."

One further difficulty has already been mentioned earlier in discussing access to news. It is that worthwhile background material would have to contain facts and statistics which, for one reason or another, are often not available.

ii. Geographical Unevenness of Coverage

From all sides suggestions were made that more attention should be paid to what was going on in the Middle East outside the main countries—Egypt, Iran and Israel. The British press, for example, was strongly criticised on the ground that Britain prided itself on creating a creditable new country in the Sudan ; but so little had been reported from that country that the British public was quite unable to arrive at any well-founded conclusions in the Anglo-Egyptian quarrel over its future.

Similarly, there were requests for more news about Libya, Jordan, Iraq, Syria and Lebanon.

The picture of coverage given earlier shows why this unevenness exists. Most Middle East bureaus of world agencies are centred in Cairo ; most permanent correspondents of the large newspapers are based there or in Beirut. Teheran is treated as important and covered as well as the restrictions there will allow. Israel has a strong representation of correspondents and stringers.

But suppose the agencies were to review their Middle East coverage, they are entitled to ask what demand there is for more news from the smaller centres. The principle on which a news agency works was explained at the London assembly of the IPI in May 1953 by Mr. Pipal, of the United Press.[1] Agencies, he said, were the most sensitive organisations in the world on editors' interests and, whenever they found that any story interested a reasonable number of editors, it became a competitive story which the agencies would cover. An agency's effort to improve the quality of its report should not be directed at forcing on a newspaper a fixed daily quota of news from, say, Bombay, if the reader was more interested in news from Berlin —or, he might have said from Amman or Khartoum if there was greater interest in Cairo or Teheran.

The problem is different for the Middle East correspondent of a newspaper. Large though his beat is, he could, according to many reporters serving in the area, visit the smaller countries more often. Instead there is a tendency to circulate mainly round the larger and more comfortable capitals on the argument that these are the places where the main news is made. An American correspondent said that it was the very rarity with which the foreign correspondent shows himself in countries like Jordan that creates suspicion of him when he does arrive. If he goes only to cover a major story sensationally and ignores all the surrounding circumstances that have led up to the story, the official assumption is that he is there to exaggerate and distort and the official reaction is to place obstacles in his way.

A British foreign editor with experience of Middle East reporting commented : "Many correspondents will not leave the towns and explore the country. They prefer to rely on second-hand information which is largely government handout material."

iii. Kinds of News Reported

Middle East coverage is strongly weighted towards politics, and economic and social news tends to be ignored even though political developments very often have direct economic and social causes. Human interest stories are virtually non-existent. The result is an unbalanced picture of the area and several correspondents fastened on this as an explanation of why the public outside the Middle East finds life there inexplicable.

---

[1] See *IPI Assembly 1953 : The Proceedings,* page 63.

"Coverage is too selective," said one correspondent, "and it has a strong bias towards political news. I think that more space should be devoted to economic analysis, news of cultural life and the life of the ordinary people in the village who are, after all, the real Middle East. Many of the glib dispatches about 'xenophobia' in various parts of the area would, I believe, never have been written if the correspondent had had some contact with the mass of the population."

Various examples of important economic and social stories which were ignored or inadequately covered by the press abroad were given :

Economic Stories

"The cotton scandals of 1950 and 1951 were, with rare exceptions, inadequately reported from Egypt. It was only after the fall of the Wafd Government that the economic condition of Egypt focussed attention on the mishandling of the cotton market, but even then it was inadequately explained. Yet this affair of the cotton market was a major factor affecting almost everything which has since happened in Egypt politically and economically.

"Again, in 1952, the Egyptian Government's failure to sell the cotton crop produced an economic situation in Egypt almost comparable with that caused in Iran by the failure to sell its oil. The analogy, which had obvious political implications, was given little space in the world press."

"Economic developments in Iraq, arising from the immense oil revenues now flowing in, have never been adequately reported outside the more weighty world newspapers."

"Insufficient attention has been paid in the world press to the recapture by the Germans of important economic markets in the Middle East."

"Newspaper reports in recent years have given a totally distorted picture of the population movements in the Middle East. It is grasped that the Middle East is overpopulated in many regions and is daily becoming more overpopulated. This is the crux of the problem in Egypt, Jordan and Israel. It is sometimes reported in a few newspapers that development schemes are being prepared to deal with this problem, but it is not underlined that these schemes cannot bring any alleviation for another ten to 15 years and it is during that period that the problem will come to a head."

"That feudalism still exists in some places in the Middle East is true. But that feudalism is definitely on its way to extinction in the Arab Middle East is equally true, as recent events in Lebanon, Syria, and Egypt can illustrate. In Egypt the agrarian reform law is already being implemented. Some 600,000 acres of land, formerly owned by rich landlords, the royal family and pashas and operated as feudal domains, are today in the process of being distributed to the landless peasants. How this destruction of feudalism is taking place and how the new land reform law is working seem rarely to have inspired an inquiring American correspondent or editor."

Social Stories

"Little has been said about the three-quarters of a million Arab refugees from Palestine, for whom life stands still in the tented camps in the deserts across the Israeli frontiers."

"Reactions of Israeli immigrants towards their new home and the fact that 40,000 of them (5 per cent of those who have entered the new state in the past six years) have left again, have been little reported. Equally little has been said about how the Arabs who remained in Israel are faring."

"Educational developments, including the astonishing decrease of illiteracy in recent years, have been ignored—for example, the establishment of a Unesco centre of fundamental education in Egypt."

"Little or nothing appears in the world press about important social reform movements, such as the growing emancipation of women and public hygiene experiments in backward villages."

Some of these subjects are topics for feature rather than news treatment. Some may be regarded as too dull or too specialised for the general reader. But, one Egyptian correspondent asked, how much real reporting has been done on the extremist movements in the Middle East ? For example, the bazaars of Teheran, which have been repeatedly said to shelter the ringleaders of Iran's political underworld, have often cropped up in stories of rioting in Teheran ; Ayatollah Kashani is said to be the ruler of the bazaar underworld, but the real story has not yet been told. Again, how much really authoritative reporting has been done about the Moslem Brotherhood movement in Egypt ?

Instead of these stories, this correspondent pointed out, newspapers often receive a great deal of political copy which has little interest outside the Middle East : too much repetition day by day of inconsequential developments in the Anglo-Egyptian negotiations, Arab League discussions and so on.

iv. Distortion and Bias in Reporting

Contributors to this report agree that examples of distortion of Middle East news by deliberate use of false information are rare. Nevertheless, they said, distortion does occur and its principal causes are two.

First, there is the distortion that springs from ignorance on the part of the reporter, or from his inability to get at all the facts, or from restrictions imposed on his reporting the facts once they are ascertained.

Common reasons for this innocent distortion, according to an experienced French correspondent, are :

(a) a desire to exaggerate the picturesque ; (b) the tendency to adopt a romantic view of everything that happens in the Middle East, and to attribute events exclusively to motives of personal revenge, fanaticism and so on ; (c) the representation of secret forces such as intelligence services, the Cominform, religious sects and arms merchants as the sole arbiters of events in the Middle East ; and (d) the absence of any kind of reliable statistics or representative facts.

The preoccupation with sensationalism leads to over-simplified reporting. "For example," said this French correspondent, "most French newspapers have taken the easy line of attributing all developments in Iran to Communist propaganda, usually without seeking to distinguish between the effects of Communist scheming and genuine national aspirations. Consequently, French opinion has not always understood the importance of Middle East nationalism."

Another example of the same type of distortion, according to a British correspondent in Egypt, was the so-called attempted coup d'état against the Neguib régime in January 1953. "The story," he said, "was really that a few dissident elements had been interned by the régime, but it was represented in the foreign press as an actual plot to overthrow the régime. Two factors contributed to the false impression. One was censorship, which prevented the truth from being told early enough; the other was the desire of visiting journalists, who had come for Sunday newspaper stories and were only staying for a few days, to sensationalize the event. One correspondent managed to evade censorship with a grossly overwritten account of what had happened for a British Sunday newspaper."

Misunderstanding of the way political forces work in the Middle East was suggested by an American specialist as another cause of distorted reporting. "It is impossible," he said, "to compare 'majorities,' 'forces,' 'underground movements' and 'oppositions' in the area with corresponding groupings in western countries. Therefore the views of opposition groups and the influences of underground currents are often neglected, although they determine trends within Middle East governments and changes of government more than all the official declarations. The case of Egypt seems to have been a lesson to western correspondents, but reporting in Iran, Syria and Jordan shows that correspondents too often are the mouthpieces of the government of the day. The same is true of Israel. So the coups d'état of Neguib and Shishakly and the resignation of Ben Gurion came as great surprises and were wrongly interpreted."

The second main cause of distortion is more serious. It is the deliberate slanting of news to produce a certain effect in the reader's mind. It may be caused by a prejudice on the part of the reporter or by the policy of his editor.

A prime example of distortion quoted by British specialists was the case of "The Dancing Major." It was interesting because it could have arisen either from the desire on the part of the reporter to make a graphic headline or from the political impulse to represent Egyptian behaviour in the Sudan in an unfavourable light.

Major Saleh Salem, Egyptian Minister of National Guidance and a close associate of General Neguib, visited the Sudan in the summer of 1953 to promote Egypt's case in the forthcoming elections. During his tour in southern Sudan he took part in a "fantasia" (celebration) and was photographed during the ceremonies dancing in déshabille : whereupon part of the British press nicknamed him "The Dancing Major" (one referring to him as "Underpants Salem"). Of this reaction one British observer commented : "Apparently no British paper thought it worth while pointing out that British officials in the Sudan have often themselves taken part in these ceremonial dances with the Sudanese tribes as a complimentary gesture." Another added : "In western eyes the exhibition was neither dignified nor decent, but in the eyes of the Sudanese and of the Arabs generally, it was little more remarkable than would be, for instance, the 'exhibition' of the squire or parson taking part in a game of darts at the village local.

"But these reports and comments came back to the Sudan at once and were published and broadcast all over the Arab world. In many quarters they were represented as a subversive attempt by the British to discredit their opponents on lines that were neither justified by the past nor pertinent under any conditions."

Bias does not always spring from a newspaper's policy. Several correspondents admitted that the atmosphere in which they work in the Middle East is so heavily charged with emotionalism about rights and wrongs—for instance, of the semi-colonial Arab country asserting itself against its former "protector" and of the Arab versus the Jew—that it is difficult to remain objective.

Of reporting from Israel, an American correspondent wrote : "The Americans appear to be sending a well-rounded picture from most parts of the Middle East except Israel ... Here most correspondents are won over by the Israelis because of the little state's valiant struggle for existence and they give little emphasis to the bleaker side. For example, one seldom reads about sub-standard living conditions, exorbitant prices, black markets, inefficient and insulting municipal workers, discrimination against Israeli Arabs and the lack of religious devotion except among the Orthodox minority. Instead we get a picture that is all milk and honey."

The major subjects on which observers have noted bias in the British press in recent days are the disputes between Britain and Egypt over the future of the Suez Canal zone and the Sudan and between Britain and Iran over the oil question. Israeli relations with the Arab world are a familiar bone of contention but, now that Britain is no longer responsible for administration in Palestine, much of the heat has died away. [1]

"There is the undoubted development in reporting from the Middle East," said one veteran British correspondent, "that some newspapers act according to a set policy, either expecting the corre-

---

[1] According to one British observer, the way in which the British press has tired of the Arab-Israeli question has led it to underplay the issue. "I cannot understand," he wrote, "why no newspaper that I have seen has yet described the intensity of feeling in the Arab world against Israel. For some reason neither the correspondents nor any of our politicians seem to have appreciated what some of my colleagues and myself have found to be our most striking impression on visiting the Arab world today."

spondent to send news which suits the policy or else partially ignoring or presenting inconspicuously the news which conflicts with its policies. Thus one mass circulation London newspaper has consistently presented the news regarding the Anglo-Egyptian question in a manner which shows the Egyptians in an untrustworthy light and a settlement based on evacuation as unwise for Britain."

"The British press," commented a specialist, "gives a reasonably accurate picture of Egypt and Israel when there are no direct British interests at stake. But, as soon as these come on the scene, reporting is more in the nature of political warfare than objective coverage."

Another British specialist added : "Probably as much attention is given by the British press as a whole to Arab as to Israeli news, but one has the impression that the Arabs seldom appear to advantage —and that through no fault of their own. Sensational stories receive more attention than the serious aspects of Arab affairs. Statements by Arab statesmen and leaders get a good show if they are violent attacks on the British or if they lend themselves to disparaging treatment."

In the American press, on the other hand, the Arab-Israeli question is still said to be the major cause of bias, but, as the United States has been drawn deeper and deeper into Middle East politics, other questions have roused strong feelings. "The present coverage of the Middle East by American newspapers," said one of America's foremost experts, "is defective in being slanted toward pro-American, anti-British, anti-imperialist, anti-communist, pro-Israeli and any other number of points of departure."

An American correspondent said bluntly : "The main 'restrictive practice' does not exist in the Middle East at all but in the United States itself. American editors are nearly all afraid to tell the truth about the Israeli-Arab controversy because of the Zionist lobby."

Another American specialist commented : "Not many editors of American newspapers are really impartial in the treatment of news concerning the Middle East. If Arabs are involved in events contrary to western policies or western interests, such stories are generally amply covered and displayed prominently in the American press. But if events happen that are favourable or in line with policies of the Middle Eastern states, these are often ignored.

"Then there is the technique of slanting the news against the Middle East. I have seen stories from the Middle East in the American press that were favourable to the Middle East government's point of view but with headlines that are certainly misleading, and also contrary to the contents of the news stories. The reporters told the truth but the headlines were slanted contrarily.

"For example, if a story from Tel Aviv accuses the Arabs of a frontier violation, it will have a headline of from 16 to 48 point type, depending upon whether the headline is one or more columns wide. Just the opposite happens when a story, datelined Amman (Jordan), accuses the Israelis of a frontier violation. The Jordan story will rarely carry a headline of more than one column width, and generally the heading is either an eight, ten or twelve point boldface type. With such a situation existing, how can American correspondents or editors expect government authorities in the Middle East to be friendly to an obviously one-sided and often slanted coverage? The story of the Qibya massacre might seem to disprove this contention, but the size and drama of the incident were such that the American press could not play it down."

One American observer thought that the American press had sided too much with Britain on the AIOC oil dispute. "Most readers of American newspapers," he said, "know that Iran seized the holdings of the company. They also know about the antics of former Premier Mossadegh, but that American is indeed a rare individual who can say that his newspaper provided him with the pros and cons of both the Iranian and British positions in the oil dispute. Most American newspaper readers know that the Tudeh Party in Iran is either Communist-inspired or Communist-controlled, but few know the causes that make possible the existence of the Tudeh Party.

"Again, most Americans have read something in their press about the Middle East Defence Command proposed by the U.S. Government, but it is a rare newspaper which explains what reasons Middle East leaders give against agreeing to such a command. In the American tradition of giving 'both sides of the story' it would seem that an editor would have his curiosity stirred even to the small extent of wanting to find out why the Middle Eastern states opposed the plan.

"I do not believe that any reputable American newspaper editor or reporter deliberately distorts the news from the Middle East. I do think that their coverage is often naïve and ill-balanced. For example, many American newspapers and magazines ran full accounts of progress made in Israel on the first, second and third anniversaries of the new state. But it never seemed to occur to the editors that progress is not the exclusive possession of one particular group of people or of one country. One might have thought that some correspondent or editor would ask and try to answer the question : 'What have the Arab states done in a comparable period of time ?' "

According to a French correspondent, "significant distortion occurs in the French press when it touches on events in Lebanon and Syria, the reason being the memory of and hankering after the former privileged position occupied by France in the Levant."

Another French correspondent said that the generally fair picture of the Middle East in the French press was marred by political bias in certain newspapers. The principal causes of bias, he thought, were

(a) the belief of certain newspapers that the Jews, because of their persecution, had a right to a territorial asylum, which led them to adopt an *a priori* defensive attitude on behalf of Israel ;

(b) the natural sympathy of France for other great powers in conflicts with semi-colonial countries. Thus, with the exception of the French left wing press, newspapers as a whole supported Britain in her disputes with Egypt and Iran. On the other hand, there was a growing trend on the part of certain Conservative newspapers, such as *Figaro,* to modify this attitude towards French North Africa and consequently to give a more favourable reception to the arguments of Middle East nationalism.

Another cause of bias is the frequency with which Middle East news is reported not through the eyes of an impartial professional observer on the spot but through the diplomatic channels of foreign embassies. For this governments in the area are often to blame themselves, because they close ordinary channels of news and invite the world press to seek the story from foreign offices. When that happens the foreign case is inevitably played up and the point of view of the Middle East country involved played down. The good diplomatic correspondent prides himself on knowing the amount of salt to add to any official version, but his capacity for scepticism has limitations, especially if he has no firsthand experience of the area. London in particular ranks as a major source of news on the Middle East not only for the British press but also for many foreign newspapers. Britain's traditional position as paramount power in the Arab world makes it inevitable that her Foreign Office should be a speedy and important news centre, but if, as sometimes happens, a European newspaper presents what is reported in London as straight Middle East news, the risk of bias in the reader's mind is obvious.

News from interested sources outside foreign offices can also mislead. A British specialist commented : "During the quarter century preceding the establishment of the State of Israel, it was almost universally believed in Britain and the U. S. that there were great tracts of empty land in and around Palestine which could be made available for new settlers but for Arab obstruction. I would not lay responsibility for this on the press. It was a case where the press reported on information given to it by those who appeared to be best informed and most strongly represented in Britain and the U. S. A. and they happened to be those who had a motive for getting that point of view accepted.

"My belief is that distortions and inaccuracies have had their origin mainly in the sources from which the press draws its information and views, rather than in editorial offices—except where the latter are themselves governed by interested parties."

Some correspondents spoke of a further source of bias within the Middle East. The large oil companies maintain public relations departments which are usually well equipped and helpful. It is their legitimate task to present the companies' activities in a favourable light, but it seems that on occasion their pressure on the correspondent to send "the right story" can exceed reasonable bounds.

For example, one correspondent reported of Saudi Arabia : "Virtually the only way to get in is through sponsorship by Aramco (the Arabian American Oil Company). If the company likes you, you get in. If not, you've had it." Another said : "Visas for Saudi Arabia are very difficult to obtain and can be got only through the aid of Aramco. Once there under the oil company's wing, a reporter finds himself under considerable pressure to be nice to the company in print."

A similar dilemma was reported from Iran during the dispute between the Anglo-Iranian Oil Company and the Iranian Government. "In 1951," wrote a correspondent, "at the height of the crisis, correspondents at Abadan had unusual difficulties to face. Abadan has grown up around the refinery and is rarely visited by Europeans in large numbers, so that the only tolerable accommodation in that tough climate was the AIOC guest house. The company offered correspondents a free bed, meals and drinks and any attempt even to pay for the latter was refused. For those who stayed only a short time the position was acceptable, but it was difficult for a correspondent who stayed throughout the months of the crisis and tried to remain impartial. A reputation for impartiality did one harm with the company

77

and no good at all with the Persians, none of whom believed that a western correspondent would try to be impartial and certainly not when living at AIOC expense . . .

"The situation in Abadan was exceptional but worth recording as a perfect image in miniature of totalitarian régimes as they affect the press. Pressure was exercised on the correspondent with greater or lesser degrees of obnoxiousness according to the official involved, but as tensions rose towards the end and the evacuation, it became unwise for a correspondent even to hint aloud that the Persians had perhaps something of a case and that the company was anything but immaculate."

Perhaps the most powerful cause of bias is the attitude of the newspaper reader. He wants to believe, whenever possible, that his country and therefore he himself is in the right in any international dispute. This feeling is a major consideration in Britain, which has played a predominant role in the Middle East for as long as most newspaper readers can remember.

A British foreign editor commented : "There are certain firm prejudices in the West about some Middle East countries which influence editors in their briefing of correspondents and in their selection of material. So far as Egypt and the British press are concerned, a contributing factor was the wartime experience of the British army which saw often only the seamier side of Egyptian life ; it was a side which could hardly have been worse, but it was only one element in the picture."

A British specialist added : "Few would deny that the (British) man in the street is puzzled and hurt when, after 'defending Egypt from Rommel,' Britain is hysterically and monotonously vilified by Egyptian spokesmen ; when, after having to all intents and purposes created the geographical and national entity known as the Sudan, Britain's political enemies win the recent elections ; when, after having created and subsidised for years the Kingdom of Jordan, Britain's reputation is so low in Amman ; when, having risked a quarrel of historic proportions with her neighbour and traditional ally, France, to ensure for Syria and the Lebanon their national independence, these two countries join the other Arab states in attacking Britain."

For readers who start with that attitude (and many editors share their view) the story they want to read is not a complicated explanation of why there is something to be said on the other side but a short clear vindication of their own national integrity in a world of wilful misunderstanding.

The development of the Anglo-Iranian oil dispute in the British press was cited as an example of this tendency by a specialist who otherwise championed the performance of the British press on its Middle East reporting. It was doubtful, he said, whether the British public ever understood from its newspapers the basis on which the Iranian Government claimed £49 millions from the oil company ; it was enough that the sum seemed excessive in British eyes. Further, the story that Iran would reject any official British representative who spoke Persian was widely believed in Britain, though it was apocryphal. It gained currency because it was a simple example of the kind of foolishness into which excessive nationalism might lead a country ; so the exact facts did not matter.

v. Calibre of Reporting

The volume of good reporting of the Middle East which the interested reader can find in the press is a proof of the high calibre of the senior foreign correspondents who write with experience of the area, but it must be admitted that the ideal Middle East correspondent has yet to be born and the conditions in which he can do his best work have yet to be created.

The ideal reporter would have to be a first-class political analyst who can grasp the real trends in an area where signposts are few and the bypaths innumerable. He must also be a good military strategist and a shrewd economist who can sift the truth from insufficient data about population trends and budgets. He should have Arabic and Persian (and Hebrew) as well as French and English as his familiar languages. He must be deeply read in the history of the Middle East and have a grasp of its tribal organisations and religions. The wonder, as one observer remarked, is that, with so many qualifications required, there is so much clear and competent reporting from the area.

But critics drew clear lines of distinction between various types of Middle East correspondent. In contrast with the solid, and sometimes brilliant, work being done by the permanent and experienced men is the shoddy work often turned in (and readily splashed by the employing newspaper) by the visiting correspondent and the rank-and-file local correspondent and stringer.

Visiting Correspondents

Several correspondents thought that, in the highly suggestible atmosphere of the Middle East, the quality of reporting was affected by the length of time a reporter stayed there. But opinions differed widely on the ideal.

One correspondent said : "Personally I think a rapid turnover is healthy. I do not favour leaving a man in one spot for more than two years or at the most three. This of course does not apply to the heads of the large agency bureaus, whose contacts become more valuable as the years pass."

Another correspondent with long experience of Middle East coverage gave a further strong reason for limiting a correspondent's stay. "Many reporters," he said, "especially those who have been in the Middle East for several years, lose their sense of proportion and give too much importance or too much detail which is of no interest outside the country itself. I found this myself when, after a long stay, I got so close to political detail as to lose perspective. On the whole, the agencies face up to this task without falling too often into the trap."

There is, however, much to be said on the other side. A correspondent who arrives in the Middle East without previous experience of the area undoubtedly sometimes sees stories which his older colleagues have missed, but the "fresh look" which he can put on a story may have to be paid for in accuracy.

The permanent correspondent had some hard things to say about the special correspondent who flies in and flies out in a space of days or weeks. "It is one of the curiosities of foreign reporting today," said one British correspondent, "that special correspondents are frequently rushed round the world, arriving on the heels of the news and presenting an angled and tendentious story based on inadequate time and study. The fault lies in the newspaper system and is particularly heinous in the case of some popular British Sunday newspapers. French newspapers are also given to this kind of foreign reporting. The Middle East has suffered gravely by it."

This same correspondent thought that the frequent changing of correspondents also led to poor results. "For example," he said, "one London daily has had four changes of correspondent in Cairo in two years. Another has frequently changed its correspondent, although nominally retaining the same man. Thus, through no fault of their own, correspondents have difficulty in acquiring more than a superficial judgment of the situation in the area. It seems that the popular newspapers do not expect their correspondents to find time to master their area. The latter know that their sojourns will be so short that the effort is not worth while."

An American specialist commented: "The overwhelming majority of the American public has a woeful misunderstanding of the Middle East and it is due to a large extent to the kind of non-resident correspondent which the American press sends to that area. Rarely does an American editor choose his correspondent on the basis of his knowledge of the Middle East. Too often 'name correspondents' are sent to cover a short assignment which they do with the air of an expert, but how can a Westerner, with no experience of the traditions and philosophy of the Middle East, expect in a matter of hours or days to interpret intelligently for his audience back home exactly what is happening in the Middle East ?"

Agency Coverage

The foreign staffs (American, British, French, German and Indian) of agency bureaus in the Middle East are generally acknowledged to be doing a sound and conscientious job. Nevertheless, the handicaps under which news agencies must work have to be recognised.

One observer said : "It seems very ungrateful for anyone interested in newsgathering to criticise the news agencies. The newspapers depend on them heavily for the solid body of news—the statistics, the quotations from local papers, the public statements and so on—which the special correspondent seldom has time for and anyway knows is being covered for him. The agency men work hard, continuously and competitively for 24 hours a day and rarely miss a beat... But they have the defects of their virtues. The pressure of competition means that it is dangerous for them to spend too much time on checking their stories—and that, in the Middle East, almost invariably means that some vital detail is left out or left in wrong.

"Their effort to serve the newspapers 'by putting the lead in the lead' sometimes results in their tearing the heart out of a story to make a headline. Quotations from the local press are selected not so much for their objectivity as for their provocativeness, as this assists the agency in its useful function of 'getting a reaction.'

"During the period of tension between Britain and the Middle East these peculiarities of agency reporting can cause trouble. During the Anglo-Egyptian negotiations on the Sudan and later on the Suez Canal zone a number of misunderstandings on both sides were engendered by over-enthusiastic transmissions that tended to make the worst of any situation.

"All that having been said, it still remains true that the news agencies perform an indispensable service and that they do it with great efficiency and completeness. They fill innumerable gaps where there are just not enough newspaper correspondents to go round and everywhere they supply a constant stream of basic news that no newspaper could match from its own resources."

All contributors agreed on the truth of this qualified tribute to the agencies. They agreed further that the weaknesses inevitable in agency reporting anywhere are increased by the extent to which agency coverage in the Middle East is left to local correspondents and stringers.

Local Correspondents

One agency executive said of local correspondents : "They inevitably have faults. The following gives some idea of working with them in an agency :

1) They are seldom objective about conditions in their own country.

2) They are usually anxious not to quarrel with the authorities, so that they are inclined to apply a censorship of their own.

3) They lack western news standards and methods and are usually incapable of producing reliable reports on such matters as economic developments. They will, for example, publicise extravagant plans for some development without pausing to examine the probability or even possibility of their execution.

4) They have a passion for the interview, irrespective of whether the interviewee or his opinions have any topical news value."

Yet this is an area where the local correspondent is a key man. As was pointed out earlier, the fact that speedy movement is often difficult for a foreign correspondent means that the first—and most vital—coverage of a major story has to be left to the local man. Secondly, as the man on the spot in a complicated situation, the local correspondent can claim a validity for his views which is hard to check independently. Thirdly, the coverage of news between crises, which is often the most difficult copy to write, is left to the local man—whether or not, as an editor in the Middle East commented, he has the time, ability and knowledge of language (that is, English) to do it properly.

"Most stringers," commented a British journalist who has worked with them for many years, "are handicapped by government pressure because they have other and more important financial interests. This applies even to foreigners like myself. When the stringer tries to present a reasonably objective picture, he often finds himself being bulldozed by officialdom into producing a piece of propaganda. Foreigners in these circumstances just drop the piece altogether, but local stringers may have to go on and write something which is untruthful.

"Some form of training for stringers is essential. In the Middle East many of them have not got the faintest idea of accuracy or indeed of what goes to make up a news story."

Another correspondent who has made periodic tours of the Middle East for years said : "Most local correspondents have their own jobs from which they derive their regular livelihood and what they earn as correspondents is often regarded as pocket money. When I was last on tour I found that many of them were so insignificant personally and professionally that they were of no assistance for making contact with local opinion of any value.

"But there is this excuse for them. Their position is often very delicate. They are quite safe so long as they confine their activities to the automatic dispatch of official or social news. But, when it comes to views—except of the propaganda type with which their national press is saturated—those who have any views think twice before sending them abroad. If their views are untimely or, worse still, officially unwelcome, their shrift will be very short.

"Most of the local personnel who used to be employed by agencies and newspaper correspondents lacked professional training. Although the situation has considerably improved in the past few years, stringers, who are being increasingly relied upon, often tend to take a passionately unobjective view of affairs, even if they do it unwittingly."

An experienced British observer commented : "Things are less happy when an important newspaper relies for some reason—financial or organisational—on a 'stringer,' sometimes British, sometimes a local national, not always a professional newspaper man. Much misunderstanding is caused when 'Our Correspondent' expresses opinions that are much more a reflection of the local marketplace than of a detached and independent point of view.

"What is an exception for the newspapers is, in some important centres of the Middle East, the rule for the agencies. It is sadly often the case that all the authority and reputation of a great international agency are placed at the disposal of a local correspondent who has yet to learn the very first lesson of agency work—impartiality. Of course, nine times out of ten, a biassed dispatch is filtered out at one end or the other ; but some are not, and they contribute their mite to the confusion of nations."

It must be said that these general impressions seem unfair to the individual correspondent who stands out against pressure and does his utmost to provide an impartial account of events. In such a case his close links with the area can make him a more valuable channel of news than the foreign-born reporter.

Nevertheless, the unanimity of every contributor to this report in stressing the weaknesses of reporting by native correspondents and stringers was too impressive to be disregarded.

These reporters have, however, one tremendous advantage over the foreign-born correspondent and many specialists and correspondents laid great emphasis on it. They know the language of the country—Arabic, Persian and Hebrew—whereas the foreigner does not.

Problem of Language

Estimates vary among correspondents about how great an obstacle ignorance of Arabic is, but one, with experience going back over a decade, described it as "the main barrier between the West and the Arab world."

To appreciate the size of the barrier, he pointed out, it is necessary to remember that there are in effect three Arabic languages in use. The first is the "literary Arabic" of the Koran, which is also the official language. The second is the "vulgar Arabic" spoken in the street and the bazaar. It is not a written language at all, nor is it exactly a dialect. It is rather the formal language with its complicated grammar simplified and with many foreign terms taken over almost literally (such as 'el telefoun' for telephone). This is the kitchen Arabic which most foreigners with any length of residence learn fairly fluently. Finally, there is "newspaper Arabic" standing midway between the other two, but nearer the pure than the vulgar language. It is this Arabic which anybody who wishes to read the newspapers and official handouts or listen to speeches must have—and very few foreign correspondents possess it.

In recent years the language barrier has grown greater. In former days, when French or English was considered an official language in most Middle East countries, the foreign correspondent (even from another oriental country like India, where Arabic is little understood) had direct access to official proceedings. In Egypt, for example, the "Official Gazette" was published in French as well as Arabic and was a faithful translation of the original. Today, there is still a French edition, but it is less reliable and increasingly different from the Arabic edition. Texts are often omitted from the French edition and if they appear at all they are given months later—a reflection of the growing coldness to the West and neglect of press relations.

Another interesting source of information, the meetings of learned societies, are steadily abandoning French in favour of Arabic for purposes of discussion and record. Even in banks and financial houses, which have the strongest reason of all for maintaining close relations with the West, Arabic is perforce replacing French and English.

Ignorance of Arabic is therefore gradually closing channels of information to the foreign correspondent, though there are still several ways in which he can obtain some idea of the movements of opinion.

His best source consists of those newspapers still published in a European language. They usually try to be objective and to hold aloof from partisan quarrels ; they summarise comment in the Arabic press ; and they normally have their own reporters at the ministries and in parliament. Nevertheless, the European-language press also faces the same two obstacles as the correspondent—censorship and the language problem. Further, its appeal is to the foreign resident and its news selection and treatment is determined by its readership, so that it often ignores what is going on in many important spheres of Arab life—the theatre, the cinema, belles lettres and even sport which has no European angle—and gives its readers a partial view of the local scene. From the correspondent's point of view, it also has the disadvantage of being a day late with its reflection of the Arab press.

These drawbacks are to a certain extent offset by the fact that the newspapermen working for the European-language press, like their colleagues throughout the rest of the world, usually know a great deal more about what is going on than appears in the columns of their paper. This knowledge, if it is available to the foreign correspondent, is often of the greatest help to him.

The correspondent has another valuable source of information— the press digests which have sprung up in the past few years as a special service to interested foreigners, such as newspapermen and business men. They have the disadvantage, however, of usually being too small to give more than a very broad idea of the Arab press—the title of the main articles in the leading dailies and weeklies, a brief news summary, a translation of the main leaders and so on. They also suffer from the specialist nature of their readership, so that they also give only a partial picture. For example, a press digest may report in detail Arab League decisions on Morocco and pass over League decisions on equally important questions of political relations among the member states ; or it may quote an unimportant writer because he is talking about relations with the West and ignore much more significant material because its immediate interest is strictly Arab in character.

Finally, the correspondent can, and usually does, hire a local reporter to read the Arabic press for him. Many of the translators employed are excellent journalists and often hold important positions on large local papers ; but the best of them can hardly avoid a tendency, conscious or unconscious, to guide the correspondent along a certain line of thought. Of these translator services, one correspondent said : "The practice of having a local newspaperman read the newspapers isn't too good because they are frequently hip-deep in local politics. Sometimes, they just do not read you everything in the papers ; at other times they tip you on false rumours. They are, of course, under heavy pressure because they could be punished severely by the local authorities."

Again, even if a completely impartial translator could be found, the correspondent is still faced with the task of deciding what is or is not reliable in the material read to him.

One contributor to this study, with a wide and sympathetic interest in the Arab press, said of it : "It is extremely unreliable as a source of information. Not that Middle Easterners cannot make good journalists—far from it. But, whether from lack of tradition or experience or from a superabundance of misplaced patriotism, they do seem to find it much harder than most to exercise those virtues of restraint and impartiality, to say nothing of careful attention to the facts, without which all reporting is largely a wasted exercise ... Without a reasonably honest indigenous press, the task of the foreign correspondent is very much harder. Further, where the local press has lost or never acquired its self-respect, the governments find it much easier to treat it with contempt and to extend their interference to foreign correspondents. There are many Middle East journalists who are well aware of this and greatly deplore the local lack of standards, but they are still a minority."

One pitfall for the correspondent who does not understand Arabic, according to observers well qualified to judge, may have serious results for relations between Middle East countries and the outside world. This springs from the fact that Arabic is a very different medium of expression from western languages. In the earlier days of Islam there was a ban on the representation of the human figure and all artistic endeavour was canalised in language. The result is that ideas in Moslem countries are apt to be expressed more forcefully and vividly than in the West. Rhetoric, therefore, needs careful interpretation as well as translation if undue importance is not to be given to inflammatory speeches and bellicose resolutions which in their original Arabic are, in fact, nothing but words, words, words. The correspondent is under a special obligation to make a real distinction between what is just plain demagogy, political irresponsibility and sheer ignorance of diplomatic procedure on the one hand, and acts and statements of real consequence on the other.

The damage that ignorance of the language can do extends into the day-to-day legwork done by the correspondent. A correspondent with long experience of reporting and editing in the Middle East said that he had taken part in press conferences, conducted in both Arabic and English or both Arabic and French, at which the Arabic version was deliberately different from the English or French ; the spokesman would tell his Arabic listeners in an aside that there were certain things it was pointless to reveal abroad.

The fact that most Middle East leaders have a good knowledge of English or French is naturally a considerable advantage to the foreign correspondent without Arabic, though, when both interviewing reporter and interviewed leader are making contact through a language which is native to neither of them, such as French, the value of what passes between them must often be dubious.

The language problem, it should be remembered, often exists also for the eastern correspondent. An Indian observer, commenting that his own press did not give a very clear idea of the area, said : "Too few newspaper correspondents know the right language and have the requisite knowledge. The newspaperman must not only obtain his information from the chancelleries and the clubs where the upper classes are to be met ; he must also find a way to tap opinion in the cafés, mosques, and bazaars."

Foreign P. R. O. s.

In an area where the native languages are Arabic, Persian and Hebrew, the importance to the foreign correspondent of the public information departments of foreign embassies and legations is obviously increased. Correspondents whose experience of the Middle East is confined to the postwar years expressed qualified satisfaction with the help given them by American and British public information officers.

"Many correspondents," said one, "resort mainly to the American and British Embassies. The Americans are too often on the defensive to justify themselves—unless you are lucky and find a really friendly professional who doesn't care where the chips fly. The British likewise have to justify, but much more ; yet the high calibre ones make a very good case for their side."

Newspapermen with experience dating back to the period between the two world wars think that there has been a marked deterioration in the quality of work done by the British public information offices— which, with the French, were until recent years the principal foreign sources of official information in the Middle East. This was how one British correspondent summarised the position. "Before World War II," he wrote, "official contact with foreign correspondents and the Middle East press was handled by the oriental secretariats in each mission. There were few communiqués and fewer press handouts, and the calibre and personality of the individual official responsible were the all-important factors.

"During World War II the British Ministry of Information introduced into the diplomatic missions a new machinery in the shape of press officers and information officers. Many of the holders of these new appointments had had previous personal experience of the Middle East newspaper world and knew how to explain local conditions and politics to foreign correspondents. But, as the war progressed, they found their time more and more occupied by paper work—communiqués, handouts, censorship and so on—with the result that less and less time became available for personal contacts.

"After 1945, the British press and information services in the Middle East were overhauled and reduced ; and, unfortunately perhaps, the control of these offices was gradually transferred from trained journalists to *de carrière* Foreign Office officials, few of whom had any journalistic experience or previous acquaintance with the special problems of the Middle East. The result was that many of these offices became more and more mechanical Civil Service offices and more and more defensively aloof, impersonal and official."

vi. Handling the News

One of the greatest weaknesses of the presentation of Middle East news is its handling by the individual newspaper. It was pointed out above, when comparative coverage was being discussed (see page 61), that often the most competent treatment occurs on newspapers which have apparently slender extra resources of news from the area. The knowledge which the foreign editor brings to bear in directing his correspondent and which the foreign sub-editor shows in handling the news can go a long way to remove the greatest defect noted in Middle East coverage—its patchiness and lack of continuity.

For the facts that space for news from the area is severely limited and that the newspaper cannot afford special coverage no editor can be blamed. But apathy on the desk in the attitude to the Middle East is something that can be combated ; until it is overcome, the apathy of the reader is understandable.

There is no doubt that, on its long journey from reporter to page, Middle East news can produce some striking grotesqueries. One prime example occurred in the summer of 1953 when an agency distributed a report from Cairo in which preparations for general elections in Lebanon were inextricably mingled with General Neguib's Egyptian régime, so that the latter, a one-party affair, was reportedly facing a challenge from the Lebanese opposition party.

The report said : "The Egyptian Government will impose strict security measures to maintain order during the next election campaign, which might well produce trouble, in the opinion of some observers. Kamal Jumblatt, leader of the Opposition (*Lebanese* [1]), has called a conference of all Opposition candidates to discuss plans for forcing the resignation of the Neguib Cabinet... Yesterday the Neguib Cabinet decided not to resign at a meeting called to solve the ministerial crisis caused by the resignation of the *(Lebanese)* Minister of Defence Rashid Beydoun. It is thought that Lt-Col. Saleh Salem, chief of staff of the army *(should have been Saeb Salem, the Lebanese Premier)*, has asked the ministers who seek a mandate to resign in order to assure complete governmental neutrality. But the ministers have told Lt-Col. Salem that General Neguib should set the example in this. Faced with this dilemma, General Neguib has decided to retain the Cabinet in existence and Mr. Beydoun has changed his mind."

The example is extreme, but when the sub-editor is presented with that jumble of Middle East news, what is he to do ? Even some of the details are erroneous in places. The Egyptian Saleh Salem was neither a lieutenant-colonel nor chief of staff at the time but a major and Egyptian Minister of National Guidance.

Another example occurred during the treason trials in Cairo when, in autumn 1953, a large German newspaper splashed a report of the trials in which the members of the tribunal, all leading henchmen of General Neguib, were firmly placed in the dock and the accused on the tribunal. The observer who drew attention to this instance added : "This was an extreme case, but the wrong use of names is frequent even in the most reliable newspapers."

A British observer commented on this tendency : "The careless slips and mistakes of detail which all newspapers seem to make whenever they get on to your own special topic are multiplied manifold when they deal with the Middle East. There is almost complete ignorance of the Islamic religion in particular and of the background of Muslim culture in general. When Ibn Saud died one paper announced that he had once declared his fondness for three things in life—women, prayer and perfume. In fact, this is a quotation from the Prophet. Perhaps Ibn Saud did say it, but what would be thought

---

[1] This and the following italicised words in brackets in this paragraph have been inserted by the editor of this report as explanations.

of a French reporter who wrote that Churchill had once said, 'A little learning is a dangerous thing' ? These mistakes are not important in themselves, but they symbolise inaccuracy and produce distrust."

Other criticisms of the handling of Middle East news by the newspapers most commonly made were :

(a) that the desk man asks that the news should conform to his own stereotyped ideas of what makes the area interesting. Glamour and bloodshed are the keynotes, so either the news source dresses its stories accordingly or sees the space go to a rival who does. One contributor gave an example in which a sub-editor took the newspaper's own correspondent's story and warmed it up by adding sensational but inaccurate detail from an agency reporter.

(b) that, as was mentioned earlier, many newspapers turn to their own country's sources of diplomatic news to an extent that often makes the diplomatic correspondent chief Middle East correspondent. Though they usually do this in self-defence because adequate news from the area is not forthcoming, it does tend to make the foreign office the real source of information and comment.

(c) that the constant cutting of even reasonably comprehensive and concise stories from the agencies from force of habit has discouraged the agencies from trying to provide a properly backgrounded service.

(d) that, even when the story is factual and not distorted, headlines are forced.

vii. What Editors Think

Criticism of present reporting of the Middle East has been aired at considerable length in the previous pages, since it was the object of this study to gather as wide a volume of opinion on the subject as possible and present criticism as fully as possible. Some of the views expressed will be dismissed as too academic, others as too much like special pleading.

It is important, however, to know what newspaper editors think about the points raised, since they are the filters through which news services reach the readers.

An appreciable number of editors approached by the IPI agreed broadly with the agency executive who said that coverage just about matched the importance of the area. But most of them also indicated that they regarded the problem as too specialised for their capacity of criticism. This gives all the greater weight to the criticisms voiced by some of the editors.

Comment revolved round four points :

1. Quantity of news received : British editors thought the quantity generally satisfactory. Some American, Indian and European editors agreed (one editor in India describing coverage as "sometimes excessive") ; others did not. "The volume of news," said one Indian editor, "is woefully poor. Except from actual trouble spots like Teheran and Cairo there is very little to be heard from the Middle East. Even from these centres the flow is regular only when trouble is taking place. There is in short a noticeable lack of continuity. Many countries do not even get mentioned as far as their political developments are concerned. After reporting the accession of the new king in Jordan, nothing was said about what he has been doing, what happened to the old cliques, how the people feel and so on. Syria and Iraq are practically blind spots. Saudi Arabia burst into the headlines for a brief moment when King Ibn Saud died ; then there was silence again. Even the Sudanese elections did not get comprehensive continuous coverage, in spite of the fact that an Indian was chairman of the Election Commission." A Norwegian and an American editor considered agency coverage most defective on Iran and Egypt.

2. Quality of news received : Editors who thought the quantity sufficient criticised the quality of reporting. A German editor said : "The volume does not matter, but coverage of the U. S., Britain and France is better in every instance because it is more concrete, precise and to the point." An editor in India commented : "I am not conscious of any real scarcity of news from the area, though the quality of some of it is open to question. The information I should really like is rarely obtainable except in the form of intelligent guesses which perhaps are just as likely to be accurate if made from a distance." "The quality leaves a lot to be desired," wrote a British editor, "but this would seem to be due as much to the dubious motives and tactics of official sources as to the quality of local stringers and agencies."

3. Types of news : Two American editors suggested that they would like more background on non-political subjects. An Indian editor said : "Hardly ever does a social, cultural or human interest story escape from the Middle East, even from Egypt or Iran." A British editor criticised "the general lack of situationers from the agencies. What situationers there are," he said, "are never political because the agencies will not stick their necks out."

4. **Bias in reporting :** This complaint was confined to India and Europe. One Indian editor, however, pointed out that while the western agencies failed to assess news from the Indian viewpoint, "the faint undercurrent of bias in many of the stories appears magnified to Indian sub-editors because India is biassed the other way round." A German editor commented : "I have not been in Egypt since 1947, but I have a strong impression that many correspondents are not independent in their attitude . . . I believe that correspondents are wooed to bring them 'into line.' For instance, reports about the attempts of the Arab states to play off the West against the Soviet Union are abrupt and never touch the core of the problem." A Norwegian editor thought that, though the world was getting a fairly true picture of the Middle East, there was occasional bias, as for instance in reports on the Anglo-Iranian oil dispute. Generally, he felt that western correspondents tended to get their stories too much from European sources in the area.

Chapter IV

CONCLUSION

CONCLUSION

Any critical estimate of Middle East coverage in the world press would be unrealistic if it did not take full account of the difficulties involved.

Some of the difficulties are inherent in the character of the region. The great distances between the main centres of population, the trying climate, the complicated ethnic composition of the Middle East and the languages spoken by its peoples, all make high demands on the energy and capacity of the men reporting it. These initial difficulties are increased by the primitive nature of the sources of information in many of the countries.

A different set of problems are the product of deliberate policy on the part of Middle East governments. They arise from the occasional determination of this or that government to prevent the facts about it being fully reported.

A correspondent may find his entry to a country delayed or indeed barred altogether by the use of the visa system. Once he is in a country, his departure to another country where news is breaking may also be delayed by visa trouble. His movement inside a country may be restricted by the declaration that certain areas are out of bounds. Even in the capital his efforts to gather news may be frustrated by the refusal of the authorities to allow him access. Anything he writes may be subjected to overt or covert censorship. His cables may be delayed for a period which renders them useless. Even if his reports are not stopped, he may be subjected to a campaign of pinpricks because his version of events has upset officialdom. In Iran and Egypt the record of expulsion of correspondents is a constant reminder that the same fate may overtake him.

These are formidable obstacles. Restrictions tend to operate at just those periods when events of international interest are happening. They weigh most heavily on the resident correspondent—that is, among others, on the agency reporter who is responsible for the bulk of the Middle East news reaching the world's press. If he is a national of the country he is reporting—and agency coverage in the area is largely done by nationals—he runs a particularly serious risk in incurring his government's displeasure.

But the effects of restrictions are limited. They do not prevent the news from getting out. At most they merely delay it. Often they do not even achieve that, because the resident reporter may find his way round the obstacles. If he does not, there is often a rover correspondent on the spot who can move across the frontier to a point from which he can break the news. The only result achieved is to give the world a distorted version of the facts which harms the government concerned more than the truth would have done.

Other difficulties in the way of adequate reporting of the Middle East are presented by managerial problems, which once again affect the news agencies particularly. The fact that the Middle East consists of a group of at least a dozen independent countries means that, if the capital of each were to be covered by an office headed by a full-time correspondent of foreign nationality, the outlay for maintaining 12 such correspondents would be uneconomic in terms of the column inches of Middle East news published by client newspapers. This is a worldwide problem for the agencies, which meet it by employing, wherever possible, nationals of the country being reported. It is a workable solution in countries where press traditions are high, but it cannot be so satisfactory in the Middle East where the standing of the press is comparatively low and nationalism is intense.

The present network of telecommunications in the Middle East also creates problems. In most capitals the communications are not designed to carry the volume of traffic imposed on them when an event of international importance draws the world's press to the spot. Competition for priority on the wire often means that cables have to be sent at high 'urgent' rates, which in turn leads to an understandable tendency on the part of the correspondent to limit his story to the barest essentials. Middle East governments, by using telecommunications as a source of revenue and increasing cable charges to a rate which sometimes seems to bear no relation to the figures established by international agreement, help to prevent adequate reporting of their countries.

The difficulties presented by the triple handicaps of censorship, costs and communications to the news agencies have been underlined because the great majority of the world press relies virtually entirely on the agencies for its Middle East service. Only a handful of newspapers consider the area important enough to justify the maintenance of one or more permanent staff correspondents there and the cost of a daily news service from them.

What is thought of the calibre of Middle East coverage ? All contributors to this report drew a distinction between the volume of good reporting reaching the newspapers which make serious efforts to cover the region and the poor performance of the rest of the press.

The superiority of the small group of newspapers was said to lie in a combination of continuous news reporting, containing adequate background explanation, and informed editorial comment. The principal criticism made against them was that their coverage is often too narrowly political and too much confined to one or two countries of the area, but within these limitations conscientious reporting by the correspondent and intelligent interest in his reports on the part of his editor earned them high praise.

By contrast general coverage in the world press was criticised as superficial, incomplete and sensational. Its main defects were said to be :

1) lack of material explaining the background of events reported.

2) geographical unevenness of coverage ; comparatively too much attention to Egypt, Iran and Israel, too little to the other countries in the area.

3) too great concentration on political news, too little on economic and social news which often shapes and portends political developments.

4) distortion and bias in reporting and comment, partly through ignorance, partly through deliberate policy.

5) too thin coverage by experienced senior foreign correspondents; too much of the news gathering left to less well qualified local correspondents, who have the additional disadvantage of being nationals of the extremely sensitive countries they are reporting.

6) insufficient grasp of problems by foreign correspondents who suffer, in particular, from ignorance of the key languages.

7) poor handling of the news received on the desk and consequent lack of stimulus to the reporter in the field.

Insofar as these criticisms apply directly to the calibre of reporting from the Middle East, it might be thought that the distinction between the few newspapers reporting the area well and the rest of the press lies solely in the fact that the first have their own correspondents whereas the second do not. This, however, cannot be entirely true because, as examination of coverage showed,[1] some newspapers with comparatively extensive representation are not ranked as authoritative reporters of the Middle East while others with virtually no representation have a high reputation.

This enables us to put the estimation of agency services in better perspective. Some of the shortcomings attributed to them are based on the assumption that an editor without correspondents of his own, whose newspaper makes a poor showing on Middle East news, can shift the entire responsibility on to the agencies. This seems unjustifiable for two reasons. First, there is the question of what the newspaper does with the agency messages it receives. Agencies complain that often a well backgrounded story, obtained at considerable expense, is cut to an extent which makes it barely intelligible. Secondly, there is the question of what efforts a newspaper makes to supplement the agency spot news service.

Much must depend on the interest and initiative shown within the newspaper office in handling the news received from the agencies and amplifying it from other sources. The editor of a newspaper which does this with acknowledged success, explaining that it was done by means of special background features and leading articles, added : " In the Middle East what is really wanted is interpretation rather than a flow of spot news."

If his formula is correct, the improvement to be sought in Middle East news lies rather in the field of feature articles than of spot news. The same argument was advanced by an agency correspondent, who expressed the view that some of the spot news from the Middle East appearing in newspapers was a waste of space. Money and newsprint, he said, were being thrown away in attempts by newspapers to report day by day developments in political problems in which significant progress could be better assessed in terms of weeks or even months—for example, in the drawn-out Anglo-Egyptian negotiations. The result of fragmentary day-to-day reporting, in his view, was to give the reader dull, indigestible material which repelled him.

The correspondent added his own formula for better coverage. It would consist of three kinds of article—a) periodical political

---

[1] See pages 55-58.

roundups every time an important development called for it ; b) a regular supply of feature articles on non-political subjects, such as social and technical changes, and on prominent people (not only such obvious choices as Neguib and Zahedi, but also men less well known abroad but influential in their own countries) ; and c) letters from roving correspondents.

But, granted that these proposals are sound, how is a newspaper to obtain such material ? One of the greatest problems about news from the Middle East, as evidence in this study has indicated, is the comparative scarcity of journalists on the spot who combine the special knowledge required with the necessary degree of impartiality.

Contributors suggested various ways in which this problem might be tackled. For example, it was urged that the system, widely practised in Europe, of forming pools of newspapers to share the cost of a joint correspondent is capable of development for the Middle East. It was also thought that existing methods of syndicating articles from specialist journalists who tour the area from time to time might be expanded.

But, said observers, it is not enough to arrange intermittent feature coverage. Considerably better use could also be made of material already available (for example, from the agencies) if those in the home office of the newspaper knew more about the subject. There is, however, an obvious limit to the number of problems on which any editorial staff can be expected to be well informed. It was this human factor which led contributors to a previous IPI study "The News from Russia" to urge that editors, wherever possible, should enlist the aid of an expert in interpreting and supplementing the bare facts of the current news. The same suggestion was frequently made for improving the presentation of news from the Middle East. In many cities there are university departments of oriental studies from which specialists go regularly to the area ; among them are men and women ready and able to contribute information and articles to the local newspaper once contact with the editor is made.

These suggestions amount to saying that the key to better coverage of the Middle East lies in greater concentration by newsgatherers and newspapers on background articles that would explain the peoples of the area and their problems and less preoccupation with spot news developments which, without their context, may be meaningless to the reader, if not actually misleading.

If this advice were followed, qualified observers believe that in the long run it would also help to solve the abiding problem of Middle East coverage presented by governments hostile to any external criticism.

At present, one of the reasons why newspapers accept lower standards of reporting from the Middle East than they would from other parts of the world is the feeling that the hostility of the governments of the area to full and impartial coverage would frustrate any effort to report them better. This attitude was summed up by the correspondent who said that it was impossible to write "frank interpretive pieces" for long about any Middle East country without getting into trouble. [1]

The absurdity of some grounds on which Middle East leaders have chosen to take reprisals against newspapermen tempts the conclusion that they are always and everywhere wrong in their quarrels with the press, but several experienced correspondents say that this is not so. This is how a British foreign editor, who served in the area for a long time as a correspondent, described the position :

"The reporting of the Middle East has grown worse since the last war. There is a serious lack of confidence between the Middle East governments and the press of the world for which the governments are not wholly responsible. Western editors and agencies have their share of responsibility. The Middle East as a whole is ignored except when things go wrong and then is very often misreported. Reports are slanted according to the prejudice and the national interests of the countries concerned.

"There has been a great deal of progress in the whole area and there have been revolutionary changes in the past twenty-five years, but these have gone relatively unnoticed because there are not enough reporters with the span of experience or sufficient perspective to assess these changes. Twenty-five years ago the Middle East was 500 years behind Europe. Now the gap has been reduced to about 70 years."

Views expressed in the course of this report by other newspapermen show that this editor is not alone in his view that, in the "crisis of confidence" between Middle East governments and the press abroad, all the fault is not on one side.

As long as this crisis continues, the good correspondent risks

---

[1] See page 67.

having to pay for the sins of the bad ; and, even worse, he is threatened with retaliation for writing the truth as he sees it because, in an atmosphere of distrust, any criticism is likely to be regarded as prompted by illwill.

Contributors who noted and deplored this problem could see no quick and easy remedy for it, especially since it has become aggravated by the division of the area by the Arab-Israeli quarrel. As was pointed out earlier, [1] one important effect of the Palestine war has been to deny free movement to the correspondent between Israel and the rest of the Middle East, so that he is unable to obtain an overall picture of the area. In this situation the tendency of the world press is to leave Israel to be covered by Israelis and to send the foreign reporter into the Arab world. The contrast in the tone of reports from the two areas has embittered Arab leaders and peoples.

Yet there are one or two signs that, as political problems are settled, conditions of reporting the Middle East may improve. There are, for example, grounds for believing that governments in the area are learning by experience that freedom to report conditions in their countries is better for them in the long run than reporting muffled and distorted by censorship and secrecy. It is to be hoped that this is true. The greatest sufferers from the policy of restrictions on newsgathering are the governments and peoples of the Middle East.

---

[1] See page 34.

APPENDICES

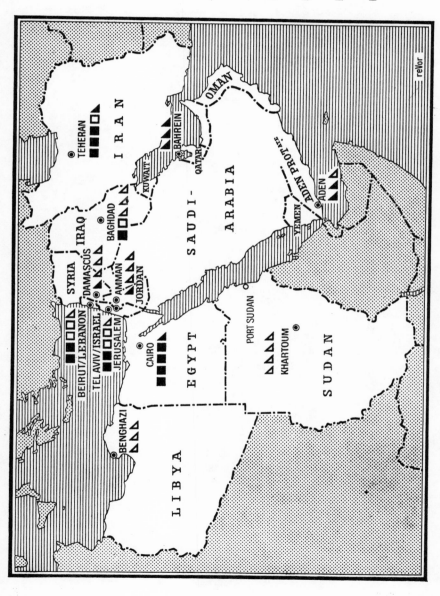

APPENDIX A

Coverage of the Middle East by
the major western News Agencies

Key to chart:

■ Fulltime correspondent who is not
  a national of country reported.

□ Fulltime correspondent who is a
  national of country reported.

▲ Parttime correspondent who is not
  a national of country reported.

△ Parttime correspondent who is a
  national of country reported.

APPENDIX B

CORRESPONDENTS EXPELLED OR PUT UNDER OTHER FORMS OF PRESSURE

The following list of correspondents expelled or threatened with expulsion by the authorities in Egypt and Iran is based on news reports issued at the time of each occurrence. The list starts with the year 1951.

Egypt

1951 November. Kurt Emmenegger, correspondent of the *Neue Zürcher Zeitung* and other Swiss newspapers, was expelled because of the "obvious dishonesty shown in his articles." The article objected to appeared in the *Neue Zürcher Zeitung* on November 1 and was headed "The foreign policy diversion manoeuvres of Nahas Pasha." It contained references to the growing opposition in Egypt, general "discontent" and "sharp criticism of the government." Mr. Emmenegger gave as reasons for criticism of the government not the failure of the British negotiations but the poor economic position of Egypt, the open failure of economic policy and governmental corruption "with consequent scandalous enrichment of powerful politicians," which "even by oriental standards was hardly tolerable any longer."

The *St. Galler Tagblatt* of November 21 reported that Mr. Emmenegger had been called on November 7 to the Egyptian Foreign Ministry. He was told that a telegram from the Egyptian authorities in Berne declared that he was writing pro-British, anti-Egyptian articles in Swiss newspapers, that he must be watched, given more accurate information and, if necessary, have his visa withdrawn. An official of the press department gave him to understand that Egypt was dissatisfied generally about Swiss reporting from Egypt.

Three days later the correspondent was called to the passport office of the Ministry of the Interior, his visa was cancelled and he was told to leave within three days. This action was taken independently by the political police without consulting the Foreign Ministry and its press department tried, unsuccessfully, to reverse the decision.

December. Fred Zusy, Associated Press correspondent in Cairo, was ordered to leave the country. It was later announced in Washington that the order had been cancelled. The explanation given for the expulsion order was "numerous serious offences against the laws of the country and a reprehensible attitude on Egyptian national aspirations," but the head of the Ministry of the Interior's press department said that it was not in the general interest to divulge the offences at that moment.

1952 August. Reuter reported the arrest on August 20 of Roger Vailland, a French writer and journalist, in an Egyptian village where he was alleged to have taken part in a Communist meeting. His Cairo hotel room was searched. M. Vailland had been sent to Egypt as a special correspondent for the review *Défense de la paix*, whose editor denied that he had been sent for Communist papers. M. Vailland said that he had arrived in Egypt on August 12 to write for the weeklies *Les Lettres Françaises* and *La Tribune des Nations.* He met an Egyptian writer and asked to be taken to a village to interview fellahin on the projects for limitation of landed property. He had just started his interviewing when he was arrested. Protests were made by both Egyptian and French journalists' unions. The correspondent was released in under a week (announced August 27), following a finding that he had attended the meeting as a simple observer. Reuter reported on August 27 that, despite his clearance, Vailland was still under police surveillance and that telephone communications with his room had been cut.

October. Alan MacGregor, of the *Egyptian Gazette* and Kemsley correspondent in Cairo, was detained for questioning and his office and home were searched. He was later released. Thomas Clayton, *Daily Express* correspondent, was questioned but not detained, and the office and home of Michael Clark, *New York Times* correspondent, were also searched. The events were connected with an army investigation into the activities of a publishing house, the Société Orientale de Publicité, publishers of the *Egyptian Gazette, Le Progrès Egyptien* and *La Bourse Egyptienne.* The authorities alleged the uncovering of an "espionage network," denied that any foreign correspondents had been arrested and stated that the search of the home of one journalist was made because an Egyptian journalist was believed to be staying with him. The nature of the alleged espionage was not explained, but it was believed that the authorities felt that correspondents had shown too great interest in the question of German officers training the Egyptian army. (In May 1953, an Egyptian newspaperman, George Fahmy, who had been taken into custody the previous October in connection with the army investigation, was acquitted. The defence pleaded that he had gathered information on the role of German military experts in Egypt purely for journalistic purposes.) Etienne Deloro, editor of *Le Progrès Egyptien,* was also detained and later released.

October. Michael James McGee, South African free-lance journalist from Johannesburg, was held and questioned in connection with an alleged espionage network.

1953 May. Jacques Maleh, Cairo correspondent of the *Jewish Chronicle*, was expelled as "undesirable" because he was a British subject and the correspondent of a foreign Jewish newspaper. He was held in prison for six days.

Iran

1951 May. Haig Nicholson, Middle East manager of Reuters, and Sefton Delmer, *Daily Express* chief foreign correspondent, were ordered to leave within 24 hours.

July. Rawle Knox, *Observer* correspondent, was given 12 hours to leave before the date of expiry of his transit visa. The order was withdrawn the next day.

December. Michael Clark, *New York Times* correspondent in Teheran, was called before Dr. Hussein Fatemi, Dr. Mossadegh's assistant, and told he had 48 hours in which to leave the country because of a dispatch of a few days before. The report had said that Dr. Mossadegh's "remarkable 90 to nil vote of confidence in the Majlis" on his return from the United States was helped by "incipient terrorism, i.e. the threat of assassination held over Mossadegh's opponents." Clark was told that he had insulted the government and was an agent of the Anglo-Iranian Oil Company. When the U. S. Ambassador Loy Henderson intervened, he was told that Clark was guilty of criminal libel and could stay only if he either published a retraction or if the Ambassador did so publicly. This alternative was rejected and Mr. Clark left the country.

December. Dr. Fatemi announced at a press conference the expulsion of Leopold Herman, Reuters correspondent, who had been in Iran 10 years. He was given 48 hours to leave the country. The reason given was "exaggerated reports" about opposition demonstrations in parliament. (*The Times* said that the reason alleged was a trivial slip in reporting Dr. Mossadegh's speech to the Majlis as reproduced from Reuter in a Arabic newspaper.)

1952 February. Phil Clarke, Associated Press correspondent in Teheran, was accused by a Teheran newspaper (edited by Dr. Hussein Fatemi) of "intriguing against the government and security of the country, and of falsifying reports in the interest of foreign elements." The paper demanded that he be put on trial. On December 18, 1951, Dr. Fatemi had told a press conference that Clarke was being given a "last warning" and would be expelled if he did not change his methods of reporting. Mr. Clarke left Teheran after these threats.

1953 January. Keghám Megerdichian, Reuters stringer in Teheran, was sent to prison charged with having reported false news. He was released on bail for medical treatment on March 18 ; he died in September.

April. Basil Bunting, correspondent of *The Times* in Teheran, was told that he must leave within 15 days. No official reason was given and no serious criticism of his dispatches was ever made publicly.

May. Marc Purdue, Associated Press correspondent, was given three days to leave the country for "false and provocative news against the interests of Iran." He was later informed that he could remain another month.

October. David Walker, *News Chronicle* correspondent, was ordered to leave Iran within 24 hours for dispatches sent to his paper. Officials refused to identify which dispatches were offensive. On October 28 the order was revoked by General Zahedi, but Mr. Walker left the country.

1954 January. Gaston Fournier, AFP correspondent, was told to leave by February 4. The offence was his reporting of fatal casualties in a clash between police and demonstrators during elections at Abadan and refusal to give the source of his information. His wife, correspondent for *Le Monde*, was also expelled. They had been there for two years.

APPENDIX C

PRESS CABLE RATES per word from nine Middle East countries to London, Paris, Rome, Hamburg, New York and New Delhi. Rates are converted into U. S. cents from other currencies and the figures below are therefore only approximate.

	LONDON		PARIS		ROME		HAMBURG		NEW YORK		NEW DELHI	
	Press	Urgent Press	Press	Urgent Press	Press	Urgent Press	Press	Urgent Press	Press	Urgent Press	Press	Urgent Press
	Cents	Cents	Cents	Cents	Cents	Cents	Cents	Cents	Cents	Cents	Cents	Cents
EGYPT Cairo	3.80	11.70	4.09	12.28	4.09	12.28	4.09	12.28	5.85	19.89	6.43	25.14
IRAN Tehevan	10.50	52.20	16.70	50.10	16.50	49.50	14.90	44.70	12.46	37.38	14.43	43.29
IRAQ Baghdad	6.35	23.05	24.68	68.26	24.45	68.26	30.18	68.26	12.31	50.51	10.45	44.46
ISRAEL Jerusalem	1.17	8.88	8.77	21.65	6.66	21.65	10.83	21.65	6.61	30.00	1.17	8.88
JORDAN Amman	1.17	7.00	6.72	19.55	6.72	19.55	6.72	19.55	5.07	16.33	1.17	7.00
LEBANON Beirut	9.87	29.61	10.41	31.32	11.09	33.27	11.09	33.27	18.30	54.90	22.60	67.80
SUDAN Port Sudan	5.26	15.78	5.55	16.65	5.55	16.65	5.55	16.65	7.29	24.57	6.43	25.44
SYRIA Damascus	8.50	25.50	8.96	26.88	9.45	28.35	9.45	28.35	15.96	47.88	13.16	39.48
ARABIA Aden	1.17	7.00	7.00	30.04	9.92	30.04	9.05	31.50	4.68	16.04	1.17	7.00

APPENDIX D

TELEPHONE RATES from the Middle East to London, Paris, Rome, Hamburg, New York and New Delhi. Rates have been converted into dollars from other currencies and the figures below are therefore only approximate.

Per three minutes

	LONDON	PARIS	ROME	HAMBURG	NEW YORK	NEW DELHI
	$	$	$	$	$	$
EGYPT Cairo (Flat rate of £3)	8.40	8.40	8.40	8.40	8.40	8.40
IRAN Teheran	12.60	13.10	14.17	14.20	16.07	6.75
IRAQ Baghdad	8.40	9.24	8.40	10.08	10.50	—
ISRAEL Jerusalem	8.40	8.83	10.33	9.72	12.00	10.50
LEBANON Beirut	10.15	9.45	11.02	10.39	16.06	—
SYRIA Damascus	through Beirut	7.70	6.58	7.19	12.85	—
ARABIA Aden	10.50	11.34	—	—	10.50	—

GOVERNMENT PRESSURES

ON THE PRESS

Published by
The International Press Institute
Zurich 1955

The English version of this Study
is a translation from the French original

Printed for the International Press Institute
by Imprimerie Ganguin & Laubscher S. A., Montreux

CONTENTS

THE VIENNA RESOLUTION

The General Assembly of the International Press Institute meeting in Vienna has been informed of the relations between press and government existing in different lands of the free world and has discussed present facts and tendencies. It has noted with great concern that even in countries which uphold democracy and whose governments would reject the thought of applying dictatorial powers, there exist trends which limit the freedom of the press through new laws or the application of existing laws.

The leading editors of the free press, united in the International Press Institute, declare that the limitation of the freedom of the press at any time and anywhere paves the way to the establishment of the rule of despotism and injustice even where restrictions were imposed for worthy reasons.

The Assembly warns the authorities in all free countries against any attempts to undermine the freedom of the press since they would destroy the basis of their own existence, freedom and justice. It calls on the press to defend its freedom with the greatest vigilance.

It demands that its Secretariat should report regularly any attempts, direct or indirect, to influence the freedom of the press.

May, 1954.

INTRODUCTION

It has been said that the press is one of the greatest forces in the world. The risks to which it is exposed are commensurate with its power. It is an inconvenience or an embarrassment to many who wish to diminish its power or even reduce it to impotence. And when these are governments, they have a thousand and one means of achieving their purpose. It is these means which are of concern here.

In publishing this Study, the International Press Institute seeks to reach not only jurists and specialists, but all those who are interested in information problems, as well as the members of the profession and political circles in general. It is hoped that this work will show them the gravity of the attacks which can be made on an essential freedom, even outside the totalitarian world, and that at the same time it will indicate to them the means by which the press can defend this freedom, supported by an informed public opinion. That is why the Study deals not only with defects in laws and various discriminatory and arbitrary practices, but also presents examples of good legislation and practice.

The conflict between government and press is not insuperable. In a healthy democracy there should be peaceful relations between them. The press has a natural function in society : it is the interpreter of public opinion. The government which recognizes this function will find ways to establish a *modus vivendi* with the press, even a collaboration freely entered into on both sides. Such a collaboration, in which the press guards its independence and all its critical powers, can work only to the profit of the people as a whole.

This Study is the outcome of a decision of the third I.P.I. Assembly, which met in Vienna in May 1954. At this assembly newspaper editors from free countries of the five continents spoke of the government pressures to which their national press is subjected. The members of the conference were deeply impressed by the evidence that such serious attacks on the freedom of the press occurred in free countries. They therefore instructed the staff of the I. P. I. to publish a detailed study of the different forms of pressure to which newspapers can find themselves subjected in countries which ostensibly accept the traditional democratic principle of the freedom of the press.

The term pressure should be taken here as meaning any regulation or discriminatory procedure which prevents, or might in any way prevent, a journalist from carrying out his professional duties normally. Behind the pressure lies the threat of sanctions in some form or another. This is where the real attack on the freedom of the press lies. There are other restrictions to freedom of information, but, however aggravating they may be, they do not constitute a genuine menace. In some countries the problem of access to official sources is a constant preoccupation, but it is not dealt with here unless the restrictions imposed in this field discriminate against particular sections of the press.

As the Study is concerned with government pressures within each country it does not touch on pressures exerted on foreign correspondents, except indirectly in so far as they are native journalists working for the foreign press.

The period studied is from 1951 to 1955 (the lifetime of the Institute). An occasional glaring case of government intervention in press affairs before this period is mentioned, but not earlier than the end of the Second World War.

A certain number of countries have not been studied :

1. Countries of totalitarian ideology, where the press is a government instrument, and those where the regime has been an absolute dictatorship throughout the period of the Study (e. g. San Domingo and Venezuela).

2. Countries where a state of war for the major part of the period would have made the evidence misleading (Korea, Viet Nam, Formosa).

3. Non-self-governing territories (even if the metropolitan country recognizes the freedom of the press).

4. Countries where the press is more or less non-existent (Afghanistan, Saudi Arabia, Ethiopia etc.).

Some countries where the freedom of the press was in abeyance have been retained, however, for instance Argentina, Colombia, the Arab States and Thailand. In these are to be found the most extreme forms of pressure and in addition they show the battle for freedom of the press still being waged ; the issue there is perhaps still in doubt. In each of these countries a marginal independent press has survived throughout the period under review.

In this Study the following premises have been borne in mind :

1. The press is not above the law. There is therefore no suggestion of indicting governments for not granting absolute liberty to the press or for not tolerating attacks which might endanger their existence.

2. As totalitarian countries are excluded, there is no discussion of measures taken for security reasons against organs preaching violent revolution in the free countries, except in so far as these measures may jeopardize the freedom of the press in general.

3. Even though the freedom of the press should ideally be complete, it is realized that in practice this has to be qualified. A violation of the principle in a country with a long democratic tradition is more sinister than is one where democracy is in its infancy. It would be too much to expect a calm and detached attitude from either government or press in Asian countries which have achieved independence since the war or in countries which have lived a long time under a dictatorship.

The present work is in two parts. The first analyzes pressures based on the law, the second those of an economic, administrative or purely political nature. This division seemed the most logical. It is true that it is sometimes necessary to come back to a topic ; for instance, the problem of security occurs in the section devoted to security laws proper, again in the section on penal laws and a third time in that on extra-legal political pressures. The question of defamation occurs both in the section on press laws and in that on penal laws. Cross references will reduce the inconvenience of this arrangement, which seemed preferable to the alternative one of dealing with questions topic by topic. This would have led to a blurring of the legal considerations, which are all-important.

It would also have been possible to deal with the situation in one country at a time. At first sight this might seem a good solution, but it would not square with the object of this Study, which is the systematic analysis of types of pressure on the free press. However, a geographical approach is made possible by the index, where all references in the text are entered opposite the name of each country.

The Study is based on a number of sources : the records of the Institute ; the proceedings of its 1954 and 1955 General Assemblies ; the monthly bulletin, I. P. I. REPORT ; the publications of other bodies, especially the Inter-American Press Association. In addition inquiries were carried out in 36 countries, either by letter or through roving correspondents who traveled over Latin America, Southeast Asia and Western Europe and made investigations on the spot. The I. P. I. received as a result 72 reports specially written by experienced journalists for the purposes of this Study.

Part One

Pressure
based on the law

I

Constitutional laws

In all the countries covered in this Study, where there is a Constitution, it guarantees the freedom of the press, or, in more general terms, freedom of expression. The shortest statements, those which merely establish the freedom of the press as a principle, are generally considered the most satisfactory. Such a one is the First Amendment to the Constitution of the United States of America : " Congress shall make no law... abridging the freedom of speech, or of the press...," or Article 55 of the Swiss Federal Constitution : " The freedom of the press is guaranteed." As soon as States start elaborating the conditions under which the freedom of the press is recognized, then the principle itself is liable to be watered down. For instance, in several countries, particularly in the Middle East, the Constitution specifies that the freedom of the press is guaranteed " within the limits of the law." The implications of such a formula, when the law itself is restrictive of freedom, are obvious. It is for the law to obey the principle inscribed in the basic charter, and not vice versa.

It is possible, however, to have constitutional articles which get down to detail yet are not restrictive in any sense. An example often quoted in this connection is Article 21 of the Constitution of the Italian Republic of December 27, 1947. " The press," it says, " may not be made subject to licensing or censorship. Confiscation may be carried out only on an order from the judicial authority accompanied by a statement of reasons in the case of offenses for which the press law expressly authorizes such action." Provision is made for emergency cases, but in such cases the judicial authority must be informed immediately and must give its decision within 24 hours. Another clause provides that the press make public its financial sources.

Conversely, concise articles may not be an efficacious safeguard of the freedom of the press. One of the most precise constitutional articles on the freedom of the press, guaranteeing liberty of expression in the fullest sense, was to be found in Argentina.

Article 32 of the National Constitution of 1863 (superseded five years ago) went so far as to stipulate that Parliament was " forbidden to pass laws calculated to restrict the freedom of the press and to submit them to federal jurisdiction." What became of this freedom, at a time when this Constitution still applied, is common knowledge.

During the period covered by this Study the most flagrant threats of restriction of the freedom of the press by constitutional means have taken place in India and in Colombia.

In 1951 there was added to Article 19 of the Constitution of the Indian Union (the article dealing with freedom of expression in all its aspects) an amendment enabling the imposition of " reasonable " restrictions on the press in the interests of public order and the maintenance of good relations with foreign powers, and also to prevent incitement to violence. Article 19, before this, already authorized restrictions in the interests of the security of the State, public decency and protection against libel. The press reacted vigorously, as it seemed evident that the loose wording of the amendment constituted a potential threat to freedom of expression. And in fact, the amendment, once passed, made possible the adoption of a law with powers to restrict this freedom pretty seriously (see p. 27).

It is interesting to note that in its report published in 1954 the Indian Press Commission raises no basic objection to this constitutional amendment.

In Colombia, Urdaneta Arbalaez's authoritarian government attempted in May 1953 to introduce a new constitution in which the press and the radio were decreed to be " public services." This sentence occurred : " The liberty of the press must be exercised in a responsible manner and in conformity with Christian truth and morality, in such a way as not to mislead or pervert public opinion but, on the contrary, to contribute to the public weal." The editors of liberal newspapers saw in this document not only a threat of expropriation but also one of permanent censorship. One of them described it as a " super-falangist " act.

Even though this new constitution never became fact, owing to the overthrow of the Arbalaez government, it is unfortunately true that the principles which inspired it have not been given up and in 1955 the idea of giving the information services the status of public services was again raised.

II

Laws on security

The laws on security are particularly feared by the press. The Constitution or the Penal Code generally contains measures designed to protect the security of the state and its institutions. It is a bad sign when a government thinks it necessary to promulgate a special law.

As their aim is to reinforce ordinary legislation, laws on security or the defense of the regime are inevitably severe and lead to a stringent control of the press. They often allow the executive to act in an arbitrary way, because most of these laws do not offer the same guarantees of defense as ordinary laws.

Since the war, several laws of this type have been added to the legal arsenal of the democracies to strengthen their defenses against hostile or revolutionary forces. The Cold War must be blamed for this highly regrettable development. Thanks to these laws in defense of democratic institutions, the countries concerned possibly avoid the necessity of passing emergency legislation or suspending constitutional guarantees. Nevertheless, by adding to the legislation dealing with information media, they do represent a step in the direction of control.

It is perfectly understandable that a state should be anxious to improve its safeguards against revolutionary violence. The Weimar Republic and other democratic states went under before the totalitarian wave precisely through failure to do this. But even though the intention of these laws is justified, their terms, and especially their application, often overstep the original conception. As a result they come to represent a latent threat not only to extremist papers but to the press as a whole.

This situation is particularly well illustrated in the Union of South Africa. The government there has, during the past few years, promulgated several laws which are a sword of Damocles for the entire press.

The Public Safety Act of 1953 allows the South African government to declare a state of emergency in regions where racial riots

break out. The press may then be censored and papers may even
be suspended. On top of that, under this law protesting, or inciting
to protest, against the established order becomes an offense. The
maximum penalty for " protest " is a fine of £ 300, three years in
prison or ten lashes (or any two of these), but incitement can be
punished even more severely :— £ 500 fine, five years' imprisonment
or 15 lashes. Up till now, it should be said, this law has not been
applied.

Another law, the Riotous Assemblies Act, makes it possible to
prevent papers from reporting racial riots without previous permission
from the police. Failure to get this official " permission " can lead
to the conviction of a newspaper editor who has merely reported
without comment that the riots took place. If he is convicted of
incitement to racial hatred the journalist can be sent to jail, heavily
fined, or even deported.

Finally a law against Communism, the Suppression of Communism
Act of 1950, represents, according to several South African editors,
a definite danger to the press in general. Under it, the government
can stop a journalist from exercising his profession, banish him, and
even suspend the paper, if anything published by him seems to be
" revolutionary " or even merely calculated to propagate Communist
ideology. As an editor from the Transvaal points out, the mere
reporting of a remark by Stalin brings a journalist within the scope
of this law. It was invoked to suspend the left-wing *Guardian* in May
1952. A week later the paper reappeared as the *Clarion,* and later
it emerged once again as the *Advance.* In October 1954 this publication was finally suppressed with no reason given. Commenting on
the suspension of the *Guardian* at the I. P. I. Assembly in Vienna
in 1954 Morris Broughton, editor of the *Cape Argus,* deplored the
fact that South African opinion had failed to react, though this
Act had aroused the indignation of the press elsewhere.

Public apathy a danger

In his view it is precisely this lack of interest on the part of the
public which makes the position of the press precarious in his country.
It explains why in the last 20 years, and especially in the last five, the

encroachments of the South African government on the freedom of the press have become increasingly serious. There is, it is true, no censorship as such, nor does the government issue directives to the press, but nevertheless it exerts pressure by virtue of a body of laws often laudable enough in intention, but which complicate the journalist's job, intimidate him, or even directly threaten him.[1] " Editing a newspaper under these conditions is like walking blindfold through a minefield," as the editor of the Johannesburg *Star* wrote to the I. P. I. in 1952. He went on to say that the restraints on publication in the Union of South Africa are so complex that in few countries in the world this side of the Iron Curtain is a greater strain imposed on newspaper editors.[2]

Pakistan is another of the free countries whose security laws cause journalists great anxiety. On the one hand the Press (Emergency Powers) Act of 1931 is in force and considerable use is made of it in times of trouble. Then there is the 1952 Public Security Act, which has a national application, and in addition its replica at the provincial level, the 1950 Public Safety Act. These two contain similar clauses, regarded as very dangerous to the press :

a) The government is the sole judge of what is prejudicial to the defense and security of Pakistan, and to its relations with foreign States.

b) It may order the seizure of an issue of a paper infringing the law and search its offices ; it may also temporarily suspend publication of a paper or submit it to censorship.

c) It may require the editor of a paper to disclose his sources.

d) The accused has no right of appeal and cannot be released on bail except at one stage of the hearing.

These laws constitute above all a potential threat, as they have not often been applied. The case of the Lahore *Star* may be mentioned, which in 1952 was prosecuted for casting aspersions on the Army by criticizing the organization of the King of Iraq's visit. Then, in 1953, at the time of the troubles fomented by the Ahmediya sect, several papers in different provinces fell foul of these security laws.

---

[1] *I. P. I. Assembly 1954, Proceedings*, p. 30 ff.
[2] See I. P. I. REPORT, January 1953.

The most notorious case is that of the Dacca *Pakistan Observer*. In February 1952 this paper published an editorial criticizing the Prime Minister of Pakistan in vigorous terms. The authorities deemed this article liable to cause public disorder. By virtue of the local Public Safety Act the editor, one of the owners and the head printer were arrested. The government opposed bail. They were released after a certain time, but within a week they were back in jail on orders from the government, this time on the trumped-up charge of having tried to set fire to a rival journal's premises. The police dragged the case out for over a year and it was not until June 1954 that the courts ruled the accusation to be unfounded. However, during all that time the paper had not been able to appear, its presses had been impounded, 150 persons had been deprived of employment and the publishers had lost about 300,000 rupees.

Although the security laws are not often invoked, they are regarded by the Pakistani press as a whole as an intolerable means of pressure. On repeated occasions during the last few years the publishers' and journalists' associations have clamored for the repeal of the present laws. A resolution of the Pakistani Journalists Federal Union Congress of 1953 went so far as to pillory the Security Act as the most abominable law passed since the country achieved independence.

Japanese law on subversion

In Japan the law on the prevention of subversive activities, in force since 1952, is regarded by the press as dangerous to freedom of expression. The Japan Newspaper Publishers and Editors Association criticizes this law on the following grounds :

a) It fails to establish exact and proper standards, using a weak definition which could cover non-subversive acts.

b) Under the law a " subversive terroristic act " is punishable even when it is merely assumed that it will be committed.

c) A mere administrative agency of the government may decide that an act is subversive and may apply the punitive measures provided for. This agency can dissolve an organization whenever it has grounds for thinking that it may pursue such activities in the future.

d) Furthermore, although an organization has the right of appeal to a court, the court cannot quash the government agency's ruling if the Prime Minister objects.

In the opinion of the Association this law introduces limitations to fundamental rights which may be used by the government for purposes of domestic policy.

Up till now, it is true, the Japanese government has not abused its powers under the law on the prevention of subversive activities. From its promulgation in July 1952 until the beginning of 1955 there have been 56 prosecutions under this law and only 15 resulted in convictions. In every case the proceedings concerned extremist plots. Nevertheless a less liberal government might use its powers less reasonably, to the detriment of the press.

It must be pointed out that the present law might have been much worse if the press had not been very much on the alert in defense of its freedom. Already in 1951 the government began to consider the desirability of a law against extremist activities. First it tabled a proposal for a law on public security, then one on the control of organizations. Under the terms of the latter, newspapers themselves could be described as " organizations " and thereby subjected to such threats that, according to the newspaper editors, any form of criticism would have become impossible. The press protested and a more moderate proposal was accordingly drafted, but even this contained dangerous features : compulsory filing of newspaper copies, the possibility of suspension of papers and of dissolution of publishing houses, plus the fact that individuals might be held responsible for acts not specified in the Penal Code and loosely interpreted as subversive.

The reaction of the press once again forced the government to put its proposal back on the stocks. A new proposal was again condemned by the Association, as " liable to revive the political police and government interference in the public's political activities on the pretext of controlling violence." In the end the government put forward a proposal for a special law on security, as a substitute for the proposed Organizations Control Bill. But this formula was no better received than the one before. The press perceived in it the same danger of censorship and suspension and the same threat to the citizen's fundamental political rights, particularly in the proposal to institute a Special Inquiry Commission with discretionary powers and in the introduction of new "infringements" not found in the Penal Code.

So yet again the government had to modify its plans. It tabled a new law in the Chambers on the prevention of subversive activities, and this time it was passed. It is much less dangerous to the freedom of the press than the previous proposals, even though there are still grounds for criticism. In this welter of proposals and counter-proposals it is interesting to follow the successive attempts made by a government still hankering after authoritarianism to dominate the press, and the unremitting efforts of the press to safeguard its independence.

In Burma the 1947 Public Order Preservation Act authorized detention under remand for up to two months, banishment, search and sequestration. One clause stipulates that a police inspector can, without a warrant, arrest anyone *suspected* of endangering public order. Several Burmese newspaper editors have been convicted under this law for more or less pettifogging offenses. This has not prevented them from resuming cordial relations with the authorities afterwards.

One of the victims of this law was E. M. Law Yone, editor of the Rangoon paper *The Nation* and chairman of the Burmese committee of the I. P. I. In his paper he carried on a vigorous campaign against irresponsibility and incompetence in high places, which galled the government considerably. After an attack on a high official, whom he accused of malpractice and inefficiency, E. M. Law Yone was arrested and sentenced in March 1953 under the terms of the law to a heavy fine and a month in jail. However, the case boomeranged on the government. As the editor of *The Nation* was about to go on trial, members of the Burmese Press Association stepped forward and placed a garland of flowers on his shoulders. All over the country E. M. Law Yone became the symbol of freedom. This is what he himself wrote to the I. P. I. : " The government lost face because it became an honor to be arrested under Sect. 5 of P. O. P. A. In jail journalists were special-class prisoners, good food, no work, etc. When released they were treated like heroes. This added to the prestige of newsmen, and in the end the government found there was nothing to be gained by jailing them. I'm one of those jailed under Sect. 5 and privileged to live at government expense for a period of time."

Since then arrests have to all intents and purposes ceased in Burma. But as long as the law on the preservation of public order remains on the statute book it represents a potential threat. It must be realized, in addition, that judges in Burma do not enjoy complete independence. They are nominated by the Executive for five years, subject to the approval of Parliament, which means in effect that they are appointed by the party in power.

Latin American examples

In Latin America too there are to be found several laws on security or the defense of democracy which constitute either a direct or a potential threat to the press.

In Argentina, the Security Law of October 1950 contains a number of cunning paragraphs which may well be used to justify extremely severe verdicts against journalists. Article 2, supplementing an earlier article of the 1945 decree, provides that distribution of political, military, economic or social data, documents or information, which must remain secret in the interest of national security, is subject to imprisonment of from one to ten years. Article 6 states that " whosoever passes on, communicates, publishes or distributes, without authorization, economic, political, military, financial or industrial information, which—*without being secret or restricted*—is not intended for publication . . ., will be punished with imprisonment of from one month to four years." Under Article 8, a maximum penalty of eight years in prison can be imposed on persons " who, *by whatever means*, cause the public to get alarmed or depressed."

In Cuba a law on security was in force from July 1953 till January 1954. This law was based on the Spanish law of 1941 on the defense of the State, particularly in the creation of a new offense, " dangerous thinking," to which a whole section was devoted. It also punished the publishing of reports which might reflect on the " dignity of the nation," an elastic concept under cover of which the government could crack down on any independent paper. The law also contained a new and particularly harsh clause ; the government might imprison the writer of an article and the editor of the paper in which it had been published merely on the strength of a charge. They could only be released, even on bail, if the Public Prosecutor expressly demanded it.

Peru has had a law on security since 1949 which represents a threat to the press, even though it has not often been applied. It allows the censoring of both internal news and news sent abroad.

In Brazil the 1938 decree on security is certainly the law which holds the greatest menace for the press. The police can seize an issue, the Minister of Justice can suspend a paper, and a newspaper editor can be arrested on a trifling pretext. This fate befell Carlos Lacerda, the editor of the *Tribuna da Imprensa,* in December 1952. He had hinted that the police accepted bribes to tolerate prostitution. The police hit back. When summoned as a witness, Carlos Lacerda was arrested under this law, but released after two days. This incident was luckily exceptional. In fact the decree on security has been little used since 1950.

In this category of security a law passed in 1954 in the United States should also find a place. It makes it compulsory to register printing and duplicating equipment belonging to organizations classed as suspect by the Attorney General's office. This law has been criticized by several papers ; while admitting its laudable intentions, they are afraid that, once the principle of Federal control is accepted, the press will be subjected to a latent threat. In this connection the St. Louis *Post-Dispatch* said : "Any registration by the Federal Government of printing facilities, whatever their use, is a potential threat to freedom of the press and yet the bill slipped through. The American press need shed no tears over the troubles of subversive groups ; the sooner they collapse the better. But our journalists and publishers must keep a close watch on the framing of laws, however well-intentioned they may be, which run the risk of putting the American press in a strait-jacket."

In Europe the case of Italy may be mentioned, where Fascist laws on security are still in force and seem to be in flagrant contradiction to Article 21 of the Constitution. The relevant provisions are Articles 112 and 113 of the 1931 law on Public Security which were partially amended in 1946 but not in the essential provisions. These enable the police to forbid, confiscate or censor any written matter liable to disturb public order. In fact this law is clearly designed to deal with propaganda tracts and pamphlets, but newspapers might well become its victims if an anti-liberal government came to power. As written matter contrary to political and social principles is considered illegal under Article 112 of the Public Security Law, it might well be thought illegal to conduct through the press a vigorous opposition campaign against the government.[1]

[1] See article by Professore P. Nuvolone in the *Bollettino dell'Associazione per la libertà della cultura*, February 1954.

III

Press laws

Is legislation specifically on the press either desirable or necessary? A number of countries manage quite well without, for instance the United States, the United Kingdom and most of the Swiss Cantons. Belgium's Constitution provides for the drafting of a press law, but for almost 150 years it has never seen the light of day. The Belgian Parliament doubtless has seen that the gap is purely theoretical, experience having shown that no vital interest is imperilled.

Conditions governing publishing

In fact there are very few countries which have not laid down a special law at least governing the actual publishing of newspapers. The Commonwealth countries, which are generally averse to this type of legislation, nearly all have Licensing or Registration Acts. These are purely formal regulations dealing with such points as registration, designation of a responsible manager and filing of newspaper copies. Nevertheless, these regulations may include certain conditions which allow licensing to creep in by the back door. (In Part Two administrative pin-pricks and the political conditions attached to the grant of publishers' licenses will be dealt with.) Thus, what appear to be purely formal regulations may turn out to be hindrances, or positive threats, even in countries where freedom of the press is solidly based.

In Australia, for instance, in the course of a campaign against obscene literature and Communism, new regulations have been introduced during the last few years in several States. Editors have by and large found no cause for complaint, but there are some who do find these new regulations disturbing.

The Printers and Newspapers Act of the State of Queensland, amended in 1953, makes newspapers register afresh every year and allows government officials to inspect printing presses and to seize material. Some newspaper editors consider that this gives the State authorities excessive powers to meddle in press matters.

A 1954 regulation in the State of Victoria providing for the obligatory registration of distributing agents is also regarded as disturbing. Under this regulation, which aims at preventing the circulation of " indecent " literature, a second infraction leads to the loss of the agent's license. He may appeal, but for a number of weeks he is off the circulation list, which involves considerable financial loss. It has been pointed out that this new regulation was unnecessary, as the Police Offenses Act already had enough teeth in it.

Another cause of complaint in Victoria is that, by virtue of a regulation going back to 1677, newspapers may not be published or distributed on Sundays. Victorian editors point out that papers from other States are on sale on Sundays at the Melbourne airport and railway station and other places. The complaints of the local press have never been satisfactorily answered, the government preferring to turn a deaf ear, for political reasons, including the fear of antagonizing the clergy.

In Canada, in 1953, the Federal Supreme Court invalidated various municipal regulations, particularly in Quebec province, which made a police permit necessary for the distribution of publications. The terms of these regulations were regarded by lawyers as so lacking in precision as to constitute a possible threat to freedom of expression.

In several countries, particularly in Asia and Latin America, in addition to the routine formalities a deposit or " caution " has to be made. This requirement may occasionally be justified by local conditions, but in Western legislation it is regarded as a form of censorship incompatible with a genuinely liberal conception of the press.

It will become evident later in this Study that laws on the press impose all sorts of other conditions on the grant of a publishing license.

* * *

Press laws as generally understood do not confine themselves to the conditions of publication. Their main function is the regulation of press offenses. This is the point where real controversy begins.

Some hold that common law should suffice. Others hold that separate legislation is called for owing to the special nature of offenses committed by the press (a summary procedure may, for example, be justified for dealing with those offenses which are obviously flagrant). Press laws do not necessarily entail restrictions on the freedom of the press, although in fact they generally do.

Liberal press laws

As an example of what a press law should be the new Swedish press law of 1949 might be quoted.[1] Its very title is propitious : " Constitutional act relating to the freedom of the press " ; and it is clear throughout that the Swedish Parliament has had the protection of the freedom of the press in mind rather than the punishment of abuses of that freedom. It is worth summarizing its main features.

First, freedom to print is guaranteed in a variety of ways, and so is freedom to disseminate ideas. It is forbidden to hamper the circulation of printed matter in any way. (A regulation tending to prevent the distribution of certain newspapers during military religious services was deemed to be incompatible with the law !) The law even provides for sanctions against indirect restrictions on the freedom of the press such as inequitable allocation of newsprint or the granting of special transport facilities to printed matter according to its contents. Freedom of information proper is protected by a very wide right of anonymity and by the rule that information is without prejudice unless it bears on official secrets or makes allegations of a defamatory character. As regards offenses, the chief merit of the law is that it explicitly refers them to common law. The law does envisage the use of emergency measures to stop the circulation of a piece of printed matter at once, but there are numerous guarantees against the exaggerated use of any such exceptional procedure. Finally, in proceedings against the press, the law makes use of the jury system. This is the only sphere in which the jury is used in Sweden and, what is still more remarkable, Swedish juries have even wider powers than Anglo-Saxon or French juries. If a Swedish

[1] Cf. *Freedom of Information* — A compilation of texts communicated by governments. Department of Social Affairs of the United Nations, 1950, Vol. II, p. 69.

jury decides that the article in question is legally innocuous its decision is final and the accused is released. If the bench disagrees, fresh proceedings must be instituted and the case tried again *ab initio.*

So liberal in fact is the law that it seems positively to lean over on the side of the press. As regards the disclosure of official secrets it goes beyond what even journalists might reasonably claim, and as regards defamation it must be admitted that the Swedish citizen has little legal defense. The libeller has the enormous initial advantage that proof of untruth is not admitted as evidence. Swedish lawyers have reached the conclusion that it is high time this overly lenient aspect of the law was modified.

Since 1916 Sweden has also been fortunate in possessing the so-called Press Fair Practices Commission. This is a private body, to which the three main press associations belong and which acts as a buffer between press and public.

The laws of the other Scandinavian countries on the press are conceived in the same liberal spirit. For instance in Denmark a law of 1938 provided for the setting-up of a Board of Denials and Corrections. This institution smooths out such matters as a newspaper's refusal to publish a private citizen's reply to matter appearing in the paper which he regards as prejudicial to himself. The Board functions to the entire satisfaction of both the press and the public. In recent years the Danes have even contemplated widening its scope and turning it into an institution analogous to the Swedish Press Fair Practices Commission .

Another law which may be regarded as liberal is the French law of 1881, on which several others in Europe and Latin America were later based. However, this law is now somewhat suspect as later amendments have introduced some features which are unfavorable to the press. The most serious defect is in the treatment of defamation. This will be dealt with more fully in the section on penal laws.

The entirely satisfactory law from the point of view of the press is unfortunately the exception rather than the rule. By and large these laws, particularly outside Europe, contain clauses which are a serious handicap to freedom of expression.

It must, however, be remembered that in certain countries a press law which is far from embodying the older democracies' concept of freedom may nevertheless mark an advance. It may curb an executive which has hitherto had matters all its own way. It may also offer the press a status more enviable than that it enjoyed under a previous out-of-date or Draconian law. It may also represent a necessary step towards complete freedom. An example is the Iranian law of 1952 which replaced that of 1908. This law was passed under the Mossadegh government and is still in force. It has been vilified repeatedly but it did introduce the jury system in litigation concerning the press—a democratic procedure *par excellence*— and makes a passable attempt to define the exceptional circumstances in which a paper may be banned without the sanction of the judicial powers. Unfortunately, as Teheran is under permanent martial law, its palliative effect cannot make itself felt.

In the course of the period under review two laws containing restrictive clauses have caused a great deal of discussion. They are the Indian Press Act and the Turkish Law of 1954.

The Indian Press Act

In 1951 the New Delhi Parliament passed a law on the press, the Press (Objectionable Matter) Act. In spite of its restrictive character, this Act was accepted by the press, for want of anything better, for a trial period of two years. In 1954 it was extended for two years, despite the press, and indeed, two of its clauses were amended.

In its first form this law was criticized for certain provisions not to be found in the legislation of traditionally democratic countries, i.e. the printer or publisher of a paper is required to deposit a sum which is forfeit if the newspaper publishes anything objectionable. Within the meaning of the Act, "objectionable" is something "grossly indecent, or scurrilous, or obscene or intended for blackmail." A second offense makes the newspaper's presses liable to seizure. Such action, however, may only be taken by a magistrate with a jury. There is right of appeal.

This obligation to make a deposit is a dangerous measure. It means that the printer or publisher, for fear of forfeiting his deposit, may be led to interfere in editorial matters and seek to prevent the editor from printing matter which he considers perfectly "legitimate." Here is a case of pressure exerted through a third party ; the printer or publisher assumes the role of unofficial censor.

The Act has been brought to bear upon a number of newspapers which had published gross or obscene matter. The infringement was in most cases obvious and the jury returned a verdict of guilty. Only one case is recorded where the law has been applied with seemingly excessive severity. It is that of *Spotlight,* a Calcutta weekly, against which proceedings were taken at the end of 1953. This paper had published a series of articles on Iraq and Iran which, according to the Calcutta Commissioner of Police, contained passages which were clearly gross and indecent, with particular reference to King Feisal and one of the Shah's sisters. The editor, the publisher and the printer were convicted.

The press considered the conviction to be improper. In the profession doubt was expressed as to whether the definition in the Act of what constitutes objectionable matter could in effect be applied to articles such as the ones in question. It appears that the offending passages caused the authorities to react chiefly because they might jeopardize the good relations between India and the countries concerned. Yet, when the article on the press in the Constitution was amended, the Prime Minister and other members of the government had given an assurance that there would be nothing to prevent criticism of a foreign government. The Indian press has expressed the fear that the *Spotlight* case was a means seized upon by the government to evade its promises by imposing restrictions on such criticism, using the notion of grossness and indecency as a convenient pretext.

As mentioned previously, this law was given a further lease of life from 1954 to 1956 in spite of the rough handling it received at the hands of a section of the press. Indian press circles assert that it had signally failed to prove its usefulness and that, far from being prolonged, it should have been annulled. To make matters worse, the government has introduced two modifications, ostensibly of a purely formal character, but which the press regard as sinister. The first amendment limits the powers of the jury, which can now only pronounce on the issue of " objectionableness." In other words the jury cannot now judge the seriousness of the offense or decide whether proceedings are justified. The second amendment gives each State of the Indian Union right of appeal against a verdict,

which means that it can henceforth go on harassing an editor who
has won his case in the lower courts.

The Indian law on the press raised a storm of protest from the
outset, largely because journalists consider legislation in this sphere
to be unnecessary. They claim that the normal law should suffice.
It must nevertheless be admitted that this law has not in fact impaired
the freedom of the press. It is at worst a potential threat. Furthermore, most of the Indian editors whose views have been canvassed
for the purposes of the present Study have expressed themselves as
satisfied by and large with the conditions in which the press can
operate in India. At the Fourth I. P. I. Assembly in Copenhagen, in
1955, Sookamal Ghose, editor of the Calcutta *Jugantar,* went so
far as to say that neither the Press Act nor other laws relating to
the press are of a nature to cause grave disquiet.

The Turkish law of 1954

The situation in Turkey is very different.

To understand the present situation it is necessary to recall that
in Turkey the freedom of the press does not rest on solid foundations.
In the past this principle has been only intermittently recognized.
A. E. Yalman, editor of *Vatan,* said in I. P. I. REPORT: "Freedom of the
press could not take root in Turkey because it was excessively abused
each time, so that dictatorial measures followed each short period of
freedom." In fact, dictatorship in Turkey ceased only after the last war.
The era of true freedom seemed to have dawned when the 1950 elections returned the Democratic party to power. Respect for civil liberties,
those of the press in particular, had been the main plank in the
party's platform, and the press law of 1950 is certainly one of the
most liberal ever known in Turkey. Even though one or two of its
clauses might be regarded in the West as somewhat too restrictive,
it did not in any event prevent opinions being expressed, and even
passions running high. This alarmed the government and caused
it to go into reverse gear ; liberty was becoming license.

At the beginning of 1954 the law was amended, the new
provisions being of considerable severity. The new law provides for
heavy fines and prison sentences for defamation, and the penalties

are far more severe when the victims of the attack are political personalities or public officials. In the latter case the public prosecutor can act without a complaint from the person libelled. The fines go up to 10,000£ Turkish, i.e. about $3570.

Another article provides for equally severe sanctions against the publication of inaccurate news of such a nature as to weaken the State's political or financial credit or to cause public alarm. The punishment is doubled on a second offense.[1]

The implicit threat to the freedom of the press lies in the loose definition of the offenses. A journalist who has criticized a Minister may be sentenced for a minor verbal imprudence. A paper which, for instance, reproduces under a banner headline an agency report on inflation in Turkey may be prosecuted, and this did happen to the daily *Yeni Sabah* in October 1954.

The most sinister aspect of the situation is the way the law is applied. Journalists under suspicion are generally arrested before the case is tried ; hearings take place behind closed doors ; proof of truth is no defense and newspapers are not allowed to comment on the verdict or on the proceedings (Article 30 of the Law on the Press).

Finally, it is a matter for speculation whether the judges enjoy full independence. A law was passed in May 1954 which reduces judges to the level of civil servants by authorizing the Minister of Justice to retire them after 25 years' exercise of their functions. Naturally it is the judges in the highest courts who are the most threatened as they only reach that position at a late stage. In addition, the Minister of Justice has the power to transfer judges. At least one case is on record when, during a press case, the independence of the Bench was tampered with. The editor of the *Yeni Sabah* had to appear before the courts after publishing an open letter to the Prime Minister. In it he said that, as the result of activities organized by hooligans against the paper because of an article on the U. S. S. R., the personnel of the *Yeni Sabah* would have to take their defense into their own hands if the authorities were incapable of affording

---

[1] When the Turkish press law was revised in 1954 it included an amendment to Article 161 of the Penal Code making it a punishable offense in peace time to spread "inaccurate or tendentious news," especially when it may have a prejudicial effect on the national interest ; this conception is particularly vague.

them protection. The government elected to regard this letter as harmful to its prestige. When the case reached the Supreme Court two judges declared in favor of the accused. They were replaced by two others whom the government knew to be more ready to cooperate.

Since the new press law came into force and up to the time of writing a score or so of journalists have been prosecuted. The most conspicuous cases were the proceedings against the dailies *Halkci* (the chief organ of the main opposition party, the Popular Republican Party) and *Dunya* (independent, but favorable to the opposition), and the weekly magazine *Akis*.

In the first case proceedings were taken mainly against the *Halkci*'s chief editorialist, Hüseyin Cahit Yalçin, the doyen of the Turkish press. He was accused of being too severe in his criticisms of the Prime Minister and the Foreign Minister. Here, from an editorial of April 3, 1954, is an example of Yalçin's theme : " To observe our Foreign Minister's activities ending in a leprous incapability surely has not created sympathy in the hearts of the people toward these incapable persons." The Head of the Turkish diplomatic service was then described as a man whose understanding of current events would just about pass muster at the local tavern. An editorial of April 26 advised Prime Minister Menderes to apologize to the nation and retire from public life, after all the harm he had done to Turkey's prestige abroad.

For these and other articles H. C. Yalçin was sentenced to 26 months in prison and the editorial board, whose chairman is Nihat Erim, former Vice-Premier, was very heavily fined. H. C. Yalçin went to Scutari jail at the beginning of December but, in view of the state of his health and his age—he is over 80—he was transferred to another prison after a short time and was in the end pardoned in March 1955.

In the case of the *Dunya*, proceedings were taken because of articles slandering the Minister responsible for press affairs, Mukerrem Sarol. The author of the articles, Bedi Faik, one of the editors, was imprisoned. His colleague, Rifki Atay, a well-known novelist and publicist, and the manager of the paper also received the attentions of the police. Bedi Faik had insinuated in his articles that Mukerrem Sarol had been guilty of making illegal profits and of maladministration of justice. For instance, it was said that he had promoted the sale of the newspaper which he now publishes, the *Turk Sesi*, by obtaining about 35,000 accommodation subscriptions from the education department of the province of Ankara. In addition Bedi Faik accused Mukerrem Sarol of sharp practice in that he was alleged to have intrigued against the *Dunya* and impeded its radio publicity service. The articles also cast doubt on the Minister's competence.

The case against Bedi Faik was in fact dropped, as the paper apologized and the Minister withdrew his charges.

The last conspicuous case is a double-barrelled one against the *Akis*. Metin Toker, publisher of the *Akis* and son-in-law of ex-president Inönü, was sentenced in the spring of 1955 to nine months and ten days in prison and also to a fine of about $3400, on a charge of discrediting Minister Sarol by false allegations. The tribunal set up a commission of experts to give an opinion on the articles in question. This commission, which included the Dean of the Faculty of Law at Istanbul University, a professor from the Faculty of Arts and the president of the Press Association of Istanbul, who is also a professor at the Institute of Journalism at the University, reached the view that the articles were severe but not defamatory. Thereupon the composition of the tribunal was changed and the new judges ignored the findings of the commission of experts.

A little later the managing editor of the *Akis* was imprisoned because his magazine published anonymous articles on Turkish internal policy containing allegedly libellous remarks about the Premier. He has since been released on bail, after being detained for four weeks. Both these proceedings against the *Akis* were pending at the time of writing.

Although the action taken against Turkish journalists under the new laws has been pilloried in the free countries, the Turkish press has not been at all unanimous in its reactions. It is true that, apart from the government organs, the entire press castigated H. C. Yalcin's prison sentence. As regards the application of the law as such, however, it is by no means only the government press which shows approbation. For instance A. E. Yalman said at the I. P. I. Assembly in Copenhagen in 1955 that the present state of affairs, however unsatisfactory, was inevitable in view of the political climate. In his view, and his colleagues, he said, by and large thought

A delegation from the Burmese Press Association
pay tribute to E. M. Law Yone, editor of *The
Nation* (Rangoon) as he is about to go on trial (p. 18).

In the central prison of Ankara, Cüneyit Arcayürek (left), editor of *Akis*, whose head has been shaved during his imprisonment, confers with the former President of the Turkish Republic, Ismet Inönü (p. 32).

the same, passions would have to cool down and the difference between liberty and license would have to be learned, otherwise the young democracy of Turkey would be sapped at the base.[1]

It remains true, however, that Turkish journalists are exposed to risks which prevent them from expressing their opinions as freely as would be desirable in a healthy democracy. As Cemil Said Barlas, former Minister and Republican deputy, wrote in his Ankara daily *Son Havadis* on April 18, 1955 : " One cannot really speak of freedom of the press in Turkey ; the existing laws allow no true criticism. I must add that I do not confuse freedom of the press with the right to defame and slander... Far be it from me to speak of the existence (in Turkey) of a ' peronista ' regime or of heavy pressures on the press. But if, in a country which calls itself democratic, someone claims that a minister is incompetent, it should not be considered punishable."

The Middle East

In the Middle East, all the countries which have a press of any importance have a press law which in general lays down strict rules of publication. Apart from the " caution," or deposit, these laws hedge the granting of a license to publish with all sorts of conditions.

In Lebanon, under the press law of 1948 the responsible editor must produce evidence of university studies and various other certificates. He must deposit security. The license may be cancelled if the paper temporarily suspends publication within a period of six months or if, for 20 days, the circulation falls below 1500. A reason must be given if the license is refused or withdrawn and an appeal may be lodged. But as a paper cannot appear until the tribunal dealing with the case has given its verdict, the damage may be considerable.

In Syria the law of 1949, which remained in force until 1953, and the main features of which are again to be found in the new law of May 11, 1954, gave the government powers to control the number of copies printed, and their lay-out, and to force papers to amalgamate. The regulations go into the smallest details. At one time in Damascus it was compulsory for a paper to have at least

---

[1] *I. P. I. Assembly 1955, Proceedings*, p. 28.

three members on its editorial staff and a reporter and to subscribe to two foreign news agencies.

These regulations often stem from the most laudable motives. The government is anxious not so much to persecute the press as to help it maintain a certain level, even to reform it, in the best sense. Many journalists in these countries would be the first to admit that a certain measure of control is necessary and that the time is not yet ripe for such sweeping freedom as the older democracies enjoy.

This type of regulation is unfortunately a double-edged weapon. Laying down the minimum number of copies to be printed and similar rules prevent a pullulation of newsheets, which would debase the journalistic currency. But it comes in handy for preventing the growth of an opposition press. Thus, towards the end of 1954 every newspaper publisher in Iraq found himself obliged, by virtue of a new decree, to apply for a fresh permit to publish. The new license was only handed out to eight dailies and one weekly, i.e. scarcely half the existing regular papers, and the result was the virtual wiping out of the opposition press overnight.

Press offenses are also severely dealt with under the laws in the Middle East. In Iraq the press law of 1933, still in force after the war, made it an offense to publish news of the government which did not stem from an official source. It also laid down that a warning would be sent by the Minister of the Interior to any editor publishing any article " tending to bring discredit on the government or to reflect on its prestige." In addition the Minister of the Interior acts as both prosecutor and judge in legal proceedings.

The Egyptian press law of 1941, amended in 1949, allowed of *administrative* control over publishing houses. Further, a newspaper was automatically suspended if it fell foul of the regulations. The government sometimes made the proceedings drag out so that an " awkward " newspaper should remain out of action. This happened, for instance, to the opposition paper *Saout El-Omma* towards the end of Farouk's reign.

In Thailand the 1941 press law is very restrictive. The official responsible for its application has wide and almost discretionary powers of censorship. He is sole judge of whether an article offends public order or morals, and decides whether the offending paper shall be suspended or seized. The newspaper can appeal within seven

days, but the high official in charge of press matters turns out
to be Vice-Minister of the Interior as well. The paper may sometimes
win out in spite of everything by virtue of a clause in the law which
prescribes, in somewhat vague terms, that a paper must be warned
before it is censored. In 1952 a newspaper brought an action to have
a censorship order annulled, and claimed damages, on the grounds
that the official in charge of press matters had omitted to send a
warning and to indicate which article was in question. The tribunal
found for the newspaper, a rare occurrence. The press has several
times, particularly since 1952, tried to get the law amended, but
unsuccessfully. In fact the government's reply was to propose a still
harsher press law. It alleged that censorship continued to be necessary
because the newspapers in Bangkok were not accurate enough and
were not run as the national interest required.[1]

The Western Hemisphere

In Latin America several countries have press laws which inflict
considerable restrictions on newspapers. Brazil is a happy exception,
the new law of November 1953 being more liberal than the previous
law of 1934.

At the other extreme is Colombia. The 1944 press law, passed
under a liberal regime, already contained clauses which threatened
the free expression of opinion. Subsequent laws have made matters
considerably worse. The nadir was reached with Decree No. 2835
of September 24, 1954, which luckily never came into force. This
decree began by giving the status of law to the code of professional
ethics passed by the first national congress of the Colombian press
in 1953. This code was never intended to be more than a general
guide to the profession. It then abolished the measures dealing with
press matter of a defamatory character and introduced much harsher
ones in their stead. Right of appeal was whittled down. Worst of all,
press offenses were to be dealt with by civil servants and not the
judiciary. Commenting on this decree the Bogotá *El Tiempo* said :

[1] Albert G. Pickerell : *The Press in Thailand*, to be published shortly by the
University of California (Berkeley).

" There is no cause to treat journalists as a class dangerous to society. By what right is it assumed that a journalist is a potential criminal ? And why, if he is so considered, is he denied the means of defense granted to the worst criminals ? What has happened to the equality of all citizens before the law ? "

Decree 3000, which came into force at the end of 1954, though less Draconian, is still pretty severe. It re-establishes normal judicial procedure ; it allows the possibility of a case being dropped after a correction has been published ; it no longer provides for the suspension of newspapers guilty of infractions, but it does retain fines on such an astronomical scale that obviously most Colombian newspapers could never pay them. These fines are increased by a third or even a half when the newspaper's target is a political figure, a civil servant, a member of the Armed Forces or the Church, or when a public body is attacked. At its congress in 1954 the Colombian Press Association asked that this decree be amended, and the I.A.P.A. associated itself with this request.

Protection of prestige

In many other press laws, the provisions which most endanger freedom of expression are those covering attacks on the prestige of the government.

In Nicaragua the 1953 law on freedom to express and disseminate opinions rates as an offense the publication of matter " denigrating " the State authorities or reflecting on the " good name of the nation," whatever those terms may mean. An editor remains in the dark, but if he is judged to have transgressed his paper is confiscated. The daily *La Prensa* was prosecuted under this law for having criticized working conditions in a firm managed by President Somoza's sons.

The Chilean law of March 20, 1925 is considered locally to be not liberal enough and out of date. The main defect is the clause on *desacato*, i.e. disrespect towards the authorities. Most Latin American countries have a provision of this type, incidentally. It is clearly highly dangerous, as any fairly frank press criticism of the government can lead to a prosecution.

Four journalists were arrested in March 1952 and sentenced for publishing remarks about a minister's somewhat equivocal activities. However, the Supreme Court quashed their sentence. The Santiago Press Circle induced a number of deputies to table a new and more liberal press law, but up till now Parliament has not debated this proposal.

In the meantime other journalists have been victims of the *desacato* clause. The most striking case was the arrest in August 1953 of Alfredo Silva-Carvallo, editor of the main daily in Valparaiso, *La Union*, and a member of the I. P. I. Executive Board. He was accused of having insulted President Ibañez and three of his ministers. What his paper had done in fact, was to publish, *without comment*, extracts from speeches made by some Radical deputies at a banquet celebrating the party's 60th anniversary. These speeches denounced the infiltration of Perón men into the government and the shocking morals of high officials. The press objected to Alfredo Silva-Carvallo's arrest with vigor and he was released after 24 hours. In January 1954 the tribunal which dealt with the case dismissed the charge.

In the spring of 1955 both the publisher and the editor of the Santiago daily *El Debate* were arrested. They were accused of *desacato* towards the President of the Republic, having credited him with dictatorial ambitions. However, a few weeks later, the Supreme Court in Santiago caused them both to be released unconditionally. It ruled that it was illegal to imprison journalists because the articles published in their papers were not to the liking of the authorities, and that their refusal to divulge the source of their information did not justify their imprisonment.

To come back now to Europe. The Greek Chamber adopted in July 1953 a decree which reinforces previous measures against press offenses, particularly those relating to defamation of public notabilities (protection of prestige including heads of parties) and the dissemination of false or tendentious news (including matter liable to shake faith in the currency). Fines are steeper and prison sentences longer. A new sanction has been introduced, which a paper might not survive—the withdrawal of rights to duty-free newsprint, for periods of anything from two months to a year. Both the independent and the opposition press objected violently to this decree and several staged a one-day strike when it was passed by Parliament. Nevertheless freedom of expression does not appear to have suffered greatly since the law came into force, though a fairly serious potential threat for opposition papers remains. One of them, the daily *Eleftheria,* had a brush with the authorities in January 1955, but without very serious consequences.

In Italy the press law of February 8, 1948 contains several clauses whose severity constitutes a threat to free criticism. In particular the penalties for *vilipendio* (defamation) are even stricter than they were in Fascist legislation. Anyone guilty of defamation in the press is liable to from one to six years in prison. As roughly any criticism of authority can be construed as *vilipendio,* everything depends on how the law is applied. This will be dealt with further in the section dealing with political pressure.

In 1951 a new draft press law was tabled by the De Gasperi government. This provided in particular for even greater liability on the part of the editor and the tightening up of confiscation measures, allowing the executive in certain cases to suspend a publication before the court had pronounced judgment. An issue could be seized if democratic institutions or their representatives were attacked. This proposal met with a very hostile reception both from the press and a large section of the public, and seems now to be completely dead.

Still-born laws

In the course of the last ten years the vigilance of the press, with the help of enlightened public opinion, has succeeded in killing at birth various attempts by governments to introduce anti-liberal press legislation in several other countries.

A case in point is Japan, where after the end of the occupation the government tried to insert in the national legislation the Press Code imposed by S. C. A. P. (Supreme Command of Allied Forces in the Pacific) after the capitulation. This was a very severe code which laid down, among other things, that news should be in strict accordance with the truth and forbade all propaganda, as well as " destructive " criticism of the occupying powers. To put still more teeth into this code the Japanese Attorney General was given the job of drafting a law on the control of publications. It has been seen how this proposal fared in the section on laws dealing with security. By dint of a prolonged and bitter struggle the press, with the aid of the liberal element in public opinion, succeeded in forcing the government to rework the project four times, something being whittled away from it each time.

Much the same happened in the Federal German Republic after the Minister of the Interior, Robert Lehr, tabled a draft Press Bill in 1952. This measure involved a number of dangerous provisions restricting freedom of expression, such as a ban on the publication of anything likely to affect the reputation of the Federal Government. The most dangerous clause laid down that " the press must publish only what corresponds to the truth. It must not garble news either by leaving out important details or by any other procedure. News items which prove false or ambiguous must be rectified immediately."

This proposal was withdrawn following a storm of protest from the press, which regarded a Federal press law as undesirable anyway, particularly as almost every *Land* already had its own. In general there are few complaints about *Land* laws, though some editors find the compulsion to correct irksome, where such provision exists, as they are usually not permitted to contest either the contents or the length of the replies.

IV

Penal laws

In theory, the press should be subject only to the ordinary penal law ; such is the general desire of the profession and indeed, when it is well organized, its demand.

When they are not specifically based on common law, as in Sweden, the penal provisions of press laws sometimes overlap or duplicate the penal code, or else increase the number and extent of the possible restrictions on the freedom of the press, often excessively. As has been seen, their object is to cover the entire field of press offenses and provide for a more expeditious procedure than that of common law.

Almost every penal code in the world contains provisions which have the press in view, even in countries which have a separate press law. These provisions are usually regarded as perfectly normal ; the press has no right to be above the law. They are the provisions relating to the rights of the individual and his reputation, public health, breach of the peace, crime and national safety.

However, even " legitimate " clauses of the penal side of common law may sometimes constitute a threat to the freedom of the press. They may be couched in over-elastic or over-severe terms, i.e. they may offer loop-holes, or the penalties laid down may be so crushing that the press simply dare not risk infringing the law ; this automatically and severely restricts its freedom to criticize. This has been the result of the 1954 amendment to the Turkish press law, as was seen above.

The aspects of the penal code which affect the press most are those on defamation in general, incitement to disorder, inaccurate news and disclosure of official secrets.[1]

[1] Cf. F. Terrou and L. Solal : *Legislation for Press, Film and Radio* (UNESCO, 1951) for a comparative study of penal legislation on the press.

Defamation

It is most important to the press that the articles of the law on defamation should be clearly and accurately worded and applied with impartiality. If they are too severe and if the door is left open for arbitrary application, then any genuine freedom of criticism becomes impossible. If on the other hand they are too flexible the irresponsible press can get away with the most venomous and vicious abuses of its freedom. Until, that is, the authorities clamp down on the press as a whole. When at the beginning of 1953 the government of Ecuador banned several papers it justified its action by claiming that, owing to the deficiencies of the law, no proceedings against the journalists who had overstepped the bounds would have succeeded. This does not excuse the illegality of the government's action, but it does show the need for properly drafted laws, a point which I. A. P. A. also underlined.

Iran may be quoted as another country where prosecution for defamation is so fraught with snags that newspapers can indulge in personal attacks in the most uninhibited way and normally hope to get away with it. When the authorities do react they sometimes bring pressure to bear on the judges or resort to other arbitrary methods.

One of the latest laws in this field, and probably one of the best, is the Defamation Act passed in the United Kingdom in late 1952. The press as a whole regards this law as a definite advance. Compared with previous laws of libel it reduces the possible repercussions of an unintentional libel ; it gives more weight to a defense of " truth " or " fair comment " and finally it draws up a precise and extended list of " privileged " subjects which may be reported fairly and honestly without risk of libel actions.

In general a newspaper risks the most serious consequences when its target is a public authority. Defamation of a minister or a high official is regarded in quite a different light from libel of a private individual. However, the former are by the very nature of their functions more open to criticism, and it is sometimes couched in somewhat sharp or even personal terms. Public authorities are quick to take umbrage and are not always particular in their methods of self-defense.

In the analysis of press laws it was seen that the most threatening measures were generally those against attempts to discredit government personalities and officials (Turkey, Greece, Italy, Colombia, Chile). The same is true of most countries' penal laws.

In the Federal German Republic, Article 187a of the penal code was amended to increase the penalties when public figures are involved.

In India, Parliament passed a law late in 1954 allowing the public prosecutor to initiate proceedings against editors or journalists who publish attacks on servants of the State. The press organizations and the Press Commission protested against this law, which is clearly apt to hamper freedom of comment.

In the Philippines the Supreme Court, in December 1951, ruled that any attack on the government may be slanderous and as such liable to prosecution. The following year the government tabled a law providing for the deportation, without a hearing, of any foreign journalist guilty of slandering the rulers of the country or members of Parliament. The American editors of three Manila dailies would have been very much in the line of fire. The proposal was rejected, however, and since then the right to criticize public figures in the press has not again been queried.

In Indonesia during the summer of 1953 the editors of two Bandjarmasin newspapers in Borneo were arrested for publishing articles which were allegedly insulting to the local authorities. One of them, Asnawi Musa, editor of *Tekad,* was kept in prison for several days before being brought to trial. The other, A. Djohansjah, editor of *Tugas,* was sent to a forced labor camp along with ordinary criminals. They were both freed, thanks entirely to the violent uproar raised by the Indonesian press. This shows what an excessively severe law, coupled with an out-of-date procedure going back to colonial times, can lead to.

In Latin America the crime of *desacato* (disrespect towards the authorities) crops up in several legislations, either in the press law as in Chile (see p. 36) or in the penal law as in Argentina. In the latter the chief instrument of pressure is the 1949 amendment to Article 244 of the Penal Code, which deals with *desacato.* It is one of the worst examples of this type of restriction. Any unfavorable comment on a magistrate or a civil servant is actionable. The accused is not allowed to prove that the facts as stated by him are accurate. He finds himself stripped of any means of defense, and prosecution automatically leads to conviction. Numerous papers have been hit by this article of the Penal Code, including *La Prensa* and *El Intransigente* of Salta.[1]

In Peru Article 299 of the Penal Code treats as a crime all disparaging comment on governments with which Peru has good relations. This Article was applied in 1952 to the editor of *La Prensa* of Lima because of an article deemed insulting to Argentina. The press has long been agitating for its repeal.

Another danger must be mentioned in connection with the law on defamation in certain countries, and that is the frequent absence of any distinction between wilful, conscious, even systematic libel on the one hand and involuntary or unpremeditated libel on the other. This is particularly true in France, and Claude Desjardins, assistant to the editor-in-chief of *Le Parisien libéré*, speaking at the fourth General Assembly of the I. P. I. in 1955, characterized it as the worst form of legal pressure on the press in France at the present time. Under the present system bad faith is automatically assumed in libel cases. Unwelcome allusions to persons in high places can lead to the journalist being brought before the court, with no right to present the proofs of his assertions, with good faith counting for nothing, and with the probability that he will be asked to name his sources. Finally, he will be convicted. In such circumstances, said M. Desjardins in conclusion, it is understandable that the newspapers have a tendency to caution, even if this is unfortunate for freedom of expression.[2]

The French press has attempted to get the law modified. Since 1952 a bill has been before the National Assembly which stipulates that before a suit is brought against a paper and where truth is no defense, the libelled person make use of his right of reply to the libellous statements. Insertion of the reply in the paper would constitute a legal presumption of good faith unless there was proof to the contrary.

This bill has not been passed by the National Assembly. In the meantime the public authorities continue to have a dangerous weapon

[1] Cf. this paper's case in the section on political pressures.
[2] *I. P. I. Assembly 1955, Proceedings*, p. 21.

at their disposal, and they can harass a newspaper which displeases them. In fact they do not, but if a government hostile to the press were returned to power, the legal armament for muzzling the press would be ready to hand.

Incitement to disorder

Even in the most advanced democracies the expression of certain opinions is still an offense. Condoning crime and propaganda which undermines public order, are punishable offenses. So far so good— freedom of expression must not become license. But how the need to put the brake on obnoxious or subversive propaganda can be reconciled with freedom of opinion is a delicate question.

As has been seen [1], a number of governments have passed special laws on security which are particularly ominous for the press. However, even when the repression of incitement to disorder comes within the framework of ordinary penal legislation there is still sometimes a threat to the press. For the freedom of the press to be safeguarded the law must limit intervention by authority to clearly defined situations. In the United States, for instance, for proceedings to be possible there must be " clear and present danger," and this criterion is final.

Newspapers have obligations on their side. " It is for the press to realize its power over the masses, and to see to it that the law, which is so dangerous to its freedom and yet so necessary, does not have to be called into play." [2]

In the older democracies these conditions are in general pretty well met. In the young democracies the situation is sometimes less satisfactory. Several of them, for instance, have retained penal codes introduced by a colonial power. Repression of " sedition " is as a result often harsher than the circumstances warrant.

An example is Article 124 a of the Indian Penal Code which provides penalties for publication of matter liable to incite hatred and contempt for the government. In 1953 several journalists in the Punjab were arrested by virtue of this article for violently criticizing

---

[1] See p. 13 ff.
[2] F. Terrou and L. Solal. Op. cit., p. 303.

the government's attitude towards the Sikh troubles. Part of the press regards this measure as justified but the dangers to freedom of criticism seem clear. In its report in 1954 the Indian Press Commission recommended the repeal of this article on the grounds that it is incompatible with the guarantees in the Constitution. Article 153 a concerning incitement to hatred between different classes of citizens constitutes another threat. The same Commission suggested it be amended to give a more exact definition of its scope.

In Pakistan the same articles, which date back to the rule of the British, give rise to the same recriminations. In this country they seem to be applied with greater severity. One of the victims was Z. A. Suleri, editor of the Karachi *Evening Times* (now the *Times of Karachi*). He was imprisoned, together with the paper's publisher and its cartoonist, at the end of December 1952 and kept in jail until the following March.

The charge was occasioned by an article and a cartoon which in effect accused the government of plunging Pakistan into chaos. They occupied the whole front page of a special supplement of the *Evening Times* published on December 25, 1952, Jinnah's birthday. Bail was refused, as was a request that the hearings be public. The defense maintained that the proceedings were deliberately dragged out, the longer to keep Z. A. Suleri and his colleagues in *preventive* custody. The cartoonist, N. M. Kutpal, was the victim under examination of a brazen attempt at blackmail. He was invited to sign an affidavit to the effect that Z. A. Suleri had insisted that he should draw his cartoon so that the ministers from Bengal should appear as the incendiaries of the nation. Finally, after 83 days in prison, the three accused were released on bail and a little later the charge itself was set aside by the Supreme Court of Sindh. Most Pakistan papers and journalists considered that the government's action gravely undermined the freedom of the press and that the penal provisions concerning the press should be revised and brought " into line with the requirements of modern times." As a protest the two main Pakistan press organizations staged a one-day strike. In a special statement the president of the Pakistan Newspaper Editors' Conference said : " Mr. Suleri's arrest is in reality a challenge to the journalistic profession of this country. This is an attack on the freedom of speech and the liberty of the press which no democratic government worth the name would dare to make." Moreover, many large newspapers throughout the world and international organizations such as the International Press Institute and the Commonwealth Press Union protested against the jailing of Z. A. Suleri and kept the subject alive in the minds of the public until he was released.

In Indonesia the press lives in fear of an article of the colonial penal law of 1848 which allows the authorities to take preventive measures if they deem that a crime *may be* committed or public order *may be* disturbed. The public prosecutor in Djakarta used this article in October 1953 as a pretext for imposing restrictions on the publication of inflammatory speeches made in public sessions of Parliament or in public trials calculated to excite public opinion. The indignant protests of the press caused the restrictions to be removed. Indonesian newspaper editors regard this as the most flagrant attempt to intimidate the press recorded since the country achieved independence.

Laws do not need the ancestry of a colonial regime to be dangerous. The penal code of Thailand, which never was a colony, contains a clause like the " seditious libel " clause in force in India, except that its loose wording makes it perhaps even more dangerous. To become liable to a prison sentence one need only publish matter likely to foster public discontent which in its turn would be liable to cause disorder.

This form of pressure caused by legislation on incitement to disorder is not by any means confined to Southeast Asia. It is rife in the Union of South Africa and is even to be found in Western European countries, though in attenuated form.[1]

Inaccurate news

Inaccurate news, particularly the systematic distortion of truth, may have very serious consequences. As it is almost impossible to intercept such news in time it might seem plausible to legislate for penalties of some sort. Some countries, however, have managed to avoid doing so. The United States, Great Britain, Denmark and Belgium have no law on the subject.

[1] See Section II — The laws on security.

The countries which have legislated on inaccurate news have adopted various formulae. Turkey's solution has already been dealt with in the section on press laws.

Certain countries do not lay down bad faith as a deciding factor. In these, inaccurate news is punishable as soon as, or if, it becomes liable to disturb public order. It makes no difference whether the author or the editor published it knowingly or not. Good faith is not an excuse. This is so in Mexico, for example.

This conception may help the maintenance of public order but its possible repercussions on the press need no underlining. Journalists are forced into excessive caution, news is reduced to a trickle and as a result the normal dissemination of information is strangled.

Another possible criterion, also open to objection, is that of grave prejudice caused, *or liable to be caused,* to public order. It is not necessary for news to be harmful to the maintenance of public order, it is enough that it *might* be harmful. In France the 1945 order modifying Article 27 of the press law of 1881 punishes the spreading of inaccurate news in bad faith if " it disturbs or is calculated to disturb the peace." The judge has almost unlimited powers to decide whether the report might or might not do so.

In Indonesia journalists have a similar cause for complaint. The terms of Article 171 of the Penal Code are by no means clear-cut. Anyone is liable to penalties who is responsible for spreading news which is inaccurate and might create disorder and which he might have known was inaccurate. The editor of a Djakarta paper writes that this article is known as the " india-rubber " law as it does not define either inaccuracy or what is liable to create disorder. Such interpretation is left to the discretion of the authorities. A perfectly straight item of news might be judged to be liable to create disorder.

Disclosure of official secrets

Legislation on this subject poses a number of thorny problems, particularly in relation to defense secrets. In June 1955 the Institute of Criminal and Penological Science of Strasbourg University organized study courses on this aspect of penal law. Seven countries of Western Europe were represented. The conclusion of the study

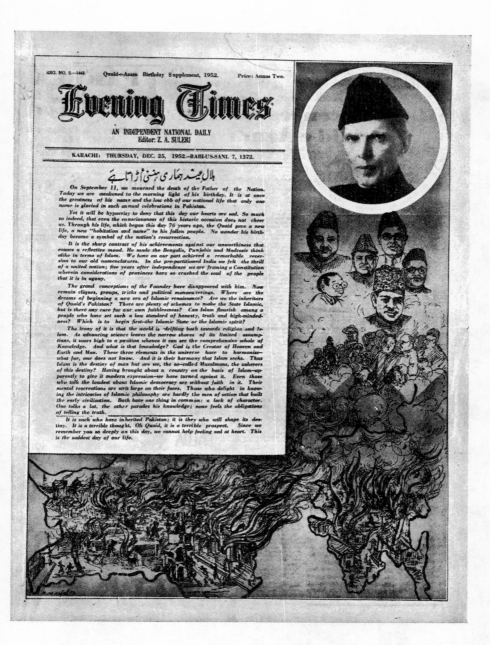

Front page of the Karachi *Evening Times* for December 25, 1952. This cartoon and the accompanying editorial brought the artist and the writer 83 days in prison (p. 46).

Roger Stéphane (center) of *France-Observateur* is conducted to prison by two police inspectors (p. 50).

groups was that it is impossible to arrive at a precise legal definition of defense secrets, and that progress is only possible in the direction of safeguards to persons convicted of violating such secrets .

The legal systems of all countries contain restrictions on freedom of information concerning national defense secrets, sometimes very severe ones, either in the penal code or framed as separate laws. However, the penalties for journalists vary considerably. There seem to be two different conceptions of information in this field. According to one, when information reaches a paper through normal channels it ceases to be secret. According to the other, even if information comes through normal channels it may be punishable to publish it if it concerns national defense, owing to the fact that its appearance in the press automatically gives it wider currency. The Netherlands and Italy, for instance, take the latter view.

Since the last war there have been brisk skirmishes between the press and the public authorities, particularly in the Federal German Republic and in France, on this question of the penal law and the disclosure of official secrets.

In the Federal German Republic journalists are agreed that Article 353c of the Penal Code is the worst of all existing legal threats. This article was introduced by the Nazis and was not repealed in 1945. It punishes the publication of official news which is supposed to be secret (the Minister of Justice deciding what news comes within this category) and obliges a journalist charged under this law to disclose his sources. This article has only been applied once since the war, in the Platow case, which raised a considerable stir in press circles and among the general public between 1951 and 1953.

Robert Platow, a Hamburg journalist who specialized in economic matters, was arrested in 1951 on a charge of having obtained information from officials by illicit means. This was shortly followed by the arrest of a Bonn journalist, Albert Schulze, on similar charges and of the officials concerned. The press agitated vigorously against Article 353c and some deputies of the Federal Parliament also urged its repeal. These attempts were unsuccessful but an amnesty bill was tabled in Parliament. For months this proposal was bandied between the Bundestag and the Bundesrat and was passed only in 1953 in the shape of a more general amnesty covering various other classes of delinquents as well.

Article 353 c has not been applied since, but the fact of its existence continues to represent a threat to journalists. They have continued to clamor for its repeal, and a draft bill to that effect is waiting in some government pigeon-hole. A number of eminent jurists have stated that the article is inconsistent with the Constitution.

In France the Penal Code contains two articles providing for sanctions against newspapers publishing military secrets. Article 81 provides for the punishment of the disclosure of defense secrets, and Article 86, amended by the Daladier decree of 1939, the disclosure of military information *of any type* not cleared by the government. The second article obviously admits of a very wide interpretation and is highly dangerous to the press. Though Article 86 has rarely been brought into play, Article 81 has been used to belabor journalists in 1954 and 1955 in circumstances which gave rise to serious altercations between the press and the public authorities. In both cases the charges were clearly inspired by political considerations.

The most striking case was the arrest and imprisonment of Roger Stéphane, editor of the neutralist weekly *France-Observateur*, in March 1955. The charge was "attack on the external security of the State," based on articles on the war in Indochina which he had written on July 30, 1953 and May 27, 1954 i.e. 20 and 10 months earlier respectively.

He was released three weeks later. However, this case raised a wave of protest in the press, especially as it came soon after some highly questionable proceedings against other members of the same paper's editorial staff. The French National Press Federation protested indignantly both against the charges and the attempt to make the journalist divulge his sources, as being "unjustified by any national interest and a direct attack on the freedom of the press." The National Journalists' Syndicate, an independent body, stated : "The lawfulness of bringing a charge is one thing, imprisonment quite another. The arrest of a journalist on a question of professional ethics is completely unjustifiable."

In Japan, too, the press is taking alarm at new penal measures which are in the wind. They prohibit disclosure of " the principles and achievements of national defense," and it is feared that this vague phraseology might be judged to cover the political, diplomatic, financial and economic aspects of national defense.

Criminal procedure

There are provisions which constitute a threat to the press, not only in the penal codes themselves, but also in the codes of criminal procedure. They are not aimed at journalists specifically, but journalists are the first to suffer from them.

One of the most feared by the press is that which permits the preventive arrest of the author of an offending article or of the paper's editor. The press rightly objects very strongly to such a measure which is just a glaring form of intimidation. In the opinion of the press there is no justification for thinking that any journalist would attempt to refuse to answer a summons. However, this procedure has been used against journalists, for instance in France against Roger Stéphane, and also in Turkey since 1954, where Article 104 of the code of criminal procedure has frequently been interpreted to the disadvantage of the press. This article provides for the arrest of the accused only if there is danger of his escaping or if public order is jeopardized. A similar procedure has been known in Lebanon. Cases in the same category which have already been mentioned in other contexts are those of Z. A. Suleri in Pakistan ; the two editors in Bandjarmasin in Indonesia (by virtue of an old colonial law permitting imprisonment without proof of guilt) ; Carlos Lacerda in Rio and Alfredo Silva-Carvallo in Valparaiso.

* * *

Another very widely feared provision of criminal procedure is that which obliges a journalist to reveal his sources. If he is a defendant the journalist usually enjoys the right of any accused to refuse to depose. If he is called as a witness the law in many countries denies him the right to refuse to disclose his sources, which is accorded to priests, lawyers and doctors. The press is unanimous in demanding that their rights in this respect be recognized, at least when the public interest is not at stake.

Sweden, Austria and 12 States in the United States already accord the journalist this right, and Chile and Indonesia are moving in the same direction ; but in many other countries it is denied him.

Penalties for refusal to reveal sources

Here are some outstanding examples :

Federal German Republic : In 1950 a Hanover journalist called Kallenbach was arrested for refusing to disclose the name of a police officer who had given him information on a mysterious fatal accident. In 1953 a correspondent of D. P. A. got a prison sentence, commutable to a fine, for withholding the source of some information concerning a group of Czech spies.

Netherlands : In 1952 a journalist called Hommerson of *Het Vrije Volk* was sent to prison for refusing to testify.

Norway : In 1952, the editor of the *Harstad Folkeviljen* was sentenced to three months in prison for the same reason.

Japan : In 1950 a reporter of the *Asahi* was sent to prison.

Philippines : In 1949, the Supreme Court sentenced a journalist to a month in prison. In 1954 three journalists of *News behind the News* were involved in a similar affair.

Indonesia : In 1953, sentence was passed on Asa Bafagih, editor of the *Pemandangan* of Djakarta, but a demonstration by the press secured his release. The following year two journalists from Kalimanthan were imprisoned on the same grounds.

The absence of a special privilege exonerating a journalist from revealing his sources is one thing ; the pressure of a law forcing him to reveal them is something infinitely worse. As has been seen, the security law in Pakistan imposes this condition. The same was true in New South Wales in Australia under a law passed in December 1953 and entitled " Sydney City Council (Disclosure of Allegations) Act." Its aim was to force journalists to divulge their sources for some articles on corruption alleged to exist within the Sydney City Council. It was directed virtually against only one daily in Sydney and its application could be retrospective. Not only the local press but the press of the whole world rose up in indignation over this law. Luckily the Supreme Court found a legal flaw in it and threw it out.

In certain countries criminal procedure contains various other provisions liable to restrict freedom of expression. Here are three examples :

An article of the code of criminal procedure of the Federal German Republic lays down that " objects likely to constitute important evidence in a legal investigation are subject to confiscation. They must be deposited with the authorities or put in a safe place." If the object is a newspaper, the application of this law should involve the confiscation of only a few copies and not an entire edition. There have been no concrete cases, but it is superfluous to stress the abuses to which such rules of penal procedure might lead to serve political ends.

In Italy there is a permanent conflict of jurisdiction between civil and military justice. Journalists are liable to trial by military courts even when they are not on active service, for the simple reason that they can, if need be, be called to the colors. The most striking instance of this paradoxical situation is the Renzi-Aristarco affair. These two journalists were charged in 1953 with undermining the army's morale ; they had published an article in a film magazine on the behavior of the Italian expeditionary force in Greece.

Early in 1955 two Bologna left-wing journalists were given prison sentences by a military court for having criticized some policing operations by the army. Another journalist was prosecuted in his capacity of head of the information service of the Bologna edition of *Unità,* which had carried an anonymous article siding with the accused journalists. The upshot of these measures was that the executive committee of the Italian Press Federation stepped in with a proposal for a new law which would remove journalists from military jurisdiction.

In 1953, in India a number of Calcutta reporters who were covering a banned demonstration were involved in a raid by the police. Some were wounded and 15 were arrested. A commission of inquiry ruled that the terms of the code of criminal procedure justified the action of the police. The Indian press is of the opinion that this interpretation is highly prejudicial to the reporting of certain events of public interest.

V

Laws on immoral publications

The penal codes of all countries contain clauses designed to prevent the distribution of publications which offend public morals. Not satisfied with this, many countries have special laws on publications calculated to pervert young people. In theory nothing is more defensible than the protection of minors against pernicious literature, but in practice certain laws are so drafted as to represent a serious threat to freedom of expression and even of information.

It is often clear that the drafters have made a great effort to reconcile satisfactorily the general interests of the press and the need to protect young people. One of the first steps is to distinguish between information destined to be read by adults and " literature " designed to be read by young people, with the object of legislating only for the latter. Another essential point is precisely who is going to apply the law and exactly what their powers are. It is hard to arrive at the ideal formula.

One of the most recent laws in this field is the " Children and Young Persons (Harmful Publications) Act," passed in Great Britain in March 1955 after much debate. It is aimed at " horror comics," which are defined as follows : "Any book, magazine or other like work which consists wholly or mainly of stories told in pictures (with or without the addition of written matter) being stories portraying a) the commission of crimes or b) acts of violence or cruelty or c) incidents of a repulsive or horrible nature in such a way that the work as a whole would tend to corrupt a child or young person into whose hands it might fall, whether by inciting or encouraging him to commit crimes or acts of violence or cruelty, or in any other way whatsoever."

Several newspapers, notably *The Times* and the *Manchester Guardian* felt that the text of the bill " is not quite tightly enough drawn " (to quote the latter). The expression " would tend to corrupt " could be interpreted in a variety of ways. There was speculation as to whether the bill would not prevent pictures or a written description of the effects of napalm bombing, which would be instructive for adults, but might be considered harmful for minors. Another criticism was that *intention* to corrupt had not been kept as the main criterion.

At the last moment a Labor M. P. tried to bring in an amendment to extend the bill to include newspapers, particularly the Sunday press. But his suggestion met with a rough passage and was finally rejected.

This British bill is in effect a compromise, or a half-measure. But it does have the merit of steering clear of certain snags which in other countries legislators have not managed to avoid.

The State of New York also passed a law on the suppression of " horror comics " in 1955. Previously the magazines themselves had tried to operate a voluntary censorship, hoping to ward off government intervention. The " Comics Magazine Association of America " got a judge to act as censor and to draw up a kind of code. The New York State authorities, however, decided that this kind of censorship was open to objection, and inadequate, and proceeded to draft a very carefully worded law which avoids tampering with freedom of expression but does make it possible to punish publications calculated to corrupt young people.

In Italy the press law contains a good clause designed to hit publications for minors which describe or illustrate, with horrific or sensational details, events either real or imaginary in such a way as to disturb morals or family life or to incite corruption, crime or suicide. In 1951 this law was reinforced by a special law on the type of pernicious publications which go by the name of *fumetti*. It arranges for the setting-up of "vigilance committees." The Italian press has had to take energetic action against an attempt to slip in a clause in the pre-censorship regulations which might have been applied too widely.

In the Federal German Republic the law on indecent publications, the *Schmutz- und Schundgesetz* (dirt-and-trash law), has been a bone of contention between the public authorities and the press for years. It spent three years travelling to and fro between the Lower House and the Upper House before finally being passed in 1953. This law forbids the sale to young people of any sort of literature which clearly and seriously endangers morality *(Offensichtlich sittlich schwer gefährdet)*. The decision whether a publication comes within this definition rests with a federal control commission, the *Bundesprüfstelle,* which consists of 12 members, representing the authorities, the press, youth organizations, the teaching profession and the Church.

This arrangement did not work out entirely satisfactorily. A year after it got under way one member of the commission, who represented the book trade, resigned, complaining that the commission was exercising a kind of ideological censorship. The press, particularly the weekly and the illustrated press, had fought the law from the start, arguing that it duplicated part of the penal code. Magazine publishers have denounced cases of unjustified confiscation and have asked for a precise definition of the nature of the crime so as to avoid the charge of " obscenity " being used as a cover for driving out of circulation publications criticizing certain authorities. The daily press has not been affected (except, once, a prominent Hamburg newspaper), but many editors regard the law as a potential threat.

Irish commission

In Eire, the law on immoral literature is extremely drastic, both in its terms and in its application. The body which decides what is indecent is a commission appointed by the government. It can ban publications which " unduly " emphasize sex, crime or violence. The war against allegedly indecent publications is mostly waged against publications from abroad. They are subject to an import ban and, since 1929, the regulations have been applied in the narrowest spirit. In 1953, the London magazine *Illustrated* was banned for three weeks and the *Sunday Times* for three months, and in the same year no fewer than 765 books were refused entry, including works by Hemingway, Steinbeck and Graham Greene.

In the Union of South Africa, a considerable number of publications have been put on the index on the pretext that they were immoral. Anyone found with one of these in his possession is liable to a fine of up to £1,000 or up to five years in prison. In addition the press is prevented from reporting cases of immorality, indecency, blackmail, extortion or brutal assault without written permission from a magistrate. At the I. P. I. Assembly in Vienna in 1954, Morris Broughton, editor of the *Cape Argus* showed how these regulations, though praiseworthy in intention, can hinder faithful and complete reporting of local events.[1]

In 1954 the States of New South Wales, Victoria and Queensland in Australia, adopted new laws on immoral publications. These laws are so full of pitfalls that, according to the trade journal, *Newspaper News*, they represent the most serious threat to freedom of expression in the annals of the Australian press. The laws are so loosely worded that a mildly frivolous illustration which most papers would publish without a second thought can easily get the paper using it into trouble with the censors. It is true that newspapers are theoretically outside the scope of these laws ; but as they are aimed at matter which " corrupts," it is feared that this general term will allow over-zealous censors to stamp on any anti-government opinions which they choose to regard as falling within that definition.

In fact, in New South Wales, a member of the government did write a letter to an opposition paper threatening to bring the obscene literature law down on it if it did not stop attacking the Labor Party. This resulted in a question in the Parliament in Sydney and some liberal M. P.'s pointed out how dangerous the law was to freedom of expression.

In New South Wales and in Victoria the chief editor of a paper finds himself having to do his own censoring. He has to guess at a court's probable reaction to a doubtful passage or illustration and in the event he may well over-censor himself. A number of editors would prefer a proper censorship board on the Eire model, as in Queensland. However, that is not the ideal solution either, as the workings of the Queensland " Board of Literature Review " are too far removed from legal processes. Of the five members, all nominated by the government, not one is a judge.

Up till now no newspaper has been the subject of a prohibitive order by this Board. But certain editors are apprehensive. This is what one of them said, on being approached by the I. P. I. : " In a limited way the Objectionable Literature Act of 1954 is considered to contain an inherent threat of censorship to newspapers... Objectionable literature is an abstract term that could be regarded by all sorts of people in all sorts of ways. Against this, however, the Act sets

[1] *I. P. I. Assembly 1954, Proceedings*, p. 31.

out that nothing in it shall apply to any newspaper containing only public news or political matter. Objectionable literature is defined as that which unduly emphasizes matters of sex, horror, cruelty or violence ; or is blasphemous, indecent, obscene, or likely to be injurious to morality ; or is likely to encourage depravity, public disorder or any indictable offense ; or is otherwise calculated to injure the citizens of the State. It must be admitted that this last phrase and the concept of encouraging public disorder, would appear to provide the government, through a pliant Board, with a weapon to stop publication of newspapers whose critical attacks on some matter of grave and urgent interest it resented." [1]

In New Zealand, a 1954 law on immoral publications is generally considered both obnoxious and threatening by newspaper editors. It extends the definition of indecency to include any literature with an "immoral or mischievous tendency." However, it is aimed at publications which harp unduly on sex, crime and violence and hitherto it has left newspapers alone.

In Japan, too, the press has complained of attempts to restrict its freedom, ostensibly in order to protect young people against immoral publications. The main newspapers do not deny the existence of a small group of papers which go in for exploiting an obnoxious type of literature. The profession spurns these papers and tries to eliminate them by a process of voluntary censorship. But when the government tries to help, the press is suspicious. The normal penal and police regulations available should be adequate to cope with the problem. A special law, applicable to the whole country, might easily overstep the mark. Such a law has actually been considered since 1953 but it is thought unlikely that it will ever be passed. However, this left-handed threat to the freedom of the press was regarded as sufficiently real for Susumu Ejiri to denounce it in the name of the Japanese Newspaper Publishers and Editors Association at the I. P. I. Assembly in Copenhagen in 1955.[2]

---

[1] It has been seen that in India the text of the Press Act is based on the concept of objectionable matter (see page 27).

[2] *I. P. I. Assembly 1955, Proceedings*, p. 33.

Part Two

Economic and political pressures

I

Subsidies and bribes

Economic and political pressures are just as effective as pressures deriving from the law, often more effective, and much more insidious. Sometimes in fact they appear in legal guise and, when that happens, it is less the spirit of the law or regulation which is important than the way it is applied.

Economic pressures are almost always dictated by political considerations and the two forms of pressure are sometimes almost indistinguishable.

* * *

As regards economic pressures it must be observed at the outset that in almost all countries the State accords the press a special status. Australia and Pakistan are among the few countries that do not regard the press as serving the public interest. In most other countries the State grants the press all sorts of facilities : reduction of or even exemption from taxes, especially customs duties on the import of paper ; transport facilities, subsidies to the national news agencies, etc.

The country which goes to the greatest lengths in granting this kind of favor is Italy. Journalists enjoy considerable privileges even in their private capacity. For instance, the insurance regulations have been waived on their behalf by creating the Istituto di Previdenza.

This solicitude is generally in inverse proportion to the financial strength of a country's press. Precisely because of its weakness, the press might feel indebted or obliged to the government. It knows that all these privileges may at any time be withdrawn by the State. In this way the authorities are in a position to exert indirect pressure. It is to the credit of a large number of governments that they make no use of their opportunities for blackmail of this sort.

At the General Assembly of the I. P. I. in 1955 Robert Salmon, publisher of *France-soir,* spoke in defense of indirect subsidies to the press : When such economic conditions prevailed that newsprint prices and labor costs forced newspapers to sell at a high price, it appeared to him that a democratic government should help by general means, and only in cooperation with the profession, so that the price of papers might be lower than the cost. It had been a long battle in all democracies to keep newspaper prices as low as possible. At the same time the battle for free compulsory education had been waged. So far as a general subsidy helped to keep newsprint prices down in a period of crisis, and to maintain the low level of newspaper prices, it was no more than honest for editors to recognize that the government had helped the press and did not seek to exert pressure on it.[1]

Unfortunately certain governments give a discriminatory twist to their assistance to the press and thereby in effect apply serious pressure on certain newspapers. Economic pressure may take various forms :

A number of countries subsidize their national agency. The most striking case is that of the Agence France-Presse, whose head is appointed by decree. He is at times presented with embarrassing demands by the government and may even be suspended or dismissed, as happened in 1952 and 1954 to Maurice Nègre.

Even if subsidization of a national agency or radio is accepted, at least in principle, government subsidization of a paper or papers is iniquitous. It is not only an attempt to guide public opinion, it is a form of unfair competition with independent newspapers and an encouragement to corruption.

Many governments make no attempt to tamper with the independence of the press in this way, and some have specific regulations designed to preserve this independence. For instance, Article 21 of the Italian Constitution lays down that " the law may, under general regulations, require periodicals to declare how they are financed." In Iran the 1952 Press Law provides for the auditing of newspapers' accounts. This new tendency towards governmental control of the financial resources of the press is encountered in several post-war laws.

---

[1] *I. P. I. Assembly 1955, Proceedings,* p. 31.

However, the subsidizing of pro-government papers occurs on quite a large scale in certain parts of the world. This is so, for instance, in Latin America.

In its statement to the United Nations before the 1948 Geneva conference on freedom of information the Argentine government declared that it " does not own either wholly or partly, or control either directly or indirectly, press enterprises, inside or outside its territory." Yet from 1947 onwards, by means of all types of economic pressure, including the rationing of newsprint, the Perón government drove independent newspapers like *Critica* and *La Razon* into bankruptcy and bought them up afterwards. Until Perón's fall, out of 11 Buenos Aires dailies, only *La Nacion* and *El Clarin* were genuinely independent. All the others were in the hands of organizations directly linked with the government. The Perón family had an interest in several.

During the last few years the Brazilian press has had to take energetic action to defend itself against the same kind of thing. The Vargas government, which already owned the daily papers *A Manha* and *A Noite,* tried to acquire a hold over several others. The most glaring case was when the Bank of Brazil financed the publishing and radio firm Emprezas Erica, whose main shareholders were relatives of President Vargas. This loan went beyond the statutory limits and infringed the bank's regulations. The firm's chief publication was the daily *Ultima Hora,* which became an unofficial organ of the government. Several editors, led by Carlos Lacerda of the *Tribuna da Imprensa,* launched a violent campaign in 1953 against this irregular situation. They succeeded in having a commission of inquiry appointed which established the facts. The *Ultima Hora* had to repay part of its illegally acquired funds and reconstitute its board of management.

This struggle between the free and the government press in Brazil was destined to have a tragic outcome in the second half of 1954. Some relatives of President Vargas instigated an attempt on Carlos Lacerda's life. He escaped almost unscathed, but the opposition's campaign rose to such a pitch of violence that, as a direct result, the President committed suicide.

In 1954 the Colombian government decided to launch a semi-official newspaper which was to cost a third of the price of any other paper. This plan has not yet materialized, although enormous sums have already been spent, the most up-to-date equipment bought, agreements made with the main agencies and foreign specialists engaged. If it should come off the independent press would receive a possibly mortal blow, as it would clearly be unable to compete.

Subsidizing pro-government papers is a fairly common practice also in the Middle East. A survey published two years ago in the United States shows that only 26 out of a total of 110 Arab dailies are paying concerns, and over half work at a loss. The remainder just manage to make both ends meet. In order to keep going many papers in that part of the world have to rely on hidden funds, particularly government subsidies granted to them when they toe the line.[1]

In Thailand, out of 20 or so dailies, six or seven are owned by members of the government or senior state officials or financially supported by them. The only paper receiving a regular subsidy is in fact the one belonging to the Minister for Economic Affairs, but others receive subsidies from time to time, drawn on the police's secret coffers.[2]

Other financial pressures

It goes without saying that the corruption of the press by government subsidies is not confined to the Middle East and Latin America, though it assumes its most virulent form in these areas. It can take more subtle forms, e.g. when governments grant papers favorable to them more generous financial terms than to the others. In Greece, for example, the pro-government press, unlike the independent and opposition press, enjoys fiscal advantages, bank loans and facilities for funding its debts.

In Pakistan the Federal Journalists' Union, in a resolution adopted in 1953, complained that heavy security deposits are asked by the

---

[1] Tom J. McFadden : *Daily Journalism in Arab States*. Ohio State University Press, Columbus, 1953, p. 30 ff.

[2] Albert G. Pickerell : *The Press in Thailand*, to be published by the University of California Press, Berkeley.

government in order to strangle small papers, and also that attempts are made to corrupt papers with favors and financial baits.

Similar methods are common in several Middle Eastern and Latin American countries. For instance, in Colombia in 1955 the government imposed on a small newspaper in Cali a security deposit far in excess of what the paper could possibly raise and out of all proportion to what was expected of other provincial papers.

In Indonesia, the financial support given by the government, in theory to all papers regardless of their views, tends to be granted, especially since 1955, only to those supporting government policy. Thus, the *Indonesia Raya* did not in fact get the full amount of credit that it had been granted in principle to bring its equipment up to date.

Furthermore, the government has decided not to help any longer those newspapers whose supplies of newsprint it has subsidized in recent years. Instead, it will help those newspapers which have received little assistance hitherto. At first sight this seems an eminently fair arrangement, but in point of fact, as the pro-government papers are the more recent, it works to the disadvantage of the opposition press, as the press organizations were not slow to point out. In addition the Minister of Information can waive the rule if he wishes, and if he thinks a paper is still deserving of help. This clearly puts a premium on playing ball with the government. The major part of the Indonesian press has protested, pointing out that *all* newspapers need help from the State.

Mention should be made of another form of indirect government pressure. The authorities sometimes invite concerns whose directors are favorable to them to help papers supporting their policy. This practice has been reported from Mexico.

Graft and sinecures

Apart from the granting of subsidies and other financial facilities to newspapers by governments, newspapermen themselves may be given bribes and other favors. This practice is rife in Cuba where the bribe goes by the name of *botella* and usually takes the form of direct payments made to newspapermen to keep them friendly to the government. In addition they are often awarded fictitious functions and sinecures. The *botellas* received by certain Havana editors are tantamount to a regular subsidy. It is estimated that the government spends about $ 1,000,000 a year in this way. Havana newspapers receive *botellas* ranging from $ 2,000 to $ 20,000, while individual reporters get from $ 100 to $ 300 a month, their salary being barely $ 100 a month.

Some Cubans regard this form of corruption as the symptom of a real national moral crisis. One of the causes is the plethora of newspapers. Havana has 17 dailies, of which only four or five are thought to pay their way. A multitude of pamphlet-type publications appear, their continued existence being entirely dependent on the *botellas* they can attract.[1]

Naturally Cuba has no monopoly of these practices. It has been cited because there the corruption of the press seems to reach enormous proportions. But the corruption of the press by the authorities is endemic in Venezuela, in the whole Caribbean area and in some other Latin American countries.

The same is true of the Middle East, where the causes are the same as in Cuba : too many papers, underpaid journalists, and over-flexible rules of morality. Editors and journalists whom the governments want to woo receive more or less fictitious, but well paid, official or quasi-official offices. Governments may also bring them in on lucrative deals in the financial sphere. These favors may even be extended to cover relatives or friends of a newspaper editor whom the government wishes to " oblige." [2]

It is naturally very difficult to find positive proof of these practices, but the Egyptian Republican Government, which set about cleaning up the press early in 1954, did meet with some success. It exposed 14 newspapers and several journalists who had been fattening on secret government funds under the monarchy. Among the names revealed were the brothers Abul Fath, owners of *Al Misri* and of the Société Orientale de Publicité.

It is plain that similar practices exist to a smaller or greater extent in other countries, perhaps in most countries. And it must

[1] Cf. the article by Robert Hallett of the *Christian Science Monitor*, in the I. P. I REPORT for July 1955.

[2] Cf. Tom J. McFadden, op. cit., p. 32.

be recognized that when public authorities use this kind of pressure to win newspapers to their cause it is not they who are necessarily the villains of the piece. The publisher or journalist who accepts bribery, who may even make the overtures, is even more to be despised.

II

Newsprint distribution

Paper allocation is strictly controlled in a number of countries owing to the world shortage of newsprint. The system hinges mainly on exchange control and it also affects other imported raw materials, e.g. printer's ink and equipment. The press usually has a say in the control but, when it does not, the government can allocate paper or grant foreign exchange to buy raw materials exactly as it thinks fit, and the opposition papers are the first to suffer. Moreover, when the State grants reductions of, or exemption from, customs duties on imported paper, the way is open for all sorts of abuses. Privileged papers may receive more tax-free paper than they themselves need, and they can sell the surplus on the black market.

The " selective " distribution of newsprint was one of the Perón government's principal weapons against the press. In addition there were arbitrary restrictions on the granting of foreign exchange for buying equipment and printing materials abroad. *La Prensa* and *La Nacion* were two of the main victims. At a time when newsprint was duty free, *La Prensa* was requested to make back payments on paper imported between 1939 and 1948, on the pretext that some of it had been used for commercial purposes and not solely for the publication of news. Until the Perón regime was overthrown, the original owners were still being dunned for back payments of customs duties amounting to about $ 1,300,000. Their lawyer was arrested in September 1953 and kept in custody for 62 days without a charge being preferred against him.

Sometimes a publication which was out of favor found the arrival of its newsprint delayed and it was therefore unable to appear for a period. Paper rationing also was a convenient excuse for preventing a newspaper which was hostile to the regime from increasing the number of copies it printed and even the number of its readers. Even foreign correspondents, for instance, had the greatest difficulty in taking out a subscription to *La Nacion*. On the other hand the pro-government papers were favored. A decree of October 8, 1948, limited the number of pages of dailies owing to the paper shortage. But this restriction did not apply to the publication of statements, information and pictures emanating from official sources. Which meant, in effect, that " peronista " papers, which published quantities of this sort of material, were unaffected while only the opposition press was penalized.

These methods found willing imitators elsewhere in Latin America, and in other fields besides the distribution of newsprint.

In Bolivia, too, the importing and distribution of newsprint is a government monopoly, and here also it is unfairly administered. For instance, Fernando Sinani, editor of *Pueblo* (a Left-wing paper) has had to abandon publication because his allocation of paper was reduced, for no valid reason, from 50 reams to 15. Then *Los Tiempos* of Cochabamba, whose printing shop had been gutted by hooligans in 1953, never succeeded in obtaining the necessary foreign exchange to buy new equipment.

A few years ago the Chilean government set up a commission, consisting of civil servants, to supervise the rationing of newsprint. This body's view of its duties was the reverse of impartial. The press succeeded in 1954 in having it declared unconstitutional. However, in the 1955 budget the government materially reduced the amount of paper which publishers could get at a preferential rate of exchange.

In Ecuador, the opposition daily *El Dia* was forced to pay more than the normal price for its newsprint.

Even in Brazil the press finds the conditions attached to the allocation of newsprint cramping, if not discriminatory. Brazil, together with four other Latin American States, requires duty-free newsprint to be watermarked. This regulation is supposed to prevent a black market, but the press claims that the customs control ought to be enough. Furthermore the watermark *(Linha Dagua)* increases the cost of the paper and the regulation prevents Brazilian papers from obtaining stocks of non-watermarked newsprint at favorable prices. As the unsubsidized opposition papers are the chief sufferers, this can fairly be described as a form of indirect pressure.

In Indonesia, Dutch papers have to pay three times more for their newsprint than the other papers. This could be explained by their being foreign publications, and the government does not extend to them the favorable exchange rate accorded to native publishers.

In Pakistan, the editor of the *Times of Karachi*, Z. A. Suleri, said in a paper given at the Muslim World Press Exhibition at Lahore in 1954 that the decree on paper control is seriously restricting the growth of the Pakistan press. He likened it to the kind of decree made by totalitarian regimes. It is furthermore administered in a very arbitrary manner at times, as is shown for example by the drastic treatment meted out in 1952 to the Lahore *Nawa-i-Waqt* (see below p. 82).

In Egypt under the monarchist regime the distribution of newsprint was far from impartial. A case in point is that of the pro-government *El Kotla,* owned by a past Minister of Finance. It claimed to be printing 200,000 copies when the real figure was about a tenth of that number. It sold the surplus paper on the black market. Under the revolutionary regime the opposition party's newspapers were from the outset simply not allowed to appear.

Similar practices occur in other countries of the Middle East.

In Greece the suspension of the privilege of exemption from customs duties on paper is a measure much dreaded by newspaper editors. The cost of paper with duties is very high and, as in general papers are none too prosperous, the threat to withdraw the exemption is very effective. It has been applied on several occasions, for instance against the *Athinaiki* (opposition independent), the *Ethnikos Kiryx* (right wing) and the *Avghi* (left wing).

In Israel complaints were voiced a few years ago about the allocation of newsprint, but instead of these coming from the opposition press, as might have been expected, they came from the *Hador,* the organ of the chief government party, which complained about the inadequacy of its own share.

III

Official advertising

Theoretically the allocation of government advertising should be governed by its commercial effectiveness alone, assessed in terms of the paper's circulation, distribution and so on. In some countries, however, this rule is not strictly observed. The allocation of state publicity is used as a means of pressure, pro-government papers being favored at the expense of the others.

This tendency and its iniquitous consequences have been the subject of resolutions passed at several national and international journalists' conventions. The French National Press Federation, for instance, has repeatedly protested against the use of any yardstick other than commercial effectiveness.

In Austria one paper, the *Wiener Zeitung*, is owned by the government and is given preferential treatment as regards state advertising.

In Australia, a few years ago, the Victoria State government withdrew all its publicity from a newspaper which had been particularly critical of official policy and transferred it to a rival paper. This boycott lasted only a few months, however, and since then there has been no repetition of such an incident.

In its issue of May 14, 1954, the *Cape Argus* showed how far the South African government was favoring nationalist newspapers by means of copious official publicity. In Cape Province the *Cape Argus* carried official advertising worth £820, and the *Cape Times* £854, while *Die Burger's* was worth £1248. In the Transvaal the figures were £2548 for the *Transvaler*, the main nationalist daily, and £1790 for the *Star*. In the Orange Free State, £1058 for the *Volksblad* and £514 for the *Friend*. These figures bore no relation to those for circulation and distribution.

In Turkey, up to the concordat concluded in 1953 between the press and the government, the authorities used the State's publicity funds to subsidize papers supporting their policy, thus giving them an unfair advantage over independent and opposition papers. The most glaring case was that of *Son Saat,* which is owned by a Democratic member of parliament and which, in spite of an absurdly low circulation, pocketed a very sizable sum from the State's publicity budget. Since the concordat the budgets have to be allocated according to purely technical criteria. Nevertheless, instances of discrimination continue to be reported.

In Pakistan the government uses the withdrawal of government publicity to try and bring to heel newspapers whose political line it dislikes. In 1950 the *Pakistan Observer* found itself the victim of this technique for several months because it had attacked the government for not devaluing the rupee at the same time as the pound sterling. Similarly at the end of 1953 government publicity was withdrawn for several weeks from the dailies *Dawn* and *Evening Star* of Karachi because of an article criticizing the conduct of the inquiry into the assassination of Liaquat Ali Khan. In the summer of 1955 the same step was taken against three Karachi papers, the *Pakistan Economist,* the *Mirror* and *Variety,* and several other papers, for criticizing in varying degrees either the government's policies or the conduct of one of its members.

In Burma the withdrawal of government publicity can have disastrous consequences for the smaller papers. As the Socialist government has a large number of public works in hand it also has numerous notices to publish, and the revenue from these is some of the smaller papers' life blood .The government therefore has them at its mercy.

In India, too, the problem appears in an accute form. In 1953 the government of the State of Bombay withdrew its advertising from the *Times of India* because of an article which was too critical of the local authorities. Two years later this measure had not yet been rescinded. As a result of this boycott the *Times of India,* which is one of India's foremost English-language papers, and its associated papers have suffered a loss of 2.2 per cent of their total receipts from advertising.

Nor is this particularly conspicuous case an isolated one. A Madras weekly, *Swatantra,* was for similar reasons deprived of official advertising for several years. Two Bihar papers have met with the same treatment. The situation has improved, however, thanks to the intervention of the All-India Newspaper Editors' Conference.

It is not unknown for small pro-government newspapers to get more official publicity than a fair allocation would warrant. Local authorities are responsible for pressure or discrimination of this nature rather than the central government.

In several American countries too, particularly Mexico, pressures of this kind are exerted by the provincial governments. According to informants, a certain number of publications, generally not dailies, are kept going only by the allocation of government advertising or by advertising from firms closely connected with the government. As a *quid pro quo* they have to reflect the official line, although some latitude in the matter of criticism is allowed.

IV

Trade union pressures

This form of pressure is mid-way between economic pressure and purely political pressure. It affects newspapers on the financial plane but it is of a more markedly political character than the discriminations dealt with above.

It should be stated straightaway that this form of pressure is studied here only in so far as it is used by the authorities ; in other words, only where the government controls the trade unions, or can at least influence them. Where that is the case the government can use the typographers' and newsvendors' unions to silence papers it does not like.

This situation is chiefly to be met with in Latin America. The fate of *La Prensa* of Buenos Aires provides the best-known illustration of this form of pressure. This story is too well known to be repeated here.[1] However, it is not the only case worth noting. In 1952 the editor of the *Argentino* was compelled to resign owing to pressure from a trade union. In 1953 a Rosario daily was forced to accept a manager appointed by the typographers' trade union. Early in 1955 the newsvendors' union refused to handle the Rosario *La Capital* and demanded its suppression.

In Bolivia, when the National Revolutionary Movement came to power in 1952, the trade unions became the tools of government policy. The same year they compelled the main La Paz daily, *La Razon*, to cease publication. In 1955 the trade unions demanded the expropriation of the premises of *La Razon*. They are now occupied by the Ministry of Mines.

In Brazil, although the government has no direct control over the trade unions, it has been able to put pressure of a social character on newspapers under the pretext of satisfying trade unions' claims.

---

[1] Cf. the book published by the editors of *La Prensa : Defense of Freedom,* John Day, New York, 1952.

These claims, instigated by President Vargas in 1952 and pressed by demagogic means, would have fixed typographers' and journalists' wages at such a high level that newspapers' budgets would have risen astronomically and some papers might have been compelled to suspend publication. The newspapers protested against this attempt at pressure and it has since been declared unconstitutional.

V

Discriminatory practices

In this class of pressures or restrictions on the press exerted by the public authorities can be listed various measures of an administrative nature which are either specifically directed against certain papers or give the executive a loophole for unfair practices. They almost all mark an abuse of a government's legitimate powers.

Restrictions on the right to publish

In all the countries which were occupied during the Second World War, the newspapers which continued to appear and kowtowed to the enemy regime were not allowed to reappear after the liberation, at least under their old mastheads. The press is practically united in admitting that this measure was right and morally sound. In a book published under the auspices of the Belgian Press Association the debarring of journalists guilty of unpatriotic or unworthy behavior during the war is described as " a restriction on the freedom of the press which journalists who believe in the civic worth and dignity of their profession cannot but approve." [1]

In France the problem was solved provisionally by the law of May 11, 1946 and finally by the law of August 2, 1954, which provided for the confiscation and disposal of press property. It should be noted, however, that there were cases of discrimination up till February 28, 1947 in the publishing permits granted by the Ministry of Information ; and some glaring inequalities in sentences and clearances are on record too.[2]

---

[1] J. Demarteau and L. Duwaerts : *Droits et Devoirs du Journaliste*, Brussels, 1952, p. 22.

[2] The Study takes no account of restrictions imposed by an occupying power on the right to publish, as for instance the post-war system of licensing in Germany.

In several countries restrictions on the right to publish are in force against the papers of banned political parties. In Peru, for example, against Aprista and Communist papers ; in Chile and in Greece against Communist papers (though in these two countries extreme left-wing papers manage to survive, albeit with difficulty). This ban is of course dictated by circumstances which do not affect the press alone.

In Syria, the last press law of May 11, 1954 compelled all publishers to apply for a new publishing license. This could be refused to papers which had supported " anti-constitutional " regimes.

Some much more arbitrary uses of pressure can be instanced, however. In Pakistan, in 1952, the Lahore daily *Nawa-i-Waqt* was subjected to all sorts of politico-administrative pin-pricks by the Governor of the Punjab, whose policy it had been attacking. To punish the editor, Hameed Nizami, the Governor began by withdrawing all official publicity from his paper and putting obstacles in the way of his getting his share of newsprint. Then he arbitrarily impounded the paper's printing presses and withdrew Nizami's license. The latter requested permission to use another printing press, which was ignored. As a paper loses the right to its title if it fails to appear for two months, Hameed Nizami, when this time had elapsed, again lodged his paper's title with the competent authorities. He was informed that his paper's title had been transferred a few hours earlier to another applicant. Undeterred, Nizami submitted an application for another title. Once again his request was ignored. He applied to the provincial courts but failed to get satisfaction. It took months, and the intervention of the central government, which disavowed the Governor of the Punjab, to restore the situation to normal.

This case is an extreme and striking illustration of the injustice of the license system when its application is left to the discretion of the executive authority. That a publisher should be asked to satisfy certain entirely non-political formalities, such as the regulations mentioned in Part One, is natural enough and acceptable ; but that the right to publish a paper should depend on the whim of a public servant is outrageous.

There are a hundred and one other ways of preventing a newspaper from appearing by means of indirect pressures of this kind.

General Perón's government was an expert at this game. In 1947 the Buenos Aires Socialist daily *La Vanguardia* was closed down because the vibration of its presses disturbed the neighbors and the unloading of its newsprint supplies held up the traffic. The paper was refused permission to transfer to other premises. In 1952 two radical papers in the provinces were closed down because they were printed " in unsanitary conditions."

Restrictions on distribution

When a newspaper is authorized to appear, in principle nothing should hamper its free distribution, unless it contravenes a specific aspect of the law. In practice that is not always the case. In several countries the authorities find more or less insidious ways and means of making things difficult.

Such restrictions affect foreign publications especially. It would be tedious to enumerate all the countries where they occur and the countless cases known to the I. P. I. Even the most developed democracies are guilty at times, and invoke the most disingenuous pretexts ; the allegedly obscene nature of such and such a publication, for example.

What is of concern here are the obstacles to the distribution of domestic publications, often without the backing of any regulation. Not unnaturally the authorities prefer not to come into the open, and in any case the damage is often done by local or subordinate officials acting without the knowledge of their superiors. Or a certain political climate may be the cause.

This is one of the most subtle forms of pressure and therefore very difficult to prove.

In a letter of June 6, 1955 to the Director of the I. P. I. the managing editor of the New York *Daily Worker,* a Communist organ, wrote that " large areas of the American people, teachers, public employees of all kinds, workers adjudged to be in defense industry, those in the military reserve, are debarred from reading the *Daily Worker* in particular, and other Left publications generally, on pain of loss of employment or other disability. A bill pending in Congress, urged by the federal administration, would extend this ban to workers in all industry. In effect then, the people of the U.S. are denied the right to read the *Daily Worker* without suffering martyrdom. Where the penalties are not immediate, there is always the danger of future reprisal. The files of the secret police contain information as to the readership of Left publications."

An American judicial expert, when consulted on this point, stated that this proposed law (the Defense Facilities Protection Act) had absolutely nothing to do with publications and was only concerned with access to installations vital to national defense. Nor is there anything in the existing law to prevent citizens in the categories given above from reading the Communist press. " In practice, however, there are indisputably several categories of people whose employment might be jeopardized if it were officially known that they were on the *Daily Worker* distribution list or read the paper." This form of pressure, if it can be established that it exists, is a border-line case as it results at least as much, or perhaps more, from the prevailing political climate as from deliberate and systematic intervention on the part of the public authorities. In practice a private individual would not have a brush with the authorities from the sole fact that he read the *Daily Worker*. It might constitute a contributory factor if other charges were made against him.

It is true, however, that the postal services in 1955 did seriously consider refusing to accept the *Daily Worker* for distribution. This suggestion was hotly attacked by the American press. In this connection it should be noted that the United States postal authorities have the right to prevent the distribution of a newspaper if it is obscene or seditious, pending a ruling by the legislature.

Then there is the situation in Greece, where Left-wing publications seem to run into distribution snags in the provinces. Clearly this is less the result of the application of regulations than of the fears of both distributors and buyers. The latter may run into difficulties if they are denounced as suspects.

In Iran some publications at times never reach the newsstands. They are not officially seized but spirited away. This applies usually to pamphleteering material rather than to established newspapers, though even such a sober paper as the *Kayhan* has at times not reached its readers in the provinces when it contained criticism of government policy.

The *Bangkok Post* of June 2, 1952 stated that the police in Thailand had instructed the postal authorities to examine all publications sent through the post and to hand over to the police those which might be "harmful." The police defined as harmful any publication containing articles against the government or the laws, or articles calculated to compromise Thailand's foreign relations.

In Indonesia the delivery of opposition newspapers in the provinces is sometimes impeded. The Masmuji party, for instance, complained in 1953 that its papers did not reach their readers regularly.

Even in Australia this kind of pressure is to be found, at the local level. A newspaper editor from the State of Victoria declares that from time to time members of the Melbourne City Council have threatened certain papers which were in their view overcritical. Municipal by-laws could be invoked which would hamper the sale of papers in the streets. In fact by-laws relating to obstructions to the traffic were invoked against newsvendors belonging to a certain political party, but have not been used against newsvendors of other papers.

Restrictions or pressures of the same type are frequently met with in Latin America. In 1953, for instance, dispatch by air of copies of the Bogotá daily *El Espectador* to the provinces was prohibited on some trivial pretext. This adds up to censorship pure and simple.

The same procedure was practiced under Perón in the Argentine on a large scale. In 1950 the postal services suspended the distribution of about 20 papers. In 1953 they refused to accept two provincial opposition papers. In Buenos Aires the municipality banned the public sale of certain provincial newspapers. And so on.

Access to official sources

In a certain number of countries, especially in the most developed, editorial staffs complain that the public authorities are making access to information increasingly difficult. This problem exercises the press in the United States in particular. It is certain that restrictions in this field do sometimes considerably impede free access to information. However, it is not intended to deal with this subject in itself in the present Study. Indeed, a general restriction on a certain category of news is one thing, but a similar restriction applied only to certain newspapers is something else. Here it is of concern only in so far as the existing restrictions can be said to be applied in a discriminatory way, i.e. to certain papers only.

It must be recognized that political authorities are very inclined to " punish " newspapers whose attitude they dislike by withholding information from them, or by giving it to them incomplete or late. This can be a convenient way of penalizing a paper which cannot be attacked by orthodox means, or it can be used as a way of favoring the pro-government press by enabling it to get better and quicker information on questions of internal policy. In either case it is a method to be condemned.

Sometimes this discrimination takes a fairly mild form. In Norway, for example, there is no restriction on information and the worst that happens, according to some newspaper editors, is that the Socialist government sometimes gives its own side a helping hand by letting them in first on official news. Much the same thing occurs in Finland, and probably in many other countries.

What happened in France to one daily is rather more serious. For purely political reasons, for about a year not a single reporter from *Le Parisien libéré* was allowed inside the Elysée Palace to cover presidential activities (1950-51).

More recently, in March 1955, a regrettable incident of the same kind occurred in the Netherlands. Six of the leading Dutch newspapers were asked to nominate a reporter for a tour in New Guinea organized by the government. The independent socialist daily *Het Parool* was then given to understand that its nominee was not acceptable. It is true that he was on bad personal terms with the then Governor-General of New Guinea, but this official intervention in a purely professional matter was criticized in the Netherlands. In the event the editor of *Het Parool* decided not to send a representative at all. The other journalists invited signified their disapproval of this step on the part of the government, as did the editors of other papers.

Several West German newspaper editors and journalists complain that in Bonn the opposition papers are not always treated on a par with their pro-government colleagues when it comes to availability of government sources. In 1954, a Bundestag deputy of Chancellor

Adenauer's Christian Democratic party went so far as to ask the editor of the *Bremer Nachrichten* to dismiss his correspondent in the Federal capital. This suggestion was indignantly rejected. At the municipal level similar cases of discrimination have been reported.

In February 1953 the acting Prime Minister of Australia barred correspondents of the *Sydney Daily Telegraph* from his press conferences, because it had criticized his policy. This form of blackmail is also practiced locally, especially in States with a Labor government. Public servants, even departmental heads, are forbidden to make any statements to the press. This means that journalists have to approach the minister direct. His reply to questions often contains much that is sheer party propaganda, according to an editor from Adelaide. And when a journalist fails to play ball, ministers threaten that future stories will go to the opposition. The same methods are frequent at the municipal level, particularly in the States of Victoria and Tasmania. At the federal level again, in Canberra the official services tend to fall back to an undue extent on press communiqués, a procedure which the press naturally dislikes.

In the Union of South Africa similar cases have been reported. In 1953 the Minister for Economic Affairs refused to give information on his department's plans to the correspondent of the *Cape Argus*, an opposition organ. In 1954 the *Cape Argus*' right to Parliamentary privilege was challenged. Furthermore, in Parliament the lobby correspondents of the English-language press are at a disadvantage as compared with their colleagues on Afrikaans newspapers, who receive fuller information.

The divorce between government and opposition has got so much worse lately that reporters on opposition papers hardly have any normal contacts with ministers or with the administration, said the editor of one of these papers. Worse still, there have been cases when the authorities have deliberately misled a reporter, in order to be able to give him the lie afterwards and accuse his paper of printing tendentious news. A case in point was the " news " that South Africa intended to leave the United Nations.

In Pakistan in 1953 access to public buildings in Karachi was refused to reporters of *Dawn* and the *Evening Star* by way of reprisal for their criticism of the authorities. In India, for the same reason, the correspondents of the *Times of India* were for two years (1953-55) refused the right to attend sessions of the Bombay Parliament. The measures against these three papers coincided with the withdrawal from them of official publicity (see p. 76).

Other newspapers have from time to time found their access to information similarly hampered, for instance the *Madras Mail*.

Finally, Iraq and Peru may be mentioned as two further examples of countries where news from government sources on internal policy is imparted direct to certain newspapers and withheld, or given late, to those who are not in the good books of the rulers of the day.

Other forms of discrimination

There are a certain number of other discriminatory practices which escape exact classification. They will be mentioned as they occur in reports which have reached the I. P. I., and even then the list will be far from exhaustive.

In Austria there is a peculiar situation in that two-thirds of the press owe allegiance to one or the other of the two main parties in the government coalition. The independent papers which form the minority are not always afforded the same treatment as their colleagues in, for instance, the matter of news handouts, obtaining licenses and other more minor points.

At the I. P. I. Assembly held in Copenhagen Josef Felder, present editor of *Vorwärts* of Bonn, explained how certain indirect pressures stemming from local authorities had compelled him to abandon publication of the Bavarian newspaper of which he had been the editor. This paper had taken a political line which displeased certain powerful local interests. Josef Felder felt that these influenced the owner of the plant where his paper was printed to refuse to renew his lease, in order to stifle a warning and critical voice.[1]

In Israel certain opposition journalists have the feeling of being as it were ostracized on the occasion of government functions.

In Pakistan " conformist " journalists are more likely to be asked to take part in government committees and delegations sent abroad. This is a way of " seducing " the other journalists by dangling before

[1] *I. P. I. Assembly 1955, The Proceedings*, p. 29-30.

them prospects of favors obtainable if they will only drop their critical attitude.

The same practice obtains in Burma and Turkey. In the Arab countries and in Latin America it is particularly rife. These forms of " moral " pressure, with their appeal to honor and patriotism, even to the crudest flattery, are carried to their wildest limits in the patronage traffic. This culminates in the system of *botellas* or bakshish which was discussed earlier (see p. 67).

The same kind of pressure, in a gentlemanly form, is not unknown even in very developed and very democratic countries. A newspaper editor or a journalist allows himself to be " persuaded." He is flattered to stand well with the powers that be. He likes being asked to their houses, gets a few minor advantages, perhaps eventually a decoration. All very innocent and above-board, but it is a dangerous course.

VI

Direct political pressures

In every country in the world the public authorities canvass the press, or some papers at least. This may take any form from an informal approach to a newspaper editor by a minister on a man-to-man basis, to the sending of regular directives to editorial staffs, who are expected to obey them or else. Between these two extremes there is room for a wide range of intervention : suggestions, recommendations, warnings, instructions, refusals to communicate. Sometimes the directives come from a special government information office set up for the purpose. Nothing makes the press more suspicious. The idea of a government information office is too reminiscent of the censorship and methods of press control which prevail in totalitarian States and which obtained during the war even in democratic countries.

In general these directives are concerned with questions of national security. Journalists everywhere are unanimous in objecting to the growing tendency of governments to abuse the concept of security. When the I. P. I. some time ago solicited views on freedom of access to information the editor of the *Sunday Sun* of Sydney wrote : " In the democracies some controls on information which were instituted during World War II still remain. Worse still, security practices which were no doubt necessary during the war created a state of mind among bureaucrats. These men now believe that agencies of news dissemination should rely on the handout. They discourage and avoid on-the-record interviews, and actively resent inquiry by newsmen who are seeking after the truth."

Replying to the same question the editor of the *Yedioth Chadashot* of Tel Aviv said : " In reality ' security ' means the wish of governments to sit more securely and to be able to govern without the interference of a free press." [1]

[1] *Improvement of Information*, I. P. I. Survey, Zurich 1952, p. 10.

Cases of these different types of intervention, pressure or restriction are legion.

From recommendations to orders

In the United Kingdom, notes requesting papers not to carry news endangering the national interest—the D (Defense) Notes—are sometimes sent to newspaper offices. These emanate from a commission on which the press and the ministers concerned with national defense are represented. In this particular case the authorities appeal to the civic sense of newspaper editors and there is no compulsion to comply. To the best of knowledge no British journalist has ever complained of this practice, but some feel that the abuse of the system might curtail freedom of expression.

In Switzerland journalists as a whole have long complained of the Federal Government's reluctance to give access to information and some parliamentary correspondents point out that papers are sometimes "recommended" to use certain bits of news with "prudence."

In the Netherlands in 1954, at the suggestion of the Court, a group of editors asked all journalists to submit articles and illustrations concerning the Royal Family to a form of official censorship. This request, which was motivated by the excesses of certain sensation-mongering papers, drew unfavorable reactions from some sections of the press, and particularly from foreign journalists.

In Finland, newspaper editors sometimes complain that the government tends to impose a blackout on subjects which might affect relations between Finland and the U. S. S. R. One editor writes : " These restrictions on information which the public ought to have distort the interpretation of events and are equivalent to a censorship."

In Australia, journalists for some years have been complaining increasingly of what they call " censorship by request." The worst example was the request by the Prime Minister to abstain from publishing photographs or descriptions of Vladimir Petrov, the U. S. S. R. embassy official in Canberra who in April 1954 " chose freedom." What galled Australian journalists most was that foreign correspondents were not obliged to comply with this request. An Australian newspaper editor said that in certain States the authorities have tried to influence the local press by appealing to its " loyalty."

For instance it is frowned upon to criticize a measure which would procure for one State an advantage over others, say in such a matter as federal credits. The suggestion seems to be that such a revelation shows disloyalty on the part of a paper to the interests of its own readers.

The Executive Order issued by President Truman in September 1951 which placed information from 45 government departments in classifications from " restricted " to " top secret," might also be considered as a form of censorship. The aim was, of course, to protect the security of the State, but many editors felt that this measure went too far, that the idea of security was wrongly interpreted and that it was almost equivalent to the censoring of news which the public was entitled to know. Professional organizations protested strongly against this Order. After Dwight D. Eisenhower was elected President, the Order was not revoked but it was toned down in December 1953. The category " restricted " was abolished and 28 of the 45 departments lost their right to withhold information from the press. Nevertheless, some editors consider that the situation is still not satisfactory.

The press in the United States is particularly sensitive on the question of access to official sources and the least restriction immediately gives rise to protests.[1]

However objectionable they may be, the various types of government directives mentioned above do not constitute a serious attack on the freedom of the press. But in certain free countries the insidious and systematic use of directives by the government does at times represent a very serious pressure on the press. It is interesting to note that, during the period studied, this threat was most felt in two countries ruled by out-and-out totalitarian regimes before 1945. The danger was averted by the vigilance of the democratic forces.

In 1952 the government of the Federal German Republic planned to set up a ministry to " co-ordinate " news. This was regarded in professional circles as nothing less than an attempt to control the press and the radio. These joined forces with other interests and, faced with this combined opposition, the plan came to nothing. Nevertheless, it was brought up again in the following year in the form of a " Co-

[1] Cf. Harold H. Cross : .The People's Right to Know, Columbia University Press, 1953.

ordinating Committee " for the Federal Republic's Press Service, but this move was no more successful than the first.

A similar attempt was made in Japan, also in 1952. The government decided it would set up an official information bureau. Here, too, the press saw a risk of return to the control of information media and offered stout resistance to the plan, which had to be dropped. The government next hit on the idea of enlarging the Cabinet Research Office and linking it to an information bureau, but this move had no greater success.

* * *

In other countries where there is an independent press, "regulated" information is a latent threat. This is so in the Union of South Africa, where press circles are apprehensive that the Press Commission will recommend the adoption of controls.

Elsewhere in the free world public authorities, even during periods of calm, sometimes resort to measures more appropriate to dictatorships.

In Pakistan, so the I. P. I. has been informed, side by side with the official censorship, which was imposed in exceptional circumstances, there is a kind of unofficial censorship. It consists of a recommendation to the newspapers to take a certain line and not to publish or, on the contrary, to play up certain varieties of news and editorial comment. A minister or a high official of the government meets the newspapermen, individually or in a group, and lays down before them the viewpoint and the stand of the government on a certain issue and then asks them to adopt a certain line or refrain from a certain kind of approach to that problem. This advice has no legal sanction behind it, and the newspapermen will ordinarily be free not to follow it. In practice, however, such is not usually the case and the newspapers bow to government wishes. They know that otherwise they may be in trouble with the authorities.

Much the same practice obtains in Turkey. The I. P. I. has been informed that it is not uncommon for opposition newspapers to receive phone calls from the attorney-general's office in Istanbul, advising them to keep off such and such a subject.

Compared with the above, the official censorship which has existed in Israel since 1948 as a result of the Palestinian war seems to compromise the freedom of the press far less. Israeli newspaper editors describe it as having become a matter of simple routine. Papers submit to the censor's office anything they want to publish which concerns national defense, taken in its widest sense. Editors are entitled to appeal immediately against any censorship decision to a mixed committee which was set up under an informal agreement negotiated in 1949 between the editors' committee and the armed forces. This committee is comprised of a representative of the army, a newspaper editor and a neutral president representing the public. Under new legislation, drafted in 1954 but still to be enacted, this agreement would receive the force of law, the committee being replaced by a tribunal headed by a judge.

As the censorship in Israel is generally exercised intelligently, newspaper editors rarely have occasion to appeal against its decisions. In several cases it has been admitted that the censors had erred through an excess of zeal and the ban on publication was immediately lifted.

Instructions and warnings

On the fringes of the totalitarian world the use which public authorities make of instructions and warnings to newspapers becomes one of the principal means of muzzling the press.

In Thailand, although the Constitution explicitly forbids admonitions to the press, the public authorities quite often resort to this method to bring the press to heel. In 1954, 31 warnings were issued to various papers. Those who repeated their offense were censored.

In Peru, although there is no official censorship or ruling as to what papers may or may not say, there are, according to one of the I. P. I.'s correspondents, "invisible limits" which it is as well not to overstep, particularly in the field of domestic affairs. Another correspondent states that, even though direct censorship is still illegal in theory, in practice newspaper editors are advised, by phone or personally, to abstain from political comment on such and such an event, usually something connected with the political life of Peru or of a friendly country like Argentina. In cases of non-compliance with this rule the editor responsible is summoned to appear at the Press and Propaganda Office and threatened with sanctions. The important Lima daily *La Prensa,* among other papers, has several times been a victim of this procedure. One of its editors, Eudosio Ravines, was deported because he ignored instructions by the Odria government. The same paper reported a strike in 1952, whereupon the government immediately published a *démenti* and severely censured the paper.

The situation is far worse in Colombia, which has been under martial law since 1949. Between then and now a succession of authoritarian governments has alternated between actual censorship and control of the press by the technique of issuing instructions. When they are not censored outright, newspapers receive regular warnings. They must abstain *by order* from publishing certain items and commenting on them, especially news about dissension among the Conservatives (the party in power), student demonstrations, and in general all matters relating to public order. Occasionally the ban has included information on the country's economic situation or its foreign policy (the sailing of a battalion for Korea, for example). When the control was complete the censors were very strict. Even a poem could sometimes only be published with the overstamp " read and approved." The mere mention of the literary worth of an exile or praises of freedom, even without any allusion to local circumstances, might make the censors crack down on a paper.

Much the same situation has reigned in Egypt ever since the Second World War—a combination of directives to the press and of censorship, capriciously administered, in an atmosphere of martial law. Under the Farouk regime the directives mostly concerned Court news, the Army, social demands and Anglo-Egyptian relations. Under the dictatorial regime which succeeded it, the same types of news continue to be affected, the Court being replaced by the political parties and the relations between General Naguib and Colonel Nasser. The Egyptian censorship has functioned very erratically at various times and even according to the mood of the officials in charge. In 1955 it became extremely strict. An editor who has worked under both regimes, said in reply to the present inquiry that it was often possible to outwit the censors and that indigenous editors were past masters at the game. Another journalist has pointed out that the press has the right of immediate appeal against decisions by the censors. At the present time the appeal is lodged first with the Minister of National Guidance, then with the Premier. This defense is in fact more apparent than real and the government does not hesitate to threaten with reprisals a journalist who fails to obey the directives. Thus in September 1953 the Director of the Press Control Office announced that, " should certain papers or journalists *stray from the straight path,* the Minister of National Guidance will not confine himself to censoring them but will take other more serious measures. These are, first, a *warning* to the offending paper and its *closing down* for a month ; and second, if the offense is repeated, the *withdrawal of its permit* and its *closing down* for good."

Pressures through devious channels

One type of pressure which is perhaps more sinister than the normal type of directive is pressure resulting from representations by a foreign power. Many countries treat as a crime anything which compromises good relations with foreign powers. This is understandable where abusive language is concerned, even though the normal measures against defamation should be enough. But when reasonable criticism of a foreign government's acts is objected to, then freedom of the press is jeopardized. A country's press cannot be turned into an instrument of diplomacy and any attempt to do so is unhealthy and contrary to the role the press must play.

It was seen in a previous chapter how the Indian press reacted to the interpretation of the article of the law which relates to the maintenance of good relations with foreign countries, particularly in the *Spotlight* episode. Similar cases in other countries could be quoted.

In Thailand the press was prevented from reporting adequately on the evacuation of Chinese Nationalist troops from Burma and on events in Indochina. This was because foreign powers intervened with the Bangkok government, which in its turn gave the newspapers rigid instructions.

In 1952, Peruvian Foreign Minister Gallagher sent Washington a diplomatic note couched in somewhat sharp terms on the subject of a dispute about coastal fishing rights. The Lima daily, *Ultima Hora*, carried the following headline : " Gallagher slaps Uncle Sam's face." The next day the newspaper's manager and the head of its news service were thrown into prison for compromising the good relations prevailing between Peru and the United States. After a few days in a cell in company with common criminals the two men were set free. The United States Embassy had intervened and said that in a country where freedom of the press is recognized nobody would take umbrage at such a headline.

In another case, in 1951, Leonidas Rivera, editor of the weekly paper entitled *Buen Humor*, got four months and a heavy fine for publishing, in translation, an article from *Life* magazine on Eva Perón. The government of Argentina had made representations to Lima against this article, and it was judged to compromise the good relations between the two countries.

As a matter of fact Leonidas Rivera is far from being the only victim of the activities of General Perón's ambassadors. Not only in Peru, but also in Chile and Colombia and other Latin American countries, journalists have suffered as a result of protests of the same kind. In Colombia a decree forbidding criticism of heads of friendly nations was the direct result of representations of this nature by the ambassador of the Dominican Republic.

Examples of similar situations could be multiplied. They occur particularly in small countries exposed to pressure from the great powers. Their very weakness often causes these governments to leave their press only relative freedom.

These pressures emanate especially from totalitarian states, which are adepts at intimidating their neighbors and whose enormous propaganda machines manage to corrupt democratic institutions even in surrounding countries. It is only necessary to recall the ravages caused by Nazi propaganda in Europe before the war and the attempts made by Goebbels' organization to intimidate journalists who, outside Germany, did not paint that country in the roseate hues which Berlin would have liked. A similar state of affairs is to be found now in Latin America. Dictatorships exercise a nefarious influence on the entire continent, as the preceding examples show.[1]

---

[1] See article in I. P. I. REPORT, May 1953 : " Contagion of censorship in South America."

Pressures may also work outwards from within, and governments may try to influence journalists who work both for the local press and for foreign papers or agencies. A government is anxious to have a good press, or at least to avoid having its actions criticized, and so it urges the journalist who is in this dual position to be " conformist " in what he writes for foreign consumption. It appeals to his patriotism. It butters him up, or else it waves a big stick or resorts to blackmail. These methods are to be found particularly in the " new " countries, which takes umbrage easily, and also in the Union of South Africa.

In an I. P. I. study on *The News from the Middle East* several correspondents testified to this sort of pressure. A Briton stated that when the local correspondent (who is also working for an agency or a newspaper abroad) " tries to present a reasonably objective picture, he often finds himself being bull-dozed by officialdom into producing a piece of propaganda." If the local authorities cannot stop an awkward piece of news by appealing to his patriotism they can effectively frighten him out of strict objectivity by threat of reprisal. This is true, apparently, not only of Arab countries and Iran, where restrictions are generally more onerous, but also, to some extent, of Israel. An American correspondent commented that in the latter country local men are inclined to close their eyes to things displeasing to their country. " I know of cases " he wrote " in which excessively objective Israelis have been made to feel the displeasure of the Public Information Office and of the Foreign Ministry." [1]

Obligation to publish government material

Compelling newspapers to publish official handouts or any other material inspired by the government is certainly one of the worst abuses of power. It is current practice in totalitarian countries. In Spain, for example, papers are bound to publish material issued by the government, but have to pretend that it is put out by the newspaper office itself. In the free, and even in the semi-authoritarian, countries this practice takes a less flagrant form but it is none the less reprehensible for that.

[1] *The News from the Middle East*, I. P. I. Survey, Zurich 1954, pp. 83 and 41.

At its mildest it takes the form of getting the country's press as a whole to chime in on some press campaign launched by the government on a question of national interest, or to write polite bromides on such occasions as visits by heads of foreign states. All this is merely a variant of the system of " recommendations " or " directives " mentioned earlier. The pro-government newspapers are naturally only too glad to oblige, and the independent press sometimes allows itself to be cajoled. The opposition papers, on the other hand, see an obligation thrust upon them possibly to perjure their consciences, but they can only draw back at the risk of inviting reprisals. The government's request thus automatically becomes a form of pressure.

Here are a few examples :

When Marshal Tito visited Burma in 1954 officials of the Ministry of Information insisted, it appears, that all newspapers should publish pro-Yugoslav propaganda material.

Arab governments are not averse to inviting the local press to inflame public opinion against Israel. In 1952 the Lebanese government tried to go one further. A dispute arose between the Executive and the Press Syndicate over a new press law, and the newspapers gave their objections tangible form first by going on strike and then by refusing to publish any matter from official sources. Whereupon the government, by way of reprisal, decreed that under penalty of a fine or a prison sentence newspaper editors must publish all official communiqués and all official material in general. The press reacted so strenuously that the decree had to be rescinded within a short space of time.

In 1953 the Ecuadorian government ordered the closure of the country's main daily, *El Comercio,* because it had refused to insert a communiqué criticizing the behavior of the press. Other newspapers which had also refused were more leniently treated. In the end *El Comercio* was permitted to reappear after having been suspended for 43 days, on condition that it publish as an insert in one of its issues the communiqué issued separately by the State printing press.

In Argentina this type of pressure was used several times during General Perón's period in power—in 1950, for instance—on a large scale. A decree of January 1 obliged all papers to carry under their title the legend " Year of the Liberator General San Martin." This was tantamount to a declaration of loyalty to the regime, and so any paper failing to comply from the outset was liable to suspension on the orders of the Visca commission, a body whose function was to punish anti-Argentinian activities. More than a hundred papers were suspended in the country. According to circumstances, and the influences brought to bear, the suspension lasted days, months, or even years. The important point is that a paper could not be reinstated unless the editor signed a written undertaking to abstain from publishing news or articles directed against the government.

Within the period under review this procedure was used to silence the liberal Colombian daily *El Tiempo,* generally considered the most important Spanish-language paper in the Americas since the expropriation of *La Prensa* of Buenos Aires. This occurred at the beginning of August 1955. The paper's editor had addressed a message to a Quito (Ecuador) newspaper, complaining of the censorship inflicted on the Colombian press. The police handed him the text of a correction, written at government headquarters but purporting to come from the newspaper's own offices, with instructions to publish it on the front page for 30 consecutive days. If the paper refused, it would not be allowed to appear. The editor refused to knuckle under and the paper was duly banned.

Harassment and violence

The pressures of a political nature which have been described so far, whether they stem from the law or from a regulation of some sort, compromise freedom of expression to an unfortunate extent. They can also seriously damage the interests of newspaper owners and do grave harm to their editors. But there has been no suggestion of threats to life and limb. Political pressure can, however, take far more disquieting forms and affect journalists directly and brutally. There are countries, even free countries, where a man by exercising his profession as a newsman runs the gauntlet of the public authorities' vindictiveness and actually risks his life, and that not only in times of revolution or war.

Examples can be quoted even from such a well-policed country as Brazil. They should be laid at the door of local subordinates rather than of the central government, but, however unrepresentative or exceptional they may be, such cases of this reprehensible type of pressure must still be reported and branded. In 1953 a reporter in the provinces was killed for having uncovered a scandal in the local administration. It was the head of the administration who instigated the murder. Neither he nor the actual murderer suffered in any way. In 1954 Nestor Moreira, a reporter on *A Noite* (Rio) died from a beating he received in a police station for criticizing police inquiry methods.

In April 1953 the premises of *La Nacion* and *La Hora*, two big opposition dailies in Guayaquil (Ecuador), were attacked by pro-government demonstrators and ransacked. The police arrived on the scene when it was all over. The government's defense was to allege that someone had fired on the crowd from the newspaper building. The publisher, the manager and three of the staff were arrested without further ado and the premises occupied by the police. To show their solidarity several papers suspended publication, whereupon the editor of the principal one, *El Comercio*, was jailed on a charge of organizing a token strike. He was freed within 24 hours. The five journalists arrested were first of all sentenced to five years in prison and a heavy fine for unlawful possession of firearms. In July 1953, however, the case was re-tried and the sentence quashed. A few weeks later *La Nacion* and *La Hora* were both authorized to resume publication.

Before being suspended in the circumstances outlined above, the great Bogotá liberal daily, *El Tiempo*, was the victim of several attacks. The most savage took place on September 6, 1952. That day a group of demonstrators attacked the buildings housing *El Tiempo* and another liberal daily, *El Espectador*, and set fire to them. This assault was just one episode in the battle then raging between the liberal party and the conservative government party, whose authoritarian tendencies had been sharply denounced by these two papers. In spite of official denials, there is evidence of government complicity in the attack. For one thing the police made no attempt to stop the demonstrators. A photograph taken during the disturbance showed policemen standing with arms folded at each end of the street while the populace stormed the *El Tiempo* building. The I. A. P. A. branded this event as " an abominable and obviously premeditated crime." Colombian journalists have been the victims of violence at other times too. Sheriffs, particularly in the provinces, act in a very arbitrary manner and editors are often imprisoned without legal cause.

It has already been mentioned that in Bolivia the most important paper in La Paz, *La Razon,* owned by the tin magnate C.V. Aramayo, was forced to close down through trade union pressure. When in 1952 demonstrators attacked the building the government refused to send the police to protect it. The following year the daily *Los Tiempos* of Cochabamba was also attacked by demonstrators, led by government officials. The paper's offices and printing works were completely gutted and its editor, Demetris Canelas was arrested on the pretext that he had fomented a plot to overthrow President Paz Estenssoro's regime. This accusation was shown to be pure fabrication and after a certain time Canelas was set free, but to this day he has received no compensation for the losses sustained by his paper. Since President Estenssoro assumed power it is quite normal for Bolivian newspaper publishers and editors to be arrested without rhyme or reason or threatened with reprisals if they do not stop criticizing the government.

In Peru, Francisco Igartua, editor of a magazine and of the daily *La Libertad,* now suspended, was arrested and put in solitary confinement for a week in 1952 because of an editorial which displeased the government. He then had to live in exile for some time. In the same year *Jornada,* published by the writer Mayos Osorio, was suppressed as a result of publishing a series of articles unfavorable to the Odria government.

This kind of pressure has naturally occurred most often in Argentina. When the Perón government made up its mind to give the death blow to Gainza Paz's *La Prensa,* there was bloodshed, it will be remembered. On February 27, 1952 when the paper's staff and employees arrived at work they ran into a sharp volley from peronista union strike pickets. One typographer was killed and 14 wounded. The remainder managed to get into the building and set the presses going. At that point the police, who had been noticeable for their absence hitherto, intervened—to close down the paper and to take its entire personnel into custody. A British and an American reporter, who were on the spot and witnessed the whole scene, were arrested with the rest and kept in prison for 36 hours.

In 1950 the radical daily *El Intransigente*, published in Salta, was suspended by the Visca Commission for criticizing the authorities. It was next expropriated and handed over to the Salta prison. Its editor, David Miguel Torino, was for some reason not arrested until May 28, 1951, but when he was no charge was brought against him and there was no trial. Over a year later, on October 23, 1952, he was accused of *desacato* (disrespect) and also of two other offenses in connection with a so-called misappropriation of a legacy. No member of his family took part in the trial. On March 31, 1954 a court of appeal acquitted D. M. Torino on the two counts of testamentary fraud, but upheld the *desacato* charge. He was set free, however, having in effect already served his sentence. The two judges responsible for this verdict were immediately discharged, arrested and accused of abusing their functions.

In 1953 the editor of *La Ley* of Mercedes was arrested and his paper suppressed for publishing the text of a motion tabled by some radical deputies in Parliament on the subject of police strong-arm methods. Two other provincial newspapers got into hot water with the authorities for the same reason. In 1954 a journalist was arrested for writing that there was an electricity shortage in the town of Lincoln, and another, from Junin, for complaining in an article that meat was too expensive.

Asian examples

This kind of persecution and violence is not peculiar to Latin America. Examples can equally well be quoted from Asia.

In Indonesia professional circles complain of arbitrary arrests carried out under obsolete colonial laws which do not require proof that persons arrested are guilty of an offense. In the analysis of penal laws in Part One mention has already been made of two newspaper editors in Borneo who were arrested in this way, one of them being imprisoned with common criminals, because of articles regarded as offensive by the local authorities.

It is the Dutch papers and journalists, however, who in Indonesia suffer most from the authorities' arbitrary use of their powers. On several occasions Dutch newspaper offices have been attacked and the local police have by no means always taken the necessary steps to protect the papers and their personnel. In November 1952 the editorial staff of the *Malang Post* (Eastern Java) was attacked by a mob of students who were incensed at having their behavior at a football match criticized in the paper's correspondence columns. They caused so much damage that the paper was unable to appear for months. At Jogjakarta the daily *Nasional* was also attacked, and the authorities apparently did not lift a finger.

In February 1954 the Indonesian authorities ordered the arrest and expulsion of E. Evenhuis, editor of the Surabaya daily *Vrije Pers* and correspondent of the Amsterdam *Algemeen Handelsblad*. He had written a report of an attack on a Dutch business concern which was deemed liable to stir up trouble among the population. In it he said that the Surabaya government was carrying out a policy hostile to the Dutch element which was living in a state of permanent anxiety. He was also accused of endangering public order by his attitude and his writings as a whole, which were described as tendentious and offensive to the Indonesian people. While the events culminating in E. Evenhuis' expulsion were in train, demonstrators attacked the paper's offices. The police did not intervene. The Indonesian Committee of the I. P. I., when it was apprised of the treatment meted out to this Dutch journalist, formally denounced the government's actions as contrary to the freedom of the press.

During the first few years after Burma achieved its independence the government was very sensitive to criticism and sometimes treated the press very high-handedly. It has already been seen that it misused the Public Order Preservation Act by having journalists arrested on trivial pretexts. These arrests, about ten all told, were of a palpably arbitrary nature. In addition, men in government pay ransacked the printing works of opposition papers on no fewer than three occasions. In one case the paper had accused the Minister of Agriculture of "moral depravity." The editor refused to retract his words, and hired thugs came and destroyed the paper's printing presses and offices. The press unanimously demanded an inquiry, which established the government's guilt. The Prime Minister, U Nu, indemnified the three papers whose premises had been wrecked and adopted a more conciliatory and tolerant policy towards the press.

In Iran, in December 1951, about 40 journalists took refuge in Parliament and sent the U. N. Commission on Human Rights a memorandum affirming that their safety was in danger. In 1952 the premises of the main Teheran daily, *Ettelaat,* were ransacked by Mossadegh supporters. The police failed to cope with the situation. In 1953, under the new regime, another prominent Teheran paper, *Kayhan,* wrote that the press was being persecuted by the police. There are relatively frequent suspensions of papers and arrests of journalists based on martial law. One article of this law stipulates that newspaper editors can be summoned to appear before a military tribunal when they publish matter calculated to rouse the public against the authorities.

In Egypt, both under the monarchy and under the revolutionary regime, suspensions of newspapers and arrests of journalists with no legal justification have been relatively frequent. In 1951 the Press Guild protested against the arbitrary detention of two of its members. In 1953 two of the staff of *Misr el-Fatat* were arrested for " dangerous thinking." Their writings were regarded as being " contrary to the social order." Even reporters of the great daily *Al Ahram* got into trouble over their reports on the Anglo-Egyptian negotiations. Under the dictatorship a number of journalists found it impossible to carry on their profession and some, fearing for their lives, preferred exile.

VII

Indirect political pressures

Public authorities exert pressure on the press not only by the direct methods which have been discussed so far, i.e. laws dangerous to freedom, arbitrary or discriminatory application of laws or regulations, directives, or even violence. There is also a form of pressure, more subtle and no less dangerous, which results from a certain political climate. Though legal obstacles or economic and administrative pressures may not exist in their countries, publishers and editors, especially of independent and opposition papers, are hampered in saying what they think by the general political background against which they work.

This kind of indirect pressure is sometimes combined with direct pressures, and not only in the semi-authoritarian countries. The harshness of recent Turkish press legislation, the way it is applied, and the other forms of intimidation to which Turkish journalists are subjected are a consequence of both the extremist threat hanging over the country and the gradual worsening in the relationship between the party in power and the opposition.

During the troubles fomented in various parts of Pakistan by religious sects, and when the discussions on the future constitution took a violent turn, the Pakistan authorities tended to abuse their powers. Even if they did not always impose a censorship or take emergency measures, the conditions in which independent journalists had to work deteriorated rapidly. The whole apparatus of security laws, always a potential threat, weighed on them more heavily and partly paralyzed them.

For an explanation of the laws, regulations and other measures which encroach on the freedom of the press in the Union of South Africa the political climate prevailing in that country must be considered. The conflict between the Nationalist government, which wants total racial segregation, and the opposition automatically has repercussions on the press. What makes matters worse is that, roughly speaking, all the Afrikaner papers support the government while the entire English language press is on the side of the opposition. As nearly all the correspondents of foreign papers are English speaking it follows that reports abroad on South African affairs are fairly one-sided. As the Nationalist government is hyper-sensitive to criticism by the press, particularly the foreign press, there is now an almost complete rift between the authorities and journalists of the English-language papers. Quite apart from the laws and regulations mentioned in previous chapters, these journalists feel themselves exposed to the ill-will of the government, which in turn accuses them of maliciously distorting the facts and running down the country in the eyes of foreigners. Ministers have no scruples about holding out the threat of sanctions.

The methods used by the commission of inquiry on the press constitute one of the most unpleasant forms of this intimidation. This press commission was set up in 1950 and has, at the time of writing, not published its report. The very fact that after all this time it still has not published its findings can be regarded as a form of pressure, because the uncertainty in which journalists find themselves easily turns into fear. Though there is no report, alarming rumors have filtered through about the commission's methods of investigation. Journalists are cross-questioned behind closed doors and dossiers assembled on their careers and activities. Every press cable sent abroad is seized. Some 35,000 cuttings from foreign newspapers have been classified by the commission, a list drawn up of " distortions," and the authors of them traced. Commenting on this body's activities the correspondent in Johannesburg of the London *Daily Express* stated in June 1955 that English-language journalists were in the grip of a " sinister 20th Century inquisition " and the only outcome could be " a creeping stranglehold over news reporting so that criticism of Nationalist policy is impossible."

There is no need of harsh regulations or arbitrary treatment for a newspaper editor to feel frustrated, or for him simply to feel that he is having to work in an antagonistic atmosphere. India may be taken as an example. In that country newspapers constantly mention the relationship between press and public authorities as a problem. This insistence reflects an uneasiness which has political origins.

The genesis of the problem was explained in an article which appeared in the *Hindustan Times* of November 15, 1953. After recalling that during the period of struggle for independence the Indian press was solidly behind the Congress party and vigorously attacked British domination, the author went on :

" With the coming of freedom, there was a complete transformation ; the barrier between the government and the governed disappeared ; and the press renounced its age-long role of critic and became instead the advocate and protagonist of Authority. This transformation has not been without its dangers. During the struggle for freedom, the leaders of the nation had found in the press a powerful ally. Not unnaturally, when they took over the reins of government, they looked for a continuance of that alliance.

" The desire was not articulate ; it was not as if the government openly demanded that the press should fall into line with the government policies now that government and people were one. On the contrary, there was an almost exaggerated notion of the importance of the press, a feeling that the press as a vehicle of popular opinion was closer to the government, as an instrument of the popular will, than ever before.

" Curiously, it is precisely this increased (even exaggerated) awareness of the role of the press that holds a threat to the freedom of the press."

Conscious of their role as watch-dogs and spokesmen for the various currents of opinion, the newspapers were not slow to show that they had no intention of merely bolstering up the authorities. The more critical the press becomes, however, the less willing the authorities seem to be to concede it the right to be critical. They appear to find difficulty in understanding that the press which was so united behind the Congress Party during the struggle for independence is not so willing to follow the official line eight years after independence has been achieved. The authorities, especially in the provinces, either make no secret of their contempt for the press or else go on urging it to conform. It follows that the press must always be on its guard against encroachments on its freedom. It is a question of adjustment which time will no doubt solve, but it remains true that the transition period is difficult for some newspaper editors.

It must be said, however, that no Indian editor has painted this picture in particularly sombre lines when replying to the present inquiry ; not even Frank E. Moraes, editor of the *Times of India,* which has been the main victim for years now of a two-fold piece of unfair discrimination. They were all satisfied that the present situation was not unacceptable. Recognizing that many Indian newspapers naturally tend to support the government, A. D. Mani, editor of the Nagpur *Hitavada*, went so far as to write, in 1952, in *Far Eastern Survey :*

" It is perhaps true that some Indian newspapers are generally amenable to suggestions from ministers, not in order to support the ministers, but in the broad interests of the country. Doctrinaire believers in freedom of the press would no doubt resent such suggestions from ministers on editorial policy. But when it is remembered that the Indian democracy was almost engulfed by communal fanaticism in 1947 and by external troubles like the war in Kashmir and the intransigence of the Nizam of Hyderabad, one can sympathize with the majority of the Indian newspapers in their desire not to embarrass the government. This does not mean, however, that the Indian press has been adopting a subservient line. On occasions it has been extremely critical of the government, and it has been responsible for exposing a number of scandals in internal administration."

In Peru the situation is certainly much graver. Although there is no suggestion of a state of emergency or of civil war, as for instance in Argentina or Colombia, the press is hardly better off in Peru than in those countries. Since 1948 the country has been under a semi-authoritarian regime led by General Manuel A. Odria. The Peruvian press does not apparently labor under any serious restrictions. As has been seen, the security law, the chief threat to the freedom of the press, is rarely invoked, and in principle censorship is illegal. But by all sorts of indirect means—unfair distribution of paper and of news on domestic affairs, instructions, arbitrary arrests of journalists, suppression of papers etc.—the government has succeeded in muzzling the press just as surely as if it had used legal methods. The papers which have survived have had to fall into line. Their editors respect certain taboos. They know that if they publish anything unfavorable to the government, or even to certain foreign governments such as Argentina, they are in for trouble. They end up by submitting themselves to a kind of unwritten censorship and the more independent among them are working in an atmosphere which they are bound to find stifling.

Effects of the Cold War

In Greece too there is a peculiar situation. Although the Communist revolt ended as far back as 1949 its aftermath still lies heavily on the political life of the country. The Communist party is still outlawed and its press is therefore banned. Leftist papers and journalists are the object of constant surveillance. As has been seen, opposition papers do not enjoy complete equality before the law, particularly in the financial sphere. On the other hand every newspaperman must in principle hold a " certificate of loyalty " from police headquarters. This requirement could be a source of pressure. However, what might seem outrageous about this situation is considerably mitigated by the local circumstances, which lend themselves to special arrangements. This goes far to explain how it comes about that some journalists who were with Communist papers are now on the staff of right wing journals and enjoy almost complete independence.

In Italy newspaper work is by no means uninfluenced by the very polarized political situation. In its struggle with the strongest Communist party in Western Europe the government has been forced to adopt measures which could threaten the press as a whole. It has been mentioned previously what use the Italian government makes of its powers under the penal laws on the repression of *vilipendio* and of the procedure which sanctions bringing before a military court any person liable to be called to the colors. The Italian National Press Federation and other organizations such as the Association for Cultural Freedom constantly remind the authorities of the dangers democracy will run if they abuse these powers, which in any case are incompatible with the Constitution.

It is certain that in Finland the press does not suffer from any abnormal restrictions based on the law or on arbitrary measures taken by the authorities. However, newspaper editors do not feel entirely at ease, owing to the country's political situation. Their civic sense enjoins upon them reasonable tact towards the U. S. S. R., and the government would not hesitate to remind them of their duty should they forget it. In fact, the Finnish press can say a great deal, provided it obeys the forms. But the result is often a distortion of the news or comment. Some information never sees the light of day and some editorials are excessively watered down. Many newspaper editors feel restricted by these circumstances.

Even in the United States it may be wondered whether the Cold War climate has not affected freedom of expression to a certain extent. The Congressional investigating committees, especially the Permanent Investigations Subcommittee of the Senate Government Operations Committee as presided over by Senator McCarthy, bred an atmosphere of suspicion towards political non-conformists. During a certain period of tension, which reached its climax in 1953, some journalists may have become fearful, and in consequence have expressed themselves with unusual restraint. Some journalists stated that at that time there did exist a subtle form of intimidation arising out of the methods of these Congressional investigations. The question came up in 1953 in clear-cut terms in the case of James A. Wechsler, editor of the *New York Post*, who was summoned to appear before the McCarthy committee. He subsequently complained that his examination was due to his criticisms of the Committee and maintained that this constituted an attempt to intimidate American newspaper editors. The question was referred to the American Society of Newspaper Editors (A. S. N. E.), but this body did not adopt a definite position. A minority report of the ad hoc committee set up to consider the case nevertheless affirmed that the Senate Subcommittee's methods constituted a threat to the freedom of the press. In this report it was argued that the freedom of the press is diminished when " a single newspaper, however worthy or unworthy, is subjected by one Senator, however worthy or unworthy, to inconvenience, expense, humiliation, ridicule, abuse, condemnation and reproach, under the auspices of governmental power."

For the purposes of the present Study the I. P. I. sought the views of ten eminent American newspaper editors and journalists in late 1954 and early 1955.

Some of the newspapermen consulted categorically denied the existence of any unease in the American press resulting from the

This front page appeared in *El Tiempo* of Bogotá the day
after a mob attacked the newspaper plant on
September 6, 1952 (p. 102).

Djakarta : the demonstration for the release of the journalist Asa Bafagih (p. 116).

government's attitude in the Cold War. The editor of a leading Washington publication affirmed that there was no pressure or braking influence of any sort, and even seemed to suspect the inquirer of being ill-informed or ill-intentioned. An editor from North Carolina also saw little to fear. He did not regard the attacks of a Congressional committee against certain newspapers as improper pressure, however ridiculous the charges may have been. Attacking the press is just as proper and just as essential as the press attacking anybody else.

However, some of the other replies were less categorical. The Washington correspondent of a New York paper who felt that the Cold War situation did affect the way editors presented news and comment said, in substance : Although the McCarthy influence is waning, there is a " hangover " from it which restrains editors from saying certain things which might leave them vulnerable to charges of being " soft on Communism." This newspaperman felt that the general atmosphere of conformity definitely had an adverse effect on the flow of news. The general atmosphere in which a government operates is more important than any specific regulations that may be passed from time to time.

Another journalist, who also regards the Cold War as a cramping factor, wrote that Congressional investigations as they had been recently conducted did constitute a pressure on the press to some degree, but that the whole subject was very complex. In his opinion, Senator McCarthy's crude attempt to blackmail the press into submission failed, but it could be demonstrated that the kind of investigations conducted by the Senate Internal Security Subcommittee had a restrictive influence on the press.

Finally, an editor of a Washington newspaper saw a subtle form of intimidation in the way Senator McCarthy has succeeded in making unpopular the use of the Fifth Amendment of the Constitution. " In the temper of the times it is usually necessary to establish one's own anti-Communism before criticizing abuses in the name of anti-Communism."

He went on : " Certainly the Cold War situation does affect the way editors present the news and comment on the news. We are all conscious of the effect of what we say, and this tempers very considerably the way we say it. A number of Congressional committee investigations, including those by McCarthy as well as that recently conducted by the Reece Committee, in my judgment have been intended to constitute pressure on the press. Fortunately, I can see more and more evidence that the press is speaking up and refusing to be intimidated. But so long as we are in the Cold War and the consciousness of security remains as great as it is, it seems to me that there will be a considerable degree of restriction on press freedom. Some of this restriction undoubtedly is necessary, but it seems to me that the prime duty of the press is continually to question it."

CONCLUSIONS

Having read this study, the reader might be tempted to conclude that government pressures on the press are tending to increase in countries which have remained free. It is true that censorship is contagious. The control to which newspapers in authoritarian States are subject has an unfortunate influence even in neighboring democracies. This was seen in Europe before the war ; it is a fact today in Latin America. There is, however, no need to be too pessimistic.

If the struggle for freedom of the press has perhaps sharpened in the free world, this is also due to the fact that the number of free countries has increased. Before the war some of these countries had colonial status, or lived under a dictatorship ; they have since gained their independence and are attempting to make democracy work. This is a development which does not take place overnight. Unfortunately it must be noted that in these new countries the rulers too frequently do not respect the freedom of the individual. They have thought primarily of national freedom. Once this has been acquired, and they themselves have reached the top, they tend to abuse their power.

What is more serious is the emergence of new forms of government pressures in countrie which are democratic by tradition and which have a long history of freedom and of parliamentary life. Such is the case in the Union of South Africa and to a lesser degree even in Australia and France. These pressures are all the more disastrous because of their insidious nature. They are often the result of an atmosphere of tension, the consequence of an unhealthy political climate which affects a journalist mainly intellectually ; his freedom of expression may suffer just as much as when the pressures are of a more direct kind.

The free press therefore has a long fight before it. It has taken some crushing blows. The expropriation of *La Prensa* in Buenos Aires and the muzzling of the entire press of Argentina under Perón, the banning of *El Tiempo* in Bogotá in 1955, the imprisonment of some 20 Turkish journalists by virtue of some highly dubious legislation adopted in 1954, the arbitrary arrest or the detention on suspicion of journalists in Germany, France, the Netherlands, Brazil, Chile, Indonesia, Pakistan and elsewhere ; the continuance of Nazi and Fascist measures in the press laws of Western Germany and Italy, and also the adoption of laws of authoritarian tinge in certain countries, the abuse of the campaign against " corruptive " writings in Australia especially, and lastly the deliberate use of intimidation in South Africa and elsewhere—these are the heaviest blows dealt to the freedom of the press during the post-war period.

But the free press can also boast of some resounding victories. Its vigilance, together with that of a section of public opinion, enlightened by it, led to the crushing in the Federal German Republic, Italy, Japan, Brazil and elsewhere of a resurgence of some forms of authoritarian control. The demonstration organized in Djakarta on behalf of the journalist Asa Bafagih not only led to his release but also obliged the government to recognize the journalist's right to professional secrecy. It should be stressed that these victories were won thanks to the combined efforts of the local press, public opinion and to a greater or lesser extent, the foreign press. The solidarity of the press at the international level has developed considerably in the course of the last few years. The protests voiced by the most influential papers against violations of the freedom of the press in any country sometimes carry more weight with the governments concerned than the protests of their own national press. It is a safe assumption that editorials appearing in the foreign press were a sizable factor in the Federal German government's decision to drop its project of a news " co-ordination " bureau, in the Pakistan government's decision to drop the proceedings against Z. A. Suleri, and in the Turkish government's reprieve of H. C. Yalçin.

When the great international press organizations rise up and voice the solidarity of the profession against any attack on the fundamental principle which is presumed to govern all its members, that too carries weight. In the first five years of its existence the International Press Institute has seen evidence of the truth of this more than once. It has worked for a development of the spirit of solidarity between newspapers and it has gauged the effect that protests can have against measures which destroy freedom. The measures may not always be repealed, but evidence of solidarity puts fresh heart into those who are battling on the spot, strengthens the will to resist in those who are exposed to the same dangers, and increases the vigilance of opinion everywhere.

Nothing can be more important for the safeguarding of democratic freedoms, and the freedom of the press in particular, than a watchful public opinion. Silence or indifference is the greatest danger. This has been seen in the Union of South Africa, where the ostracizing of the English-language press by government circles produced hardly any reaction from the general public.

It is therefore of capital importance to keep public opinion in the free countries constantly on the alert, and at the same time to strengthen the bonds of solidarity within the profession.

* * *

What are the main tendencies towards control of the press to be met with at the present time ?

The most widespread is that which derives from the needs of national security. Governments make exaggerated use of this argument. The tendency to do so is an aftermath of the Second World War and has been increased by the Cold War. In a number of countries, laws relating to national security in fact represent the most present danger to the freedom of the press. This is so in Italy, the Union of South Africa, most of the Latin American countries and also in Asia. In Japan the press has waged a long and fierce battle on this point. In Pakistan, Burma and Indonesia emergency laws on security weigh on journalists like a perpetual threat. This is also the case in all the Middle East, even in Israel, where, owing to the Palestine war, censorship sometimes trespasses outside the military matters with which it should be solely concerned.

Parallel with this tendency is another, the regrettable proliferation of laws and measures directed against papers deemed to be attacking the " national interest " or " national prestige." This is to be found particularly in the " new " countries, where national pride is sensitive ; especially in new Turkish legislation on the press, in new laws in several countries of the Middle East, Southeast Asia and Latin America. Particularly deplorable examples were the laws of the Perón regime, and a Cuban law which fortunately did not last long. The concept of national interest or prestige is far too imprecise and it easily becomes a pretext for muzzling papers which are too out-spoken.

Nevertheless, the expression of anti-government opinions is regarded by certain governments as an unpatriotic attitude. And when legal methods fail to reduce a non-conformist paper to silence, public authorities sometimes resort to violence. Their thugs destroy news-paper offices and printing presses ; this happened in Argentina, Bolivia, Colombia, Ecuador, Burma, Indonesia and Iran during the period under review. Or else journalists guilty of " anti-national " activities are arbitrarily arrested and the newspapers expropriated after a parody of justice. This has occurred particularly in Argentina and Bolivia.

There is also a tendency, which is becoming more widespread, to shield public personalities from overly brisk criticism by the press. It is only right that these people should be protected against calumny and libel, but criticism, even harsh criticism, should not be obstructed. Unfortunately, a number of laws, especially among the most recent, are so severe that they intimidate journalists. This is particularly the case in Turkey, since 1954, and in several Asian countries. In several Latin American States *desacato*, i.e. attacks on the authorities' reputation or prestige, constitutes an offense, and freedom of criticism is compromised. In Italy the similar offense of *vilipendio*, i.e. vilifica-tion, is exploited for political ends. Legislation in several countries, e.g. in France, fails to recognize inadvertent defamation, and this too has a cramping effect on journalists, who are driven to excessive caution.

It would be wrong to think that pressures on the press are con-fined to the law and its application. The present Study has shown that governments make use of a host of other means. They are so numerous and so varied that they have taken up as much space here as pressures based on the law ; nor is the list exhaustive by any means.

In the countries where democracy is still in its infancy, or else in temporary suspense, the rulers are experts at ringing the changes between both legal and extra-legal pressures. In the more developed countries, where opinion is usually quick to react to the adoption of laws dangerous to freedom, and also to the abuse of existing laws, the main pressures on the press (fortunately exceptional) tend to belong to the extra-legal category. Under this head come administrative orders which hamper the distribution of papers on fallacious or flimsy grounds, the activities of inquiry commissions which create an oppressive atmosphere for journalists, the vexations of all sorts to which they are subjected in such matters as access to information, and finally the " recommendations " and " advice " lavished on them from above. Public authorities, avoiding a frontal attack, sometimes also try to bring a paper to heel by other means : the " old boy " technique, the offer of material advantage and various forms of the art of seduction, often more difficult to resist.

It cannot be stressed too often that infringements on the freedom of the press, whatever form they may take, and also lapses from high professional standards are more serious when they are committed in a country where the tradition of freedom and democracy is firmly rooted.

* * *

What emerges from the present Study in the last analysis is that the cases of pressure enumerated are usually the outcome less of the application of a principle fundamentally hostile to the freedom of the press than of an abuse of power on the part of the public authorities. Instead of maintaining an impartial attitude towards the press, as towards any other element of the social body, governments discriminate against the press in the political, economic and administrative spheres. Instead of relying on the common law in their dealings with journalists, governments impose special laws upon them which generally are defective through looseness of definition of the offenses or provide for over-severe punishments. A further hazard is that they too often authorize arrest on suspicion and proceedings *in camera*, even when they do not go to the lengths of removing the accused from ordinary jurisdiction.

The safeguarding of the freedom of the press thus depends on two conditions of primary importance :

> All papers in a country should receive equal treatment, not only vis-à-vis the law but also in political, economic and administrative matters.

> Journalists should come under the same laws as other citizens in principle, and they should enjoy the same legal safeguards.

It should be added that the laws must be good laws. They must not for instance be based on notions such as " prejudice which might be caused," nor must they allow guilt to be established on presumptions. And if there is reason to depart from the letter of the law at any time it should be in favor of the journalist, in recognition of his right to err through imprudence and also to refuse to divulge his sources when it is legitimate to do so, i.e. taking into account the conditions in which a journalist works in mid-20th century and the role which the press has to play in the present-day world.

It is also certain that freedom of the press must be exercised within certain limitations, but, as Salvador Lopez wrote in his report to the United Nations in 1953, only those limitations, clearly defined in the law and applied in conformity with the law, which are necessary to preserve the rights and good name of others, to safeguard national security, to prevent disorder or crime, or to protect public health or morals.

When the problem of freedom of information—how it should be protected and how far limited—came before the United Nations, no solution was reached. As the United Nations is an inter-governmental institution no positive result could very well be expected. It is for the press itself to fashion its own future. It alone can apply the brake to pressures it is subjected to on the part of public authorities, on the one hand by establishing its true status and demanding from its members a high sense of responsibility, and on the other by jealously defending its independence.

In the last resort the best safeguard of the freedom of the press will be the solidarity of the free papers of the world.

It should be emphasized that this freedom is the corner stone of all freedom. It is the private individual's best guarantee against the whim or injustice of the all-powerful State. That is why in defending its freedom, the press is assuredly defending not only its own interest but also the public interest.

INDEX

IPI SURVEY No. 5

THE PRESS
IN
AUTHORITARIAN COUNTRIES

Published by
The International Press Institute
Zurich, 1959

PREVIOUS IPI SURVEYS

The English version of this Study
is a translation from the French original

Printed for the International Press Institute
by Imprimerie Ganguin & Laubscher S. A., Montreux

CONTENTS

INTRODUCTION

The aim of this survey is to give an account of the position of the press under all the authoritarian regimes existing since the Second World War. No enterprise of this kind has previously been attempted. It appears all the more opportune to fill this gap because the publication of the present volume coincides approximately with the fortieth anniversary of the Soviet regime in the U. S. S. R., the thirtieth anniversary of the Salazar regime in Portugal, the twentieth anniversary of Franco's rule in Spain, and the tenth year of the People's Democracies of Eastern Europe. Moreover this study was being prepared just at the moment when the movement towards "liberalization" made its appearance, not only in the Soviet sphere following the death of Stalin, but also in the dictatorships of the Iberian peninsula.

The survey is divided into two separate sections, one of which analyzes the position of the press in countries whose governments are inspired by Marxist-Leninist ideology, and the second which deals with the press under other authoritarian governments. More particularly the survey examines two principal phenomena :

— The enslavement of the press by authoritarian governments, and especially the methods used to censor and control it, and to suppress opposition newspapers.
— the development of "liberalization" occurring at the time when this study was being prepared, its fluctuations and its consequences.

In order to avoid unnecessary repetition and duplication regarding the countries with Marxist-Leninist regimes, only one chapter, that dealing with the Soviet Union, describes the conception of the role of the press held in Communist countries, and the resulting methods employed. In the case of the other countries, the emphasis has been placed on specific and important aspects of the press which do not fall within the framework outlined in the first chapter.

The chapter on Communist China examines more particularly the utilization of newspapers to indoctrinate a nation of 600,000,000 people. The chapters on Rumania and Czechoslovakia provide two examples of the suppression of press freedom—by radical methods in the first case and by progressive means in the second. The chapter on Eastern Germany examines the fate of a press in subjection and draws a contrast between the press in the two different sectors of Berlin. The chapters on Hungary and Poland describe the experiments of "liberalization" of the press in these two countries, their tragic end in the first and their decline in the second. Finally, the chapter on Yugoslavia both reviews some unusual factors of the Tito experiment and describes the development of Belgrade's press policy as affected by the fluctuations of relationships with Moscow.

The study does not include Albania, North Korea, Outer Mongolia or North Viet Nam, Communist countries where the position of the press does not offer any peculiarities of special interest

The second part of this study deals with all the other authoritarian States of the world which existed during the period in which the study was being prepared (1956-1958). While no claim is made of giving a scientific definition of an authoritarian regime, the choice of the regimes studied for the purposes of this survey has been governed by the existence of a permanent censorship or a constant and general control of the press.

In a previous survey published in 1955 under the title of *Government Pressures on the Press,* the IPI studied the different kinds of pressure to which newspapers could be subjected by government authorities in States subscribing to the traditional conception of freedom of the press. This study was concerned with all forms of pressure, from the mildest to the most serious. Only in the most serious cases, of course, does the situation occasionally resemble that which exists permanently in the authoritarian States.

With these two studies, the IPI has now examined the situation of the press in practically all the States of the world.

* * *

The defense of the freedom of the press is the primary concern of the International Press Institute. The preamble to the Statutes of the Institute declares that it has been founded primarily with a view to "the furtherance and safeguarding of freedom of the press, by which is meant : free access to the news, free transmission of news, free publication of newspapers, free expression of views." This conception of the role of the press provides a constant background to the present study which, however, seeks to abstain from all polemics. Considerable attention has been given to explaining the authoritarian conception of the role of the press, and there are included also a number of quotations from the arguments put forward by those who promote or defend the various policies and doctrines concerning the press in the authoritarian countries.

In view of the extreme difficulty of obtaining correct and complete information about the methods of control of the press just in those countries where freedom of information is not to be found, there obviously exists a certain danger of error. Every chapter, however, has been written on the basis of several reports furnished by experienced journalists who have lived in or visited the countries in question and who are considered as specialists in their field. These documents have been further completed and verified by other experts. In other cases the text is the result of an investigation on the spot made by a special envoy of the Institute. All contributions have remained anonymous, in accordance with the usual practice with IPI surveys. To the authors of these reports who have so generously contributed to the present publication the International Press Institute wishes to express its deep gratitude.

Part One

Communist Countries

Soviet Union

On July 8, 1956, at the height of the de-Stalinization period, Moscow's *Pravda* categorically stated that no liberalization of the press according to the standards of the Western democracies was taking or could ever take place in the Soviet Union. By way of emphasizing this statement, the central organ of the Soviet Communist Party quoted some of the most relevant passages from Lenin on the subject. In a pamphlet on the press published in 1921, the father of the Bolshevik Revolution wrote : "Freedom of the press is freedom for the political organizations of the bourgeoisie and their agents the Social Democrats and the Social Revolutionaries. To give these people such a weapon as freedom of the press would mean facilitating the task of the adversary, helping the enemy. We do not wish to find ourselves committing suicide, and for this reason we shall not introduce freedom of the press." Lenin goes on to say : "In the capitalist world, freedom of the press represents the freedom to buy the newspapers and those who edit them, as well as the freedom to buy, corrupt and mould public opinion in the interests of the bourgeoisie."

Stalin made a number of similar statements on this subject. Andrei Vyshinsky, one of the Soviet Union's most eminent jurists, says in his manual on the law of the Soviet State : "In our country there is obviously no freedom of the press and freedom of speech for the enemies of Socialism and in fact there could never be. All attempts on their part to set themselves up against the State, which means against the bulk of the working class, must be considered as counter-revolutionary crimes punishable according to the sanctions outlined in the Penal Code."

What has the Penal Code to say on the subject ? The famous paragraph 58 stipulates that anti-Soviet agitation and the diffusion of anti-Soviet literature is punishable by at least six months' imprisonment and, in the case of more serious circumstances, by five to twenty-five years' internment in a labor and re-education camp. Such treatment is meted out to those whose offenses are judged likely to weaken the strength of the Soviet Union or the conquests of the proletarian revolution. In other words, any writing containing the slightest criticism implying the modification of the foundations of the Soviet regime is a criminal act and is punishable as such. This would be the case, for instance, with an article in favor of abolishing the kolkhoz, affecting the discipline of work or questioning any decision of the party which becomes a dogma.

The Constitution of the U. S. S. R. and that of each federated republic contain clauses concerning the freedom of the press. This freedom is in every case expressly limited in the interests of the Soviet regime and in favor of the regime's supporters. Paragraph 125 of the Federal Constitution of 1936 states : "In conformity with the interests of the working people, and in order to strengthen the Socialist system, the citizens of the U. S. S. R. are guaranteed by law : a) freedom of speech ; b) freedom of the press..." This formula limits freedom of the press according to the statements of Communist leaders mentioned above. The "interests of the workers" are determined by the Communist Party. This is in accordance with another provision of the Constitution in which the Communist Party is described as the vanguard and nucleus of the working class. The other limitation, by which freedom of the press must serve the "strengthening" of the Socialist regime, means in effect that the press must never be used for criticizing the Soviet State—which is the embodiment of the Socialist system—or the Communist Party, the system's basic foundation stone.

Paragraph 125 goes on to say that "these rights (to freedom of expression) are ensured by placing at the disposal of the working people and their organizations printing presses, stocks of newsprint... communication facilities and other material requisites for the exercise of these rights." According to the Soviet law of 1932 on associations, the constitutions of these depend on the approval of their statutes by the administrative authorities. The same law stipulates that printing presses can be put into service only by government authorities, corporations and mass organizations. As these are all in the hands of Communists the use of a printing press by a non-Communist group is out of the question.

In practice, Soviet newspapers are edited only by federal ministries, Supreme Councils of the federated republics, committees of the

Communist Party, the Komsomols (Communist youth organizations), trade unions and other organizations dominated by the Party. Moreover, there are also State publishing houses.

In these circumstances, it is clear that what is called freedom of the press in the U. S. S. R. is very different from the formula as conceived in the West. Freedom of the press is freedom for the newspapers of the Communist Party and for those of the organizations directed by it, including the organs of the State.

Developments of the post-Stalin era

During the years following the death of Stalin, especially from 1955 to 1957, the Soviet press became considerably transformed and in a certain sense, liberalized. Its past shortcomings were resolutely denounced by both high party officials and by some prominent journalists.

At the end of 1953, the Central Committee of the Communist Party called a conference of newspaper editors which was addressed by the First Secretary Nikita Khrushchev. His speech marked a new turning point in the regime's information policies. On December 4, 1953, *Pravda* reported him as saying : "Firmly rooted stereotypes and well-worn methods whereby everything is written according to a single pattern must be vigorously driven from the newspaper pages... Material must be more varied and more thought must be given to content and form of presentation." [1]

Since this speech, criticism of the dullness of the Soviet press has become more widespread and vigorous in the U. S. S. R. In April 1955, the authoritative Party magazine *Kommunist* published a critical survey by Mr. Strepukhov, a high official in the Central Committee's propaganda and agitation department in Moscow. In this article he stated that Soviet newspapers were dull, stereotyped, superficial and feeble from an ideological point of view. He said : "Before me lie

[1] This quotation and most of the subsequent extracts from the Soviet press reproduced in this chapter are taken from the *Current Digest of the Soviet Press,* a weekly publication of the Joint Committee on Slavic Studies at Columbia University. Its founder and editor, Dr. Leo Gruliow, is preparing a book on the Soviet press which is due to appear in 1959.

several issues of province and territory newspapers published on the same day. Above all, one is arrested by the striking similarity of the papers. Like twins, they can hardly be distinguished from one another. If it were not for the names of the papers and the names of districts, factories and collective farms which are mentioned in them, any one of the papers could be substituted for another and neither the readers nor the staff itself would notice."

On May 5, 1956, celebrated as the Day of the Press, Moscow's *Pravda* wrote : "The Central Committee's report to the Twentieth Congress has underlined the necessity of devoting particular attention to the reinforcement of the role of the press in all political and ideological work as well as in all organizational work. It is thus essential to improve seriously the operation of newspapers. Such faults as the superficial and insipid manner of describing life in our country, the clichés, the generalizations and the political jargon must be resolutely suppressed."

Nevertheless, a year later, the same paper still had to point out that "Soviet newspapers are insipid, lifeless, deadly dull and difficult to read."

The most vigorous of all criticism was published at the beginning of 1956 in *Kommunist*. Its author, E. A. Lazebnik, was the then Deputy Director of the propaganda section of the Ukranian Communist Party's Central Committee. He expressed himself as follows : "The clichés and stereotyped patterns ever recurring in the press have a dulling effect on readers and thus increase their isolation from real life... Here in the Ukraine, we have good newspapers which are in touch with their readers. But one must frankly admit that journalists (not only in the Ukraine) often deal superficially with the most important problems. The serious analyses of industrial and agricultural development have practically disappeared from our papers. In the editorial offices one finds a large number of dilettante journalists who are ready to discuss anything, even subjects of which they have only the vaguest notions. It is in fact difficult to find in Ukranian editorial offices a journalist capable of writing a leading article on economic affairs, analyzing the activity of an industrial enterprise, or of a kolkhoz.

"The editorial staffs of local papers are in the habit of passing over in silence all new problems until the papers of the capital have pronouncèd on them. There is a tendency to repetition and to restate truths that have long been known.

"If one were to conceal the names of newspapers, it would be almost impossible to tell which is the republic and which the local district paper, and where they have been edited... They are all presented in the same manner, since they all copy the capital's press...

"If a journalist shows signs of independence and tries to write an article which, through its style and form, stands out against other articles, the editor-in-chief usually disapproves of it and advises him to rewrite it according to the established pattern."

Most editors are in fact nothing more than copiers and bureaucrats. *Kommunist* also quotes the following admission by a journalist : "I know how to administer, but I do not have the slightest talent for writing." The important papers have been blamed for not having produced able columnists enjoying popular esteem and authority.

Soviet journalists have tried to do something about this state of affairs so vigorously denounced by party officials. At the beginning of 1956, the assistant editor of *Izvestia*, A. G. Baulin, outlined in *Sovetskaya Pechat*, the organ of the new Journalists' Union, certain changes that had taken place concerning the appearance of his paper. He invited his colleagues to follow suit. After having praised the way in which Western newspapers were presented, Baulin expressed the hope of seeing all Soviet newspapers change their outward appearance. "Each newspaper," he said, "must cater for the taste of its readers ; up till now, one sees too often the tendency of newspaper staffs to turn out the same copy."

In its issue of June 1956, *Sovetskaya Pechat* discussed the public's interest in its newspapers. It asked itself whether the Soviet journalist wrote for his public or for the benefit of the authorities of which his paper was the organ. Here are some of its conclusions :

"These discussions among newspapermen clearly reflect the reading public's obvious dissatisfaction with many of our newspapers... The Soviet people see that the life around them is fuller, more interesting and more complex than appears in the papers. That is why the reader is not satisfied with the papers. We journalists cannot be satisfied, either...

"Just pick up a newspaper and see for yourself ! All too often the editorial is not complete without several stereotyped paragraphs.

Editorials on the same topic are repeated year after year, season after season ; even the headlines over them are the same. Articles sometimes still consist of quotations, with or without quotation marks..." In short, the article points out, the editors are concerned with making a good impression on officialdom, losing sight of the interests of their readers.

A more lively press

Since the campaign against monotony in the press began, the presentation of Soviet newspapers has become generally more lively and their contents more varied. Regional newspapers now hardly ever publish editorials from *Pravda*, but instead, print their own original texts. In Stalin's days, all papers were obliged to publish government decrees and every sort of official announcement on the same page and in the same typography. Now, however, editorial staffs enjoy a much greater freedom of choice in the publication and presentation of decrees and announcements of lesser importance. In the past, perhaps the most grotesque example in this sphere was the publication by Soviet dailies of the list of organizations and prominent individuals who sent greetings to Joseph Stalin on his 70th birthday, December 21, 1949. In Moscow's *Pravda*, the list ran serially for 22 months... till October 1951.

Since the change referred to above, one finds quite often in the Soviet press serial stories and light or humorous articles on the more negative aspects of Soviet reality. Crime reports have become more frequent and newspapers briefly report the condemnation of thieves, murderers, speculators and "hooligans." This is still, of course, in accordance with the official information policy dictated from above and having as its object the combatting of crime, more especially juvenile delinquency. For this reason, news of this kind is chosen taking into account the psychological effect it might have on the public ; it disappears completely from newspaper columns at times when the government is seeking to create a solemn atmosphere as, for instance, during the celebrations of the first of May.

Accidents and disasters are still reported only on exceptional occasions ; stories of every day life in different parts of the Union, however, have become more numerous and less stereotyped But one still finds virtually nothing about prominent personalities, officials or even artists unless their conduct is criticized by the Party. Newspapers now also publish more letters to the editor, which are more varied in style and content ; a larger number of letters from factories and agricultural organizations are also published. The institution of rural and worker correspondents (rabselkor) which once used to play a big part in Soviet journalism but had fallen into disregard at the end of the Stalin era, is now once again assuming considerable importance.

As for foreign news, it is now more topical. It is generally published more rapidly than it used to be. In accordance with the policy of peaceful coexistence, TASS News Agency has often proved to be more objective. On April 25, 1953, the Moscow papers published the whole text of President Eisenhower's speech of April 16, in which he called for an agreement on a world-wide scale. During the summit conference of 1955 at Geneva, the speeches of President Eisenhower and other Western statesmen were reproduced in the Soviet press. Dispatches on the congress of the Socialist International at Vienna in 1957 or on the annual conference of the Labor Party included the main resolutions of these anti-Communist organizations, without any alterations.

An important factor in the transformation of the Soviet press after the death of Stalin was the foundation of a Union of Journalists which began operating in 1956. This was the first time that members of the profession were able to organize themselves in this way in the U. S. S. R. The aims of the Union provided a curious mixture of professional preoccupations and ideological anxieties. As regards the former, the statutes of the association include the study of problems of Soviet journalism with a view to developing form, style and variety ; the strengthening of links between the press and the mass of the workers ; the defense of rights of journalists within the framework of labor legislation. As for the ideological anxieties, the statutes declare that the Union aims at :

1. Encouraging the maximum participation of Soviet journalists in the mobilization of the workers in their determined struggle for the victory of Communism in the U. S. S. R.
2. Raising the ideological standards and professional ability of Soviet journalists.

3. Training journalists in a spirit of loyalty to the country and to the
Communist Party.

* * *

Certain papers or certain kinds of papers are distinguished by
a more audacious editorial policy. This is especially the case of
Sovetskaya Rossia, a new daily founded in 1956 for the Russian
Federated Republic, which became, after *Izvestia,* the second newspaper of Russia, reaching a circulation of over 1,700,000. Its policy
is to concentrate on news, keep all articles brief, to carry many photographs and to try to write simply and popularly.

These are also the characteristics of evening papers like
Vechernyaya Moskva. During the Stalin era, these only appeared in
several large towns but their number has increased since, especially
in 1957 and at the beginning of 1958. These papers do not carry much
Party propaganda and hardly any articles on agricultural problems.
Instead, they publish more news of local events, theater, films, sport,
and give more importance to serial stories and light or humorous
items. They are, moreover, quite well illustrated and also include a
large number of advertisements some of which come from private
sources. In a general way, apart from the political line, these papers
bear considerable resemblance to their Western counterparts in both
appearance and content. Contrary to the rest of the Soviet press, they
are sold chiefly in kiosks, the number of which have greatly increased
since 1957 in the large towns of the country. However, the circulation
of the evening papers remains weak. In Riga, a town of 600,000
inhabitants, it amounts to only 50,000 copies for the Latvian edition
and 30,000 for the Russian edition.

The *Literaturnaya Gazeta* and other literary papers are also
more lively than the rest of the press. Their articles are neither too
long nor too specialized. These papers are also glad to open their
columns to discussions on cultural subjects.

It is above all the youth papers, notably Moscow's *Komsomolskaya
Pravda* which have distinguished themselves most amongst the great
mass of Soviet newspapers since the death of Stalin. Their circulation,
however, does not represent more than eight per cent of the whole
press, less than four million copies. Their editorials are concise, the
ideological articles not too numerous and one finds in them more

travel accounts, short stories, news items, poems, serial stories, humorous features and drawings and a considerable amount of sporting news. The headlines are sometimes flashy. The *Komsomolskaya Pravda* was, for instance, the first paper in the U. S. S. R. to publish a report on the "abominable snowman" and the only one to give a certain importance to this subject. It has published interviews with artists and writers as well as open discussions of readers' letters about the problems of young people. In November 1957, it printed an account of the heroism of soldiers who de-mined a German munitions dump that lay buried under a new quarter of the city of Kursk and threatened to blow up part of the town. Later the paper replied to numerous letters from readers who expressed astonishment that such a situation could have arisen.

The youth papers are better illustrated than the others. While *Izvestia* publishes about two or three illustrations per issue and *Pravda* generally a few more, *Komsomolskaya Pravda* prints a dozen every day. Moreover, it chooses the most interesting pictures and other youth papers follow its example, though not always with the same skill. Thus it occurred that in February 1958, *Pravda* published an article deploring the misuse of photographs in certain parts of the press. The organ of the Central Committee denounced "the blind imitation of scandal newspapers" when photographs of persons condemned as "hooligans" were published. It also deplored the use of illustrated advertisements "in the style of the bourgeois press."

At the beginning, the innovations of *Komsomolskaya Pravda* and of other similar papers were encouraged in official circles as well as by official papers. In December 1957, *Pravda* published a laudatory article on the occasion of the 10,000th edition of the central organ of Communist youth. Among other things, it said : "It has a happy combination of lofty ideological aim in its copy and brightness in its presentation. There has been heated discussion among newspapermen in recent times about the question of newspaper individuality ; they speak justifiably of the monotony of some papers, of their resemblance to one another. There are more and more searches for new topics and new approaches to the presentation of newspaper material. *Komsomolskaya Pravda* sets many papers an example of such creative effort... The staff seeks new forms of newspaper make-up, although not everything here can be considered beyond dispute ; sometimes it is hard to find out what is more important on the page. But more and more often there appear colorful, concise headlines. The paper is better illustrated than it used to be, live reporting appears in photographs, with close-up techniques; drawings and cartoons appear more and more frequently."

However, this new style was not always the subject of unstinted praise. In 1957, the Central Committee of the Komsomol complained of the decline in the ideological level of the youth papers. It reproached them with not publishing enough propaganda articles and with tending towards bad taste in the manner of the sensational bourgeois press. *Sovetskaya Pechat,* the organ of Soviet journalists also reproached its colleagues for adopting "a sensational tone" and pointed out that such a way of editing a paper "was totally out of place in Soviet journalism." The youth paper was accused of having lost all sense of proportion in its efforts to attract attention. Was it really necessary, asked some critics, to know, for example, which football team was supported by such and such an artist ?

In 1957, *Sovetskaya Pechat* also opened a discussion on the changes to be brought about in the Soviet press. Some journalists expressed wishes going beyond what the authorities had hitherto sanctioned. Some of these demanded among other things "a reduction in the number of official speeches to be published and permission not to have to reproduce in full all Soviet diplomatic documents and reports on different conferences and meetings." In the place of these items, they suggested the appearance of short and lively articles of entertainment interest on a variety of subjects.

The detente during the period that followed the death of Stalin, encouraged Soviet journalists to pursue further those reforms sanctioned by the authorities. There were several journalists who were not content to stop half way. They wished to produce attractive newspapers in which the Party's propaganda and official announcements should be reduced to a minimum. Until now, however, these wishes have only been partially fulfilled in the youth papers and in the evening papers. Although the post-Stalin period has brought important changes in the Soviet press, it has nevertheless failed to bring about a fundamental change in its structure or any revolutionary transformation of its style.

The press as an instrument of propaganda

The primary concern of the Soviet press remains that of propaganda and agitation. In accordance with Soviet doctrine on information, the first mission of the press is not to inform but to propagate Communist ideas and popularize the measures of the Soviet government. Even news itself must be used to this purpose. Objectivity is therefore no valid criterion.

A Soviet specialist in press affairs, D. Kuzmichev, once made the following statement : "The purpose of information is not that of commercializing news, but of educating the great mass of the workers, and organizing them under the exclusive direction of the Party according to clearly defined objectives... Information is one of the instruments of the class war, not one of its reflections. As a result an objective concern with events prevents information from being used to its true purpose, namely to organize the workers."

The Director of TASS Agency, N. G. Palgunov, lecturing at the Institute of Journalism at Moscow University in 1956, resolutely denied that news could have a purely informative character. He said : "News must be organized ; otherwise it is news of mere events and happening... News should not be merely concerned with reporting such and such a fact or event : it must pursue a definite purpose... News is agitation via facts. In selecting the subject, the author of the report must above all proceed from the realization that the press should not simply report all facts and just any events... News must be didactic and instructive."

In order to attain this end, the Soviet press has recourse to various methods : a one-sided choice of news, the deliberate holding up of news, silence on certain events, and falsification of others.

The news of the capitulation of Italy in 1943 was held up for a long time. Great Britain's decision to grant independence to India was never published as news. The death of Andrei Vyshinsky in 1954 appeared in the Soviet press two days after it had made the round of the press of the rest of the world. Some important information has had to wait several years before reaching the public. In 1944, the autonomous republics of the Crimean Tartars, the Kalmouks and two smaller nationalities in the Caucasus were abolished, and their populations deported. Yet only in 1946 did *Izvestia* publish news of the event ; it was the first paper to mention it in the U. S. S. R. There are also major national events that have never been reported. At the end of 1957, for instance, the West learned through a Russian naval officer who had fled to West Berlin that, in 1955, one of the most important units of the Soviet fleet had sunk off the coast of the Crimea, and that this disaster had cost the lives of 1,500 victims.

In 1956, the whole of the Soviet press had to hold up for five days, from January 29 till February 3, President Eisenhower's reply to Prime Minister Bulganin's proposed non-aggression pact between the United States and the U. S. S. R. In 1957, the decision of the Central Committee of the Soviet Communist Party to dismiss Molotov, Kaganovitch, Malenkov and Shepilov was held up for four days, from June 29 till July 3. In October of the same year, the news of the exclusion of Marshal Zhukov was held up in the same way. Even when the Soviet radio had announced the nomination of Malenkov as Director of the hydro-electric power station of Ust-Kamenogorsk in Kazakhstan, no newspaper in the U. S. S. R. published this news on the same day.

The Soviet press has never mentioned the massive deportation of populations in the Baltic countries which took place especially in 1941 and 1949. The strikes and other incidents which occurred in the spring of 1953 in the prison camp of Vorkuta and in other centers of internment were completely ignored. After the amnesty of September 17, 1955, the press has never mentioned the number of political prisoners set free, although these included hundreds of thousands of persons. In fact, the subject has only been touched upon very generally in some literary works. In 1956 and 1957, when politicians, generals and writers executed under Stalin were being rehabilitated, the papers never explained what had actually happened to them. They simply evoked their memories in historial articles. This is, for example, what occurred in the cases of Rudzutak and Eikhe, old members of the Politburo of the Soviet Communist Party, of Marshals Tukhatshevski and Iegorov, and of the writers Kolzov and Kirshon. When silence over such "negative" facts as these is no longer possible, they are dealt with in a Communist sense, that is to say they are presented in a way that fits into current propaganda. One of the world's most glaring examples of news distortion is furnished by the treatment of the revolt of June 17, 1953 in East Berlin and other parts of East Germany. After remaining silent for five days, the press reported these events as "a Fascist putsch prepared over a long period of time by the agents of Wall Street." The strikers were described as "a horde of pillagers and Fascist incendiaries" which the Soviet army had to disperse in order to save the German People's Republic. Thus no Soviet reader is aware that German workers revolted against the Communist regime.

The Soviet press treated the Hungarian revolution of 1956 in the same way. Except for the four days during which Moscow appeared to hesitate, the Hungarian rebels were systematically described as "hostile elements, counter-revolutionaries and reactionaries" whose object was to restore the dictatorship of Admiral Horthy, the landed gentry and capitalism. According to the Soviet version, the revolution had been launched from abroad and hundreds of ex-officers of the old Horthy army had returned to Hungary equipped with foreign arms. The Soviet reader was told that Russian troops intervened on the appeals of the Hungarian working class in order to save the country from reaction.

After the revolt had been suppressed, the Soviet press went on talking for weeks on end of the "reactionary putsch" and presented the Kadar government imposed by Soviet troops as the authentic "revolutionary government of workers and peasants." The Soviet reader was completely misled over the situation in Hungary. He was kept completely ignorant of the aims of the insurgents which included the restoration of political liberties and democratic institutions, the maintenance of agricultural reforms and the nationalization of factories.

In the same period, the Sinai campaign was reported in the most tendentious manner. The capture of large stocks of Egyptian arms by the Israeli army was never mentioned, and the Egyptian defeats were covered up.

Among the important events of 1957 which were passed over in silence by the Soviet press at the time they occurred, can be mentioned the acceptance by Poland of American aid, the revolutionary discovery of two Chinese physicists living in the United States who reversed the "law of parity" for which they were awarded the Nobel prize. Other events were reported very briefly such as, for example, the abandonment of the current Five Year Plan. Finally, on many occasions between 1956 and 1958, speeches and interviews of

Khrushchev have been cut or modified before being published in the press.

The functions of the Soviet press

The treatment of news is determined by the general objectives of the press as determined by the Party. According to the Communist conception, reaffirmed every year on the occasion of the Day of the Press, May 5, the Soviet press exists only to carry out these prescribed functions. In this context, no fundamental change has taken place during the post-Stalin period. The press has always remained in the words of Lenin, "not only a collective propagandist and collective agitator but a collective organizer" in the service of Communism.

The first and most important function of the Soviet press is the Communist education of the masses. At the same time, it seeks to make more popular the internal and external policies of the Soviet government. This is the agitation and propaganda function described and illustrated above.

The second function of the press concerns economics. In this field, newspapers carry out a ceaseless campaign of agitation. They campaign daily for the rapid and anticipated realization of five-year plans and for the increase of production. They describe the working methods of "innovators" and the records of the best workers and engineers. They encourage "Socialist emulation" between different enterprises and regions in order to achieve the best results in production. The Soviet press thus performs the function of mobilizing and organizing the masses for the economic development of the Soviet Union.

Two further functions also have an organizational character : every newspaper devotes an important feature to the affairs of the Party. It aims at stimulating interest in its organizations and showing that its activities are followed in the press. Furthermore, every newspaper publishes decrees emanating from the Praesidium of the Supreme Soviet, resolutions, instructions and announcements from the Central Committee and other committees of the Party, as well as from the Soviet government, its ministries, the government of the federated republics and the governing bodies of mass organizations. The press is used to communicate all these orders and notices to lesser authorities and to the public, who are invited to put the new measures into practice.

A fifth and very important function of the press is that of supervising and criticizing. As a result of readers' letters, reports from correspondents in factories and agricultural enterprises, as well as by inquiries carried out by the editorial staff itself, the shortcomings in the work of administrative and economic organs are revealed and denounced along with other negative aspects of "socialist reality." This criticism, however, is never concerned with political matters ; the party line is never questioned [1] This function of the Soviet press is important since the press is obliged to investigate complaints from readers or reporters and to report to the complainant on the results of the investigation. This is the reason why the personnel employed on Soviet newspapers is so large compared with the staffs of Western newspapers. The number of letters from readers received by the principal newspapers is reckoned at over a million a year. Only a small fraction of them ever get printed in the paper, but they all have to be examined and dealt with. One can say in this respect that the Soviet press assumes the role of public ministry, of jury and judge and that its power therefore surpasses that of the courts. It functions to a certain extent as an extra-legal court of appeal.

Such are the principal functions of the Soviet press. From the Soviet point of view, one can understand why objectivity is not fundamental criterion of journalism, and why there is relatively little news in Soviet newspapers. Actual news consists of less than a third of the contents of newspapers, and of this third, almost half is devoted to the communications of official bodies ; the other half mainly includes foreign news. Soviet newspapers are concerned with what they would like to see take place rather than what actually does take place and they base their policies on the means of achieving the former.

In a speech on art and literature delivered in the summer of 1957, Nikita Khrushchev said : " Just as the army cannot fight without arms, so the Party cannot carry out its ideological mission without that efficient and powerful weapon, the press... We cannot put the press

---

[1] cf. below (under "Marginal freedom") details of the scope of authorized criticism.

in unreliable hands. It must be in the hands of the most faithful, most
trustworthy, most politically steadfast people devoted to our cause [1]."

Control through planning

In order to carry out its functions of agitation and propaganda,
the Soviet press has to be very strictly controlled. In the U. S. S. R.
everything is controlled : the circulation of each newspaper, its format
and size, its distribution and the section of the public to which it is
devoted. New papers appear by order of the competent authorities of
the Communist Party and suddenly cease publication in the same
circumstances.

Thus in 1939, *Krestianskaya Gazeta,* a paper published three
times a week devoted to the rural population (circulation 300,000)
ceased publication because the authorities considered that it had
accomplished its task, the campaign for collectivization having come
to an end. In April 1953, *Krasny Flot,* the organ of the naval forces
published by the Ministry of Defense, ceased publication due to an
administrative reshuffle, but reappeared again in October 1954 under
the new title of *Sovetsky Flot.* As mentioned above, a new paper was
created for the Russian Federated Republic in 1956, which soon
became one of the most important newspapers in the country.

The distribution of newspapers to the appropriate sections of
society is very closely regulated. Only ten per cent of a newspaper's
edition is sold in the streets. The rest is distributed according to a
detailed plan. Each republic and region of the country receives a
fixed quota of papers appearing in Moscow. Local distribution is
organized as follows : Party and Komsomol authorities are the first
to receive newspapers, then come the administrative and economic
units. It is rarely that a private person can subscribe to one of the
chief papers. Thus a Soviet citizen cannot simply buy or subscribe to
the paper of his choice ; he receives the paper that is specified for him
according to the plan.

[1] This ideological role of the Soviet press, and of the Communist press in
general, has been well described in two important works which have appeared in
the last few years : *Public Opinion in Soviet Russia, A Study in Mass Persuasion,* by
Alex Inkeles (Harvard University Press, 1950) and *Der sowjetische Propagandastaat,*
by Bruno Kalnins (Ed. Tiden, Stockholm, 1956).

The work of editors and journalists is also determined in advance, according to a monthly plan. The person responsible for each feature has to present every month a plan of the articles and reports to be published in the inside pages. Editors are guided by the directives of the propaganda and agitation department of the Communist Party, by themes suggested in the "manual of the agitator" which the Party publishes every ten days, and by the speeches of leaders. In this work schedule, Communist holidays and anniversaries play an important part. The monthly plans of the various feature editors are discussed and co-ordinated by an editorial committee consisting of the editor-in-chief, his assistant, the secretary and all the feature editors. The plan is then usually presented to the competent Party committee for its approval. This is a fixed rule for less important papers, but central papers, such as *Pravda* do not have to abide by it. Once the plan is approved, the feature editors go back to their departments and give the relevant outlines of chosen subjects to be written up by their staff. Thus the editorial work in a Soviet newspaper proceeds according to a fixed plan in harmony with the instructions of the Party and under its control.

The monthly plan is by no means rigid, but often undergoes revision week by week. It is usually not planned in detail until two or three days before going to press and minor changes are still possible at the make-up stage.

The choice of editorial staff is also very closely controlled. The editors are nominated or approved by the competent committees of the Communist Party. Paragraph 36 of the Party statutes adopted in 1952 stipulates among other things that "the Central Committee of the Communist Party... nominates the editorial staff of the central organs and confirms the appointment of editorial staff of Party organs in large local organizations." Other paragraphs (43, 48 and 51) lay down the same procedure for the staffs of republic, regional and local newspapers.

The procedure, from a formal point of view, is slightly different as regards the papers of ministries and mass organizations ; here the editor-in-chief chooses his sub-editors and the Party merely ratifies his choice. In practice, however, it is the Party that governs everything. The Party statutes affirm that the Party "directs the work of councils and social organizations through its militants." These are directed by the corresponding Party authority, from the Central Committee at the top to the department committee at the bottom of the hierarchy. They must be "constantly and strictly guided in all things by the leading organs of the Party" (paragraph 68). This article of the Party statutes is translated as follows in Soviet practice : The committee of a trade union, for instance, chooses the editor of its journal on the recommendation of the militants, but must have its choice confirmed by the competent committee of the Party. Thanks to this system of confirmation, the Party holds in its hand the whole of the editorial apparatus of 7,500 Soviet newspapers. Only journalists approved by the Party committees can become editors.

Most of the editors-in-chief and feature editors must be members of the Party. Moreover, the editors-in-chief of Party organs are always ex-officio members of the committee of the Party corresponding to their position, and of its Bureau. For example, the editor-in-chief of a party organ in a federated republic is ipso facto a member of the Bureau of the Committee of the Party in that republic. This has occurred since 1930, and the procedure was formally legalized by a decision of the Soviet Communist Party's Central Committee in March 1937. In this way, the Party has created very effective links between its committees and the editors-in-chief of its newspapers, which obviously greatly facilitate the task of using the press intensively as an instrument of Party policy.

This manner of selecting the editors-in-chief and other editors of newspapers has allowed the Soviet regime to resolve the problem of censorship in the most effective way possible. The knowledge that these people are completely subservient to the Party line is a guarantee in itself of the conformity of the publications which they produce. However, even if they are entirely devoted to the Party, the editors, especially those of provincial papers, do not always find it easy to follow the Party line. They are constantly being subjected to a double pressure, on the one hand from the higher authorities, and on the other hand from provincial organizations. Moreover, there is so much coming and going of personnel in the provincial press, that editors rarely have the time to get familiar with local conditions. According to an article in *Partiinaya Zhizn* appearing in 1956, a journalist's average period of employment on one local newspaper is no more than two years. In 1954, 66 per cent of the newspaper staff changed jobs and positions during one year in the autonomous republic of Daghestan (Caucasus). In the regions of Rostov and Tomsk, the corresponding figures were 30 to 40 per cent. Moreover editors are often required by the Party to carry out extra-editorial duties, for instance, in the sphere of agitation and oral propaganda. The above-mentioned journal revealed among other things the case of an editor in the Ivanovo region (Russia) who could be at his desk only ten days a month because of his multifarious other duties. After denouncing this state of affairs, the responsible authorities have made efforts to improve them and in fact the situation did improve after 1956.

In the planned work schedule of Soviet editorial offices, there is one factor which is still little-known—the role of the "instructors." Their importance, which was considerable in the years which preceded the last world war, has considerably declined. The "instructors" are neither journalists nor censors, but liaison officers between editorial staffs and enterprises, offices, kolkhozes and other organizations. Their role has been described more particularly by a former member of the staff of *Pravda* and *Izvestia* who fled to the West, Arkadi Gayev [1]. He gives as an example the campaign for the development of the collective rural economy. An instructor is charged with revealing the weaknesses in the working organization of the kolkhozes. He chooses certain kolkhozes of modest dimensions where the organization leaves much to be desired. He then organizes a meeting in one of them, and later writes up a report of it for his paper, taking the opportunity of underlining the failures and low production of some of the kolkhozes. This is the signal for a campaign on this theme in several newspapers. A few months later, when the campaign has grown to the desired extent, a government decree orders the fusion of the several small enterprises. This is the way the instructors launch a campaign to bring about a decree which is then presented as "the expression of the wishes of the kolkhoz workers."

According to Gayev, the instructors, always members of the Party, are sometimes more numerous than the editors and other journalists on the paper.

---

[1] A. Gayev : *Tsensura sovetskogo pechati* (Censorship of the Soviet Press) published by the Institute for the study of the U. S. S. R., Munich 1955.

However, in the post-Stalin period, the number and importance of instructors considerably diminished. In several newspaper offices, their existence is even unknown, while in others they simply act as filing clerks, perhaps also investigating letters of complaints from readers. Discussions on general subjects such as the proposal to sell tractor units to the collective farms in 1957 or on the educational reforms of 1958 are no longer conducted according to the procedure described by Gayev, but are now prepared by lectures of experts and speeches by leaders as well as by the publication of surveys in specialized journals. However there still exists in Soviet newspapers a personnel with no editorial or reportorial functions whose task is an organizational one, mainly to develop contacts between the newspaper and the public.

Instructions and orders

The work of Soviet editors is guided by directives from the Party. Numerous congresses, conferences and sessions of the Central Committee and other organs of the Communist Party have pronounced upon the functions of the press and criticized the newspapers. A volume of 220 pages which appeared in 1940 contains all the principal pronouncements of the Party concerning the press made until then [1]. They are mostly general directives of a political character which Soviet papers were called upon to follow. The post-war edition of 1954 contains 675 pages.

In spite of the tendency towards liberalization which characterized the beginning of the post-Stalin period, the Party continued to guide the press through its directives which were just as detailed and numerous as before. There is in fact no fundamental contradiction between the new tendency towards diversity described above and the maintenance of standards of uniformity in other spheres, namely, those which concern the Party line. The diversity in matters of content authorized and even recommended in high places, does not necessarily imply any concessions in the political and ideological sphere.

---

[1] *Rechenia partii o pechati.* There is also a book by Professor L. Fogelevitch on "General directives and legislation concerning the Press" published in Moscow in 1935.

Conversely, uniformity in this sphere does not in any way exclude variety in the appearance of newspapers and in the choice of subjects dealt with.

Instructions are constantly being issued by the Central Committee and its Praesidium. These are chiefly concerned with three spheres: the general political line of the Party, official information from home and abroad and material originating in the editorial office itself. Policy is devised in the Kremlin. Newspapers cannot give their own versions of it; they must confine themselves strictly to the directives of the Central Committee. The second sphere concerns news of conferences, meetings and discussions. Reports on these are edited by high officials of the Party and then given to TASS News Agency to be redistributed to the whole of the Soviet press. Newspapers must publish this material without the slightest alteration. The official version of a speech or interview of Khrushchev, for instance, must be reproduced in its entirety even if it spreads across several pages of the paper. The third sphere consists of articles, serial stories and correspondence dealt with by editors and their staff. It has already been pointed out that the editorial staff's monthly plan must be submitted for the approval of the competent committee of the Communist Party. However, part of the copy prepared in the editorial offices is in fact inspired by directives emanating from higher party authorities. These decide what subjects must be treated by the press at a given moment. One therefore finds identical articles appearing in different newspapers. This is particularly the case when Moscow is engaged in a propaganda campaign.

Organs of the Party also occasionally decide how copy is to be published in the press. They decide, for example, that certain news will be published first in *Pravda* and *Izvestia,* only later in other papers. In other cases, they decree that certain news must be published only in the local press.

In the summer of 1957, for instance, *Pravda* published at the bottom of its front page, in the form of a short news item, a report from the TASS Agency announcing the promulgation of a decree against speculation. The report did not specify details of the offense nor the sanctions to be applied to offenders. The following day, all newspapers reproduced exactly the same text in the same place. Several days later the daily *Sovetskaya Rossia* was the only paper to give details of the decree. In this particular case it was evident that well-defined instructions had been given to the press as to the manner of treating this news, bearing in mind the psychological effect to be produced on readers.

"AGITPROP"

The Communist Party has created special organs for controlling the press. These are the press sections of the department of agitation and propaganda of the Central Committee at Moscow as well as the corresponding sections of subordinate committees. In Moscow, there are three of these sections of the so-called AGITPROP. One of them takes care of central papers, the second is concerned with papers of the Federated Republics and other territories while the third deals with the local press. The press sections of the subordinate committees control the press within their appointed territories, and supervise that of the category immediately inferior to theirs. For example, the press section of the Central Committee of the Soviet Republic of Latvia is concerned directly with seven of the Republic's newspapers published at Riga. It examines and approves the editorial staff's work plans, issues instructions and criticizes the shortcomings of each edition of each newspaper. At the same time, this section supervises the work of 57 regional and local papers in the republic. It points out the mistakes and weaknesses which it finds and lays down the manner in which different questions are to be treated. The editors of these papers are regularly summoned to meetings in the capital in order to receive their instructions. The section of AGITPROP in a Federated Republic also controls the activities of subordinate sections but is itself directly responsible to the central department in Moscow.

The central sections of AGITPROP in Moscow exercise continual supervision on all matters. They embark on inquiries and from time to time screen particular newspapers. Sometimes the results of such screening is communicated only to the paper concerned. At other times, they are published in the Party press to serve as an example for other editorial offices. From time to time, inspectors are sent to different parts of the country. Conversely, the editors of different groups of newspapers are summoned to meet in Moscow. The central sections of AGITPROP regularly transmit directives to subordinate sections, indicating how certain questions are to be treated.

AGITPROP directives are kept secret. They contain notably a list of subjects which must not be mentioned in the press. Forbidden subjects include news of internal opposition. Generally speaking, nothing must be written about strikes, agitation in university and agricultural circles, concentration camps, the flight of Soviet citizens abroad, attempts on the lives of officials and other similar events. Exceptions to this rule are all the more remarkable. Such exceptions were very rare during the Stalin period but have become slightly more numerous since then. After Stalin's death, the press has been known to allude to forced labor camps, as well as agitation amongst the students, resistance against the authorities, especially in the Ukraine and the flight of citizens abroad—always, of course, with the object of condemning such occurrences, never with the intention of merely informing the public. These examples, however, only reflect a less rigid information policy and do not allow one to conclude that there has been any weakening of the control exercised by the agitation and propaganda sections of the party. These have maintained their full importance and continue to be the main instrument of press control in the U. S. S. R.

The role of certain publications specializing in the orientation of the press should also be mentioned. These in particular include the "manuals of the agitator" which appear in every republic and in most other territories. Editorial staffs must of course follow attentively the articles on ideological and practical questions which appear in the doctrinal reviews *Kommunist* and *Partiinaya Zhizn. Sovetskaya Pechat* is also important from this point of view. Finally, the speeches of leaders, in particular those of the first secretary of the Central Committee, serve the editorial staffs as a guide to the government's intentions, the themes that it would like them to develop, and the campaigns that are to be organized.

"GLAVLIT"

Apart from the direction and control exercised by the Party, the Soviet press is also subjected to direct legal censorship. Before appearing, the newspapers are examined by the officials of a government censorship office. Its visa is required before a newspaper goes to press. It is called GLAVLIT, the Russian abbreviation of "Chief Administration for Literary Affairs and Publishing." Officially, GLAVLIT forms part of the Ministry of Education, but in practice, its officials belong to the committee of State security.

According to a decree of 1931, GLAVLIT is primarily charged with controlling the content of newspapers from the point of view of the military, political and economic security of the country. This institution's main task is thus to make sure that no State secret appears in the press.

However, GLAVLIT's competence has become greatly diminished as far as the Party press is concerned (i. e. all papers directly edited by the Party) as well as in the case of a certain number of other papers such as *Izvestia*, the central organ of the Supreme Soviet of the U. S. S. R., the newspapers of the Republics' Supreme Soviets, and most of the reviews published by the Academies of Science. In actual fact, the editors themselves are responsible for making sure that no State secrets appear in their newspapers.

As the Soviet press is very largely the press of the Communist Party, it is evident that the role of government censorship must be limited, and that it cannot but play a relatively minor part. Political and ideological guidance is so overwhelming that such an instrument as State censorship can have only subsidiary functions.

Details of the way GLAVLIT functioned were revealed during the last war, thanks to the discovery of the so-called Smolensk archives, seized by German troops during their occupation of the town. These documents, which include all the reports from the local offices of GLAVLIT for the period 1931 till 1939, are now in the hands of the American Army at Alexandria, Virginia. These reports show that officials of GLAVLIT compiled a regular index called "peretchen" enumerating all the items to be censored. They also issued a confidential bulletin setting out all useful working rules for censorship.

According to several Soviet journalists who have fled abroad, GLAVLIT's censorship during the Stalin period was very fastidious [1]. There were at least two censors on the editorial staff of each paper.

---

[1] cf. in particular A. Gayev, op. cit.

These examined thoroughly the paper's proofs at the make-up stage, especially making sure that units of the Soviet army were never referred to by their number nor mention made of their garrison towns, eliminating all information of enterprises concerning national defense or secret inventions. Censorship went as far as including questions of production capacity and the size of the labor force in factories. Moreover, censors used to scrutinize each illustration of a paper to make sure that there were no swastikas or any other "counter-revolutionary" signs, or in fact anything else considered to compromise the security of the State. They also used to examine each text in order to detect all allusions judged inopportune from a political point of view.

In the period that followed the death of Stalin, the importance of GLAVLIT as an organ of censorship diminished to the same extent as the responsibility of editors of newspapers increased. This is indicated by evidence from Soviet journalists. Censorship by this organ became more or less a formality, at least in the case of the central newspapers. The only real function of GLAVLIT officials is now to stop State secrets from appearing in the press. The main question is to know what these secrets are. There is no recent document that defines them. The law of 1947 on State secrets covers such a vast area that anything not specifically mentioned as approved for publication could be considered as secret. But during the first years of the post-Stalin period, the situation became less rigid and newspapers have published detailed accounts of the production capacity of certain enterprises or the size of their labor forces.

There is, however, one sphere in which GLAVLIT continues to function with uncontested authority : in supervising the export of Soviet publications. It is very interesting to note that even in the years following the death of Stalin, newspapers and magazines published below the central republic level are in theory not allowed to be exported. (While Stalin was alive, the ban also applied to the central newspapers of the federated republics.) This has the curious effect of eliminating foreign access to such important newspapers as those of Leningrad or other major cities, while allowing a capital paper such as the central organ of the obscure Moldavian republic to be exported ; Leningrad is not the capital of the Russian republic although being the most important city after Moscow (which can export its papers, being the capital of the Russian Federated Republic as well as the Soviet Union). This might suggest the higher authorities' lack of confidence in the powers of judgment of local editors and censors, in particular in the effectiveness of the control system below the level of the federated republic—although all this may be no more than the results of pure bureaucracy.

It must also be remembered that in addition to the censorship of GLAVLIT, there is another form of control exercised by the editors themselves : the "visa from the source." Most Soviet editors will require a "visa" from the source where the information was gathered. An interview with a high official, for example, generally requires the official's signature or initials on the manuscript which is called the "visa." An article on foreign affairs requires the "visa" of the Foreign Ministry, a crime report requires the "visa" of the police or court authorities, etc. An editor generally expects that his reporter or writer will obtain this "insurance" for him.

Failures of control and marginal liberty

GLAVLIT's censorship has not always found it possible to have its orders enforced. Even during the years of terror (1934-1939), its directives were not always acted upon. Evidence of the resistance it encountered is to be found in the Smolensk archives, and especially in a confidential bulletin, which is the internal organ of GLAVLIT's services [1].

Editorial offices have often showed astounding indifference towards the censors. An "ultra-secret" report dated March 20, 1934 contains the following passage : "In many places, the results of censorship can hardly be regarded as satisfactory. In the district of Nevilsk and Sychevsk, military units engaged in secret works were referred to by their numbers ; P. and N. (censors) allowed reports of highways of strategic interest to be mentioned... A certain number of districts have not as yet nominated their censors..."

GLAVLIT's bulletin found at Smolensk also mentions several times the difficulties encountered by censors who tried to impose on

---

[1] See especially the article by Merle Fainsod on Soviet censorship : *Problems of Communism*, March-April 1956.

editors a silence on certain subjects which they considered intolerable. In the last resort they appealed to the "peretchen" (index). It has sometimes occurred that complaints were lodged by the newspapers against censors who were subsequently condemned for showing too much zeal. However, the publication of information that should have been kept secret has always been considered a much more serious offense.

Different newspapers have shown in various ways their general irritation with censors who interfere too much in editorial matters or who carry out their tasks in the spirit of rigid bureaucracy. Sometimes the cuts demanded by the censors have been ignored. When a dispute broke out, the censors would appeal to the superior authority of their own organization while the journalists would have recourse to the Party Committee at the level corresponding to that of their newspaper. This would often result in long controversies which became conflicts of authority. It has even happened on rare occasions that a newspaper has made fun of GLAVLIT officials who were taking their jobs too seriously. This was a particularly serious development as the "peretchen" distinctly forbids all references to the rules and methods of the censorship. Another way of showing their annoyance with the censors has been the editors' practice of purposely introducing misprints into their work. For example, "capitalism" would be printed instead of "socialism," "glorious danger" (slavnyi) instead of "principal danger" (glavnyi), etc.

Such exceptional occurrences are of course only revealed by accident. Thus there have been no examples of the press's resistance to censors during the post-war period. Nevertheless, experts agree that the importance of censors has diminished at the beginning of the years following the death of Stalin.

Despite the extent and complexity of the control apparatus imposed on it, the Soviet press does nevertheless enjoy a certain margin of freedom which has been slowly developing since 1953. This freedom is on the whole a freedom to criticize, or more precisely the freedom of self-criticism, in Communist terminology. This criticism originates in the first instance from each paper's special correspondents in the principal centers of its circulation. The same applies to correspondents of agricultural enterprises and factories. The main task of these reporters is to inform the newspapers of the shortcomings and mistakes which come to light in their spheres of activity. The satirical serial features which have acquired special importance since the death of Stalin tend in particular towards self-criticism. They also point out certain negative aspects of daily life in the U. S. S. R. The same thing is done in many letters to the editor. These are not always written spontaneously ; they have often been inspired by the "instructors" attached to the editorial staffs or by organizations of the Party. Most of these letters concern cases of disorganization, corruption, and bureaucratic abuses. For example, there are complaints concerning the bad organization of the sale of cinema tickets, ridiculous bus time-tables, the lack of provision for children's playgrounds, bad food, the ill-mannered behavior of certain officials, the scarcity of certain consumer goods, and bad organization in the shops. Some letters even go so far as criticizing court verdicts considered to be unjust. In most letters to the editor criticism involves a person, a group of persons or an institution which has failed in its duty. Usually, criticism has a local character and tends to be concerned with the defective application of policies emanating from higher quarters. But in no circumstances does criticism challenge the general policies of the Soviet Communist Party, nor the Soviet government, nor the activities and behavior of current leaders. Whatever has been decided by the Party is taboo. The execution of the plan can be criticized, but never the plan itself. On the other hand, letters to the editor may contain to a limited extent criticism of local authorities, which give a certain section of the population the opportunity to air some of their grievances. Moreover, letters to the editor also represent one of the Soviet regime's instruments for dealing with bureaucracy. Self-criticism is a tolerated freedom which is generally considered as a safety-valve for public opinion. But according to certain Western experts, after the death of Stalin, freedom of criticism developed to such an extent that it no longer simply served as an outlet for discontent but even went so far as to stimulate a real spirit of criticism.

As far as the scope of criticism of subordinate authorities is concerned, the November 1956 issue of the doctrinal review *Partiinaya Zhizn* offers some interesting information. In reply to readers' inquiries as to whether local newspapers had the right to criticize local leaders of the Party, the review said : "The writers of these letters realize that each newspaper (at the district level) is the organ of its Party committee, expresses the views of this committee and operates under its guidance. This is the organizational expression of Lenin's principle of the partisan nature of the press. There was once a case in which the editor of a provincial newspaper printed a decision of the provincial Party committee bureau and accompanied it with editorial "comment," initiating a polemic against the provincial committee in the pages of the newspaper. If the editor disagrees with the Party committee, he is permitted, under the Party statutes, to raise the question in the committee and, if necessary, in a superior Party body ; but he has no right to use the newspaper to settle personal differences with the Party committee."

Nevertheless, went on *Partiinaya Zhizn*, readers ask : But the district committee officials are not the district committee—does the newspaper not have the right to criticize them ? *Partiinaya Zhizn* replied somewhat ambiguously that the newspaper "has the right to criticize anyone, but in doing so it must not oppose itself to the district committee." The article went on to emphasize the harm wrought by "inconsiderate criticism."

The Party condemns the practice of requiring editors to submit all copy to the Party officials for approval, said *Partiinaya Zhizn*, citing a 1954 instance in which the Central Committee in Moscow had rebuked the secretary of the Kromy District Party Committee in Orel Province for requiring the local editor to submit all critical readers' letters for approval ; "but," added the magazine, "cases will arise in which the editor must submit critical material for collegial discussion by Party agencies before publishing it."

Results of the "thaw"

The margin of freedom conceded to the press after the death of Stalin was evident in the development of discussions in newspapers as well as between different newspapers. Formerly, polemics or simple discussion between newspapers was rigorously forbidden, even on non-political subjects, with the sole exception of certain scientific and literary themes such as the great debate on biology in 1947. The change is significant, even though controversies between newspapers are still rare and rather reserved. In 1954, for example, *Literaturnaya Gazeta* declared itself against the official policy of separate boys' and girls' schools. The paper upheld its point of view in spite of several reprimands from the teachers' journal and even from *Pravda*.

However, this kind of discussion is still far from becoming part of the traditions of Soviet journalism. At the beginning of 1957, the professional organ *Sovetskaya Pechat* expressed astonishment that a district newspaper and a provincial newspaper should have both criticized the same factory in very different terms, one of them severely and the other with a sense of balance. And the author of the article went on to raise the question of whether the two papers should not have consulted each other in order to adopt the same attitude.

In the middle of 1956, real polemics took place between *Voprossy Istorii*, a historical review, on the one hand, and *Pravda* and the doctrinal journals of the Central Committee on the other hand. The editorial staff of the first review had gone much further in their history of the Party's "destalinization" than the Party leadership itself was prepared to approve. It had attempted to present in a more favorable light the Social-Democrats (mensheviks) and some Western anti-Communist marxists like Karl Kautsky. The review upheld its point of view in the face of criticism from Party organs. After several months of polemics, in the spring 1957, the Party leadership intervened and dismissed the editorial staff of *Voprossy Istorii*. This is a good illustration of the extent to which the regime is prepared to tolerate free discussion on a political subject.

One result of the post-Stalin "thaw" and the new if restricted possibility of discussions between newspapers was the slight eclipse of the hitherto overwhelming authority of Moscow's *Pravda* ; at least a slight modification in its accustomed pre-eminence. During the Stalin period, it had been usual to see complete editorials from *Pravda* reproduced five or six times a month in regional papers. Between 1955 and 1957, this practice ceased completely. Papers at the republic and regional level published only articles prepared by their own staff. Of course they followed the Party line but they no longer imitated the Moscow press slavishly. One of the most typical examples of the decline of *Pravda*'s paternal role among the rest of the Soviet press was that of the unprecedented dispute between the latter and its principal Muscovite colleague, *Izvestia*. *Pravda* had criticized its colleague's agricultural story on the production of maize, while *Izvestia* replied by accusing the central organ of the Party of having altered the text in question. However, in the end, the Supreme Soviet's paper admitted that *Pravda* had been right in its original remarks.

* * *

During the years following the death of Stalin, there were indisputable signs of "liberalization" in the Soviet press. This above all affected the appearance of newspapers and to a lesser extent also their content. However, "liberalization" never diminished the control exercised over newspapers ; in fact, not only was it authorized, but also encouraged along lines dictated by the regime's highest control organs. Thus the most recent Russian manuals on journalism show that the new tendency to replace the long regular editorials of newspapers by two more concise ones was dictated by a recommendation of the Central Committee.

In fact the purpose of the changes brought about in Soviet journalism after Stalin has not been to diminish the control over the press, but to make newspapers more readable, thus turning them into more effective instruments of mass-persuasion in the service of the regime.

Chinese People's Republic

In Communist China, the press assumes an even more vital role as an instrument of mass persuasion than in other Communist countries because of the country's immense population. It is true that total circulation figures do not reach an average of more than 12 million, which at first sight appears to be low for a population of more than 600 million inhabitants ; however, given the system of public reading groups, the press represents in actual fact one of the most powerful instruments which the regime possesses to carry out its avowed task of moulding the Chinese people to the tenets of Communist ideology.

On seizing power, the Communists proceeded to turn the press into an elaborate, diversified and highly specialized apparatus, each of its parts being devised to influence definite groups of readers, each carrying out a specific and defined function. At the same time, schools have adopted newspaper reading as part of their official curricula, while government agencies, mass organizations, military units, commercial firms, industrial enterprises and collective farms have organized "newspaper reading groups" in which literate persons read the papers to those who are illiterate. Periodically there are tests to make sure that in fact the newspapers are being effectively read.

In order to ensure the efficiency of this machine of indoctrination, government officials have subjected the press to the most rigorous control. Such control is evident, as in other Communist countries, in four main spheres : organizational, personnel, editorial and operational. In each of these, Peking has introduced certain original features to which this study will devote particular attention.

Organizational control

In Communist China, the government decides when, where and how many newspapers should be founded. The government also decides who or what organizations are to be responsible for editing them. It therefore goes without saying that the press exists solely to serve the interests of the government. The survival of certain privately-owned newspapers—a special feature of the Chinese Communist press—does not in any way detract from this statement, as will be shown below.

One of the primary aims of the new regime has been to eliminate the opposition press.

Since the Kuomintang was regarded as the arch enemy of the people, it was only natural for the Communists to ban all of its newspapers on the mainland once they seized power there. Actually, most of the official newspapers of the Kuomintang, including the 44 daily papers (one of them had editions in ten major cities) published by the central and provincial headquarters of the Party, suspended publication on the eve of Communist occupation of their respective cities or towns, as they were fully aware of what their destiny would be after the Communists' arrival. Thus the newly-arrived Communist authorities found that what remained to be done with regard to the Kuomintang newspapers hardly involved any more effort than confiscating the properties of such papers. This, of course, was done quickly and thoroughly. As part of the campaign for the suppression of "counter-revolutionaries," the Communist regime also liquidated or sent to forced labor camps a good many former Kuomintang newsmen who failed to flee from the mainland. Those authorized to continue their work after a rigorous examination of their political past were obliged to attend special indoctrination classes.

Privately-owned newspapers

The Communists' policy toward privately-owned newspapers, however, has not been so simple or straightforward. In this field it has been far more subtle and complex, a practical consequence of the intricate Chinese version of the Communist theory concerning the State at the transitional stage of "people's dictatorship." According to the Chinese theory, all elements of society other than the "bureaucratic-capitalists," "feudal landlords" and the "lackeys of foreign imperialism" are legitimate components of the People's Republic of China and therefore entitled to enjoy all political rights including the one to have their own newspapers. Consequently, outright banning of all privately-owned newspapers has not been considered by the regime in Peking an advisable or expedient policy during this first phase of revolution.

On the other hand, there has never been any question of giving completely free reins to any privately-owned newspaper ; for Communist theory asserts that, during the stage of "people's dictatorship," the Party and the government must effect, among other things, an ideological transformation of the population as a whole and that, in order to do this, it must assume the role of teacher, guide and leader of the people. In this connection, the Party and government have both the right and responsibility to direct the flow of ideas and information through all sections of the mass communication media. This, of course, implies governmental regulation of privately-owned newspapers.

The first step taken by the Communist regime in this connection was to announce that while privately-owned newspapers of "counter-revolutionary tendencies" would be outlawed at once, "progressive" ones and those without definite political leanings might apply for new licenses to continue publication. Thus, quite a number of privately-owned newspapers were able to coexist together with newspapers owned by the Communists, although subject to strict control and supervision by the regime.

But, late in 1951, the regime began to put into effect a policy aimed at reducing the number of privately-owned newspapers as well as changing the nature of those which were to be retained. Many privately-owned newspapers were therefore closed, others amalgamated, and still others "reformed" and "reorganized."

Since 1953 there have been only five important privately-owned newspapers left in the country, none of which retains any of its former identity and independent status. In addition to having Communists and pro-Communists as their staff members, these four newspapers have been charged by the regime with specific responsibilities in the conduct of propaganda and indoctrination. The *Ta-kung pao* in Tientsin, once the most influential independent newspaper in China, now concentrates on news and comment concerning financial and economic matters—the sphere it specialized in before the Revolution. Its editor's conversion to Communism in 1949 greatly facilitated the Party's task. The *Kuang-ming jih-pao,* nominally a joint organ of all the "Democratic parties," specializes in reporting and discussion of cultural and educational affairs. As for the other privately-owned papers, the *Wen-hui pao* primarily serves school teachers and senior high school students in Shanghai, the *Hsin-min pao* devotes its space largely to sports and recreational activities in the same city, and the *Sin-wen jih-pao,* one of the oldest dailies in China (founded in 1893), caters specifically for the "capitalists" tolerated by the Communist regime. It has a circulation of about 100,000. (The *Jen-min jih-pao,* principal organ of the Party, has nearly a million.) It is therefore quite clear that these papers have practically become an integral part of the official press apparatus and that the fact of their private owner-ship no longer has any significance other than an indication of the Chinese Communists' continued adherence to their above-mentioned political theory.

The development of the Communists' own press of course flourished long before the victory of the Communist regime in 1949. During the early 1930's, the Communists were already publishing no fewer than 34 newspapers in the Kiangsi Soviet district alone. *Hung-se Chung-hua* or *The Red China,* then an official organ of the Central Committee of the Party, had a circulation of some 50,000 copies per issue—a highly impressive record considering the restricted limits of the territory in which the newspaper was able to circulate.

Upon their reconciliation with the Kuomintang following the outbreak of the Sino-Japanese War in 1937, the Communists were allowed by the National Government to publish a newspaper in Wuhan and later in Chung-king, wartime seat of the National Government.

Meanwhile, the Communists founded more than one hundred newspapers in the units of their armies and in the so-called border regions in North and Central China then occupied by their guerilla forces behind the lines of Japanese troops.

Expansion of the press

Since they conquered the entire mainland, the Communists have expanded this more or less localized press into a nation-wide apparatus. The most important fact about this expansion is the kind of control exercised over it by the central authorities of the Party which decides not only when, where and how many newspapers should be founded but also the question of among what groups of people the various newspapers should respectively seek circulation. A typical example of this control is a directive issued by the Central Committee of the Party in January 1956, calling for the establishment of 360 new regional newspapers as a means of strengthening the Party's ideological leadership over the rural population at a time when agricultural collectivization was being vigorously put into effect.

With such centralized direction and supervision the regime has been able to make highly efficient use of the somewhat limited number of trained journalists and inadequate publishing facilities. Unlike the state of affairs before 1949, which was marked by undue concentration of newspapers in large cities, the geographic distribution of Communist newspapers is so carefully planned that at each level of the territorial-administrative hierarchy there is generally an appropriate press to be used by the Party, government and other public organizations in influencing the minds and activities of the masses.

According to Communist statistics, there were in 1955, 392 newspapers above the administrative district level. The total number of regional newspapers was estimated as 1,000 in 1951. Even though since then the government has not disclosed any more systematic figures on this score [1], unofficial sources suggest that there has been a considerable increase in the total number of papers on the regional level.

Most of the above-mentioned newspapers are printed, but some are lithographed or mimeographed. In addition to these printed, lithographed and mimeographed papers, which, by the end of 1955, had a total circulation of approximately 12 million copies per issue, there are countless handwritten wall news-sheets and blackboard news-sheets in small villages, factories, schools, public organizations, co-operative farms, and all units of the armed forces. All of these special "newspapers" are also organs of the government, Party or other public organizations in their respective localities and therefore ultimately as subject to the control of the central authorities as the regular newspapers.

---

[1] Up to the time of writing this chapter.

Control over personnel

Closely related to organizational control is the control over personnel. This control is designed to ensure that the press is in the hands of persons who are above all politically trained and ideologically indoctrinated. Such selection of newspaper staff provides the regime with a far more effective guarantee of the political reliability of newspapers than a conventional censorship system can possibly do.

The regime effects its personnel control largely by enforcing a Party rule that the publishers and editors of the official newspapers on various levels shall be appointed by the corresponding Party committee with the approval of the next higher Party unit in the case of appointments made by Party committees below the national level. Thus, as in U. S. S. R., while the Central Committee has full power to appoint publishers and editors of newspapers on the national level, appointments by regional committees of editors of regional newspapers require the confirmation of the administrative district committees or the Central Committee of the Party. Similar rigid control is exercised by the Party committees over the dismissal and promotion of newspaper publishers and editors.

To be sure, these personnel controls are not imposed merely upon the official organs of the regime. They are applied to all newspapers and journals in the country irrespective of their formal auspices. The editor of the journal of a provincial women's association, for example, while appointed by the association, must first be approved by the provincial Party authorities and then confirmed by the Central Committee of the Party.

Immediately after its seizure of power in 1949, the Party heavily relied upon Communists and fellow travelers who had worked either on Communist newspapers in the border regions or on non-Communist papers in the territory then under the control of the Kuomintang regime. But the great expansion of the press apparatus quickly made it clear that these limited resources of journalistic personnel were inadequate to meet the increasing demand for press personnel. To cope with the situation, the Party appointed people as newspaper editors from among reliable Party members who had experience in some kind of propaganda work.

In the meantime, Party schools on various levels offered special short courses to train press personnel. Shortly afterwards, the Peking College of Journalism was established, offering courses both on school and university levels.

In both the Peking College of Journalism and the special classes of the Party schools, political indoctrination rather than professional training comes first in importance. The political indoctrination courses include such subjects as dialectical materialism, the theory of the State and revolution, imperialism, political economy, history of social development, history of the Communist Party of the U. S. S. R., the thought of Mao Tse-tung, history of the Chinese Communist Party, and current affairs.

The emphasis on the journalist's political training is aimed at developing and heightening his Socialist consciousness so that he may be unquestionable loyal to the Party and capable of correctly interpreting and carrying out the current Party line in his journalistic activities.

Editorial guidance

Important as they are, personnel and organizational controls, however, create only the physical conditions in which the regime can make use of the press. To ensure that this vast press apparatus performs its specific functions under ever-changing circumstances, it is necessary for the regime to give concrete editorial guidance to the press and to see to it that such guidance is always thoroughly understood and scrupulously followed by the newspapers on all levels.

Since 1949, when it seized power, the Chinese Communist regime has used several devices for exercising editorial control over the press.

A. Rules

In the first place, there are a number of standing rules setting forth the fundamental points that are to guide the newsmen in their editorial work. Some of these rules are found in the constitution of the Party. The "General Provisions" of this constitution states, in effect, that the Party press, as part of the Party organization, must always report news and discuss problems from the viewpoint of Marxism-Leninism, consequently denouncing all opinions of or tendencies to idealism or "bourgeois objectivity." The Party constitution also stipulates that newspapers, like individual members of the Party, shall never openly make any statement or express views on any issue relating to Party policy without awaiting instructions from the appropriate authorities of the Party (Art. 25-26).

Article 27 of the same constitution provides press personnel with more general guidance for the formulation of editorial policy. The essence of this provision is that editors of newspapers on various levels must keep the content of their newspapers in line with the immediate tasks and the long-range goals not only of the Party organizations on the corresponding levels but also of the higher Party organizations including those on the national level.

More standing rules governing the editorial policy of the press are to be found in government legislation. The Provisional Regulations on the Protection of State Secrets and the Regulations of the Chinese People's Republic on the Punishment of Counter-Revolutionaries, for example, roughly indicate the kind of news items that the press must refrain from featuring.

According to the provisions, no newspaper may carry any material calculated to disseminate counter-revolutionary propaganda, to spread rumors detrimental to the prestige of the People's government, to incite people to obstruct the enforcement of laws and decrees including those concerning grain requisition, taxation, and military and labor conscription ; nor may any newspapers disclose political, military, economic, financial, and diplomatic secrets. Penalties for those violating these provisions range from three years' imprisonment to death.

B. Directives

In addition to the standing rules, the Party and the government, from time to time, also issue directives to newspapers, providing either general or specific lines of policy which the regime wishes the entire press or particular groups of papers to follow. As a matter of fact, it has been largely through the guidance provided by such directives that newspaper editors have endeavored to adapt their papers to changed conditions and responsibilities. Moreover, through such directives the regime has also found a way of correcting the errors and inadequacies of newspaper editors, which are bound to occur at one time or another since newspaper editors, no matter how carefully selected and trained, are as fallible as any other human beings.

The regime also controls the content of the press by controlling the supply of news and important feature articles. This control is exercised primarily through the Hsin-Hua or New China News Agency. With the exclusive right to gather news on a nation-wide basis and with the so-called "large newspapers" in the country legally obliged to print verbatim its important news releases and special articles, this official news service is in a position to determine not only what kind of material the newspapers may get to fill a large part of their daily pages but also in some instances the exact wording of such material.

In these circumstances, newspapers themselves are not given much freedom of action in gathering and selecting those news and feature stories which are supposed to be gathered or prepared by their own staff members. They are required to make quarterly and monthly plans on editorial topics and feature articles and to submit these plans to the appropriate Party authorities for approval. They are prohibited from gathering news from sources other than those organizations or individuals directly involved in the news. Before publishing a news story or a feature article, they are obliged to have the manuscript examined by the organization or individual who features prominently in it, so as to ensure "completely accurate and responsible news reporting."

Once again, as in the case of the Soviet press, it seems not to matter much whether subjects treated are topical from a chronological point of view. The essential point is that they should be topical in a political sense. Thus, for example, only in February 1953 did the Chinese Communist press launch its vast propaganda campaign for the collectivization of agriculture when in fact the decision to this effect had been taken by the Party over a year before.

C. Scrutiny

Once printed, the newspaper is carefully read and scrutinized by the press section of the Party committee on the corresponding level of the territorial-administrative hierarchy. In the case of newspapers below the national level, they are also subject to periodical scrutiny by the press sections and the newspapers of the Party organizations at higher levels. Such scrutiny or review is designed to discover ideological deviations or editorial shortcomings that all the pre-publication control might have failed to detect. This post-publication examination has, therefore, quite frequently resulted in criticism of erring or offending papers or groups of papers. The system is the same as that existing in the U. S. S. R. In important cases, the Party authorities issue formal directives or may call conferences of newspaper editors for direct discussion and instruction. There have also been occasions when officials of Party press sections have found it necessary to go so far in helping some newspaper editors "improve their work" as to write editorials or draw up editorial plans for them.

All these different controls, however, do not prevent gross errors from appearing in the Communist Chinese press. For instance, it once reported that 370 wells had been sunk in ten days in a certain district, when in fact no such work had ever been undertaken. The only work contemplated had been a railway line over a bridge, but this had not yet been constructed. Again there had been descriptions and photographs of the introduction of a mechanical plough in a collective farm at a time of the year when such work would have been unthinkable. This kind of practical error probably saps public confidence in the press more thoroughly than the ideological zig-zags of which it is often the mouthpiece.

Businesslike management

In addition to controlling the structure, personnel, and content of the press, the regime also directs and supervises its business management, especially circulation and finance. (In this respect, the Chinese system differs almost completely from most other Communist countries.)

Prior to 1950, all Communist newspapers almost completely relied upon Party subsidies. As the number of newspapers was increasing rapidly following the Communist conquest of the mainland, the Party found that continued financial subsidies for the press would not only put a great strain on the national budget but also might strip the newspaper managers and editors of all urge for making ceaseless efforts to improve their own work as an essential means of assuring the survival and development of their papers.

Toward the end of 1949, the Information Administration convened a national conference of newspaper managers to discuss possible changes in newspaper financing. The conference decided, among other things, that henceforth all newspapers should begin to operate on a businesslike basis with a view to attaining financial self-sufficiency. Since then, newspapers have taken the following principal measures to introduce more businesslike management : 1) fixing sub-scription fees high enough to cover the cost of newsprint ; 2) reducing the number of employees to a minimum ; 3) adopting the system of cost accounting ; 4) strictly enforcing the rules of budgeting and auditing ; 5) enacting rules governing the upkeep of equipment ; 6) rewarding employees for elimination of waste and for high produc-tivity ; 7) using inexpensive, homemade newsprint ; 8) improving services to the reader by getting papers printed and delivered promptly every day ; 9) engaging in profitable sideline activities such as using idle presses to print posters or handbills for commercial and government agencies ; and 10) carrying advertisements for publishing houses, "cultural organizations" and certain commercial enterprises. Here it should be noted that a newspaper is not allowed to carry ordinary commercial advertisements unless it has failed to achieve self-sufficiency by other means. Even in the latter case, a newspaper is still under obligation to ensure that such commercial advertising does not take up too much of its space, thus adversely affecting its discharge of propaganda and agitation functions. As a result of these measures, newspapers, especially national dailies, have been able to support themselves financially, and some of them even are making considerable profit.

However, it should be stressed that the achievement of financial self-sufficiency by some newspapers has not had the slightest effect of lessening their dependence upon the regime. The regime still maintains strict financial control over the newspapers by periodically reviewing the latter's budgets and final accounts.

Control of distribution

Closely related to financial supervision is the control over the newspapers' circulation. By controlling the circulation the regime hopes to make the newspapers steadily enlarge their readership, thus enhancing their influence upon the masses. One of the major steps taken by the regime to promote newspaper circulation was its decree, in 1950, calling upon the post offices to deal with newspaper subscriptions. Like its Soviet counterpart, a model which it has considerably perfected, the Chinese Communist regime regarded the post offices as a convenient network for the distribution of newspapers on a nation-wide basis. As a result of a joint conference between the postal authorities and newspaper executives held in December 1949, newspaper personnel specializing in distribution were transferred on a large scale to the post office. Since then, postmen do not simply deliver newspapers to readers ; they are also charged with renewing and opening subscriptions and are even given the task of organizing newspaper reading groups. With the help of this giant network, which often applied undue pressure on the people, most of the newspapers quickly began to increase their circulation. On July 22, 1955, the Minister of Postal and Telecommunications was able to report that since 1950 there had been a 408 per cent increase in the total number of newspaper subscriptions. In the rural areas alone, there was, according to subscription figures, one newspaper for every 274 peasants ; five years later there was one paper for every 74 peasants.

However, the minister also indicated in his report that up to the summer of 1955 nearly one-fourth of the nation's administrative villages (an administrative village is made up of several smaller villages) still did not have any postal service while in the remaining three-fourths of the administrative villages, post offices had to ask civilian travelers to bring newspapers to subscribers living outside the administrative villages. Due to these and other inadequacies of the post offices, the regime was led to effect, in 1954, another change in its policy regarding newspaper circulation. Instead of relying exclusively upon the post offices, the regime now ordered the establishment of special agencies to help handle newspaper subscriptions. Meanwhile, Party committees on various levels were instructed to "mobilize" consumers' cooperatives and retail stores to erect newsstands for selling newspapers on the street. Since 1954, newspapers have been sold in the streets, stations and restaurants.

Effects of the control

Having described the unique nature of the Chinese Communist regime's unfailing and ever-present control over the press, it is now necessary to analyze the effects of such control. Undeniably, such control has enabled the regime to make the entire press a politically reliable instrument to be used in remolding the ideology of the people and mobilizing public opinion to ensure popular support for its policies. At the same time, this control system has also had certain adverse effects on the regime. In the first place, the regime's ideological control has resulted in the press's over-emphasis on propaganda and complete negligence of human interest. This, in turn, has made the content of newspapers dull and monotonous. During the brief period of the "thaw" in 1957, the students of a school in Peking unanimously decided to stop subscribing to newspapers and indeed to stop reading them. Needless to say, the regime's ever-increasing effort to "organize" people to read newspapers has been partially necessitated by such examples of popular aversion.

Another adverse effect that the control measures have produced is their sterilizing effect upon the press itself. As Dr. Franklin W. Houn, an expert on Chinese Communist propaganda, already pointed out in an article published in 1956 in the *Journalism Quarterly* (33/IV), editors of Chinese Communist newspapers, restricted as they are by multifarious directives and fearing that they might commit ideological deviations, have been strongly inclined to play safe. They are reluctant to take any initiative in expounding the regime's policies or in elucidating the Party line, even though this is part of their assigned duty. The Communists themselves have confessed that many editors, especially those on the provincial and local level, tend to avoid responsibility simply by filling their pages with material taken from the New China News Agency wires or from such leading news-papers as the *Jen-min jih-pao* of Peking. This attitude of the editors, if left unchecked, will tend to disqualify their newspapers from performing their various specific functions for the Party and the government.

The central organs of the Party have more than once complained at the small number of original editorials in the provincial press. For instance, an important regional newspaper, the daily of Chekiang, had not published more than 12 editorials during the first half of 1954. Even some of the major national papers are not beyond reproach in this matter. During the same half of 1954, the *Kuang-ming jih-pao* had produced 31 original editorials ; in addition, it had also printed 19 which had first appeared in the central organ of the Party and seven from *Pravda*. During one period of 111 days it published no editorials at all. As for the *Ta-kung pao* which used to be famous for its outspoken views, in six months it published 75 original editorials while taking 23 from the central organ of the Party and eight from *Pravda*.

From the "thaw" to "rectification"

Press control is in fact so strict that newspapers have been prevented from carrying out their function of *self-criticism* as author-ized by the regime.

In April 1950, the Central Committee of the Communist Party took several decisions regarding "the conduct of criticism and self-criticism in newspapers and other periodicals." This document invited the press to ask the public for open criticism of failings and errors in the affairs of the Party and government, and encouraged the press to do the same. But the authors of the document were careful to stress that the press should distinguish between "constructive" criticism and "negative" criticism, which for the Central Committee meant any-thing liable to harm the people's dictatorship and to destroy "social discipline by sapping the nation's confidence in their leaders and spreading pessimism and discord amongst the masses." In effect, the criticism to be tolerated was not to go further than the denunciation of the mistakes, failings and deviations of the lower hierarchy.

Suddenly in 1956, a new wind began to blow on the Chinese press. The central organ of the Party and other official papers admitted that current criticism lacked bite and the press continued to be so dull that the Party could not expect to achieve the propaganda successes that it had planned. In June of the same year, this new tendency became crystallized in Mao's famous slogan "Let a hundred flowers blossom, let a hundred schools of thought contend." It was the signal for a new outburst of freedom of expression which during a certain period was unequalled in other Communist countries, with the exception of Poland.

As regards the press, the *Jen-min jih-pao* set the example by making its contents more readable, broaching previously forbidden subjects and introducing satirical features on day-to-day affairs. Satire, which had from the start been allowed in the U. S. S. R., had hitherto been almost unheard of in Communist China. The Party's principal journal, considered until then to be above all criticism, went so far as to publish letters to the editor criticizing inaccuracies. One of these letters declared that a photograph of Ibsen published a few days before was in fact not Ibsen. Another correspondent criticized the paper's lyrical description of a cooperative farm where "a happy cow lies suckling its calf." The reader said that in more than twenty years' experience with cows, he had never seen one suckling its calf while lying down.

This "thaw" reached its climax during the first months of 1957. At the beginning of May, a meeting of journalists took place at Shanghai in the course of which strong complaints were voiced at the restrictions imposed on them by the authorities. The journalists also condemned the interference of Party officials in editorial affairs and went on to claim greater freedom of expression and criticism, as well as regular government press conferences during which reporters would be able to ask questions and obtain specific answers. The assistant editor of the principal Shanghai daily denounced the pseudo-journalists installed in executive positions who merely acted as camouflaged censors. One of his colleagues accused the government of having raised a barrier between the Communist journalists and the others to whom official authorities often denied news which was released to the Communists.

At the beginning of June, one began to find direct criticism of President Mao Tse-tung and Premier Chou En-lai in *Kuang-ming jih-pao*. The paper reproached the two politicians for not having kept their promises to the leaders of the non-Communist democratic parties about their participation in the government. This was the first time that in a Communist country a newspaper had dared to criticize the heads of State and government.

During the same period, a large number of unorthodox articles appeared in the press, some of these going so far as to question the basic foundations of the regime. Thus the central organ of the Party did not think twice about reproducing the text of a lecture given by Professor Ko Pai-chi of Peking University which included the following passage : "China has a population of 600 million inhabitants, including the counter-revolutionaries. This country does not belong to the Communist Party alone... If you Communists are working for the general good, all is in order. If not, the masses will kill you and overthrow the regime. This will not be considered as an anti-patriotic act since you will no longer be able to claim to be serving the people. And the downfall of the Communist Party will be far from implying the end of China."

A reaction was bound to follow. From the middle of 1957, the Party unleashed a vast campaign of "ideological rectification." In June the Central Committee severely condemned the *Kuang-ming jih-pao*, and the *Wen-hui pao,* the teachers' journal, for having advocated bourgeois views, and appealed for an all-out struggle against deviationism in the press.

At the end of June, the chairman of the administrative board of the *Kuang-ming jih-pao*, the Minister of Communications Chang Po-chun and the newspaper's editor were sacked for having attempted to give the paper an anti-Socialist line. This decision was taken by the committee of the Society of the Third of September, one of the non-Communist parties of which the editor was a member and the paper a mouthpiece. In a public confession in July, the editor accused himself of publishing lies fabricated by non-Communist ex-ministers, of reproducing tendentious news and of sending reporters to several towns in the interior in order to foment disorders.

Later, the purge spread and reached among others a certain number of journalists working in the New China News Agency. At the end of the year, the Communist Party appointed a thousand of its officials to impose or strengthen the guiding role of the Party in the cultural and educational field. Several of these men were appointed editors of newspapers and other publications.

Thus ended the brief "thaw" of the Chinese press, which soon fell back completely into the clutches of the Party and the government.

Rumania

At the end of the Second World War, it was assumed that the nations of Eastern Europe would enjoy a new era of freedom, in particular freedom of expression which most of them had never fully experienced, even before the war. The appearance of several newspapers immediately after the retreat of the Germans was thought to be one of the signs of this new era. But such illusions were not to last long. In the countries which had been at war with the Allies, freedom of expression was soon limited by Russian censorship, and when this was lifted after the signature of the peace treaties in 1946, a new apparatus conceived on the same model was ready to take over. In the other countries, there was a period of freedom of the press until the Communists seized power, but from the start, this freedom was only relative.

For countries of the first category, Rumania has been chosen as a particularly significant example which moreover disposes of abundant sources of evidence, notably some sworn testimony from Rumanian editors-in-chief and journalists which has been collected by the U. S. State Department. [1]

It can be maintained that the censorship, seizures and suspensions of Rumanian newspapers by the Soviet Armistice Commission was justified by the prolongation of the state of war until 1945. But at the end of that same year, after the conclusion of the Moscow agreement which provided for the restoration of democratic liberties as well as the handing over of the powers of censorship to the Rumanian authorities themselves, the situation got no better. On the contrary, it grew worse and gradually in two years resulted in the total suppression of freedom of the press.

From the beginning, previous authorization was required before a newspaper could be published. This was not merely denied to

---

[1] Evidence of violations of Human Rights Provisions of the Treaties of Peace : Vol. I, Rumania — Department of State of U. S. A., 1951.

"Fascists." While the organs of the Communist Party began to multiply, the National Peasant Party, numerically the stronger, obtained only two licenses for publication. The Ministry of Interior rejected all requests for the creation of organs of this party in the provinces. It based these refusals on the shortage of newsprint, the need for an inquiry and reorganization of the press. The request for a license for the Liberal Party's organ—suppressed in 1945 by the Soviet Armistice Commission—was rejected on the pretext that the population lacked interest in such a paper. [1] However, from February 1946, the party managed to publish another paper, *Liberalul.*

A publication license included the right to have full use of a printing press, but it should be noted that as all the printing industry was nationalized, the non-Communist papers were at a disadvantage because of the discriminatory distribution of their equipment. Later, a decree of June 9, 1950, required that all types of reproducing machines including typewriters be subjected to the control of the Ministry of Interior. The license for publication also carried with it the allocation of a certain amount of newsprint. In fact independent newspapers and those of the opposition (to the Communist Party) usually did not receive the quantity of newsprint to which they were entitled, while the Communist organs and those affiliated to them received more than their fair share. "All our protests were in vain," declared the managing director of the Peasant Party's publications in his testimony ; "we were forced to turn to the black market, which was supplied by the excess supplies of the Communist newspapers. As black market prices were four or five times higher than official prices, the production costs of the Communist press were practically being covered by the publishers of independent and opposition newspapers."

From the beginning of the new regime, restrictions and control affected not merely the means of production, but also the means of information. The News Agency Rador (Agerpress since 1949) acquired the monopoly of the distribution of news and became a Communist-controlled instrument of information. Important news, such as a

---

[1] This paper, *Uiitorul,* was suspended on February 17, 1945, apparently because of a use of initials which was considered questionable. It had published the letters C. B. E., D. S. O., M. C. after the name of the British Vice-Marshal Stevenson, according to his titles. (Cf. R. H. Markham : *Rumania under the Soviet Yoke.*)

speech by President Truman or Prime Minister Winston Churchill, was not distributed, and papers that published it, after hearing it from foreign radio stations, rendered themselves liable to considerable unpleasantness.

Newspaper reporters who sought to work in an independent fashion were subject to intimidation which ranged from moral pressure to acts of violence. The notions of espionage, treason and actions prejudicial to the interests of the State were so widespread that very ordinary news, the publication of which might have appeared perfectly legitimate from a Western standpoint, could become an offense in the eyes of the regime.

Furthermore, the exercise of the profession of journalist was subject to limitations. Journalists who had collaborated with the Antonescu regime were the first to be disqualified, but subsequently when the press syndicate passed under Communist control, disqualifications also began to weed out democratic journalists. In 1945, for example, a contributor to the paper *Universul* was excluded from the profession for having defamed the U. S. S. R. by spreading allegedly false information about social conditions in that country. In September 1947, the purge reached several editors of opposition organs who were reproached for their "anti-democratic attitude" and accused of having put themselves at the service of reactionary circles in the country and abroad.

Assuming that a paper had managed to surmount the various obstacles mentioned above, assuming, in other words, that it had managed to obtain a license, equipment, sufficient newsprint, more or less adequate information sources, and a homogenous staff able to work with sufficient independence, this paper had still to face the censorship.

In this connection, the editor of *Timpul* said in his testimony : "Every word of a newspaper including advertisements and other publicity was required to have censorship approval before publication. Censorship cut any material not favorable to Communism or the Soviet and much material basically favorable to the Western Allied powers... It held up the examination of non-Communist papers, thus delaying their publication until competitors had been selling for some time on the streets."

In a letter addressed to the Ministry of Information on December

19, 1946, the publishers of *Dreptatea*, organ of the National Peasant Party, complained of the abuses of the censorship : "There were days when practically everything was marked with blue pencil and editors had to have alternative texts at hand. Sometimes it happened that pages which had been emptied by the censor's suppressions could not be made up again."

"Later on, new methods were used against *Dreptatea* : Although the censors had granted their visa for the publication of certain resolutions of the Central Committee of the National Peasant Party, the editions containing the declarations of Iuliu Maniu (the party's leader), and the party's manifesto to the nation (on December 5 and 18, 1946) were confiscated. Since that last edition, the paper has remained suspended. A police officer informed the printers that on orders from above, the paper could no longer be printed."

Transgression of the censorship's orders could result in a warning for minor offenses, temporary suspension in other cases and the withdrawal of licenses in the case of repetition of offenses or a very serious misdemeanor.

Moreover, as the censorship formed part of the propaganda services, it did not limit its activity to suppressing texts. It also imposed them on editorial staffs. In his testimony, the editor-in-chief of the *Jurnalul de Dimineata* declared : "On several occasions, we were forced to publish articles praising the merits of Stalin and the Soviet paradise. We were even given instructions as to how the article was to be published and where it should appear in the paper."

"As a newspaper was not allowed to appear with blank spaces," said Mr. Farcasanu, editor-in-chief of the Liberal Party's organ, "the government obliged us to publish pro-Communist material furnished by the Ministry of Information in the place of the suppressed articles."

Once past the hurdles of the censorship, an independent or opposition paper had still to face the pressures of the typographical unions dominated by the Communists before it could appear. On several occasions, these exercised their own particular control, reinforcing and supplementing the official censorship. Their intervention, dictated by Communist leaders, was particularly manifest at the time when the Communists had not yet imposed total control over the press.

As it was difficult for the censorship to ban the texts of declarations made by Western statesmen, the authorities overcame the difficulty by advising the Communist leaders of the printers' union to see to it that these texts were not published. It was practically impossible to dismiss the responsible typographers since they enjoyed the protection of the Ministry of Labor.

In a letter of April 2, 1946, to the Prime Minister, the Minister of State Romniseanu, wrote: "...Although the official censorship of the daily *Liberalul* is no longer so strict, the indirect censorship exercised by the printers has been intensified. Not only have compositors refused to set certain totally inoffensive articles, but they have gone so far as to make partial cuts and even changes in certain articles."

On August 1, 1946, a gang invaded the printing works which published the organ of the Peasant Party, sacked it and obliged the workers to assemble at the headquarters of the printers' union to sign a declaration undertaking not to work for the paper any more. Although alerted, the government took no notice of the whole affair. In other similar cases, the authorities simply refused to assure the necessary protection to newspapers against the acts of violence of their printing personnel.

Even the paper that managed to go to press without too many obstacles had still to be distributed, and here was again one more occasion for the Communists to exercise their control. Since 1950, a decree has conferred on the government the monopoly of newspaper distribution. But since 1945, the government already exercised a virtual monopoly indirectly. Opposition newspapers sent from Bucharest to the provinces often never reached their destination : bundles of them were thrown along the roadside and railway track. At other times postmen would refuse to distribute them. Those who subscribed to the papers were under pressure to cancel their subscriptions. Obstacles to the proper sale and distribution of newspapers were even applied in the capital. The Communists often molested the sellers of opposition newspapers.

In spite of all this pressure, there were some papers that survived. As these would not abandon their struggle, the government had to resort to more drastic measures.

In July 1947, *Dreptatea*, the organ of the National Peasant Party, was suspended indefinitely by order of the government. In the same month, the independent daily *Jurnalul de Dimineata* was forced to cease publication after having declared in a report that Bessarabia (annexed to the U. S. S. R.) was Rumanian territory. In August of the same year, the daily *Liberalul* was seized by the police. Its editor-in-chief states that he was forced to publish an article explaining that financial difficulties prevented the newspaper from continuing publication. Towards the end of 1947, the papers *Argus* and *Timpul* were confiscated by the police. One independent paper, *Semnalul,* continued to appear in Bucharest until October 1, 1948, when the censorship authorities refused to receive it for censorship. This was the equivalent of a death sentence, as no newspaper can appear without obtaining the censorship's visa. (The same procedure was used against the *Jurnalul de Dimineata* after its publication of the report concerning Bessarabia.)

In February 1949, a decree legalized the Communist government's control of information by authorizing the Ministry of Arts and Information "to direct and control the press and all publications".

It is true that two further Rumanian newspapers theoretically not in the category of Communist or affiliated organs still continued to exist in the Rumanian capital. In actual fact they had no more independence than the others. *Adevarul,* a "Democratic" paper which had made its first appearance before the war, had to cease publication in 1951, after announcing that its mission had been accomplished. *Universul,* the most important paper of Rumania even before the Second World War, was not suppressed until the beginning of 1953. It differed slightly from the other papers as it was intended to reach the old bourgeois and conservative elements, for whom marxist-leninist doctrine was served and distilled in small doses by Communists who were experts in this field. In order to make a change, from time to time it broached religious questions. Furthermore, it was the only paper to go on printing "Mr." and "Mrs." before a family name instead of introducing the formula of "Comrade." But when the authorities considered that the category of citizens towards whom the paper was directed no longer needed special treatment and guidance, *Universul* (which had belonged to the State since 1945) ceased publication.

Czechoslovakia

An entirely different evolution from that of Rumania took place in Czechoslovakia, yet in the end it led to the same results. Czechoslovakia was a country possessing certain special characteristics which make its experience all the more instructive. In the first place, it was the only country of Eastern Europe that had enjoyed a continuous period of press freedom before the Second World War ; journalism could look back to some solid traditions embodied by some of the best Czech writers, such as Jan Neruda and Karel Capek. In the second place, Czechoslovakia as an allied and victor nation did not have to suffer from Soviet censorship after its liberation.

However, with the advent of peace the freedom of newspaper publication was not completely re-established. It was understandable that parties which had collaborated with the enemy had their organs banned and that other newspapers of similar tendencies were also refused publication. Yet the new restrictions went further than this. Only authorized political parties forming part of the National Front and official corporations and other organizations were given the right to publish newspapers. Private persons no longer possessed this right. It is thus clear that in the years that preceded the seizure of power by the Communists, the press was limited in character and variety ; although newspapers expressed themselves freely in various manners, not a single one took up the role of an actual opposition paper.

The post-war character of the Czechoslovak press was defended in particular by Dr. Benes. In a statement made in July 1945, the Czechoslovak President said : "In my opinion, journalism is a public service. Unbridled freedom to publish newspapers should not be re-estabished. We all know what the yellow press meant before the war. This, to be sure, is a restriction of personal liberty, but the public interest must come first. That is why with us newspapers are published by public corporations, which alone have the right to freedom of publication... We must to a certain extent admit that Liberalism has been discarded. This is a fact, and we must realize that one of the factors in public life that is above all subject to today's socializing trends is journalism. How to harmonize this fact with freedom of speech is another matter. But here, too, the principle that the freedom of the individual must be subordinated to the freedom of the whole holds good."

At first sight this might appear an attractive theory. It has been held by convinced democrats. A distinction is made between freedom of the press and independence of the actual publishing house with the implication that control can be imposed on the latter without its affecting the former—at least in theory. [1] In his book on "The Press the Public Wants," Kingsley Martin speaks of the Czechoslovak 'experiment' as follows : "This seems a natural pattern for a free press in a socialist society. I gather that the change has given greater freedom to journalists, improved their professional status, and not deprived the public of news or protected the government from criticism." [2]

On the other hand, it is perhaps a trifle arbitrary to assume that a newspaper in private hands will inevitably put the interests of the public in the background. In fact, in the first Czechoslovak Republic the yellow press was more often the exception than the rule, for the majority of newspapers had a very high conception of their duty to the nation.

It is still more arbitrary and dangerous as well to allow the State to decide which corporations shall have the right to publish a newspaper. In this context the closed shop represents a grave threat to democratic principles. It is significant that in Czechoslovakia the corporations and official organisms authorized to publish a daily newspaper have remained more or less the same since 1945, before the Communist seizure of power and after the coup d'Etat. In fact they were the same corporations that are authorized to publish in any Communist country, namely, trade unions, rural co-operatives, the

---

[1] Jacques Kayser, *Mort d'une liberté*, Plon, 1956, page 63 and seq.
[2] *The Press the Public Wants*, Ed. Hogarth, 1947, page 107.

army, the national youth organization, large cultural associations and certain ministries, as well as the recognized political parties.

However, such a system does not rule out the possibility of a corporation's organ taking an opposition line to the government. But as the newspaper is in fact published by permission of the State, the latter will necessarily have the last word. Moreover, in order to counter such opposition, the Czechoslovak Communists from the beginning sought to introduce definite rules. They wanted a new press law to legalize the post-war de facto situation of the press which was in part without a legal basis. A draft law prepared by the Ministry of Information, which was dominated by the Communists after 1945, provided for total control and organization of the press. It sought, notably, to exclude the possibility that a group might constitute itself as a new company and claim to be allowed to issue its own paper and solicit a license for publications. It was, however, impossible to find a legal formula satisfying both the Communists and the Democrats to embody the principles announced at the liberation. It was only after the assumption of power by the Communists that the whole planning of the press found a legal basis.

It is true, as Kingsley Martin has said, that until the coup of February 1948, Czechoslovak newspapers were able to inform their readers and comment on events with complete freedom; it is not quite correct to say that the post-war changes gave journalists greater freedom than they had enjoyed before the war. There was, in the first place, a vast purge in professional circles led by the Communists, who dominated the Ministries of Information and Interior as well as the different professional organizations and then a single trade union was formed to which all journalists had to belong in order to exercise their profession. In practice this meant that a journalist could only work subject to the approval of the Communist Party.

Thus before 1948 freedom of the press in Czechoslovakia was already considerably restricted, by the licensing system, the "closed shop" of organizations authorized to publish newspapers, the controls over means of publication and supplies of newsprint by a ministry dominated by the Communists and the compulsory incorporation of all journalists in a single association. What occurred later can well appear as a logical consequence of the press's evolution from 1945, supported by statesmen whose democratic convictions are above all suspicion but whose foresight turned out to be singularly defective.

The Prague coup d'Etat and its consequences

During the fateful days of February 1948 the Communists soon managed to muzzle the newspapers that were opposed to them. Some of these found their newsprint supplies cut off. Others were censored by typographers or were occupied by workers' militia and changed name from one day to the other.

On the instructions of the Communist Party the typographers of *Svobodne Noviny*, the organ of the Federation of Cultural Organizations, refused to print the paper so long as Ferdinand Peroutka remained its editor-in-chief. The latter was one of the most eminent figures of contemporary Czech journalism. He had been a victim of Nazism but subsequently did not hesitate to oppose all Russian interference in his country's internal affairs. As a result, he was condemned to forced labor, which he was able to avoid by fleeing the country.

Out of the ten Prague dailies, the editors-in-chief of half of them were forced to resign in more or less analogous circumstances to those which led to the removal of Peroutka.

Soon after their successful coup the Communists suppressed a certain number of papers, and about fifty editors-in-chief and journalists were expelled from the press union.

The number of dailies, 44 at the beginning of 1948, was reduced by half at the end of that year while the number of political weeklies dropped to a quarter of the previous total.

The press's alignment to the Soviet model proceeded at a rapid pace. A few weeks after the Communist revolution a new constitution was proclaimed which, while guaranteeing to everyone the right to express his own opinions, at the same time declared this right to be limited by the law and consideration of the public interest.

The main constitutional clause concerning the press was the following : "Freedom of the press is guaranteed ; *thus in principle it is forbidden to subject the press to pre-publication censorship.* The law decides who has the right to publish newspapers and reviews, and under what conditions, particularly in order to ensure that profit should not be the aim of publishers."

This law came into force on December 20, 1950. Its first article states : "It is the duty of the press to assist in the constructive efforts and struggle for peace of the Czechoslovak people *and to contribute to their education towards Socialism.* Press publications, newspapers, magazines, and other periodicals may not be objects of private enterprise."

The law also states that it is the function of the Ministry of Information to control the publication and distribution of periodicals, and goes on to enumerate the categories of organizations which can be authorized to publish a paper : political parties forming part of the National Front, public services, and the principal cultural, economic and social organizations.

To the legal restrictions imposed by the above measures, there can be added the practical control stemming from the choice of editors-in-chief and executive editors of papers. Most of these are members of the Communist Party from where they receive their instructions. The editors of the organs of minority parties depend entirely on the approval of the Communist Party, thus their independence is just as limited.

In addition to its control of the press, the Communist Party has in fact taken over control of all means of information. Already since 1945 it had almost absolute power over the radio and all other information services, but after its coup d'Etat it further assured its complete domination over the news agency C. T. K., which since 1948 has, like TASS, enjoyed the monopoly of all news distribution. Slowly but surely, the former became the simple extension of the latter, and the Czechoslovak press became permeated with texts from Russian sources to such a point that it has been possible to speak of a real Russification.

In an article on the "Russification of the means of information in Eastern Europe," [1] the Yugoslav journalist Vladimir Dedijer, member of the United Nations Commission on Freedom of Information and of the Press, quotes some eloquent statistics resulting from an analysis of the principal Czechoslovak daily, *Rude Pravo,* central organ of the Communist Party. These include the following :

[1] *Etudes de Presse,* Paris, Vol. V, No. 6.

From the middle of 1947 till the middle of 1948, 80 % of the news published in *Rude Pravo* on foreign affairs came from national sources, only 3 % being supplied by TASS News Agency. But from June 1951 till June 1952, 43.6 % of foreign news published in the paper came from national sources while the percentage from TASS had risen to 46.4 %.

While in March 1946, *Rude Pravo* had published 27 editorials on foreign affairs written by Czechoslovak journalists and three by Russian journalists, in March 1951, 41 out of the 82 editorials published during the month, in fact one half of them, came from the pens of Soviet authors.

In February 1946, *Rude Pravo* devoted 8.1 % of its columns to news of the U. S. S. R. In February 1951 this percentage had doubled.

At the end of his analysis Vladimir Dedijer says : "*Rude Pravo* is today from the first to last page a faithful copy of Moscow's *Pravda*. Even the typographical arrangement of its articles seeks to be a complete imitation of *Pravda*."

Thus the whole press became assailed by a flow of copy from Russian or Russian-inspired sources which proved impossible to curtail. At the beginning of 1952 the review *Tvorba*, although edited by Communists, was suppressed. It was accused among other things of having published only 180 articles on Soviet affairs out of a total of 617 during the course of 1951. Although of the remainder, 98 articles on foreign affairs reflected the Soviet and anti-Western line, none of the 322 texts devoted to national affairs mentioned the U. S. S. R. as a model.

As far as internal news is concerned, only items from official sources are published. Restrictions are very severe. The list of State secrets which appeared in the Official Gazette at the beginning of 1953 mentions, apart from military secrets (which also include news of food reserves and transport), a series of political and economic secrets. The first of these includes news of negotiations and treaties between Czechoslovakia and other States, as well as other events concerning foreign affairs and external commerce, so long as these have not been made public by the government itself. Economic secrets comprise facts about agriculture, commerce or communications which the government had decided not to make public. These also include information relating to the amount of money in circulation and provisions concerning the import and export of individual products.

Since these rules apply to foreign correspondents to the same extent as to the Czechoslovak press, it becomes impossible for a journalist accustomed to Western standards of reporting to carry out his job without perpetually running the risk of breaking the law.

This fundamental divergence between Western and Communist conceptions of reporting was at the root the trouble afflicting William Oatis, correspondent of the Associated Press in Prague, who was accused of espionage and imprisoned from April 23, 1951, till May 17, 1953.

However, even among Czechoslovak journalists who had rallied to the regime there were some who found these restrictions intolerable. The more courageous of them aired their grievances during the brief period of the "thaw" in the first half of 1956.

A brief "thaw"

In a bold piece of self-criticism, the editorial staff of the *Pravda* of Pilsen admitted that newspapers had become propaganda organs of unsurpassable boredom and that journalists had imitated Soviet methods in the most servile fashion. "Our press has kept quiet about things that were common knowledge. For example, last year Pilsen suffered from a flood that even reached our offices : but there was not a word of this in the paper !" In the Prague weekly *Literarni Noviny*, a journalist told the truth about the failure of an industrial combine in Slovakia, a failure which led to the condemnation of innocent engineers. In an article entitled, "What the newspapers did not say," the author admitted : "I have known this for a long time, but I can only write about it today : my professional honor is tarnished by conformism, silence and cowardice."

However, even during this period of the "thaw," the Czechoslovak press made no mention of a very important press conference given for foreign correspondents in Prague by Arthur London, one of several others accused in the Slansky trial. On this occasion he revealed the manner in which false confessions had been extracted from him. In October 1956 all the local press published an identical communiqué announcing the liberation of Madame Svermova, another of the accused in the same trial. This communiqué is typical of the Communists' conception of the role of information in the State : it contained no indications of who, in fact, Mme. Svermova was, why she had been condemned, or why she had been liberated. During this same period the correspondent of A. F. P. in Prague was able to find out, incidentally, in the course of an interview with the Minister of Religious Affairs that Mgr. Beran, the archbishop of Prague, was no longer in prison but under house arrest, and that two Slovak bishops had been released·"some time ago." This news, which was immediately reported to the whole world, was not taken up by the C. T. K. News Agency and was not published in a single Czechoslovak newspaper, even though it originated from the country's own Ministry of Religious Affairs.

In the summer of 1956, while the new trend of liberalization was only beginning to reach its climax in Poland and Hungary, the "thaw" in the Czechoslovak press was already coming to an end.

In the month of June the First Secretary of the Communist Party issued a severe warning to journalists which came as a blow to those who had been looking forward to a certain liberalization in the press along Polish lines. Since then the Czechoslovak press has once again become more or less as rigid and conformist as before the "thaw." Certain nonconformist opinions which had been expressed especially in some literary reviews thus remained efforts without any further consequences.

In June 1957 the Second Congress of Czechoslovak Journalists adopted a resolution calling on journalists to "fight more energetically against liberalism devoid of principles, especially against open or diguised revisionism." The resolution went on to say: "It is impossible to become a good socialist journalist if one is not convinced of the justice of our struggle for the victory of Socialism and prepared to devote one's work and whole life to this struggle."

Eastern Germany

At the end of the Second World War, most of the press that was still active in Germany either belonged to the National Socialist Party or was directly subjected to State control. Since the Nazis seized power in 1933, the whole of the country's press had been transformed into what Goebbels called a "guiding instrument in the service of the nation's political education." [1] The levelling-out process was complete ; the press and radio were subjected to the direct control of the government and a journalist could exercise his profession only after official authorization. The law of October 4, 1933, known as " Schriftleitergesetz " defined the activity of an editor as a public activity regulated by the State. The only example of resistance to the Third Reich in the German press was a certain satirical form of writing, very much disguised and reaching only a small audience of intellectuals.

It is evident that the occupying powers could not tolerate such a state of affairs and thus after 1945 immediately set about transforming the German press. The United States, France, Great Britain and the Soviet Union agreed among themselves that the new press should seek to open the eyes of Germans to the crimes committed by Hitler and help to create the necessary conditions for the peaceful and democratic development of their country. In order to ensure that newspapers were managed by reliable people, it was decided to apply a system of registration before publication, and it was at this point that the first open differences occurred in the methods adopted by East and West. The three Western Powers granted licenses not only to newly established democratic parties, but also to private individuals as well as independent groups of individuals. In the Soviet-occupied zone, however, licenses to publish

---

[1] In *Mein Kampf*, Hitler said : "The State must unhesitatingly assure itself of the complete control of the press, as an instrument for educating the people which must be placed at the service of the State and the Nation."

were given almost exclusively to parties and mass organizations. Moreover, right from the beginning, censorship in this zone was very much stricter than that existing in the Western zones. In fact censorship in Western Germany imposed at the beginning of the occupation, was abolished after a few years before the Federal Republic had become a sovereign State. On the other hand, in the East, censorship was never relaxed. Thus this part of Germany has not known freedom of the press for a quarter of a century.

Structure of the press

The German People's Republic has inherited what used to be the Soviet-occupied zone constituted in 1945. A new kind of press created by the occupation authorities has remained more or less unchanged during the post-war years. Its structure is the equivalent of that existing in every Communist People's Republic. All the principal newspapers are the central organs of the various parties and mass organizations : *Neues Deutschland* (Socialist Unity Party—i.e. Communist), *Neue Zeit* (Christian Democrat Union), *Der Morgen* (Liberal Democratic Party), *National-Zeitung* (National Democratic Party), *Bauern-Echo* (Democratic Peasant Federation), *Tribüne* (Trade Unions Federation), *Junge Welt* (Free German Youth). Only one of the main papers, the daily *Berliner Zeitung*, is not published as the official organ of a party or organization. However, it is edited in an office of the Socialist Unity Party, which also publishes the only popular paper in the Republic : *BZ am Abend*. Its precursor *Nacht-Express*, tried for many years to keep its readers informed as objectively as possible, but was forced by the authorities to close down in 1953. All the above newspapers appear in East Berlin and are distributed throughout the Republic, except for the last. In addition to these, the parties and other organizations edit a series of local and regional papers.

There are no official statistics concerning the circulation of newspapers in East Germany. According to reliable sources, the total circulation of the 39 papers (with their 277 local editions) reaches between $3 \frac{1}{2}$ and 4 millions thus providing an average of one newspaper for every five persons. According to unofficial

sources, the circulation figures are divided as follows : Socialist
Unity Party: 2,600,000 ; Christian Democrat Union: 200,000 ; Liberal
Democratic Party: 200,000 ; National Democratic Party: 150,000 ;
Trade Unions Federation: 125,000; Free German Youth: 150,000.
The ratio between the Communist or Communist-controlled press
and the so-called bourgeois press is four to one.

The situation in Berlin

The differences between this controlled press and the free press
·according to Western democratic standards appear in their most
striking form in the politically divided city of Berlin. West Berlin
has nine dailies of which the following six are morning papers :
Der Tagesspiegel, Telegraf, Der Tag, B. Z., Berliner Morgenpost
and *Spandauer Volksblatt*. The evening papers are : *Der Kurier,
Der Abend* and *Nachtdepesche*. In addition to these, local editions
of the Hamburg papers *Die Welt* and *Bild* are also published in
Berlin. In their level, style, make-up, illustrations, format and
contents, all these papers differ greatly from each other and appeal
to a wide circle of readers, not to specific social groups. They all
have their own political line without being subject to parties,
organizations or the government.

Although the newspapers of West Berlin are completely cut off
from the Federal Republic, where they hardly penetrate, they are
of the same style as those of Western Germany. Like these, they
developed after the war under the tutelage of the Western Powers.
But both West Berlin and West German papers have remained
attached to the German traditions of journalism that existed before
Hitler and they resemble their counterparts in other Western
countries much less than the East Berlin and East German press
imitate their Soviet model.

There are no contacts between the press of the two sectors
of Berlin. Newspapers of the Western sector have been banned in
the Eastern sector and in retaliation, the Senate of West Berlin
has taken the same action with respect to papers from the Eastern
sector. Whoever goes from West to East Berlin has to hand in his
Western newspapers to the control posts of the German People's

Republic. However, many East Berliners go to the Western sector
to buy the newspapers which are sold at a discount for those living
in East Germany.

Thus in the old German capital there is no real coexistence
between the two press systems. Western and Eastern newspapers
can never be found side by side in kiosks. The only means of
observing the differences is by crossing from one sector to the other.
Moreover in ·Eastern Germany not only are West Berlin papers
banned but also papers of the Federal Republic and those of other
Western countries with the exception of certain Communist Party
papers. To be in possession of Western newspapers can lead to severe
penalties for inciting hatred, imperilling the security of the State
and other analogous offenses.

Exterior appearance of the press

Contrary to the Berlin tradition, the principal newspaper of the
German People's Republic, *Neues Deutschland,* is printed in large
size with seven columns. It has the same format as the old *Völkischer
Beobachter,* the central organ of the National Socialist Party.
The other papers of East Berlin are smaller in size. In its make-up,
Neues Deutschland tends to be fairly sensational : each issue contains
glaring headlines well spaced and heavily underlined. The front page
often gives the appearence of a manifesto.

Pictures are particularly poor in the East German press, due
in part to the poor quality of the newsprint. The Party papers
publish long editorials and reproduce if possible in full the speeches
of Party leaders. In the inside pages, usually copious commentaries
prevent a lively make-up ; moreover, all news is long-winded while
brief light news items play only a minor role. Advertising is
almost negligible compared to that of Western newspapers. The
only slight exceptions to this general picture are *Berliner Zeitung*
with its evening edition and *Junge Welt.*

Contents of newspapers

As in the case of the press in all Communist countries, the contents of the newspapers in East Germany are largely determined well in advance. Planning includes three phases : a three-monthly plan of " perspectives " which is inspired by general directives from the authorities ; a monthly plan which concerns in more detail the subjects to be broached as well as the authors and dates of publication of the principal articles ; finally the weekly or daily plan which deals with latest developments and allots the space for each item. These plans emanate from the " editorial college " which consists of the manager of the establishment, the editor-in-chief and his assistant as well as the two other principal editors.

The principle of topicality which in the Western press determines the choice of articles and headings, plays only a secondary role in the East German press as in the press of other Communist countries. The front page headline and the make-up depend solely on political criteria. Sensational news which has nothing to do with politics is not published though occasionally it is to be found in the inside pages of the paper. When in October 1957, the Deutschland-halle, the largest sports stadium in Europe, was reopened for the first time after the war, the press of East Berlin did not breathe a word of the event, a good example of the disregard shown by East German editorial staffs towards the interests of the readers and their efforts to ignore non-political events which nevertheless are of great local importance.

Periodical content analyses have shown to what extent the reporting of the East Zone's newspapers is systematically tendentious. One of these analyses dealt with the press of East Berlin in 1946. [1] During the period under study, 55 to 70 per cent of news about the United States and Great Britain appearing in the newspapers of the Russian Sector was unfavorable to these countries, while only 10 to 30 per cent was favorable. The principal cliches used were the following :

---

[1] An Analysis of the Soviet-Controlled Berlin Press, by W. P. Davison, in *Public Opinion Quarterly* (II/1), 1947.

The American economy is constantly in a state of crisis ;
Policy-making in Washington is in the hands of reaction-
aries ;
With its dollar diplomacy, the United States pursues im-
perialistic aims ;
All reasonable Americans want to cooperate with the
U. S. S. R ;
The British Empire is disintegrating.

A more recent content analysis of the East German press was
made in January 1957, under the auspices of the Infratest Institute
at Munich, and dealt with six dailies considered as the most
representative of the press as a whole in the German People's
Republic.[1] According to this inquiry various types of items were
distributed among each paper as follows :

	Neues Deutschl.	Volks-stimme	Die Union	Sächs. Tagebl.	Junge Welt	Tribüne
	%	%	%	%	%	%
Political	29	20	23	18	17	24
Ideological	16	10	5	3	19	14
Economic	18	14	4	6	8	24
Topical	3	3	2	2	3	1
Other events	2	9	5	5	1	1
Culture and entertainment	18	16	30	31	34	19
Sport	8	9	7	10	11	8
Readers' letters	1	0	0	1	4	3
Advertising	4	17	23	22	3	4
Other items	1	2	1	2	0	2
	100	100	100	100	100	100

In addition to the kind of items current in the Western press,
East German papers lay particular stress on ideological items.
Their coverage in this field varies between 3 and 19 per cent of that
of the whole newspaper. It is especially important in the organs

[1] *Analyse der sowjetzonalen Presse,* Infratest-Institut, Munich-Hamburg, 1957.

of the Socialist Unity Party and its dependents, but it does not play such a large part in " bourgeois " papers where controversial or light material takes precedence. Another revealing result of the inquiry is the particularly low proportion of readers' letters in the newspapers examined.

An analysis of non-political news items shows that 40 per cent of these are concerned with presenting the West in as bad a light as possible—i. e. suicides for economic reasons, accidents at work due to lack of protection measures for workers, lack of traffic discipline, etc. This sort of news is used by the press to " unmask " capitalism without adding any further comment.

A survey of coverage of the Federal German Republic reveals that almost all news about the country is based on one of the following themes :

Bonn conducts a militaristic policy ;

German youth refuses to do military service ;

Fascism is once again raising its head ;

Workers are exploited ;

Monopoly Capitalists reign supreme behind the scenes ;

" Good patriots " are imprisoned.

Although the flow of the news is directly controlled in the press of East Germany—as it is in all other Communist countries—it would be wrong to assume that apart from the ideological sphere, the press lacks all elements of diversity. The Infratest Institute reached the following conclusion : " Here, it is not a question of uniformity. Uniformity does exist but only so far as sources of information are concerned. However, the actual individual newspapers differ from one another quite considerably."

These differences manifest themselves according to the class of readers the paper is designed to serve. Thus the readers of the "bourgeois" press have smaller doses of political and ideological material to swallow than do those of the Communist press. Moreover, the cultural and entertainment sphere is more developed in the " bourgeois " newspapers and in those belonging to mass organizations than in the organs of the Socialist Unity Party. The trade union organ *Tribüne* contains the largest coverage of economic affairs. The Youth paper offers the best coverage of sport and also has the best pictures.

Choice and preparation of items

The students of the Institute of Journalism at the University of Leipzig have to learn the following rule : " News must serve the purpose of agitation through facts. This form of agitation is particularly effective because it appeals directly to the reader's need for information."

Precise rules have been devised for the manipulation of news in the above sense. Thus the soldiers of the N. A. T. O. countries are always called " mercenaries." The principal Conservative politicians of the West are referred to as "warmongers" or "Fascists." All opinions or actions that are not in accordance with the Communist line are termed " counter-revolutionary." Reports and comment on Western Germany and the West in general, place second rate personalities in the limelight and play up minor events when these can serve the purpose of Pankow's information services. News of second rate interest which can be used for ideological ends serve as the pretext for commentaries and are in this way developed into significant events. On the other hand, actual falsehoods are rarely found. The principal methods used are the tendentious presentation of facts and exaggeration.

It is by such methods that the press of East Berlin has been able to convey a very negative impression of the West even while using Western sources. The above-mentioned analysis of contents of 1946 also established the following: "*Nacht-Express* then controlled by the Soviets and precursor of *BZ am Abend* published on its front page, during the period under review, 70 per cent of its news from Western sources (A. P., U. P., Reuter) and only 30 per cent from Eastern sources. (The monopoly of the East German agency A. D. N. did not exist at the time.) Even so, in this paper, items unfavorable to the West by far exceeded favorable references. This inaccurate picture of the West was not due to deliberate falsification but to the partial selection of news."

Control of the press

Theoretically, freedom of the press is guaranteed in East Germany. Article 9 of the Constitution says : "All citizens enjoy the right to express their opinions openly and publicly, within the limits of the laws applicable to everyone. No one should be hindered while making use of this right. There is to be no censorship." In practice this fundamental principle is deprived of all substance by laws and restrictions which classify all expression of opinion contrary to the government as " attempts to boycott democratic institutions," " attempts to restore militarism " or " manifestations of hatred of peoples," all of which are punishable offenses.

Furthermore, newspapers are subjected to six forms of control by government and Party organs, in the first instance by the "Presseamt" created in 1947 and attached to the Prime Minister's staff on December 29, 1952.

1. In the German People's Republic, a licensing system is maintained. The only papers that can appear are those authorized by the " Presseamt." This institution continues the policies of the Soviet military administration introduced in 1945, by which licenses were granted only to parties of the "democratic bloc" and to mass organizations under the auspices of the Communists.

2. The " Presseamt " regulates the distribution of newsprint. During the first years after the war, when the allocation of quotas was in the hands of the Soviets, several newspapers which had strayed from the official line were obliged to cease publication because they were denied their ration of newsprint. Even today, a deviationist newspaper can be brought into line by the cutting down of its newsprint supplies.

3. The Central Committee of the Socialist Unity Party, or to be more precise, its " agitation and propaganda " section, sends a confidential report several times a week to all Communist editors which fixes down to the last detail the political program from day to day. These directives state which events have to be played up and which have to be played down. They

act as the basis of editorial conferences. Furthermore, the editorial staffs are constantly in touch by telephone with the Central Committee's press section, and every so often conferences are called for Party officials concerned with press affairs, and editors-in-chief. These conferences are the occasion for discussing and criticizing the work of newspapers and for letting the editors know the "material for argumentation" that is to be used. At times, the Party authorities also prepare articles which the newspapers are obliged to print. As the *Neues Deutschland* is run directly by the secretariat of the Central Committee of the Socialist Unity Party, it often happens that this paper is charged with issuing instructions to other papers. In exceptional cases it even controls the entire foreign news coverage for the whole of the East German press. Thus during the Polish crisis of 1956, correspondents in Warsaw were instructed to channel all their messages through this paper.

4. For the non-Communist newspapers, control is exercised through the " Presseamt." It operates in exactly the same way as the press section of the Central Committee of the Socialist Unity Party except that its directives assume the more moderate form of " recommendations." Because of the close links between government and Party in the German People's Republic, the government press bureau is responsible not only to the Prime Minister but also to the central committee of the Socialist Unity Party. Thus in practice, the " bourgeois " press is also directed by the Party.

An example

In a special interview for this present study, the ex-editor of the Dresden daily *Sächsische Neueste Nachrichten,* Walter Ulbrich, who fled from East Germany at the beginning of 1957, gave an account of the controls to which his paper, an organ of the National Democratic Party, was subjected. First of all the "Presseamt" informs the Party authorities of the themes to be given greatest importance and those to be kept in the background. The Party authorities then send these

directives to the newspapers adding their own particular comments. The contents of the papers are systematically examined
and analyzed by government officials in charge of press control.
If they find any failings or deviations from the official line,
a meeting is called to discuss these points with the Party
executive. In fact, it is the latter and not the chief editor of the
newspaper which assumes the primary responsibility for the
current political line. In general, according to Mr. Ulbrich,
the " Presseamt " tries to avoid giving an editorial staff the
impression that it is being supervised. When from time to
time, one of its officials visits a newspaper office, relations are
usually courteous.

The Presseamt's "recommendations" can, for example,
appear as follows : [1]

— Publish several items on the economic crisis in West Germany;
  allude to the burden of defense expenditure and its contribution to this crisis.
— Draw attention to the divergent opinions within the Coal
  and Steel Community—stress these differences.
— In Churchill's speech emphasize especially the passages in
  which he calls for equal treatment of China.
— Publish a series of photographs of fighters for peace imprisoned in West Germany.

Instructions are also sent by teleprinter from the A. D. N.
News Agency. These, however, are concerned only with news,
they never deal with comment and rarely with the presentation
of news. However, they generally indicate the degree of
urgency of particular news items.

5. The choice of editors of the Communist newspapers and those
of mass organizations is in the hands of the personnel section
of the Central Committee of the Socialist Unity Party. Nobody
can be officially employed without the assent of this organ. In
the case of the "bourgeois" newspapers, work permits are issued

[1] The example is taken from directives issued between May 9 and 16, 1953.

by the "Verband der Deutschen Presse"—a unique institution
under Communist direction. A candidate for an editorial post
must be first and foremost reliable from a political and ideological
point of view ; this is a *sine qua non* for his admission. In
principle, every regular journalist must have followed an official
course in journalism under the auspices of the Party. The aim of
such a course is to strengthen an editor's ideological background
and to give him a better conception of the usefulness of news to
the State. A government decree of October 20, 1953 in fact
obliges all new editors to attend the courses in the faculty of
journalism at Leipzig University for three years.

Methods of recruitment and training of editors also seek
to eliminate the conception of pure journalism ; in other words
they discard those who believe that the main function of a paper
is not to serve the Party but to inform the public. East Germany's
journalists' publication, *Neue Deutsche Presse* states in its issue
of April 1950 : "One of our colleagues affirmed that he thought
that as a reporter, he should only describe actual facts and should
tell the truth. We had to make it clear to him that the role of
journalists nowadays consists in forming public opinion, thus
participating positively in the realization of our aims." The
recruiting authorities also consider it of great importance that
at least half of the journalists on editorial staffs should come
from the working class. One of the rules of the "Verband der
Deutschen Presse" issued on March 27, 1950 stipulates that it
will recognize as professional journalists only those coming from
the working class or the peasantry.

6. Perhaps the most effective of controls is the monopoly of the
News Agency A. D. N. (Allgemeiner Deutscher Nachrichten-
dienst). It was founded in 1946 and is the only news agency in
East Germany since the Sowjetische Nachrichtenbüro ceased
operating in 1950 ; it became a State institution on May 1, 1953.
It is under the orders of the Prime Minister and depends financially on the State. The manager, editor-in-chief and principal
assistant editors are members of the Socialist Unity Party. The
A. D. N.'s wire service is in fact the only source of information
for the press of East Germany apart from local news. Inside the

country, the agency has offices in 14 districts ; abroad it has correspondents in all the capitals of Communist countries. However, the largest part of A. D. N.'s foreign service is taken from TASS and from other agencies of the Communist bloc. At times, news from Western sources, for example, the West German D. P. A., is also used. By selecting all information, the A. D. N. in practice acts as a censorship. It should be stressed that the distribution of Western newspapers inside editorial offices is so strictly controlled that even feature editors often have to depend entirely on the A. D. N. service.

Effects of the "thaw"

In the German People's Republic, the so-called "new look" became apparent long before the XXth Congress of the Soviet Communist Party in 1956 and even before the "thaw" which began in Poland the previous year. It was one of the consequences of the revolt of June 17, 1953 and thus brought about the first example of liberalization in the press of a country in the Soviet orbit.

Putting on one side official directives which were being issued at the time by the "Presseamt," Fred Oelssner, one of the secretaries of the Socialist Unity Party (who was later disgraced) advised newspapers to break the monotony of their contents by offering their readers, apart from political propaganda, a certain amount of entertainment reading. As a result, home news became more comprehensive and comment was slightly freer. But the promoters of this new look were careful enough to stress that the current efforts to make newspapers more attractive should in no way alter the fundamental character of the "popular press." Thus in East Germany, liberalization in the press never reached the degree of freedom achieved at certain periods in Hungary and Poland.

The press began to make amends for its past behavior by admitting that it had represented events too optimistically and even confessed to having falsified news and readers' letters. Not only did it begin to publish items of greater entertainment value with official approval, but also printed news of accidents, disasters and other various events in the country.

The editors of the satirical magazine *Eulenspiegel* were able to write : "As long as there exist so many shortcomings around us, we are not able to fight capitalism with enthusiasm." In an effort to win back the public's confidence in the government and the Party, newspapers have been made more attractive while new publications have been created in which political news is presented less dogmatically and in smaller quantities. One of these publications, *Wochenpost*, devotes whole pages to news stories, cultural affairs, fashions, short stories and humorous features. Another one, *Das Magazin*, publishes accounts of criminals, light articles on films and the theater, and even photographs of "pin-up girls." However, the general policy of news reporting and selecting has not been altered.

Readers of the East German press have been very badly informed of developments in countries of the Eastern bloc, especially in Poland and Hungary. *Neues Deutschland* once gave the following explanation : "Our reports from Poland and Hungary deliberately concentrate on everything that reinforces socialism in these countries and the cause of socialism in general. These are the criteria we use." In October 1956, a whole edition of *Wochenpost* (amounting to 850,000 copies) had to be destroyed on orders from the "Presseamt" because its Warsaw correspondent had reported too openly on the Poznan trial. The Infratest Institute's survey of 1957 shows that news about "revisionist" tendencies in the Eastern bloc represented only a meager fraction of total coverage. During the period under examination, news of the discussions concerning a revision of the line of the Socialist Unity Party did not include more than 2,2 per cent of the contents of the group of newspapers studied. [1]

From the second half of 1957, controls on the East German press became once again more rigid. The weekly satirical paper *Eulenspiegel* has repeatedly run into trouble over its indiscretions which have been condemned as "infamous defamations of Socialist reality." It has changed its editor-in-chief twice during the period of about a year. In October 1957, the weekly literary paper *Sonntag* was seized for having made fun of a plan for the intensive cultivation of maize and having implicated Khrushchev.

In the same month, Albert Norden, member of the Central

---

[1] *Analyse der sowjetzonalen Presse*, Infratest-Institut.

Committee of the Socialist Unity Party expressed his indignation at the fact that it had been possible for East German newspapers "to publish Socialist policies on their front page, while introducing 'bourgeois' politics in the features section and praising the promoters of the counter-revolution and their deeds."

Finally, the conception of the press that continues to exist in East Germany is illustrated by the definition of a newspaper given by Rudolf Herrnstadt, ex-editor-in-chief of the *Berliner Zeitung* and *Neues Deutschland* as follows : "Our newspapers are not published to entertain the public nor to earn money, but for political reasons. They are a political institution which assumes the form of a newspaper for reasons of convenience."

* * *

It is thus easy to understand how under these conditions, the exercise of their profession has become intolerable to many journalists and why as a result, a large number of these, who at the beginning had accepted the rigid system imposed on them, later from 1946 onwards decided to flee from East Germany, often to escape grave penalties for small failings. Such was the case of Walter Ulbrich of Dresden, whose crime was to have been the only editor-in-chief to publish the exchange of letters between Premier Eden and Marshal Bulganin in November 1956 over the affairs of Suez and Hungary.

Hungary

The post-Stalin phenomenon of liberalization, known to many as the "thaw," began to develop after the XXth Congress of the Communist Party of the U. S. S. R. in February 1956. It was at this Congress that the Party's First Secretary, Nikita Khrushchev, presented his famous report on the faults of the Soviet dictator. From this time onwards the "thaw" became a general phenomenon spreading throughout the Communist world. However, its first symptoms appeared as early as 1953 and its effects and consequences varied from country to country.

As seen above, in Czechoslovakia and East Germany liberal tendencies in the press were brought to a halt by the summer of 1956. The following year only a few literary reviews tried to steer timidly in the direction of further emancipation, but the Party's leadership soon put an end to such stray impulses. Yet the frequency of official warnings showed that the taste for greater freedom had by no means vanished from the editorial staffs of these countries' newspapers.

An analogous situation had also developed in Bulgaria.

During the first half of 1956 journalists had managed to assert their right to give their readers better information, about the regime's weakness and to make newspapers more lively in their presentation and content. Vladimir Topencharov, the chairman of the Bulgarian Press Association, who was at the time also editor-in-chief of *Otechestven Front,* organ of the Patriotic Front, published a severe article of self-criticism decrying his paper's past failures in the sphere of news reporting. "Contact between the paper and its readers has been lost," he wrote. Original ideas were replaced by repetition of what had already been said. Difficult questions were avoided... Statistics were never revealed. This meant that our press never talked of any failures, except those of minor importance. Since the press has failed to tell the whole truth, it has failed to carry out its role of agitator, propagandist and educator of the people." This same journalist went so far as to publish during the same period a story presenting May Day as a fancy dress parade for "bureaucrats, informers, careerists and other impostors." After this tirade he was severely reprimanded and was obliged to issue an apology.

In the first half of 1956 the government relaxed its control over the press and in particular lifted some of the restrictions concerning internal news. A decree of April 24 made less rigid the legislative provisions affecting State secrets, abolished numerous restrictions and recognized that certain statistics should not necessarily be classed as confidential. But already in the latter half of the year, especially after the Hungarian uprising, control of the press reverted to its former rigidity. Many journalists had, however, acquired a taste for freedom, and since then there have been repeated warnings on this subject from the Party leadership.

In March 1957, during the Congress of the Press Association, a certain number of these were reproached for having mis-understood the meaning of " democratization" and sowing con-fusion in the minds of readers. In June the Party's doctrinal review violently attacked half a dozen publications whose editorial line was judged not to be rigid enough. It declared : "The press must on no account allow the publication of anything liable to introduce an element of confusion in public opinion or to shake its faith in the Party's cause." In January 1958 the new editor-in-chief of *Otechestven Front* as well as Topencharov, his above-mentioned predecessor who had since become his deputy, were both dismissed for "revisionism." In April of the same year the Congress of the Press Association heard a report by its committee urging the members to "work for the greater improvement of the socialist press by following the directives of the Central Committee of the Communist Party."

One of the secretaries of the Central Committee seized this occasion to condemn violently the abuses of criticism that had been appearing in the Bulgarian press, reminding the latter that it should never pass judgment on the Party or its policies. He went on to say : "Working under the constant vigilance and direction of the Communist Party, the press must serve its readers through its propaganda and agitation functions... and through its criticism of anything that is decadent and liable to hinder the people in their struggle for Socialism and Communism."

* * *

In two countries, Poland and Hungary, the "thaw" reached such considerable proportions that it merits special attention. While it lasted a long time in the former country (and therefore prompts a special chapter devoted to Poland), it ended most tragically in the latter.

During the Stalinist period the press in Hungary was as muzzled and controlled as in every other country of the Eastern bloc. In 1953 a railway disaster near Budapest claiming many victims was not reported, but some time later the papers published the news of the execution of the man suspected to have been responsible for this accident—which had never before been mentioned.

In 1950 the Politburo decided to construct an underground railway in Budapest. For technical reasons the enterprise was a failure. Some accidents occurred involving the death of numerous workmen. The press was silent. A number of houses collapsed. The press said nothing. Some engineers who had been opposed to this absurd venture were arrested as saboteurs. The press printed not a word of this either. Suddenly the truth came to light, but only in 1954 under the government of Imre Nagy.

The "Petöfi Circle"

This was the first time that a wave of freedom swept over Hungary. It was heralded by a movement of "democratization" led by writers and journalists. From 1954, and in particular in November 1955, *Irodalmi Ujsag* (Literary Gazette), the organ of the Hungarian Writers' Association, protested against the censorship. The Party tried to control the situation. It decided to oblige certain editors-in-chief to attend ideological courses and pass examinations in subjects relating to these courses. But this did not put a stop to mounting popular ferment. Several journalists in the company of other intellectuals began to attend meetings of the "Petöfi Circle" in Budapest. Their most important meeting took place on June 27, 1956 and was devoted in particular to problems of the press. On this occasion a certain number of journalists who had lost their jobs during the Stalin period were rehabilitated.

Contrary to a widely held view, the "Petöfi Circle" was not a brotherhood of agitators, but included also Communists and invited strict Stalinist members of the Party to its debates. One of these, Marton Horvath, editor-in-chief of *Szabad Nep,* the central organ of the Communist Party, was invited to preside at the session of June 27. However, he soon rapidly lost control of proceedings. Some journalists and writers impetuously demanded freedom of the press. Tibor Meray, known for his reports on bacteriological warfare in Korea, admitted that he had lied from beginning to end, by orders from above. The poet Kuczka declared : "Nationalization of the press is responsible for its decline and its incredibly low standards in Hungary."

At the beginning of autumn the emancipation of the press made fresh progress. On October 6, 1956, the Executive Committee of the Federation of Hungarian Journalists meeting to pay tribute to the memory of Minister Rajk and his companions, who had been victims of a faked trial, adopted a resolution proclaiming the right to truth. "We will never in future permit the press to abandon its role of defending truth by becoming an instrument for slandering and persecuting innocent people."

A general assembly of the Federation was convened in Budapest on October 28, with a view to standing up against "the system which hitherto has been based upon lies" and to "take account of this crime committed against the people." The assembly was also expected to draw up a text which could serve as the draft of a new law guaranteeing the freedom of the press and the status of journalists.

This assembly, however, never met, for several days before it was due, the revolution broke out.

The press during the revolution

During the last week of October 1956, Hungary, ravaged by fire and blood, had once again a free press. The blossoming of numerous newspapers both in the capital and the provinces, appearing in such circumstances, shows to what point the thirst for a free press is apparent in a country where all traditional liberties had been curtailed. Robert Kroon, special correspondent of the N. B. C. and the Netherlands Radio, reported that one could see all over Budapest newspaper vendors in kiosks installed amongst the ruins to cater for the new demand for newspapers.

It is important to note that this free Hungarian press suddenly blossoming out in the midst of the insurrection and reflecting diverse tendencies was to a large extent the work of journalists who had once belonged to the Communist Party or who had been prepared to co-operate with it.

The role of journalists in the preparation of the Hungarian insurrection has been widely recognized, and nowhere more so than in Communist ruling circles themselves. In 1957 the Minister of State Marosan stated that they (the journalists) had been primarily responsible for the "counter-revolution" the previous autumn. It is true that certain individuals of a doubtful past had infiltrated as new members into the union of journalists.

All that is known of the Hungarian press during the insurrection makes it possible to affirm that this press was really authentic and democratic. Not one of these newspapers appearing from one day to the other advocated the return of property to the landlords, or factories to the capitalists. Instead of appeals to Fascism and reaction, they contained policy statements of liberal and Socialist leanings. The one and only openly extreme right-wing paper did not manage to publish more than one issue: for on the following day the typographers refused to print it. [1]

In the first editorial of *Nepszava*, the organ of the reconstituted Social-Democratic Party, Anna Kethly wrote amongst other things : "Today we have managed to leave one prison, and we will not tolerate efforts to turn our country into yet another prison of just a different color." Another paper, *Magyar Fuggetlenseg*, took exception to TASS Agency's distortion of events and suggested that next time it expressed an opinion, it should first send a correspondent to Hungary with instructions to report objectively and comprehensively. One of the first new independent dailies which appeared at this time, *Magyar Szabatsag*, chose freedom of the press as the subject of its first editorial, demanding the complete restoration of this freedom.

[1] IPI REPORT, December 1956, « A week of freedom of the press in Hungary.»

After the revolution

Hungarian journalists were to pay a heavy price for their activities after the suppression of the revolt. Many of them were arrested, some were deported to Russia, others were summarily judged and condemned to long terms of imprisonment or even sentenced to death, while still others waited for long months before any judgment was passed. More than 150 journalists were excluded from their professional activities. Many others went on strike or preferred to take up another career.

One of these many tragic cases is that of the journalist and playwright Joszef Gali and his colleague Gyula Obersovsky, who, during the insurrection, had edited a paper called *Igaszag* (Truth) and later a clandestine organ containing, according to the accusation, "articles against the government and the U. S. S. R." After a court of first instance had sentenced them to terms of imprisonment, the Supreme Court sitting in June 1957 reconsidered the sentence, subsequently invoking the death penalty without any new facts having been advanced. The indignation which this provoked in the outside world led the Kadar government to revise its judgment. Obersovsky was finally condemned to life imprisonment while Gali received a prison sentence of 15 years.

Trials were still taking place well into 1958. In July the International Press Institute delivered an indignant protest against recent condemnations of Hungarian journalists "who, during the revolution in October 1956, pursued their calling in accordance with the principles of freedom of information which the Institute is set up to defend."

Miklos Gimes, who was executed at the same time as Imre Nagy and General Pal Maleter, never took up any official position during the revolutionary period. He participated in the creation of the paper *Magyar Szabatsag* and served on its editorial board. This paper, like others that were founded in the same period, defended the principle of freedom of expression. After the suppression of the revolution Gimes continued to form part of the Hungarian Journalists' Association, and on November 12, 1956, at one of the latter's meetings, he made a speech in favor of the restoration of freedom of the press and against Soviet intervention which earned him the wrath of the Kadar government.

Miklos Vasarhelyi, condemned to several years' imprisonment, had been a longstanding publicist right up to the time of the revolution. He then became head of the press office of the Prime Minister Imre Nagy.

Pal Locsei, condemned a few days before to eight years' imprisonment, worked mainly as a journalist during the revolutionary period. After the suppression of the revolution in Budapest he continued publishing in Sopron a weekly supporting the ideals of the revolution, particularly freedom of expression.

In spite of this persecution a number of journalists continued to oppose the regime after the revolt had been suppressed. Those of the news agency M. T. I. announced that they would only go back to work on condition that standards of honesty and accuracy in news reporting were respected. Editors and typographers of *Nepszabadsag* went on strike on November 28, 1956 after the government had forbidden the publication of an article expressing the point of view of Marshal Tito in a polemic with Moscow's *Pravda;* on several occasions during the rest of the year newspapers in Budapest failed to appear in these circumstances. Even as late as the beginning of February 1957, Communist editors of the trade union organ *Nepakarat* left the paper because their freedom of expression had been too greatly restricted. Often the government had to turn to officials without the slightest experience of journalism in order to ensure that their papers appeared.

For its part, the population expressed its feelings by boycotting the press of the Kadar regime. On various occasions right up to the end of 1957, Communist Party papers were burnt in the streets of Budapest. At the end of November the Central Workers' Council of the capital advised its members not to buy newspapers until free publications were once again allowed to appear.

In fact, since the beginning of 1957 some so-called independent papers have received publication licenses, in particular two Catholic organs. Generally speaking, the Hungarian press has not reverted to its pre-revolutionary type. At least from the point of view of presentation, newspapers published since 1957 came to resemble much more closely their Western counterparts. More space began to be given to recreational subjects, and an effort was made to entertain readers.

At the end of 1956 the Press Federation demanded the abolition or at least the easing of censorship, the authorization to publish new newspapers, and in particular the release of imprisoned journalists. The government rejected these demands and a little later, on January 23, 1957, ordered the dissolution of the Federation. The communiqué published on this occasion stated that "this measure had been indispensable for the maintenance of public order." In its place, the government created an Information Office with the object of guiding newspapers, distributing newsprint and granting publication licenses. It also nominated a commissioner to look after the affairs of the dissolved Federation provisionally. His principal task was to prepare the plenary session of a new Press Federation "to elect democratically a new management which would enjoy the confidence of the large majority of journalists, would be composed of journalists faithful to the regime of the Democratic People's Republic, and would carry out its work in this spirit."

This meeting took place from May 31 to June 3, 1958, and the Press Federation was then reconstituted with a new management reflecting the views of the government. According to a progress report its total number of adherents is 2,200, about a thousand less than those registered in the autumn of 1956. In a speech delivered to this first post-revolutionary congress of the Hungarian press, Gyula Kallai, the Minister of State, defined the aims of this new Press Federation, declaring amongst other things : "There should never be any question of criticism that is not based on the construction of Socialism. The press has the duty of defending the policies of the Communist Party and the interests of Socialist construction against their enemies and against those who do not carry out the policy of the Party or distort it. The press thus has the duty of criticizing those who seek to retard our progress. There is no place for any other kind of criticism in our regime."

Poland

In March 1953 the Catholic weekly *Tygodnik Powszechny*, of Cracow, was suppressed by the government authorities for having refused to print a eulogy of Stalin. Thus disappeared the last periodical in Poland that did not follow the line of the ruling Party. At the end of 1956, *Tygodnik Powszechny* resumed publication under its former editor-in-chief Jerzy Turowicz and most of his former colleagues who had lost their jobs three years before. This was a consequence of the new turn of events marked by the return to power of Gomulka at the head of the United Workers Party (Communist) in October 1956. In July 1957 the Cracow weekly experienced its first open difficulties with the censorship, and in August of the following year the Polish episcopate was obliged to submit all its religious publications to the government's pre-publication censorship. This brief story of the paper's experience well summarizes and illustrates the situation of the Polish press between 1953 and 1958. [1]

* * *

The first signs of emancipation appeared almost immediately after the death of Stalin, first of all in the literary magazines. The guiding role of the Communist Party in cultural matters was questioned. So-called " social realism " was attacked, as was the servile imitation of other Soviet forms. Articles were published giving a fairly bleak picture of Polish life. This literary "Fronde" reached its culminating point when *Nowa Kultura* published the famous "Poem for Adults" by Adam Wazyk on August 21, 1955.

At this time, during the summer of 1955, most other newspapers were following the example of the literary press. In the beginning the transformation of the daily press was almost imperceptible. It became more apparent with the publication of the results of an enquiry into

[1] It is true that from July 12, 1953, to May 16, 1955 a weekly paper appeared with the title *Tygodnik Powszechny*, with the same format and presentation as the former one but edited by a completely Stalinist team, affiliated to the "Pax" group.

what readers thought of *Zycie Warszawy,* by this paper itself, on November 14, 1955. Most of the replies, even the most pointed criticism, were signed.

For instance, a Warsaw reader wrote : "Up to now, the 'chewed up' and 'digested' news has been published in a manner far too one-sided (and often neither very cleverly nor convincingly). It is high time to let the readers draw their own conclusions on the basis of information which is honest, objective and as complete as possible..."

A Poznan reader who preferred to remain anonymous stated : "More objectivity is needed in international reporting and in editorials. Exact factual information is lacking on the life of Western European countries and America.." A Warsaw reader also asked for more reports from abroad. He wrote among other things: "Why didn't *Zycie Warszawy* send anybody to the last U. N. session ? We know that interesting events take place not only in the countries of the People's Democracies but also in the West."

A reader from Labork made the following remark : "It is a shame that the Poles know so little of the outside world ; but this is chiefly the fault of the press, which has so little to offer that the citizen who wants to be informed must listen to Radio Free Europe..." In another reply along the same lines, it was said : "When a citizen commits a crime of common law or when he undermines the structure of our society and seeks asylum in the 'free world', why must the man in the street be informed of this by the London or New York radio instead of by *Zycie Warszawy* or *Trybuna Ludu* ? It is true that in this respect things are a little better now, because there was a time when the press was completely silent about such events inside our borders. From the political point of view this is clumsy, because it shakes confidence in the national press and at the same time favors the spreading of hostile and frequently fantastic rumors."

The publication of such views was of course completely unprecedented in a country of Eastern Europe at the time. The event was all the more significant in that these views were expressed in one of the leading Warsaw dailies, published by a Communist-controlled co-operative.

Were the complaints of readers heard ? Certainly a large number of them were heard. Since 1955 the Polish press as a whole has considerably improved its reporting of news, both in the case of national news as well as news from abroad. The reporting of news from the Western world has become more complete and objective, especially news concerning the United States and the German Federal Republic. In many cases the Polish press has been the first Communist press to recognize the progress achieved in many fields by these countries. The experiences of Yugoslavia's Titoist regime have been analyzed objectively, and the conditions of the countries in the Eastern bloc have not always been presented in the most favorable light.

As far as internal news was concerned, this began to be reported with fewer delays and omissions. A large number of subjects, until then classed as secret, were offered to the public, some, for instance, concerning economic questions. A typical example was the circulation of newspapers, which was revealed to the public only from 1955 onwards. Several newspapers began to broach the most delicate national questions frankly and realistically. They even broached prohibited subjects. For example, they described the poverty of workers, the increase in juvenile delinquency and alcoholism, treated such subjects as anti-Semitism and prostitution, reproduced texts that had appeared in the emigré press, wrote impartially about the army and the anti-Communist resistance during the war, and revealed the truth about the Warsaw insurrection of 1944, a subject that had remained taboo for more than ten years.

One weekly paper published by students called *Po Prostu* distinguished itself by this kind of reporting and enquiry. At the beginning of 1955 this was an obscure journal with a circulation that did not exceed 15,000, but several months later it became one of the most popular papers in Poland and increased its circulation tenfold. It will be discussed in detail below.

A new press policy

In the spring of 1956 problems concerning news reporting gave rise to very interesting debates in the Polish Parliament.

Prime Minister Cyrankiewicz declared in the course of these: " We are going to keep the press and the radio better and more widely informed of the decisions, activities and plans of the government, perhaps also passing on this information more rapidly. A citizen carries out his duties all the better, and with all the greater sense of responsibility, when he is better informed of events... It must be pointed out that, apart from some blunders and other failings, the press is carrying out its functions better and better, and particularly in recent times, has made very definite progress." On the same occasion the Prime Minister criticized some faults springing from the unnecessary exaggeration of the conception of official secrets and suggested that it would be useful to organize regular press conferences in which he would participate.

During the debate a deputy belonging to the United Workers Party (Communist) reminded his audience that "the press and radio must express dominant and healthy public opinion, not just any public opinion." Nevertheless he went on to say : "It seems to me that things have reached the point where the entire responsibility of the press should, from now on, rest on the shoulders of the editors alone. For until now, the Chief Press Control Office has in certain respects borne this responsibility."

The most important speech in this debate was made by a Catholic deputy, Edmond Osmanczyk. He recalled that during the first years of the new regime both the government and Party's attitude towards news reporting was fairly enlightened, journalists were adequately informed at press conferences, thus making for good relations between the press and government ministries and other authorities. "Then, for some reason, there came a change...

"A considerable amount of interesting news from the highest sources of the community manages to find its way into the columns of newspapers only after having come up against unimaginable difficulties, and when it does appear it is, from a psychological point of view, too late as well as being disagreeably laconic in style.

"...The only form of contact between the authorities and the press and radio that survived took the form of instructions given to editors-in-chief concerning subjects which, at a certain moment, had to be dealt with in the form of long voluminous articles...

"Things developed to such a state that newspapers, especially those of the provinces, had to renounce the very 'raison d'être' of a daily newspaper, i. e., the reporting of news... It was no exception to find one of the papers of the coastal region publishing the following statement in 1952 : 'The Polish Press Agency informs us from Warsaw that the day before yesterday a heavy storm raged on our coast...' "

Speaking of the progress made in the development of good mutual relations between the government and public opinion, the Catholic deputy expressed his regret that "anachronistic forms of propaganda should still be in vogue ; as in the old days, truth is filtered through a dropper, the caliber of this varying according to the circles concerned ; the larger these circles are, the smaller the drops."

Still speaking in the Sejm (the Polish Parliament), the same deputy attacked those who held that the press and radio should not exert pressure on the government to speed up certain decisions or to publish information, the lack of which might tend to encourage rumors. "Our State," said Osmanczyk, "is a State in which the workers are fully justified in demanding that the government adopt such and such a measure, and provide such and such an item of information. A government that does this is not capitulating to anybody... These things have to be made clear : Our press should not be, in the bourgeois sense of the word, a pro-government press. Our press is a popular press... thus its role is to serve the people." [1]

Poznan riots and trials

The reporting of the riots of Poznan at the end of June 1956, as well as that of the trials that followed in September and October, gives a good idea of the degree of freedom enjoyed by the Polish press at this time. The press, in fact, reported and commented with remarkable objectivity on these tragic events. Significantly enough, one of the first actions of the rioters was to destroy the jamming station of foreign broadcasts. While Moscow was busy attributing the riots to the activities of foreign agents, most Polish newspapers, including *Trybuna Ludu*, the central organ of the United Workers Party, saw them as the result of the miserable conditions of the proletariat. Such an admission cost Jerzy Merawski, its editor-in-chief, his post. It also cost him his position as the member of the secretariat

---

[1] This parliamentary debate, of which brief extracts have been quoted above, has been published in full in the May 1956 issue of *Prasa Polska*, the organ of the Polish Association of Journalists.

of the Central Committee specially in charge of the press and propaganda. However, he remained a secretary of the Central Committee where he played a prominent part in bringing Gomulka back to power. Newspapers also gave copious reports of the Poznan trials. Among the omissions from these reports were the revelations made during the proceedings regarding the anti-governmental and anti-Soviet character of the demonstration of June 28 which degenerated into a riot, as well as the fraternization between soldiers and rioters. One of the counsels for the defense reproached some papers for having distorted certain facts of interest to the defense. However, Western journalists who were allowed to follow the proceedings declared that on the whole the Polish press carried out its functions very well.

An event without precedent in a Communist country took place on October 3 when *Glos Wielkopolski,* one of the two Poznan dailies, apologized to its readers for not being able to present the proceedings of the previous day in any form other than the shortened version of the P. A. P. Agency. In an editorial the paper complained that "there is still not sufficient freedom for us to be able to publish these proceedings without their being subject to pre-publication censorship."

Censorship attacked

Since the end of the summer of 1956 the question of censorship had provoked many a discussion. The most significant progress in this field was the fact that the subject could be mentioned openly.

Censorship in Poland is exercised by the Chief Press Control Office, an organ attached to the Prime Minister's Office and created by a law of July 5, 1946. This law stipulates that "the Chief Office (i. e., the censorship) has the task of supervising the distribution of all kinds of works executed, among other things, by means of the printing press, in order to prevent : a) attacks on the system of government of the Polish State, b) disclosure of State secrets, c) damage to international relations of the Polish State, d) violations of law and order, e) misleading of public opinion by the publication of inaccurate information." It should be noted that in the Stalinist period, censorship exceeded in scope both the letter and spirit of this text.

Alongside the Chief Press Control Office, which is a governmental organ, there also exist two parallel organs belonging to the Party charged with supervising and guiding the press. These are the press commission of the Central Committee and the propaganda department of the same committee.

On September 20, 1956, the executive committee of the Polish Journalists' Association voted a resolution against " the unjust and unjustifiable interference of the Chief Press Control Office" and demanded the creation of a committee of journalists whose function would be to keep an eye on the activities of this Control Office and to determine the scope of its prerogatives.

On the same occasion this committee of the Press Association denounced the interference of certain Party organs in editorial affairs, their lack of comprehension with regard to the new role of the press, and above all their frank aversion to journalists.

The Plenary Assembly of the Journalists' Association meeting in Warsaw from November 30 to December 2 adopted resolutions in the same sense. (This important Assembly will be discussed below.) In the meantime voices were again raised against the press control that was still in operation outside professional circles. On October 18 the Vice-President of the Peasant Party, Stefan Ignar, called for the abolition of pre-publication censorship, and analogous demands were formulated by the Warsaw committee of Communist Youth, which also declared that the reform of news reporting was not making sufficient progress.

These views even had sympathizers within the Chief Press Control Office itself. After the incident involving *Glos Wielkopolski*, the censors of Poznan voted a resolution urging that they be disbanded. The Warsaw censors did the same, but the notice of their resolution was censored from the newspapers to whom they had delivered it for publication... on the orders of the higher censorship authorities. At the end of the year the struggle for the suppression or the considerable relaxation of press control was still indecisive. In December the director of the Polish radio's news service was dismissed for having deliberately disobeyed orders from the censorship. At the beginning of 1957 the editor-in-chief of *Po Prostu*, Eligiusz Lasota, who was elected as a Communist deputy in the elections of January 20, was again calling for the abolition of censorship. "Censorship," he declared, "is anti-democratic, and without democracy there can be no Socialism."

In fact, the Chief Press Control Office was never suppressed. However, during the most liberal phase of "Gomulkism" its attributes were considerably limited.

In general, censorship was restricted to the three following items:

1. Military information, in particular anything concerning troop movements and new armaments.

2. News concerning foreign affairs liable to provoke the Soviet Union, thus exposing Poland to pressure on the part of Moscow. For instance, it was forbidden to criticize the Soviet-Polish agreements.

3. Expressions of opinion openly opposed to Communism as a philosophy and a political system, as well as attacks against the government and its members. On the other hand, it was possible to say almost anything in the form of suggestions purporting to reform or improve Communism.

"Censorship," declared the editor-in-chief of *Po Prostu* to the correspondent of *France-soir*, "stops articles that are written explicitly against the government, but it cannot intervene in discussions which are ideological or which are considered as such."

In an article published by *Kwartalnik Prasznavczy*, the Polish press science review (I-2, 1957), Andrzej Lam analyzes the new freedom of the press vis-à-vis the authority of the Communist Party. He reaches the following three possibilities:

1. The Party permits a free exchange of views on certain subjects and, as far as these are concerned, freedom of the press is complete. For example, this applies to the sphere of the arts, which has been entirely freed from politics.

2. The Party leadership accepts certain general principles, but allows some leeway in the interpretation of details. This occurs in the philosophical sphere or in the appreciation of the Yugoslav way to Socialism. Thus "independent" newspapers can indulge in broad discussions.

3. The Party takes up a firm and unequivocal position as regards certain subjects, such as the necessity of the Soviet alliance or the prohibition of all attempts to form new parties. In these matters the whole press is obliged to accept the official line; the guiding

role of the Party must necessarily entail a limitation in freedom of expression.

Emancipation of the press

From the autumn of 1956 the very foundations of agricultural and industrial policies were questioned, some newspapers expressing their preference for the Yugoslav system of workers' councils ; these sometimes went so far as to reproduce theoretical articles appearing in the Polish emigré press and even some in Western reviews, such as *Preuves,* the review of the Congress for Cultural Freedom. During the Hungarian Revolution most of the Polish press supported the cause of the insurgents, often with very few reservations. In *Nowa Kultura* the brilliant young revisionist philosopher Leszek Kolakowski dared to question the fundamental tenets of Marxism, in particular determinism in history. But the most audacious expressions of the new trend came from *Po Prostu,* the weekly of the young intellectuals. For example, one of its contributors, Roman Zimand, broached the question (which he admitted was frankly reactionary) of whether it would not be advisable to liquidate the Party and begin at scratch in creating a new Communist Party in Poland.

Such language could not fail to provoke violent reactions from the authorities in Warsaw, and even more so in Moscow. During the bloodless revolution which brought Gomulka to power in Warsaw, Moscow's *Pravda* published on October 20, 1956, a violent diatribe against the Polish press, which it accused of sapping the foundations of the People's regime. *Pravda* quoted several examples of this so-called anti-Socialist campaign and declared : "The press, whose mission is to reinforce the people's democratic order, now daily publishes articles shaking the pillars of this system, sowing distrust and polluting readers' minds with the imported poison of an ideology alien to the workers." Attacks in this vein multiplied as time went on. Moreover, from the summer of 1956 the distribution of Polish newspapers was practically banned throughout Eastern Europe. The Russians sent formal protests to Warsaw pointing out that even the press in a bourgeois country like Finland did not indulge in such violent and partial attacks against the U. S. S. R.

Once the enthusiasm of the revolution had abated, the Polish leaders began to take greater heed of Moscow's recriminations. Gomulka and his colleagues considered it necessary to discipline some of the more outspoken journalists. But the press defended itself, since it wished to continue along the road of greater emancipation.

In fact, the "thaw" in Poland assumed different characteristics from those evident in other Communist countries apart from Hungary. It represented much more than a calculated policy of concessions granted and regulated by the central authorities. It was in fact the result of an action led from below, by the people themselves and in particular by the journalists. The press in fact played a considerable part in preparing the public for the events that led to the revolution of October 1956. However, such a role was possible only because of the differences of opinion which at the time existed amongst the leaders themselves.

For the first time in a Communist country, the task of educating the masses according to the Party line was no longer considered as the principal function of the press. But another function had now emerged alongside the official one : that of accurately reflecting the state of public opinion. According to this new conception of Polish journalism, the mission of the press was no longer viewed as serving as a one-way channel from the authorities to the people, but was now regarded as a two-way channel also keeping the authorities informed of the conditions and opinions of the people. For this reason the papers published abundant opinion polls, and were encouraged by the authorities to do so. They also offered prizes for the best letters from readers.

The adoption of this new conception had as its corollary the partial "depolitization" of the contents of newspapers. According to the orthodox Communist conception, nearly all items to a greater or lesser extent have the aim of indoctrinating the reader. According to the Polish conception—which is similar to the Yugoslav view—there should be more space for non-political items. The best example here is that of cultural articles, which have become much freer compared to the time when they, like everything else, had to follow the Party line. To this development must be added the tendency of commentators and editorialists to express their sometimes heterodox personal opinions.

Not only the role of the press has changed, but also its structure. A large number of publications appeared between the end of 1956 and the beginning of 1957, many of which included newspapers suppressed during the Stalinist period, such as *Dziennik Ludowy*, the daily organ of the Peasant Party, and *Tygodnik Powszechny*, the Catholic weekly of Cracow. On the other hand, the episcopate was not authorized to publish a daily paper, and thus the only Roman Catholic daily was *Slowo Powszechne*, which remained in the hands of the Stalinist "Pax" group, a group that cannot claim to be representative of Polish Catholicism.

Moreover, a certain number of papers became independent in that they became detached from the organization that published them. One of the first periodicals to achieve this end was *Nowa Kultura*. One fine day in the second half of 1956 this weekly officially renounced its subtitle of organ of the Polish Writers' Union and proclaimed its editorial independence. Its new editor-in-chief, Victor Woroszilski, was elected through a secret ballot by the paper's personnel and, since then, he has become responsible solely to his editors and other colleagues. This example was followed by such reviews as *Przeglad Kulturalny* and *Po Prostu* and later by such dailies as *Sztandar Mlodych*, which ceased appearing as the organ of the youth movement. It is true that the independence of these papers was never absolute. Most of the editorial staff continued to be members of the Communist Party and were thus subjected to Party discipline, in the last resort being responsible for their actions before the press and propaganda department of the Central Committee's secretariat. Nevertheless, the new situation enhanced the freedom of newspapers, allowing the element of personality to assert itself, and tending to transform the old system of pre-publication censorship into post-publication control.

The development of editorial independence was paralleled by the growth of financial independence. As is the case of certain newspapers in Communist China as well as most of the press in Yugoslavia, most Polish newspapers became financially autonomous and proceeded to balance their budgets in the same way as newspapers in capitalist countries always have to do. Such changes made for competition and led the Polish press to adopt all the techniques of Western newspapers. The papers that were nominally independent of the Communist Party distinguished themselves in this sphere. This was particularly the case of the Warsaw evening paper *Express Wieczorny,* which increased its circulation by over 80,000 copies. On the other hand, the Party organs which were less adaptable—and which had always been less palatable to the public—saw their circulation decline as soon as the system of obligatory subscription was abolished. The Polish journalists' review *Prasa Polska* revealed that between December 1956 and May 1957, subscriptions to Party papers declined by 51 per cent, from 936,000 to 457, 000 copies.

Precarious and relative freedom

In spite of all these changes, the Polish press was still far from becoming absolutely and completely free, even though the new freedom of expression was fairly comprehensive. In fact, apart from the Chief Press Control Office, which went on functioning, the government still had control over publication licenses, the allocation of newsprint and the distribution of papers through the official agency "Ruch." Moreover, it possessed the publishing house "Prasa," the largest and best equipped in the country, which published 128 newspapers. This press, which was subsidized and which benefited from various other privileges, could, in theory, compete advantageously with those publications which had become autonomous. However, in 1957 the total circulation of papers published by "Prasa" amounted only to 1,700,000 copies while the previous year it had reached the figure of 2,637,000.

Thus even during the phase of greatest emancipation, the Polish press never managed to extricate itself from the tutelage of higher authorities. Its relative freedom had been the result of precarious compromises between concessions acceptable to the governing circles and to the aspirations of journalists which surpassed by far the limits of these concessions. In fact, from the beginning of the process of liberalization the Press Association was dominated by the most liberal elements.

The third Congress of the Polish Journalists' Association, which took place in Warsaw from November 30 till December 2, 1956, reflected the greatest aspirations of the profession. Some of the resolutions voted by the Congress included the following :

1. The inclusion of editors and other journalists in the press commission of the Central Committee of the United Workers Party, as well as in regional commissions. The role of these commissions should become strictly consultative.

2. The supplying of the press with current news concerning Poland's foreign policy, the organizing of regular press conferences, the preparation of foreign broadcasts over the Polish radio which give a true picture of Poland, not excluding the unfavorable side of the country's everyday life.

3. Limitation of the activities of the Chief Press Control Office, which henceforth should concern itself only with military and State secrets.

4. The elaboration of a press law and a statute for journalists.

Although the first two demands were almost completely satisfied, the third was ignored and the fourth was discussed endlessly.

Legislation on the press in the Polish People's Republic includes several scattered texts. This legislation is not comprehensive and possesses gaps which offer possibilities for arbitrary action ; on the other hand, there are clauses that have been deliberately ignored. One of the most interesting of these is the decree of December 12, 1950, which imposes on the authorities the obligation to verify all news published by the press concerning their sphere of activity or the sphere of activity of subordinate institutions. The officials are also required to take the necessary measures to fill in any gaps in the reports concerned, to eliminate all mistakes and to communicate the results of the inquiry and the measures taken to the editorial department of the newspaper which originally published the report in question. This communication must be sent to the newspaper within a month of the publication of the item concerned. If the authority fails to carry out this obligation, the newspaper can report the matter to the superior authorities and, if necessary, to the Prime Minister. The decree goes on to say that any attempt to muzzle criticism must be punished as a criminal offense. Newspapers were themselves under an obligation to publish criticisms which they received concerning the functioning and administration of the economy. In fact, this system has only begun to function adequately since Poland entered its phase of liberalization.

Since 1955 Polish journalists have called for a comprehensive press law. They considered this the best means of forestalling arbitrary action and held that this law should fix the status of a newspaper, provide a definite list of press offenses, and define the rights and duties of journalists. The elaboration of such a law has made very slow progress and up till 1958 has not moved further than the draft stage. However, in the meantime interesting progress has been made in the sphere of the rights of the press. Thus the courts have recognized the right to professional secrecy as conceived in the West. Moreover, on March 12, 1958, a Warsaw court acquitted the correspondent of *Paris-Match* and another journalist accused of "having collected and reported information concerning State secrets and published false information abroad with intent to harm Poland." But experts managed to persuade the court that these accusations had no foundation since "a journalist has the right to collect information by all possible means" and the accused had acted within the strict limits of correct professional behavior.

Rise and fall

The third Congress of the Polish Journalists' Association (November 30 - December 2, 1956) more or less represents the heyday of press freedom in Poland. At the same time the Polish Writers' Union ended its congress, having passed a resolution demanding the abolition of all pre-publication censorship and the elaboration of a press law, as well as the suppression of measures forbidding the distribution of the emigré press in Poland.

However, just at this time the higher authorities began to be seriously alarmed at the scope of journalists' emancipation. The Hungarian revolution and its tragic end prompted an attitude of prudence. These events were generally reported in the Polish press according to Western sources and by some special correspondents who did not hide their sympathy for the insurgents. *Nowa Kultura* went so far as to publish an interview with the rebel leader Josef Dudas.

Zycie Literackie of Cracow reproduced in full an article originally appearing in *Kultura,* an emigré review published in Paris, on the role of the intellectuals at the beginning of the Hungarian revolution. The source of the article was also published. On his part, Gomulka tried to make editors understand that "reasons of State" demanded that at least the U. S. S. R. should not be provoked.

It was still possible for the election campaign of January 20, 1957, to take place in an atmosphere of considerable freedom but, from spring onwards, control of the press once again began to reassert itself. On several occasions Gomulka summoned editors-in-chief, whom he called upon to obey Party instructions. The threat of economic sanctions was just as effective as that of censorship, for since the abolition of government subsidies newspapers had become extremely vulnerable in the economic field. They had been obliged to double their prices, and from the beginning of the year competition had forced some papers to cease publication.

The weekly *Polityka,* the mouthpiece of Gomulka, published several articles urging the more outspoken journalists to moderate their tone and to limit themselves to "constructive criticism." In its issue of the middle of May the paper attacked certain journalists "who have adopted a favorable attitude to the bourgeoisie and to capitalism," as well as the tendency of certain newspapers to consider themselves as autonomous. "Some of these," said *Polityka,* "have regarded the press as an independent political force, distinct from the Party, the nation and its institutions... There is no point in referring to that famous independence of the press in capitalist countries where it is generally a lucrative capitalist enterprise. In socialist countries the press cannot play a completely independent role."

These warnings, however, soon passed beyond the sphere of words. In March 1957 the editor-in-chief of *Trybuna Ludu,* the central organ of the Party, was dismissed for having shown favor to excessive liberalism ; several editors resigned as a sign of protest. In April, Eligiusz Lasota resigned from the editorial staff of *Po Prostu,* apparently to show his disapproval of the tightening of controls, but was replaced by his deputy Turski, who continued to steer the weekly in a "revisionist" direction. During the same period the Warsaw daily *Sztandar Mlodych* found itself saddled with an official from the Communist Party who installed himself in the editorial offices of the paper. In May, Mme. Edda Werfel, a prominent journalist, was deprived of the right of occupying a responsible post because she had refused to obey the censorship. She had been the deputy to the editor-in-chief of the weekly *Swiat,* which imitates the style of *Life* and which had distinguished itself by publishing extracts from George Orwell's "1984" emphasizing the de-personalization of the individual in a totalitarian society. In July the censorship forbade the publication of a statement by Cardinal Wyszynski condemning the "Pax" group. The issue of *Tygodnik Powszechny* which proposed to reproduce this statement was suspended. After this incident a Catholic deputy protested in the Diet against the censorship and other various pressures to which Catholic publications were subject, in particular the discrimination practised in the allocation of newsprint, he also protested against the government's opposition to the founding of a new Catholic daily. *Tygodnik Powszechny* was not allowed to publish this speech in full. At the same time it is interesting to note that the censorship also acted against a review of the Communist Party which claimed to have unmasked an anti-governmental campaign organized by the Catholic Church. This article was never published.

At the beginning of the autumn the *Po Prostu* affair took place. This paper was having perpetual difficulties with the Chief Press Control Office, which had suppressed a number of its articles. The first issue of September was entirely censored. This was in fact the last issue, for the Chief Press Control Office decided to suspend the weekly indefinitely. The secretariat of the Central Committee approved this measure and on October 4 issued the following statement : "The editorial staff of *Po Prostu,* which includes a certain number of Party members, has for some time been engaged in opposing the resolutions of leading Party organs : its attitude has been sterile and negative ; it has presented the present economic and political situation of Poland in a false light ; it has published texts repudiating Socialism and, in many spheres, has in fact adopted bourgeois views."

The suppression of *Po Prostu* provoked demonstrations of protest in the streets of Warsaw. These demonstrations were brutally quelled by the militia. The censorship then proceeded to stop the publication of resolutions condemning the paper's suppression, notably a resolution adopted by the Polish Writers' Union. Ten editors of *Po Prostu* were expelled from the Party following two open letters addressed to

Gomulka protesting against the suppression and the violence of police reaction to subsequent demonstrations. In answer to these protests, *Trybuna Ludu* recalled on October 11 that "the Party had never proclaimed freedom for any kind of criticism ; it had certainly not proclaimed unlimited freedom of discussion."

During the final months of 1957 attacks on the freedom of the press multiplied. The review *Europa,* which had the aim of encouraging cultural exchanges between East and West, found that its authorization to publish had been withdrawn while its first issue was going to press at the beginning of November. During the same period the weeklies *Kronika* of Lodz and *Przemiany* of Katowice ceased publication, officially for financial reasons, but more probably for their outspoken attitude and their critical reports on the conditions of workers in the mines. Other periodicals had to change their editors-in-chief or else cease to appear ; the tenth issue of the literary review *Tworczosc* was confiscated ; editors were dismissed from the staffs of several papers and from the radio.

During the tenth plenary session of the Central Committee in October 1957, Gomulka served one of his most serious warnings on the press. "The press," he said, "has the right to criticize all negative elements.. All we ask is that criticism should emanate from creative standpoints and should contribute to the construction of Socialism... The press has the duty to come to the aid of the authorities and to popularize the policy of the Party and government."

Reasons of State

The Journalists' Association, which met in the middle of November, tried to find a compromise between the demands of freedom and "reasons of State." Some courageous members still sought to affirm the ideal and principles that had triumphed the year before. One of these was Marian Bielicki, who declared that the essential problems were those of freedom of the press and the defense of the rights of journalists. In this context he denounced the measures taken against thirty of his colleagues and the dismissal of 386 others since the beginning of the year. Bielicki also deplored that the press should have reverted to its old practice of referring to problems only after they had been resolved, instead of reflecting and forming public opinion. Finally, he condemned the suppression of *Po Prostu,* whose existence, he contended, could not be considered dangerous and could only serve as a stimulant to discussion. "But," he added, "in the place of discussion and polemics, one finds that the right of free expression has been withdrawn from various newspapers and from those who produce them."

The resolution finally adopted by the Congress contained side by side both an appeal to the ideals of the previous year and an acceptance of the government's point of view. The Association recalled that the freedom of speech, criticism and constructive research in the field of theory and the construction of Socialism were some of the most important acquisitions emanating from the political developments of October 1956, but that these liberties should in their turn "contribute to the reinforcement of Socialism and not to its weakening." It admitted, however, that the Polish press had not explained the policies of the government and of the United Workers Party as it should have done and had not been willing to "defend and support the measures which, although unpopular, were necessary in view of the country's difficult position." Moreover, it went on to express its "misgivings at the decline of constructive criticism in some newspapers as well as the manifest indifference evident in the attitude of certain authorities and certain governmental organs as far as criticism in the press is concerned." The resolution again invited "all journalists to do their utmost to overcome all factors tending to prejudice the creation of a political atmosphere that will help in dealing with the present situation," and concluded, "The Polish press... will support the Party in its proper line in combating at the same time tendencies hostile to Socialism and attempts to revert to old methods."

Although the setback to freedom of expression was only too evident, one year after the rise to power of Gomulka this freedom had by no means declined into the conformism of former times. During the last months of 1957 the philosopher Leszek Kolakowski could still proclaim his audacious revisionist theories. In *Nowa Kultura* he published a series of articles on "Responsibility and History" in which he rejected all forms of determinism and the idea that the means justifies the end. Such examples of audacity were also still to be found in the daily press. The satirical review *Szpilki*, widely read throughout the country, often lashed out fiercely at the failings of the regime. At the end of 1957 an important daily of the coastal region, *Glos Szczecinski,* published the results of a public opinion poll. These included such statements as the following : "It must be remembered that 80 per cent of the population has had enough of your type of democracy," and "... I hope that we will be liberated by the Americans. Long live the liberty of the United States." An official, who was moreover a member of the Party, wrote on the subject of Communism : "It is a Utopia based on an economic idiocy. It has led to slavery unequalled in antiquity or the Middle Ages. It kills human pride, it produces the thief, the spy." [1]

During 1958 the press has been subjected to new attacks. In January a conflict broke out between the Central Committee of the United Workers Party (Communist) and the editorial staff of *Sztandar Mlodych.* The Central Committee had ordered the dismissal of the paper's editor-in-chief and other editors, accusing them of "revisionism." This measure, however, was revoked, thanks to the determined opposition of all the rest of the editorial staff and a formal protest from the Journalists' Association. But on January 10 the Central Committee renewed its attack using different tactics. It decided that the daily, having become independent since October 1956, should subsequently pass under the control of the reconstituted Socialist Youth Organization. This time it achieved its purpose, but most of the editors then handed in their resignation.

In February the editor-in-chief of the weekly *Nowa Kultura,* Victor Woroszylski, was forced to resign. He was reproached for having published too many texts of "liberal" or "revisionist" tendencies as well as a series of cartoons making fun of certain aspects of life in Moscow. In May six of the principal contributors of the paper were dismissed and replaced by journalists devoted to the Party. Among those who "resigned" was the philosopher Leszek Kolakowski. During the same period Western correspondents in Warsaw learned of some new secret directives concerning the press, issued by the Central Committee of the United Workers Party. These directives among other things prohibited the publication of texts not serving a constructive political purpose.

[1] Quoted by the *News Chronicle,* London, December 31, 1957.

Finally, during the summer the conflict between Church and State ended with a settlement by virtue of which the ecclesiastical authorities agreed to submit all religious publications to government censorship.

* * *

Thus, two years after the Polish October revolution the press, which, with the writers, had been one of the major factors in this peaceful and hopeful movement towards liberalization, found that its freedom of expression was progressively contracting more and more. Reason of State took precedence, and so did the Marxist-Leninist conception of the role of the press in Society. Since it still rested on authoritarian foundations, and on account of the situation with regard to Moscow, the regime of Gomulka could not successfully embrace complete emancipation. At all times it could not but be tempted to withdraw the concessions it had granted to a greater or lesser extent of its own accord. However, this experience did reveal that the great majority of Polish journalists aspired to freedom of expression, whether or not they happened to be members of a party based on a totalitarian ideology. And the courage with which they fought—and perhaps are still fighting—for this freedom of expression must remain as one of the bright episodes of contemporary history.

Yugoslavia

On June 28, 1948, a resolution of the Cominform expelling from its midst the Yugoslav Communist Party and accusing its leaders of "deviationism" precipitated a long and serious conflict between Belgrade and Moscow. Before this date the post-war Yugoslav press scarcely differed in any respect from the press of any other Communist country. After the end of the war as a result of nationalization the government had acquired the monopoly of the whole press industry, and all attempts to obtain equipment, newsprint and other necessary facilities for publishing a newspaper had to be made through government offices. In practice, these facilities were granted only to institutions or groups giving evidence of loyalty to the authorities. The only opposition newspaper to be published in Belgrade after the war, *Demokratija*, the organ of Milan Grol's Serbian Democratic Party, had an extremely ephemeral existence during which it encountered all kinds of difficulties.

As we go to press, no newspaper at variance with the Party line has been able to appear, and all attempts to publish such papers seem to be doomed to failure. The press law of July 8, 1946, which is still in force, prohibits anything liable to question the established order. Yet Mosha Pijade, the theorist of Yugoslav Communism, had this to say of the law : "It gives almost unlimited freedom of expression through the press, excluding from this liberty only quislings. It protects the benefits of democracy against those who, by abusing civil liberties, seek to violate the constitutional order with anti-democratic aims in view. Through its just distribution of newsprint and its nationalization of the large printing works, the State has given the press real material aid and the possibility of developing itself into a really free press."

In fact, the law denies the right of being a publisher, editor, or any other kind of journalist on a newspaper to all those who do not enjoy political or civil rights and to those who in one way or another collaborated with "Fascist" organizations. Another clause prohibits the distribution and the sale of publications if these encourage revolt, diversionary activities, sabotage, the violent overthrow of the constitutional order, or violate this order for un-democratic purposes. It also prohibits the spreading of false or alarming news liable to threaten the national interest, as well as all injurious or defamatory references to the country's supreme representative organs.

Up to the time of going to press, this law has not been modified. There has been talk, however, of amending a clause which permits the authorities or private persons to demand before a court the publication of a correction when they consider that they have been slandered by an article. As the law does not call on the court to verify the facts contained in the article or the correction, the press has considered this clause as a hindrance to its function of criticism. It seeks to have the text amended in such a way as to permit courts to verify the facts before demanding the publication of a correction. In practice, this now happens but only following a ruling from the Federal Supreme Court.

The Federation of Journalists has also been demanding for several years the modification of some clauses in the Penal Code concerning defamation in such a way as to allow true facts to be alleged. It holds that considerations of honor should not be an obstacle to the publication of "constructive criticism" with regard to an institution or an individual.

Financial independence of newspapers

Although the press law has remained the same since the advent of the Communist regime after the Second World War, another more recent law has effected profound changes in the structure and organization of Yugoslav journalism. This is a decree adopted on June 26, 1956, which defines the status of press enterprises and institutions. It had been drawn up in close collaboration with the Federation of Journalists. This document has no equal in any other Communist country, nor anywhere else in the world. Its originality lies in the fact that it applies to the press a certain number of principles that have characterized the social and economic evolution peculiar to Yugoslavia since 1948.

In the first place, each newspaper possesses a workers' council which appoints an executive committee comprising delegates of journalists, of administrative employees and of workers. Secondly, the publishing company (State institution or else a social group : a trade union, youth organization, co-operative of the paper's employees, etc.) appoints a special publishing council, a special body which comprises intellectuals and personalities from the circles for which the publication is destined. This council has nothing to do with administrative questions but is charged with watching over the publication's line, advising on matters of editorial policy, and seeking to raise the standard of journalism. It assumes the character of an organ of social control but can also at the same time be used as an instrument of political control, as will be seen later.

By way of example, it is interesting to examine the application of this system to *Politika,* the paper which in 1958 had a record circulation (250,000 to 280,000). Before the war *Politika,* the property of the Ribnikar family, was the principal independent daily in Belgrade. This tradition of independence was maintained as far as possible up to the time of the occupation in 1941. During the troubled times that followed, the attitude of Vladislav Ribnikar, editor-in-chief and proprietor, and most of his colleagues earned them the goodwill of the Communists. When these nationalized the press, they allowed Ribnikar to remain as editor-in-chief of his paper, which subsequently appeared under the auspices of the Popular Front. Ribnikar remained as nominal editor-in-chief of his paper until his death in 1955, although he had in fact handed it over to the State. Since then *Politika* has become an enterprise like other papers, operated by its employees.[1] It is no longer the organ of the Popular Front nor, as it became after 1952, that of the latter's substitute, the Socialist Alliance. It is a paper that claims to be independent. In fact, *Borba,* originally the organ of the Communist Party, has in the meantime become the organ of the Socialist Alliance of the Working People of Yugoslavia.

By virtue of the new law, the employees of *Politika* elect a

---

[1] *Politika* is operated by its employees but, like all other newspapers in Yugoslavia, it is owned by what Yugoslavs call "society." They insist that "ownership by society" is not the same thing as ownership by the State.

workers' council of 25 members, which in its turn appoints an executive committee of five. This committee deals with all administrative and editorial questions. It naturally always includes the editor-in-chief and the managing editor. A possible conflict between them and other members of this committee is settled by the arbitration of the trade union executive. As far as social control exercised by the publishing council is concerned, *Politika*'s committee is made up of nine members which include the editor-in-chief and the managing editor. The others are notable personalities of public life. In the council formed in May 1957, one finds among others the private secretary of the Minister of Foreign Affairs, an army general, and a woman author.

The system of self-administration applied to the press by the law of June 26, 1956, has had the effect of freeing the Yugoslav press from the financial tutelage of the State which originally, as in every Communist society, provided the necessary funds and equipment for the press enterprises. In fact the Yugoslav newspapers are now managed on a purely commercial basis and the majority of them balance their budget with the aid of the revenue from sales and advertising. This transformation had taken place already some years before the entry into force of the law on press enterprises. It has resulted in an intensification of competition between the newspapers, which have attempted to attract readers through the full range of subjects for which authority has left the field open.

Thus at the time when the press in other Communist countries was still rigid and monotonous, reflecting the Soviet model, the large-circulation newspapers in Yugoslavia were using nearly all the techniques of the popular Western press : lively make-up, cartoon strips, and serials of detective or even somewhat spicy love stories. This tendency grew through the years. In 1957, for instance, *Borba* and *Politika* reproduced texts of Agatha Christie and Peter Cheyney.

Moreover, the Yugoslav press gives a considerable amount of space to general interest items. There is copious reporting of certain crimes, and some papers sometimes tend towards sensationalism. This periodically brings forth warnings from the authorities.

An analysis of crime reporting in the Yugoslav press gives an interesting indication of the degree of freedom of information it enjoys. The murder of an ordinary person can be reported immediately and in full detail, whereas an actual murder of a member of the Central Committee of the Communist Party was passed over in silence for a long time. In the latter case, the murder was only briefly reported several months later when the accused was brought to trial.

In their rival efforts to win the favor of the public, several papers have gone so far as to introduce competitions with prizes. Naturally the effects of these efforts have been reflected in the papers' circulations. *Borba*'s circulation, which was over 500,000 in 1950, diminished to half this figure five years later. Yet, *Politika,* without direct links with the ruling party, has exceeded the circulation of *Borba.* There was also the case of one paper which disappeared because it was not able to compete on the commercial level. This was the weekly *Republika* of Belgrade, which ceased publication in October 1956. The strictly financial reasons given for its disappearance have, however, been questioned, since this paper was the organ of the Republican-Democratic Party, one of the satellite parties authorized by the Communists. Although this party never played any very active role, its paper, which had a circulation of about 20,000, was appreciated by a certain section of the public because it was edited in a certain manner which differed appreciably from that of most other papers. For instance, a certain amount of news about Western countries was to be found in it at a time when most of the Yugoslav press was not yet giving much space to this subject.

Effects on reporting of the break with Moscow

The above evolution was not the only change to affect the Yugoslav press after 1948. In the sphere of news reporting and comment there were the two successive phenomena of "derussification" and liberalization. The latter, after reaching a certain stage, began to decline. In order fully to understand this development, one must bear in mind the basic role of the Party. Contrary to events in Poland during the first post-Stalin period, the press in Yugoslavia did not take the initiative as regards its own liberalization. To a certain extent it accepted it passively, although a number of journalists did not fail to make the most of their opportunity. But on all points where Party policy remained rigid, the press went on being strictly conformist. It became emancipated only insofar as the Party line became more flexible and thus attained greater freedom of expression only in the spheres in which the authorities had on their own accord renounced the imposition of any directives. On certain occasions, in particular during the first Djilas affair and the Hungarian revolution, part of the Yugoslav press was able to give the impression that it enjoyed considerable editorial independence. In reality, however, it was only able to express itself with a certain freedom because the Party line was fluid at the time. As soon as this line became fixed, all newspapers observed it, even if it meant adopting from one day to another the opposite point of view from that held the day before.

* * *

The process of "derussification" had already begun in the second half of 1948. Yugoslav information media soon began to put aside material coming from the Soviet Union, with which until then they had been swamped. In 1952 Vladimir Dedijer told the U. N. Committee for Cultural and Humanitarian Affairs of his experiences when he was at the State Information Office. He said that in one single month of 1947, 150 articles written by Russian journalists had been sent to him by the Soviet Information Office's representative in Belgrade. This representative appeared very surprised when Dedijer refused to accept a certain number of them. Dedijer explained that if he had accepted the whole lot, *Borba* would not have had space for a single article by a Yugoslav journalist.

The Yugoslav News Agency, Tanjug, soon ceased to draw almost all its foreign news from the TASS Agency. Instead, it extended its network of correspondents abroad and resorted more frequently to Western news agencies. At a certain moment after 1950 the percentage of news from TASS, which had previously represented 90 per cent, had dropped to less than 10 per cent, while the services of A. F. P. alone exceed 50 per cent.

International affairs which had previously been looked at through the eyes of the U. S. S. R. were now regarded from the new point of view of Yugoslavia, committed to a policy of active coexistence between the two blocs of East and West. This new policy first became evident in reports on the U. S. S. R. and the People's Democracies. which, having formerly been tendentious in favor of these countries, were now hardly more objective, indeed often just as tendentious in the opposite sense. But here one must take into account the violent polemics that for years characterized the relations between these countries and Yugoslavia. On the other hand, it must be remembered that since the beginning of the conflict with the Kremlin, the Yugoslav press has almost always published in full the main texts of its adversaries, who in their turn failed to observe the same courtesy.

The first kind of news to become more objective in character was that concerning the United Nations. This objectivity was gradually extended to news and articles on the capitalist countries. Here a significant turning point was the appearance of some articles of remarkable impartiality in several Yugoslav papers, including *Borba,* on the electoral campaign in Great Britain at the beginning of 1950. In December 1951 the Tanjug News Agency and *Borba* sent a correspondent to join the anti-Communist forces in South Korea, whose reports were considered to be as conscientious as those emanating from the most conscientious of the Western journalists.

Next to the sphere of foreign news, the most striking transformation in the Yugoslav press after 1948 concerned cultural items. The ideas of Zhdanov on "social realism" disappeared from literary and art reviews. A number of works on the Moscow index were given serious and often laudatory reviews. Surrealism, jazz, abstract painting and other artistic forms considered by the Soviet Union as an illustration of the "decadence of the Bourgeois West" were extolled in the columns of Yugoslav newspapers.

The press's evolution with regard to news and comment on internal Yugoslav affairs was less marked. Long after 1948 accidents and natural disasters remained subjects that were best passed over in silence. For example, the fire on board the steamer "Partizanka" in the harbor at Split in 1949 was not reported in the press ; neither were the subsequent arrests of suspected saboteurs, until it was established by an inquiry that this fire had been caused by a short circuit. However, reporting of this kind has made some progress, especially since the creation of the Yugopress News Agency in 1952. This agency, which was created by journalists as a co-operative, has for a long time complemented especially as far as internal news is concerned, the services of the official Tanjug News Agency, whose council of management is appointed by the president of the Federal Government's Cultural Council. However, Yugopress ceased to function as a news agency in June 1958, while a features service was created in its place. In recent years the Yugoslav press has reported disasters and other important general interest stories objectively and without too much delay, although some restrictions still remain concerning the reporting of internal news, even spot news. Thus, for instance, there is the decree of July 17, 1957, concerning the activities of foreign correspondents in Yugoslavia, which formally prohibits them from contributing news items or other articles on events in Yugoslavia to Yugoslav newspapers or news agencies or even to private persons.

The press's freedom of criticism in internal matters thus remains limited. However, by 1950 it was already greater than that obtaining in most other Communist countries. Although it was impossible to criticize the regime and its leaders, it did become possible to judge the administration and the management of economic institutions up to quite a high level of the administration. Such criticism became increasingly outspoken. On several occasions the press went so far as to attack high-ranking enterprises and private persons. At times the controversy that followed such attacks would end in the courts with the newspaper winning its case. Some provincial newspapers, in particular the principal Zagreb daily, *Vjesnik*, managed to distinguish themselves in this sphere.

In the spring of 1951 a controversial question concerning national policy was for the first time discussed in the press. It was precipitated by the anniversary of the coup d'Etat of March 27, 1941, which overthrew the pro-Hitler government and was the signal for the invasion of Yugoslavia by Axis forces. Sava Kosanovitch, then Minister without portfolio and Secretary General of the Independent Democratic Party, published an article in *Politika* refuting the official thesis which attributed the entire resistance to Hitlerism to the Communist Party. *Borba,* the organ of the Communist Party, replied, and then followed a polemic which represented the first discussion of an internal question of this kind in the press.

After this, discussion in the press of internal questions had its ups and downs. Freedom of expression did make some progress, chiefly in the form of cartoons and light articles. In a serial called "The Heretical Story," the writer, Branko Chopich, dared to ridicule with considerable zest certain characteristics of the new society, in particular the new ruling class. He was, however, called to order by *Borba* and then by Marshal Tito himself.

In 1952 the editorial staff of *Politika* was purged. The paper had made some notable attempts to promote more comprehensive discussion of internal questions, as well as publishing reports that were favorable to certain Western countries, in particular the German Federal Republic. The Central Committee of the Serb Communist Party thereupon intervened in editorial matters and attempted to impose controls on the editor-in-chief, Bogdan Peshich. As a result, the latter abandoned his post and became his paper's correspondent in a Western capital.

From liberalization to renewed control

Freedom of expression reached its climax during 1953. During the VIth Congress of the Communist Party (which from then onwards was called the Communist League) in November 1952, Milovan Djilas, then a member of the Politburo in charge of propaganda, announced that freedom of information and criticism would be extended in scope. Several months later he himself set the example in a series of articles, some of which were published in *Borba* between November 1953 and January 1954, and others during the same period in the cultural and doctrinal review *Nova Misao*. The last and the most outspoken of these appeared under the title "Anatomy of a Morality." It caused a real sensation, for the man who was still considered at the time as the successor of Marshal Tito bluntly denounced the dictatorship of the Party as well as the hypocrisy and snobbery of the ruling caste. He called for an authentic democratization of public life and freedom of expression. On December 20, 1953, he wrote in *Borba,* the central organ of the Party : "The first duty of a socialist democracy, and indeed of any democracy, is to permit the free expression of ideas, and to guarantee that no one will be persecuted for his ideas."

The shock caused by these articles brought sanctions to their author, who was excluded from the Central Committee of the Communist League, and a tightening up on the press, and especially *Borba*, whose management was rebuked for its lack of discernment.

The whole press was then advised not to publish any more articles likely to be prejudicial to the nation and not to fall prey to sensationalism. The review *Nova Misao* ceased publication, and so did the weekly *Naprjed*, organ of the Croatian Communist Party, whose editor-in-chief had made common cause with Djilas.

When at the end of 1954 Milovan Djilas once again sought to express his political ideas, he found that not a single Yugoslav paper would accept his articles. In the end he had to turn to the foreign press. In a statement to the Belgrade correspondent of the *New York Times*, he reiterated his attacks against the lack of democracy in his country and called for the creation of another party which could confront the Communist Party with a clash of ideas and experiences. This outburst not only brought about his exclusion from the Party but also cost him two and a half years' imprisonment, which was suspended for a period of three years, a sentence that was prompted not so much by the opinions expressed as by the fact that the foreign press had been used to denigrate the Yugoslav regime. Furthermore, Milovan Djilas was excluded from the Serbian Association of Journalists and so was Vladimir Dedijer, the ex-editor-in-chief of *Borba* and author of the official biography of Marshal Tito, who had declared his support for Djilas. On this occasion the Federation of Journalists sent a letter to Edvard Kardelj, Vice-President of the Federal Executive Council, stating that it considered the press as an organ of the social order and not as a forum for the airing of opinions which were opposed to this order.

Milovan Djilas was condemned a second time on December 12, 1956, to three years' imprisonment for an article on the Hungarian Revolution which appeared in the *New Leader* of New York, and for having made a statement to the Agence France-Presse ; then on October 4, 1957, he received another seven years as a result of a secret trial called to pronounce on his book "The New Class." Each time he was condemned by virtue of Article 118 of the Penal Code of 1951, which reads as follows :

" Whoever with the intent to undermine the authority of the

working people, the defensive power of the country, or the economic basis of socialist construction ; or with the intent to destroy the brotherhood and the unity of the people of the Federal People's Republic of Yugoslavia *by means of cartoons, writings or speeches before a gathering or in any other way,* carries out propaganda against the governmental and social order or against political, economic, military, or either important measures of the people's authority shall be punished by imprisonment."

After the reconciliation between Belgrade and Moscow in 1955, the change in the relations between the governments and Communist Parties of the two countries was reflected in the Yugoslav press. TASS once again became an important source of foreign news. Criticism of the U. S. S. R. and the People's Democracies considerably diminished, even though from time to time a fairly sharp polemic took place. All the press manifestly obeyed orders from above. Newspapers systematically avoided headings, editorials and drawings likely to hurt Soviet susceptibility. Western countries, on the other hand, were not always granted similar favors. A typical example is furnished by the Belgrade evening paper *Vecernje Novosti.* During 1957 this paper had published in serial form the memoires of Viscount Alanbrooke, in which, as it is known, neither Western statesmen nor the Communists are spared their share of criticism. No one was offended by what was said of the former, but as soon as the paper printed an account of Marshal Voroshilov as a drunkard, the Soviet Embassy immediately protested. Some time later the editor-in-chief of the paper was replaced.

An indication of this change is the Yugoslav press's treatment of the Poznan riots and then of the subsequent trials. The little that the newspapers said of these events was a rehash from the TASS Agency. Other important events were passed over in silence or else simply mentioned in brief. A speech delivered by Vladimir Dedijer before an international congress of jurists at Dubrovnik in 1956, which received great attention in the Western press, was completely ignored by the papers of his own country because of its anti-Leninist conclusions.

Control of the press further increased after the events in Poland and Hungary of the autumn 1956. At the beginning the most influential Yugoslav papers, such as *Politika, Vjesnik* and even *Borba,* expressed their sympathy towards the movements for democratization.

This they were able to do while the Party line was still fluid. Rejecting the Soviet thesis of a counter-revolution fomented by imperialist agents, the Yugoslav correspondents in Budapest did not attempt to hide the fact that the Hungarian Revolution was spontaneous. On the other hand, the papers violently denounced the Anglo-Franco-Israeli attack on Egypt and did not hesitate to publish both false and tendentious news on this subject. As after the first Djilas affair, there followed a tightening of press control. The authorities particularly made use of the newly-created publishing committees to impose the Party line. Announcing the formation of these committees at the beginning of 1957, *Borba* wrote : "It is necessary to develop the sense of political responsibility of journalists... In this respect the most important role should be played by the publishing councils, through which the Socialist Alliance can best exert its influence on the press."

During the IIIrd Congress of the Yugoslav Press Federation, held at Zagreb in March 1957, tendencies favoring and opposing greater press control came out into the open, and the former won the day. V. Vlahovitch, the delegate from the Central Committee, launched an attack against the deviationists, while emphasizing that in no other profession was the number of Communist militants so high as in the press. At the conclusion of the Congress, resolutions were adopted urging the elimination of the weaknesses and ideological and other failings of Yugoslav journalism. At one point during the debates Milojkovitch, the president of the Serb section, complained of the impediments to the gathering of internal news, which, he said, had the effect of obliging journalists to resort to doubtful sources, thus prejudicing the general information of the public.

The following month, during the plenary session of the Socialist Alliance, Marshal Tito and the Deputy Prime Minister Rankovitch took a firm stand against the lack of ideological background evident in part of the press which, they considered, behaved in a way likely to prejudice the government's foreign policy.

"We are not against the free expression of ideas," declared Marshal Tito, "but... we want to build Socialism. Everything must be subordinated to this end. We cannot allow our foreign policy to be obstructed by certain journalists who imagine themselves to be above everything, and who act against the will of the majority of the nation."

On his part, Rankovitch pointed out that for several years there had no longer been a controlled and centralized press. The progressive development of freedom of expression had brought about many positive results. But it had also led "to some ideological aberrations and to some negative tendencies." In conclusion the Minister said : "The fact that our newspapers and radio stations are independent does not mean that they can consider themselves completely independent from Society."

* * *

During the VIIth Congress of the Communist League, which took place in April 1958 at Ljubljana, Marshal Tito had more to say on the press :
"...The press can do a lot of harm if journalists do not write in conformity with the country's interests and the interests of socialist construction... During our country's revolutionary period of transition, *the press cannot be considered as an independent and autonomous factor in society,* since all the actions of society as a whole must converge towards one aim : the construction of Socialism.
"...The press is responsible before Society for correctly informing the public and educating public opinion in a Socialist sense, but it does not have the function of interpreting social events and the most important issues of foreign policy independently and without regard to responsible social institutions. I underline this as there have been and still are journalists in our country who have the wrong idea about the freedom and independence of the press here. Freedom of the press in their opinion tends to give them the monopoly of the interpretation of events and the formation of public opinion. Such a conception derives from an erroneous idea of the role and responsibility of the Socialist press, as well as, to a large extent, the ideological backwardness of certain journalists."
The fresh conflict between Belgrade and Moscow arising from the Ljubljana Congress did not specially modify the situation of the Yugoslav press. However, the latter did abandon its reserve in the treatment of news concerning the Soviet Union and the countries of the Eastern bloc. One of the most significant events at this time was a confession of *Politika*'s correspondent in Peking, in June 1958. In an article published by his paper, he apologized to his readers for

having in the past given a too flattering picture of Communist China. He admitted that his conduct had been a violation of the profession's rules of impartiality, but explained his attitude by his desire to understand Chinese realities in a constructive manner and to serve the cause of co-operation between his country and the country he had been sent to cover. However, Peking's violent anti-Yugoslav campaign had made him change his mind.

* * *

At the time of writing, the Yugoslav press is still muzzled, although its possibilities of expression are considerably greater than in other Communist countries, apart from Poland. Generally speaking, one can say that restrictions are rare as far as news is concerned. These chiefly affect political comment. Although it is impossible to criticize the regime itself and the Yugoslav brand of Socialism, there is a fairly wide margin for criticizing the way Socialism is applied in particular cases. For instance, even in the spring of 1957 the official *Borba* published a series of critical articles denouncing all sorts of failings in contemporary Yugoslav society. Furthermore, the policy of decentralization, which has been a landmark of the regime, has tended to favor a certain degree of autonomy in the provincial press. In the second half of 1957 texts appeared in the principal paper of Slovenia which would never have found their way into the dailies of Belgrade.

There is one sphere, that of culture, where freedom of expression has remained considerable. Literary and art reviews include the texts and objective, even laudatory, appreciations of authors who, in the Soviet world, are judged as decadent and anti-Marxist : namely, James Joyce, Ezra Pound, T. S. Eliot, Upton Sinclair, Sartre and Anouilh. Moreover, "social realism" and the control of culture in the U. S. S. R. are often attacked.

The extent of this freedom, however, does not appear to satisfy all the public. A public opinion poll was carried out in the spring of 1957 by the Zagreb review *Krugovi*, asking the following question : "What do you think of the literary and art reviews in the Yugoslav press ?" There were many replies from readers who were dissatisfied. A well-known actor was not afraid to declare : "The cultural part of our newspapers is in the hands of an irresponsible clique," while an equally prominent composer said : "There should be much greater freedom in the cultural pages of our newspapers." The publication of these replies provoked a strong reaction from official organs, especially from *Borba*. They blamed the editors of the review for their conduct, which they termed "irresponsible and shamefully reactionary." However, no measures were taken against them, and the review *Krugovi* continues to appear.

Part Two

Other Authoritarian Countries

Spain

More than twenty years after the "National Revolution" in the summer of 1936, the Spanish Press was still being governed by the same restrictive laws and subjected to almost the same controls as those in force during the civil war.

The victory of the movement headed by General Franco was fatal to freedom of the press. There was a vast purge of journalists ; a large number of them were arrested and about forty were condemned to death. There was also a wholesale elimination of newspapers. The number of daily papers dropped from around two hundred and fifty to about one hundred. Among those that disappeared were some newspapers of old liberal traditions and long-standing editorial integrity such as *El Heraldo* of Madrid, *El Sol* to which Ortega y Gasset was for a long time a regular contributor, *El Pueblo* of Valencia, founded by the famous writer Blasco Ibañez, *El Diluvio* of Barcelona, and finally *El Debate,* inspired by Mgr. Herrera who became bishop of Malaga, and the ex-monarchist deputy Gil Robles.

These newspapers and many others were suppressed and their assets confiscated. This was particularly the case as regards the Catalan press. The printing press of *El Sol* became that of *Arriba,* the central organ of the Falange ; that of *El Heraldo* was turned over to *Madrid,* and the press of *El Diluvio* published the weekly of the Penitentiary of Alcalá de Henares. All the installations of old Republican newspapers were handed over by the State to the one and only Party, the Falange. The party press, comprising thirty out of the 109 newspapers is thus strictly dependent on the higher authorities which, conversely, favor them by fiscal and postal privileges and a ready supply of newsprint.

Other authorized newspapers that have remained in private hands, as well as the Falangist press, are subjected to a system of pre-publication censorship which derives from a curious conception of the role of information in the State.

General Franco, who from time to time has written editorials for *Arriba* signed Hispanicus, has often declared that he does not consider freedom of the press as an absolute principle.

Franco's doctrine of information is based on the condemnation of "liberalism devoid of principles" and on the idea that the press must serve the "common good" of which the State is in some measure the supreme incarnation. According to this doctrine, Authority has "two heads". The formula is expressed as follows : the newspaper enterprise gives guidance [1] insofar as it proposes the editor ; the State guides insofar as it accepts the editor. These ideas have been expressed on several occasions by Don Gabriel Arias-Salgado, the Minister of Information and Tourism [2] :

" People keep on talking, with almost morbid insistence, of public opinion... This has been and still remains the myth of liberalism... To bestow on public opinion the role of judge and supreme arbiter on all questions of common interest seems a subversion of values and the negation of reason...

" You journalists cannot blindly follow the opinions of the public. You have to sift them, you have to guide and assist the public. You must speak up when necessary but you must also know how to keep quiet when necessary. You must win the battle of truth in the face of error, educate opinion, work for the preparation and the consolidation of peace between peoples... For this reason it is necessary that you know the limits of public opinion." [3]

"Freedom of information has installed the freedom of error... The consequences of libertinism of information in Spain during the period of political liberalism, and today in the world at large, are bitter and visible signs of social and political decomposition..."

From this follows the need to eschew liberalism, "which does not mean the renouncing of liberty, but on the contrary, enables the people to enjoy a liberty that is more authentic." [4]

---

[1] Statement of the Minister Arias-Salgado at Barcelona, on the occasion of the second National Council of the Spanish Press in December 1954.

[2] Gabriel Arias-Salgado : *Política Española de la Información* — I Textos, II Antología sistemática (Madrid, quinta edición, 1957-1958).

[3] Speech delivered on December 4, 1955 at Valencia, on the occasion of the third National Council of the Spanish Press.

[4] Above-mentioned speech delivered at Barcelona.

On September 20, 1957, the important Madrid daily *ABC* published an editorial which began with the following peremptory assertion : "The free press does not exist ; it does not exist in any country in the world, has not existed and will never exist." The author continues by examining one after the other the roles of the press in totalitarian and liberal regimes. In the latter, he considers that the press "conceived in tragic adultery, loses its original functions of discussion and information and turns into the protector of some private interests which are opposed to the general interest." The editorial goes on to say : "As against the delirium of different forms and contradictory concepts, the anarchy and tyranny which nowadays afflict the majority of other countries, there shines the clear Catholic doctrine of information according to which, Authority, the guardian of the common good, must watch over the press—which is an integral part of Authority—in order to guarantee that all members of the community are served by true information. The function of Authority is to harmonize two principles which are often in opposition to one another, namely : a maximum of press freedom, and a maximum of common good... In this way, the Catholic doctrine which condemns the excesses of both the liberal and totalitarian press, is in complete accord with the Spanish doctrine of information. Here lies the one and only possibility of real freedom of the press..."

The Decalogue of the Spanish journalist drawn up by the General Directorate of the Press in co-operation with the Federation of Press Associations and proclaimed in 1955 officially confirms this doctrine of information. Its main points are as follows :

1. As Spaniards professing the Catholic religion and subscribing to the principles of the glorious National Movement, we have the duty to serve in all earnestness these religious and political truths as we carry out our functions of information and guidance.

2. All news must be judged according to its real value, while as far as its presentation and headings are concerned, these must respect truth and justice taking into account all necessary prudence, given the influence that news has on public opinion. All conscious alteration of the content of news items as well as all equivocal opinion and sensationalism must be avoided.

3. Journalists are strictly required to resist all illegitimate pressure having as its object the distortion of truth in respect to Catholic morals and the common good.

Press legislation

This doctrine obviously carries with it the seed of every kind of control and restriction. It in fact inspired the press law of April 22, 1938, promulgated before the end of the civil war and still in force without any modifications. According to its first article, this law confers on the State the tasks of organization, supervision and control of the press. The State is required to :

1. regulate the number and circulation of periodical publications; 2. intervene in the appointment of editor-in-chief ; 3. regulate the profession of journalist ; 4. supervise the activity of the press ; 5. exercise censorship so long as this remains in force.

The editor-in-chief of each newspaper must be approved by the Minister of Information who can have him dismissed (Articles 8 and 13).

Apart from the offenses and faults specified in penal legislation, the Minister in charge of the National Press Service is enabled to punish with administrative sanctions all writings which directly or indirectly reflect on the prestige of the nation or the regime, defame the work of the government in the New State, or spread pernicious ideas among weak intellectuals (Article 18). Similar punishment is also decreed for faults, disobedience, passive resistance and generally speaking for all cases of non-observance of the orders emanating from the competent authorities concerned with press affairs.

The sanctions that can be applied by the Minister of the Interior include the following : fines, dismissal of the editor-in-chief, his dismissal accompanied by the elimination of his name from the register of journalists and suspension of the paper. This last measure can be taken only in the case of a serious offense against the regime and the recurrence of past offenses, which has to be decreed by the head of the government. There is no appeal.

A circular order from the Minister of the Interior of May 1, 1941 required that the press of the Falange be exempt from censorship. But it reaffirmed that in principle this should be exercised on all other newspapers by the General Directorate of the Press, which should also send out directives for their guidance.

Mention should also be made of the law of 1941 on the security of the State which contains several clauses affecting the press. These provide for sanctions of between one and five years' imprisonment and a fine of between ten and fifty thousand pesetas for the publication of any kind of text liable to encourage acts against the security of the State, or liable to prejudice the prestige or authority of the State, or likely to compromise the dignity or the interests of the Spanish nation. The distribution or possession of such publications are also punishable according to the same sanctions (Article 27).

Those who, in any way, communicate or distribute false, distorted or tendentious news or rumors, or commit acts liable to prejudice the prestige and authority of the State are to be punished by three to ten years' imprisonment and are to be barred from holding any public function for a period of five to ten years. The sentence can be commuted in the case of a lesser offense (Article 25).

Towards the end of the regime's first decade, which coincided with the end of the Second World War and the collapse of most of the existing fascist or neo-fascist regimes, General Franco thought the time had come to offer his people a Charter : El Fuero de los Españoles. This constitutional document of July 13, 1945, states in its article 12 : "All Spaniards will be able to express their ideas freely, so long as these do not affect the fundamental principles of the State." Earlier paragraphs show that this freedom of expression as far as the press is concerned remains singularly limited by the law. It is also limited by other means.

Censorship and directives

Let us examine the machinery of control applied to the Spanish press.

First of all censorship and directives. In Madrid, all newspapers must submit their galley-proofs to the General Directorate of the Press. In Barcelona and other towns, the provincial representatives of the Ministry of Information act as censors. However, the editors-in-chief of newspapers themselves practise self-control or self-censorship. The threat of sanctions and dismissal which is constantly facing them, is sufficient to dissuade them from committing any blunders. According to a statement from the Minister of Information in 1954, 85 editors-in-chief of newspapers (out of 109 dailies plus 30 Monday papers) and a dozen editors-in-chief of reviews are exempted from pre-publication censorship. "They decide what and what not to publish, with complete freedom, yet always in accordance with their sense of responsibility." In actual fact, previous directives contribute largely in determining what the decision will be.

There are a certain number of subjects that remain taboo : the regime, the succession to General Franco, certain activities of members of the government, the intrigues of separatists, strikes and other forms of political and social agitation, indecent behavior, and generally speaking everything already condemned by the Roman Catholic Church.[1] It is equally impossible to report a scandal or discuss a trial in which government circles are involved. It is also dangerous to report certain news items which give an unfavorable impression of the country's affairs.

Examples of some of these limits are the following : The National Press Congress of 1952 revealed that one newspaper had run into trouble for having mentioned a bad orange crop and the editor-in-chief of a Malaga paper had been arrested and later released on payment of a fine for having reported a polio epidemic in Andalusia. Another year, a Barcelona journalist was arrested for having criticized in one of his articles some defects in the construction of workers' houses for which the governor of the province was responsible. He was released after having proved his good intentions and his past services to the Falange, but nevertheless he was obliged to publish a humiliating rectification of his original article.

Permitted criticism is in principle restricted to the administration of municipal affairs. It can concern town planning, street lighting, public transport, etc. At the beginning of 1957, the new mayor of Barcelona even asked newspapers to furnish such criticism.

---

[1] The State adopts the general interdicts of the Roman Catholic Church. Nevertheless, the Church itself exercises special control over the papers published under its auspices.

It is true that there are exceptions. In 1951, during a wave of strikes, *Arriba* published some articles which in no way minimized the plight of the working classes. In the spring of 1957, newspapers were for the first time in twenty years allowed to comment on the strikes in the coalmines of Asturias. This was interpreted as a sign of a general relaxation by the regime.

As far as foreign news is concerned, the problem is much more simple. The E. F. E. News Agency, which is a public institution, (decree of May 5, 1954) has for all practical purposes a monopoly. Its news dispatches are carefully controlled in the first place by the Ministry of Information and then, if necessary, by other authorities. By the time they reach the newspapers they have often lost both their objectivity and topicality.

The other news agencies, numbering about half a dozen, are concerned only with national news and are obliged to observe the same rules of prudence as the newspapers. It is true that in addition there are special reports from foreign correspondents, but as these belong to Madrid newspapers, which sometimes share them with large provincial papers, the copy to be published is censored along with the rest of the paper when the proofs are submitted to the General Directorate of the Press.

As for comment, editorial staffs are required to conform strictly to directives. In this way press campaigns are well organized, for instance, against France and England or in favor of the Arab countries or against the United States, according to circumstances.

Directives are also sent to editorial staffs to kill or else to treat in a certain way internal developments. This happens regularly to inspire the editorials which have to celebrate the 18th July, the anniversary of the "National Revolution." It also happens in special circumstances regarded as of particular importance by the authorities, who then proceed to regulate the most minor details. The death of Ortega y Gasset, for example, prompted the following circular : "Every newspaper can publish up to three articles concerning the death of Don Ortega y Gasset : one obituary and two articles of comment. All articles on the philosophy of the writer must underline his errors in religious matters. It is permitted to publish on the front page photographs of the mortuary, the death-mask or the body of the deceased, but on no account of Ortega when alive."

Directives are sometimes capricious or contradictory. In the spring of 1958, when the Madrid monarchist newspaper *ABC* had been authorized to give a detailed report of the meeting that took place in Portugal between the wife of the Caudillo and the Pretender to the throne, the weekly *SP* was forbidden to report the same event on the pretext that the paper appealed to a different class of readers than that of *ABC*.

This same reason was given in 1957 when morning newspapers were told to touch up the photograph of a trapeze girl by painting a small skirt on her, while the evening papers were allowed to publish the original picture showing the artist in her tight-fitting shorts. The reason for this distinction was the fact that the morning papers have a larger family audience than the evening papers.

The General Directorate of the Press does not, however, limit its activities to giving out directives. It sometimes hands over to newspapers ready-made texts which it requires to have published as if these had been written by the editorial staff of the newspaper. These texts are prepared by a special body of officials and then sent to the newspapers with a note labelled "obligatory insertion," sometimes also accompanied by instructions concerning the make-up and type. Such a text can, for instance, be a simple news report about a demonstration by students which would then be carried by all the press in exactly the same manner. It can also be an editorial imposed on one newspaper for special reasons. Thus the weekly *Destino* of Barcelona whose editorial staff is composed of ex-republicans, known for their admiration of Ortega y Gasset, was ordered to publish an editorial violently attacking the philosopher and accusing him of responsibility for Spain's misfortunes. During the last few years, *Destino* had often suffered this kind of humiliation as it was well known in ruling circles that the paper had not become sincerely reconciled to the regime.

Other methods of control

The government also uses other means of controlling the press, for example, its distribution of newsprint. It can regulate the price of newsprint as well as the circulation of papers and their number of pages. It has regularly used these methods for favoring the Falangist press, which also enjoys fiscal and postal privileges ; it has also used these methods on several occasions for silencing non-conformist publications. In fact it used the pretext of infringement of newsprint regulations in order to close down the literary reviews *Indice* and *Insula* at the beginning of 1956. Among other sins, these reviews had published laudatory reviews of the works of exiled Spanish writers.

As with other newspapers, these reviews used to submit their copy to the censorship in Madrid which would take its time and send it back censored to a greater or lesser extent. Some anonymous officials from the General Directorate of the Press would warn the editors of these two reviews what they could or could not publish. But *Indice* and *Insula* would defy the censorship by proposing to publish the texts that had been refused the previous month. Finally on the death of Ortega y Gasset, the homage rendered to the great philosopher by these reviews exhausted the patience of the censors. In order to suppress them they pointed to the fact that the reviews had exceeded their authorized number of pages.[1]

At the beginning of the summer of 1958, the traditionalist monarchist paper of Madrid *Informaciones* was advised by the Ministry of Information that its ration of newsprint for the month of July would be reduced by ten per cent, representing a cut of 6,000 tons of newsprint for the paper. The Ministry justified the measure by claiming that the paper's "political nuances" were offensive to the government. It went on to say that the 6,000 tons of newsprint denied to *Informaciones* would be equally divided between two other papers, *ABC* (monarchist) and *Madrid* (independent), which were carrying out a policy of which the government "highly approved."

The control exercised on the recruiting of journalists is another powerful instrument in the hands of the government. After the civil war, the professional associations of journalists were purged of the most politically dangerous elements, and even today a journalist not giving sufficient proofs of loyalty to the regime will not be employed by a newspaper. In order to exercise the profession of

---

[1] At the end of 1956, *Indice* was allowed to reappear and *Insula* followed suit in 1957.

journalist, one has to be inscribed in an official register controlled by the General Directorate of the Press. Recruits are trained at the official School of Journalism. This is run by the above Directorate which appoints all its professors. Students are admitted on presentation of a school certificate, a clear court record and a certificate of adherence to the regime. It must be admitted, however, that ideological education is not pushed to extremes and that students enjoy far greater freedom of expression in their seminars than would be expected for an establishment ruled by an organ in charge of muzzling the press.

With so many means of control and censorship available, one might assume that the Spanish press is a completely passive instrument in the hands of the authorities. In fact, however, the law of 1938 is rarely applied. There are very few examples of dismissal of editors-in-chief and punishment for the non-observance of directives from the General Directorate of the Press. This organ prefers to act in a roundabout manner, for instance, by suppressing a paper's ration of newsprint, as mentioned above.

Diversity of character

Thus in spite of all its fetters, the Spanish press does present a certain diversity of character. This is particularly the case with Madrid newspapers and also applies to a lesser extent to those of Barcelona (in fact the principal papers of the country). Beside *Arriba,* the central organ of the Falange which has an extremely poor circulation, one finds *Ya,* virtually the organ of Catholic Action and the unofficial mouthpiece of Martin Artajo, the Foreign Minister from 1945 till 1957. *ABC,* which enjoys the largest circulation of approximately 100,000 copies, reflects the views of liberal monarchist circles. The evening paper *Informaciones* serves the traditionalist monarchists and Carlists. Another evening paper, *Pueblo,* is both a trade union organ and a popular paper. In spite of these different tendencies, the possibility of expressing definite opinions remains so limited that Madrid newspapers fail to interest a large public. It is said that just one of the big pre-war Madrid newspapers had a larger circulation than all present-day capital papers together, while in the meantime Madrid's population has almost doubled.

The most courageous and least conformist of present-day newspapers is *ABC,* which also is the most important of them. Its conflicts with the General Directorate of the Press have been numerous. In 1953, its editor-in-chief, the Marquis Torquato Luca de Tena, son of the newspaper's owner, was dismissed for having defied the censorship by announcing, in spite of official denial, the arrival in Spain of Beria who was said to have escaped from the U. S. S. R. In actual fact, the real reason for his removal was apparently quite different : *ABC* had published some time previously an article on the Kremlin's personality cult making some obvious allusions to the same situation in the Pardo. It then subsequently refused to publish an extravagant eulogy of the Caudillo prepared by the General Directorate of the Press which was required to appear as an original text emanating from the paper's editorial staff.

It is interesting to note that the action taken against the Marquis de Tena was no simple formality. He was first of all suspended, then dismissed, then once again reinstated to his editorial post, only to be finally dismissed some time later. He finally became his paper's commentator on foreign policy.

At the end of 1954, *ABC* ran into more trouble after having criticized the conditions in which the municipal election had been held. It had its general exemption from taxes on newsprint provisionally withdrawn on all consumption exceeding the limit of 50 tons a month. In order to maintain its circulation, the paper was obliged to spend an additional 400 dollars a month in order to pay for this new burden of taxation.

Resistance to control

However, it is evident that the Spanish press is far from being completely muzzled. In fact on the contrary, there are signs of new forces tending towards greater freedom of expression. These new forces emanate partly from the Church and partly from the profession itself.

Before discussing the role of the Roman Catholic Church in favor of a relaxation of State control over the press, it is only fair to point out its past compromises. In 1947, several bishops had supported the catechism of Father Ripalda which was used in Spanish schools. This catechism included freedom of the press among what it termed "fatal" freedoms. There is a strong current running through the Spanish Church chiefly represented by the secret secular society of the Opus Dei, which is anxious to impose on the press a religious censorship which is just as, if not more, intolerant than the present political censorship. But there also exists a more liberal current. This is particularly evident in the review *Ecclesia*, the official organ of Catholic Action, which by virtue of a "gentlemen's agreement" with the Cardinal Primate and the Caudillo, remains the only publication in Spain that is completely exempt from censorship. This weekly has on several occasions raised its voice against the abuses of the censorship exercised by the General Directorate of the Press, although this voice was never raised too strongly. It also called for a new press law. However, one of its most courageous articles which appeared in May 1954, aroused such displeasure in higher circles, that a few months later *Ecclesia*'s editor-in-chief, Father Jesus Iribarren, was forced to resign. Amongst other things, he had written: "How can we consider our press regime as ideal when it obliges people to look elsewhere for the news that is the newspaper's 'raison d'être' ?" Furthermore he raised the question of whether the government would not do better to trust the judgment of some 115 editors-in-chief of Spanish papers rather than rely on about fifty more or less educated censors.

In spite of this outburst, the review continued to publish some more moderate articles under its new editor-in-chief but still called for an improvement in the treatment of the press. At the beginning of 1955, an article appeared demanding an end to the system of directives which "oblige newspapers to publish as their opinion the views of ruling circles, a practice that is an outrage to the rights of a human being."

This editorial started a polemic in the press between Mgr. Herrera, the bishop of Malaga and ex-editor-in-chief of the daily *El Debate*, and Don Gabriel Arias-Salgado, the Minister of Information.

In an open letter, Mgr. Herrera admitted the principle of censorship. He maintained that in order to serve the common good, the government was justified in applying censorship to all sorts of news items, even true ones, as well as to editorial comment... However, although censorship was legitimate in itself, it should be exercised in a legitimate fashion ; in other words, this right should be used judiciously. It did not include the right to issue directives obliging a journalist to publish what he did not believe "which is contrary to the natural law that upholds the right of personal judgment." In conclusion, Mgr. Herrera proposed the following points as an outline for a new press law.

1. The maintenance of pre-publication censorship but sanctioned by a decree-law which should limit its scope.
2. The reorganization of censorship in such a way as to prevent it from causing harm to the newspaper.
3. The creation of a special tribunal for press offenses.

These points coincide exactly with the demands submitted to the government in 1952 by the National Council of the Catholic press with the object of reforming the legislation concerning the Spanish press as a whole.

Apart from the Church, some liberally-inclined personalities have also had the courage to criticize the regime's press control publicly, with special regard to the practice of sending out directives. One of these individuals was the writer Dionisio Ridruejo, one of the former leaders of the Falange. In an open letter addressed to the government at the beginning of 1956 following the suppression of the reviews *Indice* and *Insula*, he denounced the defects of the system.

In the strictly professional sphere, voices were also raised in protest against censorship and directives, in particular during the National Congress of the Spanish press held at Valladolid in 1951 and Madrid in 1953. During the latter Congress, the editors-in-chief of newspapers vehemently denounced the abuses of the censorship as exercised not only by the General Directorate of the Press, but also in the provinces by local civil and military authorities. Speaking in the presence of Arias-Salgado, the Minister of Information, the editor-in-chief of *El Pueblo Gallego*, the Catholic daily of Biscaya, complained of the extension of censorship to non-political news items, stated that there was a widening gap between public opinion and the press and, with the full support of his colleagues, strongly insisted on the elimination of controls and the elaboration of a new law. The Congress ended by passing a resolution urging the creation of a National Press Council, having as its object the defense of the right of journalists to freedom of expression.

These protests and demands, however, were never acted upon. At the end of 1954, it was announced that General Franco was putting the final touches to a new press law, but so far it has not materialized and what is known of its broad outlines does not give an impression of particularly generous legislation. It seems to be concerned with reinforcing the independence of the editor-in-chief vis-à-vis the publisher, but at the same time placing the former directly under the authority of the government, in return for which the censorship is to be limited. In 1956 the Madrid correspondent of the *New York Times*, Camille Cianfarra, ran into serious trouble for having revealed one of these broad outlines of the law and issues of the paper containing articles on the subject were seized.

In July 1957, a National Press Council was officially formed. It is composed of journalists but is presided over by the Minister of Information and officially represents a consultative organ attached to the Ministry of Information. It thus brings no relief to the current system of control.

In spite of this, the breath of freedom continues to permeate the editorial offices of Spanish papers. It is easy to see from any on-the-spot visit that a large number of journalists, many of whom favor the regime, are unhappy about the situation of the press and are anxious to secure a much greater freedom of expression.

Attempts to defy the censorship have become more and more frequent and audacious. In the summer of 1957, the review *Signo*, organ of Catholic Action Youth, was suspended because of an editorial criticizing social inequalities, affirming that "the Communist danger is best combatted by respecting to the maximum the rights of individuals" and concluding that contemporary Spain was suffering from a "crisis of leadership and of the system." The greatest examples of audacity are to be found above all in the satirical publications, especially in the principal one, *La Codorniz*, appearing in Madrid. These are always running great risks. At the beginning of 1958, a cartoonist of the above paper was condemned by a court of assizes to two months' imprisonment and a fine of 1000 pesetas for a "grave insult to the State." He had published a cartoon representing Justice with a pair of scales in her hands ; one of the scales was weighed down by a bill of five pesetas.

Portugal

For over thirty years Portugal has been ruled by an authoritarian regime based on a single party, the National Union, and censoring all means and sources of information. Before the military coup of May 28, 1926, the prelude to the personal rise to power of Dr. Oliveira Salazar, the Portuguese press enjoyed unlimited freedom, a freedom which was at times abused. In fact, the Republic's legislation concerning the press, especially the repression of libel, was not very comprehensive. Liberty tended to become license. Impartial historians admit that the press must bear a heavy responsibility for the disorders that preceded the advent of the dictatorship. Consequently one of the first acts of the authoritarian government was to impose press censorship which has never since been lifted and to place government officials on the editorial staffs of the leading Lisbon newspapers. Next, the State virtually took over some of these papers, notably *O Seculo*. It owns practically half the shares of *Diario de Noticias*, a daily enjoying the record circulation of 120,000.

In a speech delivered on July 1, 1958, Dr. Salazar justified his press policy as follows :

"From some monarchical extremists to the democrats and the Communists, the present press law or the existence of previous censorship has been considered as a contradiction of the constitutional principle of the freedom of expression. This is inaccurate, but the question has been left open. Let us note from the beginning that the censorship is so benevolent in our country that it allows itself to be discussed, not just in the mistakes it may make but in its principles and its function.

"I can realize that the censorship inconveniences newspapers a little, even independently of any slips or faults in appreciation, but there can be no doubt its existence has permitted a security of work and even a liberty of action—seemingly contradictory but not really so—that we do not find in other supposedly more liberal regimes. There is now no case of seizure of a newspaper, much less of assaults or wrecking newspaper offices as in the past, and it can be said, neither suspension of publication nor crimes to be judged in courts. There are monarchical newspapers and republican ones, Catholic and Protestant, political or simply factual, neutral, favorable or obstinately in opposition, and everyone knows that they can only be what they are because they are not dependent on the government. Already well informed of the limits as they are, they do not in any way feel hampered in their activity either. The press must know that there are many possible paths of administrative activity by which their legal liberty can be "innocently" denied, diminished or distorted in practice ; but that is a sphere forbidden to us.

"Governments like ours, by which opinion is granted a constitutional function as a social force, have to prevent it from being distorted. And they also have to defend the national interest. The journalist's or writer's recognized privilege cannot be absolute and has to be framed within these two essential needs."

The Constitution of April 11, 1933 recognizes freedom of expression in all forms, but goes on to stipulate that "precautionary and restrictive measures will guard against the perversion of public opinion in its function as a social force, and shall protect the character of citizens..."

The status of the Portuguese press was defined by the decree-law of July 29, 1926, one of the first laws to be passed by the new regime, and one that is still in force. Article 1 of the decree affirms that "all persons are allowed to express themselves freely through the press independent of guarantee or censorship and without having to seek previous authorization or agreement." Article 9 declares that no authority has the right under any pretext whatsoever "to stop or hinder the free circulation of any publication... except in the following cases : if guarantees are suspended or if the newspaper has been suspended, if it has published texts or comments against republican institutions, the person of the President of the Republic, military discipline, national independence, as well as publishing information tending to alarm public opinion or liable to prejudice the State, or else a statement offending national dignity or honor, or finally when the publication is pornographic, directed against the security of the State and public order and tranquility." Special note should be taken of the vagueness of some of the clauses such as prejudice to the State and offense against national honor. Some of these are also to be found in certain laws of traditionally democratic countries.

According to Article 12 of the decree, "it is not forbidden to discuss or criticize legislation, political and religious doctrines and government actions, etc., so long as the object is to educate public opinion and to prepare it for reforms...", but "the publication by the press of any insult, defamation or threat against the public authorities is considered as an offense against the dignity of these authorities (Article 13). Any newspaper condemned on three occasions for defamation is suspended and its editor forbidden to hold a post on any newspaper for five years.

The Board of Censors

While the decree of July 29, 1926 was above all repressive in character, the much more effective decree of May 14, 1936 was essentially preventive : it gave legal sanction to a state of censorship which had existed since the advent of the new regime although only as an exceptional measure.

A board of censors was set up with headquarters at Lisbon but with branches in all towns to which all texts including advertisements have to be submitted. No paper appears in Portugal without the censors' official stamp on the first page *(visado pela comissao de censura)*.

The board of censors wields wide powers of discretion. Not only does it cancel texts but it also alters them ; it permits items to appear in some papers which it suppresses in others ; it sometimes holds up the granting of its visa quite arbitrarily thereby retarding the publication of the paper and causing serious financial losses ; it also decides on the sanctions to be applied against offending newspapers, being empowered to suspend them or even close them down permanently according to the gravity of the offense. There is no appeal against its decisions.

This board used to work in close co-operation with the Ministry of Interior, later coming under the surveillance of the Prime Minister's office. Its duties also include the sending of instructions to editorial staffs as circulars which editors are obliged to act upon. These instructions concern the subjects that can be mentioned and those that must be avoided. The board of censors obliges newspapers to print all notices from the government and the national information office, especially communiques and official speeches. As far as it is known it does not actually impose its own prepared texts on newspapers as part of their own editorial material. Nevertheless there is no doubt that it favors all pro-government propaganda.

Another task of the board of censors is to keep a list of the newspapers that are allowed to have official advertising allotted to them. This kind of control springs from the decree-law of May 14, 1936. Its preamble says the following : " There have been occasions when certain public enterprises have had advertisements published in papers which hold views that differ from those of the State, and which have been continually seeking to destroy the fundamental principles of the Constitution. This not only brings profit to the enemies of Society and the State, but also indirectly obliges all those interested in those advertisements to read those newspapers. However great the tolerance of the authorities as regards those persons who remain unconcerned with political issues or those who adopt views opposed to the new regime, there are limits which cannot logically be surpassed without the government appearing to show inexcusable favor towards those who seek to destroy its own institutions." Thus any civil servant publishing an official advertisement in papers that do not figure on the list drawn up by the board of censors is liable to disciplinary sanctions.

The board of censors must furthermore approve the nomination of assistant editors of newspapers. This function dates from the post-war period and has no legal foundation at all. It arose out of an incident concerning an opposition weekly called *O Sol*. The paper's owner and editor, Colonel Lelo Portela, died suddenly and neither his widow nor the newspaper itself could obtain government approval to continue publication under a new editor. Thus in order to avoid similar plights, several newspapers appointed assistant editors after having consulted and obtained the approval of the board of censors.

In addition to these controls, serious enough in limiting freedom of the press, one must add other restrictive or discriminatory measures such as subsidies to government papers and the inequitable distribution of newsprint. The decree of May 14, 1936 limits the number of pages of newspapers. Yet exceptions can be granted by the authorities and these obviously tend to favor government organs since these papers can claim a special allowance of pages in respect of space occupied by official texts. Finally, the State controls the National Union of Journalists, membership in which is obligatory for all those in the journalistic profession.

The margin of liberty

It might be thought that such restrictions have reduced the Portuguese press to complete subservience. In fact this is not quite true for there have always been some independent newspapers, indeed opposition ones, which are regarded as some of the most important papers of the country. They include the dailies *Republica, Diario de Lisboa,* and the monthly review *Seara Nova* in Lisbon ; the dailies *O Primeiro de Janeiro, Jornal de Noticias* and *O Comercio do Porto* in Oporto.

Most news is supplied by the semi-official news agency A. N. I. but the principal world press agencies can also run their services with hardly any restrictions, although their news has to pass through the hands of the censors. Banning of foreign newspapers is rare. It is above all internal news that is subject to severe censorship. This, on the one hand concerns news that can be judged to be unfavorable to the regime, and on the other hand news regarding public morals (scandals, suicides, indecency, crime, etc.).

Comment is relatively free so long as it does not touch the regime or its representatives. In Lisbon, *Republica* shows considerable courage by expressing democratic opinions.

Independent or opposition newspapers are naturally closely watched and have had trouble with the board of censors. For instance, *Republica* and other papers, especially some of Oporto and some literary reviews with strong views, have sometimes been suspended. More often they have been fined for having infringed the censor's prescriptions. The board of censors at times can behave extremely capriciously. The editors of *Primeiro de Janeiro* and *Republica* were once accused of having failed to abide by the censor's instructions when in fact the texts concerned had mistakenly been passed by the censors themselves. In 1942, the editor of *Comercio* was ordered to stop the naval articles by Commander Moreira de Campos whose articles were subsequently refused by other papers yet he was able to contribute the same articles to a semi-official review devoted to the instruction of naval officers.

At the end of the war, press restrictions in Portugal were to a certain extent relaxed. In October 1945, censorship was practically abolished for a brief period before the elections for the National Assembly. However, this experiment was judged unfavorably by the government, for the newspapers immediately went further than the limits which the authorities considered justified. Prime Minister Salazar thus thought it necessary to return to the old system of direct control.

Even so, censorship has become less rigorous. Its field has been narrowed down to comment on international politics affecting Portugal, news or opinions tending to sap public confidence in the regime, and news that can be exploited in a sensational manner. For instance, the censorship suppressed passages from a speech delivered at a Congress of university Catholic youth in 1955 which described the pitiful economic and social conditions of the working classes.

Opposition to the censorship

Newspaper editors in recent years have appealed regularly for the relaxation of restrictions, at times going so far as to ask for the abolition of censorship altogether. Within government circles there have also been those in favor of such abolition. There were even suggestions of this kind at the Congress of the National Union held in July 1956 which coincided with the thirtieth anniversary of the Salazar regime. Father Urbano Duarte was one of those who spoke against the control of the press suggesting that the government should find other means of reconciling the need to safeguard freedom of the press with the need to prevent its abuse.

In May 1957 on the occasion of an international congress of journalists meeting in Lisbon, several local newspapers raised the question of press freedom in Portugal reproaching members of the congress for not having dared to broach the subject. *Diario Ilustrado* said : "A press law replacing the system of pre-publication censorship would be the best thing that could be offered to Portuguese journalists." Its editor, Miguel Urbano Rodriguez, went so far as to repeat his views in a letter published a few days later in the Paris daily *Le Monde*. The editor of *Diario de Lisboa* also appealed to the authorities in an editorial which concluded with these words : "Give us back our right to fulfill our mission and thus to assume the full sense of responsibility which has been lost. By so doing you will have taken a big step towards the pacification of sentiment as well as the actual consolidation of the regime."

This vigorous spirit continued to manifest itself in part of the Portuguese press, especially in the *Diario Ilustrado*, one of the more newly-established evening papers of Lisbon which has no financial or other connections with the government. However, in September the editorial staff of the paper was completely reshuffled following a crisis which involved the resignation of the editor-in-chief and most of his colleagues.

Before the legislative elections of November 3, 1957, press censorship was again lifted. Non-government newspapers published the programs and propaganda of those opposition groups which dared to make their timid voices heard. It was possible to criticize the government fairly directly on condition that nothing was said of Dr. Salazar personally, and in fact several articles were written deploring the lack of respect for individual liberties as well as criticizing the regime's economic policy.

Newspapers most openly reflecting the views of the opposition, such as *Republica* of Lisbon, found that their circulation rose, yet became subject to all kinds of interference on the part of the authorities which sought to hold up their publication timetables and disrupt their distribution in the country. Moreover, the censorship although technically relaxed, continued to cut out passages in political articles considered abusive. While, for instance, it was possible to print an article in *Republica* on October 29 saying that "there is no sincerity in the protestations of those who maintain that the National Union will return to democratic traditions," in the same article (by Commander J. Moreira de Campos) the following passage was censored : " If I have decided not to go to the polls, it is not because I am an abstentionist but because these are not elections. Elections cannot take place in the midst of threats, and if we ourselves are subjected to pressure we can well imagine the intimidation to which the humble defenseless elector is exposed. Civil liberties must first be restored before the citizens are invited to go to the polls. Any other procedure would be a fraud."

The press was not allowed to publish the statement of an opposition candidate who claimed that at the previous election he had been expelled by the police from an electoral meeting without any reason being given, while the Ministry of Interior turned a deaf ear to his protests, adding that the same sort of thing was happening during the current electoral campaign.

On October 11, *Republica* published the text of an appeal to the highest administrative court by an opposition candidate whose candidature had been refused. However, the censorship banned the following passage : " The penal code has been revised ; new violations of laws have been defined, but these are so arbitrary that they are beyond discussion or alteration, even beyond constructive criticism... In fact once again, the odious security measures have had the effect of doubling the already existing sanctions ; people can be sent to prison not only for doing something but for the act of thinking ; a citizen can be liable to imprisonment for life for simply following his own political opinions..."

After the elections of November 3, which resulted in the victory of 120 government deputies, the press was once again subject to the full force of official censorship. This was once more relaxed before the presidential election campaign in May 1958, although General Delgado, the main independent candidate, had reason to complain several times at the restrictions imposed on his propaganda campaign. The government replied that press censorship had been applied only "insofar as it was necessary to put an end to all attempts to mislead public opinion with the object of disturbing social order."

Latin America

Latin America has always been peculiarly prone to dictatorships and authoritarian regimes, but these regimes have rarely been stable. They have come and gone. Their leaders have usually been ambitious military men, not ideologists of the European kind, although they have often borrowed relevant techniques from the past totalitarian dictators of the Old World.

As for the press, it has suffered as it is bound to suffer under any kind of arbitrary ruler, yet government interference has tended to be negative rather than positive. It has simply prevented newspapers from functioning or from functioning properly ; it has not, on the whole, used the press consciously as an instrument to mould the mind of the public—a possible exception being the Argentine.

After the Second World War, Latin America suffered a fresh spate of dictatorial regimes, the most important being Argentina under Perón, Colombia under Rojas Pinilla, Venezuela under Jimenez and also the Dominican Republic under Trujillo (in power since 1930). Since 1955, however, the first three have collapsed one after the other, while Trujillo still remains.

In addition to these four, Bolivia and Paraguay must also be included, though perhaps in the slightly less rigid category of authoritarian regimes. Their leaders (Paz Estenssoro up to 1956 in Bolivia, and Alfredo Stroessner in Paraguay) were both frank imitators of Perón and maintained special relations with Argentina's deposed dictator. No study of the press in authoritarian countries could be complete without mentioning these six countries, and perhaps certain others of minor importance in Central America. However, Argentina, Colombia and Venezuela having rid themselves of their dictators, can no longer be classified as authoritarian countries in 1958 ; they will nevertheless be discussed, and the role and condition of their press described from 1955 as a sequel to the accounts given in the previous IPI Survey *Government Pressures on the Press.*

Argentina

Juan Domingo Perón's dictatorship in Argentina from 1946 till 1955 was the fiercest example of authoritarianism and the nearest approach to totalitarianism that Latin America had ever experienced. Consequently it was in Argentina that the most drastic bullying and muzzling of the press took place. Perón in fact adopted the fascist technique of taking over newspapers in order to use them positively as government organs or as the mouthpiece of the Peronista Party and its auxiliary the C. G. T. (General Confederation of Labor) for the propagation of the Peronista cult and the so-called doctrine of " Justicialismo " (Details of Perón's treatment of the press are discussed in the IPI Survey *Government Pressures on the Press*).

After the fall of Perón, the provisional government pledged itself to restore full freedoms, including freedom of the press. Many people, especially foreign observers, looked upon the restoration of *La Prensa* to its original owners, the Paz family, as a test case. This in fact took place at the beginning of 1956, after the cautious right-wing military government of General Lonardi was replaced by a more radical group of army and navy officers headed by General Aramburu.

Freedom of the press was almost fully maintained by the two provisional governments with hardly an exception throughout the period of transition to representative government —a notable achievement when it is borne in mind that constant trouble making and sabotage by Peronistas was taking place inspired by their chief in exile. The elections for the Constituent Assembly in July 1957 and the General Elections of February 1958 which resulted in the victory of Frondizi (the most outspoken critic of the provisional government) were held without a state of siege and with the press and the radio free to express all ideas, except for those of the deposed regime and its party.

Indeed a varied daily and weekly press flourished in Argentina after the September revolution, although most of the dailies backed the government fairly steadily, perhaps through a mixture of habit and conviction. Opposition views were loudly expressed particularly in the weekly papers such as *Palabra Argentina* which was the principal mouthpiece of left-wing (some said neo-Peronist) views.

Indeed anyone walking down the main shopping street of Buenos Aires, Calle Florida, could not fail to notice headlines of papers, reviews and pamphlets extremely hostile to the government. Even during the state of siege re-established in 1957 because of repeated acts of sabotage, it was specifically stated that the suspension of constitutional guarantees in no way applied to the freedom of the press—and it did not.

Colombia

In Colombia, the great champion of freedom of expression, comparable in prestige and independence to Argentina's *La Prensa*, was *El Tiempo* of Bogotá. As in the case of *La Prensa*, *El Tiempo* came into headlong collision with its dictator, Gustavo Rojas Pinilla, and in August 1955 suffered a similar fate amidst equally widespread national and international consternation.[1]

There were other closures and suspensions which took place after the closure of *El Tiempo*. These affected amongst others *El Espectador* and *El Independiente* (the latter, as in the case of *El Tiempo*, for refusing to publish a confession of an offense of which it was not guilty). However, after this wave of direct assaults, the dictator chose quieter and more subtle methods of muzzling his press, notably through his control of newsprint and a particularly capricious form of censorship.

By a decree of August 23, 1955, all orders for the importation of newsprint had to have the approval of the Empresa Nacional de Publicaciones which issued licenses. If these were granted, the orders could be made at the official exchange rate of 2.50 pesos per dollar with a stamp tax of 3 per cent. On the other hand, without licenses the tax automatically rose to 30 per cent and the rate of exchange to 4.00 pesos per dollar. Moreover, after the approval of the Empresa Nacional de Publicaciones, the demand had to pass through the Oficina de Registro de Cambios where there was

---

[1] For the suppression of *El Tiempo* and other attempts against freedom of the press up to 1955, see IPI Survey *Government Pressures on the Press*.

perpetual disorder as Rojas Pinilla himself liked to decide personally how and when licenses should be granted. For example, *Intermedio,* a daily replacing *El Tiempo,* in February 1956 was threatened with extinction because import licenses were withheld by this office " on orders from above." It was in fact saved by the revolution of May 1957 which ousted Rojas Pinilla. At the same time, the Empresa Nacional de Publicaciones hoarded more newsprint than it could use for its own official publication *Diario Oficial.*

As for the censorship, its particular characteristics included the following : there were three successive stages of examination—those of originals and proofs, individual pages and the complete newspaper, all of which had to be sent to censors, working at an often considerable distance from the newspapers, before midnight. Material that was censored was simply not sent back and there were sometimes instructions as to the form of make-up. Not only was all political comment forbidden, but at times official news was banned in favor of the government paper. At other times, some papers could print items which were banned from other papers.

It must be stressed that this peculiarly capricious system, like the arbitrary distribution of newsprint, was consciously designed not only to control opinion, but to constantly prejudice the circulation of independent newspapers in favor of the *Diario Oficial.* For instance, *La Republica* was forbidden to print an account of the escape of a famous criminal, while *Intermedio* was not allowed to report news of the disaster of Cali (the explosion of a munitions dump in August 1956). Both incidents naturally received copious accounts in other newspapers. *Intermedio* in particular suffered from this kind of underhand discrimination. It was not allowed to publish national news on the front page, regardless of its importance, it was denied official bulletins, and once an interview with the Foreign Minister was held up for a week. Yet another technique used by the censors was to forbid all mention of certain names in all papers, thus decreeing what became known as " civil death " on some prominent personalities.

At the fall of Rojas Pinilla, all censorship came to an end and old newspapers previously suppressed reappeared with added prestige, while the *Diario Oficial* was closed down. Radio censorship was imposed for a period in 1957 following outbreaks of violence which the Military Junta claimed had been exaggerated unduly by radio broadcasts. However, newspapers remained unaffected.

Venezuela

Under the late dictatorship of Marcos Perez Jimenez, rigid censorship existed ever since the general came to power through a military putsch in 1948. It was exercised by a central office headed by a Director of Information and local offices in other towns to which all political and economic news had to be submitted. No political comment was allowed, although this did not apply to foreign affairs.

The only exception to an otherwise strictly muzzled press was the Catholic daily *La Religion* under Msgr. Jesus Maria Pellin as editor-in-chief and Father Hernandez Chapellin as acting editor. Its thinly-veiled opposition included the practice of criticizing other dictatorships and their methods in a way that was obviously designed for local consumption. Msgr. Pellin was offered thousands of dollars as a bribe to stop this criticism and support the regime, which he firmly refused. He managed not to publish a word about the faked election of December 1957, simply ignoring it as not worthy of attention.

The story of the press in Venezuela is remarkable for the part played by the newspapers in ridding the country of the dictator while his power was waning a month before his fall. Apart from *La Religion*, the most active opponent of the regime in the pre-revolutionary period was Miguel Angel Capriles, the owner of *La Esfera* and *Ultimas Noticias*. He was an expert at getting innuendos past the censor and reached the point of mimeographing wire stories critical of the government and passing them on to restive officers before the New Year's day abortive air force revolt at Maracay air base.

Jimenez' downfall can be dated from this abortive revolt of January 1, 1958. After its suppression, the dictator ordered all newspapers to print daily front page editorials condemning the attempt. Individual columnists were also ordered to prepare at least one article of condemnation. Four papers refused to obey the order and decided to suspend publication until two arrested publishers (Capriles and Pellin) were released and the order to condemn the revolt withdrawn. The government was forced to give way, for a suspension of newspapers would have openly proved false the government's assertion that all was peace and harmony after the Maracay uprising.

However, one paper, *El Universal*, was singled out for special punishment for it had protested particularly strongly against the condemnation order and had published news of the arrival of the rebels in Colombia on its front page. It was prohibited from distributing its copies until noon for nearly a week. The government hoped that this eight-hour delay would ruin its circulation and advertising, but the effect was just the opposite. In fact people fought to buy copies when they arrived, and advertising demands increased beyond all available space.

During the next two weeks, the constant arrest of newspapermen and orders to sack certain employees in various newspapers considered to be anti-governmental as well as recommendations as to who to employ, solidified the press's opposition to the government. Newspapers subsequently played a leading part in the general strike called by the Junta Patriotica on January 21, 1958. In fact they gave the signal by having their technical and editorial staff out of their offices the previous evening at 6 p.m. melting down type and in some cases breaking machinery so as to avoid being forced to work. Even the government paper, *El Heraldo*, was forced to suspend publication. This strike accompanied by an ultimatum from the armed forces and the civilian Junta Patriotica finally forced Jimenez to flee the country.

After the revolution, liberty was immediately restored and Venezuelan newspapers more than doubled circulation. *El Heraldo* was closed down and a new paper, *El Mundo*, founded by the veteran publisher Capriles. In June 1958, a rebellious faction of officers headed by the Defense Minister General Castro Leon sent an ultimatum to the provisional President, Admiral Larrazabal, demanding amongst other things the reimposition of press censorship. But the attempted coup was unsuccessful and their demands were rejected.

Paraguay

Of the authoritarian regimes that still exist in Latin America in 1958, Paraguay is the least interesting and the most negative as far as the role and condition of the press is concerned. There are in any case only four newspapers in the whole country, reaching a total circulation of about 45,000 in a population of one and a half million, a large percentage of which is illiterate.

There is no freedom of the press. All news is handled by an Under-Secretariat of the Press patterned on the old Peronist model, the Secretaria de Prensa. In fact twelve Paraguayan newspapermen were awarded scholarships by Perón to go to Argentina and three Peronista technicians were sent to Paraguay. Even foreign correspondents cannot transmit news not approved by the government, one of the main reasons why so little is known of Paraguay.

There is only one non-government paper, *La Tribuna*, but it has not published editorials for fifteen years. A newly-founded paper, *El Orden*, was closed down in February 1958 after only 26 issues for commenting on the government's one-party election which gave Alfredo Stroessner an extra term of office. In fact, editors take the line of least resistance : they either openly support the government or keep quiet. It is "insinuated" to them what news can or cannot be printed.

Bolivia

In Bolivia, the government's most favored technique for bullying the press is officially inspired hooliganism. Moreover, as in Perón's Argentina, the State controlled Trade Unions (COB) have been pitted against non-conformist newspapers, and it is often from this quarter that demands for suppressions and closures are made. The Unions have also been the direct inspiration of mob action against such papers as *La Razon* of La Paz and *Los Tiempos* of Cochabamba (described in the previous IPI Survey).

In 1956 there was a new president, Siles Zuazo, apparently not as harsh as Paz Estenssoro, the previous Peronist-inspired strongman, for on several occasions he announced his intention of restoring

constitutional guarantees. An amnesty was proclaimed for Demetrio
Canelas, the exiled editor of *Los Tiempos,* and the new president
promised to "co-operate" in reaching an equitable settlement of
indemnification (for the paper had been gutted by hooligans). Canelas
in fact returned to Bolivia in September 1956 but three days after
he had presented his claim for compensation, his arrest was once again
ordered and he was saved only through the intervention of the Papal
Nuncio. Thereafter he fled to Buenos Aires where a year later he
received more protestations of goodwill and leave to return home
from the Minister of Foreign Affairs and others. But so far there
have been no deeds to match these words.

As for *La Razon,* the other important paper closed down by
Paz Estenssoro, the new president, after reviewing the case decided
"not to grant" legal guarantees for its resumption of publication
because it had belonged to one of the expropriated mining enterprises.
There has been evidence of conflicting opinions concerning the future
of *La Razon.* For instance the attack on an official paper, *La Nacion,*
(partly sacked by a mob) was explained as being the work of an
extremist faction in the government whose object was to warn the
president against any intended appeasement of opposition parties and
thus to prevent *La Razon* from being restored to its original owners.
It has for some time been coveted by the powerful Trade Union
Organization (COB).

However, *Los Tiempos* and *La Razon* are not the only papers to
have suffered under Bolivia's authoritarian regimes. Other papers
seized or mobbed include *Antorcha* and *La Noche* of La Paz,
Trinchera of Trinidad, and *La Patria* of Oruro. There is no independent or opposition press except for a Communist weekly, *El Pueblo,*
which criticizes the government for want of revolutionary zeal, and
a fairly impartial Catholic weekly called *Presencia.* The only papers
left in La Paz are the morning daily *El Diario* (a government paper)
and *Ultima Hora,* a syndicalist-controlled evening paper which
collaborates fully with the government. *Antorcha* which had been
previously suppressed, was allowed to reappear as the Falange Socia-
lista's organ for an electoral campaign.

The government's actual control of newspapers is chiefly
exercised through its control of newsprint which is used as a Sword
of Damocles over the heads of editors who might be tempted to

criticize the government and its officials. There is also a government office for the co-ordination of news called the Departamento de Prensa e Informaciones de la Presidencia. It is based on the similar institution created by Perón and copied by Paraguay's Alfred Stroessner.

Dominican Republic

Generalissimo Trujillo, autocrat of the Dominican Republic since 1930, has boasted of the freedom of the press in his country, maintaining that there is no censorship there. Censorship indeed does not exist, but for the simple reason that there is no need for it. There is no independent or opposition press since all newspapers (six main dailies in the country) belong directly or indirectly to the government or to friends of Trujillo and his brother. The only exception to this rule was *El Popular* which was founded as an organ of the so-called Socialist Party at the end of 1946. It lasted only six months.

Of the important papers existing before 1930 when the dictator seized power, only *La Informacion* of Santiago de Caballeros remains. This paper had always maintained a policy of supporting the government in power. However, it must be noted that the disappearance of the other pre-1930 papers is not of any great significance as they closed down for financial rather than political reasons. One of these, *El Listin Diario* did oppose Trujillo openly for a short time until May 1930 when it suddenly assumed a cautious attitude and two years later became a champion of the regime. Other important pre-1930 papers which have now disappeared include *La Opinion* and *Diario*, both ardent supporters of the dictator, the latter's editor having suggested that the country's capital of Santo Domingo be renamed Ciudad Trujillo. Only the disappearance of one paper, the satirical *Cojanlo*, coincided with the inauguration of the Trujillo regime.

As for the Dominican press during the Trujillo regime, it has come to consist of two main capital papers, *La Nacion* and *El Caribe*, both founded by Trujillo himself in 1940 and 1948. Their joint circulation accounts for 61,000 out of the Dominican press's total circulation of 73,500.

The only incident to trouble this virtual ownership of the country's press by the dictator has been the so-called Ornes affair in 1957. It concerned the editor-in-chief of *El Caribe*, German Emilio Ornes, once highly favored by Trujillo for his absolute co-operation with the dictator, who later fell out with his master for reasons of personal antagonism according to Ornes, and financial irregularity according to Trujillo. At any rate, this case appears to have had nothing to do with political opposition.

The best description of the press in the Dominican Republic was given by Trujillo himself in an interview accorded to Daniel Morales of *Mañana*, Mexico, for the latter's report to IAPA's Freedom of the Press Committee in October 1956. After claiming that there was freedom of the press in his country, the Generalissimo said : "I can boast to the opposition of having created the press in the Dominican Republic ; the modern newspaper, with an abundance of national and foreign information edited with patriotism rather than the spirit of serving the end of a few or party interest, was established in this country when I founded the newspaper *La Nacion* on February 19, 1940, and later when I supplied the necessary funds for the appearance of the great newspaper *El Caribe* on April 14, 1948."

He went on to admit that other newspapers did exist before the two he founded, but these had only "purely local circulation" or fulfilled political or "purely literary ideals." As for the opposition he said : "In the Dominican Republic, the opposition is shown by newspapers with a moderation that belongs to a responsible press with a constructive orientation." In fact there is a column in *El Caribe* called "Public Forum" where criticism of officials takes place with every appearance of free discussion. Nevertheless, according to IAPA, it is said that these letters come from the presidential palace.

Cuba and Nicaragua

Stability in Central America is even more fragile than elsewhere in the Western Hemisphere. A regime can become more or less authoritarian overnight and the condition of the press will vary accordingly. The usual criterions of press freedom are difficult

to apply because of constant internal disorder and the virtual ownership of the press either by the government (as in the Dominican
Republic) or by other equally formidable powers in the land. Moreover, the press itself as a medium of expression is undeveloped due to
the large percentage of illiteracy in these countries.

At the time of writing, Cuba and Nicaragua appear to be the
most authoritarian of the countries in this area, insofar as restrictions
on the press are concerned, apart from the Dominican Republic. In
Cuba, constitutional guarantees (including Art. 33 on freedom of the
press) were suspended in some provinces at the end of 1956 after the
landing of Fidel Castro and his rebels. From this date, censorship
has been applied for successive periods of 45 days with varying
periods of respite in between, as regularly as if impelled by clock-
work. President Fulgencio Batista often assured representatives of
IAPA who have protested against these suppressions of guarantees,
that they are only due to the rebellion which had in fact dragged on
and off for several years until the sudden fall of the Cuban strongman at the end of 1958.

In Nicaragua, the assassination of President Anastasio Somoza
in September 1956 suddenly transformed the situation from complete
freedom of expression to rigid censorship and a state of siege. Editors
were imprisoned, papers failed to appear, and all journalists were
held incommunicado. Then as the situation became less tense, new
permanent restrictions were imposed which included censorship of
political news and comment. In particular, Nicaraguan censors were
concerned that no blank spaces be left after a paper's ordeal. Thus a
picturesque example of Nicaraguan censorship was the policy of
Prensa Libre which replaced all items cut out by the censors by
photographs of Ava Gardner. It was therefore not surprising to find
several photographs of Ava Gardner in one issue of *Prensa Libre*.

At the end of 1957, on the request of President Luis Somoza,
the Nicaraguan Parliament repealed a restrictive press law passed in
1956 after the above restrictions concerning censorship were decreed.
Letters of congratulation were sent by both IPI and IAPA. The
situation nevertheless was far from ideal, two prominent editors
of opposition papers being still in exile.

In conclusion, it must be said that in the fluid situation that characterizes politics and therefore press freedom in Latin America, one of the positive factors in this field is the work of IAPA, the Inter-American Press Association. Apart from the actual role of the press in countries like Venezuela, where it contributed directly to the overthrow of a dictator, IAPA has acted tirelessly on behalf of press freedom in countries that directly or indirectly challenge it. At times, its roving representatives have been banned by the official decree of a guilty government. At other times, the organization has acted as a forum for airing the cases of the victims of authoritarianism—and has been recognized as a formidable opponent by Latin American dictators.

Egypt

After the abdication of King Farouk in July 1952, the new regime slowly but surely began to develop its own policy on the press. At first there was much hesitation and fumbling, as the junta of young army officers who had seized power had only the vaguest ideas as to what the press really was. They did not appreciate the vital role which the press might have played in the revolutionary period which ended in the dictatorship of President Nasser, who combined the offices of President of the Republic and of Prime Minister, that is, of the Executive.

The first concern of the revolutionary government in its policy towards the press was to put an end to certain abuses current under the monarchist regime. In the first place, it set about ending the practice by which considerable funds of the Ministry of the Interior were distributed to a large number of journalists and newspapers. More than 100,000 Egyptian pounds a year had been distributed in this way to organs favorable to the party in power. During this period, party newspapers were often in a considerably more healthy state when the Minister of the Interior was a member of their party.

During the war, the royal government facilitated the provision of newsprint to certain newspapers through the Secretariat of the Order of Journalists or the Ministry of Supply which distributed newsprint at a tenth of the price of the free market. This permitted certain government papers to prosper by operating their own black market.

In the course of the Revolutionary Tribunal's inquiry concerning the daily *Al-Misri*, it was established that through being the organ of the Wafd Party at the time of Nahas Pasha's ministry, this paper came to some very favorable agreement with the Treasury by which it obtained much larger supplies of newsprint than it could possibly use for its daily circulation.

The suppression of *Al-Misri* in May 1954 caused a stir in the country and abroad because of the paper's importance. The Revolutionary Tribunal had accused its co-proprietors, Mahmoud and Hussein Aboul-Fath, of conspiring against the security of the State. Found guilty, their license of publication was withdrawn and *Al-Misri* ceased to appear.

However, Mahmoud Aboul-Fath still remained the proprietor of the Oriental Publishing Company, which published *La Bourse Egyptienne* and *Le Progrès Egyptien* as French-language papers, as well as the English-language paper *Egyptian Gazette*. All three papers and their parent publishing concern were subsequently taken over by the government-controlled Gomhouriah publishing house.

Al-Misri was not the only paper to disappear at this time. The dailies *Al-Gamhour al-Misri* and *Al-Ikhwan al-Muslimin* also suffered the same fate.

These first changes in the Egyptian press were accompanied by a purge of the Order of Journalists (or Press Union). At the beginning the purge rooted out only those who had profited from secret funds but later the exclusions began to apply quite arbitrarily to journalists who were hostile to the new regime. At the end of 1956, the Committee of the Order met to examine the case of 38 journalists whose exclusion had been recommended without any reason being given. This was the third purge since 1952.

The Order of Journalists was thus completely subjected to the revolutionary regime and this state of affairs was confirmed by the Law of March 30, 1955, which placed most professional and trade union organs of the press under the direction of the new Ministry of National Guidance. A symptomatic consequence of the Press Union's subjection to the new authority is its unstinted praise of President Nasser. In a telegram addressed to him, the union used the terms "Al-Zaim" (Leader) and "Al-Caed" (Supreme Chief) though his official title as head of State is "Al-Rais" (President).

The Press Statute has been modified giving some real material benefits to journalists. Their salaries have been increased and their social conditions as well as their retirement conditions have been ameliorated. However, in order to benefit from these advantages, they have to conform to the regime's politics. Since 1954, more than a hundred journalists have been excluded from the profession for not showing the necessary loyalty towards the regime.

Severe censorship

After seizing power, the new regime imposed severe censorship. It is true that censorship already existed in the days of the monarchy. It was attached to the Ministry of Interior. The Minister appointed a chief censor who, in his turn, designated the censors for each newspaper. The newspapers at this time used to complain that the censors not only stopped certain news unfavorable to the government, but also cut news items from independent papers in order to give them to papers friendly to King Farouk. It often happened that news was held up for a week so that it could first appear exclusively in *Akhbar-El-Yom*, a weekly which was then devoted to the Palace. Moreover, newspapers were censored inconsistently according to their attitude towards the government. It even initiated campaigns against offending papers, demanding their suppression. *El-Ishtirakeya*, the Socialist Party's fortnightly paper which was violently opposed to Farouk, often suffered from these campaigns, as did the Nationalist Party's paper *Misr-el-Fata*. Even influential dailies with large circulation such as *Al-Misri* and *Al-Ahram,* also suffered from time to time from difficulties of this order.

When General Neguib came to power, censorship was assigned to the Ministry of National Guidance, a new creation, the first head of which was Major Salah Salem. Censors were attached to all newspapers. These were handed two copies of the proofs of every news item or article before publication. The censor then returned one copy signed and approved or else refused. He kept the other copy for his Ministry as a reference.

At first, things were a bit chaotic, as the censors were young officers who had never had anything to do with the press before. One of these once told the paper to which he had been posted : "Do not include anything about cotton. I don't know a thing about it and I prefer to avoid errors." Thus important news concerning the possibilities for cotton exports was never published in this paper for the simple reason that the censor knew nothing about the cotton question.

The nomination in 1953 of Major El-Hamawi as head of the censorship marked a strengthening of press control. He held this position until his death in 1958 and during this period he gave precise orders, justifying and explaining his ideas and policies to the editors of newspapers. The press could theoretically appeal against the decisions of the censors to the Ministry of National Guidance and then, if necessary, to the Prime Minister. Sometimes it managed to do so successfully.

In a country emerging from a state of revolution, the government habitually tries to justify the control of information by considerations of public order. The Republican Egyptian government in fact considered that the ordinary laws of the country were not sufficient to restrain the press, for these laws made themselves felt only after publication of the newspaper, when some more or less erroneous information might have already caused grave harm to the national interest as conceived by the new regime. The resulting control, of course, could not but be harmful in itself, but after the creation of a permanent Censorship Bureau in the Ministry of National Guidance, the harm was, so to speak, 'generalized.' "Equality in injustice is justice," says an Arab proverb.

Censorship has, from the beginning, shown itself to be very touchy especially concerning anything to do with the regime. It does not tolerate any allusions to rivalries among various leaders. It even went so far as to forbid the publication of the name of General Neguib in a death notice announcing the decease of his sister. It bans anything that could be interpreted as an attack, even an indirect one, against the dictatorship.

Other forms of pressure

Apart from censorship, the revolutionary government has also resorted to many other forms of pressure in order to put the press in its power. For instance, in September 1953, editorial staffs were advised that "in the event of certain newspapers or certain journalists deviating from the right road, the Ministry of National Guidance will not limit its action to censorship, but will take other more serious measures. These include, in the first instance, a warning to the news-paper in question and its closure for a month ; secondly, in the case of a relapse, the withdrawal of its permit and its closure for an indefinite period."

With the coming to power of Colonel Nasser, the government further reinforced its tutelage of the press. The Director-General of the Information Department gradually took precedence over the Minister of National Guidance. At first in the hands of Colonel Abdel Kader Hatem, now in those of Colonel Saad Afra, this agency began to assume very extensive powers of control, going so far as granting or refusing the right to exercise the profession of journalist. Moreover, the government has taken over a certain number of newspapers and placed its own men in others. One has therefore seen colonels, lieutenant-colonels and other officers suddenly become journalists, installing themselves in the editorial offices of newspapers.

In 1956, the menace of nationalization hung over most of the Egyptian press. Several papers supported this measure, notably the semi-official revue *Al-Hayat,* which opened its columns to the ex-president of the Press Union, Hussein Fahmi, so that he could conduct a vigorous campaign in favor of it. President Nasser himself favored the project. In fact he declared at the time : "It would only require Beshara Takla of *Al-Ahram,* the brothers Zaidan of *Dar-El-Hilal* (the large publishing house of the main weeklies and illustrated reviews) and the Amin brothers, proprietors of *Al-Akhbar* and *Akhbar-El-Yom,* to launch a campaign all together against the government, for the whole of Egypt to be inundated from one day to the other with articles which could be very prejudicial to public order. This is the reason why I would like to see all newspapers belong to collective organizations with part, at least, of their shares in the hands of a certain number of people, in order to avoid the possibility of certain individuals being able to create movements of public opinion in the country."

However, no action was taken to enforce this point of view.

Towards the end of the same year, 1956, it was proposed that an office be created for the prevention of deviationist publications. The Minister of Labor and Social Affairs was charged to elaborate the project, but this also has remained a dead letter.

Up to the time of writing, no new press law has been elaborated, although such a law was forecast in the new Republican Constitution of January 1, 1956, in which Article 45 stipulates : '"Freedom of the press, freedom of publication and copyright are assured in the interests of the public welfare within the limits prescribed by law."

A good reason for not enforcing these measures was the fact that the government of Colonel Nasser had been able to muzzle the press sufficiently by other means.

The creation of the Middle East News Agency (MENA) at the beginning of 1956 tended to make the Egyptian press increasingly government-inspired and stereotyped. This agency was created with the participation of all the newspapers and especially the government. In the summer of 1956 the English business manager of the Arab News Agency, which distributed Reuters, was arrested on espionage charges. ANA was later put under sequestration at the time of the tripartite attack on Egypt. Realizing the importance for propaganda purposes of a well-run news agency, the Egyptian government began to build up a network of MENA correspondents at first in the Middle East and then in Europe. However, dispatches from Western agencies have by no means vanished. Items from UP, AP, and Reuter are common in the columns of newspapers. Frequently, these dispatches carry headings that have nothing to do with their contents, sometimes actually distorting them.

The development of a semi-official press has done much for the new regime. Three big daily newspapers have appeared since the revolution. Two of these are edited by high-ranking officers closely connected with the ruling junta.

The first of these newspapers was *Al-Gomhouriah*, which tried for a certain time, in vain, to supplant *Al-Ahram* and *Al-Akhbar*. It was launched with a circulation of 160,000, but at the end of 1957 this had dropped to 40,000. The preceding year its deficit was reckoned at 2,400,000 dollars.

To enlarge the government-controlled press, certain military leaders decided to launch another paper, *Al-Shaab,* in February 1956. It was first published and edited by Major Salah Salem, in disgrace since 1956. Just before the first publication of *Al-Shaab,* its editor announced his intention of revealing certain official secrets of affairs in which he had been concerned. Such prospective revelations in a

dull press which consciously or unconsciously was obliged to avoid
even the most harmless political issues, in particular anything to do
with rivalries within the military junta, were eagerly welcomed by the
public. The first issue was awaited with considerable impatience,
particularly when this was postponed several times. But when the
paper finally appeared the public found that it had been cheated—
for Major Salah Salem judged it more advisable not to disclose
anything at all.

Another paper, *Al-Messa*, appeared in 1956, published by left-
wing military elements. This is the only evening paper of any
importance. Its editor-in-chief is Major Khalil Mohyeddin, a cousin
of the Minister of Interior.

As the editors of *Al-Gomhouriah*, *Al-Shaab* and *Al-Messa* were
all ex-military men, at the time of the 1957 parliamentary elections
possible trouble could come only from *Al-Ahram* and *Al-Akhbar*. However the latter was, until July 1957, edited by a close friend of President
Nasser, Mohammed Hassanein Heikal, who after August 1, became
the editor-in-chief of *Al-Ahram*. Attempts were made over several
years to strangle *Al-Ahram* and later certain military circles planned
to buy it up. However, the above-mentioned nomination of Mohammed
Hassanein Heikal as editor-in-chief and managing director of *Al-
Ahram* convinced the government that there was no more to fear
during the elections from any real opposition in the press. Those
government circles who had considered buying up the paper, gave
up the idea, apparently alarmed at the high sums demanded for the
purchase of this doyen of the Arab press.

Al-Ahram, *Al-Akhbar* and the last minor publications to remain
more or less independent no longer represent a serious danger to the
regime. These withstand as well as they can the competition of a
semi-official press which enjoys enormous privileges. The latter
spends freely without bothering to balance a budget. It attracts the
reader by running competitions and giving prizes. It is distributed in
the provinces by special lorries or by plane, while the other papers
are sent by train and arrive with considerable delay. The reduction in
the size of papers to six or eight pages has adversely affected the
large independent dailies which used to publish over 20 pages. These
no longer offer special pages, they publish fewer reports from
special correspondents abroad. Like other newspapers which support

the regime, these more independent ones are obliged to sing the praises
of the leaders of the revolution, in particular those of President Nasser.
Twenty-five different photos of President Nasser have been found
in the same edition of one Cairo daily which is not even semi-official.
The King of Egypt in all his glory never had his photograph in the
press as often as the President of the Republic in 1957.

In these circumstances, nationalization of the press did not
appear to be necessary to the regime. In 1955, President Nasser told
journalists that so long as the press was in the hands of private persons
rather than groups and collectivities, it would be difficult for him to
envisage the suppression of censorship. Censorship of the Cairo press
was lifted for a few months in 1957 only to be reimposed by government decree.

Diversity of expression

Although the whole of the Egyptian press has been in tutelage
since 1957, there still exists a certain diversity of expression. It is
still possible to read from time to time in Cairo newspapers some
comment that could just as well have appeared in independent
Western newspapers. In April 1957, the daily *Al-Messa* energetically
attacked the government on account of a proposed law concerning
industrial development. Although maintaining that it favored a
planned economy, the paper declared that the government's law tended
"to control totally and arbitrarily the industrial life of the country"
and reproached the government for envisaging "excessive measures of
control." The same year, *Al-Ahram* and *Al-Akhbar* accused four
deputies of having received payment for technical advice given to the
higher authorities of Liberation Province, the province won from the
desert and regarded as a show case in the new regime's program of
land development. The deputies concerned appealed to the President
of Parliament, Abdel Latif Boghdadi, to defend them against the
attacks of the Cairo dailies. Mr. Boghdadi, however, replied that the
Egyptian press was entirely free, not being subject to any kind of
censorship.

This press campaign has shown that the government sometimes
allows newspapers to investigate the doings of political personalities

without interfering with the result of the inquiry. This gives the public
the impression that the press defends their rights and allows the
authorities to claim that journalism in Egypt is free. Such an example
appears real enough to the mass of the population. In practice,
however, a hidden threat constantly menaces journalists. Without any
given reason, anyone accused of having spoken unfavorably about
the regime can be punished. At the beginning of 1957, the editor-in-
chief of the Catholic weekly *Le Rayon d'Egypte* learnt to his cost
what were the limits to freedom of expression when he allowed
himself to condemn the discrimination suffered by the country's
important Christian minority. A member of the Security Service
visited the newspaper to warn him against the dangers inherent in
the publication of "tendentious" news. Father Victor Gohargui, the
editor-in-chief, however, refused to be intimidated. The following
week, he invited his readers to send him all the information possible
showing how the Christians of Egypt were affected by the government's "Islamization" policy. As a result, the issue of the paper in
which this information was due to appear was confiscated, while a
priest who had written some of the incriminating editorials was
expelled.

At the time of writing, criticism of the regime is still inconceivable
in Egypt, and editorial policy is rigorously controlled by the government.

In actual fact, there no longer exists in the Egyptian press a
single newspaper which could really constitute a menace to the new
regime, and one can go so far as to say that all the press has become
an instrument of propaganda for the regime. In this respect, Egypt's
newspapers have the mission of supporting and supplementing the
intensive propaganda campaigns of Radio Cairo in the Arab countries.

The alignment of the Syrian press following the integration of
Syria in the United Arab Republic at the beginning of 1958 is a good
illustration of the role of Egyptian newspapers, as well as being
characteristic of the press policy of the government of Colonel Nasser.
After March 1958, the kiosks in Damascus and other large towns in
Syria were swamped by newspapers imported from Egypt, of better
quality than those of the local press, yet selling at the same price. The
first editions of Cairo dailies arrived by plane at Damascus at about
seven o'clock on the morning of their publication and were on sale

one hour later. The Syrian press soon found itself incapable of facing such competition. Ironically enough, most of the editors of local papers affected by this competition had eagerly campaigned for the union with Egypt. Their situation was made even more difficult by the dissolution of political parties, which had represented for many of them their principal source of revenue.

Representations made in Cairo by the proprietors of Syrian newspapers led to the visit of Abdel Kader Hatem, President Nasser's press advisor, to Damascus. As a result, a plan for the reorganization of the Syrian press was elaborated at the end of April with the co-operation of a committee composed of the Syrian Ministers of Interior and of Justice as well as the Syrian chiefs of propaganda and information services. This plan provided for the reduction of the number of Syrian newspapers through the fusion of some and the simple elimination of others in return for government compensation. As for the personnel of the newspapers ceasing publication, some of these were pensioned off while others were integrated in the government information services. Thus at the beginning of the summer of 1958, more than a third of some twenty dailies appearing in Damascus disappeared. An even worse purge affected the press of Aleppo and other large provincial towns. Nevertheless, there were some newspapers in the capital which decided at their own risk to continue publication despite the new press created by the fusion of certain newspapers and the imported press from Egypt.

Far East

In several countries of the Far East, the press has been sub-jected to government supervision which has remained more or less strict and constant during the time of writing this Study. An extreme example is represented by the Chinese People's Republic, to which a whole chapter is devoted in the first part of the Survey. An identical situation is to be found in North Korea and North Viet Nam, which are Communist States. Moreover, in certain non-Communist countries, governments have also burdened the press with very severe controls and restrictions. These governments may justify their actions by invoking a state of war or a state of civil war with the after-effects that these involve, or else the existence of a grave external or internal threat, of Communist or other origin. The best examples of such countries are South Korea, Nationalist China (Formosa), South Viet Nam, Indonesia and Thailand. In South Korea, however, a non-Communist opposition press has been able to make headway without too many impediments after the end of hostilities ; in Indonesia and Thailand, it is only on occasion that the freedom of the press has been suppressed.[1]

But in the case of Nationalist China and South Viet Nam, gov-ernment control of newspapers and of information media in general have displayed more constant and systematic characteristics. For this reason it has been thought useful to devote some attention to the position of the press in these two countries in this Study. Furthermore, it has also seemed interesting to make a rough comparison between the present regime of Peking and that of the Kuomintang, first of all on the mainland, before the Communist victory, and later in Formosa.

---

[1] Various attempts against freedom of the press in Indonesia and Thailand until 1956 were dealt with in the IPI Survey *Government Pressures on the Press.*

Nationalist China

In a preceding chapter on the Chinese People's Republic, it has been shown that the Communist regime exerts both an extensive and a severe control over the press. Such a control is without precedent in China. Before the Communists took over, the policy of the Kuomintang with regard to the press, although restrictive according to Western standards, was, however, less severe than that of the Communist regime. In the first place, the Kuomintang never considered the press as a political instrument for its own exclusive use or for that of its allies, so that unlike the Communists, it never tried to turn the newspapers of the country into its own official or semi-official organs. On the contrary it permitted the existence of a large number of opposition publications. Although there are no precise statistics to show the exact relationship between the newspapers of the Kuomintang and the others before 1949, the available information indicates that the former never amounted to more than a small proportion of the Chinese press.

In the second place the control over the press exercised by the old regime did not seem so systematic or severe as that installed by the Communists, although opinions vary as to its efficiency and its severity. This control had been justified by the Japanese invasion and Communist intrigue, but often it went beyond its purpose. The Kuomintang has been considerably criticized for restricting freedom of expression in the press. In the book "Press and Public Opinion in China" (Chicago University Press, 1936), Lin Yutang gives a very unfavorable account of the press policy of the Kuomintang : suppression of newspapers, arbitrary arrests of journalists and their prolonged imprisonment without trial, the censoring of harmless news and economic pressure on independent publications. In October 1947, the American magazine *World Report* published an enquiry into these same grievances, supported by many topical examples. For example, in Shanghai three of the principal newspapers had been suspended. One of them was able to reappear after its proprietor had signed a "declaration of repentance" (recantation) and had engaged a new editor acceptable to the Kuomintang. Two other private newspapers had been closed down because of collaboration with the enemy but were able to reappear under the control of the Kuomintang which seized the opportunity of getting hold of most of the shares. The independent *Ta-kung pao* was especially opposed to the petty interference and threats from the government party, which undoubtedly partly explains the capitulation of its editor to the Communists and the fact that the latter subsequently allowed this big paper to remain in private hands.

Though the Kuomintang bullied the opposition press, it rarely obliged it to mirror its views. The system of directing editors was far less forceful than under the Communist regime. The control acted above all in a negative way, by censorship. Moreover it was generally as clumsy as it was capricious. For example, once it prevented the newspapers from reporting the arrival of an important official in a town where he had been officially welcomed with great display. However, the newspapers often managed by subtle allusions to discuss any subject or any person, including General Chiang Kai-shek.

Even the Kuomintang's control over its own organs was fairly loose and irregular. With the exception of editorials, the editors of the party's newspapers were free to choose their own texts. And even as regards the editorials, the instruction given by the principal members of the party was unsystematic. The control of personnel and the administration of publications of the regime were hardly more severe. Once nominated by the party, the publishers and editors had practically a free hand, as much in the choice of their collaborators as in the direction of their newspapers, so long as they made no outstanding blunders.

* * *

The situation is more or less the same in Formosa. Although the freedom of the press is limited, one speaks more often than not of the Nationalist Chinese press as being "inspired" and not "controlled." Firstly, alongside the official press (the chief government paper is the *Central Daily News*), there are a dozen private newspapers, some of them in sympathy with the regime and a very few in more or less open opposition. Some, such as the *Kung-lun pao,* are not over-moderate in their criticism, and often denounce the abuse of power and cases of corruption. However, with very few exceptions, private newspapers are owned and edited by members of the Kuomintang.

However, it must be remembered that martial law exists and the government therefore has wide powers, direct or indirect, to suppress papers. But on the whole, whenever there has been any repression of the press, it has come from the Party (KMT). Section Four of the Party organization deals with the press and issues "friendly" warnings to those editors or publishers who offend. There is also a Secret Advisory Committee which advises the Central Committee of the KMT on the press and all media of publicity. Although its existence is kept secret, it has great power. Some of the newspaper publishers are members of the Committee.

The most recent controversy concerning press freedom in Formosa was the new press law (the third revision of an old publication law) passed in secret by Nationalist China's Legislative Assembly on June 20, 1958, after more than two months of bitter dispute between newspaper publishers and the government over the constitutionality and political wisdom of the measure. Opposition to the law also came from a substantial minority in the Parliament, and reportedly even from some members of the party itself.

This legislation empowers the Minister of Interior to close, confiscate or suspend for a specified period not exceeding one year (after three warnings for minor violations) any publication if it is considered guilty of sedition or treason or of "instigating others to sedition or treason." Such powers also concern those who "commit or instigate others to commit offenses of interference with the lawful exercise of public functions or with voting, or offenses against public order or offenses against religion and the dead or against public morals" (Art. 32).

The Ministry of Interior can take these disciplinary measures without trial, although it is stated in Article 41 that in the case of revocation of registration (i. e. closure) of newpapers for "serious cases of sedition or treason or of instigating others to sedition or treason," offenders must be found guilty "by law."

Similar action is threatened if the publication "continues to publish as its essential contents indecent articles that are offensive to public morals or incite others to commit offenses against public morals after having been thrice subjected to suspension for a specific period of time" (Article 41). In fact the government's main published argument for the law was that it served as a check to the irresponsibility and excesses of the so-called yellow press. (General Chiang Kai-shek himself, however, was reported to be chiefly concerned with the prestige of the army. More will be said on this subject below).

Another provision of the law was registration or licensing. This existed and had been acted upon under the old publication law. However, the new law specifically gives the government the right to revoke a newspaper's license by administrative action. This was in fact one of the clauses of the law that was most fiercely resisted by the independent newspapers.

Measures that were regarded with less disfavor by the opposition concerned the stipulations that persons or organizations demanding corrections or rebuttals of certain articles should be satisfied in their demands within three days after their demands had been received, and the publication of such corrections should be made on the same page as that carrying the original article in question.

Moreover, no publication was to comment on a law suit currently under investigation or pending judgment.

One of the most controversial aspects of the new press law was the manner in which it was passed. Three parliamentary committees had approved the bill in a speedy vote taken before most of the legislators had arrived for the meeting. Then the government extended the Parliament's spring session into the middle of the summer to assure time for the passage of the bill, and when Parliament met, its proceedings were conducted in secret. Daily petitions from Chinese editors were ignored as were all other expressions of public opinion. The *Hongkong Standard* and the *China News* published in Taipeh spoke of a "rubber-stamped" bill and "steamroller tactics."

In commenting on the government's assertion that the press law was primarily designed to deal with abuses in the gutter press, the *Hongkong Standard* in its editorial of June 20 maintained that there already existed ample provisions in the existing civil and criminal codes as well as the law of libel which would give protection to those who felt they had been injured. The authorities had in fact closed down several "yellow" magazines prior to the revision of the law.

The *Hongkong Standard*'s editorial also stated : "Actually, as the situation now stands (just before the adoption of the new law), the amount of freedom enjoyed by newspapers and other publications in Taiwan is qualified and circumscribed to such an extent that the free press is already an illusory thing. There is of course no open censorship. But every editor and writer knows how far he can go without getting himself or his publication into serious trouble. The pressure under which the fortnightly *Free China* operates because of its outspoken comments is an outstanding example while the detention some time ago of two editorial writers of newspapers in Taiwan furnished another case in point."

It seems that one of the sins of the fortnightly *Free China* had been the open criticism of Chiang Kai-shek's proposed third term of office. It is a generally accepted taboo in the Formosan press not to level criticism at the person of the Generalissimo. Another example of this unwritten rule was furnished by an editorial of unprecedented vigor appearing in January 1958 in the *China News*, which lashed out at what it termed the lack of "broadminded, enlightened and forward-looking leadership" in Nationalist China, accusing the leadership of holding back "the progress or the nation," yet never mentioned the name of the leader, Marshal Chiang Kai-shek.

Indeed the question of press freedom in Formosa is paradoxical. On the one hand, the fact that a restrictive press law was passed, and passed in secret sessions of parliament, would suggest that the freedom of the press is severely limited. On the other hand, the violence of the Formosan press's reaction to the new law before it was passed indicates that newspapers have never been muzzled in the classical sense of the term.

* * *

This paradox is in part explained by the special circumstances of Formosa's existence. As the Chinese Nationalists consider themselves the representatives of Free China, it is natural that they should be concerned in maintaining as sacrosanct the actual principle of press freedom. This principle is in fact upheld with evident sincerity. It means more than just a question of lip-service, for its ruthless suppression on the Communist mainland cannot but be constantly before their eyes. Yet in time of war, principles are sometimes diluted or shelved.

Although there are plenty of examples of various types of criticism, it is significant how often this criticism only fully manifests itself just "after the event," once it is too late to have any practical consequences.

A good example of such tactics occurred during the quarrel between Taipeh and Tokyo over the flying of the Red flag in Japan to celebrate a commercial agreement between the Chinese Communists and some Japanese firms. The Chinese Nationalists' immediate reaction was to break off all commercial relations with Japan, a radical step to take because of the considerable importance of such commerce to Formosa. In this, the Formosan press backed the government, but when an assurance from the Japanese Premier was considered acceptable by Taipeh, and good relations were restored with Japan, some newspapers immediately attacked the government, maintaining that it was hardly worthwhile to deprive Formosa of vital commerce for several weeks for just a mild assurance on the matter. This opinion had not been heard while the crisis was raging.

Thus this curious habit of criticizing after the event must be added to the other restraints such as the tacit disinclination to criticize Chiang Kai-shek (mentioned above) and the virtual impossibility of founding new publications due to the need of government registration and licenses which in fact have not been issued for a long time. And in addition to these burdens, there is the new press law of 1958.

It has been said that the key to the motives prompting this law, as indeed the key to most Nationalist Chinese concern and interference with the press, is to be found in Chiang Kai-shek's particular insistence that anything to do with his army must remain sacrosanct. As his whole "raison d'être" in Formosa is, as he sees it, the reconquest of the Chinese mainland, the morale of his army must necessarily assume very special importance. The whole regime is geared to this one objective, and the press must therefore renounce any part of its freedom that may conflict with it.

Chiang Kai-shek himself has offered an explanation of the motives behind the new Publication Law which largely confirms what has been said above. In an interview with Dr. Howard Long in May 1958, he said : "The proposed Publication Law is a practical gesture of good faith to the press, because it is an attempt to avoid application of martial law to offending publications which undermine the national objectives by tampering with the morale of the people and of the

Army. In reality we need no change in the laws to accomplish this purpose. There are many provisions of martial law which could be invoked to hush those who employ divisive tactics.

"It has been our policy to be lax in the enforcement of any measure directed toward the press. It has been our purpose to allow free discussion, even criticism of the government. But we will not permit tampering with the morale of our Army."

South Viet Nam

At the Geneva Conference of July 1954 Viet Nam was divided between the Communist Vietminh and the State of Viet Nam which remained part of the French Union. North of the 17th parallel, the Democratic Republic of Viet Nam under Ho chi Minh, is today a State on the familiar Communist pattern. The State owns and controls all organs of the press and other means of mass communication.

Since the time of the Geneva settlement, the southern half of Viet Nam has evolved gradually from a chaotic remnant of the French Empire in the Far East into a nationalist republic with its own Constitution, Parliament and most of the other external attributes of democracy. However right from the beginning, the Republic of Viet Nam found itself assailed by the propaganda and criticism not only of the Communists but also of Western liberals who reproached President Diem with an intolerant attitude towards the opposition and marked authoritarian tendencies.

South Viet Nam has a strong Presidential regime which considers that a fairly strict control of the press is necessary in order to deal successfully with disorder and "Communist subversion." This policy is explained by the particular situation of the country. It also stems partially from previous French domination ; the colonial authorities hardly ever encouraged the development of a national press able to discuss government measures freely.

Restrictions governing the press were very strict at the beginning of Ngo dinh Diem's regime. All the press was subjected to censorship. Officials from the Ministry of Information examined the galley proofs of newspapers with utmost care. Their editors-in-chief were forbidden to leave blank spaces giving evidence of the censor's intervention.

Censorship was abolished by Decree No. 13 of February 20, 1956, but this was replaced by strong sanctions applied after publication. Fines ranging from 25,000 to one million piastres (600 to 24,000 dollars) and prison sentences from six months to five years can be served on persons spreading tendentious news or comment tending to favor Communist or anti-national activities, whatever the means employed. Less severe sentences are also served out in cases of offenses against morals, defamation and insults through the press. Any newspaper guilty of such an offense is liable to have its license withdrawn and the court can also order the closure of its printing works. In the case of a second offense, the paper's license is withdrawn ipso facto.

This decree has been in force up to the time of writing this chapter, but it is to be replaced by much more comprehensive press legislation now in the course of preparation. The new legislation is inspired by the French law of 1881 in addition to which it prohibits all propaganda in favor of Communism.

The Republic of Viet Nam's Constitution is more recent than the Decree No. 13 described above. It came into force on October 26, 1956, one year after President Diem had dethroned the ex-Emperor Bao-Dai and proclaimed a republic. Freedom of the press is guaranteed on paper, but the relative clause of the Constitution includes a dangerously vague qualification.

Article 16 of this Constitution reads as follows :

"Every citizen has the right to freedom of expression. This right may not be used for false accusations, slander, outrages against public morals, incitations to internal disturbances or for the overthrow of the republican form of government.

"Every citizen has the right to liberty of the press in order to establish a truthful and constructive opinion which the State must defend against all effort to distort the truth."

Mention should also be made here of Article 98 :

"During the period of the first legislature [1] the President of the

---

[1] From October 26, 1956 to September 30, 1959.

Republic may provisionally decree the suspension of the freedoms of circulation and residence, of opinion and the press, of assembly and association, trade union freedom and the right to strike, in order to satisfy the legitimate claims of collective security, public order and national defense."

* * *

In South Viet Nam, most questions concerning the press are dealt with by the State Secretariat of Information and Youth. This Secretariat issues the authorization for the founding of a newspaper, distributes newsprint and is used to disseminate the anti-Communist message of the Diem government. For administrative questions, it acts in co-operation with the State Secretariat attached to the President of the Republic.

The State Secretariat of Information and Youth examines all the publications appearing in the country, and when necessary, takes appropriate measures when a newspaper publishes news or comment which it judges to be harmful.

Sanctions take the form of the seizure or suspension of a paper, or of court action being taken against it. A distinction must be made between legal control (which allows for the right of appeal) and administrative control (without appeal) which is concerned with political questions.

There are a certain number of subjects which remain taboo. All praise of Communism, in particular that of the regime of North Viet Nam, is strictly forbidden. This is an officially recognized taboo. Furthermore, the actual foundations of the South Viet Nam regime and its overall policies are not to be questioned. Nor can criticism be levelled against the personality of President Diem or his immediate entourage.

At the beginning of the Diem regime, it was practically impossible to discuss and criticize the functioning of the administration or economic policy. But during the later period covered by this Study, a certain amount of criticism on administrative and economic problems was permitted. Embezzlement was publicly denounced. There was strong criticism of the nature and methods of American technical and economic aid.

Although comment has become freer, news is still very one-sided. Both home and foreign news is released exclusively by the Vietnam-Presse news agency which was founded at the end of the French colonial regime. Vietnam-Presse subscribes to the main world news agencies but reproduces in its bulletins only the copy it considers politically adequate for reproduction in the local press. Newspapers in Saigon are not allowed to subscribe directly to a foreign news agency.[1]

Vietnam-Presse has greatly improved its services from a technical point of view since Nguyen Thai, a young Vietnamese journalist with some United States educational background, became its director. Nevertheless is still presents all the characteristics of a State information agency and obeys all government directives.

Apart from this control of news at its source, mention must also be made of the monopoly in the distribution of newspapers. In December 1955, the State Secretariat of Information gave the monopoly of the distribution of all newspapers published in Viet Nam to the War Veterans Association. At the time, this association was headed by General Nguyen Ngoc Le, chief of the police and security forces. There is no evidence of the interference of this organization in the distribution of newspapers although the potential danger of such a system is obvious.

* * *

Since 1957, as has been noted above, government control of the press has tended to become less rigid. However one experiment in liberalization was brought to a sharp halt. The episode in question illustrates the atmosphere of restriction and intimidation in which South Vietnamese newspapers are edited—even though most of these are in favor of the regime.

For about six months, during 1957, the weekly *Thoi-Luân* was permitted, unmolested, to report all manner of news unflattering to the government. Besides touching on subjects normally taboo, such as arbitrary acts of provincial officials, corruption, etc., *Thoi-Luân*

---

[1] A similar situation is to be found in India where there is freedom of the press.

became the vehicle for vehement commentary and criticism of the government from the pen of its editor and publisher, Nghiem xuan Thien, and its leader writer, Phan quang Dan, head of the "Democratic Bloc" which purports to be a coalition of all non-Communist, anti-Diem forces.

Thoi-Luân rapidly became the most popular newspaper in South Viet Nam and its circulation, officially admitted as 25,000, was thought to be much higher—probably about 50,000, though the publisher claimed the figure of 80,000.

The first blow was struck against *Thoi-Luân* in September 1957, while President Diem was abroad. A crowd of coolies claiming to represent the Vietnamese Socialist Party and other pro-Diem organizations, attacked the printing works and burnt several thousand copies of the newspaper which were to have been distributed on the following day. The raiders smashed the presses and poured acid on the rollers. The police intervened only after the damage had been done.

The government, of course, denied all connection with this outrage and there is no proof of its having been involved. Simultaneously, however, the government brought a charge against *Thoi-Luân* for infringement of the distribution regulations and for unwarranted attacks on officials. The case was brought before a Saigon court but was adjourned and the newspaper then reappeared almost immediately.

It should be mentioned that the same gang which attacked the premises of *Thoi-Luân* also burned a few thousand copies of another less popular opposition weekly, *Tan-Dan*, published by a nationalist politician, Nguyen the Truyen. *Tan-Dan* ceased publication shortly afterwards. The gang subsequently moved on to the offices of the daily *Tu-Do* and threatened the editors with trouble if they published "any libels on the Socialist Party." In fact the premises of *Tu-Do* were sacked by the mob two days later because this paper had condemned the attacks against the two others.

Thoi-Luân emerged triumphantly from these difficulties and went on from success to success. It became the focal point of anti-government commentary. Its criticisms progressed from mild censure of the methods of American aid, a theme not wholly distasteful to the government in late 1957, to open denunciations of government activities and propaganda. This was too much for the authorities.

The police seized the edition on February 28 when it was half completed in the printing works. The newspaper's editor and publisher was charged with having published news and comments favorable to Communist and anti-national activities. The Saigon court found the defendant guilty and pronounced sentence of ten months' suspended imprisonment for Nghiem xuan Thien, fined him 100,000 piastres (about 2,800 dollars at the official rate) and ordered the withdrawal of the paper's license. It should be added, however, that Nghiem xuan Thien has been able to continue living unmolested at his Saigon residence.

There have since been other incidents involving the seizure of whole editions of various newspapers. In the spring of 1958, ten journalists were arrested in Saigon and charged with carrying on subversive propaganda. According to a police communique they admitted affiliation to a Communist network. One of these was the general secretary of the daily *Dan-Chung* whose paper commented as follows : "We are inclined to think that this arrest must be the consequence of a series of articles published by us recently on individual liberties."

Altogether, since the proclamation of the Constitution which purports to guarantee press freedom, there have been more than 25 papers suppressed in South Viet Nam. However, in 1958, a number of new newspapers have come into existence, in particular a lively and successful one edited by the dissenting nationalist and former Foreign Minister of the Diem cabinet, Tran van Do.

It must also be pointed out that many Vietnamese journalists oppose the controls to which they are subjected and resist attempts at intimidation. On several occasions, the South Viet Nam Association of Journalists has sent petitions to the government demanding the complete re-establishment of freedom of the press. In the summer of 1958, the daily *Tu-Do* published articles courageously attacking the principle of censorship in general.

In conclusion it can be said that although the press of South Viet Nam was still subject to rigid control in 1956, more liberal tendencies have been making themselves felt since then. However, President Diem and his government have made it clear that they regard newspapers as something of a necessary evil. At the time of writing this chapter, it still remains true that all systematic opposition to the government on the part of newspapers (even if this is not Communist-inspired) remains impossible. The danger of "Communist subversion" from at home and abroad is always the reason— and sometimes the pretext—given by the Republic of Viet Nam to justify its policy of constraint with regard to the press.

CONCLUSION

Any conclusions drawn from the Survey must necessarily be tentative. The regimes examined in the two parts of the study are basically very different from one another and even those which hold in common the principles of Marxism-Leninism offer substantial variations of the basic theme. It would thus be rash to establish comparisons based on similarities which are more apparent than real. Nevertheless it can be said that although authoritarian regimes often differ considerably in their press policies, they use—with greater or less severity—roughly the same methods and techniques. The range of weapons for the control of information is not a very wide one : thus there is regularly encountered the recurrent theme of censorship, directives, the intervention of government authorities in the choice of editorial staff and economic or other sanctions to bring pressure to bear on those who do not conform.

In fact, it is not so much the differences in methods and techniques of controlling information media which primarily emerge as the differences existing between the political systems which apply them. With the exception of Spain, which possesses a well-established doctrine on information, the regimes covered in the second part of this work have authoritarian information policies which are dictated solely by their own particular political circumstances rather than based on any ideology. It thus follows that the control of information media in these countries varies more often according to circumstances.

It is quite a different story in the Communist States. Their press policies derive from their totalitarian ideology. Under this system, the information media are and must necessarily be instruments for promoting the ideology embodied in the government and for guiding opinion in a direction conforming to this ideology.

The nature of the tutelage exercised over the press in Communist countries and in other authoritarian countries is therefore entirely different. In the case of the latter, the State seeks to control an instrument of which it is not generally the absolute master, while in the first case, the authorities guide and supervise an instrument which is entirely at their service.

Communist information policy has been established and tested for more than 40 years in the U. S. S. R. The Soviet archetype therefore serves as a model for all other countries with the same regime. Nevertheless there are different shades and variations which at times are quite well-defined. For example, the Chinese People's Republic admits, during the transition stage of the revolution, a sector of private enterprise in the press. Yugoslavia has applied the idea of workers' councils to newspapers which in other Communist countries are the organs of public corporations or social organizations ; Poland legally admits the existence of censorship which is denied either in the Constitutions or in the laws of most of the other countries in the Eastern bloc.

Moreover, during the period of the "thaw" which followed the death of Stalin, the "liberalization" of the press varied greatly from country to country, not only with regard to its extent but also to its nature. In the U. S. R. and in most of the States of the Eastern bloc, there was some limited relaxation of control inspired from above—very limited in East Germany and Czechoslovakia, more extensive in Communist China but followed there by rigorous repression. In Poland, on the other hand, there was temporarily a real emancipation of the press, resulting both from concessions from the authorities and a "liberal" current surging up from below. However, the control of this evolution remained always at the discretion of the government which could bring a halt to it from one day to another. The Polish experience also shows that under the Communist system, the press, even in the best conditions, can never enjoy anything more than a form of supervised liberty.

Two further general points should be made :

The first is the existence in the professional circles of all the countries studied of a spirit of revolt against the complete tutelage of the press by the State. The extent of this resistance varies from one country to another according to the circumstances. But it can be detected even in the U. S. S. R. where the control of information media is the most rigid. During the period under review there has been evidence in may authoritarian countries of the aspirations of journalists to a greater freedom of expression and a greater degree of truthfulness in news. This is true even when "liberalization" was inspired from above. A large number of these journalists both in Communist and other countries have been prepared to run grave risks in defying government authority for the sake of their aspirations. Some of them have paid dearly for their courage, in some cases at the cost of their lives.

The final important point which emerges from this Study is the public's desire for a press which gives correct information and expresses itself with freedom. This need has been voiced by the public in dictatorships whenever it has had the opportunity to do so. It was evident in Warsaw as soon as the "thaw" had got under way and later when the banning of *Po Prostu* provoked disturbances. It was also evident in Budapest, before and even more so during the revolution in the autumn of 1956, when the sale of the new free newspapers assumed the same importance as that of bread in the midst of the fighting in the streets. The same phenomenon was once again observed in Caracas during the days that preceded the fall of the dictator and again in Lisbon when censorship was relaxed during the electoral campaigns.

In the countries where information is controlled and the newspapers are in bondage, freedom of the press is seen—by contrast—at its true value. Only then is it fully realized how essential this freedom is for the human being.

IPI SURVEY No. 6

PROFESSIONAL SECRECY

AND

THE JOURNALIST

Published by
The International Press Institute
Zurich, 1962

PREVIOUS IPI SURVEYS

Printed for the International Press Institute
by Imprimerie Ganguin & Laubscher S. A., Montreux

CONTENTS

Preface

In undertaking this study of professional secrecy, the International Press Institute has turned for detailed reports to authorities within representative countries. On the basis of their own special familiarity with the indigenous conditions and circumstances, they have in each case provided information bearing upon the journalist's right, or lack of right, to protect his sources.

This information has included relevant legal texts, conditions and limitations affecting the journalist, evidences of recognition of the problem in jurisprudence, in custom, and in ethical codes ; references to important cases, and to opinions, statements or publications giving expression of relevant or significant legal, professional and public views. These reports, sometimes very extensive, have been edited and reduced in length to provide a certain uniformity of approach in the treatment of the general subject with reference to each of the countries examined.

In addition, an extensive questionnaire of 60 questions was distributed to professional journalists and professional associations in 31 countries, through the assistance of members of IPI National Committees. Of 250 copies so distributed, 123 copies were returned from 24 countries. This high response provided indications of the views of professional journalists on the subject, and these views are examined in detail in the study following.

The IPI wishes to express its appreciation to those rapporteurs who have assisted so conscientiously in making this general study possible, and to those journalists who contributed so usefully. If the country-reports that follow are in some measure repetitious this has seemed inevitable because of the existence of circumstances common to the legal systems of many nations. Yet, if this is a fault, or if other faults appear in the study, let such shortcomings be ascribed to the editor, rather than to any rapporteur or journalist responding to a questionnaire.

Introduction

The basic function of the press, where properly conducted, is to present that information required by the people if the democratic process is to operate effectively. To obtain such information, in the first place, the representatives of the press must have access to the necessary facts, and then must be free to publish them without interference or harassment.

The history of the press, since its introduction some five centuries ago, has been very largely a history of struggle to win and retain full freedom to perform that basic function. It has been a struggle against licensing and restrictive taxation, against barriers limiting its access to information, including the right to report debates in Parliament and Congress; against the concept of "seditious libel" under which the truth of a report not only was irrelevant, but wherein the courts held to a rule that "the greater the truth, the greater is libel."

In its provision of information for the people, and acting on behalf of the people, the press seeks information about the administration of government at all levels and about every sort of subject directly related to the public welfare. Although limits still exist, even in free countries, relative to access to some such information, the press organization now is sufficiently established and accepted so that most information in the area of public affairs is available to newspaper representatives through a well-established routine. In certain circumstances, however, this is not the case, and these may be important circumstances.

As might be expected, when inefficiency, corruption or selfish personal or policy interests are involved in the conduct of public or private affairs or where intolerances exist, the reporting and investigative function of the press in likely to encounter obstacles. Relevant information then becomes more difficult to obtain or to verify. Yet the public welfare may be seriously involved. If a responsible press is to perform as it should, its representatives then may be forced to depart from the more routine procedures of news-gathering to obtain information through sources not normally used, and through sources that — for their own protection —

may wish to remain anonymous. This wish derives from the fact that an individual providing information which powerful interests might prefer to have withheld could very well become a target for retaliation taking any imaginable form, up to and including murder.

The journalist and his informant

An essential element of the news-gathering process is the relationship between the journalist and his informant. The journalist seeks information from any and all sources likely to be able to provide him with that information. In the final analysis these "sources" are individuals. Many of them are public officials operating at various levels of government, and with varying degrees of authority and knowledge ; others are individuals engaged in business or professional activities, or in the arts.

In seeking information from any individual, bureaucrat or not, the journalist almost always receives his answers in a straight-forward conversational exchange. In using information so obtained, he normally credits the source by name, with such further identification as may be necessary to establish the validity of the speaker's knowledge. Very few reports appear in print without some such specific attribution to source. This is regarded as essential if the reader is to be able to form a proper judgement of the weight to be given a particular statement.

But they are exceptions. They are infrequent, but may be important. There are times and circumstances, as noted, when an informant may not wish to be identified as the source of a statement. To the journalist who has established himself as a reliable reporter, accurate and responsible in his approach to his task, the "source" may nevertheless be willing to provide certain information with the understanding that it will not be attributed to him. The informant may have good reason for wishing to remain anonymous. It may be a personal reason, but perfectly understandable and legitimate. There may even be a reason bearing some direct relation to the public welfare. The journalist might try to persuade the source to permit him to use the information with the usual attribution, or he might not. But if the source clearly wished to remain anonymous, and if the information seemed worthy of use, the journalist would use it without any such direct attribution.

The relationship, in situations of this sort, between a journalist and his source, is referred to by the term *professional secrecy*. The information is given "in confidence" or "off the record". It is received as a "confidence," so far as concerns identification of the source. The ethics of journalism, written or unwritten, are such that a journalist receiving information in confidence will respect that confidence. The occasion does not often arise to receive information in that way, but when it is so received it would be a very rare thing for the journalist to break the confidence. If he did so he would be operating quite contrary to accepted standards of behaviour for a reputable journalist whether under a formal "code of ethics" or not. If only as a matter of enlightened self-interest, also, he would respect that confidence because to do otherwise would tend to deprive him of further confidences, cause his source to "dry up," and reduce his effectiveness as a journalist.

Rare as it is for a source to convey information in confidence, most uses of such information go unchallenged. But occasionally a situation may arise wherein the journalist is asked to reveal his source of information. This demand may be made upon him as a witness in a court hearing a case in which the subject matter of the confidence is in some way involved. Or the demand may be made by some quasi-judicial or legislative or quasi-legislative body or some official or semi-official agency of government. The question then arises as to the *legal* right of the journalist to "protect his source" or to "protect his confidences".

The privileged groups

Where they claim this right, journalists naturally point out that professional secrecy is a right or privilege accorded to certain groups in almost every country. So the courts recognize that they cannot normally demand information originally received in confidence by officials in national governmental positions or in provincial or local administrations, by members of the legal or medical professions, or by members of the clergy. Through statutory provision, this privilege almost always is extended to these groups, usually to some peripheral groups such as pharmacists, medical technicians, midwives, hospital authorities, and occasionally, by interpretation, even to pawnbrokers, accountants, or business or industrial employees privy to trade secrets. But neither governments nor the legal profession have so far accepted the journalist's claim for inclusion among these special groups.

It has been argued that the right of professional secrecy, where legally recognized, is based upon concern for what is best for the general public—for the people as a whole. The precedents for restricting that recognition to those groups now generally protected by law were established before the press had grown to its present estate. Historically, professional secrecy for government officials existed from time immemorial, when it was a duty imposed upon servants for the ruling group, even though their interests did not necessarily coincide, in fact, with the public welfare. Today recognition of professional secrecy for government officials is justified as the public welfare is conceived by executives of the government to require, with the explicit or tacit consent of the Parliamentary majority.

For the clergy, somewhat the same early opportunity arose to establish a legal right to protect confidences. There was, in fact, a sound *human* reason to argue that a person in distress should have the opportunity to seek comfort or assistance, without fear of having his confidence abused. Thus he might appeal to a member of the clergy, or of the medical or legal professions.

It is a normal psychological phenomenon for a group of people with the same professional interests to develop a clan spirit. A clan spirit, sufficiently strong and well entrenched, might establish for a group certain rights and privileges—including the legal right to professional secrecy.

There is no fundamental reason to insist that the concern of the clergy, the medical profession or the legal profession—any more than of the ruling class—always has coincided perfectly with the public interest or welfare. The medical profession might be indignant if one attempted to trace their concept of professional secrecy back to the secrets of the medicine men and medieval barber-surgeons, and to suggest that their *right* to secrecy had been gained through clan pressure. The clergy might object, equally, at any suggestion that they used their spiritual hold over the people to win similar privilege. And the legal profession would dispute the suggestion that, because they *made* the law, it was easy for them to see that their own clan had such special privilege as survives to the present day.

Whatever the origins, professional secrecy for government officials, members of the clergy and of the medical and legal professions is virtually unquestioned today, and is regarded as justified as a protection to the people, and therefore correctly retained in the public interest.

Misusing privileges

Questions do arise, however, on occasions when it is demonstrated, or even believed, that individual members of the privileged groups are misusing their privileges. Questions also arise when those privileges are extended to certain peripheral groups but still withheld from other groups—such as journalists—whose functions may be regarded as bearing at least as direct a relation to the public welfare. It is on this ground that some journalists and their associations have urged that professional secrecy within their field also be given *legal* recognition.

So far, this urging has been largely in vain. The negative arguments of courts and legislative bodies, with reference to the journalist's position, tend to be one-sided, in the view of journalists. Yet, the jurists argue that an individual consulting a doctor or a lawyer is not concerned about it becoming known that he has done so, even though he may be concerned about preserving secrecy as to the precise content of the communication between them. By contrast, the journalist's informant is not concerned about the subject matter conveyed to the journalist becoming known — indeed, the whole purpose of the communication of such information may be to have it made known—but he is concerned about having his name kept secret. In short, the relationships are based on quite opposite concepts.

Not even the strongest opponents of journalistic professional secrecy deny the social importance of journalism, *in its highest expression*. While pointing to the interest that society as a whole has in granting professional secrecy to doctors and lawyers, they agree that society has an equal interest in the function of the press in disclosing abuses in the social structure or in the conduct of government at various levels. Revelation of such abuses is one of the highest public responsibilities of the press. Yet, the press has argued in vain that it cannot entirely fulfill this task if its sources are unwilling to speak to journalists out of fear that the journalists may later be forced to disclose those sources under legal demand to do so.

In judging the validity of this argument, of course, it is necessary to consider the nature and level of the journalistic profession in a given country, and its organization. In countries where the ethical and technical standards are low, arguments in opposition to granting the privilege of professional secrecy are difficult to challenge. It has, in fact, been held by officials of countries where the press is in a condition of "infancy" that there would be a positive danger in recognizing a journalist's right to withhold sources, in the face of official or court demand, since to do so might mean that an unscrupulous journalist could "protect" a source that had no actual existence, but was merely claimed to give a semblance of truth to propaganda of his own origination. There are circumstances, also, where the organization of journalism is so loose as to provide no assurance as to its integrity or its quality of performance. Where this is the case, it would be unrealistic to extend privileges to journalists of such a country on the same basis as to members of the other professions, possessing established safeguards as to technical competence and ethical standards. In an authoritarian country, finally, no journalist would have any such right or privilege. If asked to reveal his source of information he would have no choice but to comply at once.

Cases in point

There is a juridical aspect to the problem, also, bearing on how to define or determine who may properly be called a "journalist". Should anyone who asserts himself to be a journalist be accepted as such, and given the privilege of professional secrecy ? Should there be any differentiation between journalists attached to news publications, to political or to polemical publications ? Should the editor of a publication be privileged in that way ? Or a publisher ? Or a foreign correspondent ? Or a local correspondent in a small provincial town ? Or at the national capital ? Or a sub-editor on the staff of a newspaper ? Or a local reporter ? Or a printer ? Should the privilege be extended to journalists associated with news agencies ? Or with periodicals of various sorts and frequency of publication ? Or to a radio or television journalist ? In other words, who is to be regarded as a "journalist" if such a right is to be acknowledged ?

If the public welfare is to be a determining factor in evaluating the legal recognition of the principle of professional secrecy, we must consider the possible or actual clash between the administration of justice and the social function of the press even in its highest form of development. Here the *content* of information may have a very real bearing on issues affecting the public welfare.

If the informant himself belongs to a group with a recognized right of professional secrecy, but his *information* does not fall within an accepted category protected by law, *then* there may arise a conflict between the administration of justice and journalistic ethics. That is, if a journalist testifying before a court is asked to disclose his source of information—with that testimony held by the court to be essential—should the journalist refuse, or may he refuse, on the ground that it is equally essential that the flow of information from source to journalist—and so to the public—be not hampered or compromised, as it would be if he is forced to break the confidence reposed in him by his source ?

Even more—if the informant himself belongs to a group with a right and duty to maintain professional secrecy—as with a government official—*and* if the information he has conveyed to the journalist (even though concerned with the public welfare) is itself "classified," then the journalist is confronted by a doubly difficult problem. The court may wish to determine whether an official violation has occurred whereby secret information has been revealed, possibly affecting public security, or even amounting to treason. If an officer of the administration has violated his duty to guard secret information, the administration of justice and of government business becomes an issue. But so also does the activity of the journalist, whose revelation of such secret information may make him a party to an official offence. Recognition of the journalist's right to professional secrecy in such a case would be tantamount to the recognition of the informant's right to violate official secrecy.

The gravity of the issue may properly be considered, also. A slight offence is one thing. But a case that might relate to high treason, for example, would be quite another. Even where no legal right of professional secrecy exists for journalists, the courts or other officials in practice might handle a minor case with a tacit understanding of professional journalistic ethics. Where the administration of justice might be adversely affected by the withholding of information as to source, however, they might take a different position.

Because the issue of professional secrecy has not arisen very often in past generations, it has not acquired the same high value as for instance, freedom of the press, of which it is, nevertheless an aspect. Yet, however difficult it is to formulate it precisely, the issue of professional secrecy is possibly the most important problem *of a juridical nature* now confronting the press of the free world. No solution has yet been found to offer promise of any universal clarification of a situation where, even in countries with a press otherwise free, journalists nevertheless have been imprisoned because they elected to protect a person who has given them information in confidence. It is this problem which is examined in the pages that follow.

Part One

The Legal Position

Argentina

In Latin America, no country offers journalists legal protection to safeguard professional secrecy. The general attitude of courts and legislative bodies has been unfavourable to recognition of any such right. The position of the journalist in Argentina is representative, in that respect, of his position in other countries of the western hemisphere south of the United States.

Most Latin American nations make provision in their Constitutions for "freedom of the press". But those assurances have repeatedly been set aside under "state of siege" regulations suspending all civil rights during periods of emergency. Although journalists of some of the countries, through their own organizations, also have drafted codes of ethics and have proposed reforms to assure full liberty of expression through press and radio, and even though the Inter-American Press Association has demonstrated special interest in matters of press freedom, the results have been reflected only rarely in liberal official government action or policy.

On the contrary, there is (or has been) on the statute books of a number of Latin American countries a penal offence called *desacato*. This can be variously interpreted as meaning "disrespect" for the authorities, or "disobedience," "irreverence" for accepted religious or social standards, or "contempt" or merely disregard for abstract principles of the legal and administrative norm. It may not be a "crime," but it can subject an offender to a fine or to imprisonment, as a civil offence.

Governments of Latin American countries have tended to regard infractions by the press as a particularly dangerous form of *desacato* because of the influence the press may exert on public opinion, even to the point of arousing revolutionary sentiment against the authorities. Systems thus have been evolved to restrict or discourage the press from indulging in unrestricted political analysis or social criticism, and this has had its effect on professional secrecy.

It has not been uncommon in Latin American countries for a journalist who gives offence by what he writes, publishes or broadcasts to be arrested. If such an offence should occur in other countries, the journalist might be brought into court to answer charges. In Latin American countries, however, the procedure frequently has been to subject him to arbitrary imprisonment and, at times, to physical abuse. At best, he is likely to be subjected to intensive interrogation and—where the authorities find it appropriate—ordered to reveal confidential sources of information.

In Latin American countries, as in so many others, a lawyer or a doctor or a priest is entitled by law to protect the identity of those who may confide in him. But this same privilege is not extended to the journalist. If he declines to reveal a source of information, he is likely to remain in jail, he might be subjected to physical abuse, or he might be exiled as a political enemy.

While it would not be accurate to say that the more extreme actions would necessarily be taken against a reluctant journalist in Argentina, at least since the period of the Peron regime, the fact remains that there and elsewhere in Latin America, whenever the Courts or any committee of the national legislative body has had occasion to request a source of information presented in the press, the reporter or editor summoned to reply has acceded to the request with little or no hesitancy. This has been the practice without exception, so far as known, however difficult and unwelcome to the journalist, because neither law nor custom protects him in an assertion of a right to keep silent. For that reason, there is no case law bearing upon the issue of professional secrecy in Latin America.

This is not to say that the press and the journalist lack certain other forms of protection under the law. In Argentina, as an example, a Statute of the Professional Journalist, enacted in 1944, provided the journalist with certain safeguards and guarantees, and greater advantages than most groups in the country. But these all bore upon his relation to his editor and his publication. It was a labour law almost exclusively. When the National Congress voted in 1960 to give journalists even more advantages, the President of the Republic vetoed the proposed new legislation because he believed it went so far as to alter the principle of "equality before the law," specified by the Argentinian Constitution for the protection of all workers and citizens.

No assurance of professional secrecy for journalists exists, however, either in the Statute of the Professional Journalist or in the general laws. The Criminal Code does specify that a person who divulges without proper reason any secret entrusted to him by reason of his position, office, employment, or art may be punished by a fine of from 200 to 1,000 pesos and also may be disqualified from his position for from six months to three years.

Secrecy for publisher's sake

Although it has been argued that journalists might properly be entitled to maintain professional secrecy under this positive provision of the Criminal Code, such has not been the legal interpretation. It is conceded that a journalist, having obtained certain knowledge about his own newspaper enterprise, could and should keep that knowledge secret, lacking a "just reason", if its revelation would cause damage to the editors, to the publisher or to a third person. But if the same journalist were ordered by a court or other qualified body to give information about the source or origin of a report published in his newspaper, then he could not properly take refuge in the provision of the Criminal Code.

The Argentine Codes of Procedure in the law also establish that "physicians, pharmacists, midwives and any other person cannot be admitted as a witness on facts revealed to them by reason of their profession". As with the Criminal Code provision just mentioned, this article likewise has been advanced as justification for professional secrecy by journalists, but without acceptance. The legal interpretation is that, even with the unspecific reference to "any other person," it refers only to the "liberal professions" of law, medicine, and the clergy—that is, to persons who have obtained a title or diploma enabling them to exercise a certain regulated activity—but that it does not apply to journalists. Further, the judge in an action at law decides, in every case, on the scope of the law, and any person refusing to give evidence in response to a request approved by the court becomes subject to penalty.

Journalists' associations in Argentina favour a statutory guarantee of professional secrecy. The need for such a guarantee was demonstrated recently when the National Chamber of Deputies, lower house of the Congress, appointed a special committee to investigate reports published in a Buenos Aires newspaper, and the editor of that paper was obliged to give all information requested about the origins of the material presented.

This is typical of the awkward position in which journalists are forced to operate in Argentina and other Latin American countries for lack of any clear legal protection. The courts and other official groups, too, have yet to prove their concern for the ethical concept of professional secrecy as it applies to the journalist, even in the absence of any supporting legislation, in many other free countries.

Australia

In Australia, the journalist's capacity to preserve secrecy as to his sources of information rests in uneasy balance between a complete absence of any formal legal protection beyond that enjoyed by all persons equally *and* a generally liberal attitude on the part of the judiciary under which newsmen rarely are asked to break confidences reposed in them.

Professionally, the Australian journalist takes an attitude on this issue that could not be sustained in law. Article 3 of a Code of Ethics, drawn up by the Australian Journalists' Association, states that the journalist "shall in all circumstances respect all confidences received by him in the course of his calling". In practice, this position has so far been supported by the Australian newspaper proprietors. Because of an inbred suspicion of political motivation on the part of officials, also, and a reluctance to permit a situation that would afford them opportunity to operate without full critical attention, it is probable that public opinion generally supports the journalists' position as well. The fact remains that, legally, it is an untenable position.

For all practical purposes, only a court is in a position to insist that a journalist disclose the source of his information. Each state has its own special legislation, to which the journalist naturally is subject, as he is also to Federal legislation.

Broadly speaking, the journalist has no legal right in any of the states to refuse to disclose sources of information if he is requested by a court to do so. But neither is he under any compulsion to do so, provided he is prepared to take the consequences of a refusal. In practice, this means that in civil cases — such as libel — a journalist often appears as a witness when there is no question of compromising his sources. But if there is such a possibility he and his paper may elect not to give evidence. It is true that he might be required to testify, even so, but this rarely occurs because litigants recognize that the judge may decide against insisting that the journalist disclose his source of information, and also because, even having testified, he cannot be cross-examined.

Only the state of New South Wales, with a long tradition of feuding between government and press, ever has attempted to make it legally obligatory for journalists to reveal sources of their information. That legislation was passed after repeated charges of corruption within the City Council at Sydney, the state capital. These charges gained substance in 1953 when the state government, then controlled by the Labour party, "purged" Labour party members of the Council and then conducted an inquiry into their bank accounts. Following this, Sydney newspapers, including the *Sydney Morning Herald,* published accounts of improprieties in increasing detail, and sought the appointment of a Royal Commission to make further investigations.

With an election approaching, this proposal was opposed by the late John J. Cahill, State Labour party leader and State Premier. He said that prosecutions against the former Council members or aldermen, would be undertaken without the necessity of any Royal Commission action, provided the newspapers would reveal the information they purported to have. The newspapers replied that they had acquired their information in confidence and that their informants, although willing to appear before a Royal Commission, would not reveal themselves to any other tribunal.

Mr. Cahill countered by introducing into the State Parliament on November 25, 1953, a so-called Sydney City Council (Disclosure of Allegations) Bill. It provided a maximum penalty of a £1,000 (Australian) fine for a corporate body and a £500 fine or twelve months imprisonment, or both, for individuals who failed to comply with a Court order to disclose information requested. The Bill provoked criticism from journalists, educators, church leaders and even from lawyers as "unwarranted interference with the freedom of the press". The New South Wales district of the Australian Journalists' Association made its position clear on November 26, directing journalists to observe the Association's code of ethics, and particularly the obligation to "respect all confidences in all circumstances". In the State Parliament, nevertheless, the Bill was passed, and became law on December 3.

On the following day the *Sydney Morning Herald* was ordered to give to an inspector of police the names of two City Council members who had, according to that newspaper of November 17, "alleged widespread graft and corruption over a number of years and have undertaken to give evidence before a Royal Commission". The *Morning Herald* refused to provide the names and was promptly brought into court. The case was heard in the Supreme Court of New South Wales, before Justice William E. Owen.

The Solicitor-General, Mr. H. Snelling, QC, speaking in the case for the Crown, said that "There is no reason why the interests of a journalist who claims confidence should prevail over the interests of justice."

Alex Mair, a former New South Wales Premier, expressed his opposition to the legislation, describing it as "The Grafters' Protection Bill." He said :

> The average citizen shuns publicity, especially if such results in appearances before a Royal Commission or Court proceedings. Consequently a safety valve exists at present by giving a statement to the Press on the understanding that such is treated in confidence.
>
> The fear of victimization is very real among citizens today. Are we to become a race of whisperers afraid to express views for fear of being overheard by some pimp or informer ?

Victory for the press

On December 9, Mr. Justice Owen gave a verdict for the *Sydney Morning Herald* and awarded costs against the New South Wales Government. He was reported as saying in part :

> In common law a court, except for the most exceptional circumstances, will not force a newspaper to disclose a source of information. It is a rule of common law that a newspaper cannot be ordered to disclose a source of information.
>
> This Act could force solicitors, priests and doctors to disclose confidential information to police officers. It is a far-reaching Act — not limited to newspapers. No doctor worthy of his name would disclose the confidences of his patients. An Act of this kind might make him do it.
>
> The *Sydney Morning Herald* is a corporate body and as such could no more disclose information than drive a motor car. If the *Herald* had been ordered to produce documents, it would have been a different matter. The present application was for the disclosure of information, not documents. The only person who could have non-documentary information must obviously be a natural person. The names of the two aldermen to whom the article referred could be known to and in the minds of one or more members of the company's staff. There is no means by which the company could compel its employees to reveal the names, however.

The New South Wales Government made no subsequent attempt to use the legislation, and on March 2, 1954, the State Cabinet was to repeal the Act. At the time, Mr. Cahill stated that "the allegations made against the Sydney City Council in the Parliament, in the Press and elsewhere had not been supported by evidence of wrongdoing".

The State Parliament in 1959 passed an amended Defamation Act, which it described as a "codified law of libel". Assertions have been made that the Act tends to stifle the writer, in part because it specifies that defamation does not die with the defamed. On the contrary, it remains as a subject for action that may be brought by surviving relatives or even descendants. But the journalist's position with reference to protection of his sources is not affected.

So far as Federal law bears upon his position, and protection of confidences reposed in him by his sources, the journalist operates under the provisions of the Crimes Act 1914-1960, as recently amended by the Government headed by Prime Minister Robert G. Menzies, Liberal party leader. The amendments were made in the face of Labour party opposition and some community protests. The legislation is omnibus in character, dealing with offences ranging from counterfeiting to treason, and was described by Attorney-General Sir Garfield Barwick, who steered it through the Parliament, as modernizing the nation's security to meet the needs of the cold war era.

Indirect pressures

Journalists are clearly affected because, under certain circumstances, they might come under direct pressure, supported by threats of punishment, to reveal sources of information. Journalists recognize that the pressure actually is on the public official to protect information having security elements, rather than an actual threat to the journalist himself. The old Act, before amendment, contained many of the same provisions, but they were less extensive in their applications and placed far less emphasis on punitive aspects. Moreover, those sections of the old Act were never used, possibly because of the generally liberal attitude of the judiciary, and also because specific acts of suppression by government did not accord with the political climate in Australia.

While the new Act remains to be tested in practice, it is regarded unfavourably by the Australian Journalists' Association as suggesting that the Federal Government may be disposed to cut the journalist off from news sources by saying, in effect, to a public servant or other custodian of public information that "If you tell a journalist something that is not politically authorized, you will not be protected by his professional code under which he cannot disclose his source of information". Whether the government actually contemplates taking punitive action against journalists, it *could* do so within the scope of the legislation. Thus it also is saying to the journalist, in effect, "If you are asked to disclose a source of information, you either will do so or suffer a heavy gaol sentence".

The provisions of the amended Crimes Act of actual or potential importance to journalists appear in various sections of Part VI of the Act, "Offenses By and Against Public Officers", and Part VII, "Espionage and Official Secrets".

Part VII provides, for example, in its Section 79, that

> Subsection (3). If a person communicates a prescribed sketch, plan, photograph, model, cipher, note, document or article, or prescribed information to an unauthorized person ...he shall be guilty of an offence.
>
> Subsection (5). If a person receives any sketch, plan, photograph, model, cipher, note, document, article or information ...he shall be guilty of an indictable offence unless he proves that the communication was contrary to his desire.
>
> Subsection (6). If a person receives any sketch, plan, photograph, model, cipher, note, document, article or information, knowing or having reasonable ground to believe at the time when he receives it, it is communicated to him in contravention of subsection (3) of this section, he shall be guilty of an offence unless he proves that the communication was contrary to his desire.

The penalties attached to these "offences" are imprisonment, respectively, for two years, seven years, and two years. From the journalist's viewpoint, the key word in each subsection is "information". No definition of "prescribed information" appears, but "information" is defined, and covers almost anything that could possibly emanate from government sources. Officially, it "means information of any kind whatsover, whether true or false and whether in material form or not, and includes (a) an opinion, and (b) a report of a conversation".

The Australian Journalists' Association, reviewing the Act and its implications for journalists, concluded that: ·

> A newspaperman could become liable to a charge by receiving "prescribed information" (vaguely defined) from an official who had no right to give it, or indeed from an ex-official.
> He would have the defence in this case that he had no grounds for believing that the official was breaking the law in giving it to him. In such a case the circumstances could well be such that he could avail himself of this defence only by disclosing the source of his information in breach of his own code of ethics.
> It would, of course, be impossible for a journalist to prove that the communication was contrary to his desire.

The Crimes Act, nevertheless, is operative throughout Australia and even though there has, as yet, been no test of the Act in its application to a reporter, editor, editor-in-chief or any other journalist, its indirect effect on news reporting has become apparent on several occasions.

Threats that backfired

In one instance, *Truth,* Brisbane Sunday newspaper, reported an alleged improper use of a Commonwealth vehicle by the Queensland Director of Posts and Telegraphs. The report was flatly denied, and a driver for the Posts and Telegraphs department, interviewed by post office officials, was accused of having been the source of the information presented in the newspaper. He was threatened with prosecution under Section 70 of the amended Crimes Act, stating that

1. A person who being a Commonwealth officer publishes or communicates except to some person to whom he is authorized to publish or communicate it any fact or document that comes to his knowledge or into his possession by virtue of his office and which it is his duty not to disclose shall be guilty of an offence.
2. A person who having been a Commonwealth officer publishes or communicates without lawful authority or excuse (proof whereof shall lie upon him) any fact or document that came to his knowledge or into his possession by virtue of his office and which at the time when he ceased to be a Commonwealth officer it was his duty not to publish shall be guilty of an offence.

The penalty for either "offence" is specified as imprisonment for two years.

The accused driver was given the alternative of resigning, or facing a charge under Section 70. He was told that *Truth* could do little or nothing to help him, and that its reporters might possibly be required under provisions of Part VII, already noted, to name him as their informant or risk gaol sentences themselves. Unsophisticated in such matters, and also unwell, the driver resigned his position.

In this case, as it happened, Parliamentary pressure subsequently produced further investigation of the charges *Truth* had published. The accuracy of the report was established through a Public Service Board inquiry. The Director of Posts and Telegraphs was demoted, as a result, and the driver was reinstated in his position. Whether he actually had been the source of the reports appearing in *Truth* never became an official issue.

In a second instance, the Australian Broadcasting Commission, a government body under the jurisdiction of the Postmaster General, figured in an incident also relating to the indirect effect of the amended Crimes Act on the journalists' professional code calling for protection of news sources.

The Australian Broadcasting Commission, as an official agency administering both radio and television stations and broadcasts, advising on programmes, including news programmes, and sponsoring several orchestras, is an important news source in itself. News items appearing in the Australian press commonly make clear that the information reported has come from persons with intimate knowledge of the inside workings of the Commission.

Following passage of the amended Crimes Act in 1960, the Assistant General Manager of the ABC, T. S. Duckmanton, distributed a memorandum to all officers and employees of the organization headed "Disclosure of Unauthorized Material", and drawing attention to the applicability of Section 70 of the Act to all personnel.

Since a major concern of the ABC is with news broadcasts, requiring the services of journalist members within the organization itself, those members were sufficiently disturbed by this official communication to submit a statement to the Australian Journalists' Association, to which they belonged. It said in part:

The ABC is an autonomous body not concerned with the formation of government policy. Its business is the dissemination of entertainment, news and so forth.

Basically, its function is the same as that of a commercial broadcasting network. If a commercial network needs only the normal disciplinary powers of an employer to ensure the discretion of its employees, there seems no reason why the ABC should need recourse to a criminal charge.

The reminder to the ABC staff members, nevertheless, remains unmodified. One of the very real fears of the ABC journalist, therefore, must be that, with the Commission operating under the provisions of the Crimes Act, the ABC journalist may at some time be compelled to reveal the source of information broadcast, and particularly if originated by an ABC journalist. This would require him either to disregard the journalistic code of ethics calling upon him to respect confidences in all circumstances, or face the prospect of a long prison term.

A tentative legal opinion, so far untested, is that a journalist of press or radio in Australia who might become involved in receiving unauthorized information from a public official is protected to some extent by his legal right to refuse to give evidence that may tend to incriminate him. By this untested theory, such a right might derive from that reference within Section 79 of Part VII of the Crimes Act where, under Subsection (6), it is made an offence punishable by two years of imprisonment for a person to receive unauthorized information from a public official. It is argued that a journalist can refuse to name his informant on the ground that to do so *would be to incriminate himself*.

Any expectation that such an interpretation might give a journalist immunity from prosecution could quite easily prove illusory, however, if brought to an actual test. This is suggested by an experience of Rohan Rivett, at a time when he was editor of *The News,* Adelaide, and was being prosecuted on a charge of seditious libel. Mr. Rivett and the *News* had insisted upon an inquiry into the case of Rupert Max Stuart, part aborigine, convicted of killing a little girl in South Australia. The South Australian state government responded by bringing the charge of seditious libel against Mr. Rivett. A journalist witness called refused to identify the writer of a certain article on the ground that to do so might be self-incriminatory. The South Australian government, bringing the charge against Mr. Rivett, promptly granted the witness immunity so that he could no longer cite the possibility of self-incrimination as a basis for refusing to answer certain questions. As it happened, a jury ultimately found Mr. Rivett not guilty, but the precedent for granting a witness immunity from prosecution for anwers to questions that might seem self-incriminatory might also be used to set aside any such plea made by a journalist to avoid answering questions as to source in a case hinging upon the provisions of the Crimes Act.

Theoretically, a Parliamentary Committee, such as the Privileges Committee, also could force a journalist to disclose a source of information. In practice, however, the use of such Parliamentary committee power has fallen into general disuse and it is doubtful whether a committee today would ask for a journalist's source of information, except most perfunctorily perhaps. It is doubtful, also, whether the present-day political climate in Australia would permit a committee to take punitive measures, assuming that it should undertake to do so by way of attempting to force a journalist to make disclosure of a source if he refused to do so voluntarily.

Aside from possible application of the amended Crimes Act to force a journalist to speak, only a court remains in a position to insist that a journalist disclose the source of his information. Because the journalist has no present legal right to refuse to do so, if so pressed, he can only hope that the discretion of the judge might then enable him to preserve the inviolability of confidences. Either that, or he might take such measures as may be legally possible to avoid appearing as a witness when he had reason to believe he might be questioned about his sources. Or, being called, he might seek escape by pleading that disclosure of requested information would be self-incriminatory. But legally, the journalist has no rights over or beyond those belonging also to any of his fellow citizens.

Austria

In Austria, the right of professional secrecy, in its reference to journalism, is understood to mean the right of journalists to refuse to reveal the sources of their information in civil and in penal courts of justice, and also in administrative proceedings, legislative or otherwise.

The journalist's right to withhold evidence is more clearly established in Austria than in any other country of the world. It is established in penal law under Article 45 of the Federal Law of April 7, 1922 (Bundesgesetzblatt Nr. 218, or Federal Law Gazette, No 218) (Press Law). This Article, and the relevant paragraphs, valid today, reads :

> *Paragraph 1 :* Persons who are professionally engaged in the production of a newspaper are exempt from the obligation to give evidence as regards a penal action brought on account of the contents of the newspaper in all questions which concern responsibility under penal law (Article 29).

> *Paragraph 2 :* This exemption does not apply to advertisements.

In civil law proceedings this same right to withhold evidence is based on Article 321, Code 5 of the Civil Law Statute (Zivilprozessordnung, Nr. 321, Ziffer 5), which states that a witness can refuse to make a statement

> on questions which the witness cannot answer without revealing an artistic or professional secret.

Under the provisions of the Civil Law Statute, the attention of the witness must be drawn, before questioning, to this right of exemption.

In administrative proceedings professional secrecy for journalists is based on Article 49, Paragraph 1 B, of the General Administrative

Proceedings (Verwaltungsverfahren) Law of July 21, 1935, BGBl (i. e. Bundesgesetzblatt), Number 274, stating that

> a witness can refuse to make a statement on questions which he cannot answer without transgressing an officially recognized duty to reticence, from which he cannot validly be exempted, or without revealing an artistic, trade or business secret. *

In Austria the legal position of journalists is specifically defined in the law of February 11, 1920, STGBl (Staatsgesetzblatt) (Journalists' Law). This law is amended by a Supplementary Journalists' Law of 1955, the Federal Law of July 20, 1955 (BGBl, No. 158), and by the Federal Law of May 21, 1958 (BGBl, No. 108).

The provisions of the Journalists' Law, as it exists today, concern all who are engaged in editing the letter press or in drawing pictures for a newspaper concern, who are employed and paid regular salaries, and who carry on this activity as a main, rather than as a secondary occupation.

The Supplementary Journalists' Law of 1955, drafted to cover journalists engaged in activities that have gained importance since the 1920 law was approved, extends the provisions of the Journalists' Law to apply also to those who work for a news agency, in radio or television, in pictorial production, including motion pictures ; and in editing the letter press, including general periodicals ; with the proviso, again, that they carry on such activity as regularly salaried employees and not merely as a subsidiary occupation.

There is some question whether the Journalists' Law extends its benefit to journalists associated with technical journals. In fact, a decision of the Supreme Court of February 25, 1958 (Number 4, OB 152/157) indicated that the Journalists' Law applies only to newspapers, and not to technical journals. The Supreme Court interpretation was explained by saying that

> by the Journalists' Law of February 11, 1920, StGBl, Number 88 a special service legal status has been established for those paid a regular salary and primarily engaged in work on newspaper concerns, applicable to the particular situation of editors in various capacities there.

---

* It is a unanimous opinion in literature and learning that editorial secrecy comes under the concept of a "business secret".

As transpires from the argument in the government bill submitted in No. 403 of the Supplements of the Constituent National Assembly, this special regulation was intended, on the one hand, to take account of particular instances of social and political contests in the situation of editors ; on the other hand, to fill gaps left by legislation on the relationship between newspaper concerns and their employees. According to Article 1, Paragraph 1 of the Journalists' Law all those who are concerned with the editing of the letter press and with the drawing of pictures for a newspaper concern, in so far as they are regularly paid and principally engaged in journalism, come under the provisions of this law.

Whereas the Press Law in Article 2, Paragraph 3, mentions the newspaper alongside the periodical and declares both to be periodical public prints, not limited to a particular group of people, the concept of a *newspaper concern* is not so specifically defined in the Journalists' Law. By the Supplementary Law, BGBl Number 158/1955, the sphere of application of the Journalists' Law was extended to the so-called Radio journalists, and to persons engaged in film editing and with the production of topical news reels. The particular protection afforded by the Journalists' Law to newspaper journalists, in particular in connection with the liability to a change of political direction of the newspaper,* should thereby be just as much applicable to radio journalists and film reporters.

As the report of the Committee on Judicature, Number 595 of the Supplements to the stenographic minutes of the Austrian National Council, VIIth period of the legislature, points out :

"In the new paragraph of Article 1 of the Journalists' Law the definition starts with the supposition that the definition of newspaper journalists, in legislation valid today, meets the practical needs and therefore largely conforms with this formulation. All that is needed is the replacement of those distinguishing features which characterize the difference in conditions of employment between newspaper journalists, on the one hand, and radio journalists and film reporters, on the other. The application of this law pre-

* The reference here is to a certain right, also under the Journalists' Law, for an editor or other responsible member of a newspaper staff to leave the staff, without prejudice as to rights or salary, in the event of a change in ownership or political orientation of that newspaper. Austrian journalists are further protected, under the provisions of the Journalists' Law with reference to sphere of work, salary and salary increased holiday leave, period of notice for dismissal and conditions of such dismissal or severance under a variety of circumstances, including sale or suspension of the newspaper, and including voluntary departure of the journalist.

supposes that it concerns those who are employed on a regular salary basis by a broadcasting or film company and who are not just subsidiarily engaged in the editing of the letter press or with the production of pictures of topical daily events."

From the way this is expressed it transpires that the concept of a newspaper concern in Article 1, Paragraph 1, of the Journalists' Law is to be understood in the narrower conventional sense. *It is evidently not intended to extend the sphere of application of this law to those who are primarily employed by technical journals on a regular salaried basis.*

Editors ask wider coverage

The Association of Editors-in-Chief and Journalists in Austria has refused to accept this decision of the Supreme Court whereby editors employed by technical journals do not come under the protection of the Journalists' Law or the Supplementary Law.

Nevertheless, this legislative question has no influence on professional secrecy, as an issue, because that unconditional right is broadly established in Austria and extends to all persons who have a part in the production of periodical public prints, whether in the editorial department, in the mechanical department, in circulation or in advertising,** and including those employed by news agencies or special correspondence services, or engaged as foreign correspondents.

Since the Press Law was established in 1922 and, in fact, since the Journalists's Law was established in 1920, there has been no known case in Austria in which the right of a journalist to withhold evidence was questioned. Even though the Press Law of 1922 remains unchanged, several modifications have been *proposed.* The Federal Ministry of Justice drafted an additional Press Law in 1948 (No. 13, paragraphs 442-448), while in 1954 another article was prepared by that same Ministry (No. 11, Articles 343-349, 354). Article 45 of the 1922 Press Law was to be replaced by Article 60, the first paragraph of which was phrased somewhat differently from the first paragraph of Article 45. It read :

** For members of the advertising department professional secrecy exists only in civil and administrative proceedings, but not in criminal proceedings, as expressly specified in Article 45, Paragraph 2 of the 1942 Press Law.

Persons who are professionally engaged in the production of a *periodical public print* are exempted from giving evidence on a penal proceeding in regard to *offences arising out of the content of a Press item or from negligence of the necessary accuracy,* namely in all questions which do not concern only responsibility, as defined in Article 47.*

The Austrian Journalists' Trade Union interpreted this paragraph as providing "immunity from giving evidence in all questions which do not concern responsibility as defined in Article 47". The second paragraph in the renumbered draft article of 1954 remained similar in sense, if not in precise wording to the second paragraph of the old Article 45, reading :

This immunity does not extend to proceedings which concern advertising.

Another redraft of the Press Law was produced in 1955 (No. 10, Article 265, Code 9/55) by the departmental specialist of the Federal Ministry of Justice. Also based upon the old Article 45, but still numbered as Article 60, the two relevant paragraphs remained the same in essence, but Paragraph 1 was even more specific. They read:

Paragraph 1 : Persons who are professionally engaged in the production of a periodical public print have immunity from the requirement to give evidence in a penal proceeding which is brought on account of the content of this periodical public print or on account of neglect of the necessary accuracy in regard to such content, in all questions which do not concern responsibility as defined in Article 47.

Paragraph 2 : This immunity does not extend to questions which concern advertisements.

---

* Article 47 specifies that, in a case where printed matter is deemed offensive in the eyes of the law, but where neither author nor collaborator can be punished, other persons specified may be held responsible for neglect of proper duty. In cases involving periodicals, posters, and pamphlets, accordingly, punishment then may fall upon
(a) the responsible editor if, through his exercise of proper care, publication of the material found offensive might have been avoided ; or
(b) the publisher, if he neglected to appoint a responsible editor, or if he knowingly appointed a person who did not meet the legal specifications, and therefore could not properly be held responsible.
The same provision for punishment applies with reference to printed matter judged to constitute a crime within the meaning of the Federal Law relating to obscene publications and to the protection of the morality of youth.

Extension of rights sought

The Association of Austrian Newspaper Publishers, commenting on the 1955 draft, felt that it should be still more specific. It was said that:

> It would be desirable to make clear that the exception for editorial secrecy is limited to statements required under responsibility as defined in Article 47. It does not permit substantiating facts raised in a question of a Press offence nor the situation of an individual as culprit nor as concerned in complicity.
>
> The general allusion to Article 47 could give rise to misinterpretation. It would be desirable that editorial secrecy in the Press Law should be extended also to civil and administrative proceedings. Persons who are engaged professionally in the production of a periodical public print should be given immunity from giving evidence on all questions which concern the content of a periodical public print or the source.

Still another modification of the Press Law was drafted in 1959 by the Federal Ministry of Justice. In it, Article 45 remained unaltered from its original form, as promulgated in 1922, but was numbered as Article 59.

A commission of editors-in-chief, newspaper proprietors and legal counsel nominated by the Austrian National Committee of the International Press Institute has proposed that this Article 59 should bear the title "Defence of Editorial Secrecy," and that Paragraph 1 should read:

> Persons who are professionally engaged in the production of a periodical public print have immunity from the requirement to give evidence in a proceeding which has been brought on account of the content of a periodical public print or an account of neglect of the necessary accuracy with regard to such content.

This version would have the effect of assuring immunity, not only with reference to penal proceedings, as specified in the original Article 45 and in the other proposed modifications, but would presumably cover immunity arising in civil and administrative proceedings, as well, at present separately covered.

A professional jurists' opinion on this proposed revision was prepared by the Standing Representative Assembly of Austrian Legal Counsel and submitted to the Federal Ministry of Justice. Bearing the Number 163/60, it stated that:

> The Chambers of Legal Counsel recommend also that in general the so-called editorial secrecy should be abolished. This does not exist in other States, for instance in Germany and Switzerland.
> It must be admitted, however, that the professional right of journalists must be brought into consideration in this context. It is indeed not codified in an exact form. It is, however, regarded as defamatory and derogatory when an editor of a newspaper discloses in court the identity of a contributor on account of whose article legal proceedings have been brought.
> On the other hand there is an eminent interest of the person who has been injured in his rights, and above all in his honour, through such an article, that the name of the author of this article should be made known. Between these two directly conflicting interests a suitable agreement must be found.

Still another proposed draft, under a modified Article 86, in the Press Bill, would provide that

> 1) Persons who are professionally engaged in the production of a periodical public print are exempted from giving evidence in all administrative proceedings with regard to all questions referring to legal responsibility as laid down in the general penal laws (Article 47) for punishable acts committed through the contents of a periodical public print.
> 2) This exemption is not extended to questions which refer to paid notices.

No question has arisen, so far, with reference to professional secrecy in its application to radio news in Austria. To that extent, radio journalists share with journalists of the press of Austria a legal right to professional secrecy such as is not equalled in any other nation at present.

Belgium

In Belgium, professional journalistic organizations are unanimous in believing that sources of information should be cited in reports, as evidence of authority or proper documentation, so long as those sources are not confidential. At the same time, they favour strict secrecy as to the source when the journalist is not specifically freed by the person who has provided the information from an obligation to observe a confidence.

The Belgian journalist feels bound by the generally accepted rules of the profession to maintain secrecy, as a matter of conscience, in such circumstances. He regards this professional concept as taking precedence over demands by judicial or administrative authorities, by legislative or executive powers, or by third parties. He looks upon professional secrecy as an indispensable element in the exercise of freedom of the press and in the accomplishment of its mission.

The view of Belgian journalists on this subject has been set forth in a statement on The Rights and Duties of Journalists, issued by the General Association of the Belgian Press (Association Générale de la Presse Belge), and prepared by two former presidents of that association, Joseph Demarteau and Léon Duwaerts. This *Traité de déontologie professionnelle,* or statement of "moral obligation," says in part :

> The citizen who is aware of an error, an abuse, or an injustice causing harm to the public interest or to legitimate private interests should be able to inform the press without fear of being himself penalized; he may, indeed, have sound reasons for not disclosing his own identity, whether for the sake of his own security or to give more weight to the intervention of the newspaper as an organ of public opinion.
>
> Many revelations, spontaneous or solicited, by which the press has been enabled to redress unjust, harmful and illegal situations could not have been made if those who made or advanced those revelations had not been able to rely upon the discretion of the journalists in whom they confided.

Undoubtedly there is, moreover, a certain nobility in the attitude of the journalist who, in the public interest, assumes the responsibility for revelations in which he has not, perhaps, taken the initiative himself and which may cost him dearly. Respect for professional secrecy is a duty, but a duty which the journalist ought to be proud to perform.

Whatever the journalists of the country may feel about the importance of professional secrecy, Belgian law does not recognize any such right. Although the law (Penal Code, Article 458) grants exceptions for "doctors, surgeons, public health officers, pharmacists, midwives and all other persons who receive, by reason of their profession, secrets confided in them," so that they may keep such secrets, the law so far has refused to consider journalists as among the "other persons" thus privileged. Indeed, the journalist's situation is regarded as quite different because people are held to confide in him precisely so that the *content* of their secrets may be revealed. This is not to say, of course, that the *source* is necessarily to be revealed.

Professional conscience upheld

In practice, a Belgian journalist being questioned by a magistrate as to a source of information will reply, with the deference due a court undertaking to perform its function, that his professional conscience forbids him to provide the information requested. For several decades, Belgian journalists have followed this procedure. That they have succeeded in reconciling their position, without penalty, with the court's action, however, is explained—as Maître Paul Tapie, barrister at the Court of Appeals of Brussels, wrote in *Le Journaliste* of October 1958— by the liberal and moderate practices of magistrates rather than because of any recognition of the journalists' view in formal jurisprudence.

Jurisprudence, in fact, has not provided any examples of a formal legal demand upon a Belgian journalist to make positive response to a request as to the source of his information since sentences passed by the Supreme Court of Appeal as long ago as November 7, 1855 and April 25, 1870.* On those occasions, journalists were sentenced for their refusal

---

* These cases related to M. Outendirck, of *L'Avenir,* in 1855; and Gustave Lemaire, of *L'Etoile de Belgique,* in 1870.

to speak, under the provisions of Article 80 of the Code of Criminal Instruction, which states in part that

> any person cited for questioning as a witness is obligated to appear and to satisfy the citation. Otherwise, that person may be detained by the examining magistrate who, for this purpose, and without formality or delay and without recourse to appeal, shall impose a fine not to exceed one hundred francs, and may order the person cited to be compelled by physical duress (i.e. imprisonment) to come and give his evidence.

Belgian journalists have never accepted this law as properly applicable in cases wherein the courts may demand that they reveal a source of information. Rather, they have stood firm on their assertion of a "moral obligation" to keep silent in such instances. Not only have they, as individuals, always refused to submit to a demand upon them to reveal such a source, but their professional organizations never have ceased to press for legislation—although, so far, in vain—to establish recognition of a full legal "right of secrecy". This they regard as essential in a political and social regime appropriate to a democratic state such as modern-day Belgium.

Legal recognition sought

In 1914 and again in 1938 the annual congresses of the Belgian press adopted resolutions calling for legal recognition, through legislative action, of the journalist's right to professional secrecy. Further, on the occasion of the 25th congress, meeting in 1947, the General Association of the Belgian Press named a permanent commission on "professional deontology". It was at that time that the commission's *rapporteurs,* MM. Joseph Demarteau and Léon Duwaerts, began work, among other things, on a complete review of the question of professional secrecy. They sought opinions from every quarter, including the higher ranks of the magistrature, and arrived at two conclusions :

> 1) That, as a matter of principle, it was agreed that the right of a journalist to maintain silence about the source of information should be legally recognized. That, far from harming the public interest, such recognition was in conformity with the spirit of a democratic regime, properly understood.

2) That, in order to make this legal right effective, both considerations of legislative technique and of practical opportunity indicated dissociation of the right to secrecy from the obligation to secrecy. The obligation to secrecy, accordingly, should not necessarily be related to Article 458 of the Penal Code,* but could be incorporated in a new law recognizing the professional status of journalists. The right to secrecy, on the other hand, should be established by insertion in the Code of Criminal Instruction, and specifically in the chapter on evidence and on the duty of the witness to testify, of an Article 80 *bis* exempting the professional journalist from revealing the source of an item of information and the circumstances relevant to that which he had reported.

It was proposed that the "professional journalist" should be identified as one bearing a national press card issued by the Ministry of the Interior, but excluding as a consequence the editor, printer, and distributor of a newspaper.

The proposal that professional journalists be exempt from giving evidence, through a new law, as certain professions are now exempt through Article 458 of the Penal Code, reflects the view of journalists themselves that they are not now excluded justifiably from the benefits of that law, or indeed from its obligations.

As already noted, Article 458 not only recognizes exercise of the right of secrecy by "doctors, surgeons, public health officers, pharmacists, midwives and other persons," but specifies that secrets confided to them by reason of their "status or profession" *must* be kept secret. Penalties specified for disclosure are "imprisonment of from eight days to six months, and a fine of from one hundred to five hundred francs". The person possessed of such a secret cannot be compelled to speak if he himself believes he should not. (Supreme Court of Appeal, March 22, 1926.) On the other hand, if he is summoned to give evidence on a topic involving such a confidence, and if he himself believes it to be in the interests of justice for him to reveal such information, in that circumstance he may do so without penalty. (Supreme Court of Appeal, March 19, 1948.)

Journalists are not among the "other persons" covered by the provisions of Article 458, but it has been established that this blanket provision admits lawyers, notaries, magistrates, registrars and clerks of court,

* Granting exemptions to doctors, surgeons, and others, as noted above.

directors of hospitals and infirmaries, directors and employees of pawn offices, priests, civil servants, inspectors of the Criminal Investigation Department, judicial officers, police officers, and constables.

It would be difficult to say that a journalist is any less entitled to preserve a confidence than are many of those persons whose status or professional obligations are thus recognized in Article 458. Taking this position, groups within the Belgian press have defined the character and limits of their claimed right in justifying silence by the journalist where the ordinary citizen would be compelled to speak. Yet, at present, for lack of legal recognition, they have no such "right".

The views of Belgian journalists

The statement issued as a *Traité de déontologie professionnelle* by the General Association of the Belgian Press, and standing as a kind of code of ethics, includes the following comments upon journalistic behaviour with reference to professional secrets :

> As regards information hitherto secret, communicated to a journalist, a distinction must be drawn between what he can publicize and that which he should retain for himself only for the purpose of his personal edification in order to possess complete documentation and a reasoned view of the matter with which he is dealing. This distinction the journalist must establish when clarifying in his own mind all the information provided by the informant.
>
> His task is clear if the informant has fixed the limits of what is to be divulged. Once the promise has been made to fulfil this request on a point to be determined, the secret is rigorously inviolable whatever its object may be. All that is required is the application of the general rule of elementary honesty which prescribes fidelity to a promise once spoken.
>
> But if there are no such precise indications the conscience of the journalist then serves, governed by circumstances, and in case of doubt giving precedence to secrecy rather than to revelation of a source of information.
>
> The concept of professional secrecy is not yet generally understood by the public. That is demonstrated by the number of requests received by newspapers to make known the author of an item of information, or a correspondent's report, or of an article. But the practice of secrecy is itself sufficiently estab-

lished to enable an informant, even if he has not formally asked not to be identified, to assume that he may rely upon the discretion of the newspaper to keep his name secret. The journalist should therefore be regarded as having implicitly guaranteed such discretion to those whose information or collaboration he utilizes. Questioned about the origin of a document he should reply negatively, even though being prepared, if pressed, eventually to ask the informant if he is prepared to be identified. In the case of a negative reply by the original informant to such a question, the journalist should give a categorical and determined refusal to the questioner seeking information from him, and that without reference to who the questioner may be or what may be the consequences to him of his refusal.

In the absence of explicit indication that the journalist may reveal his source, the journalist may reveal that source only to his editor-in-chief, who then assumes responsibility for using the information. To appreciate the value of information, also, the editor needs to know whence it came, yet he too must be prepared to keep rigorous secrecy on the source of that shared knowledge.

If the journalist has been requested by his source not to reveal the origin of an item of information to anyone else, his editor-in-chief included, he should then maintain complete silence and the editor-in-chief should refrain from any insistence that the promise be broken. The editor should simply judge whether he can trust the journalist to estimate the trustworthiness of the source which he alone knows. If the editor is not assured on that score, he may then refuse to use the information so provided.

No case since 1870

The personal responsibility of the journalist to consider the reception and the use of information, secret or not, as it may bear upon the public interest is stressed in the concluding part of the statement by the Belgian press group. A disciplinary council within the General Association of the Belgian Press is designed to assure respect for the journalist's obligations to the public.

Even though Belgian journalists are themselves faithful to the concept of professional secrecy, and even though there has been no case in the Belgian courts since 1870 to test that concept—largely because both journalists and magistrates have been tactful and reasonable—the fact remains, as previously stated, that no legal support exists for the concept. If a case should arise in which a magistrate deemed it proper to insist that a journalist reveal a source of information, he would have the law on his side. Unless, and until, the law is amended in some such manner as spokesmen for the Belgian press long have urged, this will remain the situation.

The question of professional secrecy with reference to radio news treatment never has arisen in Belgium.

Canada

In Canada, journalists have little protection under the law when courts or certain other agencies possessing quasi-judicial powers wish to probe into sources of information. Despite this, such bodies have not been unreasonable in demanding disclosure of information and, in practice, there has been little harrassment of journalists. Cases have been rare in which journalists actually have been asked for information that they felt unable, in conscience, to provide, and there is no case on record where penalties, whether in the form of fine or imprisonment, have been imposed.

In the absence of any formal enactment on the subject of professional secrecy by any Canadian legislature, the Common Law prevails. Judicial approval has been given to a statement in Dean Wigmore's "Evidence in Trials at Common Law" to the effect that privilege in respect of disclosure of communication can only be recognized where (1) the communication originates in a confidence that the source will not be disclosed, (2) the element of confidence is essential to a relationship between the parties, (3) the relationship is one which, in the view of the community, ought to be fostered, (4) the injury done by disclosure would be greater that the benefit obtained from correct disposal of the litigation.*

The only relationships accepted as satisfying Wigmore's four specifications in eight of the ten provinces of Canada are those of "solicitor and client" and "husband and wife". In the province of Quebec there also is a statutory recognition of the relationship of "doctor and patient". In Quebec and Newfoundland privilege also extends to communications between "clergyman and penitent".

A journalist's sources of information may come under investigation in three circumstances: (1) where he appears to have information pertinent to a public inquiry by a Commission or Board acting under statutory or special powers conferred by Parliament, or by the legislature of a province, or by a committee of Parliament or a legislature; (2) where

---

* The Wigmore conditions are somewhat more fully presented in the examination of professional secrecy in the United States. See page 174 *infra*.

he publishes material alleging that a crime has been committed, with the published material appearing to be pertinent to the determination of the guilt or innocence of particular persons; or (3) where he is accused of libel in criminal or civil proceedings as a result of the publication of information, and bases his defence on an assertion of honest belief in the truth of the matter published.

In any one of these situations a journalist may be called as a witness and asked to disclose the source of his information. If he refuses he may be held in contempt of court and imprisoned—theoretically until he produces the information asked, thus purging the contempt. In proceedings for libel, the normal practice would be to disregard his defence so far as it might be based on his own unilateral assertion as to the truth of the statement or statements at issue.

Contemporary cases reviewed

There are, as noted, few recorded cases of demands on journalists for information they have felt honour-bound to withhold, and no cases of imprisonment. One incident of a threat of penalty occurred in 1952 at a time when Mr. Justice François Caron was a Commissioner inquiring into vice conditions in Montreal. His attention was directed to an article in the *Montreal Standard* wherein Miss Jacqueline Sirois, a reporter for that newspaper, indicated that certain persons had told her they paid protection on account of illegal activities. She was called as a witness, but refused to name those persons. The Judge held her in contempt, directing her to return the following morning at which time, he said, "If you don't change your mind I will be obliged to sentence you". The record does not show whether she did change her mind and reveal the sources of her information. Because she was not sentenced, however, it is to be presumed either that she did so or otherwise satisfied the Commission that her information was not relevant.

Privilege for journalists in libel actions has been pleaded and has drawn judicial comment, but nothing so far has established it as a right. Relevant is the case of Wismer v. MacLean-Hunter and Fraser (1954 Dominion Law Reports 501). This concerned an article by Blair Fraser, editor of *MacLean's* magazine, published in that magazine. It dealt with the conduct of the government of British Columbia and led to a libel suit brought by Gordon Wismer, Attorney-General at the time of publication. The defendants pleaded the article was "fair comment on a matter of public importance". On examination for discovery, a procedure corresponding to "Interrogatory" in England, Mr. Fraser was asked the source of his information. He refused to disclose it and the defence was struck out. The defendant appealed this ruling, but the British Columbia Court of Appeal confirmed the ruling, with one judge, O'Halloran, dissenting.

This case is significant in that it established that in the province of British Columbia, at least, journalists may be compelled to disclose sources of information at examination for discovery. This is a divergence from a rule recognized in England, which affords protection at that stage of libel proceedings, although the English courts have not held that such information could be withheld at the actual trial of a libel action. Interest also attaches to Mr. Justice O'Halloran's minority view as one of the few judicial comments on record favourable to journalistic privilege. He reasoned that a journalist has a duty to provide information to the public and so should enjoy some kind of special position, or privilege. This view, however, appears to have been rejected by the Supreme Court of Canada in two later libel actions (Boland v. the *Globe and Mail,* 1960 Supreme Court Reports; Banks v. the *Globe and Mail,* 1961 SCR). That Court, where decisions are final and binding, said a newspaper has no duty to report or comment on specific matters, and if it makes libellous statements it has no defence open to it that is not available equally to any private citizen.

The Fraser case never went to trial. The issue of the defendant's rights at examination for discovery was appealed to the Supreme Court of Canada, but that Court declined to consider a matter pertaining to the rules of a provincial court. The magazine published an apology, and Attorney-General Wismer withdrew his suit. The case, therefore, adds nothing to Canadian law on the issue of journalistic secrecy, and is notable only in that it brought virtually the only judicial comment on journalistic privilege in relation to sources of information.

As a federal state, Canada has a complicated system of constitutional law. Up to the present time, this has not been relevant to the question of journalistic privilege. It would be relevant if any attempt were made to establish such privilege by legislation, as has been done in some states of the United States where the Common Law prevails. The legislative power in Canada is unlimited. The federal Parliament and the provincial legislatures may each make any law, affecting the rights of the subject, in their defined areas of jurisdiction. Normally, "property and civil rights" are within the area of provincial jurisdiction; "criminal law" is federal. So, in theory, provincial legislation alone could establish journalistic privilege in civil proceedings such as libel, or relative to official inquiries under provincial authorities. Federal legislation alone could establish such privilege in criminal matters or federal inquiries.

Constitutional provisions

The jurisdiction of the Supreme Court of Canada extends both to provincial and federal matters. Although that Court rejected the right of a journalist to claim special privilege in its rulings in the two libel actions mentioned above, involving the Toronto *Globe and Mail,* in 1960 and 1961, it also returned a ruling more favourable to the general press position in 1938.

A statute established by action of the provincial legislature of the province of Alberta, among other provisions, required publishers to disclose, on demand of certain officials, the source of any information presented in their newspapers. Stiff penalties were provided for failure to do so, including suspension of publication. This statute was ruled unconstitutional by the Supreme Court in 1938, with a statement that a provincial legislature's right to legislate on the press was restricted, and that it could not interfere with the free dissemination of information necessary to the working of the democratic parliamentary system established by the Constitution for all of Canada. Presumably, the Alberta law would have been condemned even if it had not dealt with the source of information. But the Court's ruling demonstrates that there are constitutional limits to the power of a legislature to deal with, if not to enlarge, journalistic privilege.

Denmark

In Denmark, the Administration of Justice Act specifies in Section 168 that any person may be called as a witness in a legal case and is obligated to give evidence of his knowledge of the case or of the subject under investigation. Refusal to give such evidence makes the person subject to fine or to as much as six months in gaol.

A journalist appearing as a witness is subject to this same obligation in cases being heard in any court, civil or criminal. A number of administrative authorities—boards, tribunals, and committees—also have the task of settling legal questions, but the nature of the cases within the jurisdiction of these authorities is such that the problem of a journalist's right to withhold information as to the source of his information will not arise, nor will it arise in reference to inquiries conducted by legislative bodies. A journalist's right to keep secret the *content* of information, rather than the *source,* is a somewhat different matter, and one governed by statutory provisions, some concerning a witness' right *not* to reveal his source, others concerning his right *not* to divulge circumstances known to him.

In a civil case before the courts, a witness—journalist or not—may refuse to give evidence if it is likely to expose the witness himself, his wife, parents, or children to a "loss of general esteem or welfare," a considerable loss of fortune, or any other substantial damage. (Section 170, Paragraph 1.) In a criminal case, also, a witness may refuse to give evidence if it is likely to expose him to a loss of "general esteem or welfare". (Section 170, Paragraph 2.) He is never under obligation to give what might be self-incriminating evidence in a criminal case in which he himself appears as a suspect. (Sections 765, Paragraph 2; 766, Paragraph 2; and 868, Paragraph 1.)

Under Danish law, as under the law of most other countries, lawyers and clergymen (by provisions of Section 169), and physicians (under Section 10 of the Danish Doctors and Physicians Act) cannot normally be requested to give evidence about matters confided to them in the conduct of their professional or spiritual duties. Nor can civil servants and others performing public functions be requested to give evidence about matters considered confidential, unless their superiors give their consent.

In such instances the courts themselves follow the practice of making no request for such evidence *except* in cases where the court believes such evidence necessary to prevent a miscarriage of justice and, even then, only if the party entitled to secrecy gives his consent.

Journalists are not obliged by law to observe professional secrecy in Denmark, whether with reference to sources or to content. Nor does any Code of Ethics exist within Danish associations of journalists binding them to professional secrecy. Nevertheless, journalists of the country do consider it an unwritten law that they must observe secrecy with reference to their sources of information, and that a wish on the part of a "source" to remain anonymous must be respected, in court or out. So far as is known, accordingly, no Danish journalist during the present century has complied with a court order to reveal his source, even under threat of punishment.

How the courts draw the line

Two statutory provisions have a direct bearing upon the journalist's position with reference to observation of the principle of professional secrecy.

Liability of an editor or author to punishment because of the contents of a periodical printed in Denmark exists, generally, only under certain conditions. (Press Act, Section 6.) If proceedings are instituted, and if the author's name is attached to the offending article, he is liable. If his name is not attached, or if the article is written under a pen name, then the editor is liable. The term "editor" is interpreted to mean the person responsible for the publication of the article in question. This provision generally excludes any search or demand for the name of an anonymous source even in a criminal case being heard because of the contents of a periodical.

This general rule is subject, however, to certain limitations.

First, it applies only with reference to cases arising from the actual content of an article held to be libellous or slanderous, to invade privacy, or to be obscene or blasphemous—"press delicts," in Danish terminology. It does not apply with reference to violation of copyright, or breach of secrecy by persons in the public service or performing a public function. Thus, in the latter instance, if a newspaper has published a statement based upon information obtained through a civil servant's violation of his duty not to divulge confidential matters, the case cannot be judged under the rules on liability embraced by the Press Act, but must be judged according to the general rules of liability set out in the Penal Code. Yet, if the civil servant remains anonymous, the editor or journalist who has obtained the information and written the account may be summoned to appear before the court and there be asked to reveal his source.

Second, the rule with reference to liability of author or editor, under the Press Act, specifies that certain particularly dangerous offences must be judged according to the general principles of liability. Such offences would be those regarded as threats to the independence or security of the state, or offences against the public administration and the higher authorities of the state. In such a case, the editor or journalist may be ordered to give evidence and to reveal the identity of the author of an anonymous article containing such offensive references, or to reveal the name of the source of information contained in a published report.

Statute gives limited right

The second statutory provision bearing specifically upon a journalist's asserted right to professional secrecy appears in the Administration of Justice Act (Section 170, Paragraph 4). This holds that the editor or a sub-editor of a periodical printed in Denmark may refuse to give evidence as to the identity of the source of an article or of a statement printed without the author's name attached *unless* the case concerns a crime subject to heavy penalty—meaning something more than a brief prison sentence— or *unless* it involves a breach of secrecy by persons engaged in the performance of public functions.

This is the only special rule under Danish law on a journalist's right to refuse to give evidence, and it has strict limitations. Extending a certain protection to editors-in-chief and sub-editors, it does not provide any exemption to include editors whose functions relate to commerce and finance, for example, or to sports, theatre and the arts. Nor does it apply, as noted, if the case being heard in court is one that may bring a heavy penalty if the defendant should be found guilty under the Penal Code. Since most serious offences may carry such a penalty, exemption from a duty to give evidence is held justified only in the most exceptional instances.

In the circumstances, this particular provision of the law has been invoked in support of the principle of professional secrecy perhaps four times, in the last half-century, and only once successfully, being dismissed by the court on the other occasions as irrelevant.

When a journalist is asked to reveal a source of information to a court, whether in a civil or criminal case, and refuses to do so, the same court has the right to decide whether he shall be required to reveal that source or suffer the prescribed penalty of fine or imprisonment. If that requirement is imposed upon him, the journalist may appeal to a superior court, whose sole function then is to decide whether the lower court's decision shall be upheld or dismissed, without reference to the issues of the case itself.

A journalist might refuse to give evidence, under the provisions of Section 170 of the Administration of Justice Act, contending that for him to reveal a source of information would expose him to a "loss of general esteem and welfare," in a professional sense. No judgment is available as to how the court might receive such a plea in a civil case (Section 170, Paragraph 1). In criminal cases, there have been instances in which journalists have refused to divulge sources on the basis of that argument (Section 170, Paragraph 2), but the courts ruled against them on all such occasions.

One such case arose in 1936 before the Copenhagen City Court when an editor was ordered to reveal the source of information included in an article about a municipal problem that had been discussed behind closed doors.* The editor appealed to the High Court, protesting that he should be excused from giving evidence. Among other things, he invoked Section 170, Paragraph 2, maintaining that "to a journalist the disclosure of a source would mean that he would be expelled from his profession and lose all future possibilities of working as a journalist". To support his contention he produced a declaration from the presidents of the Association of Copenhagen Journalists and the Association of Provincial Journalists (both since combined as the Association of Danish Journalists). The High Court, however, dismissed his appeal and affirmed the decision of the City Court.

Another case arose in 1949 when a sub-editor was called upon to reveal the source of a statement made to him, and published, to the effect

---

* For details, see *UfR* (weekly publication of the Danish Administration of Justice), 1936, pp. 178 ff.

that three or four years previously a young woman had submitted to an operation by an abortionist under accusation in 1949 of a similar crime. The sub-editor refused to name his informant, also citing Section 170, Paragraph 2. He asserted that in press circles it was the general practice for journalists to keep confidental their sources of information, that any such disclosure would make it difficult for him to obtain a better position, and that this corresponded to a "loss of welfare". Both the superior court and the High Court decided against him, however, and he was fined 50 kroner.*

The question also has been raised as to whether a journalist, receiving information from a civil servant, whose revelation might itself be subject to interpretation as a breach of official secrecy, might be regarded as equally culpable and hence justified in refusing to give evidence under the provisions of the law holding that no person can be required to give evidence in a case in which he is himself a suspect. (Sections 765, 766, 868, cited above, with paragraphs.) The Danish Supreme Court has ruled, however, that the journalist's duty to reveal his source, in such a circumstance, may be enforced by the Prosecution's declaration in advance that the editor will not be held liable.**

High Court exempts daily

The one and only occasion on which the editor's or sub-editor's right to refuse to give evidence, under the provision of Section 170, Paragraph 4, was acted upon favourably by the court, under the strict limitations attached to that paragraph, occurred in 1950. This was a case in which a Copenhagen daily had published several articles about a person who had vanished and was believed dead. It appeared from the articles, however, that he was still alive. Relatives of the person concerned, acting through the courts, sought to force the newspaper to reveal the source of its information. Carried to the High Court, it was decided that the editor-in-chief of the paper should be exempted from revealing his source.***

---

* See *UfR*, 1949, pp. 112 ff. Two other decisions by the higher court on the same issue directed that journalists were under obligation to reveal their sources of information, viz. *UfR*, 1910, pp. 120 ff, and *UfR*, 1925, pp. 1004 ff.

** *UfR*, 1910, p. 120.

*** *UfR*, 1950, pp. 829 ff. The same law, but acted upon negatively by the courts, was invoked in the cases of 1910, 1936, and 1949 as noted above.

In practice, the question of a journalist's obligation to give evidence, in the sense of revealing sources, rarely arises. The most recent case occurred in 1957, and ended without any clear decision. A libel case had been brought by a barrister against the editor of the *Nordsjaellands Social-Demokrat,* Hillerod. During the hearing, the identity of the journalist who had written the article held to be defamatory, Sigvald Hansen, was established, and the plaintiff's counsel insisted that he should reveal the name of the person from whom he obtained the information held to be libellous.

When Mr. Hansen refused to reveal the source, the court ruled that he must do so. On appeal, both the higher court and the Supreme Court affirmed this ruling, holding that it was not possible to exclude in advance that a reply to the question might not be of importance to a proper judgment of the nature of the offence. While the case was still pending, however, the plaintiff died and, following the decision by the Supreme Court, his widow's lawyer declared that no further steps would be taken against the journalist. Thus, Mr. Hansen escaped any penalty for his refusal to reveal the source.

Extending the Code among journalists

Danish journalists and editors are in complete agreement on the desirability of respecting the anonymity of their sources of information. Although there is no formal Code of Ethics and no Court of Honour in being in the country, journalists regard the protection of confidences as a professional obligation. In 1957 a Joint Committee of Danish Journalists agreed to work toward a verbal alteration of Section 170 of the Administration of Justice Act to extend the exemption technically given to editors and sub-editors in Paragraph 4 to include all newspaper and periodical staff members, and also to bring about a relaxation in the limitations that have made Paragraph 4 of little practical value in assuring journalists the right to protect their sources.

The proposal for such a change is based upon an expert opinion prepared by Mr. Mohring-Andersen, Supreme Court barrister, who pointed out the discretionary character of the line drawn between editors and sub-editors and other journalists. The basis for this differentiation was attributed to the absence of a professional concept among Danish journalists until the last fifty years or so, with newspapers previously prepared by their editors and a number of anonymous workers acting on the editor's responsibility. Now, to a great extent, the editor's tasks are delegated to assistants who edit the various sub-divisons of the paper without direct supervision by the editor, assistants recognized by the public as specialists, and who, therefore, should—in Mr. Mohring-Andersen's view—be equally exempted from the duty to give evidence.

Jurists discuss the journalists' claims

Non-journalistic circles, so far, have scarcely considered the problem of professional secrecy for journalists in Denmark. Dr. Stephan Hurwitz, former professor of criminal law procedure, and present "Provost" of the Danish Parliament, has been one jurist, however, to take an interest in the subject. He recommends that journalists' rights to refuse to reveal their sources should become full statutory rights. Dr. Hurwitz has said that the present rules governing exemptions for journalists in Denmark from the duty to give evidence are not so far-reaching as those of other countries, generally, and are not in conformity with current views. He believes that the journalist's obligation to respect the secrecy of his sources, based on professional honour, should be recognized by the courts, and coercive action relaxed accordingly.

Several proposals also have been made by Dr. Bernt Hjejle, Supreme Court barrister, and president of the Danish General Council of the Bar, that journalists' rights to refuse to reveal their sources should be extended. The press, he believes, is capable of giving the public reliable information on the activities of the government and its various divisions and officials only if journalists are entitled to avail themselves of anonymous sources when necessary. If the sources run the risk of losing their anonymity, by reason of possible legal actions, they will withhold information from the press and so prevent it meeting its responsibility to keep the public adequately informed.

A subject of discussion at the 20th Scandinavian Meeting of Jurists, which took place in Oslo in 1954, was "The Right of Anonymity of the Press." Among the Danish participants, Dr. Carl Rasting reviewed the journalists' concept of professional secrecy. His concluding opinion was that the right of anonymity should be the same in all Scandinavian countries and should be extended so far as possible without doing harm to vital general interests.

An official Danish government committee was formed late in 1958, at the instigation of Hans Haekkerup, Minister of Justice, to make a careful re-examination of the rules affecting the position not only of doctors, lawyers and clergymen called to give evidence, but of journalists as well.

Minister Haekkerup had given it as his view that the problem for the journalist, called upon to reveal sources, would be substantially reduced if government services were more cooperative in revealing information through application or introduction of what was referred to as "the principle of publicity". Under practices established in Danish law, State as well as municipal services are conducted under strict secrecy. Journalists, performing their function in the modern manner to provide the public with information to which they are deemed entitled, have, therefore, been obliged to look to anonymous sources for information.

Since 1956 a committee of the government has been working on the problem of altering the older system and introducing a procedure under which government activities will be conducted with more publicity. Officials, jurists and journalists of Denmark believe that, once this committee makes its recommendations, and with possible additional recommendations by the committee formed in 1958 by the Minister of Justice, some changes in statutory provisions may also follow that will provide broader recognition of the journalist's desire and need for professional secrecy with reference to his sources of information.

The question of professional secrecy with reference to radio news treatment has never arisen in Denmark.

Finland

In Finland, a journalist can be required to divulge the source of information incorporated in a news report he has prepared *only* during the course of a case before a court of law, and, within limits, to police authorities. Apart from such occasions, he is expected to respect confidences and can, indeed, be penalized for failure to do so. A journalist is not, and may not be required to reveal sources of information to any legislative or administrative authorities.

The laws of Finland actually include no provisions specifically applicable to the journalist's right or privilege to maintain secrecy as to a source of information or the contents of information, assuming that a demand is made upon him by a court or by the police. By interpretation, however, certain paragraphs in the law of January 4, 1919, relating to freedom of the press, may be regarded as having some relevance to his position. Paragraph 11 of the 1919 law states :

> If a printer mentions the name of the writer in a printed communication, without the consent of the writer, he is to be fined up to the equivalent of fifty days daily wages.

By the same law, if a publisher or printer divulges the name of a writer, without consent, and when this occurs without any recognized legal demand, penalties are also prescribed, except in a case where an action is taken on account of the *contents* of the publication.

The general principle emerging from these paragraphs, expressed in other words, is that any person engaged in printing or publishing a newspaper or periodical is under obligation to keep secret the name of the writer of anything appearing in print, unless the writer agrees that his name may be made known. By interpretation, any person providing a news item, or information incorporated in a published report of any sort, is to be considered as sharing the same right of anonymity accorded to "the writer". There is less agreement, however, as to whether any person other than the printer or publisher, specifically mentioned in the law, can be held responsible under the law for maintaining secrecy or can be punished if he fails to do so.

The duty to keep names of writers (or informants) secret is not unconditional in Finland, however, since there may be the obligation noted to divulge such names if the writing or the information becomes a cause of legal action before a court. In such an event, the obligation to produce evidence applies to a journalist, as to other citizens of the country.

Any witness, to be sure, would be excused from such an obligation under conditions specified in the law of most countries, when to answer a question might mean that he would incriminate himself or a close relative (Chapter 17, paragraphs 20 and 24 in the law of court procedure). It also is provided that a witness may refuse to answer if to do so would reveal a business or professional secret, yet even this exemption is restricted when and if the court decides that there are compelling reasons for demanding that the witness reply. The journalist has no special privilege under this provision.

Aside from the obligation to keep the names of writers and, by interpretation, informants secret under the provisions of the 1919 law, with the qualifications applicable in a court case, there is no law in Finland having any specific application to the task of the journalist. His position is not analogous to that of the doctor, lawyer, or clergyman, whose rights to withhold information on matters falling within the areas of their professional competence is recognized by the law of Finland, as by the law of most other countries.

Few cases on record

The number of cases wherein the journalist's right of professional secrecy has come into question have been few in Finland. There has never been occasion for the Supreme Court to rule on the matter, and the question has brought little discussion outside journalistic groups. Even journalists of the country, although agreed that the source of news is not to be disclosed voluntarily and favouring a clearer statement of such a right in law, have done nothing about it. The Association of Finnish Journalists (Suomen Sanomalehtien Liitto) has not formulated or approved a Code of Ethics for the profession.

The few incidents bearing upon revelation of sources by a journalist have brought no clarification of the issue. Only three known cases in the last ten years have even approached the subject. In one, the Municipal Court of Helsinki ordered a journalist to give evidence as to whether the defendant in a libel case had provided the information forming the basis of the action — in this case, information published in a foreign newspaper. Its chief significance was that the court did not accept a plea that there were "very important reasons" for regarding the information as a "professional secret" within the meaning of the procedural law. The same Helsinki court, on another occasion, ordered a journalist to divulge the name of his informant during a criminal case where a dispensing chemist stood accused of having sold saccharine in violation of rationing rules, and of having charged excessive prices. In the third case, a journalist summoned as a witness before an assize court was ordered to divulge the name of his informant. In all three cases the journalists bowed to the court by giving the evidence required, but in the last case, which occured in 1958, the evidence was limited by the court itself to a statement as to whether the defendant before the court had given the information.

The question of a journalist's duty to guard his sources of information was discussed with reference to the Finnish situation, among others, at the 20th Congress of Jurists of the Northern European Countries, in Oslo, in 1954, Professor Kaarlo Kaira, of Finland, conceded that Finnish Law was lacking in clarity of definition on the issue of anonymity, and he expressed the hope that some adjustment would be made on that score. It was his view that protection offered by the right of anonymity should be extended as far as possible without doing harm to vital public interests, that it should be the rule, and that the freedom of the press should be furthered so far as possible through the right of anonymity, extending to persons giving information to journalists.*

The same question had been considered in 1953 by the Finnish Association of Lawyers (Juridiska Föreningen i Finland). Allan Viranko, a lawyer and also Secretary General of the Finnish Press Association, advanced the view that in a court action against a person suspected as the informant, with the information as published standing as the key to the action itself — as might be so in a libel case — a journalist called as a witness was obliged to reveal whether the person accused had provided

---

* *Forhandlinger pa det tyvende nordiske juristmote i Oslo den 23-25 August 1954.* (Oslo : Johansen & Nielsen Boktrykkeri, 1956.)

the information. For any other kind of action before a court, however, Mr. Viranko took the view that a journalist should not be obliged to divulge the name of his informant, if asked. G. Nybergh, chairman of the Finnish Association of Lawyers, and an associate justice of the Finnish Supreme Court, did not differ with Mr. Viranko's view. *

In summary, Finnish law now requires a journalist to divulge the source of his information to a court of law, if the court rules that there are "important reasons" for demanding it. The journalist himself may consider it his clear duty to do so *if* a major crime or a matter affecting the security of the state is before the court. In other cases, he may refuse to divulge information, although the court then may order him to do so. The journalist is not obligated to divulge a source to a legislative group, to administrative authorities, or to private persons. He is required by law to tell police authorities all he may know that is needed in the investigation of a crime, yet the police have no means of forcing him to do so.

* *Tidskrift utgiven av Juridiska Föreningen i Finland*, 1953, p. 105.

France

In France, a sharp contradiction between ethical and legal concepts bearing upon the issue of professional secrecy for journalists has raised problems scarcely matched in any other country. The problems have existed for years, but have been resolved without much difficulty, so far, by reason of a mutual understanding between press and bar. The critical period in which France has found itself since about 1954, however, has brought the matter into greater prominence.

The basic press law of France, adopted in 1881, assured freedom of the press. That law has been amended since and may be amended again, but it is not restrictive. At the same time, individual journalists, like other citizens, are subject to the general law of the land. This makes them subject to the provision in Article 378 of the Code of Penal Procedure, stating that any person subpoenaed as a witness is compelled to appear in court and reply to any questions asked on pain of imprisonment or fine, or both. This certainly could mean that a journalist might be asked to reveal a source of information.

Article 378 does make certain exceptions, however, such as are found in the law of most countries. Thus doctors, surgeons, pharmacists, midwives, and public health officials are excused from answering questions about matters that have come to their knowledge in the course of their work or professions, and that have been received in confidence. Beyond that, they are *required* by the law to preserve those secrets or become subject to fines or imprisonment. Statute law has extended this provision to cover lawyers, magistrates, notaries, and law officers in general.

Contrary to practice in most countries, priests and clergymen are not privileged to keep silent if confronted with a demand from the court for information. It would be impossible to insert such a principle into any piece of legislation because it would flatly contradict the 1905 Act on the separation of the Church from the State. In jurisprudence, however, application of the general principle of the "necessary confidants" has enabled priests and clergymen to be recognized among the persons bound to observe secrecy, not only in so far as confessions are involved but also with reference to any statement made to them in the course of their ministry.

One other exception exists. Article 13 of the law of October 19, 1946, known as the Statute of Civil Servants ; and Article 8 of the law of April 28, 1952, confirmed by the Ordinance of February 4, 1959, forbid civil servants and local government officers to communicate facts or information to third parties unless authorized to do so by the responsible Minister of the national government or the Mayor of a municipality concerned. Other categories of officials also are bound to complete secrecy through professional oath : postal workers, with regard to the secrecy of the mails ; civil servants employed in the Ministry of Defence, and the police, with reference to certain State secrets.

Any or all of these officials, while forbidden to reveal to third parties confidential information gained in the course of performing their duties, cannot, however, plead the same right to professional secrecy as a reason for not appearing to testify in court with reference to other matters. Legally, the only persons who can exercise this latter privilege of remaining off the witness stand altogether are those who may be engaged in a profession or a task to which the law has imparted a confidential and secret character of its own, in the general interest and in the interest of law and order. But any and every person is required by Article 62 of the Penal Code to report to the authorities any information of which he may have knowledge relating to the commission of crimes.

Until July 1960 everyone also was bound to report treasonable activities and espionage, as constituting crimes. Since that time, however, liberal trends have brought an end to this obligation so far as it might relate to those persons privileged, under the laws already noted, to preserve professional secrecy. To qualify for privilege under those laws, a person must be considered a "necessary confidant," with the secrets entrusted to him precisely because of the nature of his vocation or profession. This automatically excludes the journalist from such privilege, since his function is *not* to keep information secret, but to publish the substance of what may be told to him, even though the name of the actual informant is not revealed.

It has been traditional for a journalist, summoned as a witness and asked to reveal a source, to plead professional secrecy as justifying his silence, even though the law does not give him that specific privilege.

In practice, there have been very few cases in France since 1881 wherein journalists have been placed in such a position. In those few cases, with refusal to reply either to an examining magistrate or to a Court, they have been fined on the grounds that "the profession of journalist cannot be included under Article 378 of the Penal Code... that it cannot be upheld that journalists are necessary confidants to whom private persons are obliged to apply or that as such they would be exempted from testifying in Court". (Cherbourg Maritime Court, 1923.) But, in such cases, they usually have been fined the *minimum* amount.

The "Nouveau Candide" case

These cases have been so rare, however, that 15 years elapsed without any journalist being called upon to disclose a source of information prior to September 1961. Then René Maine, editor of the weekly *Nouveau Candide,* and Georgette Elgey, of the same publication, were called before the Military Tribunal as witnesses in an examination of a number of persons accused of complicity in a so-called "Paris Plot".

In *Nouveau Candide* they had published extracts from the "Carnets" of Colonel Yves Goddard, one of the accused, who had evaded arrest. Goddard had been one of the most prominent activist officers in Algeria. When he was the head of the "Sûreté" in Algiers, he had used rough methods of repression and had been sent back to France after the abortive civilian rebellion of January 1960 in Algeria. In Algeria once more under the orders of former General Challe, he was found to be a participant in the military putsch of April 1961. Goddard was sentenced to death in absentia on June 1, 1961.

After the failure of the putsch, a number of higher officers were arrested and arraigned before the Military Tribunal. A few days before the opening of the trial, the editors of *Nouveau Candide* received through the mails a document which later proved to be the personal diary of Colonel Goddard with day-to-day accounts of the weeks which preceded the April 21 putsch.

The names of all the participants in the plot had been reduced to single initial letters, but in presenting the diary to the readers of *Nouveau Candide* René Maine and Georgette Elgey replaced those initials with the full names of most of the officers on trial. As the disclosures threw a bad light on the defendants. M. Maine and Mlle Elgey were summoned as witnesses. They were asked how these extracts had come into their possession and how they had succeeded in deciphering certain names. Invoking professional secrecy, they replied that they were unable to reveal their sources.

In contrast to the ruling of the Cherbourg Maritime Court in 1923, previously mentioned, where minimum fines were assessed, the Military Tribunal in 1961 did no more than note the statements of the journalists and no further action was taken.

The minimum fines imposed on earlier occasions were a reflection of the fact that, in practice, magistrates generally have shown tolerance for the journalist's ethical position, and have been reluctant to force him to speak, or punish him for failure to do so, despite the letter of the law. This tacit recognition of his position has come about in part because the ethical or moral factor has been vigorously asserted by journalists themselves over a long period of years. It has been demonstrated, further, in a practice whereby both magistrates and police officers, questioning journalists about their sources of information or about facts they have learned in the course of their work, commonly accept the journalists' asserted "loss of memory" concerning essential details. If this is a mitigation of the law conveniently accepted by both parties, it seems to be the only possible way journalists can protect the concept of professional secrecy, and also continue to receive information with assurance that the identities of their informants will be protected, where that is important.

Code of ethics endorsed by the law

The somewhat permissive attitude of magistrates, particularly in the present period, also may rest in part on an apparent contradiction within the law. The French Syndicat National des Journalistes (National Union of Journalists) drafted a "Charter of Journalists' Duties" in July 1918, asserting certain rules of professional ethics. These were revised and augmented in January 1938, and continue as a professional code of ethics. An official State Decree of December 7, 1960, dealing with the status of established journalists employed by the Radiodiffusion-Télévision Française (R. T. F.) (French Radio and Television Corporation), a public body, stipulated in its Article 5 that radio-television journalists must adhere to the 1918 Charter as "the code of their professional activity". This gives actual legal sanction to the statement of principles accepted by the profession itself, including an assertion that "every journalist worthy of the name" must observe professional secrecy. Articles 36 to 38 of the official Decree of December 7, 1960, also provide that failure to comply with the provisions of the 1918 code may be punished by disciplinary action.

This could mean three things : First, that an Arbitration Committee set up under a law of March 29, 1935, establishing the status of French journalists in general, might be justified in approving the dismissal of a journalist infringing upon the rule of professional secrecy by disclosing his sources of information to the Government or to the Courts. Second, Article 34 of a Convention Nationale du Travail des Journalistes (Journalists' National Labour Agreement) of 1956 states that violation of the "rules of professional honour" is to be construed as misconduct, which might also justify dismissal under an interpretation of the law of 1935. Third, dismissal might be approved by the Disciplinary Committee of the Radio and Television Corporation, for the same reason.

It is true that, should such an action occur under any one of these three conditions, the decision to dismiss might be quashed by the Cour de Cassation (Court of Appeal) on the ground that it was based on an interpretation contrary to the general law and with no justification under Article 378 of the Penal Code. On the other hand, the very existence of the official Decree of December 7, 1960, in combination with the terms of the 1918 Charter, might equally support the journalist in asserting a moral obligation to keep secret certain facts, and especially his source of information, even though technically this would bring him into conflict with the general provisions of the penal law, wherein no distinction is made between a journalist and any other citizen in the obligation to answer a question addressed to him as a witness in court. Yet, the very presence of this contradiction supports the tendency of magistrates to give tacit recognition to the journalist's claim to professional secrecy—a tendency documented by a survey conducted in 1958 through the Association of Former Students of the School of Journalism at the University of Lille.

A typical example of the clash that can occur between the statute law and the moral code, interpreted in its broadest sense, arose in 1960.

The Arnaud case

Georges Arnaud, of *Paris-Presse,* was invited, with correspondents, to attend a secret press conference held by Francis Jeanson, a philosophy teacher and former editor, being sought by the police for activities in connection with the National Liberation Front (F. L. N.), a group charged with aiding and abetting Algerian Nationalist insurgents. Two days after publication of his report of the conference in *Paris-Presse,* M. Arnaud was arrested and imprisoned on a warrant issued by the Military Tribunal on a charge—not precisely for withholding a source of information—but for failing to report "persons engaged in activities liable to endanger national defence" — an offence covered by Article 104 of the Penal Code.

Journalists of all shades of political opinion appeared before the Military Tribunal on June 17, 1960, to state their view that M. Arnaud had acted according to his conscience and the code of journalism, and that he could not properly be expected to betray the confidence that Jeanson had placed in him.

The Prosecutor, in an address to the Tribunal, pointed out that professional secrecy is not covered by the law in France.

"You may think that having to inform on someone is an unpleasant matter," he said, and conceded that "prosecution for failing to inform is rare. But as a magistrate it is my duty to ask you to enforce the law. Legally, Georges Arnaud is guilty. The rest is a matter for you."

The Military Tribunal gave M. Arnaud a suspended minimum sentence of two years' imprisonment. This was regarded as an implicit recognition of the moral right he had invoked even as the legal limitation upon such a right was stated for the record.

Arnaud then appealed to the Cour de Cassation, which reversed the verdict and did not direct any court to reconsider the case. The Cour de Cassation accepted the plea by Georges Arnaud's lawyers, according to which the Military Tribunal had acted on inadequate provisions invoked retroactively, which is contrary to the principles of French law. The Tribunal had used the new provisions of June 1960 which had reserved the benefit of professional secrecy to certain categories, excluding journalists. Yet, since Jeanson's press conference had taken place a few weeks before, in April, this new statute was inapplicable to the case.

Thus Arnaud won acquittal through a procedural tangle which did not erase, however, the principle upon which his earlier condemnation had been based.

The political crisis in which France has been involved for some years threatens to bring a multiplication of such cases. Because of the delicate psychological climate prevailing in the country, authorities so far have hesitated to take legal action any more forthright than they did in the Arnaud case.

The only other relevant case within the provisions of Article 104 of the Penal Code occurred in September 1955. At that time, Robert Burron had published a series of articles in *France Observateur* describing a period of time he had spent with an Algerian rebel group. Burron was arrested on a warrant issued by the Algiers military examining magistrate but was released on bail. Because of an almost unanimous press protest at the time, it appears that the authorities preferred to let the case go by default ; Burron has not since been brought before the Tribunal, and nothing further has been heard of the matter.

These, of course, are admittedly borderline cases where politics plays a key role. Yet it is important to recognize that the authorities can use Article 104 and other articles of the Penal Code to discipline journalists if they are prepared to accept the risk of seeming to be encroaching upon freedom of the press, freedom of expression, and the right of the public to receive information.

Informing on criminals

If Article 104 relates to failure to report activities "liable to endanger national defence," Article 62 of the Penal Code requires any person having knowledge of a crime, whether attempted or actually committed, to notify the authorities. Occasionally this has involved a journalist in legal technicalities. The most typical case of this kind, falling within the area of the common law, and lacking in political overtones, occurred in 1948.

Police throughout France were seeking a man named Pierre Carrot, nicknamed Pierrot le Fou (Crazy Pete), who had been arrested for various offences, but walked out of a Paris gaol on June 15. Many French papers printed reports inferring that Crazy Pete was rather clever to escape and that the police were inefficient. When Crazy Pete repeated some of the same hold-ups of the same persons and at the same places as before, the press had more to say.

On July 17 Crazy Pete, well armed and accompanied by a henchman, appeared at the office of the *Paris-Presse* to protest to George Arqué, a reporter, about an article in which he had portrayed Crazy Pete as an "informer". Two days later he returned and talked with Arqué and another reporter, René Didio. On the basis of this interview, Arqué and Didio presented a story, complete with photographs and an autograph, ostensibly based upon a meeting between Crazy Pete and the reporter in a forest. They gave an advance copy of the story to the police super-intendent in charge of the case.

Crazy Pete, sometimes described as a "dangerous gangster," a "gunman," a "bandit," and as "France's public enemy No. 1," was captured shortly after the interview appeared. But the police were curious as to how Arqué had made contact with him. A few days after the story appeared, therefore, Arqué was arrested in the early morning hours, and Didio sometime later. Both were gaoled on warrants charging them with "non-denunciation," or failure to report criminals within the provisions of Article 62 of the Penal Code. Arqué was questioned for five hours by the examining magistrate, but contended that professional secrecy required that he keep silent.

Arqué also stressed that he had kept the criminal police fully in-formed of his conversations with the gangster, and the fact was con-firmed by the police superintendent.

Despite the view of the Public Prosecutor that they should have been released at once, the two men were kept in custody for eight days and then released on bail.

Journalists protest

The arrest of the reporters was protested by the Syndicat des Journa-listes. Not only was their detention held to be improper on legal grounds, but it was regarded as a kind of vengeful act by police and judicial authorities. Article 62 of the Penal Code, it was pointed out, simply obliged a person having knowledge of a crime or a prospective crime, to report the deed, not the individual. This interpretation was to be confirmed in later judgments by the Court of Appeals in two common law cases on December 27, 1960, and March 2, 1961, and also was stated in principles set out by the Cour Suprême (Supreme Court) in these words :

> It is not the identity or refuge of the criminal that must be reported to the authorities but only the crime itself so that the authorities can take steps calculated to prevent it being effective or being followed by further crimes.

It must be added that this interpretation did not go unchallenged. While Arqué had the support of the journalists' association, and the interpretation of the law did not extend to requiring that he reveal the hiding place of a wanted criminal, Maître Maurice Garçon, a member of the French Academy, for one, attacked M. Arqué's ethical position, both as a journalist and as an ordinary citizen. He wrote, in part :

> Writing an article is no justification for satisfying the public's curiosity. The journalist must not become the confidant... of a murderer. He has no professional need to rub shoulders with a gangster. Should it happen that a journalist has to meet him, against his will, then he owes the gangster nothing and under the Code he is obliged in the public interest to tell the authorities anything he may know. This is the only effective way to fight crime. Any other view belongs to a lamentable romanticism and can only deeply disturb public order which is already jeopardized unduly.

On the other side, however, Maître Henri Torrès, another brilliant lawyer, maintained that the words of Maître Garçon could not apply to a journalist who had, as Arqué did, "carried out his job, and whose duty is not to replace the police, who should do their own work."

For the French journalist, observation of the moral rule incorporated in the 1918 Charter means that he would keep his sources of information secret if he had given his word to do so, or if he considered that to reveal such sources might be prejudicial to those concerned. For the same reason, and quite apart from the matter of sources, he might refrain from publishing all he knows, in part because he might be prosecuted for libel or because to do so might violate one of the bans on publication that have become more numerous in recent years in France. Should he, nevertheless, be brought into court on a charge of libel or on a charge of disregarding some such ban, he would need to examine his conscience to decide whether he should reveal his source of information, for the sake of his defence, or suffer the consequences of refusal.

In another circumstance, a published article might throw new light on legal proceedings in progress, or on some political or financial affair. A Tribunal or a Commission of Inquiry might then ask the journalist who wrote the article to provide further details, or to reveal names and sources of his disclosures. In such a case he doubtless would consider himself bound by the 1918 Charter to keep silent, whatever the consequences.

Amending the law or not

In practice, French journalists have not been greatly concerned over professional secrecy because the compromises accepted by the courts have left it, so far, as hardly more than an academic issue.

As long ago as 1924, however, Professor Hugueney of the Paris Faculty of Law had been asked to suggest a legislative provision which might relieve French journalists from feeling the full force of the law, as in the then recent Cherbourg case of 1923. He proposed that the problem be met by amending the law in one of three possible ways: (1) To include journalists in the lists of professions bound to secrecy under Article 378 of the Penal Code, (2) to exempt prosecution witnesses from the obligation to disclose sources of information, or (3) by making it possible for the magistrate to excuse a witness from testifying if the witness requested such exemption on the basis either of ethical or of material reasons. These proposals never gained much support.

A more recent proposal was for the creation of an Order of Journalists, a professional group to be entrusted with the enforcement of a Code of Ethics comparable to that of the medical profession. This met opposition, however, from those who felt such a strict limitation upon the profession would be detrimental to its fundamental interests. Others have considered it better to face the present risks than to curtail a journalist's possible freedom of action by tying him to a code. Still others have favoured a liberal solution comparable to that provided under the laws of Austria.

A great many persons in France today, at any rate, do appear to believe that recent legislative trends and the general political situation combine to make possible and desirable a set of clear rules to govern professional secrecy. At the same time, they emphasize that such rules should not offer the authorities an opportunity to encroach on the preserves of the press, as this would mean paying a prohibitive fee in exchange for a formal recognition of the extension of professional secrecy to the journalist.

German Federal Republic

In the German Federal Republic (West Germany), journalists of the press and radio alike have had a limited right, since 1953, to professional secrecy with reference to their sources of information.

The right to refuse to give evidence is complete in the civil courts, under provisions of Articles 383 and 384 ZPO (Zivilprozessordnung) and also in the administrative courts, under Article 98 of the Administrative Courts Procedure (Verwaltungsgerichtsordnung).

Where a limitation chiefly exists is in the criminal courts and in proceedings undertaken by parliamentary investigating committees and by disciplinary courts, where the provisions of Article 53 of Criminal Law Procedure (Strafprozessordnung or StPO) apply.

A struggle for the right of journalists of press and radio to refuse to give evidence is in progress, accordingly, as that right is affected by the provisions of Criminal Law Procedure. Under that law, the right of anonymity *in personal matters* is recognized for a section of the journalistic group, it is true, but not with reference to the actual right to refuse to give evidence as requested, including revelation of sources of information.

Members of the classical professions—doctors, lawyers, and clergymen—under the provisions of Article 53, Paragraph 1, enjoy the right of professional secrecy bearing upon personal identification and subject matter alike. Members of the Federal Parliament and members of provincial parliaments as well enjoy equal status with those members of the classical professions in this respect. Journalists, however, do not share in this right.

At the same time, the journalist has seen some improvement in his status. First recognition of a limited right of professional secrecy under Criminal Law Procedure came in 1926, and a further improvement occurred through an amendment to the law in 1953, under which broadcasters also gained recognition.

Under the provisions of Article 53 of the Law of Criminal Procedure, Paragraphs 5 and 6, *the right to refuse to give evidence was extended to*

> 5. Editors, publishers, printers and others who have been engaged in the production or publication of a printed periodical, as regards the identity of the author, contributor or informant of information with punishable content, if the editor of the periodical has been punished because of publishing that, or if there is nothing in the way of his being so punished.
> 6. Superintendents, directors of transmission and others who have been engaged in the preparation or carrying out of radio transmissions, as regards revealing the identity of the author, contributor or informant of a transmission is punished or if there is no hindrance to his being so punished. Evidence may not be withheld as regards the identity of the author, contributor or informant who speaks personally over the radio.

An embarrassing quid pro quo

An essential limitation on the right to refuse to give evidence, it is to be observed, appears in the "if" clauses concluding both paragraphs, and indicating that, while the editors and others mentioned may withhold the names of informants, they themselves then become subject to punishment, personally, where the content of an article or broadcast is deemed to be of a "punishable" character.

There is less limitation on the right of professional secrecy in civil courts, as noted, than in criminal courts. Article 383, ZPO, in Paragraph 5 assures secrecy in civil law proceedings to

> persons to whom, by virtue of their office, status, or trade are confided facts which by their nature or through legal provision should be kept secret, as regard the facts on which the obligation to reticence is based.

The law further specifies that even if evidence is not refused, such persons

> are not to be questioned about facts for the elucidation of which evidence cannot be given without infringing the obligation to reticence.

Further, Article 384, ZPO, bearing upon the refusal of evidence for a "particular reason," holds that evidence can be refused:

1. On questions the answering of which by the witness or another to whom he stands in a relationship defined in Article 383... could cause pecuniary loss.
2. On questions the answering of which would bring discredit or the danger of legal proceedings upon the witness or upon someone standing in a relationship to him defined in Article 383...
3. On questions which the witness could not answer without disclosing a trade or artistic secret.

Once again, Article 385, Paragraph 2, ZPO, having to do with the release of a witness from a duty to maintain silence asserts that :

> Persons specified in Article 383... may not refuse to give evidence even if they are released from the obligation to maintain silence.

The provisions of these Articles relate particularly to Civil Court proceedings. For proceedings before administrative courts, however, Article 98 of the Federal Administrative Law Procedure states that :

> In so far as this law does not contain provisions to the contrary, Articles 358 to 444 and 450 to 494 of the Civil Law Procedure are appropriately applicable for legal argument.

For proceedings in the Disciplinary Courts, moreover, Article 20 of the Federal Disciplinary Courts Procedure (Bundesdisziplinarordnung) applies. It states that :

> For amplification of this law the provisions of *the legislation determining the constitution of the law courts* and the criminal law procedure are applicable in so far as the special form of disciplinary proceedings do not require the contrary.

By reason of these various provisions, journalists have substantially more freedom in the civil law courts and in administrative tribunals to refuse to give evidence with reference to information confided to them "by virtue of their office, status, or trade". Radio journalists as well as journalists of the printed publications are included in this category of "keepers of secrets," giving them the right to keep silent when to do otherwise might lead to direct pecuniary loss, damage to reputation, or danger of legal proceedings.

The provisions of Civil Law Procedure give journalists a reasonable legal basis for claiming the right to maintain silence as to sources of information when and if called as witnesses in cases wherein those provisions apply. Recognizing the limits and the possible penalties already noted in Paragraphs 5 and 6 of Article 53 of the Law of Criminal Procedure, journalists engaged in periodical and radio enterprises also possess a qualified right to keep silent as to sources of information.

A second-rate status

To this extent, and within these limitations, the concept of professional secrecy has been brought up to date in the German Federal Republic. At the same time, the limitations of Criminal Law Procedure continue to handicap journalists, in the matter of professional secrecy. They occupy what might appear to be a subsidiary status by contrast to those members of the classical professions and those parliamentarians whose rights are more clearly defined by law, and are more comprehensive. This privileged group also includes taxation advisers, notaries, accountants, dentists, midwives and chemists.

The position of the journalist in the German Federal Republic, even allowing for the somewhat more specific recognition of the radio journalist, nevertheless differs in no great degree from the position of the journalist in most other states. The limitations are a survival of the centuries-old contest between the desire for free expression and the concern of the State to track down those who might undermine its authority. While this contest has now been largely modified, if not wholly resolved, in favour of the right of free expression by journalists, among other members of the community, it leaves journalists in the German Federal Republic, as elsewhere, still dissatisfied with what they regard— in the context here under examination—as an unjustified denial of a full "right" to professional secrecy. More than that, they tend to resent existing limitations of that "right" whereby a journalist or publication performing a service in revealing abuses adversely affecting the public welfare, for example, may be placed in a position where he (or it) must sacrifice informants who have made such a service possible, or—as an alternative—penalize themselves, under the law.

In at least one part of the German Federal Republic this conflict has been removed. The Bavarian Press Law of 1949 places journalists on much the same footing as members of the provincial (Land) parliament, and thus gives them the same exemptions accorded members of the parliamentary body. Article 12 of that Bavarian Press Law of 1949 (GVBL. 1949 S. 243) states :

> Responsible editors, publishers and printers can refuse to give evidence concerning the identity of the author, contributor or informant of a publication in the editorial section of a printed work.

Since this law was passed in 1949 there have been no difficulties in Bavaria in assuring to the Press a full right to withhold evidence as to sources of information. The Federal Constitutional Court has more recently confirmed the validity of the Bavarian Press Law, so much more favourable to the concept of professional secrecy than the Federal Law of Criminal Procedure, for example. The advantages of the Bavarian law have not been extended to other parts of the country, however, and the national record of press difficulties with the law has presented a contrast to the relative tranquillity in Bavaria.

The procedure in criminal cases, when the authorities believe an official secret may have been divulged through publication, is to start proceedings against "an unknown person". A press or radio journalist summoned as a witness is himself liable to penalty if he refuses to divulge the identity of the author or of the informant who has provided the information brought into question. Unless he can demonstrate a clear legal right to refuse to speak, which is difficult to do in a criminal case, he becomes liable under Article 70 of the Criminal Law Procedure to a fine ranging from 1 DM to 1,000 DM as well as to punishment by detention—that is, imprisonment—ranging from one day to six weeks. In addition, a so-called corrective detention of up to six months may be imposed upon a recalcitrant journalist-witness, with the object of putting pressure upon him to speak.

German Criminal Law Procedure recognizes a right of professional secrecy only when "a publication of punishable content" has occurred, as specified in Paragraphs 5 and 6 of Article 53 of the Law of Criminal Procedure, as noted above (page 78). Even then, the right of the journalist-witness to refuse to give evidence is valid only in regard to so-called offences arising out of publication or broadcast wherein the liability to punishment is based on the *content* of the information published or broadcast.

Further, the ultimate decision as to the right of the journalist-witness to withhold evidence rests with the court. So a magistrate's court, a provincial court, or a court of appeal must determine whether the journalist, in a particular case, is entitled to refuse to give evidence. If that right is denied, the journalist has a right of appeal to the court of next highest jurisdiction.

Cases relating to professional secrecy, affecting journalists, have occurred through the years in Germany, with at least four major cases since 1950. One of the most important earlier cases arose in 1875, when the publisher of the *Frankfurter Zeitung* and four members of that newspaper's editorial staff were imprisoned for seven and a half months for refusing to give evidence as to the source of information published.

Trends in post-war cases

In 1950 a case involving a free-lance journalist, Karl-Heinz Kallenbach, was heard in the magistrate's court at Hanover (42 AR 734-50).* Kallenbach, in an information bulletin from Hamburg, had reported a traffic accident in which one person was killed. His report inferred that foul play had possibly occurred. The authorities assumed that Kallenbach obtained his information through an infringement of official secrecy. They started legal proceedings against "an unknown person" and ordered Kallenbach to appear as a witness and reveal the source of his information. This he refused to do. The court held that he had no legal right to refuse to give evidence, and imposed a fine of 30 DM. Kallenbach's appeal against this decision was unsuccessful.

In 1955 a reporter for the *Deutsche Presse Agentur,* Horst Westphal, reported in detail on the arrest of agents of a Czech espionage network in West Berlin. The authorities assumed that he had obtained his information through a breach of official secrecy, and he was sum-

* See "Der Zeugniszwang gegen die Presse" by Dr. Hans Badewitz, published by Pohl & Co., Munich, which gives a detailed round-up of this case. The author shows the whole development in Germany of the press's right to refuse to give evidence and makes proposals for a new version of all relevant regulations in the Criminal Law Procedure, the Civil Code and the Disciplinary Courts Procedure.

moned as a witness in the magistrate's court in Berlin. There he refused to give evidence as to the source of his information, and was fined 1,000 DM with the alternative of six weeks in jail. On appeal, however, the provincial court of Berlin overruled the decision of the magistrate's court, with the judges giving the opinion that Westphal was, in fact, entitled to refuse to give evidence. He had been found guilty in the lower court only because, by a narrow legalistic interpretation of the law, he was not granted the same privilege that would have been his as a member of a newspaper staff rather than a news agency staff.*

A second case arising in 1955 concerned Helmut Peitsch, editor-in-chief of the *Norddeutscher Nachrichten,* of Hamburg. On May 5, 1955, that newspaper had published an unsigned article headlined "Is Hamburg's Forged Money Case Cleared Up ?" The Public Prosecutor instituted proceedings against "an unknown person" for infringement of official duty in revealing certain published information, and Herr Peitsch, as the newspaper's editor-in-chief was called as a witness. When he refused to reveal the author of the article or the source of the information on police investigations against counterfeiters, Peitsch was sentenced by the magistrate's court of Hamburg to pay a fine of 100 DM and also to serve two weeks in "corrective detention". On appeal, the criminal law court of the Hamburg provincial court (Landgericht Hamburg) reduced the fine to 50 DM and cancelled the jail sentence (38 Qs 127/55). The case aroused such comment as to lead to a question being raised in the Federal Parliament, with the Minister of Justice, Dr. Fritz Neumayer, responding on December 7, 1955. He explained that, under 1953 changes in the penal code, newsmen were completely protected if they refused to reveal sources of information in themselves punishable, or that might lead to action against the paper or a staff member. **

An even greater degree of public interest was aroused in 1957 in a case involving Wolfgang Stiller, a free-lance journalist. In a series of articles, Stiller had reproached the head of the municipal housing office of Winsen a.d. Lühe with failure to carry out his duties. Administrative criminal law proceedings were started against that official. In the course of the proceedings, a colleague stated under oath that he had provided no material to Stiller. An action alleging perjury followed against this colleague, and Stiller was called as a witness. Because he refused to give

* "Privilege Limitations Worry Germans". *IPI Report* 2 : 1 (May 1953).
** "Disclosure of Sources". *IPI Report* 4 : 9 (January 1956).

evidence as to the source or sources of his information, Stiller was sentenced by the court at Luneburg to pay a fine of 500 DM and also to "corrective detention" of up to six months, whereupon he was immediately taken into custody. After a period of detention, the Appeal Court at Celle decided on November 7, 1957, to cancel the sentence of the court at Luneburg entirely (2 Ws 366/57), and Stiller was released. The higher court based its action on Stiller's right not to give evidence which might incriminate himself, but took care to state that it was to constitute no precedent to protect newsmen from the obligation to give evidence. *

Representatives of the press and radio in the German Federal Republic have been active in an effort to safeguard freedom of expression in the information media, and in advocating modification or elimination of those limitations on professional secrecy established in Criminal Law Procedure. While there is no code of ethics binding upon journalists of the country, there is general acceptance of the view that it is preferable to accept punishment under the law, rather than to sacrifice an informant by revealing his identity.

The German Press Council, established in 1956, with membership including publishers of newspapers and periodicals, and journalists associated with those media, adopted a resolution at a meeting on December 2, 1957, when the Stiller case was freshly in mind. The resolution stated that :

> The German Press Council stands behind all those active in the Press who refuse to give evidence in the courts in order to preserve editorial secrecy, which is a fundamental component of the life of the journalistic profession, in order to ensure confidence in carrying out its duties.
> In order to give effect to that view the German Press Council has decided to urge upon the Federal Parliament and the Federal Ministry of Justice a speedy reform of the law governing refusal to give evidence.
> The Council considers as unprofitable postponement of such an amendment of the criminal law procedure until the time when the so-called great criminal law reform occurs, and for the following reasons:
> 1. Practical experience, particularly in the instance of Wolfgang Stiller.

---

* "Court Compromises on Withholding Sources". *IPI Report* 6 : 8 (December 1957).

2. The situation arising out of the growing split in Press legislation after the Federal Constitutional Court had recently confirmed the validity of the Bavarian Press Law, and also the varied treatment of the right of refusal to give evidence in the other provinces, more favourable than that in the (Federal) Criminal Law. The situation whereby there is a marked divergence between the laws in the individual provinces and the criminal law procedure of the Federal Republic cannot be justified from considerations of uniformity and certainty of the law. The German Press Council has established a commission for the formulation of the necessary legislative amendments.

The Stiller case also provided a subject for extended discussion by a Study Circle for Press Law and Press Freedom, meeting at Hamburg on July 30-31, 1958. Here the problem of assuring professional secrecy for press and radio was considered exhaustively, and the existing state of criminal law procedure as related to that concept was judged to be unsatisfactory. A proposal by Dr. Arthur Schüle, Professor of State Law at the University of Tübingen, found unanimous support. His proposal was that both Press and Broadcasting media should have a full right to refuse to give evidence in the Criminal Law Courts and in parliamentary investigating committees.

The government's attitude

It must be said that however journalists may desire to see professional secrecy recognized as a full right, the German Federal Government so far has given no evidence of sympathy for that view. A request that such a right to withhold evidence as to sources be recognized for press and radio was rejected by Dr. Fritz Schäffer, Federal Minister of Justice, in an address to the German Journalists' Association at Bad Godesberg on March 22, 1958. If such a full right of refusal to give evidence were to be accorded to the press and broadcasting media, Dr. Schäffer said, slanderers and disloyal officials could hide behind those media, to the injury of the government's reputation and authority.

Journalists, nevertheless, do not accept this negative governmental view as valid. In refutation, they put forward several arguments.

First, journalists contend, they are not even now prevented under criminal law procedure from withholding evidence in cases involving defamation and slander because the legislative presupposition relative to "information of punishable content" embraced by Paragraphs 5 and 6 of Article 53 of the Law of Criminal Procedure (page 78 above) already gives them a certain exemption. The governmental contention that "slanderers" might hide behind a more liberal interpretation of the law, therefore, is called irrelevant, since they presumably do not hide behind the present law. Journalists contend that it is difficult to see how protection of the reputation of the government against "slanderers" would be weakened if the press and broadcasting media were to be granted an unlimited right of refusal to give evidence, so long as the media report in accordance with the true facts.

Second, governmental expressions of apprehension lest an extension of the right of professional secrecy result in injury to the government's reputation are regarded as ignoring the special system whereby the editor, in particular, is responsible for the contents of his publication, and broadcast executives for the content of their programmes. Under the old German Press Law of 1874 (Articles 20,21 R. P. G. — "Reichspressegesetz") there is a well-defined assignment of authority and legal responsibility to the editor, the publisher, the printer, the distributor, and to the author or writer or contributor, not to mention the broadcaster. Because the journalist must accept responsibility for every word published or broadcast, it is argued, this should be sufficient assurance to the government, particularly with penalties and actions in atonement for offences specified. This should justify — and, indeed, should require — the inviolability of sources of information for press and broadcast media, confidential or otherwise, so journalists insist.

Third, the government view that official secrecy is being violated, or may be violated, is not plausible, in the opinion of journalists, as a basis for denial of the right of professional secrecy in its fullest sense. Under the existing law, however, if a public official gives the press information truthful or otherwise, and if publication of that information later is regarded by other officials as of such a nature as to bring a demand for the journalist to reveal his source of information, the journalist has no protection. He cannot even cite Paragraphs 5 and 6 of Article 53, because that which might be a breach of professional secrecy on the part of the official is not information of "punishable content", as covered by the above paragraphs. So the Press is at direct odds with the State, which is taking disciplinary action to identify an official who has revealed information that should, in the view of other officials of government, have been kept secret. The journalist then either must sacrifice an official who has reported to him truthfully on some abuse that should be made known, in the public interest, or he must himself take the punishment for remaining silent. But another official may compromise the press by giving it inaccurate information and suffer no penalty because he, too, if the issue leads to court action, will benefit by the refusal of the journalist to reveal a source even at the cost of accepting punishment himself.

Fourth, journalists both of Press and Broadcasting argue that the legal compulsion to give evidence in the criminal law courts and disciplinary courts is accomplishing nothing since it is accepted as the honourable duty of every journalist to suffer the consequences of a refusal to give information, even including prison sentences, rather than to sacrifice an informant by revealing his identity.

India

In India, the Constitution guarantees citizens "the right to freedom of speech and expression," whether through the press or otherwise.

The Courts have the right, in the course of legal proceedings, to demand answers to questions which may, in the opinion of a Court, be relevant and necessary in determining issues under litigation. The Court may decide on its own authority whether a witness should be required to answer any question put to him. No exception is made for a journalist, under the law. If he is asked to disclose a source of information he cannot claim special privilege or protection, although any person aggrieved by a decision of the Court does have the right to refer the matter to a higher Court for review.

A right to withhold information is recognized by law only in a few circumstances specified in the Indian Evidence Act of 1872. So, judges and magistrates may not be questioned about their own conduct in Court or with regard to matters dealt with in their official capacity. (Section 121). Husbands and wives cannot be compelled to give evidence against one another. (Section 122). No person may be compelled to give evidence derived from unpublished official records relating to "any affairs of state". (Section 123). A public official cannot be compelled to disclose communications made to him in official confidence. (Section 124). A lawyer cannot be compelled to give evidence regarding any communication made to him in his legal capacity (Section 126), nor can an individual be compelled to disclose any communication made by him to his legal professional adviser. (Section 129).

Despite the absence of any legal protection for a journalist who might be asked by a Court to reveal a source of information, the Courts normally have not insisted upon the disclosure of sources, and neither newspapers nor journalists are commonly aware of instances in which pressures have been brought upon them to make such disclosures. In this respect, journalism in India proceeds under the general pattern of British journalism, with a tacit, if not legal, recognition of an effective right of professional secrecy, and without any formal code of ethics for journalists. In the circumstances, there has been no special study of the problem of professional secrecy, and no significant expression either by journalists or jurists on the subject.

So far as can be determined, only two major cases bearing upon the issue have arisen in the history of journalism in India, the first in 1907, and the second in 1941.

In 1907 certain articles and letters condemning the Government of India were published in issues of the *Bandematram,* of Calcutta, then edited by Mr. Bipin Chandra Pal. Mr. Pal, summoned for questioning by the Court as to the name of the person who had written the articles and letters, declined to reveal the name and was sentenced to six months of rigorous imprisonment. (*History of the Congress of Sitaramayya,* Vol. 1, p. 110.)

Case of the "Hindustan Times"

The second case arose in August 1941, when the *Hindustan Times,* of New Delhi, carried a report that judicial officers were, in effect, being required by the Chief Justice to collect war funds. This was followed by a comment several days later contending that this requirement would have an adverse effect on the mind of litigants and tended to lower the prestige of the judiciary.

The Chief Justice responded by issuing a notice to the printer, the publisher, and to the editor of the paper ordering them to show cause why they should not be punished for contempt. Mr. Devdas Gandhi, son of Mahatma Gandhi, and editor of the paper, was questioned as to the source of his information. He declined to disclose the name of the person who had given him the information on which the original report was based, and took full responsibility on himself. He was fined Rs. 1000, with the alternative of serving one month in prison. Mr. Gandhi declined to pay the fine, and served the sentence of imprisonment.

On appeal, the decision of the Allahabad High Court was reversed by the Privy Council. By that time, however, Mr. Gandhi had served the full term of his imprisonment. (*All India Reporter 1943 — Privy Council.* p. 202).

Even though the issue of professional secrecy has not been actively debated in India, the Press Commission of India, set up by the Government of India to review the entire position of the press of the country, made a report in 1954 in which that issue, by inference, was raised. It recommended, among other things, that an All India Press Council should be established, and that one of the Council's responsibilities would be to "help the Press to maintain its independence and safeguard the freedom of the Press," with proper ethical standards also to be given formal expression. However, the All India Press Council has not been established to date (May 1961).

The question of professional secrecy with reference to radio news treatment has never arisen in India. The radio is completely owned and controlled by the Government and there is no commercial broadcasting.

Italy

In Italy, the journalist has no legal right to refuse to testify, on grounds of professional secrecy, with reference to a source or sources of information in response to a demand by a court.

The legislation controlling the position of the journalist hinges upon two sections in the Code of Penal Procedure, and indirectly upon an Article in the Constitution of the Republic.

As in many other countries, Italian law excuses certain individuals from the obligation "to testify regarding any matter confided to them or which has come to their knowledge by virtue of their priesthood, office or profession." (Code of Penal Procedure, Title II, Chapter VII, Section 351). This exclusion extends to "Catholic priests or ministers of a religion acknowledged by the State; lawyers, technical consultants and notaries; doctors and surgeons, pharmacists, midwives and other persons engaged in a medical or related profession".

Journalists are not included among persons thus excused from the obligation to give testimony. There are, in fact, circumstances under which even the members of the other groups may be required to answer. Section 351 specifies that this may occur when "competent authority" "has reason to doubt the sufficiency of the grounds on which such persons claim exemption" or "deems it necessary for the preliminary investigation that they be examined," or feels it proper to "verify their claim so far as necessary" to determine justification for their exemption, or when "the grounds for exemption prove insufficient".

The second section of the Code of Penal Procedure relevant to the issue is titled "Disclosure of professional secrets" (Code of Penal Procedure, Title XII, Chapter III, Division V, Section 622). It specifies that:

> Whosoever, having knowledge of a secret by reason of his situation, office, profession or trade, reveals it without due cause, or uses it for his own profit or that of another, shall be liable, if harm may thereby be caused, to imprisonment up to one year or a fine of from 2,400 Lire to 40,000 Lire. The penalty is applicable upon legal action being taken by the aggrieved party.

This Section of the Penal Code does not specify any particular "office, profession or trade" to whose members it might apply, with a positive penalty for revelation of a secret which could presumably be a *source* of information. Read literally, this Section might appear to provide a justification for a journalist protecting a source of information. Legalistically, however, the Section has been regarded as being completed and therefore limited in its application by the more specific Section 351 of the Code of Penal Procedure, already cited, and extending exemption only to those groups noted.

Press sets views on Code

Journalists themselves have taken a position favourable to professional secrecy. In this, they have found some friendly, if theoretical, advocates within the legal profession but they have also encountered opposition.

A Code of Journalistic Ethics, published in the *Bulletin* of the Italian National Press Federation (F.I.N.S.I.) of June 8, 1957 in the form of a communiqué on "the self-discipline of the press and principles of professional ethics" includes a paragraph, noted as Point 9 :

> Journalists and publishers are duty bound to observe secrecy regarding news sources, particularly those of news obtained in confidence.

The F.I.N.S.I. itself has never debated the matter of professional secrecy in its Council or at any general meeting. No formal statement has been advanced requesting a modification of the existing law in favour of journalists as a group. Individual journalists, including members of the Federation, have done so, however.

In a report to the Seventh National Congress of the Italian Press, held at Milan and Gardone in 1958, and appearing in the F.I.N.S.I. *Bulletin* of November 1958, the Managing Director of the Federation noted that:

> Another problem closely linked with the activities and responsibilities of journalists is that of *professional secrecy...*
> The Italian National Press Federation has done its best to contribute to the publicizing of this problem and its discussion ; it

is one which merits the attention of our colleagues, particularly those versed in legal and philosophical studies, and they should endeavour to keep the debate alive in our ranks, in the press and throughout the country . .

It probably will be necessary, eventually, for the Italian National Press Council, or a National Congress, to adopt an official policy after due deliberation. As part of these hoped-for official directives for journalists as a class in our country, we must claim—as we do now—a right, a privilege which is at the same time a title of nobility: the one embodied in Point 9 of the Code of Journalistic Ethics.

In his address to the National Congress of that year, the Managing Director also drew attention to an article reviewing the position of the journalist's claim to a right of professional secrecy as prepared by Dr. Domenico De Gregorio, a member of the staff of the President of the Italian Cabinet. Published in the *Bulletin* of the F.I.N.S.I., also of November 1958, and later republished in *Methodology of Journalism* (Rome), Dr. Gregorio's article, titled "Professional Secrecy for Journalists," read, in part, as follows:

> To our mind, the journalist's right of professional secrecy is no different, in its legal nature, from the right granted to other categories: doctors, pharmacists, lawyers, priests. Nor can any special restriction be imposed on him as to the extent of that secrecy—rather the contrary, since other professional men and priests *may not speak* of facts which have come to their knowledge, whereas the journalist is *entitled to publish* what he knows, but cannot be compelled to reveal *how* he came to know it.
>
> Fernand Terrou comments, in this connection, that a difference exists between the two categories as regards the subject of the right but not as regards its nature. While their positions may seem to complement each other, in the eyes of the law they rank equally because of the element common to both: refusal to testify. The sanctions applied to a doctor or lawyer who, for any reason, voluntarily betrays a professional secret may be of different kinds, but they are usually extra-judicial or a result of private action.
>
> Having thus stated the principle of similarity of treatment for journalists and other categories with respect to professional secrecy, let us see how its internal logic can justify recognition of the desired right on the part of the law. As we have repeatedly affirmed, the press, apart from its informative mission, has a supervisory function with regard to the acts of the public powers.

It fulfills this function in a manner which may seen totally innocuous but which, in the end, is undoubtedly the most effective: It
arouses public opinion whenever the political or administrative
machinery of the country goes wrong.

Now, in order to accomplish this vital task, the press must
have its own sources of information and it is entitled to see that
these are protected. So the protection of such sources is in the
public interest. But that is not all. A citizen who has suffered
injury from an administrative body or, worse, a political authority,
or one who wishes to draw attention to some situation harmful to
the public interest, often has no chance of obtaining redress
through the usual legal or administrative channels. But he can
hope for assistance from the press. He must not, however, be
exposed to reprisals from those almost always powerful persons
who feel themselves to be the target of his accusations. The law
must safeguard him from possible persecution. Besides, it is the
facts which matter, not the person who reports them. If they prove
to be true, does it matter how they came to light?

It is in this sense that the protection of a journalist's right
to observe professional secrecy seems to us a necessary extension
of the constitutional right of freedom of the press.

Where Dr. Gregorio was arguing for the right of the journalist to
equal treatment with those other professional groups granted exemption
under the provisions of Section 351 of the Penal Code relating to doctors,
lawyers and priests, a comparable advocacy of the journalists' right to
protection under the more general, less specific provisions of Section 622
was advanced by Vincenzo Manzini, writing in *Italian Penal Law* (Vol. 8,
p. 914), as published in Turin in 1951. He taxes with superficiality and
sophism those who oppose such an interpretation of the law.

Manzini reasons that Section 622 does not require that the secret
necessarily have been "confided" to the witness—be he journalist or
other—but that it shall have come to his knowledge "by reason of his . . .
profession or trade". He presents two possible cases: That of a journalist
gaining entrance to a dwelling that has suffered damage and learning some
secret there, by chance; and that of a journalist who has gained knowledge
of some secret concerning the financial backers or owners of his own newspaper. In neither cases, Manzini argues, can the journalist be entitled to
divulge such facts and, if he did so, he would be guilty of an actual offence
within the provisions of Section 622, and might become subject to fine
or imprisonment if forced to reveal such information.

Jurists reject claims

Jurists in Italy, nevertheless, do not commonly share with these other spokesmen, whether of their own legal profession or not, the view that the journalist has a right to protect his sources of information in the face of a court demand for information.

A court decision delivered in Rome in 1904 still represents the attitude of the magistracy toward the issue of professional secrecy for journalists. The court then ruled that a reluctant journalist-witness was not entitled to

> entrench himself behind his professional secret, much less behind a mere verbal undertaking, but is bound, like all witnesses, to answer all questions put to him and inform the Court of any facts or circumstances which may serve to determine the truth, in the interests of and for the high purposes of justice.
>
> Professional secrecy . . . presupposes an intrinsic connection between the profession and the situation of the witness and the fact revealed to him, in the sense that it is disclosed to him precisely because of his said profession or condition involving both the need for disclosure and the duty of secrecy.
>
> There is no such connection in the present case, since the information which the witness is required to give was not communicated to him as a secret, nor could it be otherwise, since his profession—that of journalist—is not one which binds to secrecy the person exercising it, but rather the reverse.
>
> For all these reasons, the Court rejects the petition of the defence and orders the witness to reply to the question put to him.

This ruling of the Court was challenged at the time by Napodano in an essay on "Professional Secrecy for Journalists," Gabriele in the *Rivista Penale di Dottrina, Legislazione e Giurisprudenza* (Vol. 59, 1904. pp. 241 ff). Frequently quoted in later years by those favouring recognition of the right to professional secrecy for journalists, it was contested by jurists, and notably by Renato Lefevre, writing 54 years later, discussing "The Question of 'Professional Secrecy' for Journalists" in *Saggi e studi di Pubblicistica* (IXth and Xth Series, Rome, 1958). Lefevre wrote:

> The whole of Napodano's reasoning is based on the premise that journalists are bound to observe professional secrecy and, for that reason alone, cannot be obliged to betray secrets of which

they have knowledge. Even after a lapse of so many years, however, his argumentation is interesting not only because it enables
the problem to be formulated, but for the comparative interpretations of law cited. These showed, for example, that French
doctrine and practice already were definitely opposed to permitting journalists to invoke any claim to professional secrecy.

There were two reasons for this denial of the validity of professional secrecy in France: The nature of journalism as a profession and the nature of the facts likely to come to the knowledge of journalists. Napodano, however, considered only the
ordinary purpose of a newspaper as a chronicle of events, without considering its political function as an organ of public opinion,
possessing the right to censure acts of the public authorities. He
argued that any person coming into possession of a secret by
virtue of his profession was bound... not to reveal it and that...
a judge could not oblige him to testify. The problem, as he stated
it, was reduced only to whether a journalist could, by virtue of
his profession, come into possession of a secret the disclosure of
which could cause harm. Since this was undoubtedly possible,
Napodano considered that it followed inexorably—in view of the
theoretical duty of public censure devolving upon the press as an
expression of the supreme will of the people—that a journalist
called upon to testify could not be compelled to do so.

This proposition of Napodano's, however, is by no means
substantiated, even taking into account the changes that have
occurred in the legal system since his time.

Strongly opposed as he is to recognition of any legal right of a journalist to claim professional secrecy as justifying his refusal to reveal a
source of information to a court, Lefevre in the same article also under-
took to refute the contemporary view of Dr. Gregorio contending that a
journalist was properly entitled to the same exemption as granted to other
groups through Section 351 of the Penal Code, and challenged equally the
view of Vincenzo Manzini with reference to journalists' inclusion within
the provisions of Section 622.

As to these points, he wrote:

> Apart from the cases provided for in Section 351... the
> judge alone has full authority to determine whether any given
> profession or trade may and should be considered as coming
> within the scope of Section 622.
> A necessary, objective condition is that the professional
> man should have given personal service or attendance to the
> person requesting or in need of his services. It is obvious that

those in professions which by law or custom or by their very nature give rise to the receipt of confidential information or knowledge of the secrets of others are bound to secrecy, except of course when such professions are themselves prohibited or contrary to public order or morals.

It is also obvious that such services must be provided by persons who habitually provide them for gainful purposes, or are entitled to do so.

This definition must necessarily include, besides the professions and trades listed under Section 351, bankers, nurses, teachers, domestic servants, postmen, porters, craftsmen in general and employees of private undertakings (as opposed to public employees).

In all these professions and trades, the persons exercising them may of necessity come to know certain things which the "client" would refuse to "confide" to them if he could not rely on their absolute discretion, precisely because the category to which such persons belong is bound to discretion, and the relationship between them and the client is entered into exclusively on that understanding...

There can be no doubt... that journalists as such are not entitled to this right—a sound and logical conclusion from any point of view if we take into account the fact that any such entitlement implied specific acknowledgment of the duty of secrecy, from which duty it derives and of which it constitutes a recognition.

It is true, of course, that not all professions involving an obligation of secrecy give rise to the right to abstain from testifying, but only those in which the obligation is the most stringent and admits of no exceptions.

But it is also true that all professions and trades for which that right is automatically recognized, without exception, must consider themselves bound by the corresponding duty.

We may therefore conclude not only that journalists as a class may not take advantage of the *right* attaching to professional secrecy (in the strictly legal sense, i.e. the right not to give evidence), but that if they were allowed to do so they would automatically become liable to the corresponding *duty*. And we have already seen how this would place them in an impossible position, since it would seriously curtail if not destroy their freedom of action in their proper sphere of reporting and information. No such right exists then, since there is no corollary duty.

Even supposing Section 622 of the Penal Code enjoins it a duty upon journalists, it would have to give way before the supreme requirements of justice, which more than suffice to provide 'due cause', as referred to in the very same Section, and without which professional men not expressly named in Section 351 may still be denied any claim to a right of professional secrecy.

The Constitution and the press

While the Italian Constitution, brought into effect January 1, 1948, provides for "freedom of the press", it does not extend that concept to include any right of professional secrecy for journalists.

To prepare a draft of the purposed new Constitution, a Committee was specially appointed in 1947 by the Legislative Assembly. In that draft, as finally presented, a paragraph was included under Section 16 concerning (a) the verification of the sources of news items and (b) the financial backing of newspapers. In the general discussions within the Legislative Assembly prior to adoption of the Constitution, in its final form, this Section was debated, along with others.

The proposed Section 16 was challenged by one member of the Assembly as a potential justification for "such supervision as would eventually paralyse the life of newspapers and permit unjustifiable interference in their affairs". He argued that:

> Editorial responsibility for each newspaper is clearly indicated in the newspaper itself and covers individual items as well as the newspaper as a whole. Professional secrecy, in this case, is most strict and absolutely essential.

Noting the conflicting views within the Committee during the debate, the Committee Chairman suggested that action on the whole draft section be postponed until a general Press Law should come up for discussion. He pointed out that

> the investigation of news sources involves fairly serious implications; it might even lead to the suppression of reporting as such and reduce the newspapers to a sort of bulletin for official communications from the Government.

Disregarding this and other proposals for postponement, however, the President of the Constituent Assembly pressed for action. In the further discussion, and as a compromise, a member proposed that the provision relating to news sources, at least, be eliminated. He argued that

> it would strike at the very roots of the free press. At best, we would have a party press, and even this would be a serious limitation of the freedom of the press. In any case, the idea of verifying news sources will prove impractical... useless, superficial and harmful.

Another member, while agreeing to such an elimination, contended that a valid reason might arise for investigating newspaper financing, and he therefore proposed that the Assembly vote separately on the two parts of the proposed Section. This was done, with that part relating to news sources—and touching the issue of professional secrecy—being struck out of the draft, while that concerning newspaper financing was approved and was to be retained in the final Constitution as Article 21, paragraph 5, reading as follows:

> Measures of a general nature may be enacted to provide for the means of financing newspapers to be made known.

So far, no law has been promulgated to legalize any such investigation as would be required within the meaning of Paragraph 5.

The omission of any specific measure relative to "verification of the sources of news items"—meaning an inquiry into sources of information—was taken by Lefevre, writing in 1958, as confirmation

> that the demand for an extension to journalists of the right to professional secrecy not only clashes with Italian positive law but is contrary to a clear political and doctrinal line of conduct with regard to problems of the press and public information, since such an authoritative body as the National Assembly could go so far as to formulate a legal text aimed at exactly the opposite result.

Neither the legal interpretations of Renato Lefevre nor the omission from the Constitution of any reference to the issue of professional secrecy has been accepted by Italian journalists as necessarily meaning that, at some future date, the issue still may not gain official and legal recognition. This already has been indicated in citations from the spokesmen for the Italian National Press Federation (F.I.N.S.I.).

Even though the Federation has not actually embarked on a discussion of the central question, it did take a firm stand on two episodes in 1960. In the first, police entered and searched the editorial offices of the Italian Communist party paper, l'*Unità,* at Genoa, Milan, and Rome and confiscated documents, the one existing copy of an unpublished manuscript, and correspondence, including newly arrived mail, which was opened. In the second episode, the offices of *Il Tempo,* of Rome, were searched with a view to identifying the author of an article that had appeared in the paper.

The Federation took note that "these occurrences were made possible by the measures taken by the judiciary" within the framework of the laws and the Constitution "in order to ascertain whether a crime or offence has been committed, identify its perpetrators and obtain evidence". At the same time, it objected to the episodes at Genoa and Milan as including

> a breach of the inviolability of letters and an outrage to the freedom of the press, which is the bulwark of all democratic systems, solemnly proclaimed by the Constitution ; and to the professional secrecy of the press which, particularly as regards sources of information, is an essential part of such freedom.

Protests had been made to the Government concerning both episodes by individual newspapers and by the Regional Association. The Federation associated itself in these protests, recommended prudence on the part of the Public Prosecutor in measures adopted and executed, and due consideration for the greater or lesser gravity of any case. It expressed the hope that the judiciary, in the exercise of its powers and duties, would in the future refrain from acting

> in such a way as to encroach upon the rights of citizens, among which is the prime right of freedom of expression in speech, writing or any other form whatsoever, and not to cause newspapers to be censored or seized contrary to the laws and the Constitution.

The position of the Federation with reference to these episodes was fully set forth in the above terms in its *Bulletin* of December 1960.

The outlook

Despite the absence of any exemption for journalists in Italy, in the matter of professional secrecy, there have been few instances in the history of the press when the issue produced any serious impasse in the courts, and none whatever since the war. This is not to say that no problem exists. Some might contend that it has not seemed more urgent or more important precisely because journalists do lack any legal right to guard sources of information and, for that very reason, are not made the recipients of confidences on any great scale. This in itself is regarded by some journalists as constituting a serious check on the potential performance of the press in its function of reporting the acts of the administrative authorities, and censuring those acts when occasion warrants. Journalists view this as a proper function of all who write for newspapers, and one they should be free to carry out, particularly in those countries whose legislative and judicial procedures are not wholly in harmony with the principles of democracy. A reform of the procedural system, they reason, might even have the effect of reducing the need for professional secrecy for journalists.

It is accepted journalistic practice in Italy to indicate the source of information presented, at least in general terms. Articles often are signed either by name or initials, or are designated as "From Our Correspondent" or "From Our Mailbag," or bear the logotype of the news agency providing the report. Thus the responsibility for origin is clearly indicated. This, however, does not in itself necessarily exclude the appearance within any one of those reports of statements the precise source of which may be unreported, or withheld as a matter of professional secrecy. To this extent the potential problem survives, should a demand be made in a court for revelation of such a precise source.

Apart from the general reluctance of courts and jurists to modify their views, there exist in Italy other factors that tend to militate against such wish as the F.I.N.S.I. or individual journalists may have for full legal recognition of a right to professional secrecy. Most serious of these is the difficulty of defining the concept of "journalist".

It is true that there is a professional register of journalists in Italy, but that register itself includes five categories. Moreover, the obligation to register as a journalist is incumbent only upon publishers of daily newspapers of general circulation and their staff members. Publishers and staff members of political (or "party") newspapers are exempt from any obligation to register, and so also are those of technical and scientific publications, except, oddly, in the fields of cinematography and sports. Further, it is not uncommon for individuals of almost any profession to have occasion to publish an article, or articles, in the press, presenting information whose source the writer may wish to keep secret. Yet such a person is not a journalist, does not normally profess to be a journalist, and certainly does not appear in the professional register of journalists. Who, then, is to be considered a "journalist," or who may not *claim* to be a "journalist," if brought into court as a witness and called upon to testify as to the source of information published? This confused situation could enormously complicate the interpretation of where any legal right to withhold information might properly reside.

In the circumstances, then, the journalist in Italy has no present legal right to protect his sources of information in the face of a court demand. A practical, or expedient solution sometimes discussed would be to excuse a journalist from testifying as to his source of information *when the truth of that information is itself ascertained by a judge.* But this would cover only some situations and, even then, it remains no more than a speculative possibility falling short of full legal recognition of the journalist's right to professional secrecy, which does not appear likely at any early time.

Japan

In Japan, there is no law specifically exempting journalists from the obligation to reveal sources of information when or if called as witnesses before a court, a legislative body, or an administrative body. Nor is there any custom or written code of ethics in which the right of professional secrecy is recognized for journalists.

A journalist, however, shares a certain exemption with all citizens, as he does in other countries, in being privileged under the law to remain silent if an answer to a question might tend to incriminate him, or one close to him.* Yet such a situation rarely if ever has arisen affecting a journalist in any country.

Exemption from an obligation to respond to questions is granted, much as in other countries, to a person who is, *or was,* a doctor, dentist, nurse, midwife, attorney, notary public, or a religious functionary,** with respect to knowledge gained "in the exercise of his professional duties, and which he should keep secret". Nor may a person who is, *or was,* a public official, including membership in the Diet, be examined as a witness on matters regarded as official secrets, without approval by competent higher authority.*** As elsewhere, however, journalists are not included among these professionals and specialists as being entitled to exemption.

Article 35 of Japan's Penal Code states that an "act done in accordance with law or ordinance, or a justifiable act done in due course of business is not punishable". If a witness can establish with a court or other

---

* In Japan, Article 38 of the Constitution states that no person shall be compelled to testify against himself. Article 147 of the Code of Criminal Procedure extends this exemption to permit a witness to remain silent if his response might also incriminate a spouse or a blood relative "within the third degree of relationship," a relative "by affinity within the second degree of relationship," or a person "in any of such relationships with the witness", a guardian or "supervisor of guardianship or curator" of the witness, or a person of whom the witness is himself the guardian, supervisor of guardianship, or curator.

** Article 149, Code of Criminal Procedure; Article 281, Paragraph 2, Code of Civil Procedure.

*** Articles 144—145, Code of Criminal Procedure; Articles 272—273, Code of Civil Procedure.

examining body that information he possesses relates "to a technical or professional secret," and that he has "good reason" for withholding information, he may in the discretion of the court be excused from revealing it.* Here there remains some question in Japan as to whether journalists may be entitled to invoke these provisions of the law to justify a refusal to answer questions.

The court, or other investigating body seeking information, is solely and exclusively empowered in Japan to decide whether journalists or others appearing as witnesses are entitled to assert a right of professional secrecy. Any person who refuses to be sworn as a witness or to testify, without good and acceptable reason, is subject to penalty, specified in criminal court cases as a fine not exceeding Y 5,000 or detention in prison.**

Even for members of those professional groups normally exempt, as noted above, Article 149 of the Code of Criminal Procedure specifies that such exemption shall not apply "if the principal (client) has consented [to the granting of the information requested], or if the refusal of testimony is deemed as nothing but an abuse of the right intended merely for the interest of the accused when he is not the principal, or if there exist any special circumstances which shall be provided by the Rules of Court".

Officials, or former officials, called as witnesses, while subject to exemption *unless* competent higher authority consents to or approves their responding to questions, still may not be exempt in practice. Article 144, Code of Criminal Procedure, specifies that competent higher authority may not refuse such approval or consent "*except* in cases where compliance would be prejudicial to important interests of the state". Article 5 of the Law for the Oath, Testimony, Etc. of Witnesses at the Diet also holds that any withholding of consent by higher authority must be explained within ten days, and even then the explanation may be rejected as insufficient to justify exemption for the witness.

Only one court decision has been returned in Japan relative to the right of professional secrecy as it would apply to a journalist in his refusal to reveal a news source.

The case began on April 24, 1949, when the police headquarters at Matsumoto City, in the Nagano prefecture, asked the judge of the Sum-

* Article 281, Paragraph 3, Code of Civil Procedure; Article 149 and 160, Code of Criminal Procedure; Article 53, Paragraph 2, Law Relative to Prohibition on Private Monopoly and Methods of Preserving Fair Trade.
** Article 161, Code of Criminal Procedure. See also Article 5, Law for the Oath, Testimony, Etc., of Witnesses at the Diet.

mary Court of that city to issue a warrant of arrest against Mr. S., a tax official, on a charge of corruption. The warrant was issued on April 25 and Mr. S. was arrested that night.

The local edition of *Asahi* dated April 26 reported these events, although they had not been officially announced. The Matsumoto City correspondent for *Asahi*, Mr. Kiyoshi Ishii, was called upon by a judicial police official of the city to reveal his source of information. Article 100 of the National Public Service Law was cited, providing that "a person in the [public] service shall not divulge any secret which may come to his knowledge in the performance of his duties". *

Mr. Ishii declined to reveal his source. The judge of the Summary Court thereupon summoned him as a witness and directed him to take oath and to testify as to his source. Mr. Ishii declined to do so, contending that the concept of journalistic ethics justified him in keeping his source secret, and that his observance of that concept should be accepted as a "good reason" to refuse to answer within the meaning of Article 161 of the Code of Criminal Procedure. His attorney also argued that Mr. Ishii's action as a journalist was justifiable as having been done in the due course of business, as provided in Article 35 of the Penal Code, and was therefore not punishable.

The Summary Court ruled, however, that no Japanese law gives a journalist a right of professional secrecy, rejected the laws cited as having any proper applicability, and assessed a fine of Y 3,000 against Mr. Ishii, and the fine was paid.

High Court upholds verdict

The case was appealed to the Tokyo High Court, which sustained the ruling of the Summary Court. The High Court decision reasoned that, while the right of professional secrecy is necessary for newspapers and journalists in the performance of their functions, the obligation to give

* The relevant portion of Article 100 states in full, and freely translated, that the national public service personnel, including members of the Diet, are prohibited, whether in office or after retirement, from disclosing information coming to their knowledge specifically by reason of their official positions, and conveyed to them in confidence. A present or former member of the national service personnel, summoned as a witness by ordinance to testify on a matter involving official secrecy, may respond to questions only if he has permission to do so from his senior official.

testimony before properly constituted bodies also is highly important, and, on balance, must take precedence over the former. Carried to the Supreme Court, this same conclusion was sustained.

The petitioner, Mr. Ishii, had contended that under a democratic government the function of the newspaper is to provide the people with information necessary to them if they are to form intelligent opinions on matters of public concern. In this, a newspaper is not merely a private business but performs a public service, he reasoned, and journalists must be free to acquire information. If it is necessary to keep a source of such information secret on occasion, it was argued, this procedure is not primarily in the interest of the informant—necessary as it may be to protect such informants at times—but is in the interest of freedom of expression and of the public welfare. Refusal to reveal a news source, accordingly, should be regarded as based upon a "good reason," within the meaning of Article 161, Code of Criminal Procedure.

In rejecting this argument, the Supreme Court opinion was that Article 143 of the Code of Criminal Procedure imposed an obligation to testify by providing that "except as otherwise provided in this law, the court may examine any person whomsoever as a witness". That obligation implies that a witness may have to make sacrifices in the interest of justice. So he may sometimes be obliged to reveal matter he would prefer to keep secret, on the basis of his own moral sense, or the disclosure of which may earn him the hostility or enmity of others. Yet the purpose of the obligation to testify is to discover the truth and assure enforcement of the law, and it is essential for the proper administration of justice to compel all persons to testify.

As to exceptions to that obligation granted certain specified persons,* the Supreme Court noted that even such exemptions were conditional, being granted on a limited basis, and were not to be extended or applied by analogy to journalists. Article 21 of the Constitution, it was said, assures freedom of expression so far as that it does not interfere with the public

---

* Articles 144—149, Code of Criminal Procedure, enumerate the exceptions, as also mentioned above. Article 59 of the Offenders Prevention and Rehabilitation Law also makes provision for certain exemptions. This article states that officials or those who were officials of the welfare rehabilitation agencies, summoned as witnesses to testify according to the law, may refuse to disclose official secrets in terms of protecting and fostering the offender's rehabilitation if revelation of such secrets would transgress the privacy of the offender. Article 23, Lawyers Law, also provides a right of exemption to lawyers, or to those who were lawyers, giving them the right and the duty to preserve secrets that they could only have learned through the exercise of their profession, unless otherwise specified by law.

welfare, and it does not go so far, by interpretation, as to protect a news source at the risk of sacrificing the obligation to give testimony deemed essential to the fair administration of justice.

The reasoning of the Supreme Court, as here summarized, was not universally accepted as sound, and some members of the legal profession were among the dissenters. Thus Mr. Shigemitsu Dando, Professor of Criminal Law at Tokyo University, for one, said that the decision in the Ishii case was not to be regarded as definitely establishing the position of the journalist in Japan, in the matter of professional secrecy. It was a special case, he said, in which the ruling was made on the basis of peculiar circumstances, with the journalist as the only material witness. Whether a journalist should be compelled to testify even when he is not the only material witness, and where it is not impossible for investigating officers to obtain desired information from other sources, is a point that remains to be adjudicated.

Even though the Supreme Court decision of 1949 was not favourable to recognition of the right of professional secrecy for journalists, and the government has been generally negative, there have been no public statements or publications from any source in Japan, official or otherwise, that could be regarded as discouraging to a possible ultimate recognition of that right. Journalists and journalistic organizations are strongly in favour of such a right, even though they have given it no expression through a Code of Ethics.

Press sets up commission

The Japan Newspaper Publishers and Editors Association, in May 1950, however, established a Legal Research Commission, composed of nine prominent lawyers of the country, at least two of whom had had some active journalistic experience, to study various legal questions concerning newspapers. The Commission's report appeared in June 1952. It said in part that, although it should be for the courts to decide whether professional secrecy might be permitted under existing laws, it was highly desirable to establish such a right by new legislation. It was proposed that this be accomplished by adding to Article 281, Code of Civil Procedure, and to Article 149, Code of Criminal Procedure, a paragraph to the effect that :

> A journalist, or anyone who was a journalist, may refuse to reveal a news source from which he has obtained knowledge in due course of his business.

It was suggested that the condition be added that

> as regards the abuse of the right, the latter part of the provision of Article 149 of the Code of Criminal Procedure shall apply.*

Thus journalists would be in the same position as lawyers, doctors, and "religious functionaries," entitled, at least conditionally, to protect their sources of information.

Professor Dando, a member of the Commission, justified the extension of this right to journalists for a number of reasons, as outlined in an attachment to the Commission Report. While the exemption accorded to physicians, attorneys and others is to protect the private interests of their clients, as he interpreted it, exemption accorded to journalists would be to protect social interests as served by the newspaper. It is unreasonable to grant such protection to other professional groups, in his view, while denying it to journalists. The protection of news sources does not obstruct the investigation of offences, he contended, since investigating officers may conduct inquiries as well, and sometimes more effectively than journalists, and can get information as satisfactorily through their own efforts.

Professor Dando did not go so far as to claim that the right of professional secrecy should be accorded to journalists unconditionally, but should apply under certain limited conditions. As an example, he felt that if a journalist was the only witness to a crime, the right should not be accorded.

The Board of Directors of the Japan Newspaper Publishers and Editors Association adopted unanimously the report of the Legal Research Commission in 1952. Subsequently, representatives of the Association held informal discussions with the Ministry of Justice concerning adoption of the proposed new paragraphs for insertion in the Codes of Civil and Criminal Procedure, by way of giving recognition to the right of professional secrecy for journalists. So far, the attitude of the Ministry has been negative. This does not mean, however, that the law is beyond change. Indeed,

---

* See page 106 above for this provision.

the Code of Criminal Procedure was amended after the new Japanese Constitution came into effect on May 3, 1947. An amendment to Article 149 revoked the right of exemption previously accorded to apothecaries and druggists, while extending that right to nurses, and also added the provision noted above (p. 106) that the right of exemption for the professionals and specialists named should not apply if their principals had consented to give up their anonymity, if there seemed to be an abuse of the right, or if—in the opinion of a court—special circumstances existed.

No question of professional secrecy with reference to radio or television has so far arisen in Japan.

Netherlands

In the Netherlands, as elsewhere, discussion of professional secrecy has centred about a journalist's right to refuse to reveal sources of information when summoned as a witness before a body possessing legal powers of inquiry. Only three major cases have arisen in the last 25 years, however. These have been in courts making preliminary inquiries into criminal cases. In theory, the same question could arise in civil lawsuits or in procedures before social security courts. The journalist's right to keep secret the *content* of confidential information, as well as sources, has been claimed, but that issue remains largely academic.

A Dutch journalist has no legal right to refuse to give evidence before a judicial authority. The general obligation to testify before criminal courts, and the legal exceptions to this rule, are laid down in the Code of Criminal Procedure (Articles 217-219, 221). As to exceptions, Article 218 does excuse persons bound to keep secrecy because of their profession, public office, or social status from the obligation to give evidence before criminal courts, but only with reference to such information as may have come to their knowledge in confidence and incidental to the performance of their special duties. The law does not specify the persons entitled to such exemption, however; the court itself must decide in each particular case.

The High Court of the Netherlands has refused to recognize the journalistic profession as entitled to any such exemption for its members by a 1948 ruling in the Lunshof case, to which later reference will be made. By interpretation the courts have, on the other hand, granted exemptions to doctors, lawyers, clergymen, and notaries, and also to public officials or civil servants who have been, for example, in charge of the inspection of factories to determine observance of safety regulations or labour legislation, inspectors, and the like. In view of the modern development of confidential counselling practices, legal exemption has been claimed by bankers, accountants, and some others, but so far such claims have not been accepted. By a decision of December 9, 1960, the Amsterdam Higher Court (Gerechtshof) has granted legal exemption to a psychiatrically trained social worker, operating professionally in a team of a medical-educational bureau under supervision of a medical doctor.

Despite the unwillingness, so far, of Dutch courts to recognize journalists as entitled to exemption from giving evidence, journalists themselves deem it their professional duty to refuse to reveal sources of information when called as witnesses in cases where they are asked to do so. They base this attitude on an ethical code, as yet unwritten in Holland, but nevertheless regarded as internationally accepted in the profession. This presents a clear conflict with the existing Dutch law, whereunder refusal to give evidence is a criminal offence punishable by imprisonment of up to six months. (Criminal Code, Article 192.) Moreover, a judge has the power to keep an unwilling witness in gaol even during a preliminary inquiry or during the hearing of a case. (Code of Criminal Procedure, Articles 221-225, 289.) This coercive action has been taken twice during the last 25 years.

The Civil Code contains the same provisions as the Criminal Code with reference to granting of exemptions from giving evidence in civil lawsuits. But there is no relevant jurisprudence under this law because no such issue has ever arisen, as affecting a journalist or other person.

Because a journalist's right to refuse to give evidence on the source or content of confidential information has never been recognized by the Dutch courts, no question has ever arisen on the limitation of any such right to particular journalists, in terms of positions occupied, or to any specified investigative authority, or to a given type of case.

A court that wishes to hear testimony from a journalist, or other person, has sole discretion in determining whether such person is entitled to the right of professional secrecy, by exemption. A court's negative decision may be appealed to a higher court and ultimately even to a court of cassation. In the circumstances, there is no possibility of assigning the responsibility of making the original decision to another court or to another body. Some such proposal has been made, nevertheless, on two occasions.

First, in 1937, after the imprisonment of C. L. Hansen, of *Het Vaderland,* The Hague, as a coercive measure, when he refused to reveal the source of certain information, the Dutch Association of Journalists appointed a special committee to study the problem of professional secrecy. In its report of 1939 this committee began by assuming that the right of a journalist to claim exemption would be recognized eventually and proposed, then, that if such a claim was made, the judge of the court should seek the advice of a specially-created Council of Journalists, five in number. The Council would give an opinion as to whether a professional duty of observing silence should or should not prevail over the public obligation to testify. The judge would still be free to accept or reject the opinion.

Second, in 1949, the Federation of Dutch Journalists (Federatie van Nederlandse Journalisten) appointed a special committee to seek a solution for a possible conflict of obligations such as might arise in relation to a prospective Court of Honour for journalists, then regarded as approaching establishment through government action. Journalists saw the possibility that if one of their number, bound by professional ethics to keep confidential a source of information, were nevertheless required by a court to reveal that source, he would then perforce have to be condemned by the prospective Court of Honour for a breach of professional ethics, and possibly drummed out of the profession altogether.

To prevent any such clash, as between legal obligation and professional obligation, the Federation committee proposed that a provision be included in the draft Bill for the establishment of the Court of Honour whereby a judge should ask the advice of the Court of Honour itself when a journalist claimed an exemption from obligation to reveal a source through testimony in court. The Court of Honour then would determine what the journalist should do, and especially would decide whether the publication of the information in question might be regarded as having been made "in the public interest". If so, the journalist would be considered justified in refusing to give evidence, and the Court of Honour's advice would be binding upon the judge and would legally establish an exemption for the journalist.

Neither one of these proposals, needless to say, led to legislative action. The Bill that would have brought establishment of the proposed Court of Honour was withdrawn in 1960 without Parliamentary action.

Hansen imprisoned

The three major cases in which the issue of professional secrecy received special attention in the Netherlands during the last quarter century, as mentioned, were the so-called Hansen case of 1937, the Lunshof case of 1947, and the Hommerson case of 1952. The issues and the decisions may be stated briefly.

C. L. Hansen, a member of the staff of *Het Vaderland*, The Hague, wrote an account published in that newspaper on September 21, 1937, of a debate in a secret session of the city council of The Hague having to do with a contract with a neighbouring town to provide electricity. The Burgomaster believed one of the town councillors had broken the legally-imposed obligation to respect the secrecy of the meeting. He did not know which one might have done so, but he lodged a complaint. In the preliminary inquiry, Hansen refused to name his source, and was imprisoned, as a coercive measure, on December 7, 1937. He was released on December 31 by order of the Hague Court of Justice, which considered the imprisonment no longer necessary. The judicial inquiry later was closed, the case dismissed, and the name of Hansen's informant was never revealed. Hansen, nevertheless, then was prosecuted for failing to fulfill his legal duty as a witness under the terms of the Code of Criminal Procedure, Article 192. The Hague Court of Justice fined him Fl. 100, the Hague Court of Appeals upheld this action, and the case was never brought before the High Court of the Netherlands. The Dutch press particularly protested against Hansen's imprisonment during December, and the Netherlands Journalists' Association gathered and published numerous protests from journalists, most of whom stressed the view that revelation of a source would be justified only if the public interest would be served by such revelation.

Lunshof must pay fine

In the second case, H. A. Lunshof, editor of the weekly, *Elseviers Weekblad,* Amsterdam, presented in the issue of March 20, 1947, an article on the Indonesian situation. In it appeared an excerpt from the secret minutes of the Dutch-Indonesian negotiations at Linggadjati, in Indonesia, which brought an agreement between the two parties. Because a breach of security was involved, a criminal investigation began. In the preliminary inquiry Lunshof refused to reveal the source of his information. He was not imprisoned, but he was brought into court under the provisions of Article 192 of the Criminal Code, and prosecuted as an unwilling witness. The Amsterdam Court of Justice rejected pleas for dismissal of the case on the ground that Lunshof was acting in accordance with his ethical duty as a journalist, which he would betray if he revealed his source, and in keeping with the proper performance of the press in the service of society.

Lunshof was sentenced to pay a fine of Fl. 10 or spend ten days in gaol, with the argument that the administration of justice was the most compelling factor in the service of the public interest.

On an appeal to the High Court, a decision of December 14, 1948, (published in *Nederlandse Jurisprudentie,* File 1949, p. 95) confirmed the lower court's verdict in the Lunshof case. It held that the administration of justice should not be frustrated by the silence of a journalist with reference to his sources of information when the original disclosure of that information was itself a criminal offence committed by the informant (Criminal Code, Article 272.) The High Court did concede that publication of secret documents might serve a public interest higher than that of preserving secrecy. At the same time, the High Court reasoned that the judge of the court in which the original case might be heard was qualified to decide whether publication of such matter constituted a criminal offence, adding that a journalist cannot be impartial in judging the relative weight of conflicting interests when he is personally allied with one of those interests—his informant.

Because the entire Indonesian question was a subject of deep political controversy there was less unanimity on the part of the journalistic group in supporting Lunshof than there had been in supporting Hansen about a decade earlier. Yet the majority were agreed that, professionally, Lunshof could not properly have revealed his source.

Hommerson in gaol

In the third case, A. H. Hommerson, Zaandam correspondent for *Het Vrije Volk,* Amsterdam, had prepared a report published early in 1952, in which a defamatory reference to a retail businessman was included. The reference apparently was false, and *Het Vrije Volk* voluntarily published a correction of what it called "a painful fault". The injured retailer, however, lodged a complaint. In the preliminary inquiry, Hommerson refused to name his source when called as a witness, and was imprisoned on May 6, 1952, but was released on June 24 because the case was dismissed for lack of evidence as to the identity of the informant. Hommerson was prosecuted for having refused testimony, was sentenced to pay a fine of Fl. 25, and was placed on probation by the Amsterdam Police Court. He did not appeal the case. The falsity of the information involved cast a certain shadow over this case, but most journalists commenting on it criticized the coercive imprisonment of Hommerson for 50 days. The case also was the basis for a Parliamentary debate in 1953 on the matter of exempting journalists from giving testimony.

A fourth, but very minor case of refusal by two journalists—both editors of a professional journal—to give testimony occurred in 1949. They were sentenced to pay small fines, but their case brought no repercussions.

The three major cases mentioned as having occurred between 1937 and 1952 did produce a considerable airing of opinion in the Netherlands on the subject of professional secrecy. Indeed, for more than 50 years the question of recognition of the journalist's right to preserve professional secrecy occasionally was debated by journalists and non-journalists alike. There were proposals for absolute privilege, suggestions for conditional privilege and, of course, for no privilege at all. But the more recent debates had greater meaning because they were based on actual cases.

The Hansen case of 1937, as an example, became a topic of discussion, and one pertinent comment was made by Professor Dr. J. C. van Oven, a jurist, but also an ex-journalist, in an editorial appearing in the juridical journal, *Nederlandsch Juristenblad* (File 1937, pp. 1081-1088). Van Oven rejected any absolute exemption for journalists because, in his view, there is a great difference between the motives for granting exceptions for lawyers and certain others, as against the claims presented in justification for exempting journalists. The protection of human beings in distress underlies the traditional exemptions, in his opinion, whereas protection of a journalist's source of information appeared to him to lack equal justification. He added that the journalist could fulfill his professional duties without claiming such exemption, and that the exigencies of a good administration of justice therefore should prevail. This same view was taken by other juridical writers, with reference both to criminal and civil procedure.

The same issue was discussed with reference to the Lunshof and Hommerson cases in 1947 and 1952. The emphasis appeared to have shifted, however, from a claim by journalists for total exemption to a claim for a limited or qualified right to refuse to give evidence. Indeed, there seemed a tendency to believe that the absolute exemption for the traditional professions might also be limited as, for example, when lawyers or notaries were summoned as witnesses or experts before the post-war Council for Rehabilitation of Rights, concerned with events associated with the German wartime occupation of the Netherlands. In medical circles, also, a new awareness of certain conflicts of interests led some doctors to refrain from claiming absolute exemption.*

For a compromise

At the same time, while some journalists turned to the view that only a qualified exemption for members of the profession would be justified, some jurists now seemed inclined toward the view that the former positive denial of any sort of exemption for journalists might be modified. This was suggested, for example, in another article by Professor van Oven in *Nederlandsch Juristenblad* (File 1949, pp. 357-363).

Discussion between those opposing the journalist's exemption and those claiming such a right tended to revolve about three points:

(a) the difference of motives as between people in distress, seeking legal, medical, or spiritual advice and assistance, *and* people giving confidential information to journalists, with or without betraying confidences they are legally bound to keep;

(b) the difference of social function and of the nature of professional activities between the traditional professions and journalism; and

(c) the difference of organization between the traditional professions and journalism.

The first of these points had been stressed by Professor van Oven in his article of 1937 to which reference has been made, and also was emphasized by Professor Dr. G. E. Langemeyer, Solicitor-General in the High Court of the Netherlands, in dealing with the Lunshof case in 1948; as well as by Professor Dr. M. P. Vrip, writing in *Nederlandsch Juristenblad* in 1953 (File 1953, p. 63).

Such an emphasis on "people in distress" as a justification for exemption of the traditional professions, at the expense of journalists, was contested as a distortion, however, by L. F. Tijmstra, then editor of the *Utrechtsch Nieuswsblad,* in a lecture at the Utrecht Juridical Association in January 1956. It is not the informant's motives in speaking that is relevant,

* See, e.g. Dr. J. B. Stolte. *Het Gemenebest.* XV: 5/6 (January and February, 1955) pp. 190ff.

he argued, whether that be to find relief from distress or to convey information; there may also be differences in motive between the informant and the journalist, but it is the exemption for the journalist that is under discussion, not the motive of an informant, in distress or otherwise.

The second point of discussion found some juridical writers, while opposed to exemptions for journalists, willing, nevertheless, to take into account the importance of confidence as between a journalist and a news source. This was true of Professor Dr. W. Pompe, writing in *Nederlandse Jurisprudentie* (File 1956, January 18), and Dr. D. van Eck, professor of Criminal Law in the Catholic University of Nijmegen, writing a series of articles in *De Gelderlander* in May and June of 1952. Both men contended, however, that the nature of the profession and the function of the press were such that journalists could perform their duties without any need for special exemption enabling them to keep their sources confidential.

Extent of claim defined

Presenting the journalist's viewpoint, however, Dr. Maarten Rooij, honorary president of the Dutch Journalists' Association and then editor of the *Nieuwe Rotterdamse Courant,* replied to Dr. van Eck in a series of articles also appearing in *De Gelderlander* in June 1952. Dr. Rooij disputed the traditional arguments against exemptions for journalists, and pointed out that the confidential nature of the journalist's profession is not limited to keeping secrecy about sources of information, but also extends to confidences given by government officials as background information not for publication, yet required by journalists if they are to form adequate opinions on matters involved and so serve readers properly. Dr. Rooij proposed that the courts should be compelled by law to take into consideration whether a journalist, claiming exemption from giving evidence bearing upon something he had written, had presented such information in the public interest. If so, Dr. Rooij argued, the journalist should be held legally justified in refusing to give testimony, and should be exempted from doing so.

Mr. Tijmstra, in the Utrecht address of January 1956 already mentioned, agreed that the judge should balance the importance of the journalist's service in the public interest, in a particular case, against the service to the administration of justice that would be accomplished by forcing a revelation of the source of certain information. Although he would favour excluding cases of serious crimes, such as high treason or espionage, from the possibilities of exemption for journalists, he argued that since most of the activities of the traditional professions could be carried out without concern for any possible exemption from giving evidence, it was no more proper to apply that quantitative standard to deny the same possibility of exemption for journalists, as Pompe and van Eck had done in asserting a difference in the social function of the press as against the traditional professions. The decision on exemption, Tijmstra contended, should rest with the courts, but he proposed some advisory members, elected from a list of journalists drawn up by the professional organizations, to assist the courts in arriving at that decision.

The third issue raised by jurists opposing exemptions for journalists emphasized that members of the traditional professions were required to meet certain qualifications before entering upon their activities, and were subject to disciplinary action for offences, whereas journalists were not subject to any such standards and therefore were not equally entitled to claim similar consideration.

Journalists have been forced to concede that there is some basis for this view. It was to meet this objection in part that the proposal had been advanced for the establishment of a Court of Honour for journalists in the Netherlands, that it was proposed in 1939 that an advisory professional board be created to assist the court in judging the professional status of a journalistic witness, that it has been proposed that an obligatory training system be established for young journalists, and that an official system for registration of journalists should be evolved. None of these measures appears wholly practicable or assured at the present time, however.

In the parliamentary debate on the draft code of Criminal Procedure, now in force since 1925, the Netherlands Government had opposed any exemption from giving evidence being extended to journalists. When questions were asked in Parliament on this matter with reference to the Hansen and Lunshof cases the Government position continued to be negative. The issue was more thoroughly explored in a debate relating to the Hommerson case in 1952 and 1953, but with no clear result. So far as legislative action is concerned, therefore, the problem remains unresolved, nor has it been regarded as urgent since no new case of a journalist's refusal to give evidence has arisen since 1953.

On those rare occasions when a case has arisen, journalistic organizations in the Netherlands have taken an active role in support of the journalist's moral obligation to keep sources confidential. Although no written code of ethics exists, a special committee of the Federation of Dutch Journalists is drafting such a code and it is to be expected that the obligation to keep silent about sources of information will be restated therein.

No question of professional secrecy with reference to radio or television has so far arisen in the Netherlands.

Norway

In Norway, citizens are under an obligation to provide information to judicial, legislative and administrative authorities when called upon to do so. This requirement derives from provisions established in statutory law. Any exemption from such obligation also is based on statutory authority.

The obligation to provide the courts with information is based on the rule of compulsory evidence stated in general form in the Criminal Procedure Act, Section 171, and in the Civil Procedure Act, Section 199. The sections contain no limitations except as to the distance a witness may be required to travel to appear in court.

The Storting (Parliament) may require persons to give evidence before it in state cases, under provisions in the Constitution, Section 75, litra h. Exceptions are granted for the King and members of the Royal Family. The right to summon persons for examination may not be exercised, however, by committees of the Storting.

The obligation to give information to administrative authorities has been established in a number of laws pertaining to the administration. There is no general requirement, however, that information need be given to the police or prosecuting authorities, apart from a duty to provide facts necessary for personal identification. But if a witness once does make a statement to the police, he is obligated, under penal liability, to give a true and correct statement.

The exceptions to the general obligation of citizens to provide information are similar to those in other countries as applying to members of the traditional professional groups. In Norway, these exceptions have the force of law in that secrecy is not merely permitted, but is *required* under the Penal Code, Section 144, reading as follows :

> Clergymen, attorneys at law, defence counsel in criminal cases, medical doctors, pharmacists, midwives and nurses, as well as their subordinates or assistants, who unlawfully divulge any secret confided to them or their superiors in the course of their professional duties shall be punished by fines or by a term of imprisonment of up to six months.

A public servant also is to maintain secrecy in regard to information confided to him in the course of his service. This obligation, too, is stated in the Penal Code, Section 121, of which the first paragraph reads :

> If a public servant reveals without sound reason anything that has been confided to him in the course of his service or that is described as a professional secret by statutory or other valid provision, he shall be punished by fines or by the loss of his position or by a term of imprisonment of up to six months.

Obligations upon public servants to maintain secrecy have been further and more specifically stated in a number of special laws, including the Taxation Acts.

In addition to the actual requirement of secrecy thus imposed by statute upon persons in certain professions and positions, Norwegian law also has established a right of exemption from giving information, or a right of secrecy, for certain persons, usually with reference to special information. The Criminal and Civil Procedure Acts have provisions, too, that prohibit the taking of evidence from certain persons or about certain circumstances. Journalists have benefitted from some of these provisions.

Exemption from the obligation to give evidence, where granted, has differed somewhat as between criminal and civil cases. In criminal cases, the closest relatives of the defendant are entirely exempt from the obligation to give evidence (Criminal Procedure Act, Section 176), whereas in civil cases the exemption of relatives is limited to that bearing upon information of which the witness has been informed by the party to the lawsuit (Civil Procedure Act, Section 207), and does not extend to personal observations. In criminal and civil cases alike a witness may refuse to answer a question that might expose him or his relatives to punishment or loss of reputation. (Criminal Procedure Act, Section 177, paragraph 1 ; Civil Procedure Act, Section 208).

A *special right of exemption for journalists* was established by an Act of June 15, 1951, with the introduction of a third paragraph in both the Criminal and Civil Procedure Acts, respectively, section 177 and section 209. It provides that

> the publisher (editor) of a printed publication may refuse to reveal the author of an article or notice in the publication or the source of the information contained therein. The same

applies to any other person who has been informed of the author or of the source in the course of his work for the publishers, editors, news agency or printers concerned.

The right of exemption is not absolute, however. The court still may

decide that evidence shall be given when, after weighing the conflicting interests, it finds such evidence necessary. In such cases the court may further decide that the evidence shall be given only to the court itself and the parties in meeting behind closed doors and under an order of secrecy.

It is further provided that :

Evidence should always be required when the article or notice contains information which presumably has been supplied by a punishable breach of secrecy, or when the witness refuses to give such complete information about the matter as he is able to procure from the author or source without naming them.

These provisions form the only legal recognition of any special right for journalists in Norway to protect their sources of information, or any special exemption for journalists who may be called as witnesses. They were obtained, moreover, only after a prolonged struggle, as reflected in Parliamentary Bill (Ot. prp.) No. 28 for 1950. In presenting this Bill, the basis for the additions to the Criminal and Civil Procedure Acts, the Norwegian Government went to considerable lengths to meet demands by the press for legal recognition of professional secrecy with reference to sources of information. The phrasing of the Bill embraced principles advanced in 1948 by a committee of the Norsk Presseforbund (Norwegian Press Association) in urging recognition of journalists' rights. The committee statement had said, in part :

The protection of its sources demanded by the press is primarily motivated by social considerations. If the press is to fulfill its task not only as a vehicle of news but also as the watchful critic of society, it must be able to convey the individual citizen's observations and experiences without the citizen himself having to enter the limelight.

The objection will often be heard that anyone wishing to criticize private or public affairs, censure dishonesty or expose corruption, should himself stand forward and take the responsibility for his statements. In principle, of course, that is correct, and in most cases an editor will probably require his source to guarantee the accuracy of his own statements by disclosing his name. But cases will frequently occur where the same considerations as those which have motivated the right of anonymous authorship will apply in support of the claim for protection of press sources.

Who is a journalist?

It may be observed that, in the additions to the Criminal and Civil Procedure Acts just previously described, the word "journalist" does not appear. In Norwegian usage, however, the designation "journalist" covers all members of a newspaper staff permanently connected with editorial production, and it must be presumed that the words used in the law have the same broad application. It will be noted, too, that the provisions of the law have to do with information about the *author* of an article or notice, or the *source* of information published, but do not provide authorization for a journalist to refuse to reveal the *content* of secret information he may have obtained or received. So far as any protection attaches to content, it is no more than exists in the procedural acts applying to the general obligation to give evidence. There is some protection assured under the provisions of those acts, however.

Both the Criminal Procedure Act, Section 180, and the Civil Procedure Act, Section 204, provide that no evidence at all is to be taken by courts with reference to

> secret negotiations, consultations or decisions in matters affecting the nation's security or rights in respect of another state, unless permission is granted by the King.

Nor may a court take evidence

> in questions that the witness cannot answer without violating secrecy imposed on him as a public servant by statute or other valid provision, unless permission is granted by the competent authority.

Just as the Penal Code requires secrecy on the part of members of traditional professions and occupations, as already noted, so obligations are placed upon the courts of Norway to respect that requirement. The Criminal Procedure Act, Section 178, and the Civil Procedure Act, Section 205, provide that a court may not take evidence from any of the persons mentioned in the Penal Code — clergymen, attorneys, etcetera — without the consent of the individual having a claim of secrecy about

> facts confided to them in their profession, unless they have a statutory obligation to reveal such facts.

The statutory obligation would arise, under the provision of the Penal Code, Sections 139 and 172, only where there was a question of preventing serious crimes or preventing an innocent person being condemned for lack of relevant information.

The courts' interpretation

The content of information relating to business affairs, amounting to professional secrets, is one other area in which a witness may claim the right to withhold evidence. (Criminal Procedure Act, Section 177, paragraph 2 ; Civil Procedure Act, Section 209, paragraph 1). But, with the exception of the right of the journalist to protect a *source* of information, there is no other professional right of exemption. Even the legal *obligation* to maintain secrecy in the traditional professions does not establish any right for the witness to decide *for himself* whether he shall give evidence or not.

It is for the court to decide whether a legitimate reason for exemption exists. The decision of the court may be reviewed right up to the Supreme Court's Appeal Committee.

Prior to the establishment of a special right for the journalist to protect his source of information, by the Act of June 15, 1951, the courts had been forced to rule frequently on the question of a journalist's obligation to give evidence. The number of such cases since 1951, however, have been few. The Chief Public Prosecutor nevertheless requested, by a circular letter on May 12, 1953, that he be informed of any demands by public prosecutors for court decisions ordering a journalist to answer questions as to the name of the author of an article or notice in a publication, or of the source of information contained therein. This was done to assure uniform decisions in such cases.

Among cases affecting professional secrecy for journalists in Norway since the passage of the Act of 1951 only two have been significant enough to gain more than passing attention. One occurred in 1952, the other in 1959.

In the first of these cases, in 1952, Mr. Erling Hall Hofsoe, editor of *Folkeviljen* (The Will of the People), Harstad, was ordered to reveal the source of a report in his paper concerning two cases of attempted rape. He declined to reveal the names of two women, victims of the attempts, who were, in fact, his sources, and he was remanded into custody. The court directed him, under the provisions of the Criminal Procedure Act, Section 177, to reveal the names of his informants. When he still refused to do so he was remanded into custody for up to three months in accordance with provisions of Section 189 of the law applying to criminal cases.

Execution of the sentence was postponed when Mr. Hofsoe, with the full support of the Norwegian Press Association, filed a new appeal. He had declared his willingness to assist in an investigation of the case by serving as an intermediary in passing police questions to his informants and delivering their replies and, if desired, tape recording those replies. Thus, he contended, the police could obtain all necessary information, while the names of the women informants could be protected.

This case was brought twice before the Appeal Committee of the Supreme Court. On the first occasion the question was whether Hofsoe was obliged to name his source, and the decision was in the affirmative. Upon his continued refusal to do so, with the case before the Appeal Committee again, the question concerned what action might be appropriate—whether a fine, under the provisions of the Court Act, Section 206, or a confinement in custody, under the Criminal Procedure Act, Section 189, until he complied with the order to reveal his source. The second alternative was approved, with confinement authorized, under the law, not as a penalty, but as a means of coercing a reluctant witness, and not to extend beyond three months.

Mr. Hofsoe was taken into custody, but was released after about 14 days when his sources had themselves given the required information to the police. Meanwhile, he had directed his paper from a prison cell, and received visitors. His preference to serve a period in gaol rather than expose his source won him applause from journalists in Norway and abroad, but as a first test of the Act of June 15, 1951 the episode was not reassuring to the journalistic profession in Norway.

News agency under scrutiny

The second case, arising in 1959, brought results somewhat more gratifying to journalists. Early in the year, the Oslo bureau of the Associated Press distributed in Norway a report concerning the prospective abolition of rationing on the sale of automobiles in the country. The story was in two sections. The first reported that rationing would be completely abolished during 1959. A "spokesman for the trade department" of the government was cited as authority for the statement, but without naming the individual. The second section of the story, attributed to an "informed" source in Copenhagen, reported that the abolition of rationing would be preceded by a 10 to 25 per cent increase of Norwegian government sales taxes on automobiles. This second part, in particular, led to a heavy sale of cars, even under rationing, and prior to the tax increase, so that considerable revenue was lost to the government.

Publication of this report in *Dagbladet,* an Oslo evening paper, resulted in three members of the Oslo Associated Press bureau being summoned into court and ordered to reveal the source of information published. These were J. W. Lager, bureau manager ; H. O. Haugen, cable editor ; and J. L. Mowinckel, a reporter. The prosecution argued that the "spokesman of the trade department" cited was, in fact, the source for both parts of the story, and that, as a government official, he was guilty of a breach of official secrecy. Under the Norwegian Criminal Procedure Act, Section 177, paragraph 3 — the Act of June 15, 1951 — it was argued that the press, or agency, had no right to protect a source thus guilty of revealing an official secret. Refusal to reveal the source would make the journalists subject to three months coercive imprisonment, as in the earlier Hofsoe case.

In May the three journalists filed an appeal against the order, claiming that the Lower Court had based its decision on an unsupported supposition that the source was the same for the two parts of the story, and asserting that this was not so. This argument was upheld in July by the Court of Appeals, which reversed the Lower Court decision and released the journalists from the order to reveal the source or sources of the report.

Although a somewhat technical victory for the concept of professional secrecy, this was taken to mean that even if the Norwegian press does not have an absolute right to keep secret its sources of information under any and all circumstances, it may be regarded as having the right to do so if there is no proof that any breach of official secrecy has been an element in obtaining that information.

Prior to the amendments to the Criminal and Civil Procedure Acts in 1951, the question of a journalist's obligation to give evidence, even to the point of revealing sources, was the subject of considerable discussion by journalists and jurists alike.* The Norwegian Press Association, as noted, sponsored a proposal in 1948 to protect sources of information, and it was this which became the basis for the Parliamentary Bill No. 28, for 1950, which led to the Act of 1951. In the Bill itself, and its appendices, there is included a substantial amount of information about the subject, and about earlier cases. Even after the amendments of 1951 had become part of Norway's law, the right of the press to keep sources anonymous was the subject of a debate at the 20th Meeting of Jurists of the Northern European Countries, in Oslo in 1954. A paper on "The right of Anonymity" read by Professor Kaarlo Kaira, of Finland, served as a basis for the discussion.**

Professor Kaira's general view was that "the safety valve offered by anonymity is of the greatest value to society", presenting "opportunities of expression to those who, for acceptable reasons, cannot stand forth openly". But he insisted that the principle must be applied with a full sense of responsibility by journalists. He regarded the Norwegian recognition of the limited right of anonymity for sources as somewhat less complicated than the Swedish system and somewhat more elastic than

---

* See, for example, a discussion by Olaf Salomonsen, later a Judge in the Court of Appeals, relative to a report to the Storting (Parliament) in 1912, in which the Ministry of Justice had examined the subject, published in the Scandinavian Review of Penal Law (Nordisk Tidsskrift for Strafferett) for 1914, pp. 234 ff. See also Salomonsen's Commentaries on the Norwegian Criminal Procedure Act (1925) pp. 185-186. See also *Omriss av Norsk Presserett* (an Outline of Norwegian Press Law, 1930), pp. 51 ff., by Fr. H. Winsnes, barrister at the Supreme Court, in which a number of court decisions for the period prior to the date of publication are examined. A proposal by journalists for a law to establish their right to protect sources of information had been originally proposed in 1917, but was rejected.

** The paper and the debates were published in Oslo in 1956 by the Norwegian Executive Council of the Meeting. See: *Forhandlinger paa det tyvende nordiske juristmote i Oslo den 23-25 August, 1954.* (Oslo: Johansen & Nielsen Boktrykveri, 1956.)

the Danish. He saw it as placing a heavy burden upon the court, however, to decide whether anonymity should prevail in a given case and to be certain that a consistent policy was followed in according the right of anonymity. He felt that it left the author or source of information somewhat uncertain as to whether he would, in fact, remain anonymous.

Responsibility of the press

Norwegian journalists themselves invariably have sought to maintain a professional right, and have observed an obligation to protect their sources. This view has found expression in a general assertion of rules for correct professional conduct, as prepared by the Norwegian Press Association, and set forth in a so-called "Be Careful Code" distributed to the membership. It says, in part :

> Safeguard the sources of the newspaper ! Do not reveal the names of sources of information or names of authors writing under a pen name, unless they have given their consent or a court has issued an order of such a nature that it must be complied with.
> Be, on the other hand, particularly careful in appraising such sources and authors; in such cases the full weight of responsibility rests with the journalist. Have in mind that many would wish to employ a publication as an instrument of attack against their fellow men without having reputable reasons for doing so. Never use information or contributions from anonymous sources.

These rules, among others, together with "Directions for Press Reporting of Court Cases", as adopted in 1952 following conferences between representatives of the Norwegian Press Association, the Norwegian Bar Association, the Norwegian Association of Judges, and with the cooperation of the Chief Public Prosecutor, may be considered a "Code of Ethics" for Norwegian journalists.

Violations of the rules may be reported to the Professional Committee of the Norwegian Press Association, named primarily to deal with matters of professional conduct. The committee, consisting of three members appointed by the Central Executive Council of the Association, has final authority to deal with cases referred to it. Its statements are published in the journal of the Press Association, to which members subscribe, and may also be reported in the press if the committee deems proper or if other responsible groups within the leadership of the Press Association consider such action appropriate.

Questions have arisen on several occasions as to whether the provisions of the law might require the Norwegian Broadcasting Corporation (Norsk Rikskringkasting) to name sources of news broadcast by radio, but the matter never has reached any critical point requiring decision.

Employees of the N. B. C. have, in principle, the same obligation to give evidence as other citizens. Since the N. B. C. is an independent government corporation, however, it may be assumed that its employees are subject to the special rules imposing secrecy on public servants, as stated in the Penal Code, Section 121, already cited.

The special rules in Norway's Procedure Acts regarding the duty to supply evidence in regard to information appearing in a *printed publication* do not directly cover radio news broadcasts. Even so, the motives which have been noted as leading in 1951 to amendments both to the Civil and Criminal Procedure Acts will, no doubt, find analogous application to the protection of sources used in N. B. C. broadcasts. This would mean that employees of the broadcast media presumably would enjoy the same exemption as press representatives from the obligation to provide information.

Pakistan

In Pakistan, there is no recognition of professional secrecy for journalists, either by custom or by law, and virtually no indication of interest or concern in gaining such recognition, in whole or in part, by journalists themselves or by any other group.

Prior to the partition of 1947, by which Pakistan was separated from India to become an autonomous Republic, the British administration of the subcontinent had placed an effective control upon the press to discourage criticism of the government. This control was supported by applications and interpretations by the courts of sections of the Press Act (Act I of 1910), the Press and Registration of Books Act (XXV of 1867), the Press (Emergency Powers) Act (XXIII of 1931), the Evidence Act (I of 1872), Ordinances and Regulation (III of 1888), the Contempt of Courts Act (XII of 1926), the Official Secrets Act, as well as of the Penal Code, the Civil Procedure Code, and the Criminal Procedure Code.

Hedged by the provisions of these laws, the press had limited freedom, and any concept of professional secrecy, by which sources of information might be withheld from the courts or other authorities, if demanded, was not even a matter for serious consideration.

Following the establishment of the independent Republic of Pakistan, the major portion of the existing body of law, jurisprudence, rules and regulations was retained, with no more than the most incidental and routine modification, under the blanket designation of the Unrepealed Control Acts, issued under the authority of the Ministry of Law in 1952. By that date, there had been added, and included, the Pakistan Public Safety Ordinance (XIV of 1949) and the Security of Pakistan Act (XXXV of 1952). Broader changes, under consideration, have yet to be made, and there is no present reason to believe the concept of professional secrecy would be recognized as having any validity even when and if such changes are made.

Just as independence of press investigation and comment was limited prior to partition, therefore, it remains limited today within much the same legal structure. The only groups in Pakistan entitled to claim a right of professional secrecy under the law are lawyers, judges and magistrates, doctors, civil servants, and "informants". This latter group includes persons who might provide information to the authorities regarding offences and offenders against the law, and whose identities were to be protected as an assurance to them that they would be spared personal recriminations. These special exceptions are made within the provisions of the Evidence Act, Sections 121 through 129.

No privilege granted in court

Beyond that, however, the law is adamant. A journalist may keep a source of information secret from his readers, or from private persons, but *not* from any court, whether civil or criminal, and not from the High Court of Judicature, when and if any such court makes a demand for a source of information. Under the provisions of Sections 21, 176 and 179 of the Pakistan Penal Code, also, refusal to answer a question asked by any "public servant" — with that designation carefully and specifically established in the law — in the performance of his assigned task carries a penalty of a fine or imprisonment, or both.

A journalist, then, is subject to the same laws as any other citizen. By the provisions of the Evidence Act, Section 132, he is required, when called into court as a witness, to answer any question as to any matter at issue, whether under civil or criminal procedure. Under Section 165 of the same Act, the judge may ask any question in any form and at any time, and may order the production of any document or evidence, without objection, and without any right of appeal to another court, or to a higher court. Nor can the witness decline to answer the question, as he might in many other countries, on the ground that his reply might tend to incriminate him, directly or indirectly, or expose him to a personal penalty or forfeiture of any kind. Failure to respond would subject the journalist, or other citizen, to citation for contempt of court under Section 228 of the Penal Code, and would make him liable, under the provisions of Section 176 of that Code, to imprisonment for from one to five months, to a fine of as much as Rs. 100, or both.

Nor is it a duly accredited court alone that is authorized to demand replies from journalists or other witnesses. Under Section 176 of the Penal Code, "omission to give notice or information to a public servant by a person legally bound to do so" — which could mean any public official operating within the area of his authority — would make the reluctant witness subject to imprisonment for up to six months, or to a fine of Rs. 1,000, or both. So an editor, for example, might be asked to reveal the name of the author of a particular news story or article, or to produce the original copy used in preparing such a story or article for publication, and could refuse only at his peril.

In court cases involving libel or defamation there have been decisions giving specific denial to any right of a journalist to claim professional secrecy. So it has been ruled, for example, that "no privilege attaches to the profession of the press as distinguished from the members of the public. The privilege of a journalist is no higher than that of an ordinary citizen." (B. L. R. 544 - 41 C 1023 P. C.) ; that "an editor is bound to give evidence as to the actual printer of the paper during his absence." (1928 - A. 400 - 26 A. L. J. 746 - 50 - A 860) ; that "newspapers owe a duty to their readers to publish any or every item of news that may interest them. But this does not make every communication relating to public interest a privileged one." (43 Cr. L. J. 17 (21).) ; and "the Press, authors and publishers have no special privilege. They must show that attack on the character of another was for the public good and that it was made in good faith." (1942 No. 117-43 (aP. J. 856, 41. C 1023 (P. C.).).

Editors accept limitations

Not only is there no recognition of a right of professional secrecy in Pakistan, whether in law, jurisprudence, or custom, but there has been no disposition on the part of editors, working journalists, or press groups to insist upon such a right. Indeed, Pakistani editors and journalists generally, by a careful concern for what they write and publish, consistently and prudently avoid placing themselves in any position where they might be brought into court to face a demand that they reveal a source.

In the Pakistan press structure, the editor, in practice, is the chief figure, and the working journalists are his employees. Editors have, at times, and as individuals, been regarded as enjoying somewhat privileged positions under various governmental administrations. Any such advantages as an editor might enjoy, however, even to the extent of giving him some measure of freedom from a court summons to reveal a source, has hinged upon his own personality and ability, and on his political agreement with the administration in power. Apart from such special situations, editors as a group have undertaken to see that their news editors and staff members give no cause to invite any court summons. For that reason, editors and journalists seldom have found themselves in positions where they might even have to try to protect sources of information figuring in published reports. The general practice on those rare occasions where any such issue has arisen has been for an editor to offer unconditional apologies to the courts, and editors and journalists have responded promptly to court demands for information when questions have been asked about sources.

In some cases where questions as to source *might* have been asked they were not asked. But it was recognized in advance that they would not be asked. So, because of tensions between Pakistan and India in the period following partition, reports of alleged atrocities appeared in the press of both countries, each ascribing offences to the other, and with no concern as to determining either authenticity or sources. Indeed, so many such reports appeared, often quite irresponsibly, that a Liaquat-Nehru agreement in 1950 included a clause providing that both countries would desist from publishing such news in their press. A Code of Honour, drafted by the Pakistan Newspaper Editors' Conference, also proposed the establishment of self-restraint in the use of such reports, and their correction when errors appeared. In practice, neither agreement has been wholly observed and, in any event, had no direct bearing on the question of professional secrecy, much less on the legal factors involved.

Because the Pakistani press is relatively young in its modern period, and many of its staff members also are young, impetuous and inexperienced, there have been dangers that, in their handling of government information, they might make mistakes in judgment on sensitive points in the affairs of the nation, even to such a degree as might affect the safety of the country. In this area of news treatment there are legal hazards, also, relating to the issue of professional secrecy.

First of all, government officials are instructed that no information they may acquire, whether directly or indirectly, from official documents or in the course of official business shall be communicated directly to any representative of the press. Official information, rather, is to be channeled to the press through the Ministry of Information and Broadcasting.

An arsenal of restrictive laws

Beyond that, editors and journalists are restricted by the provisions of the Official Secrets Act of 1923, consolidating the Indian Official Secrets Act of 1889, the Indian Official Secrets Act (Amended) of 1904, and two Statutes of the British Parliament of 1911 and 1920. They also are subject to the provisions of the Pakistan Public Safety laws and ordinances presented, in essence, in the Security of Pakistan Act of 1952 and providing, among other things, that any news report or information considered by the Government as likely to endanger public order or safety may result in a demand upon the editor, printer, or other person to reveal the source of his information. Refusal to do so carries a permissive penalty even more severe than any under the Penal Code, as presented in the Press (Emergency Powers) Act of 1931 and in the Press and Registration of Books Act of 1867.

Whereas cases involving professional secrecy have arisen only rarely in Pakistan and occasioned little comment if they have because the demand for revelation of source has not been contested, one recent case arose from the application of the laws just mentioned.

The *Pakistan Times,* of Lahore, which had published a news report allegedly based upon information contained in an official classified document, received an order, directed to its editor, Ahmad Ali Khan, under the provisions of the Security of Pakistan Act, to reveal the source of his information. The editor complied immediately, replying that the information had been obtained by Salamat Ali, a reporter on the paper's staff, and also producing the original news copy as written by the reporter. Salamat Ali then was requested to reveal the actual source of the information upon which he based his report. This he refused to do. Accordingly, he was placed under detention on August 7, 1960, pending trial under the Security of Pakistan Act and the Official Secrets Act. Asrar Ahmad, also a reporter for the *Pakistan Times,* was arrested at the same time. Both men were discharged, however, in December, by the city magistrate of Rawalpindi, and the cases against them were withdrawn by the government of Pakistan. No official explanation was made for this action, but it is believed that both official and unofficial spokesmen had interceded in the matter and that the supposed offence had received reconsideration.

Philippines

In the Republic of the Philippines, the right of newsmen to observe professional secrecy is recognized in the law.

The right had been established by the passage of Republic Act 53, dated October 5, 1946, and so made effective three months after the independent Republic was proclaimed. It had been supposed by the author of that first professional secrecy law, Senator Filemon Sotto, that it would assure to newsmen the right to refuse to reveal sources of information. In 1948, however, the Supreme Court interpreted the Sotto law in such a manner as to make it, in effect, a limitation upon that right, rather than as an assurance of professional secrecy. The result was the passage of Republic Act 1477, effective June 15, 1956, as an amendment to the earlier law, to remove any limitation upon that right.

The first law, Republic Act 53, of 1946, the Sotto measure, had provided :

> Section 1. The publisher, editor or duly accredited reporter of any newspaper, magazine or periodical of general circulation cannot be compelled to reveal the source of any news report or information appearing in said publication which was related in confidence to such publisher, editor or reporter, unless the court or a House or committee of Congress finds that such revelation is demanded by the interest of the State.
> Section 2. All provisions of law or rules of court inconsistent with this act are hereby repealed or modified accordingly.

As matters developed, the weak point in this law was in the exclusion provided by the phrase, "unless... such revelation is demanded by the *interest* of the State". In 1948, Angel Parazo, a reporter for a small Manila daily, the *Star Reporter,* wrote an account in that newspaper indicating a leakage of examination questions to be asked in the bar examinations. When asked, Parazo refused to reveal the source of his information, invoking the Sotto Law, and contending that the phrase "interest of the State" had reference only to cases involving the "security of the State" or "public safety." The court ruled against him, however, and he was cited for contempt.

On appeal, the Supreme Court upheld the lower court decision, ruling that the story tended to discredit the integrity of the Supreme Court itself, which had charge of the bar examinations, that the "interest of the State" therefore was affected. The Supreme Court reasoning (In re Parazo, 82 Phil. 230) was that :

> The phrase "interest of the State" is quite broad and extensive. It is of course more general and broader than "security of the State". Although not as broad and comprehensive as "public interest," which may include almost everything, even of minor importance, but affecting the public... the phrase "interest of the State," even under a conservative interpretation, may and does include cases and matters of national importance in which the whole state and nation... is interested or would be affected, such as the principal functions of the Government, like the administration of justice, scientific research, practice of law or medicine, impeachment of high Government officials, treaties with other nations, integrity of the three coordinated branches of the Government, their relations to each other, and the discharge of their functions, etc.
>
> We are satisfied that the present case easily comes under the phrase "interest of the State".

The citation against Parazo thus stood, and he was goaled. Senator Sotto bitterly criticized the Supreme Court for its interpretation of the law, and some civil liberties groups also interested themselves in the case. The general public, however, was largely indifferent to the action, possibly because the newspaper that published the story had a reputation for sensationalism.

Seven years later, in 1955, the ruling of the Supreme Court in the Parazo case was invoked by Judge Emilio Rilloraza, of the City Court of First Instance in Pasay, a suburb of Manila. This was in a case wherein a former member of the Cabinet, Oscar Castelo, was implicated in the murder of a star witness in hearings on a bribery charge against him. The hearings had been completed and the judge was preparing his decision when Manila dailies published reports alleging that two Manila women, one of them said to be a relative of the judge, had attempted to extort 100.000 pesos (U.S. $50.000) from Castelo, with a promise of a favourable decision upon payment of that sum. Sources for this information were not specified.

The judge responded by summoning five Manila newspaper reporters, and ordering them to reveal the source or sources of information on which the published reports had been based. He contended that the "interest of the State" was involved, and cited the Supreme Court ruling of 1948 in the Parazo case as a precedent. The reporters, nevertheless, refused to name the source or sources, asserting that the original intent of the author of the Sotto law was that professional secrecy need be waived only when there was clear and present danger to the safety of the State. The judge thereupon cited the five reporters for contempt and sentenced all of them to 30 days in gaol.

Contrary to the public apathy that had attended the Parazo case, this action caused a general outcry, with an assertion that freedom of the press in the country was threatened. The five imprisoned newsmen were swamped by gifts from citizens of food, drinks, and tobacco. President Magsaysay himself went *incognito* to visit the reporters in the Pasay gaol, and Mrs. Magsaysay sent army cots with bedding and mosquito netting.

Supreme Court petitioned

The following morning, the reporters petitioned the Supreme Court for a writ of *habeas corpus,* invoking Constitutional rights as well as the Sotto Law, and the High Court freed the newsmen on 200 pesos bail bond each, pending a hearing on the merits of their petitions. Representative Floro Crisologo and several other members of Congress also made haste to prepare and introduce a new bill intended to amend and so to clarify the interpretation of Republic Act 53, the Sotto Law. This became Republic Act 1477, passed unanimously by both houses of Congress, and immediately signed by President Magsaysay, who had shown a personal interest in its passage from the outset. It became effective June 15, 1956.

The text of the new law read as follows :

Republic Act No. 1477 an Act Amending Sec. 1 of R.A. 53, entitled "An Act to Exempt the Publisher, Editor, Columnist or Reporter of any publication from revealing the source of published news or information obtained in confidence."

Section 1 of the Republic Act Numbered Fifty-three is amended to read as follows :

Section 1. Without prejudice to his liability under the civil and criminal laws, the publisher, editor, columnist or duly accredited reporter of any newspaper, magazine or periodical of general circulation cannot be compelled to reveal the source of any news report or information appearing in said publication which was related in confidence to such publisher, editor or reporter unless the Court or a House or a committee of Congress finds that such revelation is demanded by the security of the State.

The new law, as noted, specified that a newsman might be compelled to reveal a source of information only if "demanded by the security of the State," rather than by the "interest of the State," as previously. This was the first time the Congress of the Philippines passed a law that had the effect of deciding for the Supreme Court an issue pending before that tribunal. Accordingly, the five Manila reporters out on bail for several months pending action on their petitions, were removed from jeopardy, with their gaol sentences dissolved by the Supreme Court.

The Supreme Court action was taken in the following ruling :

In re Aspiras, et al., G.R. No. L. 10031, August 29, 1956.
In view of the approval on June 15, 1956, of Rep. Act No. 1477, amending Section 1, Rep. Act No. 53, which provided that the publisher, editor or duly accredited reporter of any newspaper, magazine or periodical of general circulation could not be compelled to reveal the source of any information appearing in the publication or confided or related in confidence to such publisher, editor or reporter unless the Court should find that such revelation be demanded by the interest of the State, in the sense that, unless the Court finds that the revelation be demanded by the security of the State, there can be no such compulsion ; and it appearing that the security of the State does not demand the revelation of the source of the information involved in the contempt proceedings brought in the Court below ; and that the amendatory act, being favourable to the persons charged with contempt in the Court below, should be applied retroactively, the petitioners for the writ of *habeas corpus* in G.R. No. L. 10031, José de Aspiras, et al. vs. Warden of Pasay City Jail, etc., et al. are held not guilty of contempt under the provisions of Rep. Act No. 53, as amended by Rep. Act No. 1477, and the judgement rendered in the contempt proceedings brought against them in the Court below is set aside.

The passage of the Rep. Act 1477 in 1956 settled what had been a long held dissatisfaction among journalists with the interpretation of the Rep. Act 53 of ten years earlier—an interpretation clearly at odds with the intent of the proponent of the 1946 measure and, no doubt, of most members of the Congress that passed it. The passage of the 1956 amendment, making "the security of the State" the only limitation, assures journalists in the Philippines as complete a legal right to professional secrecy as exists in any part of the world. It is in accord with an historic desire within the country for freedom of expression.

Filipino reformers of the late 19th century had advocated press freedom at a time when that was not to be enjoyed under the Spanish administration of the islands. When a revolutionary Republic was set up in 1898, with the overthrow of the Spanish regime, Article 20 of the Malolos Constitution, adopted January 20, 1898, provided that no Filipino should be deprived of the

> right of expressing freely his ideas and opinions either by word or by writing, availing himself of the press or any other similar means.

The Spanish-American war, beginning in April 1898, resulted in the Philippines being ceded by Spain to the United States. Philippine resistance to U. S. sovereignty over the islands continued for about four years. U. S. administrators then permitted the gradual extension of press freedom, however, and in 1916 the U. S. Congress passed what was known as the Philippine Autonomy Act, promising independence as soon as a stable government could be established by Filipinos. The Act included a specific provision for press freedom, borrowed from the First Amendment to the U. S. Constitution. It specified that

> No law shall be passed abridging the freedom of speech or of the press, or the right of the people peaceably to assemble and petition the government for a redress of grievances.

The present Constitution of the Republic of the Philippines, in its Article 111 (Bill of Rights), Section 1 (8), includes precisely the same provision. It is in that spirit that the Republic Act 1477, of 1956, was passed without dissent by the Congress assuring newsmen protection in the right to professional secrecy, unless the security of the State is involved.

Sweden

In Sweden, as elsewhere, a journalist's "right to professional secrecy" is understood to mean his right and, indeed, his *duty* to refuse to reveal his sources when they are confidential. He has no legal right to refuse to give information on the *contents* of information obtained in the practice of his profession. His right to protect his *sources,* while not absolute, is legally construed as a right to anonymity for the journalist's informant and a corresponding obligation on his part to respect that anonymity. This has its application in Sweden to a journalist's relation to the courts, to legislative bodies and their committees, to the administration of state affairs by executive authorities, and to private individuals. While not a specific journalistic "right", it is an effective protection.

The Freedom of the Press Act (Tryckfrihetsförordningen), one of the four Acts of the Swedish Constitution, defines "the right of anonymity", in its Chapter 3, and specifies in Article 1 that no printer, publisher or other person concerned with printing or with publishing printed matter—which includes journalists—shall reveal the identity of the author or of any person who may have provided information for publication, except with the permission of such author or informant, *unless obliged to do so by law.*

More particularly, under this provision, a journalist is legally *obligated* to refuse to reveal the source of his information either to a private person or to a person in a position of authority if (a) the source has not consented to the disclosure of his identity and, in general practice, if the source has not specifically waived anonymity, and if (b) the journalist is not required by law to reveal the informant's identity. This latter might occur by reason of the general obligation of the citizen to appear as a witness in court, as stipulated in the Swedish Court Procedure Act, Chapter 36, Article 1.

The rules of cross-examination

If a journalist is called as a witness before a court he is technically required, if asked, to reveal a source or sources of information, as any other citizen would be, under the provisions of this Act. In general, however, this has presented no great problem for journalists because, under Swedish law, cross examination of witnesses can only be held before the courts in a definite case. Then, by the rules of court procedure, a question may not be put to a journalist regarding the identity of an informant unless the answer is, in the judgment of the court, of vital importance in determining the outcome of the case in which the journalist is being heard as a witness.

Beyond that, neither Parliament nor parliamentary committees can cross examine witnesses, nor are administrative authorities of the government entitled to do so. In effect, therefore, authorities of the government are prevented from investigating a journalist's sources.

With rules as clear and explicit, nearly the only matter ever to require interpretation has been the extent to which a journalist-witness may be obliged to testify without the constitutional limitation noted being overstepped. It is not always immediately evident whether provision of the answer to a question might remove the anonymity of the source, and whether to do so would be properly relevant in that particular instance.*

The rule in Chapter 3 of the Freedom of the Press Act of the Swedish Constitution, the basis for the journalist's pledge of secrecy as to a source of information, also extends the same prohibition to the printer, the publisher, and others concerned with the production of printed matter — in reality, to all those employed by a newspaper, including foreign correspondents. Infringement of that prohibition is a punishable offence.

Even though nothing is expressly stated on the matter within the Freedom of the Press Act, it is regarded as correct to assume that it would be incompatible with a public official's duty to try to persuade another person to commit a breach of that law. Accordingly, a civil ser-

---

* To illustrate, in a 1959 libel action, a judge had permitted one of the parties to put a question to a witness on who had given certain information to a newspaper. As it transpired that the question of who gave the relevant information to the press was of no importance to the case in which the witness was being heard and, as it happened that the witness was also the source of that information, the judge who had erred in this way was censured. (Justitieombudsmannens ämbetsberättelse 1959, pp. 75-92.)

vant, being a government official, is not entitled (a) to question a journalist about his sources of information since if the journalist answered, he — the journalist — would be guilty of breaking the law. If a civil servant, or government official, alternatively, should (b) try to mislead a journalist into disclosing a source, so breaking the law, however unintentionally, the civil servant would be acting improperly, and might be subject to penalty for breach of duty. Both cases (a) and (b) are treated equally.

Despite the protection afforded by the Freedom of the Press Act it must be made clear, however, that the journalist is not exempted from appearing as a witness in a court case, or expressing himself, or even being asked to reveal a source if, as noted, the court should regard the information as being of real importance in establishing justice in the case. In this respect, the journalist does not have the sort of clear exemption granted in Sweden, as in most other countries, to public officials, doctors, lawyers, clergymen, and some others. This special exemption is made legal for such persons in Sweden in the Court Procedure Act, Chapter 36, Article 5, as follows :

> An official or public servant or whoever is ordered or elected to carry out a public service or who holds another public appointment may not be heard as a witness about a matter in respect of which in view of his position he is required to observe silence.
>
> Nor may a lawyer, doctor, dentist, midwife or their assistants be heard on a matter which, on account of their position, has been confided to them or which in connection with their duties they have learnt unless it is permitted by law or unless the person in whose favour the pledge of secrecy applies, agrees thereto.
>
> A court official, legal adviser or defending counsel may not be heard as witness on what for the fulfilment of his assignment has been confided to him unless the party concerned agrees that it may be disclosed.
>
> Without prejudice to what is laid down in the second or third paragraphs persons other than the defending counsel are under obligation to give evidence in crime cases in which the most lenient penalty may not be less than two years penal servitude.

Special provisions are laid down regarding the obligation of a priest to observe secrecy, under the Ecclesiastical Law of 1686, to the effect that he may not disclose what he has heard in the course of performing his spiritual duties.

For journalists, as already noted, the right to hold as confidential the source of information extends to all those connected with a printing and publishing enterprise, and even extends to matter printed outside Sweden. By virtue of an amendment to the Constitution in 1957, moreover, the benefits of an assured anonymity also were extended to persons providing information to news agencies, with a corresponding pledge of secrecy for news agency personnel.

Limitation of the journalists' privilege

It must be repeated, however, that a journalist cannot legally refuse to indicate his sources if that actual demand should be made upon him as a witness in a court of any jurisdiction within Sweden, whether in a criminal or in a civil case. He would, as previously noted, have no such obligation with reference to Parliament or parliamentary committees or others, under Chapter 36, Article 6, of the Court Procedure Act, by including the police. As a witness in a court, however, a journalist is under the same obligation as any other person, beyond those enjoying the special exemption noted, to tell the court everything he knows that is of importance to the case. The only exception is that also available to others, under Chapter 36, Article 6 of the Court Procedure Act, by which a witness may refuse to say anything that would reveal that the witness or someone closely connected with him had committed a crime or a disgraceful act, and that would therefore be self-condemnatory. A witness also may refuse to make a statement that would reveal professional secrets, without a special reason for doing so, but journalists' sources are not regarded as belonging in this particular category of professional secrets.

Under Swedish Procedure Law, each court itself decides upon the limits of the obligation resting upon each witness. The court decides to what precise extent a question should be answered to provide information essential to the proper handling of the case being heard. Each court is expected to give careful attention to such delimitation with a view to preservation of professional secrets and to protection of anonymity of sources under the Constitution, so far as such revelation is *not vital* to a decision in the case. This latter provision is the journalist's basis for the preservation of professional secrets, and protection of sources.

Because of this established constitutional and procedural law, under which the right of journalists to keep professional secrets has been protected even without any more specific authority to keep silent as to sources, and with no cases presenting any sort of threat to that right or privilege, the issue has hardly been discussed in Sweden. Cases where a journalist is asked about his sources appear very rarely.

Press favours amendment

Journalistic organizations do, however, favour an amendment to Swedish legislation governing the obligations of witnesses so that a journalist may have a position similar to that of a lawyer or a doctor, and thus be freed of any requirement to give testimony about matters that have come to his knowledge in the course of his professional activities. The only exception would be in serious crime cases.

A written request for such a change in the law has been submitted to the Government, arguing that it is possible to imagine a case being brought before a court with the sole purpose of having a journalist called as a witness and forcing him to disclose his source of information in a certain matter, presumably. as a means of taking retribution on the informant. Actually, this never has happened. Nevertheless, the technical legal obligation to reveal a source, it is argued by the journalists, should be restricted in application to the most serious criminal cases only. So far, this proposal by the journalistic organizations has brought no official acknowledgment or action.

No special rules exist in Sweden with reference to radio news. Most such news, as now broadcast, is delivered to the radio by news agencies, which operate in accordance with the same regulations already described as applying to the press. The position of the news agency is not changed in that respect by reason of its provision of service to radio as well as to newspapers. For such material as may be collected exclusively for radio broadcast, usually by its own reporters, there are no legal rules relative to secrecy. It may be noted, however, that a Royal Commission began investigations in the autumn of 1960 concerning the legal responsibility of the radio.

Switzerland

In Switzerland, as in many countries, statements of a witness constitute one of the most important means of obtaining evidence in a legal proceeding. For that reason, the duty to give evidence is generally obligatory. Such few exceptions as are allowed relate to the protection of interests regarded as equal or superior in importance to the administration of justice. So an official of government has a recognized duty to observe reticence, and a judge is legally forbidden to interrogate doctors, lawyers, and clergymen to the point of requiring revelation of professional secrets.

Journalists, on the other hand, have no legal right to withhold evidence. In specified instances and circumstances, however, the court itself may be disposed to recognize a higher interest in the performance of a service by the press as, for example, in the discovery of abuses of the public interest. A journalist, if he should himself be accused of a punishable offence, would share with other persons the right to refuse to make a statement, protected by the legal provision that under "the principle of accusation, the accused person contributes to the investigation of the truth only in so far as that corresponds with his interests". The reasoning here is that "otherwise there would be an inquisition in the medieval sense or as under the penal law of dictatorship states".

Such a limited right accorded to the Press, or to editors responsible for the content of newspapers to withhold evidence where a "higher interest" is recognized applies, however, only in penal law—not in civil law—and is limited even then to withholding the name of the author (and not *ipso facto* the informant). It does not authorize withholding the substance of any such information as may be requested of a witness.

The legal provisions governing this procedure appear in the General Part of the Swiss Penal Law Statute Book (StGB, or *Schweizerischen Strafgesetzbuches*), in force since January 1, 1942, and specifically in Article 27 under marginal notes designated as "Responsibility of the Press". The article has binding force not only in federal courts but in the Swiss cantonal jurisdictions.

Under Article 64 bis of the Swiss Federal Constitution, the Federation (Federal Central State) is authorized to legislate in the sphere of penal law, but the organization of courts, of legal proceedings, and the administration of justice come within the competence of the Cantons, that is, the member States of the Federation. Political offences come within the exclusive competence of the Federal Law, as determined by the Law on Federal Penal Administration of Justice, the "Federal Penal Proceedings" (BStP, or *Bundesstrafprozess*), including provisions for interrogation of witnesses. Every juridical prosecution of such offences and crimes must be undertaken, however, only on the basis of a decision by the Federal Council, the National Government. The Federal Council, under Article 18, BStP, can authorize that "a Federal penal case, for which the Federal Penal Court is competent, be transferred to the cantonal authorities for investigation and adjudication". By the provisions of Article 247, BStP, the Cantons in effect apply the Federal Law, although the actual legal proceedings and the determination of sentence are governed by cantonal law.

Application of Article 27, StGB, is restricted exclusively to instances in which "a punishable offence has been committed *by means of the printing press* and the punishable offence ends with the production of the press". In other instances, where this restriction does not apply, interrogation of witnesses is governed by the *generally* valid provisions of common law, rather than the definition of Article 27 on the "responsibility of the press". In such cases, and depending upon the circumstances, the procedure may be determined either by the Federal Penal Law or by the cantonal penal provisions.

Cantonal and federal provisions

This optional procedure has importance because there are individual Cantons which commonly accord to the Press a right to withhold evidence on a par with that right as traditionally extended to members of the clergy, the bar, and the medical profession. As an example, the Canton of Berne, in its law, provides that:

> Editors of periodical press publications are not required to divulge the names of authors who submit articles which constitute the subject of penal investigation, if the authors in question do not release the editors from the duty of secrecy.

On the other hand, the Federal Penal Law does not recognize the Press as having any special privilege in the matter of withholding information beyond that derived from Article 27, StGB, relative to a possible recognition of a "higher interest" in the performance of a public service.

Article 27, in Paragraph 3, Inset 2, specifies that :

> The editor is not required to give the name of the author. Legal compulsion may not be used against the editor, nor against the printer and his staff, nor against the chief editor or publisher in order to discover the name of the author.

But subsequent paragraphs hedge this apparently clear right with such conditions as to make it very limited in its application. The right is valid, as already noted, only when "a punishable offence has been committed by means of the printing press and the punishable offence comes to an end in the production of the press." This makes little or no allowance, under the law, for the protection of sources.

The protection of sources, and of professional secrets in general, is—as also noted—a privilege limited to officials and to the traditional group. That is, Article 320, StGB, provides that officials "cannot be required to give evidence," and Article 321 specifies the same for the "clergy, barristers, defence counsel, notaries, auditors legally obligated to reticence, doctors, dentists, pharmacists, midwives and their professional assistants".

The sharp limitation placed upon the Press and its staff members under the Swiss Federal Penal Law is further illustrated by a requirement that an editor or publisher may be freed of legal compulsion to divulge the name of the author of an offending article *only* if the author of that article cannot be traced in Switzerland, cannot be brought into court, or if the article has been published without his knowledge or against his will. Even then, "the editor who is designated as responsible is punishable as the offender". In this way satisfaction is given to the procedural need to be able to trace the offender and bring him to justice. The editor becomes a substitute offender for the actual offender about whom he has maintained silence. As such, he is treated under penal law as the offender would have been treated.

This acceptance of an obligation, alternative to identifying or producing the author of an article or of information concerning which the courts seek knowledge in a penal case, has been made by the press, in legal consultation, a kind of *quid pro quo* under which editors have gained a right, limited as it is, to refuse to name an author or source.

Exceptions listed

Even this limited right does not extend, however, to provide justification under which the Press may refuse to give evidence as to the author in cases before the courts bearing upon high treason and treason against the country, support for foreign interests that are deemed contrary to the safety of Switzerland, forbidden information or "intelligence" services, tantamount to espionage; attacks on constitutional order, propaganda dangerous to the state, illegal association, or references endangering military security.

The provisions of Article 27, with the limited and limiting rights, apply, so far as editors are concerned, in instances where a witness is to be questioned by an interrogating judge, by a judge, or by administrative or police officials. Where the provisions of Article 27 and its qualifications do *not* apply, the general provisions of the common law on statements by witnesses do apply, as they are laid down in the law on Federal penal administration of justice under the Federal Penal Proceedings or in the cantonal penal procedure ordinances.

Thus, according to Article 79, BStP, the witness

> can refuse to answer questions which expose him to legal prosecution or to grave injury to his honour; the judge should not put such questions intentionally.

In some circumstances, when there must be adjudication of a refusal of a journalist-witness to give evidence, the provisions of Article 32, StGB, in the general penal code, may be invoked for the judge's consideration. This article says that:

> The action which a *professional sense of duty* commands... is no crime or offence.

In such instance a judge *might* recognize the assertion of a need to protect journalistic professional secrecy as being a proper extension of a "professional sense of duty" and so excuse the journalist from the obligation to answer a question.

As this implies, an interrogating judge, a court, or administrative or police officials in Switzerland may make the decision as to whether

a witness is to be regarded as in duty bound to give evidence or whether
he is entitled to refuse to make a statement.

In practice, where cases have arisen outside the scope of Article 27,
StGB, governing penal law procedure, the question emerging from the
refusal of a journalist to make a statement as a witness seldom has
intruded itself. This has been true either (a) because those empowered to
question the witness, in tacit acknowledgement of the known claim of
the Press concerning the need to protect professional secrets, declined
to put to him the kind of question that might bring a refusal, *or* (b)
because the authorities simply chose not to use such powers as they
possess—the right to fine or gaol a journalist refusing to make a statement—and so, by default, permitted the potential issue to fade away.

The only case of any moment in Switzerland, in recent times, hinging upon the issue of professional secrecy was the so-called Goldsmith
Case of 1957. It was a case that evoked a lively and even controversial
discussion in Switzerland and abroad alike.

The Goldsmith case

The case began on March 20, 1957, when Michael Goldsmith, a
British subject and Geneva correspondent for The Associated Press,
reported to that agency, and so to the world press and radio, that an
official in the Swiss Federal Public Prosecutor's office was suspected of
giving confidential information to a foreign embassy in Berne, the Swiss
capital. The official, already under surveillance, was thereby warned and
the success of the investigation was jeopardized. For that reason and
because it was suspected that a third party, interested in misleading the
Swiss investigators, may have given information to Mr. Goldsmith, the
AP correspondent was questioned by a special Federal examining magistrate. Mr. Goldsmith refused to make a statement as to the source of
his information, maintaining it to be a professional secret, whereupon
he was placed in the Berne district goal for 24 hours.

The examining magistrate based his action, legally indisputable, on
the provisions of Article 88, BStP. * The action was criticized in public

---

* Article 88 BStP states : "The judge can place under arrest, for not more
than 24 hours, the witness who, for no legal reason, refuses his testimony. If the
witness persists in his refusal, for no legal reason, the judge may inflict a disciplinary punishment: up to 300 francs fine or up to 10 days' imprisonment. The witness must pay the costs resulting from his refusal."

discussion, however, as being inappropriate, politically imprudent, and practically ineffectual since, as the magistrate might have foreseen, Mr. Goldsmith would continue to remain silent despite his "disciplinary arrest".

In fact, Mr. Goldsmith lodged a complaint with the Swiss Federal Appeals Court immediately after his release, protesting the action of the judge, and citing Article 27 StGB; Article 55 of the Swiss Constitution, guaranteeing freedom of the press and also Article 79 BStP, holding that a witness can refuse to make a statement if answering can expose him to grave injury to his honour. The Appeals Court rejected the complaint, however, on May 7, on the grounds that the crime of espionage was involved, and therefore Article 79 did not apply. Mr. Goldsmith thus became liable to serve an additional 10 days in jail or to pay a fine of up to $70 for contempt of court. In September 1957, by a ruling of the judge who originally sentenced Mr. Goldsmith to disciplinary arrest, the correspondent was fined 100 Swiss francs (about $ 25) for his refusal to reveal the source of his information, and also to pay about $70 in costs.

Federal Court sets views

The reasoning of the Chamber of Indictment of the Federal Court in its rejection of Mr. Goldsmith's complaint casts light on the Swiss attitude toward professional secrecy for journalists and the position of the press in relation to law, politics, and government. The relevant decision of the highest judicial body in Switzerland dates from May 7, 1957, and appears in the arguments published in the Federal Judicial Decisions *(Bundesgerichtlichen Entscheiden)*, Volume 83 (1957), Part IV, pages 59 ff. There it is contended :

> *a)* That because the questioning of Mr. Goldsmith as a witness is directly linked with the question as to whether Max Ulrich, Federal Police Inspector, an official in the Public Prosecutor's Office, and the person accused of having given confidential information to a foreign embassy in Berne, or another unnamed person, had been engaged in a provision of information in a forbidden manner, as specified in Article 27, StGB, and had thereby committed an offence *affecting the security of the State,* Mr. Goldsmith, in petitioning for

a redress of grievances, cites Article 27 in his own behalf without justification.

b) That Mr. Goldsmith's citation of Article 55 of the Federal Constitution establishing the principle of press freedom was equally unacceptable since a journalist's right to withold testimony as a witness in a penal procedure does not emerge from that principle. Even if it were assumed that the right of press freedom, assured through Article 55, included the protection of anonymity as an essential element for the fulfilment of the special tasks incumbent upon the press, the extent of that press freedom is defined and limited by the federal legislation as represented by Article 27, StGB. This definition is binding on the Federal Court under provisions of Article 113.3 in the Federal Constitution. Only thus is it to be decided whether and to what extent press freedom confers special rights on individuals. *

c) The Chamber of Indictment of the Federal Court rejected Mr. Goldsmith's complaint with reference to the action taken against him through citation of Article 79, BStP, specifying that a witness can refuse to make a statement if answering will expose him to *grave injury to honour,* in this case his professional honour as a journalist in the matter of protecting confidences. The decision of the Chamber on this point reads as follows :

"The petitioner's argument is not to be accepted in so far as he cites Article 79, BStP, in support of his application. This provision should prevent the duty to give evidence leading to compulsion to confess his own guilt or shame. That, however, does not mean that the witness can gain immunity from his duty to make a statement if through refusal to give evidence he breaks a freely given promise (to his source of information) and thereby incurs injury to his honour. Injury to honour must arise directly from the content of evidence and not merely from the fact of a statement being made, as would allegedly have been the case had the petitioner given evidence. The plea in the complaint based on citation of Article 79, BStP, does not therefore hold good."

d) The 24 hours' detention imposed by the investigating judge is not a punishment but a means of compulsion given to the judge against a refractory witness. Whether this measure is to be used is for the judge to decide after scrupulous con-

---

* This interpretation of the effect of rights of freedom in the Federal Constitution is, however, rejected as incorrect by certain jurists, including Prof. Z. Giacometti in his standard work on the Federal State Law *"Schweizerisches Bundesstaatsrecht,"* 1949.

sideration. The Chamber of Indictment has no grounds for intervention unless the detention order constitutes an excessive judgment. The Federal Court is not required to make a pronouncement, however, about that in the Goldsmith petition.

Swiss press reacts

The Central Committee of the Association of the Swiss Press *(Verein der Schweizer Presse)*, through a special fact-finding committee named to investigate the Goldsmith case, expressed the following view on the decision of the Chamber of Indictment toward Mr. Goldsmith's petition of complaint:

> According to Swiss and international understanding of the concept of Press Freedom and its inseparable basis of defence of journalistic secrecy, the interpretation of Article 79, BStP, by the Court of Indictment misses this point entirely.
> The constitutional and legislative foundations of legal practice, valid today, permit an understanding interpretation of the right to refuse to give evidence and the defence of free information from all sides, which are closely linked with freedom of the press.
> Keeping secret confidential information sources is to be respected.
> An extensive and understanding interpretation of legal issues which concern freedom of the press and of information is urged upon the competent juridical authorities.
> *De lege ferenda* efforts should be made for the realization of the right to refuse to give evidence in the Federal Case Law. Similarly, the Press urges the Cantons in their Press laws to anchor the right to refuse to give evidence in the sense of the information right of the Press.
> The right to refuse to give evidence accorded to the editor in Article 27, StGB, is to be extended to the journalist responsible as an author.

In connection with the Goldsmith case, furthermore, the President of the Swiss Jurists' Association *(Schweizerischer Juristenverein)*, Dr. F. T. Guhler-Corti, of Winterthur, a barrister, contributed a notable essay "On the Problem of the Right of Journalists to Refuse to Give Evidence." It formed part of a commemorative gift presented to Willy Bretscher, chief editor of the *Neue Zürcher Zeitung,* Zurich, on the occasion of his 60th birthday, in November 1957. Dr. Guhler-Corti, in his conclusion, made four points:

> The precedence of defence of the State over the right of organs of the Press to refuse to give evidence is undisputed and absolute.
>
> *De lege ferenda* it seems necessary that the right of refusing to give evidence accorded to the editor under Article 27, StGB, should be extended to the correspondent liable as author, although the author is not designated as responsible.
>
> A general right for journalists to refuse to give evidence, extending beyond the limitations of Article 27, StGB, analogous to professional secrecy for doctors, is to be rejected.
>
> On the other hand, the protection in penal law of editorial secrecy should be supplemented by precautionary measures in civil law.

Apart from the accounts of parliamentary discussion evaluating relevant legislation, there are no outstanding utterances by Swiss officials of government bearing upon the refusal of the Press to make statements with references to sources of information in the process of the questioning of witnesses. The Press view, however, was effectively presented in the Parliament in 1931 when the formulation of Article 27, StGB, was under discussion prior to its enactment in 1942. The spokesman was a member of Parliament and of the advisory commission acting on that legislation, Dr. O. Wettstein, a former chief editor, lecturer on press subjects at the University of Zurich, and legal adviser of the Association of the Swiss Press.

Association intercedes

Whenever disputable cases concerning journalistic professional secrecy occur, the Association of the Swiss Press, as the representative journalistic professional organization, gives its opinions publicly or in representations made to the authorities. From time to time, the Association intervenes in the evaluation of relevant legislative definitions, and generally with success.

In this context, also, a Joint Press-Political Commission of the Swiss Press presented an opinion on the preliminary draft for a Federal law on administrative proceedings and on administrative jurisdiction, with due consideration for the protection of the position of the press.*

There is no formulated code of ethics for professional practice of journalists in Switzerland. The General Work contract of 1957, concluded between the Association of the Swiss Press and the Swiss Newspaper Publishers' Association, for the German-speaking fraction of Switzerland only, but obligatory there for the members of both organizations, specifies in Article 18 that:

> The editor is required to exercise the utmost reticence with regard to all the circumstances of the newspaper. Deviations from this basic principle are permissible only in agreement with the publishers.

It is the unwritten law that the Swiss journalist also upholds the Declaration of Journalists, as drawn up by the International Federation of Journalists, meeting at Bordeaux in 1954. Point Number 6 of that Declaration reads:

> The journalist maintains professional secrecy and does not disclose the sources of confidential information.

Although Switzerland is not a member of the United Nations, Swiss journalists consider the United Nations draft for an international code of ethics for those persons associated with the press and the dissemination of information, as prepared in August 1952, as a principle that should be voluntarily observed. The last paragraph of Article III of that draft code recommends that professional secrecy be "invoked up to the extreme limits of the law."

The "limits of the law" in Switzerland are sharply defined, however, as the foregoing examination makes clear.

---

* This appears in Bulletin No. 399 (March 1958) of the Swiss Newspaper Publishers' Association.

United Kingdom

In England and the United Kingdom generally, there is no occupation or profession whose members are privileged by law to refuse to disclose the source of information they may possess, or the *contents* thereof, if such information is held by any court to be necessary or material to the proper conduct of litigation. A witness who refuses to answer questions properly put to him is subject to punishment for contempt of court through a fine, imprisonment, or both.

Professional secrecy, in other words, has no legal recognition. Not only has the journalist no such legal right, but neither has any other person. Contrary to popular belief, the right does not even extend to medical advisers and priests. So even disclosures in the confessional are not legally protected.* As a matter of practice, however, judges have in general been averse from permitting a breach of confidence unless considered indispensable as a means of arriving at full justice.

The claim to any legal right stands or falls, in the last analysis, only in a court of law. It is within the power of the courts to require any disclosure deemed necessary. The House of Lords, sitting as the highest tribunal, has given expression to the interpretation of the law as it might apply to the journalist. Although the opinion was returned with special reference to a case more specifically involving the law of libel, the view is deemed relevant to the issue of professional secrecy : **

> Their Lordships regret to find that there appeared on the one side in this case the time-worn fallacy that some kind of privilege attaches to the profession of the press as distinguished from the members of the public. The freedom of the journalist is an ordinary part of the freedom of the subject (that is, the

---

* See Wheeler v. Le Marchant 17 Ch. D. 675 at p. 681 ; Normanshaw v. Normanshaw and Measham, 69 L. T. 468 at p. 469, both cases relating to confidences given a priest. And see McTaggart v. McTaggart 1944, Probate, at p. 97, and C. v. C., 1946, 1 A.E.R. p. 562, relating to confidences given a physician.

** Arnold v. The King-Emperor of India (1914) 30 T.L.R., p. 462, 468.

citizen), and to whatever lengths the subject in general may go, so also may the journalist, but apart from the statute law, his privilege is no other and no higher. The responsibilities which attach to his power in the dissemination of printed matter may, and in the case of the conscientious journalist do, make him more careful; but the range of his assertions, his criticisms, or his comments, is as wide as, and no wider than, that of any other subject. No privilege attaches to his position.

In the courts, and as a matter of the general law of evidence, neither the journalist nor anyone else can be required to reply to a question if the answer may tend to incriminate him by exposing him to a criminal charge, or to a penalty or a forfeiture. Similarly, husbands and wives are privileged from disclosing communications made to one another during marriage. Lawyers and their clients are privileged from disclosing confidential communications made for the purpose of obtaining legal advice, but not if the communications are made for the purpose of committing a crime, or if they are part of a criminal or unlawful proceeding. Public officials are privileged from disclosing facts or documents, the knowledge of which they declare to be potentially injurious to the public welfare. Public officials and police officers alike are privileged from disclosing the source of their information. Witnesses for the Crown in public prosecutions are privileged from disclosing the channel through which they have communicated information.

These are exceptions to the otherwise general denial of any legal right to professional secrecy. It will be observed, however, that they are exceptions chiefly operative in the criminal courts, rather than in the civil courts, and that their primary purpose is to contribute toward assuring full and fair justice. They are in conformity with the dictum, frequently quoted in England, that justice should not only be done, but should also be seen to be done. This same dictum explains the reluctance to recognize any secrecy whatever, where court action is involved, unless it be in the very pursuit of justice itself, as in the special circumstances just noted. Questions of privilege arising during the hearing of an action in an English court are determined by the court itself in application of the law of evidence.

Since there is no legal right of secrecy for journalists, it is not surprising that there is, in the United Kingdom, an almost complete lack of decided case law touching on the matter.

The Bahama Islands case

One case may be mentioned, however, because of the light it throws on the operation of contempt of court in relation to non-disclosure of information. Its application to the matter of professional secrecy is indirect and negative, rather than positive; it is a case that arose as long ago as 1893, and in the Bahama Islands, rather than in the United Kingdom itself. It is pertinent, nonetheless, because it demonstrates the principles of English law.

Contempt of court as relating to non-disclosure of information may most commonly be committed by a witness in an action before the court. But there is another form of contempt of court wherein it is not necessary for the court to be sitting, and which is constituted by a libel upon a judge, holding him up to contempt and ridicule, so that the law, of which he is the representative, is lowered in the public esteem. This form of contempt is a matter of publicity rather than of secrecy, and therefore would not normally call for consideration in a study of professional secrecy. It happened, however, that in the particular case arising in the Bahama Islands the two forms of contempt became curiously intertwined in a matter ultimately referred to the Judicial Committee of the Privy Council, in London, for a report to the Queen. *

The facts were these: An anonymous letter published in the *Nassau Guardian* contained criticism of the conduct of the Chief Justice of the Bahama Islands. The criticism was of such a nature that it might have been made the subject of proceedings for libel. This, however, did not occur. The editor of the *Nassau Guardian,* who also was proprietor and publisher of that newspaper, was nevertheless requested to attend on the Chief Justice in his Chambers. Upon doing so, he was further requested to reveal the name of the writer of the letter published, and to hand over the original of that letter. He refused to do so. As a consequence he was summoned to appear in the court, by action of the Chief Justice. There he was sentenced to imprisonment for publication of the letter, held to be in contempt of court and of the judge's official position, and was fined. He also was sentenced to pay an additional fine for his refusal to reveal the name of the writer of the letter or, alternatively, to be imprisoned. Upon his continued refusal, the editor was in fact imprisoned.

* In the Matter of a Special Reference from the Bahama Islands (1893) A. C. p. 138.

Thereupon, a deputation of Nassau residents waited upon the Governor of the Colony to urge his release. The Governor communicated at once with the Secretary of State for the Colonies in London, asking if he, the Governor, had the authority to take action in the matter. The reply from London was that he did have such power. The Governor promptly ordered the editor to be released. There the matter virtually ended, having occupied some two days of time.

In the later reference of the incident to the Judicial Committee of the Privy Council by the Secretary of State for the Colonies the Committee was asked to answer the questions: "Was the editor guilty of contempt of court in respect (a) of the publication of the letter signed 'Colonist' in the *Nassau Guardian*; (b) of his refusal to give up the name of the writer, or hand over the manuscript, of the letter?" After hearing counsel both for the Secretary of State and for the Chief Justice, the Judicial Committee stated :

> (a) that the letter, even though it might have been made the subject of proceedings for libel was not in the circumstances calculated to obstruct or interfere with the course of justice or the due administration of the law, and therefore did not constitute a contempt of court.
> (b) that the editor was not guilty of contempt of court in respect of his refusal to give up the name of the writer or to hand over the manuscript of the letter, there being no authority in point of law to require him to do either.

In so reporting to the Queen, the Judicial Committee of the Privy Council did not enlarge upon the second part of this statement—this being the part most directly related to the issue of professional secrecy. Some question might arise from the statement as to whether it could be interpreted as an admission of at least a limited legal right to professional secrecy for a professional journalist. In the view of one competent authority, the statement is *not* to be regarded as subject to any such interpretation. A prominent London barrister responding to an IPI inquiry, reasons that :

> The editor of the *Nassau Guardian* was not at any stage in court as a witness whose evidence was necessary or material to the proceedings being taken. Had proceedings for libel been brought, as indeed the Judicial Committee pointed out might have been done, and the editor had been called as a witness in

those or similar proceedings, the position might have been different. For then, if either the identity of the writer of the published letter, or the manuscript of it, had been held to be necessary and material evidence, the editor would have been compellable to produce them. As it was, he was in the position of an accused person, not of a witness for or against. All the evidence of the contempt sought to be established against him was available to the court in the form of the newspaper in which the letter was published—and was not and could not be disputed. For the purposes of the proceedings as they were brought, neither the identity of the writer of the letter nor the manuscript of it was material or necessary evidence. In sum, what might appear at first sight to establish, in the report of the Judicial Committee, some special principle of protection for the journalist, in fact does no more than delimit what are the duties and rights of the ordinary citizen (to whom the journalist must be assimilated) in such circumstances.

Through the Lord Chancellor and the Lords of Appeal in Ordinary, the House of Lords, apart from its legislative activities, constitutes the final court of appeal in the administration of justice within the nation. Largely through the same persons, it further ensures the judicial adornment, in large measure, of the Judicial Committee of the Queen's Privy Council, which (although its scope is now less extensive) continues to hear appeals from some overseas territories. But the House of Lords itself may act directly as a court of law in respect of offences against its own privileges.

The power of the courts to rule upon any issue of professional secrecy has been noted. No similar general power is enjoyed by the legislature or the administration. But there are exceptions. If, for example, the House of Lords holds power as a final court of appeal, and also functions as a court of law in respect to offence against *its own* privileges, the House of Commons likewise may act in the same fashion with respect to offences against *its* privileges, and it does so more often than the House of Lords. It may proceed against any person by summoning him to appear if "obstruction of the work of the House" appears to have been his responsibility. This is a phrase serving to cover a considerable variety of offences against Parliamentary privilege. If the person summoned is found guilty, he may be punished for contempt. So far as a journalist is concerned, actual publication of objectionable matter is deemed "obstructive", and production of the published material, with evidence that the journalist was in fact responsible for its preparation, is sufficient to constitute guilt and warrant punishment. It is not necessary to delve deeper into the matter to determine sources to which the journalist may have turned to obtain his information. Thus the legal issue of professional secrecy, in its most literal meaning, does not arise, and no cases exist.

In somewhat the same fashion, a special Tribunal of Inquiry may be set up following a resolution of both Houses of Parliament. Although not a court of law, it may "have all such powers, rights and privileges as are vested in the High Court, or in Scotland (in) the Court of Session, or (in) a judge of either such court" provided the Queen or a Secretary of State, appointing the Tribunal, specifically so directs, within the provisions of the Tribunals of Inquiry (Evidence) Act of 1921.

A Tribunal of Inquiry, in such circumstances, may summon witnesses, examine them under oath, require the production of documents or other relevant material, demand answers to any questions, and punish any refusals to abide by these requirements as contempt.

The Bank Rate leak

Such Tribunals of Inquiry are not frequently appointed, and never have had occasion to act directly on a matter involving the issue of professional secrecy for journalists. In 1958, however, a Tribunal inquired into allegations of improper disclosure of information relating to a proposed increase in the Bank Rate in December 1957, with suggestions heard that use may have been made of the advance disclosure to produce private gain. In this instance eight journalists from five British newspapers were among persons summoned before the Tribunal and asked to reveal their sources of information. Three of the journalists protested this demand; five did not, and one was compelled to reveal the name of a director of the Bank of England with whom he had been lunching, although it was demonstrated that no relevant information had been divulged on that occasion.

Iain Colquhoun, deputy editor of the London *News Chronicle,* took the view that any journalist faced with a demand to reveal a source, must make his own decision as to whether to answer or not to do so. Mr. Colquhoun wrote (IPI Report, Vol. 6, No. 11) that:

To those journalists who protested, Sir Hubert Parker, chairman of the Tribunal, expressed his sympathy for the situation in which they found themselves, but explained to them that it was his duty to direct them to answer any questions as to the sources of their information. Behind that direction lay the full force of Law in England. It would not have been possible for the Tribunal itself to commit on grounds of contempt any journalist who refused to reveal his sources of information. The Tribunal had power, however, to refer to the Lord Chief Justice any case where, in the Tribunal's opinion, information was being improperly withheld. It would have been bound to exercise that power and, in the event of a journalist continuing to refuse to reveal his sources, a conviction for contempt of court would almost inevitably have followed.

It was a matter of relief, therefore, to the British press and to the individual journalists when the Tribunal reported early in 1958 that no such referral to the Lord Chief Justice was to be made. The Tribunal asserted that:

> All the Press representatives who were seen by the Chancellor of the Exchequer gave evidence before us. We are satisfied that, although the Chancellor discussed with them in confidence the restrictive financial measures, he did not at any time discuss with, disclose or give them, either directly or indirectly, any information whatsoever about the proposed increase in the Bank Rate. It therefore follows that in respect of these persons there is no justification of any allegation of any disclosure to them or by them of any increase in the Bank Rate. We are also satisfied that no unauthorized disclosure was made by any of these persons of the information as to the restrictive financial measures given to them as representatives of their newspapers, and that no use was made of the information for the purpose of private gain.

Out of this episode, referred to at the time as "The Bank Rate leak," Mr. Colquhoun drew the deduction that the custom of advance briefing of journalists would continue, on a confidential basis, just as before, and that it *should* continue because it was a means to assure that accounts would be better prepared and more accurate than if written hastily following a last-minute report from the same source, or from some less authoritative source.

More controversial in a professional sense, was Mr. Colquhoun's conclusion that it was not necessarily correct for a journalist to refuse to reveal his source or sources of information upon proper demand by a court or, in fact, a Tribunal of Inquiry. In the case of the Parker Tribunal, he said, one of the objects was "to clear the names of persons about whom allegations had been made—or were thought to have been made— in Parliament".

> To that very proper end it was essential that the whole truth should be known about all the circumstances surrounding the rumours of a Bank Rate leak. If it was judged necessary by the Tribunal that these circumstances should include the names of informants of journalists, then in justice to those who had been maligned these names should be given. For what it is worth, I am practically certain that all the journalists concerned, foreseeing that they might be compelled to reveal sources, had approached their informants in advance and explained the situation to them...
>
> It is very widely accepted that so far as the press is concerned a journalist should protect his sources. The reasons why he does so and the value of the information that he may get because he does so are respected. Journalists have rarely been called on to reveal their sources. All of us who work for the press understand that no judge would ever lightly expect us to break a confidence. We know this from long experience and the sympathy which Lord Justice Parker expressed with the journalists who appeared before him bears out our experience.
>
> Many journalists, too, accept the view that the freedom of the press is a derived freedom. It is not to be claimed and defended as an end in itself, but as an essential pre-requisite to a much more important end—the freedom of the individual. Many of us accept that an even more important pre-requisite of individual freedom is embodied in the primacy of the rule of law—in the knowledge that the State itself cannot act in an arbitrary way toward the private citizen. If, upon a very rare occasion, the freedom of the press and the rule of law appear to conflict, then many of us—even among journalists—would declare our allegiance to the rule of law.

No privilege for the journalist

Because this general attitude is established in the minds of the British people, the position of the journalist in the United Kingdom under the common law differs in no way from the position of any other person. There is no legal problem relating to professional secrecy for journalists because there is no such principle as professional secrecy known to the law. Whether the common law could or would bring about an evolutionary change in this matter, as in some others, seems doubtful to British journalists and students of law alike. Legislation relating to the matter has not been proposed.

As for statute law, again the journalist is in virtually the same position as anybody else. Only in a few minor matters do exceptions exist. And these few, it will be noted, are designed to make it possible for the press to perform its function as a public information medium with greater effectiveness.

1. Representatives of the press, under the provisions of the Local Authorities (Admission of the Press to Meetings) Act, 1908, must be admitted to the meetings (other than certain committee meetings) of every Local Authority and every Regional Hospital Board, except when expressly and temporarily excluded.
2. Representatives of a newspaper or news agency, under provisions of the Children and Young Persons Act, 1933, have a right to remain in a court which has been otherwise cleared, while a child or young person is giving evidence in any proceedings in relation to an offence against, or conduct contrary to, decency or morality. Press representatives also have a right to be present at any sitting of a juvenile court constituted under that Act.
3. Special legal rights of the press exist relative to the law of libel, with certain statutory defences available to newspapers.

Circumstances being as they are, it is doubtful if professional secrecy for journalists is given any thought by the public as an issue of importance in the United Kingdom. Among journalists themselves the view is expressed that a legal right to secrecy would be of assistance in exposing some matters of public concern, but it is recognized, even so, that journalistic intervention is by no means the only way in which such a matter might be brought to public attention.

Journalistic standards in the United Kingdom are high, on the whole, but are established through example and precept without the existence of any formal code of ethics or court of honour. It is true that, pursuant to a recommendation by the Royal Commission on the Press in 1949, there was established in 1953 a Press Council to which complaints may be submitted for investigation regarding alleged press invasion of privacy, factual misrepresentation, or other conduct deemed objectionable on the part of newspapers or persons employed by newspapers. But the Press Council was set up by the newspaper industry itself, and is not a statutory body brought into being by legislation. Its creation was a positive acceptance of a view that certain ethical questions are of concern to the press as a whole. The ethical aspect of a right to professional secrecy, however, is quite a different thing from the legal aspect of any such right, and is beyond the scope of this inquiry.

United States of America

In the United States, the right of a journalist to refuse to reveal the source of information, as published, has not been recognized in the common law.

Such recognition of a journalist's right to professional secrecy can, however, be established through the enactment of appropriate legislation by individual states or by the national Congress. Attempts have been made to pass such a law in most of the fifty states, and have been successful in 12 states.* Bills to protect the journalist's right to preserve secrecy as to sources have been introduced in the Congress of the United States at least a dozen times, but no such Bill ever has been reported out of the committee to which it has been referred for consideration.

In those states where no specific legislation provides protection, and in the District of Columbia — that is, Washington, the capital — journalists are subject to penalty for refusal to respond to questions in a court of any jurisdiction, in a legislative body, or a committee of a legislative body, including committees of the Congress of the United States ; or in a legally constituted administrative body or committee. The penalties are fines or periods of imprisonment on charges of contempt, or both.

The right of press freedom, as specified in the First amendment to the U. S. Constitution (1791) and reiterated in the various state constitutions, is subject to judicial interpretation in specific cases, but never has been interpreted to embrace professional secrecy, even though it has been invoked, on some occasions. The Fifth and Fourteenth amendments, by interpretation, have tended to give support to the First amendment in protecting the freedom of the press. The Fifth amend-

---

* States now having statutes protecting the right of the journalist to professional secrecy within the boundaries of the state itself are Alabama, Arizona, Arkansas, California, Indiana, Kentucky, Maryland, Michigan, Montana, New Jersey, Ohio and Pennsylvania. In addition, juridical rulings in Utah and Oklahoma provide effective protection.

ment, declaring that no person "shall be compelled in any criminal case to be a witness against himself," may have technical application, again by interpretation, to a journalist seeking to protect a source of information. As with similar provisions in the law of other countries, however, the occasion on which the journalist is himself a defendant, and therefore entitled to invoke this law, is rare indeed. The Fourteenth amendment relates to the abridgement of the rights of citizens by the individual states.

The U. S. Supreme Court has ruled that Congress has the right to issue a contempt citation against a person who may wilfully refuse to produce information requested in the course of an inquiry, provided the subject matter of the inquiry is one on which either house of the Congress has jurisdiction. In certain instances, the same right may be claimed by a semi-judicial body, such as the Securities and Exchange Commission, or even by state public utility commissions, tax commissions, and others which have the power to subpoena witnesses. Since these latter bodies have no authority to do so based on common law, however, it may be necessary for them to apply to the courts for an order directing a person who has refused to answer a commission's subpoena to appear for examination. If such an order is granted, a reluctant witness may then be cited for contempt.*

Privilege of established professions

The privilege of members of the established professions to refuse to divulge information is less generally recognized as an absolute right in the United States than in some other countries. It finds no authority in federal legislation ; it is not recognized in common law, although it is supported in the statutes of individual states. The privilege of non-disclosure of information most widely recognized in practice in that area grows out of the relationship between a lawyer and his client. In all jurisdictions of the United States an attorney can refuse to divulge information provided to him in his professional capacity by a client. The contention is that this privilege is necessary to provide complete freedom for the client in consulting his legal adviser.

* Frank Thayer. *Legal Control of the Press,* 2nd ed. (Brooklyn : The Foundation Press, 1950), pp. 458-460.

The privilege of members of the medical profession to refuse to divulge information provided them by patients is less well established. The State of New York was the first to pass a statute granting such a privilege to the medical profession in 1828, and most other states recognize that privilege in practice, if not by statute. Recognition has been modified, however, in recent time in accordance with provisions of industrial accident laws that demand the appearance of physicians in court, and similar modifications are sometimes required by statutes on sanitation and as bearing particularly upon the control of venereal disease. In any event, it is contended that the communication between physicians and their patients seldom finds the patient concerned with preservation of confidence.

The privilege growing out of the relationship between a priest or clergyman and a parishoner is sanctioned by statute in 21 states. In others, the common law of England applies, and that law holds that no such privilege exists.* Both courts and legislatures have been reluctant to put the issue to a test, however, by demanding information from a clergyman of any faith. If such a test arose, moreover, it is considered probable that most clergymen would refuse to answer, despite the possible penalty that might follow.

No privilege exists in the United States by which pharmacists, midwives, nurses, notaries, and others sometimes specifically exempted by the laws of other countries may remain silent. Nor do journalists have any such exemption except in the 12 states that have statutes so specifying. In those states, however, there is no condition attached even to limit the exemption in cases that might involve serious crimes or threats to security. Nor is there any condition attached, as in some countries, limiting the right of exemption in such states to journalists bearing any particular title, such as "editor". The protection of the statutes may be invoked by any journalist employed full time or, presumably, part time, by a "newspaper". In one state, where such a statute exists, Pennsylvania, the specification is that it is to be "a newspaper issued daily, or not

---

* A privilege of secrecy attaching to confessions was recognized in English common law courts before the Reformation. During the reign of James I, however, a Jesuit priest refused to answer a question asked in court, saying that he was "bound to keep the secret of the confession." Thereupon he was asked whether, if one confessed to him today that tomorrow morning he meant to kill the King with a dagger he must conceal it. The Jesuit answered that he must do so. The subsequent ruling of the judge was that no such privilege existed. Such is the common law in the United States at present.

less than once a week, intended for general distribution or circulation, and sold at fixed prices per copy per week, per month, or per annum to subscribers and readers without regard to business, trade, profession or class". In only three states — Indiana, Montana, and Pennsylvania — does the statutory provision make specific mention of journalists employed by news agencies. Maryland extends the protection to those employed by a "journal", which might be interpreted to mean a periodical of any sort, but no other state recognizes journalists attached to periodicals by any specific mention. Nor are journalists associated with the radio or television medium mentioned in any state statutes as specifically entitled to protection, except in Maryland, where radio journalists were recognized by an amendment in 1939, and in Alabama and California, where the right was extended to radio and television newsmen in 1949 and 1961, respectively.

There had been cases in the U. S. courts at least as early as 1874 involving professional secrecy, but no "right" was recognized until 1896. The first statutory recognition was granted by Maryland in that year, but not until 1933 did New Jersey become the second state to pass such a law, with the others following between then and 1949. John Henry Wigmore, jurist and professor of law still recognized as the great authority on evidence, found no merit in the Maryland law when it was passed. He called it "as detestable in substance as it is crude in form", and predicted that it "will probably remain unique". The general principle governing the administration of justice in the United States, as elsewhere, has been that judicial and legislative bodies have a right to obtain and demand complete information. Thus there has been a reluctance, in some cases, even in states where statutes exist, to protect journalists in the matter of professional secrecy, to exempt newsmen from an obligation to respond to questions.

Dean Wigmore had contended that four fundamental conditions are necessary to justify "the establishment of a privilege against the disclosure of communications between persons standing in a given relation". These he listed * :

> 1) The communication must originate in a confidence that it will not be disclosed.

* John Wigmore, *"Evidence in Trials at Common Law,"* 3rd ed. (Little Brown & Co., New York), p. 531.

2) This element of confidence must be essential to the full and satisfactory maintenance of the relation between the parties.

3) The relation must be one which in the opinion of the community ought to be sedulously fostered.

4) The injury that would injure the relation by the disclosure of the communication must be greater than the benefit thereby gained for the correct disposal of litigation.

Dr. Fredrick S. Siebert, trained in the law, author of books on legal aspects of journalism, and Director of the Division of Mass Communications, Michigan State University, analyzed Dean Wigmore's four "tests" in an address at an International Symposium on the Professional Secrecy of the Journalist, conducted at the University of Strasbourg, in France, during October 1958, under the auspices of the International Association for Mass Communications Research.

Siebert sets views

For the first "test", Dr. Siebert said, "there is no question that the relationship between an informant and a journalist is a confidential one, based on mutual trust and respect". For the second, "there is again no question that the journalist's relation with his source meets this test". The third test, he said, "is not so readily established, but nevertheless it can be proved by evidence at hand that the public is dependent on the journalist for its information, that this information should be full and complete, and that in many cases full and complete information cannot be obtained unless the source is protected. Under our western democratic system of government, ultimate decisions are made by the community. To make these decisions, the public should have all available information even if the source is sometimes withheld for his own protection".

The fourth test was examined at greater length by Dr. Siebert. "This test", he said, "assumes that the principal function of society is litigation and consequently the need to have all relevant information available in a court of law." As to this, Dr. Siebert went on to say that the test, as stated, "neglects two important activities : The decision-making on the part of legislatures and on the part of the public in general elections". He said :

> Granted that the function of litigation is an important one in our society, it is not the sole function. A court should have access to all relevant information in coming to a decision.
> But if the requirement that a journalist disclose the source of his information before a court would seriously interfere with his ability to acquire and disseminate information, then the right of the court to demand such disclosure should be carefully questioned.
> Which is more important ? That the journalist be able to protect his informant in order to acquire the information in the first place, or that the court know the name of the informant ?
> One additional point needs clarification. What the journalist is concealing is not information in the sense that a lawyer, a doctor, or a clergyman is privileged to conceal information. It is obvious that each of these three groups of professional men have access to information which on occasion would be extremely valuable evidence in a court of law. What the journalist is concealing is not information, but the source of information, the name or names of his informers. All the information which the journalist has gathered is available in published form. His main purpose is to publish this information and make it available to everyone, including the members of the legislature, the courts, and the public. All the journalist is attempting to do is to keep open the channels of his information by protecting those sources which fear reprisal.

Dr. Siebert pointed out, as others have done, that the service of journalism to the public sometimes rests in the provision of information bearing upon incompetence or corruption in government, and upon lawless activities inimical to the welfare of the community. The revelation of such information is a first step toward correction of the faults, and such information can be revealed only through persons in a position to know about them. Dr. Siebert, in his Strasbourg address, said that :

> It has been argued that no source or informant need fear reprisal if his information is accurate and complete. This is a naive and specious argument. No police force in the world can guarantee complete protection from organized criminal elements.
> (Nor, he might have added, is any public official or civil servant safe from reprisal if he reveals information likely to bring the record of his superior into question.)

The only method by which a journalist can protect his source is to keep it secret.

It should be pointed out that the occasions when a journalist is called upon to exercise this secrecy are extremely rare. In more than nine cases out of ten the journalist can and should mention the source of his information without harm to anyone. It is only in an unusual situation that the journalist would exercise his privilege to keep silent.

Despite the fact that Dean Wigmore did not, in fact, favour the extension of any right of professional secrecy to embrace the journalist, as evidenced by his comment on the Maryland legislation of 1896, Dr. Siebert's interpretation of his "four tests" was such as to suggest that they did, in fact, justify such a right for journalists, and such was his view.

Journalists advocate protection

Journalists themselves have been extremely active in the United States in asserting the right to professional secrecy. Although formal codes of professional ethics have been drafted and approved during the last half century by newspapers, news agencies, state press associations, by the American Society of Newspaper Editors and other groups, it has not been the practice in such codes to assert the right to professional secrecy, since to do so would have been juristically unrealistic. At the same time, journalists and their organizations have insisted upon the desirability of adhering to the practice of professional secrecy, and have advocated statutes to give legal protection to journalists in that respect.

Although legislative bodies, always including a number of lawyers, have generally opposed specific legislation to protect journalists in the matter of preserving silence as to their sources, in practice the courts and other official bodies almost always give tacit recognition to the views of journalists and rarely insist upon such revelation even in states where no statutes exist to provide legal recognition of any absolute right. In instances where this was not so, and a demand was made for the revelation of a source, journalists always, so far as can be ascertained, have refused to speak, and have preferred to accept fines and periods in prison on charges of contempt of court.

In one of the first cases revolving about the issue of protection of a source, an editor of the *New York Tribune* went to jail in 1874. (People ex rel. Phelps v. Fancher, 2 Hun. 226). Similar cases arose in Georgia in 1887, two in California in 1897, and others in the present century. The first state statute had been passed in Maryland in 1896, to be amended in 1939 to give specific protection to radio reporters as well as newspaper reporters. The second state statute passed, that in New Jersey in 1933, was the direct result of a case in which a journalist's right was brought into question, with a reporter for the *Jersey Journal,* of Jersey City, held guilty of contempt for refusing to divulge to a Grand Jury the name of a person who had informed him of the presentation of a false voucher before a Board of Village Trustees. In the next decade, nine other states passed similar statutes, and Michigan followed in 1949, as the twelfth.

The negative attitude of the legal profession itself toward what might then have seemed a trend was expressed in 1938 by a committee of the American Bar Association, which reported that * :

> Of recent years, there have appeared on the statute books of several legislatures certain novel privileges of secrecy. Their history has not been traced ; but they bear the marks of having been enacted at the instances of certain occupational organizations of semi-national scope. The demand for these privileges seems to have been due, in part to a pride in their organization and a desire to give it some mark of professional status, and in part to the invocation of a false analogy to the long-established privileges for certain professional communications.
>
> The analogies are not convincing (though this is not the place for a demonstration). Moreover, the tendency is an unwholesome one. Yet it threatens to spread not only to legislatures but to other occupations. The correct tendency would rather be to cut down the scope of the existing privileges, instead of to create any new ones. We recommend that the legislatures refuse to create any new privileges for secrecy of communications in any occupation ; and particularly we recommend against any further recognition of
> A) Privilege for information obtained by Accountants ;
> B) Privilege for information obtained by Social Workers ;
> C) Privilege for information obtained by Journalists.

* Cited in Appendix D, *The Law of Journalism,* Robert W. Jones, (Washington, 1949).

This opposition from the legal profession did not obstruct the amendment to the Maryland statute in 1939 to extend the privilege of confidence to radio reporters, nor did it prevent the passage of a protective statute in Michigan in 1949, or the subsequent extension of the Alabama and California laws to protect radio and television newsmen. Other efforts, however, did fail, including a strong effort to provide protection by statute to journalists in New York State.

The history of legislation on the privilege of secrecy for journalists, in its more typical form, may be demonstrated by a sequence of events in New York. In 1935 a reporter for the *New York American*, Martin Mooney, wrote a series of articles for his paper describing aspects of a so-called "policy racket" operated by gamblers and law violators in the state. Mr. Mooney was called before the Grand Jury and there asked who the gamblers were and where they were operating. He refused to tell, since members of the gambling organization had been among his informants and he asserted a journalist's obligation to keep confidences inviolate. He was fined $ 250 and sentenced to 30 days in jail. On appeal, the conviction was affirmed.

The New York State commission

Soon thereafter, bills were introduced into the legislature of the State of New York designed to give journalists a legal right to protect their sources, but failed to pass. A number of other instances arose during the next few years in which journalists refused, as Mooney had done, to reveal the sources of information published. In 1948 the New York State Assembly authorized the Law Revision Commission of the State of New York to make a thorough examination of the problem of privilege of secrecy for journalists. This Commission produced the most complete study of the subject ever made in the United States.* It reviewed the legislation and attempts at legislation up to that time, in all the states of the Union.

---

* "Report and Study Relating to Problems Involved in Conferring Upon Newspapermen a Privilege Which would Legally Protect Them from Divulging Sources of Information Given to Them." Legislative Document (1949) No. 56 (A). (Albany: Williams Press, 1949.)

The Commission making this study consisted primarily of persons with legal training, and the report reflected that background. The recommendation of the Commission was:

1) That an unconditional privilege should not, in the public interest, be granted to newsmen who refuse to divulge the sources of information on which news stories are based ;
2) That a privilege, with safeguards essential to the protection of the public interest, may safely be granted.

The Commission indicated what it considered "proper safeguards". A Bill was presented that would have granted a journalist the right to refuse to name his source, *with the proviso* that :

> In any case where a reporter claims the privilege conferred by this section, the body, officer, person, or party seeking the information may apply to the Supreme Court for an order divesting the reporter of the privilege.

This meant the Commission recommended that if the general principle of secrecy were to be recognized, thus provisionally, the State Supreme Court would decide, finally, whether the journalist should be forced to answer.

These proposals, which as yet had no legal force, were thoroughly debated by newspaper and journalistic associations in the State of New York. It was their consensus that the proposed law would not provide the desired protection for journalists. The journalists concluded that they were better off without any law than they would be with what they regarded as half a law. The proposed legislation was not passed, partly as a consequence of the dissatisfaction of the journalistic groups with its nature, nor has any been passed in New York State since.

Marie Torre gaoled

The intervening years have brought occasional situations wherein New York State journalists, among others, again have refused to divulge sources of information. In only one instance, however, has a journalist been penalized for refusing to answer. This was the so-called Marie

Torre case, in which a special columnist for the *New York Herald Tribune* refused to reveal the source of information quoted with reference to Judy Garland, singer, who had brought a suit for libel against the Columbia Broadcasting System, Inc. Mrs. Torre was held guilty of contempt of court in November 1957. After appeals in which both the Court of Appeals and the New York Supreme Court upheld the lower court, she served 10 days in gaol.

A case somewhat comparable to that of Mrs. Torre arose in October 1960 when Mrs. Vi Murphy, a reporter for the *Colorado Springs Gazette Telegraph,* of Colorado, refused to reveal the source of information used in a news report regarding a petition filed with the Colorado State Supreme Court by a Colorado Springs attorney in which a former State Supreme Court justice was charged with taking a bribe to influence a decision in the court. She was held in contempt of court for her refusal, and the State Supreme Court imposed a 30-day gaol sentence. The United States Supreme Court declined to review the case, and Mrs. Murphy entered the Denver county jail on April 3, 1961 to serve her sentence.

A third case bearing a relation to the Torre decision arose in Hawaii in 1959. There Alan Goodfader, a reporter for the *Honolulu Advertiser,* was subpoenaed as a witness in a case wherein Mrs. Nesta M. Gallas, a former Honolulu city personnel director, had brought suit charging unlawful dismissal. Mrs. Gallas asserted that Mr. Goodfader had advance information that she would be discharged by the city's Civil Service Commission. In court, Goodfader refused to reveal his source of information and was held in contempt. The judge approved an appeal by Goodfader to the Hawaii Supreme Court, however, meanwhile postponing any fine or gaol sentence. In November 1961 the higher court, in a 4-1 decision, upheld the lower court, ruling that constitutional freedom of the press does not give a reporter the right to conceal news sources in legal matters. The one dissent, by Associate Justice Jack Mizuha, expressed the view that forced disclosure of a news source did violate freedom of the press and resulted in indirect censorship. The *Honolulu Advertiser* was considering appealing the case to the United States Supreme Court.

The problem of drafting acceptable legislation to provide for protection of journalists not only encounters legal opposition, but is far more complex than it was in 1896, when the Maryland statute was passed, or even in the decade of the "thirties". Since that time, there has been a vast increase in the number of state and federal governmental agencies possessing the right to examine witnesses. These bodies are primarily administrative in character, rather than judicial or legislative, and delve into practically all facets of public and private affairs. The problem has been complicated, also, by the growth and development of new and powerful media of communication, with magazine, radio and television reporters and correspondents added to the newspaper reporting group, which is, in effect, the only one recognized in existing legislation, aside from the Maryland, Alabama and California amendments recognizing radio reporters.

The journalistic groups, nevertheless, continue to insist upon their effective right to protect sources of information. Among such groups, Sigma Delta Chi, national professional organization of journalists, has tended to take a lead in recent years in urging the right of professional secrecy.

Reporter protects his source

The value of such a right, both to the journalist and to society, was demonstrated in 1956 in Illinois, a state without any statutory protection for journalists. George Thiem a reporter for the *Chicago Daily News* at the state capital, Springfield, became suspicious that the State Auditor, Orville E. Hodge, was living beyond the income he received from the state. Investigation produced no concrete evidence to suggest irregularity in the handling of state funds, however, until a young woman clerk in one of the state offices directed the reporter to certain records, with the understanding that he would not reveal her name. On the basis of the records, analyzed and checked, the State Auditor was brought into court, indicted for misappropriation of $ 650,000, or more, and was sent to the state penitentiary.*

The evidence of the auditor's guilt might never have been established

* See also Robert Lasch. "Crusading Journalism a Luxury, But —." *IPI Report*, 5 : 5 (September 1956), pp. 1-2.

unless the reporter had agreed to protect the name of the clerk who directed him to the proper place. The litigation leading to conviction was in no way impeded by the non-disclosure of the clerk's name, and the welfare of the people of the state was benefitted. While the courts did not question the reporter as to his informant's identity, in this case, he undoubtedly would have refused to give her name if he had been asked.

The kind of publicity made possible, in the public interest, by journalistic presentation of facts, as in the Hodge case, has been demonstrated on many occasions in the United States. Yet other situations that should be made known to the public may never be brought to light if individuals who know the facts are afraid to talk lest they be, as it were, betrayed. The possibility of unwelcome or injurious personal publicity can deter them from speaking out. If they can reveal their information to a reputable journalist, however, with assurance that he will respect their confidence and — the more so if the journalist is legally entitled to preserve an informant's anonymity — more situations can be made known and corrected.

This particular aspect of the matter of professional secrecy, although emphasized by journalists, has not as yet carried sufficient weight with courts or legislative groups, as noted, to persuade them to give a legal status to the concept of professional secrecy for journalists in the United States, except in the limited sense described. Since the United States is a federal republic, the privilege of any such secrecy, if it is to be made effective nationally, must be recognized by 50 different legislative bodies, or by an Act of Congress. It is true that 12 states already have approved such legislation in one form or another. But the fact remains that in 38 states journalists have no sure protection.

Even recognizing the consideration given by the courts and other bodies, in practice, to the journalist's ethical position in observance of professional secrecy, members of the legal profession generally are opposed to converting this tacit recognition into a legal right, such as they themselves possess. They also are disinclined to accept the public service function of the press and other communications media as a basis for the extension of such a right. Journalists themselves do not always stand firm on that right, as they did not stand firm, as a body, in the Marie Torre case. The technical problems are greater than they were, as noted, and these add to the difficulties of establishing a general legal right to professional secrecy in the United States.

A possible model statute such as might protect journalists against being compelled to testify to the source of information was presented by Dr. Siebert at the Strasbourg meeting previously mentioned. It read :

> A publisher, editor, reporter, or other person employed by a newspaper, magazine, radio or television broadcasting station shall not be adjudged in contempt of court, legislature, or any administrative body for refusing to disclose the source of any information procured for publication or broadcast.

Brief, and embracing possibilities that now exist in the media communication field, this proposed statute also employs concepts already fairly well defined by law, and covers contingencies that might arise in connection with the publication of information.

Dr. Siebert himself concluded his remarks at Strasbourg by saying that :

> It is the duty of all professional organizations in the field of journalism to agitate for the enactment of proper legislation to protect the journalist from compulsion to reveal his sources. It is my considered opinion that in the long run society will be more satisfactorily served if the various media of public information are privileged to determine when a source should be withheld and when a source should be revealed. Granted that the instruments of government should have access to all relevant information in the majority of cases, the relationship between the journalist and his sources is of such importance to our society that it should be protected by law.

This unquestionably reflects the view of many thoughtful journalists in the United States.

United Nations

The question of professional secrecy cannot be said to arise in any direct way with reference to the activities of newsmen reporting the affairs of the United Nations organization or of its various committees and specialized agencies. The reason is obvious, since the United Nations exercises no judicial functions.

At the same time, the UN itself, and the United Nations Educational, Scientific and Cultural Organization (UNESCO), as a specialized agency, both have been concerned from the outset with the flow of information throughout the world, and specifically with the issue of freedom of information. Numerous special studies have been made through the United Nations Secretariat, and that of UNESCO, bearing upon relevant subjects.

One of those studies concerned "Means of protecting sources of information of news personnel," was prepared for the fifth session (1952) of the United Nations Economic and Social Council's Sub-Commission on Freedom of Information and of the Press (E/CN.4/Sub.1/146). This study was made in the belief that the Sub-Commission "might wish to consider the protection of sources of information as constituting a fundamental aspect of the problem of the independence of news personnel," which was a general problem on the Sub-Commission's programme of work and priorities.

The Sub-Commission did, in fact, draft and approve the text of an International Code of Ethics at that meeting in 1952. It was based upon an earlier draft prepared at the fourth session of the Sub-Commission, the previous year, and revised in the light of comments and suggestions received in the intervening months from national and international professional associations of journalists and from information enterprises.

Article III of that 1952 draft code said in part:

> Discretion should be observed concerning sources of information. Professional secrecy should be observed in matters revealed in confidence; and this privilege may always be invoked to the furthest limits of the law.

This Code of Ethics, even though drafted in 1952, remains as it was then, since no action has occurred to make it in any way official. It also is to be noted that the last part of the section, asserting that the "privilege" — rather than "right" — might be invoked "to the furthest limits of the law" would mean that the Code, even if approved at the highest level in the United Nations, that is by the General Assembly, and even if then ratified by the necessary number of member countries, would still have no effectiveness, in a legal sense, by way of overriding the existing "limits of the law" in any country.

The Economic and Social Council of the United Nations, by resolution 522 A(XVII), in 1952 also requested the Secretary-General, in conjunction with the specialized agencies concerned, and in consultation with professional associations and information enterprises, to prepare a study of "means of protecting sources of information of news personnel," with that study to be submitted to the Council at its nineteenth session (1955). The Council requested member states of the United Nations to collaborate on the study. This was done, and the study appeared as Document E/2693, titled "The problem of protecting sources of information of news personnel," dated 23rd February 1955, with additions in March (Document E/2693/Add. 1 to 3). It formed part of Agenda Item 15 on Freedom of Information placed before the Economic and Social Council in 1955.

The Secretary-General's preliminary report of 1952, as prepared for the Sub-Commission, had presented the problem, with emphasis on the variations existing throughout the world in the degree of protection accorded journalists "in respect of the sources of their information". It described the relevant legislation, quoted from existing codes of ethics of professional associations, as those bore upon the subject; referred to discussions of professional secrecy at the second and fourth sessions of the Sub-Commission; and noted factors that might be taken into account, together with alternative courses of action. Information concerning national legislation and jurisprudence on the subject appeared in annexes.

The 1955 report submitted to the Economic and Social Council, although lacking any record of views expressed at the fifth (1952) session of the Sub-Commission, covered much of the same ground, and included reports not only from member states of the United Nations, but also from non-member states, so making it a world-wide study.

Since most of the substance of that report, excellent as it was, is covered in considerable detail—at least for certain countries—in the pages of this International Press Institute examination of the subject, there is no need here to repeat or recapitulate all that appeared in the United Nations document. It need only be said that no useful discussion of the subject took place within the United Nations organization in 1955, nor has it taken place since.

It might be added that brief reports appeared in the 1955 report to the Economic and Social Council relating to a number of countries and areas *not* dealt with in the present IPI study. But this need not be regarded as a serious omission here because a number of those were authoritarian countries where the concept of professional secrecy bears so little resemblance to that concept as understood in non-Communist areas as to have little significance in this report. References here presented also relate to countries where the issue of professional secrecy has special significance, with more current information and with citations of leading cases by way of illustrating the problem.

The excellent United Nations study nevertheless brought together a considerable body of factual information. It revealed, also, that most professional organizations of journalists appear to favour legal recognition of a right of professional secrecy, with 12 out of 20 such groups so recommending to the Secretary-General. In their professional view, where a right to protect sources of information exists, even by custom if not by statute, it has proved its value in producing information useful by way of protecting the public welfare. Such practice, the professional groups contend, has not appeared to obstruct the administration of justice or the conduct of public affairs. Most of the groups, even so, were prepared to accept some restrictions on an absolute right, but held firmly to the propriety of a general recognition of the desirability of professional secrecy. Governments, by contrast to professional associations, showed themselves far more generally favourable to unqualified restrictions, even though in practice many might extend a tacit recognition to newspapermen in their desire to preserve the anonymity of sources.

*   *   *

Other institutions and professional organizations, in addition to the United Nations, have concerned themselves with the problem of the journalist's professional secrecy.

Apart from the work of the International Press Institute in this field, it may be mentioned that the International Federation of Journalists has dealt with the problem. At its second congress in May, 1954, at Bordeaux, the Federation adopted an eight-point declaration on the duties of the journalist, the sixth of which read:

> He will observe professional secrecy regarding the source of information obtained in confidence.

After its foundation in 1958, the International Association for Mass Communications Research devoted its first colloquy to professional secrecy. It brought together in Strasbourg at the end of October 1958, at the International Centre for Higher Education in Journalism, some sixty newspapermen and lawyers who discussed the different aspects of the problem on a national and international level.

The views of the profession

An Inquiry by the IPI

A study of professional secrecy must necessarily include the views of journalists themselves on the protection of confidential sources.

Through the National Committees of the International Press Institute, some 250 copies of a questionnaire were distributed in 31 countries, soliciting the opinions of journalists on relevant points. While the distribution was not scientifically controlled, it was expected that the familiarity of members of the National Committees with circumstances in their own countries would result in the questionnaires reaching journalists well-qualified to answer them. The percentage of returns was gratifying, with 123 questionnaires completed by journalists in 24 countries, providing answers to no fewer than 61 separate questions grouped under 11 main headings.* Of the 61 questions, it was possible to answer 56 with a "yes" or "no". The other five called for some special comment. In practice, the "yes" or "no" questions were not always answered, so that a "no comment" entry had necessarily to be added in compiling the returns. In more than half of the completed questionnaires, also, 60 or more contained qualifications of "yes-no" answers. A half dozen or more attached supplementary letters covering points at issue, or prepared general statements rather than answering the questionnaire directly. In some instances, the answer to one question might seem to contradict the answer to another on the same return.**

* The countries from which answers were received, with the number of respondents who replied, were Australia (1), Austria (8), Belgium (2), Canada (5), Ceylon (1), Denmark (9), Finland (4), France (13), German Federal Republic (10), with separate returns from West Berlin (4), Greece (3), India (2), Israel (3), Italy (4), Japan (3), Netherlands (2), New Zealand (4), Norway (4), Philippines (3), Sweden (4), Switzerland (6), Turkey (3), Union of South Africa (2), United Kingdom (2), United States (20).

It is not without significance that most of these countries are served by newspapers largely free of interference by government or other influences tending to shape the presentation of information to suit the will of officials or other leaders, and that the general standard of press performance is good to excellent.

** In appraising such apparent contradictions, which are not surprising in a long questionnaire dealing with some difficult questions of ethics and practice, it must be recognized that questionnaires often are dealt with in haste, to dispose of them as promptly as possible in the course of a day's work.

The three-score questions, although grouped under 11 main headings in the questionnaire, may in fact be divided into three broad subject headings :

First :   What are the *reasons* for a journalist to claim the right to professional secrecy ?

Second : What should be the *extent* or *range* of that right ?

Third :   Assuming some limitation on an absolute right, *who should determine such limitation,* either in general or in particular instances ?

The questions, as set forth in the questionnaire itself, did not necessarily follow in the above order. This was intentional, as the questionnaire was prepared, to avoid even an appearance of "leading" a respondent. Analysis of the replies, however, may properly and usefully be made under those three heads.

I. Reasons for journalists to claim the right to professional secrecy

Under Question No. 5, in the questionnaire, journalists were asked to indicate the reason or reasons why they felt justified in claiming the right to keep sources of information secret—assuming they did feel that such a right was indeed appropriate. Three such reasons, commonly cited, were presented. As with other parts of the questionnaire, the responses were tallied, both numerically and in terms of percentages.

---

1. Because you feel that you must keep a promise made to your informant to keep his name secret.

    Yes : 97 (78.8 %)   *No :* 11 (8.9 %)   *No Comment :* 15 (12 %)

This, of course, is one of the basic reasons for the "ethic" of journalism by which, in practice, sources of information have traditionally been kept secret, or confidences protected in those situations where information has been imparted to journalists under such conditions as to make the confidential element important. For the journalist to abide by this promise, in such a circumstance, is a matter of simple individual honesty and integrity.

---

2. Because you feel that if you should disclose a source, after agreeing to keep it confidential, the value of that source would be destroyed for the future, and other sources also would tend to "dry up" as it became recognized that you (and journalists in general) might betray confidences.

Yes: 83 (67.4%) *No:* 23 (18.7%) *No Comment:* 17 (13.8%)

This, also, is a basic, if pragmatic reason for the protection of confidences by journalists in whom they have been reposed. It goes slightly beyond the realm of individual ethics or honesty, being rooted in an awareness of a penalty for betrayal of confidences. At the same time it is based on considerations of the public welfare, since the press cannot fulfil one of its proper functions — that of revealing abuses in the conduct of public affairs and of affairs that concern the public — if its sources of information are in any way obstructed. And they would be obstructed if sources tended to "dry up" because promises to keep them secret where necessary, were broken, or if no reasonable assurance of secrecy could be given, in the first place.

Because of the essential importance of this second reason, it may be regarded as somewhat surprising that the number of "yes" responses was 11.4 per cent below those returned for the first reason, and that the number of "no" responses — that is, those journalists who did not regard the second reason as justifying a right to professional secrecy — was 9.8 per cent higher.

---

3. Because you feel that the special character of the journalistic profession as such requires it.

Yes: 109 (88.6%) *No:* 6 (4.8%) *No Comment:* 8 (6.5%)

This question received a notably higher percentage of "yes" responses than either of the other two, and a far lower percentage of "no" and "no comment" responses.

Two other invitations to comment appeared under the same Question

No. 5. In one, respondents were invited to state any "other reasons" they might have for asserting a journalist's right to keep his sources secret ; in the other, to indicate by marginal numbering "the order of importance of the above-mentioned reasons" and to indicate reasons that might appear "equally important". A few stressed the importance of the "search for truth". One did this incisively by saying that :

> The journalist must reveal the truth for the public. Therefore it is necessary that he have all means at his disposal to discover it. When he publishes it, he does not publish the news given him by his informant, but the news which he has checked and which has become his own. This aspect of the duty—the verification—is too often overlooked. It is the obligatory counterpart of the right to professional secrecy.

The Press in a democracy

Another journalist said :

> It is indispensable to the democratic process that people can talk as freely and confidentially to journalists as to their physicians, priests and lawyers, the press being the chief guarantee for the existence of public criticism in modern society. The journalist, shouldering full responsibility for the sifting of information and for the evaluation of what is printed, he (not the source) must take the punishment if what appears in print is judged libellous or slanderous.

One European editor expressed the general view that "it is primarily in the public interest that the journalist should protect his sources. Only by doing so can the press fulfil its role in a democratic society." This he called "the most important reason for claiming the journalist's right to keep his sources secret". Valid as these reasons might be, however, he himself felt that they might not prove sufficiently convincing in a court of law.

A somewhat similar interpretation and contention was advanced by a Canadian editor, who asserted that "Responsible government in the interests of the governed is only possible when the people at large take a lively public interest in all public affairs, and are adequately informed. The people can only be adequately informed through the Press (in all its forms)." He then went on to say that :

The details of bad government, of bad management of
public affairs, or corruption and of criminal acts, are (most
frequently) known only to persons who in some way or other
are connected with the affairs in question or with persons concerned with the affairs in question.

The greatest deterrent to temptation is the likelihood of
being discovered (of the whole affair becoming known to the
public). Persons are tempted to commit improprieties mostly
when they hope that these can be kept secret. The power to keep
facts secret depends very largely upon the power of the wrong-
doers to harm persons who make known the facts of improper
conduct, so that such persons can be terrified into keeping
secret the information which they possess.

It is a fact of experience that the very vast majority
(perhaps as high as 90 per cent) of the disclosures of improper
public and criminal actions and of persons concerned therewith
comes through journalists who are absolutely relied upon by
their informants to keep secret the identities of those informants.

Only journalists with a reliable reputation for refusal to
discuss the source of their information are able themselves to
learn of, and so inform the public about improper actions, both
criminally and civilly and, above all, governmentally.

Without the informative services of The Press, responsible
democratic government in the interests of the governed is not
possible.

Without the capacity of journalists to keep secret the
source of their information, The Press cannot obtain the information which must be disclosed to the public

To destroy the capacity of journalists to keep secret the
sources of their information is to make impossible the functioning of democratic government in the interests of the governed.

The high proportion of "yes" responses to the three basic "reasons"
listed in Question No. 5 may be interpreted as an indication that such
psychological phenomena as have affected other professions also play
their role in journalism in its struggle for recognition of a "right" to
professional secrecy. In the evaluation of answers to certain other questions asked of journalists, a correlation appears between the positive views
revealed in the responses to Question No. 5 and the answers to some other
lines of inquiry. Among these, especially, are answers with reference to
the extent or range of application of the concept of professional secrecy.

II. Range of application of the right to professional secrecy

If responses to Question No. 5 indicated that 88.6 per cent of the journalists queried in 24 countries believed that "the special character of the journalistic profession" required, or justified, the protection of the source of information against revelation, certain other questions bore upon circumstances in which such protection *might* be qualified, if not surrendered. It was in an examination of such circumstances, arising in practice and in theory, that some returns were at considerable variance to those produced by Question No. 5. This was revealed in responses to Questions No. 1, 2, 3, 4, 6 and 7.

Question No. 1, in three parts, inquiring as to the precise application of a right to professional secrecy, drew these responses :

(a) Should the right to professional secrecy of journalists comprise the right to keep secret the source of information ?
Yes: 122 (99.2 %)   *No:* 1   (.8 %)   *No Comment:* 0

As the first question confronting journalists answering the questionnaire, and one of the most straight-forward inquiries, the answer obviously was quickly presented. From this point, however, complexities and complications of the issue began to increase, and the unanimity of professional opinion became less complete.

(b) Should the right to professional secrecy of journalists comprise the right to keep secret the *content* of *some* information ?
Yes: 117 (95.1 %) *No:* 5 (4 %) *No Comment:* 1 (.8 %)

In general, consideration of the right of journalists to claim professional secrecy has related only to the right to protect *sources* of information, and 99.2 per cent of the respondents indicated in the first part of the question that they subscribed to that concept. Professor Fernand Terrou, Director of the Institut Français de Presse, Paris, and President of the Association Internationale des Etudes sur l'Information, indicated in an article in the *IPI Report* of February 1958, that he regarded the

journalist's right to professional secrecy as pertaining to *sources* only,*
and this has been the usual view. Now, however, in responding to the
questionnaire, more than 95 per cent of the professional journalists
themselves were prepared to claim the additional right to "keep secret the
content of *some* information".

One respondent qualified his "ayes" vote by saying that it would
"depend upon circumstances". Another said that "if the journalist is
bound by a promise and if the disclosure would constitute a problem of
conscience or of professional ethics" he might be justified in keeping
secret the content as well as the source of information.

Qualified or not, the total answer to this part of the question came
as a somewhat surprising revelation as to the attitude of journalists since
the whole purpose of seeking information would appear to be its publication, rather than to keep it secret, even though the *sources* might be
kept secret. It raised an additional question as to what circumstances
might exist when the *content* of information obtained would not be used,
and why not. Although this question was not explored, the obvious circumstance in the minds of the respondents was that practice, increasingly
common, wherein journalists are given information relating, frequently,
to matters of government policy and intended for their background
guidance, rather than for outright publication, but nevertheless contributing usefully to the accuracy of their general reports.

The third part of the question did, at least indirectly, give added
emphasis to the importance attached by professional journalists to the
concept by which content as well as source was regarded as properly
subject to secrecy.

(c) If both (a) and (b) are answered in the affirmative [as they were
in proportions of 99.2 % and 95.1 % respectively] which of those
two rights do you feel is more important?
First (sources):   66 (53.2 %)   *Second (content):* 1 (.8 %)
Equal Importance: 47 (37.9 %)   *No Comment:*   10 (8 %)

Here, even though content was regarded by only one respondent as
of first importance, as a subject for secrecy, the fact that 37.9 per cent
of the respondents regarded it as of "equal importance" was impressive.

* Fernand Terrou. "Confidential Sources: The Protection of Sources of Information for Journalists." *IPI Report* 6 : 10 (February 1958).

The expression of views of practising journalists in responses to Question No. 1, and particularly to the last two parts of the question, (b) and (c), may be regarded as significant with reference to the range of data to be covered by the journalist's asserted right to professional secrecy, where that right *is* asserted. It also tends to counter, to some degree, the position of those who reject the idea of a journalistic right to professional secrecy on the ground that journalism, in contradistinction to law and medicine, is not a "profession of confidence," but is concerned instead with publishing, sometimes quite irresponsibly, almost all information it is able to collect, with only the name of the informant to be concealed, where secrecy is required at all.

By contrast to this view, the replies to Question No. 1 indicate that 95.1 per cent of journalists themselves would assert the right to keep the *content* of some information secret, and that nearly 38 per cent hold that right as of equal importance with the protection of *sources* of information.

Question No. 2 asked whether "the journalist's right to keep his sources secret" should apply in seven separately specified circumstances.

(a) Should the right to keep sources secret apply to sources which have (explicitly or implicitly) requested that their names be kept secret ?
   Yes: 119 (96.7%)   *No:* 3 (2.4%)   *No Comment:* 1 (.8%)

This question is not greatly different from that asked in the first part (a) of Question No. 1, which drew a 99.2 per cent "yes" response. But there, respondents reached a point of departure from the clear path, as revealed in responses to the two questions that followed :

(b) Should the journalist's right to keep his sources secret apply also to sources which have *not* (explicitly or implicitly) expressed a desire that the source's name be kept secret ?
   Yes: 99 (80.4%) *No:* 19 (15.4%)   *No Comment:* 5 (4%)

(c) Should the same right apply in cases in which journalist and informant do not afterwards agree whether or not there was originally an understanding to keep the informant's name secret :
   Yes: 101 (82.1%) *No :* 14 (11.4%) *No Comment :* 8 (6.5%)

The relatively high "yes" responses to both questions are indications that journalists tend to work with their news sources on the basis of good faith and mutual trust. No word would be broken, in the first instance (b), if a journalist did reveal the source, but 80.4 per cent of the respondents still would protect the source if they felt that to do otherwise would mean embarrassment or harm to that source. In the second case (c), the 82.1 per cent who would agree to abide by the informant's wish would be following the practice substantially approved in the second part of Question No. 5 whereby journalists who wish to keep their sources fruitful would regard it as unwise to reveal such sources contrary to the wish of the source, quite as much as because a promise has been given.

Secrecy of the Law

So far, then, the assertion of the right to preserve secrecy as to source had been only slightly compromised. But four other circumstances remained to be examined, and three of them brought a noticeable retreat in the journalists' assertion of the right to professional secrecy, or the application of that right.

First, a source may give information to a journalist, expressing no concern as to whether or not his name is kept secret. Later, however, he may raise positive objection to having his name mentioned. This is not merely a matter of journalist and source disagreeing as to whether an understanding had been reached in advance, as presented in the third part of the question (c), but represents a practical problem as to whether a journalist, having given no commitment, is perhaps under pressure to reveal a source to a court or other tribunal.

> (d) Should the journalist's right to keep his sources secret apply also in cases in which the informant *later* changes his mind and *finally* objects to his name being revealed to a court or tribunal ?
> *Yes :* 88 (71.5%) *No :* 29 (23.5%) *No Comment :* 6 (4.8%)

Second, it is possible to conceive of a situation in which an informant who had originally requested that his name be kept secret, on second thought no longer objected to his name being revealed to a court, or otherwise made known. This is exactly the reverse of the situation just previously described in (d). Not only did it bring a further decline in the "yes" vote, but the weight of the responses actually shifted to "no."

> (e) Should the journalist's right to keep his sources secret apply
> also in cases in which the informant later changes his mind and
> *no longer* objects to his name being revealed to a court or tri-
> bunal ?
> *Yes :* 54 (43.9%) *No :* 65 (52.8%) *No Comment :* 4 (3.2%)

Because of the high proportion of "yes" votes upholding the right
of the journalist to keep sources secret even when the informant had not
expressed a wish to that effect — 80.4 per cent in the second part (b) of
this question — it might have been expected that there would have been a
higher "yes" vote both under (d) and (e). Yet that percentage declined
to 71.5 per cent and 43.9 per cent, respectively. The considerably lower
"yes" vote on the fifth part of the question (e) cannot, however, be regarded as wholly inconsistent with the 80.4 per cent "yes" vote on the
second part (b), since the situation was one, under (e), where the act
of revealing the source became positively permissive, by agreement,
with no infringement of a "right" or even a "confidence" involved,
whereas, under (b), such a revelation would be, so to speak, by default,
in the absence of any agreement whatever. This is not to say, however,
that there was complete consistency on the part of all individual respondents in facing these latter two situations.

A third, and quite different circumstance was presented to respondents in the sixth part (f) of Question No. 2.

> (f) Should the journalist's right to keep sources secret apply also
> in cases in which the information provided by a source later turns
> out to have been given in *bad faith ?*
> *Yes :* 49 (39.8%) *No :* 68 (55.5%) *No Comment :* 6 (4.8%)

In a situation of this sort, where a source has deliberately misled
a journalist by providing him with inaccurate or false information, and
presumably for reasons holding some advantage for the source, something basic has happened to the moral tie presumed to exist between informant and journalist. It is not surprising, therefore, that the majority of
respondents (55.5 per cent) felt that professional secrecy need not, or
should not apply, and that no "right" survived on either side. Perhaps
more remarkable was that 39.8 per cent still believed that the source

should continue to be kept confidential. This might be explained by assuming that a journalist would not wish to admit that he had been deceived and, even if requested by a court to explain where he had obtained such information, might wish to save face, personally.

(g) Should the journalist's right to keep his sources secret apply in cases in which the information provided by the informant turns out to be *inaccurate* ?
Yes : 99 (80.4%) *No :* 16 (13%) *No Comment :* 4 (3.2%)

The difference between this situation, and the foregoing one (f), is that here the information given, although inaccurate, was not deliberately so, but was given in good faith, and so received. The moral bond between journalist and informant is undamaged, with the result that 80.4 per cent of the respondents regarded professional secrecy as properly applying, as contrasted to only 39.8 per cent in the previous instance. If the second series of questions produced some differences between practising journalists as to the proper treatment of confidential sources, succeeding questions produced even more differences.

Question No. 3, in three parts, sought to determine the views of journalists as to those precise *persons who should be entitled to assert the right to professional secrecy.*

First of all, who may be rightly called a "journalist" ? What will be the yardstick ? Who will decide ? Important in this respect is the degree of organization of the profession in the various countries. Where there is a strong organization, there may be a list or register of journalists to provide a clue for a court or other body in determining whether a person is to be considered a *bona fide* journalist. A strong organization may have set certain qualifications that must be met for admission as a fully-fledged journalist member. It may also have drafted a statement or a code in which a policy with reference to professional secrecy is presented. On the other hand, even if such an organization exists, does it legitimately represent the journalists of the country, or is it so closely related to the government of the country as, in fact, to establish a control over journalists and over the press in general ?

Whose right to secrecy?

In any case, the standing of the profession of journalism in a country
has a direct bearing on the matter of professional secrecy. In professions
that do commonly possess a legal right to professional secrecy, such as
law and medicine, the category of persons belonging to the profession is
clearly delineated. All must meet certain qualifications which, in a sense,
constitute guarantees. The absence of comparable professional groups
for journalists in free countries, with the inherent authority to designate
members and qualifications, has been cited in support of their objection
by those opposing any legal "right" of professional secrecy for journalists.
For journalists, also, the clear delineation of any group within the profession as being entitled to possess a right of professional secrecy is related
to legal stipulations as to who should be held responsible for publication
of information in a newspaper.

The International Press Institute limited its inquiry to a few simple
questions. These were intended to produce opinions as to those persons
who might, in the view of journalists themselves, be entitled to assert the
right to professional secrecy, and share in such information as to sources
as might conceivably become points at issue.

The first question, and the response, was as follows :

> For whom should the right to keep sources secret be claimed ?
> ...All journalists ?
> Yes : 102 (82.9%)
> No (not all) : 20 (16.3%)
> No Comment : 1 (.8%)

Although 82.9 per cent spoke for the right of "all journalists," there
were a considerable number of qualifications among what were nevertheless accepted as "yes" answers. These, in fact, may be said to have had a
relation to the second and third parts of this three-part question.

The replies show that 70 per cent of the publishers responding
to the question wanted the right of professional secrecy to reside with all
journalists, 83.6 per cent of the editors-in-chief responding wanted the
right for all, 85 per cent of those who combined the functions of publisher
and editor-in-chief wanted it for all, and 77 per cent of all others replying

wanted it for all. Six professional organizations of journalists responding officially * were unanimous in wanting it for all.

The second part of Question No. 3, with its uninterpreted response was :

For whom should the right to keep sources secret be claimed ?
...Certain categories of journalists only ?
Yes (certain categories only) : 25 (20.8%)
No (all, without qualifications) : 62 (52.5%)
No Comment : 33 (27.6%)

The 62 "no" votes presumably came from the 102 "yes" votes on the first question, but of the remaining 40 "yes" respondents on that question at least two must have changed their minds, more than 30 must have retreated to the "no comment" group on this question, and three were lost altogether, because only 120 answered the question (and percentages are calculated on that basis).

The second part of the question had been answered in the affirmative by 25 (20.8 per cent). The third part of the question led out of the second part.

If the last question is answered in the affirmative,
what categories should enjoy the privilege ?

	Yes	No	No Comment
Editors-in-chief	35	0	90
Editors	34	1	90
Sub-editors	24	10	86
Staff reporters	29	4	87
Correspondents			
Full-time	28	6	86
Part-time	14	20	86

The "yes" answers to the third part totalled 164 "votes," distributed as indicated. Even if all 25 who had voted "yes" on the second part of the question — the only ones properly entitled to vote on the third

* These were national associations in Austria, Belgium, Denmark, the Union of South Africa, and the United Kingdom, plus the International Federation of Journalists.

part at all — had all voted favourably on all six of the categories, the total would not have exceeded 150. For that reason, it is clear that some respondents who returned a "no" or a "no comment" reply on the second part of the question failed to notice the voting limitation on the third part, and also voted on the categories.

Whether or not this was enough to confuse the meaning of the vote on categories, there were a number of qualifications in the answers both to the second and third parts of the question by those favouring limitation of the right to claim professional secrecy to "certain categories". One respondent proposed that the right be limited to "all those for whom journalism is the main occupation," another to such as "are accredited journalists and not just casual contributors". A third commented that "if the secret is reserved for some people only, it will be too easy to get in touch with others to obtain disclosures. The secretary-typist of a doctor or lawyer is under the obligation of professional secrecy. The secret is attached to the profession and not to one or the other function of the profession."

Some inexplicable views on the optional granting of the right to professional secrecy also appeared in responses to this part of the question. Three publishers who replied would have granted the right to all journalists except correspondents, without indication as to how a correspondent was to be differentiated from a reporter. Of ten editors who responded, two would have withheld the right from reporters, normally the recipients of most confidences ; four would have withheld it from full-time correspondents, five from sub-editors, and nine from part-time correspondents.

These selective views were reciprocated in replies to Question No. 4 in which opinions were sought on those from whom "the journalist" might have the right to keep sources secret, including possibly the publisher and the editor-in-chief of his newspaper.

If journalists assert the right to professional secrecy with reference to sources of information (or, indeed, content) as indicated particularly in their responses to Questions 5 and 1, the question also arises as to the *persons or institutions with regard to whom (or which) the right of secrecy can or should be exercised.* That is, is any third person, or group or public body to be permitted to share a knowledge of the source of the information, voluntarily or upon demand, or is the confidence to be retained exclusively and completely as between the informant and the journalist ?

The right of certain groups to preserve professional secrecy — notably doctors, lawyers, and clergymen — is commonly recognized by law or by custom in most countries. Such persons may refuse, and perhaps *must* refuse, under a duty concomitant to the right, to reveal information obtained in confidence in the course of their professional activities. This right relates to relations with laymen. The right, however, to refuse to disclose such confidential information, or professional data, upon demand by a court may not be reserved for all such groups, but only for some of them and has other limitations.

Question No. 4 made five separate queries more specific in nature.

From whom should the journalist (have the right to) keep sources secret?

(a) From third persons (laymen)?
   Yes: 118 (95.9%)   No Comment: 3 (2.4%)
   No: 1 (8%)

(b) From courts in open session:
   Criminal courts?
   Yes: 118 (95.9%)   No Comment: 3 (2.4%)
   No: 2 (1.6%)
   Civil Courts?
   Yes: 117 (95.1%)   No Comment: 3 (2.4%)
   No: 3 (2.4%)

(c) Also from courts which would close the doors to hear the journalist's testimony as to his sources (in camera)?
   Criminal courts?
   Yes: 104 (84.4%)   No Comment: 9 (7.3%)
   No: 10 (8.1%)
   Civil courts?
   Yes: 106 (86.1%)   No Comment: 7 (5.6%)
   No: 10 (8.1%)

(d) Also from his editor-in-chief (if the journalist involved holds another position)?
   Yes: 32 (26%)   No Comment: 7 (5.6%)
   No: 84 (68.2%)

(e) Also from his publisher?
   Yes: 59 (47.1%)   No Comment: 7 (5.6%)
   No: 57 (46.3%)

Reviewing these expressions of journalistic opinion, it is clear that there is a strongly held belief that sources of information should be kept secret from third persons (laymen) and from civil and criminal courts in open session. Where such courts are willing to hear journalists' testimony behind closed doors, however, there is some disposition to reveal sources — not necessarily because of any readiness to depart from the basic "ethic" or the principle of personal integrity, but presumably because of circumstances that might seem to make it in the public interest for journalists to reveal certain sources. These circumstances are further explored in Question No. 6.

The reporter's dilemma

One editor, responding to these questions, remarked that he "once specifically prohibited a member of his staff to appear in a court, because the doors were to be closed during the court meeting, so that the journalist's presence behind closed doors might lead to suggestions that he had answered questions regarding sources". Thus even the *appearance* of a departure from the basic "ethic" was to be avoided.

In the last two parts of the question, (d) and (e), elements of the editor-in-chief's responsibility and the publisher's responsibility, along with that of staff members who might receive information in confidence, were re-examined. In the responses to Question No. 3 there had been a strong disposition to hold that the right of professional secrecy should be accorded to editors-in-chief and to editors. No mention was made there of publishers. The answers to the last two parts of Question No. 4 indicated that 68.2 per cent of journalists also felt that editors-in-chief might be permitted to share in knowledge of sources of information otherwise kept secret. As for sharing such knowledge with the publisher of a newspaper, however, there was far less agreement, but almost an equal division pro and con among journalists.

The general feeling, as it emerged from this inquiry, was that the fewer the number of persons who knew the source of information received in confidence, the less likely that source was to be betrayed, inadvertently or otherwise, under pressure or not. One respondent to Question No. 4, qualifying his answer and advocating no sharing of information as to source with the publisher, explained this by saying that the rule of professional secrecy should "unconditionally apply vis-à-vis the publisher, as there should be no possibility of an indirect pressure from the publisher's side on his (journalistic) employees in this matter".

Eight publishers themselves, responding to the fourth part (d) of the question, relating to the right of journalists to keep sources secret from their editors-in-chief, considered that they should *not* do so. Only one felt that they should be privileged to do so, while one abstained from comment. Among editors-in-chief, 43 were opposed to being deprived of the knowledge of sources, yet 12 rather surprisingly took the opposite view and favoured granting staff members the right to keep them in the dark, while six abstained from voting. Other respondents were about equally divided pro and con, and so were the six journalistic organizations, with three favouring the right and three opposing it. The weighting of the total responses, opposing the withholding of information as to sources from editors-in-chief (68.2%), thus came primarily from the editors-in-chief themselves, supported by a majority of the publisher-respondents.

The withholding of information as to sources from publishers, as dealt with in the fifth part of the question (e), found five publishers out of ten holding that they should *not* be deprived of that information, two prepared to be denied the knowledge, and one abstaining. Of the editors-in-chief responding, 29 out of 61 were opposed to the journalist keeping his sources secret from the publisher, but 27 favoured that procedure, and five abstained. Of seven editors-in-chief who *also* served as publishers, three were opposed to denying the publisher knowledge of source, but the other four favoured it. Of 40 others responding, 26 would keep the publisher uninformed, and five of the six journalistic organizations were disposed to this view.

On the whole, most journalists in all categories indicated a belief that they should *not* have the right to keep their sources secret from their editors-in-chief even though just over a quarter of the editors-in-chief themselves seemed prepared not to know the sources.

There was an almost equal division among all respondents on the right to keep sources secret from publishers. Aside from the publishers themselves, and slightly more than half the editors-in-chief, other groups tended towards withholding such information from publishers.

On the right, as applying both to the publisher and to the editor-in-chief, a Danish editor wrote that :

If the editor-in-chief is responsible in law for the content of the paper, he should have a right to be told in order to be able to decide for himself whether a story is sufficiently well-founded or not to reach the stage of publication. By being told, the editor-in-chief himself actually comes under the same obligation as the journalist as to the source.

If the publisher is directly responsible for the content of the paper, he should be told ; otherwise not. It is, in my opinion, not enough that the publisher is financially responsible for the consequences of a story published in the paper.

Questions Nos. 6 and 7 produced a greater difference of opinion and more general admission of circumstances that, even for a journalist, might be taken as justifying certain *limitations on the right of professional secrecy*. This is not to say that a majority conceded such limitations, but the majority holding to the asserted right to professional secrecy was not so large as might perhaps have been expected on the basis of some of the earlier responses.

This modification may be explained by the introduction of questions based upon experiences and upon theoretical considerations requiring examination in any such survey of journalistic opinion.

Question No. 6 was brief, but Question No. 7, with seven parts, presented situations that may not previously have gained full attention or careful consideration from some respondents. Faced with possibilities that might arise, however, some journalists now felt obliged to acknowledge that there might be justification for certain limitations on the complete or nearly-complete assertion of a legal right to professional secrecy concerning sources of information.

Public welfare

The general interest, or public welfare, being one of the reasons to claim the right of professional secrecy — with a free functioning of the press to permit revelation of abuses in the conduct of public affairs as essential to the performance of a public service by the press — should the asserted right to professional secrecy be limited to those publications which are, in fact, recognized as serving in the general interest, and so performing that public function ? In the context of the IPI inquiry, the term "publications" is here to be interpreted as meaning specific reports as written by journalists.

If a journalist is called upon to testify before a court on a matter in which he would be asked to reveal the source of certain information that he had produced, should any right to refuse to do so be based upon the judgment of the court as to whether his report was serving the general public interest, or was perhaps merely pandering to that element within the population responsive to sensationalized reports ? Or should the journalist have an absolute right to protect his source without reference to any consideration of the public welfare ?

In either case, would such a court, or other public agency directly concerned in seeking such information as to source, be justified in setting its own standards as to what reports are or are not to be regarded as in the interest of the public welfare, or as to whether the individual journalist from whom they seek information was observing such standards in obtaining and publishing the information in question ?

To assert "general interest" or "public welfare" as a basis for claiming the right or privilege of journalistic professional secrecy introduces a problem of judgment. Journalists write on such a variety of subjects that it is not always easy to assess the element of public welfare contained in reports, and it is obvious that some information, without being necessarily damaging to any person or interest, is intended chiefly to entertain the public.

At the same time, the occasional clash between the journalist's asserted right to observe professional secrecy with reference to his sources, and the requirements of a fair administration of justice, in the public interest, may be a serious one. If, for example, a court needs a journalist's testimony — and, in particular, the name of his informant — if it is to learn the truth in a case involving murder or high treason, should the principle of fair administration of justice outweigh the journalist's "ethical" principles and assertion of personal or professional integrity with reference to the preservation of information given to him in confidence by his informant ? Or should it not outweigh that consideration ?

Further, a journalist may have obtained his information from an official or a civil servant who is himself under an obligation to observe professional secrecy and who, by giving such information to the journalist — even though doing so in the belief that he was serving the larger public interest — was violating his technical duty to withhold such information. To assert the journalist's right to keep secret the name of his informant from a court, in such a case, might be regarded as tantamount to an assertion of the *informant's* right to violate *his* professional secrecy, and even make the journalist liable to prosecution as an accessory. But the reverse might be true, also, with the difference that, for the journalist, revelation of his source would mean the violation of a moral rather than a legal duty to keep silent. Circumstances and motives are important in such cases, and no questionnaire could take account of all possibilities.

Absolute or relative

Respondents looking at Question No. 6 and perhaps glancing ahead at Question No. 7, which introduced examples of some of these more difficult moral and legal possibilities, revealed some of the confusions that almost immediately beset them and produced answers that, as noted, were not quite so positive and affirmative as earlier ones in their assertion of the right to maintain professional secrecy with reference to sources. So Question No. 6 asked :

> Do you think that the journalist's right to keep his sources secret should apply always, and under all circumstances ?
> *Yes :* 53 (43 %) *No :* 60 (48.7%) *No Comment :* 10 (8.1 %)

This "yes" vote of 43 per cent was quite a retreat from the 99.2 per cent who had asserted in the first part of Question No. 1 that the right to professional secrecy of journalists should justify them in keeping secret the source of information, and from the 88.6 per cent who had contended in Question No. 5 that "the special character of the journalistic profession *requires* professional secrecy," or the 95.1 per cent to 95.9 per cent who had agreed in Question No. 4 that journalists should have the right to keep sources secret from criminal or civil courts in open session and the 84.4 to 86.1 per cent who made a similar contention with reference to such courts even in closed sessions.

Now, in response to Question No. 6, only 43 per cent still maintained that sources should be kept secret "under *all* circumstances" — even without the nature of any special circumstances as yet having been presented in the questionnaire. Two of those respondents also so far qualified their "yes" answers as to have made it equally appropriate to list them as "no" answers. Both wanted to leave the matter to the *discretion* of the journalist, and one made a reservation that "the exception should be the journalist's conviction that it would cover up a punishable act".

Even more striking in the response to this question was that a simple majority of 48.7 per cent, by their "no" answers, said in effect that there *were* circumstances, after all, in which the asserted right of professional secrecy for journalists should *not* apply. Also, 8.1 per cent failed to answer the question. They were not sure what to think, which meant that they, too, were wavering, at least, and might compromise any "right" they may previously have asserted, as for example under Question No. 4.

The response to Question No. 7 brought an even more marked retreat from a solid assertion of a right to professional secrecy, a scattering of opinion, and an almost sensational increase in the number of respondents who made no comment whatever, so revealing either a lack of familiarity with the issues, or an unreadiness or unwillingness to think the issue through, or to commit themselves ; and certainly an unpreparedness to stand to the defence of the principle of professional secrecy under any or all circumstances. Question No. 7 asked :

> If you feel that there should be exceptions to the rule (of professional secrecy), what should the restrictions and exceptions be ?

There then followed seven examples of such situations as might conceivably give rise to "restrictions and exceptions".

(a) Should the journalist's privilege (not to reveal his sources) be *limited* to those cases in which the journalist's publication involved is considered by a court to have been written apparently to serve the general interest ?
Yes (should be so limited): 20 (16.2%)   *No :* 61 (51.2%)
No comment: (30%)   *Answers unclear:* 3 (.2%)

Only a minority of 16.2 per cent here was prepared to limit a journalist's privilege — no longer referred to as a "right" — to those cases in which the journalist's publication was considered, by unilateral decision of the court, to have been written "to serve the general interest". Most of the respondents, although by a narrow 51.2 per cent majority, still rejected any such limitation, especially as based upon the court's own interpretation of what constituted the "general interest" or "public interest".

In the response to this question, however, the number making no comment whatever was for the first time very large, representing 30 per cent of the respondents, and three were so vague as to defy classification. One such reply introduced several "conditions". One was that a journalist, possessing voting rights, should be added to the court to adjudicate the matter ; another, that the court should ask the advice of a professional journalistic organization ; and, third, that there should be the possibility of an appeal to a High Court with jurisdiction on constitutional matters. Only if these three conditions were met was this journalist prepared to vote "yes" on the question ; otherwise he would vote "no" because, he said, "the danger of abuse by journalists is less than the danger of abuse by authorities".

(b) Should the privilege (of preserving secrecy as to source) *not* be claimed in cases in which the testimony of the journalist as to his source is deemed necessary by a court for the administration of justice and/or maintenance of security in cases of :

	Should be claimed	Should not	No Comment
High treason	33 (26.8%)	52 (42.2%)	38 (30.8%)
Murder	28 (22.7%)	58 (47.1%)	37 (30 %)
Where journalist's informant has himself violated his legal obligation to observe professional secrecy	60 (48.7%)	30 (24.3%)	33 (26.8%)

Secrecy and crime

The response to this question brought a greater division of opinion than on any previous question. An average of about 44.6 per cent of the journalists felt that the privilege of professional secrecy should *not* be asserted in cases of high treason and murder, while an average of about 24.7 per cent felt that it *should* still be asserted. About 30 per cent were unable to make up their minds, or gave such qualified answers as to make it impossible to put them in a "yes" or "no" category.*

Nearly half of the respondents (48.7%) did favour the assertion of the professional secrecy privilege, however, in cases where the journalist's informant — a public official or civil servant — had violated his own legal obligation to observe professional secrecy. Here it might be legitimately argued that only by such a departure could the public welfare be served, in some cases at least, and the informant should therefore be protected by preserving his confidence as a matter of professional principle. Among the qualified answers, also, relating to the preservation of a confidence bearing upon a murder trial, one respondent took a middle ground by saying that "it all depends. A trial for murder may be a political trial. In principle, the demonstration of truth, when the life of a man is at stake, should prevail over the professional secrecy."

The third part of Question No. 7 pursued the issue raised in the first part, in combination with various circumstances explored in the second part. This made for a complicated question put to those who had indicated themselves, in the first part of the question (a), as favouring limitation of the privilege of professional secrecy to those cases in which the the journalist's publication "was considered by the court to have been written apparently to serve the general interest". Only 20 respondents (16.2 per cent) had voted in favour of such a limitation. Here, however, in the third part of Question No. 3—respondents not properly entitled to express themselves did so anyway. In this case, *all* of them overlooked the fact that only those 20 should have replied, so that there were 123 votes, with 103 therefore representing expressions on a point with which the "voters" presumably had no sympathy in the first place, or had expressed no view.

The point at issue was whether, if the privilege of professional secrecy were to be limited in its application to cases in which the publication involved was considered by the court to have been written in the public interest, this privilege should *still* be claimed in cases of high treason,

---

* Swiss law is such that no exemption whatever could be granted to a journalist, even tacitly, in a case involving high treason. Swiss respondents were equally divided in their replies to this question, however, but since only six such replies were returned the significance of the division is dubious. In the German Federal Republic, where high treason is similarly dealt with under the law, 43 per cent of 12 respondents agreed that journalists should *not* be exempt from revealing a source in such circumstances.

murder, or violation by an informant of a legal duty to observe professional secrecy.

(c) If you are in favour of limiting the journalist's privilege in the
sense mentioned in 7a (to publications deemed to serve the public interest), do you think that (any of) the exceptions mentioned
in 7b should constitute an additional limitation so that even
when a journalist's publication is considered by a court to have
been written apparently to serve the general interest, nevertheless he should reveal the name of his informant when deemed
necessary by a court in cases of

	Yes (should reveal)	No (should not)	No Comment
High treason	35 (28.4%)	18 (14.6%)	70 (56.9%)
Murder	39 (31.7%)	14 (11.3%)	70 (56.9%)
Violation by the informant of his legal duty to observe professional secrecy	15 (12.1%)	36 (29.3%)	72 (57.7%)

German example

One thing to be observed in the response to this question was that
the journalists who made "no comment" almost doubled, in terms both
of numbers and percentages, when compared to the second part (b) of the
question. Considering, also, that only 20 (16.2 per cent), responding to
the first part of the question, had favoured a limitation on the application
of the privilege of professional secrecy to those cases in which the journalist's publication was considered by the court to have been written in
the public interest, 103 had voted "no" or had made "no comment" or no
intelligible comment. It may be assumed that most of the 70 or 72 who
made "no comment" on this third part (c) of the question had been
included in the 103. But this left 31 to 33 from this same group who,
without justification, voted on the third part to produce either a "yes" or
a "no".

The fourth and fifth parts of Question No. 7, the one related to the
other, presented still other special circumstances for the consideration
of journalists.

(d) Should the privilege (to protect the source) be granted whenever the journalist (called upon as a *witness* to reveal the name of his informant) is also the *defendant* in a trial for the publication involved ?
Yes: 79 (64.2 %)   *No:* 7 (5.6 %)   *No Comment:* 37 (30 %)

(e) Should the privilege be granted whenever the testimony of a journalist could lead to self-incrimination ?
Yes: 77 (62.5 %)   *No:* 18 (14.6 %)   *No Comment:* 28 (22.4 %)

In both circumstances, then, a substantial majority of the respondents believed that a journalist, called as a witness to reveal his source and, at the same time, himself a defendant in a trial concerning the publication involved, or awaiting trial as a defendant, *should* be privileged to assert the right to professional secrecy. Surprisingly, however, in the fifth part (e) of the question, where it was specified that the journalist's testimony might lead to self-incrimination, the percentage of those who felt the journalist then should *not* exercise the right was more than doubled, with the increase drawn chiefly from among those who had expressed "no comment" on the fourth part (d) of the question. This was even more remarkable because in such a circumstance the journalist could legitimately withhold information under provisions of law existing in most countries, specifying that no person need give evidence that might be self-incriminating.

It is to be noted that, under West German legislation, an editor can claim the right of professional secrecy only after having been sentenced for a publication. In such a circumstance, there might be an added reason for a journalist to hold his tongue, rather than reveal a source, at least until the trial concerning the publication itself is over. This may have been an element in the responses to the fourth part (d) of the question.*

Still another special circumstance, or series of circumstances, presented in the sixth part of the question, drew a variety of responses.

---

* Yet only 53 % of German respondents voted a clear "yes" on the fourth part of the question, favourable to an application of the privilege of secrecy as to source, as contrasted to a general 64.2 % vote of "yes" among all respondents.

(f) Should the privilege (of professional secrecy) *not* be claimed if the *publication involved* is deemed by the court

	Yes (should be claimed)	No (should not)	No Comment
— to be detrimental to state security	43 (34.9%)	36 (29.2%)	44 (35 %)
— to be detrimental to the general interest	63 (51.2%)	16 (13 %)	44 (35 %)
— to be detrimental to private interests, without serving the general interest	65 (52.8%)	16 (13 %)	42 (34.8%)
— to be detrimental to personal reputations, without serving the general interest	58 (47.1%)	22 (17.8%)	43 (34.9%)

Here, to sum up, between approximately one-third and just over one-half of the respondents felt the privilege of professional secrecy *should* be claimed in all four circumstances. Where state security was a factor, however, the "yes" vote was lowest and the "no" vote highest. Apart from that, there was a disposition to protect confidences where individual reputations and interests are at stake, as well as where the general public interest is concerned.

In view of the 43 per cent who responded to Question No. 6 by expressing the view that the journalist's right to keep his sources secret should apply "always, and under all circumstances," it is interesting to note that this percentage fell to 34.9 per cent where secrecy might prove detrimental to state security. But, actually, it had fallen even lower, as indicated in responses to the second part (b) of Question No. 7, where only 26.8 per cent were inclined to insist upon preservation of professional secrecy where high treason was involved — a circumstance that might be considered akin to "state security" — and only 22.7 per cent where murder cases were before the courts. These special circumstances, re-checked through responses to part three (c) of Question No. 7, found a somewhat similar readiness on the part of journalists themselves to limit the right in cases of high treason or murder. As to the attitude in circumstances involving violation by the informant of his legal duty to observe professional secrecy, however, there was considerably more disposition to stand firm. Yet, even here, the response was shadowed by the large percentage of respondents — 26.8 per cent in (b) and a high 57.7 per cent in (c) — who returned "no comment" whatever.

The seventh, and last part of Question No. 7 was an open invitation to respondents to state

---

(g) In what other cases should the privilege (of professional secrecy) *not* be claimed ?

To this there were 21 replies varying in nature and value, but carrying the inference that at least 17.8 per cent of the respondents to the questionnaire were prepared to concede that there might be reasons for compromising the "right" or "privilege" of professional secrecy.

These replies ranged from assertions that whether the privilege should be claimed, or not, "all depends on the journalist in question" to more pertinent statements, such as "privilege to withhold sources should not be claimed generally in cases where capital crimes or the clearly defined security of the state (in cases of strictly legitimate governments) are involved. And in other life and death situations, where these depend on the use of privilege, the journalist should seek the help of legitimately constituted courts in helping to decide the issue."

III. Determination of the validity of limitations of professional secrecy

Assuming that some limitations upon the right or privilege of professional secrecy are to be conceded by journalists themselves as justifiable in certain circumstances, who is to determine the validity of such limitations, either in general or in particular ? This question enters the area of juridical action.

The issues so far considered, on the basis of the IPI questionnaire, have concerned the right or privilege of professional secrecy, as viewed by journalists, with special reference to the protection of the journalist's sources of information. On the basis of the replies, and even apart from the views of jurists and officials and others, many journalists themselves apparently are prepared to agree that some limitations may exist to any assertion of a complete right to preserve professional secrecy under any and all circumstances. This was conceded by 48.7 per cent in answer to Question No. 6.

The question arises, however, as to how far any such definition of the right or privilege of professional secrecy — or to what degree modifications or limitations of such an asserted right — should be determined by law and/or jurisprudence or in some other institutionalized manner, or by journalists acting either independently and exclusively or, perhaps, in association with other existing agencies. The last four questions presented in the IPI questionnaire solicited the views of journalists on this broad topic. These are Questions No. 8, 9, 10, and 11.

---

8. Should the right of journalists to keep sources secret, subject perhaps to any of the above limitations (examined in Question No. 7), be recognized in your country (insofar as this is still not so) :

	Yes	No	No Comment
(a) by (statute) law	80 (65 %)	18 (14.4%)	25 (20.3%) (qualified reply : 4)
(b) by jurisprudence (i. e. the courts or other competent bodies to decide in each individual case)	40 (32.5%)	37 (30 %)	46 (37.3%)
(c) partly by law, partly by jurisprudence	35 (26.5%)	39 (31.7%)	49 (39.7%)
(d) by agreement between authorities and professional organizations	35 (26.5%)	40 (32.5%)	48 (39 %)

The most striking fact to emerge was the large majority — 65 per cent — favouring recognition of the right of professional secrecy by statute law, and the small minority — 14.4 per cent — in specific opposition.

One among four respondents who voted neither "yes" or "no", and therefore is included perforce among those returning "no comment," actually did propose that the right be recognized "by constitutional law, as in a material sense," he said, "it constitutes part of the fundamental right to free expression, and therefore is a human right". Another deviation from the questions as presented occurred in a "yes" response, to which the respondent added, however, that he would prefer to see the right recognized by international law.

A considerable percentage of "no comment" returns appeared on the last three parts of the question (b, c, and d), but those parts revealed no strong sentiment in favour of any one of three proposed solutions for establishment of the right of professional secrecy by jurisprudence, law and jurisprudence, or by agreements between authorities and professional journalistic organizations.

Austrian exception

The one country where the right of professional secrecy is at present assured, nationally, by statute is Austria. Swedish press legislation, also highly developed, gives journalists a considerable degree of freedom, including freedom to keep sources confidential. It is of interest, accordingly, that whereas the opinion among all respondents was 65 per cent favourable to establishment of a journalistic right to professional secrecy through statutory law, the percentage among Austrian respondents was 75 per cent favourable to such recognition, and Swedish respondents were 100 per cent favourable. The significance of these higher percentile responses may have been shadowed somewhat by the limited numerical response, with eight Austrian and four Swedish replies. By contrast, in the United States, where a dozen individual states do grant a legal protection in the matter of professional secrecy, and where journalists generally operate with a minimum of difficulty in that respect, the response by 20 journalists was only 50 per cent favourable to protection through statutory law, or considerably below the general response favourable to that means.

It is perhaps not surprising that one of the Austrian editors took an extreme position in the assertion of the journalist's *right* to professional secrecy. He considered this right to be "indispensable" to the performance of the journalist's task and to the service of the press.

"If a journalist cannot protect his sources," this Austrian editor insisted, "he is committing suicide, socially and professionally." He rejected as irrelevant any comparison with the position of the doctor, lawyer, priest or other group commonly protected in the right of secrecy by the laws of many countries. For the journalist, he said, professional secrecy was to be regarded as "indivisible, complete and absolute," with no restrictions whatever to be considered. To give force to professional secrecy, he added, not only should all journalists concerned with the editorial task possess the right, but so also should the publisher, the printer, and all employees in the mechanical department of a newspaper. Unless all of these are free to withhold a source, the Austrian editor contended, the concept of professional secrecy becomes practically valueless.

The replies to Question No. 8, as given above, and particularly to its fourth part (d), need to be viewed in the context, also, of the replies to Question No. 11, the last in the questionnaire.

Do you feel that it is for the journalist himself to decide on the limitations, if any, of his rights and duties to professional secrecy, rather than to leave this to be completely decided upon by law and/or jurisprudence ?

Yes : 72 (60.5%) *No :* 30 (24.8%) *No Comment :* 21 (17%)

With this 60.5 per cent majority preference for a decision by the journalist himself on any possible limitations to his rights (and duties) in the area of professional secrecy, respondents seemed to manifest a certain inconsistency with their earlier 65 per cent expression of preference, in the first part of Question No. 8, for a determination to be established through statute law, and perhaps with their 32.5 per cent opposition in the fourth part of that same question to "agreements between authorities and professional journalistic organizations" by way of clarifying limitations. Perhaps some respondents did not recognize the logical connection between Questions No. 8 and 11, widely separated as they were.

However that may be, a rather strong minority of 24.8 per cent rejected the proposal in Question No. 11 for journalistic self-determination of the issue, and 17 per cent did not respond at all. Even among those who voted "yes", a considerable number introduced qualifications, and six phrased those qualifications in such a way that, by some interpretations, they seemed more in favour of the minority view, or at least in favour of a kind of "mixed system," as in the case of one respondent who suggested "the rule to be recognized by law and for the rest leave it to the journalist". Another proposed a decision by journalists "as long as there is no jurisprudence on this score," but "as soon as there is one, no".

Some of the qualified answers to Question No. 11 showed that certain respondents believed the basic principle of professional secrecy could (and perhaps should) be recognized by law, but that further elaborations involving issues of high treason, murder, state security and others considered in Question No. 7, with their possible limitations and exceptions, might be left to be decided by the journalist himself.

There was apparent confusion in the minds of some respondents as to limitations to the principle of professional secrecy, on the one hand, and the journalist's conscience, on the other. These respondents appeared to regard the two as more or less synonymous. It seemed not always to occur to them that even the most refined law cannot prevent individuals having problems of conscience which, at a certain point, may force them to choose between yielding to authority *or* accepting punishment for refusal to reveal information given them "in confidence" *or* to reveal the source or sources of such information. At the same time, even an unquestioning readiness to accept punishment, because individual conscience or a sense of journalistic integrity makes that preferable to a breach of confidence, should not logically exclude a willingness to seek the most acceptable rules (even including exceptions or limitations to the assertion of a right to secrecy). Agreement upon such rules might then reduce the necessity or the occasion for some conscientious objections to revealing a source of information.

What bodies should adjudicate on a journalist's claim to keep his sources secret in any given crisis :

(a) the court which is treating the case in which it would need the journalist's testimony ?
  Yes : 40 (32.5%)   *No Comment :* 30 (24.3%)
  No : 53 (43%)

(b) another court which is not dealing with the case itself ?
   Yes : 28 (22.7%)   *No Comment :* 39 (31.7%)
   No : 56 (45.5%)

(c) one of the solutions mentioned under (a) and (b), but the court having to be supplemented by journalists,
   — in an advisory capacity ?
   Yes : 16 (13 %)   *No Comment :* 51 (41.4%)
   No : 56 (45.5%)
   — with voting rights ?
   Yes : 19 (15.4%)   *No Comment :* 48 (39%)
   No : 1 (.8%)

Although the votes on this Question No. 9 were considerably divided, with a high proportion of respondents returning "no comment", it seems clear that journalists felt no enthusiasm for any one of the procedures noted, with negative votes outnumbering the affirmative votes by from about 10 to 30 per cent.

The fourth and fifth parts of the question produced the same general line of responses, with the fifth possibility being rejected by the most positive vote of any.

(d) a special body to be set up by the profession to whom this competence (to adjudicate a journalist's claim) should be assigned ?
   Yes : 35 (28.4%)   *No Comment :* 41 (33.3%)
   No : 47 (38.2%)

(e) an already existing body organized by the profession, which would have to be given the competence in this field ?
   Yes : 12 (9.7%)   *No Comment :* 51 (41.4%)
   No : 60 (48.7%)

In view of the 60.5 per cent vote on Question No. 11, favourable to action by "the journalist himself" on the establishment of rights and duties or upon limitations, it is to be noted that the responses to parts (d) and (e) of Question No. 9, above, generally reject a journalistic handling of the problem, as a semi-journalistic handling of the problem also was generally rejected in the fourth part (d) of Question No. 8.

The number of respondents rejecting each of the above five methods for adjudicating a journalist's claim to keep his sources secret was, in every case, greater than the number in favour. The number of respondents unprepared or unready to commit themselves, one way or the other, remained large throughout — approximately 24 to 31 per cent of the entire group.

The IPI questionnaire was not intended as a "poll," in the usual sense of that word, and it would be improper to conclude, on the basis of the figures alone, that respondents rejected all the solutions mentioned. Those who voted "no" on one proposal might vote "yes" on others, and some did exactly that. Answers to a questionnaire were not comparable to votes especially not to the type of vote in which a relative preference may be given. Some respondents also did not quite realize, apparently, that every law (whatever its purview) needs to be applied and interpreted. An example of this confusion was in one qualified answer rejecting all of the suggested solutions, but then adding that "the law should apply absolutely except in cases involving high treason".

The seventh and last part of Question No. 9 invited respondents to suggest

> (f) any other system or combination of above-mentioned systems ?

There were only a few answers, or proposals, offered. As an example, one Swiss respondent said that "The decision on the journalist's claim to professional secrecy should not be left to the court which needs the testimony of the journalist. (The proposal under (a).) This should be the task of a special court which has nothing to do with the case for which the journalist's testimony is being asked, e. g. a court with jurisdiction on constitutional matters." (A variation of the proposal under (b).) This respondent also pointed out what he considered the "desirability of a court to ask the advice of existing professional organizations". (Possibly as proposed under (e), or perhaps the proposal under (c), since in Switzerland there exists a Joint Press Commission, consisting of an equal number of representatives of the publishers' organization and the journalists' organization.)

Another proposal was for "a combined body in which the working journalist, the newspaper proprietor, the legal profession, and the general public can be represented. This could be maintained as a standing committee responsible for press ethics and conduct generally". This method was somewhat as proposed under the fourth part (d) of Question No. 8, suggesting "agreements between authorities and professional organizations" for action on matters of professional secrecy, but receiving no large approval from journalists responding. It was somewhat similar in concept to the existing British Press Council. Any such body would still lack legal power, but would have moral authority.

Duty of secrecy

The *right* of professional secrecy possessed by groups other than journalists — i. e. officials of government, lawyers, doctors, and clergymen, in particular — as recognized by law in many countries, nearly always is accompanied by a concomitant *duty* to preserve that secrecy. Violations of that duty, such as revealing confidential information to third persons — laymen or otherwise — usually is punishable either under law or under some professional jurisdiction. Where considerations of public interest exist, or are advanced as the basis for assertion of a *right* to professional secrecy, such a concomitant *duty* seems to be a logical complement to the asserted, or claimed right.

This was the subject upon which journalists' opinions were sought in Question No. 10, and here a strong majority of journalist-respondents agreed, in the first two parts of that three-part question, that as a counterpart of the *right* to keep sources secret there also should be a *duty* to do so.

(a) Should the journalist as a counterpart of his right to keep sources secret have a concomitant *duty* to keep them secret ?
Yes : 98 (79.6%)   *No Comment* : 6 (4.8%)
No : 19 (15.4%)

(b) If so, should there be any sanctions against breach of this duty ?
Yes : 62 (50.4%)   *No Comment* : 29 (23.5%)
No : 32 (26 %)

The rather sharp drop in the "Yes" vote as between the first and second parts, and the sharp increase in the "No Comment" group, may be attributed, not to disagreement with the first proposition, but rather to the practical difficulty of implementing the second proposition. This difficulty was reflected in the responses to the third and fourth parts of the question.

(c) If the last question is answered in the affirmative, what sanctions ?...

(d) To be inflicted (imposed) by what body ?...

To these open questions there were varied responses. As the third part (c) was phrased, the 62 who had voted "Yes" on the second part (b) of the question, favourable to sanctions, were entitled to reply, and did reply. The proposed sanctions ranged from censure to exclusion from the profession of journalism, and from fines to imprisonment. Among the many variations, however, moral sanctions were suggested by more correspondents than any other one form.

The practical difficulty in responding to this question arose largely from the second part (d) in which respondents were invited to suggest the appropriate body to act on the enforcement or implementation of whatever sanction or sanctions might be proposed. As was to be expected, therefore, the opinions on that matter were as varied as those on the nature of the sanctions themselves, and included proposed action by the editor of the newspaper served by the offending journalist, the publisher of that newspaper, the journalist's professional peers, a professional organization, a journalistic Court of Honour, and by the ordinary courts.

In general, the proposals favoured action through the profession itself, rather than by the ordinary courts or other outside bodies. This, it may be noted, was in accordance to the responses to Question No. 11, already mentioned,* in which 60.5 per cent of the respondents supported the view that "it is for the journalist himself to decide on limitations, if any, of his rights and duties to professional secrecy, rather than to leave this to be completely decided upon by law and/or jurisprudence".

---

* See page 220 ante. But it is to be noted that this response was rather negated by responses to the fourth and fifth parts (d) and (e) of Question No. 9, as shown on page 222 ante, in which the largest groups opposed any special professional body or any existing professional body as qualified to act in adjudicating a journalist's claim to keep his sources secret.

For whatever significance it may have, also, the 60.5 percentage falls midway between the 79.6 per cent who agreed, in Question No. 10 (a), that the journalist "as a counterpart of his right to keep sources secret (has) a concomitant duty to keep them secret" and the 50.4 per cent who agreed in that same question, part (b), that there should be "sanctions against breach of this duty". Taking an average of the three expressions, there emerges a controlling 63.5 percentage of journalists who appear to favour the right of professional secrecy, recognize the concomitant duty, and believe it is for the journalist himself to control professional performance.

IV. Summary, Conclusions and Correlations

First, journalists themselves believe it important to observe the principle of professional secrecy as a matter of personal integrity, recognized in written and unwritten codes of ethics (78.8 per cent) ; as a practical matter of assuring continued confidence on the part of officials and others who are "sources" of information (67.4 per cent) ; and because they feel (88.6 per cent) that the special character of the journalistic profession, in its service to the public and in its concern for the general welfare of the community, justifies and, indeed, *requires* the existence of a right or privilege of professional secrecy for journalists quite as much as for lawyers or doctors.

Second, although journalists are quite aware that the right of professional secrecy has not as yet been generally recognized as possessing legal validity except in a few areas of the world, they nevertheless believe that such a right should exist with reference to protection of *sources,* especially (99.2 per cent), and even to maintaining secrecy with reference to the *content* of some information, in the face of official demands that it be revealed (95.1 per cent).

The journalist's insistence upon the importance of protecting sources leads him to insist that he should maintain his "right" in that respect not only where the sources have requested it, explicitly or implicitly (96.7 per cent), but also where the sources have *not* so requested it (80.4 per cent), and where the journalist and his source (or informant) do not later agree as to whether such an understanding had existed originally (82.1 per cent).

Even when a source, originally making no request for confidence with reference to his identity nevertheless later asks such secrecy, the journalist is willing to give him such protection (71.5 per cent). Moreover, a source originally asking such protection, but later withdrawing that request of his own accord, still would find 43.9 per cent of journalists even then prepared to refuse to make the revelation upon demand of court authorities. This remained so for 39.8 per cent of journalists even when it was clear that the source had deliberately given them false information, while as many as 80.4 per cent would continue to maintain silence with reference to the source when it became apparent that information received in confidence was inaccurate, but had been given without any intent to deceive them.

Third, there was no disposition among journalists to trifle with the broad claim to professional secrecy by categorizing or classifying themselves or their colleagues on any basis whatever — whether they were engaged in the profession on a full-time or on a part-time basis, for example, or earned all or only part of their livelihood from the work. The controlling figures on these points revealed an over-riding opinion (82.9 per cent) that *all* journalists should have the right to keep sources secret. Put another way, it was agreed that there should be no category more favoured or less favoured than another in that respect (52.5 per cent).

Fourth, the staunch attitude in defence of what might almost be called the sanctity of sources was even more strikingly manifested in a 95.9 per cent agreement that sources should be kept secret from third persons, or laymen. The journalist might be willing to share such information with his editor-in-chief (68.2 per cent), but there was more reluctance to share that information with the publisher of his newspaper (46.3 per cent).

Since the demand that a journalist reveal the source of his information has special relevance when certain cases are before the courts, with the courts of most countries legally empowered to insist upon such revelations, it is significant that most journalists themselves still insist, in theory and in principle at least, that such revelations of source should *not* be made either in criminal courts (95.9 per cent) or in civil courts (95.1 per cent). Even when assured that those revelations would be heard only in closed sessions, with no public naming of informants, journalists still would compromise only slightly, holding that secrecy should yet be maintained in criminal courts (84.4 per cent) and in civil courts (86.1 per cent).

Fifth, it was only when certain specific instances were suggested, involving special circumstances, that there appeared some tendency on the part of journalists to retreat from the generally strong insistence upon the protection of sources under almost all circumstances. This partial retreat was indicated when 48.7 per cent were unwilling to go so far as to say that the right to keep sources secret should apply "always, and under all circumstances". This still was no majority, and 43 per cent held to the view that the right *should* so apply — a considerably lower percentage than had appeared previously on the broad issue — while 8.1 per cent expressed no view, which added no strength, certainly, to the pro-secrecy group.

Only a minority (16.2 per cent) was prepared to sacrifice the right to protect sources if the court, by its own decision, ruled that the journalist's publication, or report, was regarded as not serving the "general interest". On the contrary, most journalists (51.2 per cent) took the view that this was not admissible as a basis for limiting the right or privilege of preserving secrecy as to source. When a further circumstance was introduced, however, questioning the propriety of preserving such secrecy in cases before the courts involving high treason, murder, and violation by an informant himself of his own legal duty to observe professional secrecy — with the fair administration of justice or maintenence of state security at issue—then there was, for the first time, a considerable divergence in journalistic opinion. Many journalists (26.8 to 57.7 per cent), responding to six relevant questions, expressed no opinion whatever, suggesting uncertainty ; 12.1 to 47.1 per cent were willing to consider some modification of the principle of professional secrecy, while almost an equal number (11.3 to 48.7 per cent) contended that the right should be maintained absolutely.

The general insistence upon the journalist's right to protect his sources was emphasized anew (64.2 and 62.5 per cent) when the question was raised as to his attitude in cases where he himself might be called as a witness in a case or even as a defendant in a case before the court. But divergence of opinion recurred promptly when a series of circumstances was introduced somewhat comparable to those that had caused the earlier split. That is, faced with questions as to their attitude when state security, injury to the general interest, and to personal reputations were involved, the proportion of those journalists making no comment again shot up (34.8 to 35 per cent), while 13 to 29.2 per cent would have refrained from claiming the right or privilege of professional secrecy. This still left a hard core, however, of 34.9 to a substantial 52.8 per cent who would hold to the principle of professional secrecy under the varied circumstances adduced.

Sixth, a strong wish among journalists to see professional secrecy established as a full legal right led 65 per cent to express their preference for such recognition through the provisions of statute law. At the same time, short of such statutory protection, there was so considerable a difference of opinion as to how the principle of professional secrecy might be made an effective "right" that an *average* of 34 per cent of all respondents, confronted by relevant questions, made no·effective comment on the possible means by which the right was to be recognized.

The response was extremely mixed, also, on various proposals for what might be regarded as a kind of interim method for adjudicating cases. Again, an *average* of 35.1 per cent expressed no view on those proposals. Considerable agreement (60.5 per cent) did appear, however, that "it is for the journalist himself to decide on the limitations, if any, of his rights and duties" in the area of professional secrecy.

Once more, this was by way of a restatement of the journalist's generally approved view that sources *should* be protected ; that a "right" of professional secrecy *should* exist, with legal authorization ; and that he himself was best qualified to guide, govern, and determine the practice, without outside interference of any sort. It was a reflection of the view held by most journalists (79.6 per cent) that they had not only a right, but a *duty* to keep the sources of their information secret when, in their own professional judgment, this was the proper thing to do. Even so, only 28.4 per cent were prepared to agree to a special professional body, and only 9.7 per cent to an existing professional body as being appropriate to adjudicate a journalist's claim to any such right or duty. This left the solution very much up in the air, unless through statute law.

Whatever the views of journalists themselves may be with reference to the issue of professional secrecy, those laws and cases in various countries providing tests in the courts shed some light on the effectiveness of the journalistic "ethic" involved. Such matters are examined in other pages of this study as they have arisen in individual countries.

Conclusions

The key issue which this survey on professional secrecy hit time
and again in the foregoing pages, is the following : should a journalist,
receiving information in confidence, be privileged to protect that confidence when or if asked by a court or other authorized body to break
the confidence and reveal his source ?

Members of the legal profession, on the other hand, both through
law associations and through representation on legislative lawmaking
bodies, have consistently turned a deaf ear to requests for extension of
the right to professional secrecy to journalists.

Journalists, on the other hand, long have asserted the ethical concept
under which they hold themselves obligated to protect those who have
given them information in confidence. A considerable number have paid
fines and gone to gaol rather than yield to court demands. Through their
professional associations, they sometimes have insisted that they should
be protected in their asserted ethical position by statute.

The journalist has a *personal* option as to whether he will choose to
reveal a source, upon demand, or refuse to do so. In either case, he can
decide whether he *should* or whether he *must* do so. In general practice,
the journalist chooses to protect his source of information, even at cost to
himself, in terms of fine or imprisonment. This attitude, while sometimes
suggesting mere stubbornness on the part of the journalist, has its justification because if the ethical concept were compromised it would weaken
the journalist's position in the struggle to obtain ultimate legal recognition
of professional secrecy through asserting a right that he does not himself
observe firmly.

A problem unquestionably exists in finding a way between the
journalist's conscience, his professional ethics, his legal obligations, the
performance of his individual function, the function of the press as
informant and defender of the public welfare, *and* the unobstructed
operation of the judicial process.

There are those in both groups, however, who would compromise the
issue. Some journalists concede that certain circumstances exist under

which professional secrecy should not be claimed ; others oppose any special legal protection for journalists. Some jurists on their side, view the journalists' ethical and moral position with understanding and sympathy. They may govern their own actions in such a way as to avoid placing the journalist-witness in a position where he would either be obliged to break a confidence or pay a penalty, or they find ways to spare the journalist from having to make a direct refusal to answer a question as to source.

If there is to be any sort of line drawn between an occasion when a journalist might legitimately claim a right to withhold information and an occasion when that claim would be of doubtful validity, it might be based upon the effect of such withholding upon the proper administration of justice. Courts commonly have insisted that the administration of justice must take precedence over any claim to professional secrecy for journalists and, in practice, sometimes even to deny the equivalent right to those other professional groups whose claim to anonymity for their informants has been so generally recognized.

If a journalist writes a report in some way critical of the administration of government, asserting in general terms, for example, that there is inefficiency or even corruption within the government, this may be resented by officials but it probably has no adverse effect on the administration of justice, and therefore would hardly warrant a demand for revelation of source. If the journalist has been able, in such a circumstance, to obtain information and to find sources providing him with such information, it may be argued that the government—holding greater power and having every sort of facility for getting that same information —has no proper cause to demand that the journalist reveal his source or sources of information. In such situations, therefore, it may be argued that a journalist should be granted the right of professional secrecy.

If the *substantive right of an individual* might be adversely affected by the withholding of information by a journalist, including information as to the source of that information, there arises a situation in which interference with the proper and full administration of justice may be a real issue. For lack of information, an individual then might be subject to imprisonment or even execution. In such a case, a journalist might be expected to respond affirmatively to the court demand for information as to source.

It has been contended that the only solution fair to all parties is for the courts to have full authority to judge whether the substantive right of an individual is going to be affected by the withholding of information. If, in the judgment of the court, such may be the case, then —but perhaps only then—would it be proper for the court to insist upon the journalist responding to the demand for information as to source, and being penalized by fine or imprisonment, or both, if he still refuses to speak.

The study shows that journalists have to operate within a wide range under widely differing legal conditions in different countries.

For instance, journalists in Austria today enjoy the almost complete *legal* right to protect confidences. That right is virtually complete, also, under the law in effect in the Philippines. Journalists in the United States are protected in the right to preserve confidences by laws in 12 states, while judicial rulings in two other states provide an effective protection. Circumstances in Sweden, in Norway, in the German Federal Republic, and in Switzerland are almost as favourable under existing laws. This, however, represents the total extent of protection under the law accorded to journalists in the world today in the area of professional secrecy.

There are other countries and states or provinces within nations, nevertheless, where the journalist's position is made almost equally secure either by *custom* or by *practice*. It is significant that these circumstances exist where the journalist has demonstrated a degree of competence and responsibility that has earned him the respect not only of those who are willing to confide in him, but of those who administer the affairs of the country. One of the best examples of this situation exists in the United Kingdom, where the journalist has no legal protection whatever against being required to reveal sources, yet where the demand to do so rarely has occurred and where journalists themselves have pressed no claim for legal recognition of a "right" to professional secrecy.

In Australia, Belgium, Canada, Denmark, Finland, and the Netherlands, also, no legal protection exists for journalists. Occupying respected positions, however, they have had little difficulty even when called upon to appear in court as witnesses. The courts generally recognize that they are responsible persons, and rarely demand that they break professional confidences. The same is true in those 36 or 38 states of the United States where no laws exist to give journalists a full legal right to protect confidences. It has been true in France, where the courts have tended to permit journalists to protect a loss of memory when asked concerning a source.

Considering the pros and cons of the argument, the reasons most commonly heard favourable to professional secrecy for journalists, legally supported, include one or more of these propositions :

1) That the journalist has a moral and ethical duty to protect the anonymity of an individual who gives him information with the understanding that it is to be regarded as confidential, as to source.

2) That the journalist must protect his sources as a practical assurance that he will continue to receive information in confidence, if need be, and so make it possible for the newspaper to obtain and publish information that should be made known to the public.

3) That the press contributes to the public welfare and performs an essential public service in gathering and presenting information that might not otherwise become known, and that keeping a confidence is an essential element in that process.

4) That the journalist, serving the public welfare, is as much entitled to special privilege under the law as is the doctor or clergyman or lawyer, all commonly recognized in law as having a right to maintain professional secrecy, not to mention other persons on the fringes of those traditional professions who also have that protection.

5) That, if a journalist can obtain information, the public agencies—including the police and the courts—with their own great powers should be able to obtain the same information after the journalist has given them a lead, but without putting pressure upon the individual journalist to do their work for them and, in the process, betray a trust.

The contrary arguments include these contentions :

1) That the function of the courts in the preservation of law and order must take precedence over any claim of privilege by the journalist, and gives any court a complete right to demand all information required, in the judgment of the court, to insure fairness and justice for all—including information a journalist might possess that could determine the legal penalty for some third person.

2) That the journalist receives information with the specific understanding that it is to be made known, whereas the doctor, lawyer and clergyman receive it with the express under-

standing that it is not to be made known. This difference removes the journalist from the traditional professional area of privilege as to source.

3) That a journalist, given a legal right to withhold a source, could then publish any sort of assertion or charge, vaguely attributed, but actually made up by the journalist to serve some purpose contrary to the public interest, and he might also be made the channel through which other persons, sure of personal protection, might seek to gain publicity for views and charges designed to serve their own selfish ends.

4) That there is no evidence to show that the press performs any better or any worse, so far as the public welfare is affected, whether it operates under law granting protection to journalists in the maintainence of confidences or does not so operate.

If there is any general solution, in law, for this conflict of viewpoint between those who favour legal protection for a journalist possessed of a professional secret, and those who oppose any such blanket protection, it has not yet appeared.

Even journalists, who might be regarded as the potential beneficiaries of such a solution, are by no means unanimous in favouring protective legislation. Some argue that the press is in a better position to perform its function without specific legal protection of professional secrecy, even if that means a journalist may occasionally be required to pay a fine or go to gaol to uphold what he regards as a moral duty to protect a confidence.

Some journalists nevertheless are prepared to concede—as indicated in responses to Questions 6 and 7 in the questionnaire summarized in Chapter III—that there may be occasions when protection of source cannot properly be given precedence over considerations of the public welfare at stake in cases involving threats to state security, treason, murder, or crime, or in cases wherein the substantive right of an individual might be adversely affected by withholding the source of certain information.

Since this is a professional journalistic problem, basically, even though possessing a clear relationship to the public welfare, it has been from journalists and their professional associations that most proposals for change have come. Jurists, although addressing themselves to the problem on occasions, have done so usually with the object of giving support to the *status quo,* under which journalists have no special right of professional secrecy.

The various proposals for change, as advanced by journalists, tend to reduce themselves to three :

1) That journalists' rights to professional secrecy be established by law or statute, as in Austria or the Philippines.

2) That journalists be included, by law, among those traditional professional groups now quite generally granted the privilege of withholding information received in confidence, or regarded as entitled to the right to protect professional trade secrets.

3) That provision be made by law for reference to a special court of those cases wherein journalistic sources are demanded, with a decision to be returned as to whether a journalist may properly be excused from answering a question that he contends would require him to break a confidence.

These are not new proposals. Some have been tested in discussions by jurists, by journalists, and by jointly constituted groups. It seems certain that there will be new efforts, chiefly instigated by journalists, to achieve a solution through statutes. Some may succeed, as some have already. The alternative is to go ahead under the existing conditions, although with journalists perhaps trying by every means to further the understanding of their ethical and moral concept of professional secrecy as an aid to the public welfare. This would be done in the expectation that the legal and judiciary group will continue to accept the validity of that concept, and so far as possible will accept it increasingly, and will refrain from harassing journalists in court. Meanwhile, in countries where the press is both free and responsible, it may be expected that the press will not be greatly hampered in the performance of its function.

Beyond that, if journalists and journalists' organizations are, in fact, to agitate for a legal or statutory recognition of a full right to protect sources it would seem probable that the measure of success to be achieved will be related to the nature of the actual cases upon which they base their claim to privilege. If those cases are demonstrably important to the safeguarding of the public welfare the claim will be far stronger, naturally, than if they are only marginally related to it.

One may well wonder in this connection whether jurisprudence through test cases, as opposed to reforms in the existing legislations, may not offer a short cut and in the long run prove to be a more rewarding way of firmly establishing professional secrecy for the journalist.

In many of the cases quoted in this study, it seems that the courts have adopted a more liberal view of the journalist's predicament than the strict observance of statute law would have normally led them to adopt. This may be because few cases involving claims to professional secrecy are so clear-cut that they can be sweepingly resolved for or against the journalist.

Statute law, is, moreover, of necessity a blanket injunction which stresses the duty of the citizen to reveal before the courts or before investigative committees all the facts of which he has knowledge. Yet, these abstract provisions are sometimes inapplicable when they are invoked in this or that concrete case. The more it appears that the law is unjust or offends the social conscience, the more it is possible that jurisprudence—that is the degree of latitude the court may have within the provisions, sometimes very elastic, of the law—may come to the defence of the journalist.

Appendix

Questionnaire

1. Should the right to professional secrecy of journalists comprise:
   a) the right to keep secret the source of information? *Yes — No* *
   b) also the right to keep secret the content of some information? *Yes — No* *
   c) if both questions are answered in the affirmative which of these two rights do you feel is more important? *a), b), of equal importance* *

2. Should the journalist's right to keep his sources secret apply:
   a) to sources which have (explicitly or implicitly) requested that their name be kept secret? *Yes — No* *
   b) also to sources which have not (explicitly or implicitly) expressed such a desire? *Yes — No* *
   c) also in cases in which journalist and informant do not afterwards agree whether or not there was originally an understanding to keep the informant's name secret? *Yes — No* *
   d) also in cases in which the informant *later* changes his mind and *finally* objects to his name being revealed to a court or tribunal? *Yes — No* *
   e) also in cases in which the informant later changes his mind and *no longer* objects to his name being revealed to a court or tribunal? *Yes — No* *
   f) also in cases in which the information provided by the source later on turns out to have been given in *bad faith*? *Yes — No* *
   g) also in cases in which the information provided by the informant turns out to be *inaccurate*? *Yes — No* *

3. For whom should the right to keep sources secret be claimed:
   a) *all* journalists? *Yes — No* *
   b) certain categories of journalists only? *Yes — No* *
   c) if the last question is anwered in the affirmative, what categories should enjoy the privilege — editors-in-chief? *Yes — No* *
   — editors? *Yes — No* *
   — sub-editors? *Yes — No* *
   — staff reporters? *Yes — No* *
   — correspondents:
   full-time? *Yes — No* *
   part-time? *Yes — No* *

* Delete whichever does not apply.

4. From whom should the journalist (have the right to) keep
   sources secret:

   a) from third persons (laymen) ?   *Yes — No* *
   b) from courts in open session :
                                         criminal courts ?   *Yes — No* *
                                         civil courts ?   *Yes — No* *
   c) also from courts which would close the doors to hear the
      journalist's testimony as to his source :
                                         criminal courts ?   *Yes — No* *
                                         civil courts   *Yes — No* *
   d) also from his editor-in-chief (if the journalist involved
      hold another position) ?   *Yes — No* *
   e) also from his publisher ?   *Yes — No* *

5. What are your reasons for claiming the journalist's right
   to keep his sources secret:

   a) because you feel that you have to stick to the promise you
      have made to your information ?   *Yes — No* *
   b) because you feel that by disclosing your source, sources
      in general might tend to dry up ?   *Yes — No* *
   c) because you feel that the special character of the journal-
      istic profession as such requires it ?   *Yes — No* *
   d) if you have other reasons please mention them here...
   e) please indicate in margin (by numbering) the order of
      importance of the above-mentioned reasons (eventually
      indicate what reasons, to your mind, are equally impor-
      tant).

6. Do you think that the journalist's right to keep his sources
   secret should always, and under all circumstances, apply ? *Yes — No* *

7. If you feel that there should be exceptions to the rule,
   what should the restrictions and exceptions be ?

   a) should the journalist's privilege (not to reveal his sources)
      be *limited* to those cases in which the journalist's publica-
      tion involved is considered by a court to have been written
      apparently to serve the general interest ?   *Should be limited to*
                                                     Should not be limited to *
   b) should the privilege *not* be claimed in cases in which the
      testimony of the journalist as to his source is deemed
      necessary by a court for the administration of justice
      and/or maintenance of security in cases of :
      — high treason ?   *Should be claimed*
                                                     Should not be claimed *

      — murder ?   *Should be claimed*
                                                     Should not be claimed *

      — where the journalist's informant has him-
        self violated his legal obligation to   *Should be claimed*
        observe professional secrecy ?   *Should not be claimed* *

c) If you are in favour of limiting the journalist's privilege in the sense as mentioned in 7a) (to publications deemed to serve the general interest) do you think that (any of the exceptions mentioned in 7b) should constitute an additional limitation so that even when a journalist's publication is considered by a court to have been written apparently to serve the general interest, nevertheless he should reveal the name of his informant when deemed necessary by a court in cases of:

— high treason ?   *Yes — No* *

— murder ?   *Yes — No* *

— violation by the journalist's informant of his legal duty to observe professional secrecy ?   *Yes — No* *

d) should the privilege be granted whenever the journalist (called upon as a *witness* to reveal the name of his informant) is also the *defendant* in a trial for the publication involved, or is awaiting as defendant a trial for the publication involved ?   *Yes — No* *

e) should the privilege be granted whenever the testimony of a journalist could lead to self-incrimination ?   *Yes — No* *

f) should the privilege *not* be claimed if the *publication involved* is deemed by the court

— to be detrimental to state security ?   *Should be claimed*
Should not be claimed *

— to be detrimental to the general interest ?   *Should be claimed*
Should not be claimed *

— to be detrimental to private interests, without serving the general interest ?   *Should be claimed*
Should not be claimed *

— to be detrimental to personal reputations, without serving the general interest ?   *Should be claimed*
Should not be claimed *

g) in what other cases should the privilege not be claimed ?

8. Should the right of journalists to keep sources secret, subject perhaps to any of the above limitations, be recognized in your country (insofar as this is still not so):

a) by (statute) law ?   *Yes — No* *

b) by jurisprudence (the courts, or other competent bodies to decide in each individual case) ?   *Yes — No* *

c) partly by law, partly by jurisprudence ?   *Yes — No* *

d) by agreements between authorities and professional organisations ?   *Yes — No* *

9. What bodies should adjudicate on a journalist's claim to keep his source secret in any given case:

a) the court which is treating the case in which it would need the journalist's testimony ?   *Yes — No* *

  b) another court which is not dealing with the case itself ?   *Yes — No* *

  c) one of the solutions mentioned under a) and b), but the
      court having to be supplemented by journalists,
                                  — in an advisory capacity ?   *Yes — No* *
                                  — with voting rights ?   *Yes — No* *

  d) a special body to be set up by the profession to whom this
      competence should be assigned ?   *Yes — No* *

  e) an already existing body organized by the profession, which
      would have to be given the competence in this field ?   *Yes — No* *

  f) any other system or combination of above-mentioned sys-
      tems ? . . .

10.

  a) Should the journalist as a counterpart to his right to keep
      sources secret have a concomitant *duty* to keep them
      secret ?   *Yes — No* *
      b) If so, should there be any sanctions against breach of
      this duty ?   *Yes — No* *

  c) If the last question is answered in the affirmative, what
      sanctions ? . . .
      To be inflicted by what body ? . . .

11. Do you feel that it is for the journalist himself to decide
    on the limitations, if any, of his rights and duties to pro-
    fessional secrecy rather than to leave this to be completely
    decided upon by law and/or jurisprudence ?   *Yes — No* *

INTERNATIONAL PROPAGANDA AND COMMUNICATIONS

An Arno Press Collection

Bruntz, George G. **Allied Propaganda and the Collapse of the German Empire in 1918.** 1938

Childs, Harwood Lawrence, editor. **Propaganda and Dictatorship: A** Collection of Papers. 1936

Childs, Harwood L[awrence] and John B[oardman] Whitton, editors. **Propaganda By Short Wave** *including* C[harles] A. Rigby's **The War on the Short Waves.** 1942/1944

Codding, George Arthur, Jr. **The International Telecommunication Union:** An Experiment in International Cooperation. 1952

Creel, George. **How We Advertised America.** 1920

Desmond, Robert W. **The Press and World Affairs.** 1937

Farago, Ladislas, editor. **German Psychological Warfare.** 1942

Hadamovsky, Eugen. **Propaganda and National Power.** 1954

Huth, Arno. **La Radiodiffusion Puissance Mondiale.** 1937

International Propaganda/Communications: Selections from *The Public Opinion Quarterly*, 1943/1952/1956. 1972

International Press Institute Surveys, Nos. 1-6. 1952-1962

International Press Institute. **The Flow of News.** 1953

Lavine, Harold and James Wechsler. **War Propaganda and the United States.** 1940

Lerner, Daniel, editor. **Propaganda in War and Crisis.** 1951

Linebarger, Paul M. A. **Psychological Warfare.** 1954

Lockhart, Sir R[obert] H. Bruce. **Comes the Reckoning.** 1947

Macmahon, Arthur W. **Memorandum on the Postwar International Information Program of the United States.** 1945

de Mendelssohn, Peter. **Japan's Political Warfare.** 1944

Nafziger, Ralph O., compiler. **International News and the Press:** An Annotated Bibliography. 1940

Read, James Morgan. **Atrocity Propaganda, 1914-1919.** 1941

Riegel, O[scar] W. **Mobilizing for Chaos:** The Story of the New Propaganda. 1934

Rogerson, Sidney. **Propaganda in the Next War.** 1938

Summers, Robert E., editor. **America's Weapons of Psychological Warfare.** 1951

Terrou, Fernand and Lucien Solal. **Legislation for Press, Film and Radio:** Comparative Study of the Main Types of Regulations Governing the Information Media. 1951

Thomson, Charles A. H. **Overseas Information Service of the United States Government.** 1948

Tribolet, Leslie Bennett. **The International Aspects of Electrical Communications in the Pacific Area.** 1929

Unesco. **Press Film Radio,** Volumes I-V *including* Supplements. 1947-1951. 3 volumes.

Unesco. **Television:** A World Survey *including* Supplement. 1953/1955

White, Llewellyn and Robert D. Leigh. **Peoples Speaking to Peoples:** A Report on International Mass Communication from The Commission on Freedom of the Press. 1946

Williams, Francis. **Transmitting World News.** 1953

Wright, Quincy, editor. **Public Opinion and World-Politics.** 1933

DATE DUE

$^{11}/_{11}/_{99}$ EC - 7 1999			
GAYLORD			PRINTED IN U.S.A.